THIRD EDITION

Physical Education Activities Handbook
for Men and Women

CONTRIBUTING AUTHORS

P. A. Lee

J. R. McCachren

E. G. Mooney

A. C. Moore

W. M. Potter

T. M. Scott

F. W. Stephens

W. R. Welsch

THIRD EDITION

Physical Education Activities Handbook
for Men and Women

Dennis K. Stanley

Dean Emeritus,
College of Physical Education,
Health and Recreation
University of Florida

Irving F. Waglow

Professor,
Department of Physical
Education for Men
University of Florida

Ruth H. Alexander

Chairman,
Department of Physical
Education for Women
University of Florida

ALLYN AND BACON, INC.
BOSTON · LONDON · SYDNEY · TORONTO

Photograph Acknowledgments

2-(top left and bottom) Courtesy Wisconsin Natural Resources Department; (top right) Wide World Photos, Inc. 5-Courtesy Colorado Department of Public Relations. 8 and 9-Courtesy Wisconsin Natural Resources Department. 14 and 17-Courtesy American Badminton Association. 20-From *Women's Basketball,* by Mildred J. Barnes. Boston: Allyn and Bacon, Inc., 1972. 25-Courtesy AMF Voit, Incorporated. 32-Courtesy AMF, Incorporated. 35-Courtesy Brunswick Corporation. 39-Courtesy AMF, Incorporated. 40-Courtesy Brunswick Corporation. 42-(left) Courtesy Amateur Athletic Union of the United States; (right) Mark Rosenberg—Stock, Boston. 50-Courtesy Springfield College. 51, 52 and 59-Allyn and Bacon, Inc. 62 and 63-Courtesy A. John Geraci. 69-Courtesy University of Florida. 78-Courtesy A. S. Spalding & Bros. 88-Courtesy Springfield College. 94 and 95-From *Men's Gymnastics,* by Leonard H. Kalakian and William R. Holmes. Boston: Allyn and Bacon, Inc., 1973. 101-Courtesy Springfield College. 106-Courtesy AMF, Incorporated. 116 and 117-Courtesy University of Florida. 124 and 131-Wide World Photos, Inc. 134-Courtesy Amateur Athletic Union of the United States. 139-Courtesy University of Florida. 152 and 153-Mark Silber. 159-Wes Kemp. 160-Allyn and Bacon, Inc. 164 and 166-Courtesy Florida News Bureau. 168-(top left and right) Courtesy Colorado Department of Public Relations; (bottom) Courtesy Sun Valley, Idaho. 172-Courtesy Colorado Department of Public Relations. 174(two)-Courtesy Florida News Bureau. 180-Courtesy The Harvard Crimson; photo by Peter A. Southwick. 199 and 202-Courtesy Amateur Softball Association. 211-Courtesy University of Florida. 220-Allyn and Bacon, Inc. 226-Robert J. Eckman—Design Photographers International. 227-Courtesy Wisconsin Natural Resources Department. 233-Wide World Photos, Inc. 242-Courtesy University of Florida. 244-Courtesy Dr. H. E. Edgerton. 249-Wide World Photos, Inc. 270 and 271-Courtesy The Harvard Crimson. 280 and 287-From *Volleyball,* by Allen E. Scates and Jane Ward. Boston: Allyn and Bacon, Inc., 1969. 294(top)-Courtesy Florida News Bureau; (bottom) Wisconsin Natural Resources Department. 297-Courtesy Wisconsin Natural Resources Bureau. 300-Wide World Photos, Inc. 308-Courtesy The Harvard Crimson. 313-Courtesy University of Florida.

Library of Congress Catalog Card No.: 72-80357

ISBN: 0-205-03640-6

Fifth printing . . . August, 1976

Contents

PREFACE   ix
INTRODUCTION   1

   Organic Efficiency; Skill in Performance;
   Knowledge and Understandings; Social Concepts.

1 | ANGLING   3

   Rules; Terminology; Equipment; Safety;
   Skills; Drills; Strategy; Bibliography.

2 | ARCHERY   7

   Target Archery; Field Archery; Flight
   Shooting; Terminology; Equipment; Safety;
   Skills; Hints; Bibliography.

3 | BADMINTON   13

   Terminology; The Game; Rules; Equipment;
   Safety; Skills; Strategy; Bibliography.

4 | BASKETBALL   21

   The Game; Fundamentals; Offense; Defense;
   Bibliography.

5 | BOWLING   33

   Terminology; Rules; Safety; Equipment;
   Scoring; Fundamentals; Bibliography.

6 | BOXING   43

   Terminology; Safety; Skills; Amateur Rules;
   Drills; Bibliography.

7 | DIVING   49

   The Three Basic Dives; Bibliography.

8 | EXERCISE   53

   Locomotor Exercises; Isometric Exercises;
   Supplementary Exercises; Figure Control;
   Helpful Tips; Bibliography.

9 | FENCING   61

   The Match; Terminology; Safety; Skills;
   Bibliography.

10 | FIELD HOCKEY   65

   Terminology; The Game; Equipment; Safety;
   Individual Skills; Strategy; Bibliography.

11 | GATOR BALL   71

   The Game; Rules; Skills; Strategy; Drills.

12 | GOLF   77

   History; Terminology; Rules; Etiquette;
   Equipment; Safety; Fundamentals; Reasons

for Incorrect Shots; Checklist; Strategy; Bibliography.

13 | GYMNASTICS   89

Nature and Values; Safety; Courtesy; Competition; Skills; Bibliography.

14 | HANDBALL   115

Terminology; Court; Equipment; The Game; Fundamentals; Drills; Strategy; Bibliography.

15 | HORSESHOE PITCHING   121

Playing Area; Rules; The Game; Skills; Safety Hints; Bibliography.

16 | ICE HOCKEY   125

Terminology; Rules; Equipment; Fundamentals; Drills; Bibliography.

17 | JUDO   133

Terminology; Rules; Safety; Skills; Skill Practice; Bibliography.

18 | LACROSSE   141

Terminology; Rules; Equipment; Individual Skills; Safety; Play of the Goalie; Attack Play; Defensive Play; Drills; Strategy; Bibliography.

19 | MODERN DANCE   151

Terminology; Movements; Values; Preparation; Technique; Choreography; Safety Hints; Bibliography; Records.

20 | MOVEMENT AND BODY
     MECHANICS   157

The "How" in Movement; The "Why" in Movement; The "When" in Movement; The Skill of Movement; Personality and Movement; Standing; Sitting; Locomotor Movements; Nonlocomotor Skills; Creativity in Movements; Bibliography.

21 | PADDLEBALL   161

Court; Equipment; Rules; Skills; Bibliography.

22 | SHUFFLEBOARD   165

Equipment; Fundamentals; Skills; Strategy; Rules; Bibliography.

23 | SKIING   169

Equipment; Safety Hints; Fundamentals; Bibliography.

24 | SKIN AND SCUBA DIVING   175

Terminology; Equipment; Skills and Knowledge of Skin Diving; Knowledges of Scuba Diving; Safety Precautions; Bibliography.

25 | SOCCER   181

Terminology; The Game; Scoring; Equipment; Safety; Fundamentals; Drills; Strategy; Bibliography.

26 | SOCIAL DANCE   189

Waltz; Fox Trot; Jitterbug; Latin American Dances; Bibliography.

27 | SOFTBALL   197

Terminology; Rules; Playing Area; Equipment; Safety; Basic Skills; Defensive Play; Offensive Play; Strategy; Scoring; Slow-Pitch Softball; Bibliography.

28 | SPEED-A-WAY   205

Terminology; The Game; Facilities and

Equipment; Skills; Rules; Strategy; Safety; Bibliography.

29 | SPEEDBALL   209

Terminology; The Game; Rules; Strategy; Players; Bibliography.

30 | SQUARE DANCE   213

Terms and Movements; Formations; Tips; Bibliography.

31 | SQUASH RACQUETS   221

Court; Equipment; Rules; Skills; Strategy; Bibliography.

32 | SWIMMING   225

Water Safety; Fundamentals; Skills; Bibliography.

33 | SYNCHRONIZED SWIMMING   235

Terminology; Sculling; Starting Body Position; Elementary Figures; Competitive Rules; Bibliography.

34 | TABLE TENNIS   241

Equipment; The Game; Rules; Skills; Strategy; Bibliography.

35 | TENNIS   245

Equipment; Terminology; Scoring; Procedure; Fundamental Skills; Drills; Strategy; Etiquette; Safety; Bibliography.

36 | TOUCH FOOTBALL   259

Rules; The Game; Individual Skills; Team Skills; Flag Football; Safety; Bibliography.

37 | TRACK AND FIELD   269

Terminology; Track Skills; Track Events; Field Events; Bibliography.

38 | VOLLEYBALL   281

History; Terminology; Rules; Rule Differences; Skills; Strategy; Drills; Bibliography.

39 | WATER SKIING—MOTORBOATING 293

Skiing Equipment; Skiing Safety; Fundamental Skills of Skiing; Bibliography—Water Skiing; Motorboating; Boating Terminology; Boating Rules; Boating Equipment; Boating Safety; Boating Skills; Bibliography—Motorboating.

40 | WEIGHT TRAINING AND
     WEIGHT LIFTING   299

Weight Training (Exercises); Weight Lifting; Progressive Weight Training for Girls; Bibliography.

41 | WRESTLING   309

Terminology; Equipment; Rules; Safety; Skills; Takedowns; Escapes; Pinning Combinations; Bibliography.

SOURCES OF OFFICAL RULES   315
APPENDIX—SKILL TESTS   321

Preface to the Third Edition

The third edition of the *Physical Education Activities Handbook for Men and Women* presents a wide range of sports and activities in physical education for both men and women. Chapters have been extended and revised in order to include the most up-to-date information concerning the activities and to emphasize the variations and likenesses in these activities for women. Additionally, chapters have been added in paddleball, movement education, speed-a-way, and speedball. Modern dance and synchronized swimming have been completely revised, with more advanced techniques included. A few chapters have been extended to include coed volleyball, slimnastics, weight training for women, and slow pitch softball. Other new and interesting revisions will also be found in this new edition.

This book is designed to serve principally as a comprehensive source of information for students in physical education activities. More specifically, however, it can serve as a coaching or teaching manual, or as a reference source for factual information on the techniques involved in any of the activities covered. In addition, it provides the more casual reader with a general knowledge of a variety of activities: sports, dance, recreational activities, aquatics, and combatives.

This handbook is organized to present the reader with enough information on the fundamental skills and technical aspects of each activity so that he can undertake a balanced and meaningful program of participation. It is hoped that the material thus presented will serve as a stimulus for continued reading, participation, and development.

The authors would like to acknowledge the assistance of the contributing authors for their contributions and technical advice in the preparation of the coverage of their fields of specialization. We would also like to thank Russell Mead, editor at Allyn and Bacon, Inc., for his help in bringing out this new edition of the handbook.

Dennis K. Stanley
Irving F. Waglow
Ruth H. Alexander

THIRD EDITION

Physical Education Activities Handbook
for Men and Women

INTRODUCTION

Never before in the history of man has there been such a great need for the individual to participate in some form of a physical fitness or sports program.

The pace and complexity of modern living impose a psychological strain on nearly everyone, while, ironically, our technological advances have minimized the need for the physical exertion that could provide a natural outlet for some of these tensions.

This unbalanced situation should be corrected by a program of athletic participation that will produce mental well-being for the participant — as well as the physical fitness that is so difficult to acquire in other aspects of his daily routine.

The many values of athletic activities should be as well known by the individual as the merits of other good practices in physical and mental health. It is the responsibility of physical educators, physicians, recreation specialists, and others in educational capacities to make their students realize the need for the beneficial effects of physical activity — and that all the benefits are not just physical.

The physical educator has the responsibility both of instructing his students about the objectives of physical education and of constructing specific programs in the curriculum by which these objectives can be achieved.

The following objectives are suggested as guidelines — the development of:

ORGANIC EFFICIENCY

Such efficiency is basic to the subsequent development of a strong supportive musculature. The person who is basically strong is equipped to undergo physical effort over a long period of time without undue tiring.

SKILL IN PERFORMANCE

Usually the desire to learn and to continue in an activity or sport develops in direct proportion to the ability to perform satisfactorily. One enjoys doing something that he can do well. The varsity athlete, facing extremely stiff competition, must achieve a high level of proficiency. Even the individual who wishes to participate in a less strenuous activity wants to perform well enough to feel the satisfaction of doing a thing well and of having others recognize his accomplishment.

KNOWLEDGES AND UNDERSTANDINGS

All satisfaction in programs of physical education, however, does not come from actual physical performance. A person can derive great satisfaction from being able to help others in learning a sport technique. He will also enjoy an activity more if he learns about its history, rules, techniques, strategies, and other aspects of theory.

SOCIAL CONCEPTS

One of the most significant values of sports and physical fitness is the way in which they contribute to an individual's social awareness. A sportsman learns sportsmanship. In team play, he realizes the cooperation that is necessary, the enjoyment of striving for *a group* goal, the ability to both lead and follow, and the pleasure and necessity of loyalty to the team. In both team play and individual competition, he comes to recognize the value of sports etiquette and thoughtfulness, of self-control, and of humility in the face of defeat.

Perhaps most important of all, the participant learns to recognize and respect the proper place of sports and physical fitness as an essential part of the total person. He discovers the need for, and value of, physical activity; and he finds out, by participation, how best to meet this need.

ANGLING | 1

One of man's oldest activities is fishing. Formerly he fished for food; now he fishes for recreation as well. By employing today's swift transportation, he may travel the entire world in pursuit of this sport. The average person will probably not play football or basketball after leaving college — not so with fishing. It is a sport in which not only the vigorous but many who are severely physically handicapped may participate. Considerable impetus has been given to fishing instruction by the American Association for Health, Physical Education and Recreation. Through its sponsorship and the support of workshops and clinics, many schools and colleges are now teaching fishing skills and appreciations.

RULES

Rules for the sport of fishing generally are found within various bodies of state and local regulations. These requirements usually include specific mention of bag limits, minimum sizes of fish, illegal methods of catching fish, types of bait permitted, those required to be licensed, seasonal dates, prices of licenses, kinds of game fish, and those authorized to issue licenses.

If use of a boat is involved, the fisherman is expected to comply with another body of rules which may include boat numbering, number of boat passengers, miles per hour, maximum horsepower, lifesaving devices, night lights, signals, rights of way, and meanings of buoys.

For the fisherman who enjoys competitive casting, rules have been established by the American Casting Association. These generally encompass such items as: rod, reel, line, target lure, method of casting, scoring, targets, determining winners, deciding ties, awards, casting distances, casting box, registration, time limits, and officiating.

TERMINOLOGY

Backlash—Snarling of the line on the reel.

Backswing—Rearward lifting of the rod after pointing it toward its intended target.

Fly casting—The type of casting that emphasizes the casting or shooting of the line instead of the lure.

Forward swing—The final effort in casting the lure toward its target.

Horsing them in—Bringing the fish in as fast as possible without regard to skillful playing of the fish.

Level-wind reel—The type of reel that has a device to control the speed and evenness of the line on the spool.

Plug—Common term for an artificial lure.

Reel seat—The section of the handle into which the reel is fitted.

Rod tip—The end farthest from the grip or handle. The entire shaft is also referred to as "the tip."

Setting the hook—Pulling the line strongly and quickly to embed the hook solidly inside the mouth of a fish.

Spin casting—A term popularly used for "push-button" casting that employs a bait-casting rod and a spinning-type reel.

Spinning—The type of casting in which the line leaves the spool on "the spindle principle" as it would off the end of a spool of thread.

EQUIPMENT

Equipment, whether for instruction or actual fishing, should be of good quality. A desirable standard for instructional classes is one rod, reel, line, lure, and target per person. Additional equipment should be on hand in case of breakage, loss, or faulty functioning of equipment.

3

For bait casting a recommended length of rod is from 5 to 6-1/2 feet. The reel should be of light or medium weight with approximately 100 yards of 10- to 15-pound test line. The lure should be of a 3/8- to 5/8-ounce weight for casting.

Spinning generally employs a longer rod from 6 to 7 feet in length, and a lighter line — usually 6- or 8-pound test. Monofilament is the most popular line material, as it is almost transparent and has great strength in relation to its diameter. A lure that is 1/4 to 1/2 ounce in weight works best with this light line and flexible rod. The reel may be an open-face or closed-face type with either a bail or finger pickup. Spin casting employs the spindle principle, usually through a closed-face push-button reel on a 5-1/2- to 6-1/2-foot bait-casting rod. The line is ordinarily the same 6- to 8-pound test that is found on regular spinning reels mounted on spinning rods. This combination works well with a 3/8-ounce lure.

Fly-casting rods are generally 7-1/2 to 8-1/2 feet in length and may have either single-action or automatic fly reels. It is recommended that 25 yards of "C" or "D" level line or 30 yards of tapered line of HCH or HDH dimensions balance the rod to the line. A nontapered leader at least 6 feet long is suggested for beginners and is also suited to several kinds of fishing. This leader should be from 6- to 12-pound test and even heavier, depending on the size and amount of taper in the line.

SAFETY

Safety on fishing trips is a matter of common sense and courtesy. When in a boat, one should look around before casting. Another occupant may have moved too close to the caster. In bait casting and spinning, the overhand cast is the safest for most casts. On windy days the fly caster must be especially careful of his safety and that of other boat passengers. Wind currents may carry the fish line to spots where other people or objects are in the way.

Hooks and lures should be in the tackle box when not in use. They should not be left on boat seats or on the floor, as they can cause very painful injuries.

A common mistake is to try to free a hook or lure by jerking it out of weeds, lily pads, or branches. Instead, the boat should be paddled to the lure.

A fisherman should know how to swim because an emergency may arise most unexpectedly. Fishermen who wade or who fish from jetties or sea walls need this skill as much as boat fishermen.

Hazards of nature should be respected by the fisherman. Lightning and signs of squalls should be heeded. Care should be exercised in situations where poisonous snakes may be present. Extremes of hot or cold weather should be prepared for in advance.

One who seeks his recreation out of easy reach of a doctor should be skilled in first aid. He should also have equipment for ordinary emergencies, including a snake-bite kit.

SKILLS

Bait Casting

To be a good bait caster, one must first of all control the line on the reel. This is accomplished by the use of the thumb. By maintaining a slight, continuous thumb pressure on the line or the metal convex part of the reel, backlashes may be avoided and the lure stopped at will.

For right-handed casting from a standing position, the right foot should be slightly forward. The right arm should be dropped naturally by the side, with the forearm and the wrist slightly above the horizontal. The cast is usually begun by pointing the rod tip at the target and then lifting the rod sharply to a vertical position overhead. Without a pause at the top of this back cast, the forward cast is made immediately. The follow-through is toward the target. Correct timing calls for the forward cast to be twice as fast as the back cast.

Bait casting is done with the wrist rather than the whole arm. The reel handles are up throughout the cast instead of out at the side. The thumb pressure is eased on the forward cast so that the line flows freely through the guides. To determine the actual release point takes much practice.

The secret of a good cast with a bait-casting rod is using the wrist as a base for the casting motion. The wrist should not be waved upward toward the ear or shoved forward toward the target. The elbow remains fixed, and there is a minimum of arm action throughout the cast.

Spinning

To be adept at spinning, the caster must master the fundamentals of range of movement, timing, and line control. Due to the more than average flexibility of the spinning rod, less range of movement is required than for bait casting. To begin the cast, the rod is elevated to a 10-o'clock (Fig. 1-1) position, and then brought back quickly to 12 o'clock. From this vertical position overhead, the rod returns in a continuous forward motion to the original 10-o'clock position. As the lure descends, the follow-through is completed toward the target.

Fig. 1—1. Ten-o'clock position.

Timing in spinning, as in bait casting, is a matter of making the forward cast twice as fast as the backward swing of the rod. Casting forward more slowly does not allow the rod to propel the lure a maximum distance with a minimum of effort. Pressing forward three times as fast, instead of twice as fast, results in the rod tip bearing down on the line; a sharp decrease in distance is then inevitable.

In line control the lure is generally lowered from 6 to 10 inches from the rod tip. The line is then held by the index finger of the casting arm, and released at the 10-o'clock position of the forward swing. To slow the line, the index finger may touch the line slightly as it comes off the spool. This is known as "feathering" and corresponds to "thumbing" in bait casting. This technique gives the caster confidence in his ability to keep out of trouble and enables him to stop his cast instantly when desirable.

Because light lines are used in spinning, the skilled use of the spinning reel's tension drag is a must. If the drag is too tight, the fish may break the line, and the result will be loss of both lure and fish.

Fly Casting

To become proficient in fly casting, the fisherman must learn to cast the line rather than the lure. By becoming expert at handling 30 to 75 feet of line overhead, he will be able to "present the fly" noiselessly and attractively to the fish.

The essentials of fly casting include the line pickup, the back cast, the overhead stop, and the forward cast. The purpose of the line pickup is to take the slack out of the line, and it generally occurs between the 9:30- and 10-o'clock positions. From 10 to 12 o'clock the rod is given a vigorous backward thrust to get the line high and behind the head. The overhead stop may best be described as a pause of approximately 2 seconds to let the line pass above the head. Accompanying this pause is a drift of the rod from 12 o'clock to 1 o'clock. As the tug of the line is felt, the rod is pressed sharply forward to the original 10-o'clock position.

The "presenting of the fly" is accomplished by following through from 10 o'clock toward the target. A sharply lifted rod just before the fly alights will insure that the fly hits first rather than the line and avoids frightening the fish away.

"False casting" is casting the line forward and backward from 10 o'clock to 2 o'clock to measure distance, dry the fly, or extend the line for casting a longer distance. To extend the line, strip off several feet from the reel and hold it in the left hand. Let it go through the guides on the first forward cast, and strip off more line for the next forward cast. Continue until the necessary amount of line is extended.

DRILLS

Drills for the development of casting techniques should follow a progression from short casts to longer ones. Beginners should not feel tense because of casting at longer distances.

Figure 1-2 indicates two suggested formations, one with the targets in a straight line parallel to the casting stations; the other shows targets set up in a "V". The former lends itself to drills common to all types of casting. The latter may be used for testing, using conventional scoring methods.

Targets placed on a straight line make it possible for a number of casters to cast identical distances at the same time. Thus, competition may be introduced into the drills in several ways.

1. Determine who hits a given number of targets first.
2. See who can hit the most targets in a given time.
3. Find who can move farthest away from the targets by stepping 1 yard backward for each target hit.

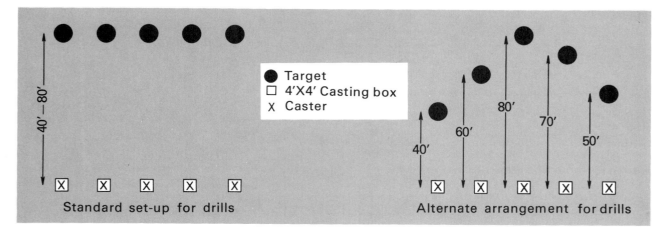

Fig. 1—2. Target formation.

The "V"-shaped formation of targets may be employed to test casting improvement. Two popular methods are widely different. One gives the caster 100 points and subtracts one point for each foot the lure lands away from the target. The other starts the caster with zero, and awards six points for a hit on the first cast and four points for hitting the target on the second cast. In the former method the caster has ten casts, while in the latter he has twenty casts. Details for these and other forms of scoring may be obtained from the American Casting Association, Box 51, Nashville, Tennessee.

STRATEGY

Strategy in catching fish has provided participants in this age-old sport with many of their greatest challenges and thrills.

Many proponents of fishing emphasize that strategy and skill far outweigh luck in achieving piscatorial success. They like to claim that ten percent of the fishermen catch ninety percent of the fish, due mainly to knowledge and skill.

Some examples of strategy employed by successful fishermen include:

1. Keep yourself and your bait moving.
2. Look for fish habitat rather than fish in barren water.
3. Keep the fish between the fisherman and the sun.
4. Change lures and methods until success is achieved.
5. Avoid frightening fish with noise, movement, or vibration.
6. Watch for signs of feeding fish.

One of the marks of a good fisherman is the strategy he uses in playing and landing a fish. He is usually careful to:

1. Keep the fish away from weeds, lily pads, logs, anchor rope, motor shaft, and even the boat itself.
2. Avoid "horsing" the fish in while he's fresh and full of fight.
3. Maintain a firm line with no slack from rod to fish.
4. Lead the fish into or over the landing net rather than thrusting the net at the fish.

BIBLIOGRAPHY

American Association for Health, Physical Education and Recreation, *Casting and Angling*. Washington, D.C.: The Association.

Bueno, Bill, *The Fisherman's Guide*. Englewood Cliffs, N.J.: Prentice-Hall, Inc., 1952.

Gabrielsen, Milton A., "Fly Casting in Your Physical Education Program," *Journal of the American Association for Health. Physical Education and Recreation,* Vol. 20 (November, 1950), pp. 32-34.

Gabrielsen, M. Alexander, Spears, Betty, and Gabrielsen, B.W., *Aquatics Handbook*. Englewood Cliffs, N.J.: Prentice-Hall, Inc., 1960. Chapter 20, Bait Casting.

Hoover, Herbert, *Fishing for Fun*. New York: Random House, Inc., 1963.

Liotta, Ernest, Jr., *The Techniques of Bait Casting*. New York: Ziff-Davis Publishing Co., 1949.

Smedley, Harold H., *Accuracy Fly Casting*. New York: Ziff-Davis Publishing Co., 1949.

The NAACC Skish Guide. Nashville: National Association of Angling and Casting Clubs.

Properly played indoors or out and year-round by all ages, archery is rated extremely high in leisure time and carry-over values. This sport attributes to the development of strength of the chest, abdomen, arms, and back, in addition to enhancing correct posture.

Historians write that archery dates back over seventy centuries, when the bow and arrow was used for warfare and as a means of killing for food.

At the beginning of the seventeenth century, gunpowder was used for warfare and archery gained popularity as a sport. More than five million people participate in target and field archery in the United States. Annual tournaments are sponsored by The National Archery Association, founded in America in 1879, and by The National Field Archery Association, organized in 1939. Annual winter intercollegiate telegraphic meets have been sponsored by the Division for Girls' and Women's Sports.

TARGET ARCHERY

Target archery involves hitting the target, preferably the "gold," with a prescribed number of arrows shot from certain distances. An *end* is a set of six arrows, and a *round* is a specified number of ends. The *Columbia round* is used in college competition. This round consists of twenty-four arrows shot from the distances of 50 yards, 40 yards, and 30 yards.

Competitive rounds are:

American Round—Thirty arrows from 60, 50, and 40 yards respectively.
Junior American Round—Thirty arrows from 50, 40, and 30 yards respectively.
Junior Columbia Round—Twenty-four arrows from 40, 30, and 30 yards respectively.
Miniature Round—Sixty arrows from 15 yards on a two-foot target.
National Round—Forty-eight arrows at 60 yards and 24 arrows at 50 yards.
Range Round—Sixty arrows from one distance (50, 40, 30, or 20 yards) on regulation targets.

Scholastic Round—Twenty-four arrows from 30 and 20 yards respectively.
York Round—Seventy-two arrows at 100 yards, 48 arrows at 80 yards, and 24 arrows at 40 yards.

An archery team consists of four archers, and individual scores are totaled for team scores.

Competitive archery for men consists of two classes of competition, the *York Round* and the *American Round*. For women the two courses are the *National Round* and the *Columbia Round*.

FIELD ARCHERY

Shooting from distances generally unknown and using the instinctive aiming method is referred to as *field archery*. Hunting with the bow, roving, and shooting at various objects or established targets while walking are examples of field archery.

FLIGHT SHOOTING

Flight shooting calls for the release of a designated number of arrows from a shooting line in an attempt to send the arrows the greatest distance. Regular flight competition is performed with the bow held in the hands. Free-style flight permits the bow to be held by the feet and pulled by the hands and arms.

TERMINOLOGY

Anchor point—Point of face at which the hand holding the bowstring is held.
Arm guard—A leather device that protects the bow arm from the bowstring.
Arrowplate—A hard material placed on the bow at the point where the arrow crosses: to prevent wear.
Back (of bow)—Part of the bow opposite the side that faces the string.

Belly (of bow)—Part of the bow that faces the string.

Bow arm—The arm that holds the bow.

Brace—To string the bow so it is ready to shoot.

Clout shooting—Shooting high into the air so arrows fall straight down into a large target drawn on the ground.

Cock feather—The odd-colored feather at right angles to the bow when the arrow is shot.

Draw—Position in which the arrow is ready to be loosed or released; bow is bent.

End—A designated number of arrows in a particular type of round.

Eye—The loop woven into one end of the bowstring.

Fistmele—Distance from belly of bow to bowstring measured by fist and extended thumb.

Footed arrow—An arrow made with hardened wood fitted into the point end for additional strength.

Free style—Shooting with the aid of a bow sight.

Handle—Middle of the bow where bow is held.

Head—Point of the arrow.

Hen feathers—Two feathers of same color, not at right angles to bow.

Holding—Hesitation at full draw for aiming.

Instinctive aim—Aiming and shooting without a bow sight or other aiming methods.

Lady paramount—The presiding official in women's tournaments.

Limbs—Ends of the bow past the handle.

Loose—To shoot, or let fly the arrow.

Nock—To fit the arrow to the bowstring.

Nocking point—Point of the bowstring to which arrow is fitted.

Overdraw—To draw the pile of the arrow back past the belly of the bow.

Petticoat—The portion of the target face extending beyond the scoring area.

Pile—Metal tip of the arrow.

Point of aim—A fixed point, on or off the target, which the archer sees just over the pile of the arrow.

Pull—Force exerted to bring a bow to full draw, using correct length arrow.

Quiver—A device for holding arrows. The quiver may be made of leather or cloth and attached to the belt or made of metal and stuck in ground.

Round—A designated number of arrows shot from designated distances.

Roving—Employing the basic archery skills over a course where the archer shoots at different targets from different distances.

Self arrow—An arrow made from a single piece of wood.

Self bow—A bow made from a single piece of wood.

Shaft—Main part of the bow.

Shaftment—That part of the arrow which contains the crest markings and the feathers.

Shooting line—The line indicating the location from which the archer is to shoot.

Tab—A piece of leather covering the fingers that pull the bowstring.

Tackle—The archery equipment.

Target face (Fig. 2-1)—The front cover of the target which contains the scoring surface.

Tassel—The cloth used to wipe soiled arrows.

Timber—The warning signal in field archery.

Toxophilete—An ardent student or practitioner of archery.

Trajectory—The path of arrow flight.

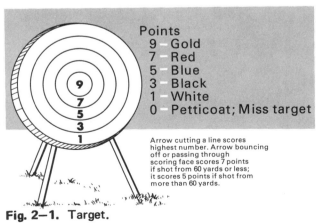

Points
9 — Gold
7 — Red
5 — Blue
3 — Black
1 — White
0 — Petticoat; Miss target

Arrow cutting a line scores highest number. Arrow bouncing off or passing through scoring face scores 7 points if shot from 60 yards or less; it scores 5 points if shot from more than 60 yards.

Fig. 2—1. Target.

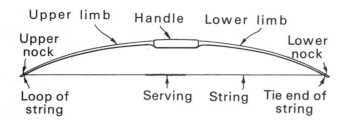

Fig. 2—2. Bow.

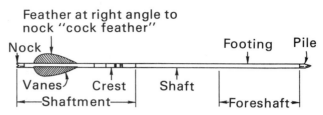

Fig. 2—3. Arrow.

EQUIPMENT

There are many types of bows (Fig. 2-2) and arrows (Fig. 2-3) that are satisfactory for the beginner; and as he learns more about the sport, the archer will become interested in higher quality equipment. Two of the most important aspects of selecting a bow are the quality of wood from which it is made and the number of pounds necessary to bring the bow to full draw. Usually a self bow, made of lemonwood, is quite satisfactory for the beginner. Most men prefer a bow that requires a 35- to 45-pound pull for target shooting. Younger persons and women prefer a bow that requires about a 25-pound pull.

Selecting Proper Bow and Arrow Length

1. *Arrow*—Extend both arms in front of the body, with the fingers extended. Have someone measure the distance from the chest (at shoulder height) to 1 inch past the fingertips. This will give a proper arrow length.
2. *Bow*—Measure the spread of your arms from fingertip to fingertip, then choose a bow from the following table:

arm spread	bow length
57 to 62 inches	4-1/2 to 5 feet
63 to 68 inches	5 to 5-1/2 feet
69 to 74 inches	5-1/2 to 5-3/4 feet
75 to 77 inches	5-3/4 feet to 6 feet
over 77 inches	not less than 6 feet

Best quality bows are made of three materials: Osage Orange, Yew, and Lemonwood. Newer manufacturing processes now permit a lower cost bow of either metal or fiber glass.

One important factor to consider in the care of any archery equipment made of wood or leather is that of moisture. Any such equipment kept in the presence of excess moisture will quickly deteriorate. Moisture will warp arrows and bows and cause leather to stiffen and crack.

Aside from the bow and arrow, other commonly used pieces of equipment are the finger tab, shooting glove, arm guard, and the quiver. Some archers prefer the finger tab to the shooting glove because it is usually more supple and thinner and, therefore, permits more "feel of the bowstring." The arm guard is a single piece of leather strapped to the lower left forearm to prevent it from being hit by the bowstring. Most experienced archers use it also, to assure a smooth movement of the bowstring and to prevent the possibility of flinching as the arrow is released. Care of equipment also includes the following points:

1. Before shooting, be sure that the bow is strung properly. The bowstring must be secured in both nocks and approximately 6-1/2 inches from the bow.
2. String the bow properly to avoid excess strain on either of the limbs. Flat bows are strung by placing the lower limb against the instep of the right foot, holding the handle with the right hand, and slipping the eye of the bowstring upward along the bow until it slides over the nock. Recurved bows are strung by stepping through the bow with the right leg, putting the lower limb in front of the left ankle. The right leg is between the bow and the bowstring, with the handle to the back of the right thigh. Pull forward against the upper limb with the right hand, sliding the bowstring into the upper nock with the left hand.
3. Do not draw the bowstring back and release it without an arrow. You may overdraw it if you don't have an arrow to measure the draw.
4. Fan arrows, or carry them in a quiver to protect the feathers from damage.
5. Try to prevent hitting solid objects with arrows. Solid resistance causes the shaft of the arrow to drive over the pile, or splinters the shaft. Check each arrow before shooting to prevent using one that is splintered or cracked.
6. When putting away archery equipment, unstring the bow by reversing the stringing procedure. Keep all your equipment together, and in a DRY place.

The bow may be hung from a rod, and the arrows should be kept in a standing quiver or a box with notches for each one. This will prevent warping and damage to the feathers.

Scoring and Retrieving

1. When withdrawing arrows from the target, separate the four fingers of one hand and place two fingers on each side of the arrow to be withdrawn, back of the hand toward the target. Withdraw the arrow and call out the score to be recorded. Start with the arrow with the highest value and proceed to the arrow with the next highest value. Continue this procedure until all arrows have been withdrawn.
2. When withdrawing arrows that have become embedded in another object, follow the same procedure. If arrows are found on the ground, partly hidden under the grass, uncover the feathers and withdraw them carefully backward. If the arrows go through the grass and only the feathers are covered, carefully pull them forward.

SAFETY

Safety in archery depends upon knowledge of the equipment used, competitive rules, and common sense. When shooting on a target range, observe the general rules that govern a firearms range:

1. When ready to shoot, straddle the shooting line and wait for the word to commence. Always check down-range prior to nocking your arrow.
2. When an arrow is nocked, or the bow is drawn, never turn away from the shooting line.
3. Never step across the shooting line until all the bows are down on ground quivers or otherwise secured, and the word is passed to proceed to the targets and begin scoring.

When roving or hunting, observe the same rules that govern the handling of firearms in the field:

1. Never shoot at an object unless it is positively identified.
2. Avoid shooting an arrow unless its destination can be clearly seen.
3. Avoid getting ahead of or behind a line of shooters. Do not permit any frivolous or dangerous behavior on the part of any member of a group.
4. Use arrows of correct length and thus avoid overdrawing. This will prevent the pile of the arrow

from coming behind the bow and snapping or splintering it.
5. Shoot only arrows that have all the feathers and a secure pile.

SKILLS

As in most sports, most of the enjoyment derived from shooting a bow and arrow comes only after the basic skills have been mastered. Composition of these basic skills is called the "shooting procedure." Steps in the shooting procedure are:

1. *Standing*—Stand at a right angle to the target, straddling the shooting line. Weight should be evenly distributed on both feet, bow held in the left hand, arrow in the right. Hips and shoulders are parallel to the ground.

2. *Nocking*—Place the arrow across the bow at the arrow plate on the left side of the bow, with the nock of the arrow at the nocking point of the bowstring, encircling the bowstring with the thumb and index finger. Slip the bowstring into the arrow nock, making sure that the cock feather is up or at right angles to the bow and bowstring. Place the index, middle, and ring fingers of the right hand over the bowstring at a right angle to the arrow so that the bowstring is held by the pad of the last joint of each finger. The arrow should be held lightly between the index and middle fingers.

3. *Drawing*—The draw begins with the left arm straight, holding the bow. The head is turned straight toward the target. Raise the left arm so that the bow is brought in line vertically with the center of the target. The bowstring is pulled back during this motion so that the string hand comes to the "anchor point." At this point the left arm, or bow arm, is extended fully but not overextended, with the bow being held in the "V" formed by the thumb and the index finger. A little practice will show that the bow may be held lightly without undue pressure from the fingers. The three fingers holding the string should lie relatively straight from the string to the hand. The thumb and little finger should be flexed inward toward the palm. The bow arm should be parallel to the ground at shoulder level. The hand holding the string at full draw establishes the anchor point, and is very important in the aiming procedure. The "V" formed by the thumb and index finger of the string hand should fit snugly at the back part of the lower jaw, just

below the ear. In order to stabilize the anchor point, the position of the string hand must be a constant factor in the drawing procedure.

4. *Aiming*—Two methods of aiming at a target are suggested here—the point-of-aim method and the instinctive method:

   a. *The point-of-aim method.* This method calls for an exact and precise point of aim in a vertical line with the center of the target. If the range is very short, the point of aim may. be below the target. If shooting from longer ranges, the point of aim may be above the target. At point-blank range, the center of the target appears to sit on the pile of the arrow. A number of arrows must usually be shot at each distance to determine the exact point of aim. In this method, the foot position and the anchor position must necessarily be constant.

   b. *The instinctive method.* In shooting a bow and arrow at objects other than targets set at specific distances, archers sometimes use the instinctive method. This style calls for a great deal of experience plus a mastery of the basic skills of archery. This method of shooting is used most often in hunting, roving, or on bowhunters' club ranges. Success depends upon the individual's knowledge of the cast of his arrows and on his ability to judge distances accurately. Greatest success is experienced by archers who pull a strong bow and whose arrows have a flatter trajectory.

5. *Releasing*—When the point of aim is reached, the arrow should be released without undue hesitation. The actual release is one of the simplest steps in the shooting procedure and yet one of the most important to execute correctly. The release is accomplished by extending or straightening the fingers holding the bowstring. AND REMEMBER:

   a. Don't pull the string hand away from the anchor point.

   b. Maintain the total body position, except for extending the three string fingers, until the arrow hits the target.

HINTS

1. Use equipment suitable to your needs and keep it in first-class condition.
2. Play it safe. A bow and arrow can be a dangerous weapon.
3. When standing on the shooting line, stay balanced and think about your shot before you begin the draw.
4. Keep your anchor point constant. *Remember:* any movement of the feet, head, shoulders, or other part of the body will change this important position.
5. Know your point of aim before you draw, then concentrate on it through the draw.
6. On the release, the only movement should be an extension of the three fingers holding the bowstring. The only movement following this should be directly backward with the string arm.
7. Take instruction from someone who is well qualified to teach archery.
8. Never draw a bow without an arrow in it. This could break the bow.

BIBLIOGRAPHY

Archery Rules—DGWS. Washington, D.C.: American Association for Health, Physical Education and Recreation.

Craft, Dave and Cia, *The Teaching of Archery.* New York: A.S. Barnes & Co., 1936.

Hodgkin, Adrian E., *The Archer's Craft.* New York: A.S. Barnes & Co., 1951.

Jaeger, Eloise, *Archery Instructor's Guide.* Chicago: The Athletic Institute, 1951.

National Archery Association, *Archery Rules—Target.* Santa Ana, Calif.: The Association.

National Field Archery Association, *Archery Rules—Field.* Redlands, Calif.: The Association. 1953.

Niemeyer, Roy K., *Beginning Archery.* Belmont, Calif.: Wadsworth Publishing Co., Inc. 1962.

BADMINTON | 3

The game of badminton, at the time of its origin in India centuries ago, was called Poona. English officers became interested in the game and brought it back to their native land about the middle of the 19th century. The game at that time was often called battledore and shuttlecock after the implements used to play it. During this period the game was often played by groups of from two to eight players, and the court varied in size from 40 by 20 feet to 30 by 15 feet. Posts for the net were set inside the court 15 feet apart, and the net was 5 to 5-1/2 feet high.

The Duke of Beaufort helped to popularize the game in 1873 at a garden party at his country estate called Badminton, Gloucestershire, England. Badminton was the name adopted by the English and in 1895, with the formation of the Badminton Association of England, a set of rules was formulated.

The game was brought to North America by way of Canada about the turn of the century, and its popularity later spread to the United States. After World War II, the emphasis on recreation, fitness for all, and the proper use of leisure time made badminton a popular family game.

TERMINOLOGY

Ace—A fair serve that an opponent is unable to hit.
All—A tie score; for example, a score of 9-all means that each side has 9 points.
Alley (side)—The oblong area on both sides of the court bounded by the singles and doubles side boundary lines.
Back boundary lines—These lines are 2-1/2 feet apart and are found at the ends of the court. The outer line designates the playing area for both singles and doubles play. It is also the long line for the singles service areas. The boundary line inside the playing area designates the long service line for doubles play only.
Backcourt—The half of the playing area that is farther away from the net.
Badminton court—See Fig. 3-1.

Bird—Shuttle or shuttlecock. The object that is struck by the players.
Dead bird—Any bird that is out of play because it hits the floor or an obstacle.
Down—A side fails to score a point when it has the serve.
Drop—To hit the bird in such a fashion that it just reaches your opponent's side of the net and then quickly loses momentum and falls rapidly.
Face of racket—The striking surface of the racket is usually made of gut or nylon. The face is open if the racket handle is held so that the face is upward, closed if the face is toward the ground, and normal if the face is perpendicular to the ground.
Fault—An infraction of the rules resulting in loss of serve if made by the server or loss of a point if committed by the receiver.
Hairpin (net) stroke—A bird barely crossing over the net and falling on the other side, resembling a hairpin.
Handout—The loss of the serve, to either your partner or the other side.
In play—As soon as the bird is hit legally during the service.
"In" side—The side that has the service.
Inning—A side's complete turn at serving.
Kill—A placement shot that the opponent is unable to return.
Let—An unforeseen hindrance that interferes with play. No penalty. Point is replayed.
Lob—To "pop" the shuttle back behind your opponent.
Love—No points. A score of love-7 means that I (the server) have no points; my opponent has 7.
Love-all—The score after a game has been set.
Match—Consists of three games, unless otherwise agreed.
Net tape—A 3-inch-wide white tape that runs along the length of the top of the net.
Odd and even courts—In singles, the left half is odd and the right half is even. The service is taken from the right-hand court when the score is love or even. The left-hand court is used when the

13

score is an odd number. In doubles, the server in the right court is called even and the partner is odd. The even player serves from the right when the score is even, and the odd player serves from the left when the score is odd.

"Out" side—The receiving side.

Out-of-hand service—A service made by striking the shuttle from the holding hand.

Out-of-play—An infraction causing play to stop.

Pace—A method to determine if a bird is suitable for play. A shuttle has correct pace if, when hit a full underhand stroke by an average player from one back boundary line, it falls 1 to 2-1/2 feet short of the other back boundary line.

Rubber—The last of three games in a regulation match, or as prearranged. Sometimes the fifth or even seventh game.

Setup—A poor return that is easily "put away" by an opponent.

Short serve (soft serve)—A service that just clears the net and just reaches the short service line.

Sling—Also called "throw." The shuttle is not hit distinctly but is carried on the racket. It is a fault.

Smash—To strike the bird very sharply in a downward trajectory.

Toss—To commence play, sides spin rackets or flip a coin.

Toss serve—A method of serving in which the bird is thrown out in front and slightly to the side of the body.

Trim—Fine strings looped into the racket face to dress it up. If loops are up, it is called "rough"; if loops are down, it is called "smooth." Trim can be used to toss and commence play.

THE GAME

Badminton can be played in either singles or doubles. The side that has the serve is called the "in" side; the side receiving the serve, or the opposition, is the "out" side.

The game is begun by a toss or racket spin; the side winning the option may (a) serve first, (b) receive, or (c) choose court.

The server shall start by serving from the right-hand service court to an opponent standing in his own

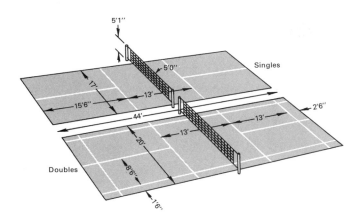

Fig. 3—1. Badminton court.

right service area. Service is made from the right service area in singles play when the score of the server is zero or even, and from the left side when the score is odd. Players, therefore, must change service area whenever a point is scored.

Once the serve has been properly made, the shuttle is in play. In the doubles game, the serve is made in the doubles court area and only the player standing in the proper service court may return the serve. The opposition partners will receive alternate serves because the "in" team is alternating positions with each serve.

The side starting the service has only one person serve during the first inning. In all subsequent innings, each partner will serve. Players continue to serve until a "handout" is made, at which point the other partner will serve until such time as the opponents win the serve.

Faults on Serve

The following seven infractions are considered to be faults:

1. Service is overhand. Shuttle is hit at a point higher than server's waist. Any part of racket is higher than server's hand holding the racket.
2. Shuttle is not hit to proper service area.
3. Server is not standing in proper area to serve or is standing on lines, or receiver is not in proper court area.
4. Server feints or balks opponent off-balance.
5. Shuttle is hit outside of court, passes under the net, or touches person, dress, walls, or ceiling.
6. Receiver strikes shuttle before it crosses the net.
7. Net or supports are touched by player or racket.

Scoring

The game consists of 15 or 21 points for doubles or men's singles, as prearranged. In a 15-point game—if the score is a tie at 13-all, the side that first scored 13 has the option of setting the game to 5 more points; or at 14-all, of setting the game to 3. The game then starts at love-all, and the first team that reaches the required points wins the game. In a game of 21, score is set at 19-all for a set to 5, and at 20-all for a set to 3.

A women's game consists of 11 points, and at 9-all the score can be set to 3; or at 10-all it can be set to 2.

If the option is rejected, a team may reset the score if the opportunity arises again; but in all cases, setting the score must be done before the service.

A set consists of three games, and teams will change ends after each game. In a three-game set, sides will change ends during the third game when the score reaches 8 in a 15-point game, 6 in an 11-point game, and 11 in a game of 21 points. Should players forget to change ends, the correction should be made as soon as it is discovered, and the score shall stand.

RULES

1. During a serve, both the server and receiver must stand in their respective courts. Touching a line with the foot is considered out of the court.
2. If the shuttle hits the net on the serve and is otherwise good, it shall be considered a legal serve.
3. A shuttle that touches the net during play is still in play if it goes into the proper court.
4. A server who misses the shuttle completely during the serve does not commit a fault.
5. A shuttle that falls on the line is considered inbounds.
6. Any accidental hindrance is considered a let.
7. It is illegal for a player to hold up his racket to block a return at the net. He may hold it up, however, to protect his face, providing he does not balk his opponent.

EQUIPMENT

The selection of proper equipment will make the game more enjoyable and will also encourage better play. It is more economical in the long run to buy good equipment. Also, a cheap badminton racket is broken easily and often cannot be restrung. In choosing a racket, the first factor—after price—should be to get a racket that fits the size of the player's hand. Handle grips come in various sizes from 4-1/2 inches to 4-5/8 inches in circumference for the average man, down to 4 inches for children. If the grip is too large, the wrist action so vitally required for proper play is impaired. The forearm and hand also get tired. A grip that is too small will prevent the individual from achieving all his power and will allow the racket to twist and slip in his hand.

The weight of a badminton racket has little bearing on a person's play, since the racket is light enough to be handled by anyone. The balance of the racket does affect the play. Rackets of the same weight will handle differently, depending upon where the weight is concentrated (center of gravity). A racket that is head-heavy will prevent quickness in returning a shot. It will also cause the player's arm to tire quickly. A racket that is handle-heavy will feel light to swing, and the player will lose the feel of the racket head and will be unable to place his shots. His timing will be poor and he will overswing and hit the bird too soon.

Select a frame and then have it strung. Laminated wood has been found to be very satisfactory. There are many factors, however, that you must carefully consider when buying a wooden racket. Examine the grain of the wood and see if it follows the racket's contour. Check for cracks and separations between the glued layers of wood. Hold the racket and turn it slowly in your hand. Look for any signs of warping. Standard brands are usually your safest if all the above conditions are satisfactory. The price for a racket frame may vary from $3 to $15.

Probably the best and most lasting string is nylon. it does not stretch and shrink like gut, and will therefore help your racket frame keep its shape. The resiliency of nylon is not as good as gut, but it does remain the same under various weather conditions. On humid days a gut racket will be much softer than on a dry day. Silk is sometimes used to string rackets, but it does not wear well.

Once you have bought a racket, you should store it in a press when it is not being used. You should also use a waterproof case to keep moisture from getting to the strings. Store your racket in a dry place and hang it up. If you follow these precautions, you will get many years of good play from your racket.

The game of badminton is quite inexpensive, since any flat area can be made into a court. The largest expense is the cost of shuttles. The shuttlecock for tourney play is made of white goose feathers and is worn out easily. It gives perfect flight, spin, and balance, but the average player will have as much enjoyment with the all-plastic birds. They are less expensive, last much longer, and perform well under the roughest conditions.

SAFETY

The game of badminton is safe for everyone to play. However, accidents *do* occur. In doubles play, partners should call out "YOURS" or "MINE" on doubtful shots that either partner could play; this should eliminate being hit by a partner's racket.

Etiquette

1. Learn to win or lose gracefully.
2. Server calls score before each serve in informal play.
3. Recover bird promptly for the server.
4. Never question official's decisions.

SKILLS

The Service

The serve in badminton must be an underhand stroke, and it therefore can put the server on the defensive. This is especially true if you are not skilled at placing your shots. Two types of serve are generally used in

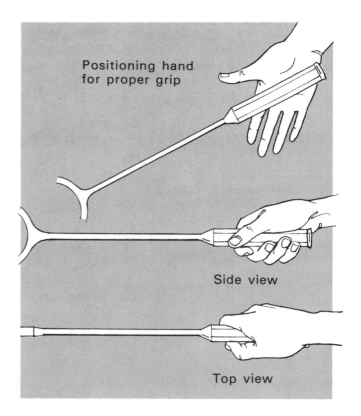

Fig. 3—2. Hand grip.

badminton: the short service, which is most effective for doubles play, and the long service, which is used mainly in the singles game.

The Short Service

This service just clears the net and falls rapidly toward one of the front corners of the opponent's service area.

The server should stand about two feet behind the short service line and about midway in the service area. Face toward the opponent's service area; place the same foot forward as the hand which is holding the bird. With the knee bent slightly and the weight on the forward foot, mentally picture where you want the bird to go. Grasp the bird by placing your index and middle fingers inside the bird, and then complete the grasp by using the thumb. The bird is then held nosedown and about waist-high directly in front of the body.

Grip the racket so that the plane of the racket head is perpendicular to the ground (Fig. 3-2). The heel of the hand and the little and ring fingers should have the "feel of the racket." The "V" formed by your index finger and thumb should be over the top plate of the racket handle. Now allow the racket to drop into a relaxed position by your side.

To deliver the serve, place the racket face in a position that has it touching the nose of the bird which you are holding in your hand. A quick flexion of the wrist drops the racket head. By snapping it back up, you hit the bird as you release it from your hand. Little body or arm movement is necessary.

The Long Service

This serve takes a high, long trajectory and falls deep toward the back corners of your opponent's service area; it is used mainly in singles play. The server takes a similar stance to that taken in the short service, except that he stands close to the center service line and about two feet back of the short service line.

The bird is held in front of the body, the holding arm pointing to the spot the bird is intended to hit. The racket is held as it is in the short service. The server "cocks" the racket by dropping his arm back behind him in pendulum fashion and cocking his

wrist. This will bring the racket into a position pointing nearly straight up.

To deliver the bird, drop it out of the forward hand and bring the racket forward in a vertical arc; a snap of the wrist at the end of the arc will impart a very high velocity to the racket head as it contacts the bird at about knee height. The weight is on the back foot to start the serve and should end on the forward foot as the serve is completed.

Basic Strokes

Forehand Stroke

This stroke is the easiest one for the beginner to master because he uses the same movements as those a person would use to hit a ball with the palm of his hand. To get into position to make a forehand return, pivot either forward or backward. A bird close to the body requires a backward pivot, while a bird away from the body requires a forward pivot. To pivot forward, the foot closer to the bird is the pivot point and the other foot takes a step forward and toward the bird. To pivot backward, the opposite is the case. The pivot foot is the one farther away from the bird, and a step backward and to the rear is made by the closer foot. In either case, after the pivot is made, the shoulders should be in line with the direction in which you wish to return the bird. At the completion of the pivot, the racket should be back and to the side with the wrist cocked. The racket head should be higher than the expected point of contact with the bird. The weight of the body is on the rear foot or foot farther away from the spot you want to place the bird. As the arm stroke is made, the weight shifts with the swing; when the arm is directly in front of the body, the wrist is uncocked to impart high speed to the racket head as it strikes the bird. It is important that you *keep your eyes on the bird at all times* when making any stroke. After the shuttle has been hit, pivot around so that you are again facing the net and holding the racket at the throat with one hand and the grip or handle with the other.

The Backhand Stroke

A bird that is hit to the side opposite the one on which you are holding your racket requires a return using the backhand stroke. To execute this stroke, make the pivot in such a manner that the shoulders are in line with the direction in which you want to return the bird. The racket is brought back as the pivot is made, and the racket head is about shoulder-high with the wrist cocked.

As the bird comes into hitting range, start the racket forward, shift the body weight forward, uncock the wrist and strike the bird at a point just in front of the forward hip. Pivot back into the ready position.

Special Strokes

The High Clear. This stroke is a variation of either the forehand or backhand and gets its name from the trajectory the bird makes in its flight. The bird is hit in a long high arc to the backcourt area of an opponent. The high clear is made on most occasions to allow you to get into a favorable position in your own court, or to drive your opponent out of a favorable position at the net. The bird is contacted about knee-high and is hit with an open face (face is perpendicular to initial phase of the trajectory). The stroke follows through in an upward arc which will lift the bird high and deep into your opponent's playing area.

The Overhead High Clear. This stroke is made when the bird is directly overhead. The return is made as one would cast in fishing. The bird is contacted slightly behind the body, and a wrist snap provides the force necessary to drive the bird deep behind your opponent.

Round-The-Head Stroke. This is a variation of the overhead stroke. The bird is contacted above the head and slightly to the backhand side. This stroke can deliver the overhead high clear or smash.

The Smash. This stroke is made when you find that your opponent has misjudged a return and set up the bird in a position that enables you to drive it down sharply into his court area.

This exciting stroke requires that the weight be on the back foot and the racket head cocked behind the shoulder blades. As the bird falls into position above and slightly in front of you, start the stroke by shifting the weight forward as the arm is brought to a vertical position. At this point, the racket is uncocked by snapping the wrist and the bird is struck downward into your opponent's court.

Note: Caution should be observed when making this shot. An overeager individual will hit the bird too soon and "pop" it up or even make a wood shot. Waiting too long results in driving the bird into the net. Getting into a position too far away results in a net shot, or too close will again cause a "pop-up".

Overhead Drop Shot. This starts the same way as the kill or smash; however, at the instant contact is made with the bird, the follow-through is stopped. This causes the bird to take a downward flight to the net and then fall vertically to the ground. Since it starts like a kill shot, the overhead drop shot is a good change-of-pace stroke to keep the opponent off-balance.

Net Flight. This stroke is made close to the net. The shuttle is hit across the court and close to the top of the net. If the bird just clears the net, it is practically impossible to return. Net flights can be used to return drop shots or if you find your opponent standing directly in front of you, waiting to drive your return back directly at you. The net flight can be made either forehand or backhand. The racket is swept across in front of the body, in a slightly upward arc that will drop the bird just over and across the net.

The Hairpin. The hairpin, as its name implies, achieves the trajectory with a short looping stroke. A flick of the wrist is all that is necessary to lift the bird just up and over the net. A drop shot or a net flight can be returned with a hairpin. Care should be taken not to hit the bird too high, or an opponent will smash it or place it out of reach with a crosscourt net shot.

STRATEGY

Singles

The serve is used mainly to put the bird into play, and it is a very rare occurrence when you are able to ace your opponent. It is good strategy to use a long serve in singles, since your opponent will be set to rush any serve that is improperly made. In singles play, you should place yourself near the center service line about four feet back of the short service line; from this spot you should make your moves to return the bird. There will be times when you will be forced to move out of this position. It is then good strategy to try to return the bird to your opponent in such a manner that he will have to move from his set position and allow you to return to your spot. If the play is at the net, this can be accomplished often by returning a net flight with a long, high clear shot. Whenever possible, hit downward on the bird, as this will cause your opponent to return the bird by hitting up at it. This lofting type of flight will often set you up for a kill or smash.

While in the ready or waiting position, always keep your eyes on the bird and do not stand flat-footed. Keep one foot advanced, with your weight on the balls of the feet.

Players who have a tendency to rush the net can be discouraged by using the high clear return; players who remain too deep should be moved out of their position with drop shots or net flights. When you have your opponent on the move, keep him off-balance by placing your shots where he isn't; seldom try to hit through an opponent. A passing shot attempt is not always the best strategy because the opponent may be able to get his racket on the bird and achieve a lucky return.

Doubles

There are four types of strategy in doubles play.

Side-by-side is used by the average players. The court responsibility is divided equally by using the center service line as the dividing line. Each partner is responsible for his half of the court.

Up-and-back divides the court at about the short service line. One player takes everything in the forecourt area and plays the net, while the other plays everything that gets past his partner.

Diagonal strategy has the court divided from the net post on one side to the back corner on the opposite side of the court. Each partner is then responsible for a triangular area. The partner who is serving or who last served is responsible for the net and area extending to the backcourt. His partner protects the back boundary line and the other half of the court almost to the net.

Rotation divides the court in the same manner as diagonal strategy, except that each player makes a return and moves from his set spot. He will move to his partner's position, and his partner will cover for him. This calls for precise teamwork, and players must practice together to make it function. It can be compared with the switch in zone defense in basketball. A player covering the bird stays with it, and his partner takes over his area and covers for him.

BIBLIOGRAPHY

American Badminton Association, *Badminton Rules.* Waban, Mass.: The Association.

DGWS American Association for Health, Physical Education and Recreation, *Tennis-Badminton Rules.* Washington, D.C.: The Association.

Davidson, Kenneth R., and Gustavson, Lealand R., *Winning Badminton.* New York: A.S. Barnes & Co., 1953.

Davidson, Kenneth R., and Smith, Lenore C., *Badminton Instructors Guide.* Chicago: Athletic Institute, 1960.

Friedrich, John, and Rutledge, Abbie, *Beginning Badminton.* Belmont, Calif.: Wadsworth Publishing Co., 1962.

Radford, Noel, *Badminton.* New York: Sir Isaac Pitman & Sons, Ltd., 1957.

BASKETBALL | 4

Basketball was invented during the school year of 1891-1892 at Soringfield College by Dr. James A. Naismith, an instructor in physical education and coach at that institution. Dr. Naismith was looking for a vigorous game to condition his athletes during the winter season and conceived the idea of attaching peach baskets at opposite ends of the gym on the track which encircled the playing floor—hence, the present basket height of 10 feet.

The game, basketball, derives its name from the original ball and basket used in the first game. Since that time the Young Men's Christian Association and the International YMCA secretaries have introduced the game to all parts of the United States and also to foreign countries. It was included in the Olympic games for the first time in 1936.

Smith College was the scene of the first basketball game for women. Even though the rules for the women's game have been altered and revised many times, the differences between the women's game and the men's game have become fewer and fewer. The Division of Girls' and Women's Sports' rules in effect at the present allow the woman to enjoy participation in this activity to the fullest extent.

The division of the court has been a center of revision as the original three-part court for women was reduced to two parts and now, to a single court.

The number, positions, and limitations placed upon the participants is a second major area of change. The standard number of two teams of six players has been altered to two teams of five players. The five players may enjoy what is referred to as *full court play,* as was the original intent of the game. The United States is the last country involved with international competition to play with full-court, five-player rules for women.

The first book of rules governing women's basketball was published in 1901. The Division of Girls' and Women's Sports of the American Association for Health, Physical Education and Recreation is the foremost governing body of basketball for women.

The Court

The ideal dimensions of a playing floor area are: 50 by 94 feet for colleges; 50 by 84 for high schools; and 42 by 74 for junior high schools. For women, the maximum size should be 50 by 90 and the minimum should be 42 by 72. The top edge of the ring or basket is at a height of ten feet for both men's and women's courts.

THE GAME

The objective of the game is to score more points than the opponent. Scores may be made from the field (a field goal) or from the free-throw line (a free throw). A field goal scores two points; a foul shot or free throw scores one point.

The number of players for a starting team in men's basketball is five. There shall be two forwards, two guards, and one center. If a team does not have enough substitutes, the game can be played with less than five but must have five to start the game.

The fundamentals of play are essentially the same for men and women.

The game is started when the referee tosses a ball between two opposing players standing in the center circle at mid-court. The rest of the players must remain outside this 6-foot restraining circle until the ball has been tapped or hit by either of the two players jumping at the toss-up. Following the toss-up, each team attempts to advance the ball to its own basket. Any player, when in range, may throw or shoot the ball into the basket; this is called a *field goal.*

A player in possession of the ball may not carry it more than one step in any direction. He may shoot, pass, or dribble the ball in any direction. To dribble the ball is to bounce it on the floor with a series of hand taps, keeping it always under control. Players may also roll or bat the ball.

A player commits a *foul* by holding, tripping, charging, pushing, or blocking an opponent. A player who is fouled is entitled to an unmolested *free throw* from the foul line. If fouled while attempting a field goal, he is entitled to two free throws if his shot misses. If he makes the field goal, one free throw is awarded.

After one team makes a goal, the other team puts the ball in play from out-of-bounds under the basket at which the goal was made. However, if a *double foul* is called (both teams foul each other simultaneously), play is commenced by a center toss, with neither team getting a free throw from the foul line.

In order to keep the game going at a fast rate, each team possessing the ball is required to advance it across the middle of the court within 10 seconds after gaining its possession.

The defense tries to counteract each move the offense makes by employing a form of team defense. These patterns are: man-to-man, zone, and a combination of these two. In *man-to-man defense* a player is assigned to guard one specific opponent. In a *zone defense* each player is assigned to guard certain areas of the court—according to the location of the ball. In a *combination defense,* a team will usually play its best guard against the opposing team's best shooter; the other four play a zone defense.

Colleges play two 20-minute halves with a 15-minute intermission. High schools play four 8-minute quarters. Boys' teams of 14 years and under play four 6-minute quarters with a 10-minute rest period between the second and third quarters. There are four 8-minute quarters in women's basketball with an interval of two minutes between the first and second quarters and the third and fourth quarters, and a 10-minute interval between the second and third quarters.

FUNDAMENTALS

Catching

When the player catches the ball at waist height or higher, his hand position is constant (regardless of whether he is standing still or moving about): palms out, fingers pointing up, and thumbs turned toward each other. If he catches the ball below waist level, his fingers point downward and his thumbs outward. Whenever the player is catching, his fingers should be well spread and relaxed. The receiver should reach for the ball with the hands and arms forward and the feet slightly apart for balance.

Passing

The *chest pass* is the most frequently used pass in basketball. Its use is most effective when making short passes. In executing this pass, the player holds the ball with both hands, with fingers well spread to cover the sides of the ball and thumbs to the rear and slightly above the center of the ball. He should hold the ball in front of and away from his body, about chest-high. The elbows should be in, but not tight against the body. He brings the ball in toward the body, cocking his wrists. When he releases the ball toward the target, he extends his arms forward, uncocking the wrists to give impetus to the ball for the forward motion. A step forward with either foot will help the coordination. He uses the same motion to execute a *bounce pass.*

The *bounce pass* should be executed with both hands or with a one-hand "push." The ball should strike the floor in front of the intended receiver so as to rise no higher than his waist, and far enough in front of him for him to have instant control of the ball.

The *baseball pass* is effective for long-distance passing. It is actually a one-handed pass, but the free hand helps to control the ball until the throwing arm is in position. To execute this pass, the player spreads his fingers under the ball and cocks his wrists. He throws the ball as a baseball catcher throws, stepping forward on the foot opposite the throwing hand.

The *underhand pass* is very effective in close quarters where a low pass is necessary. It can be hard, fast, and accurate. It is used most often when the player is guarded from the rear by a tall opponent. He holds the ball with both hands, on its sides and slightly toward the rear. He brings it back to the right hip and takes a step forward on the left foot. As the ball comes back, the right elbow extends upward and the back of the left hand rests on the body near the hip. The ball is flipped or pushed forward and the weight is shifted from the back to the forward foot as the ball is released.

The *two-hand over-the-head pass* is usually used by tall men when passing over shorter men. It is executed by bringing the ball back and over the head, the hands being over the sides of the ball, fingers well spread. As the player steps forward on either foot, he snaps his wrists so the ball moves in a forward, but slightly downward, motion.

The *hook pass* is a valuable pass for making fast breaks, getting the ball out of corners, and getting the ball out of the defensive territory. It can be made while on the run or standing. To execute the hook pass with a jump, the player holds the ball away from the body and the guard and keeps both hands on it until it passes shoulder height. He steps toward the intended pass receiver on the foot opposite the throwing hand; when he releases the ball, the elbow should be straight and the throwing arm should pass along the side of the head.

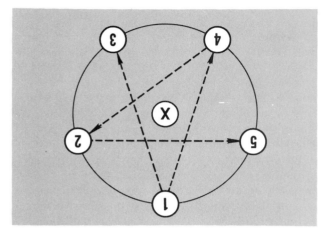

Fig. 4—1. Five-on-one drill.

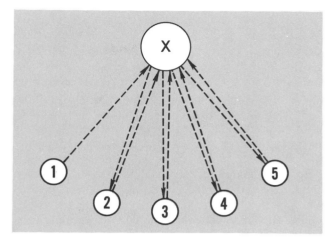

Fig. 4—2. Split-vision pass.

Passing Drills

Five-On-One (Fig. 4-1). (X) stands in a circle surrounded by five men (O). The five men on the outside pass the ball to each other, skipping a man; the middle man tries to intercept the ball. #1 passes to either #3 or #4. #4 passes to #2. #2 passes to either #4 or #5, etc.

Split-Vision Pass (Fig. 4-2). (X), the leader, stands about 15 feet from the other five men. The leader starts with a ball and #1 starts with a ball. On command, the leader passes the ball to #5 and #1 passes his ball to the leader. When the leader receives the ball from #1, he immediately returns it to #2. When #5 gets the ball from the leader, he returns it to the leader, and so on down the line.

Four-Corner Passing Drill (Fig. 4-3). #1 in squad A passes to #1 in squad B, and #1 in squad A goes to the rear of the line in squad B. This continues until the cycle is completed. Use all types of passes.

Double Ball Handling (Fig. 4-4). The inside circle moves clockwise; the outside circle moves counterclockwise. Players pass the ball from the inside circle to the outside circle, and outside circle players pass to players in the inside circle.

Shooting

The three basic shots in basketball are the *lay-up*, the *chest*, and the *foul shot*, with variations.

Lay-up Shot

The lay-up shot is the shot that all teams work to perfect. The theory behind this shot is: the nearer the

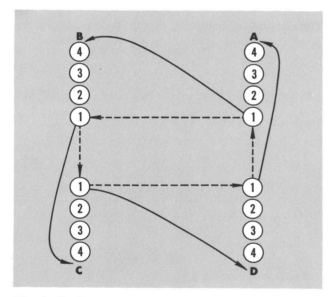

Fig. 4—3. Four-corner passing drill.

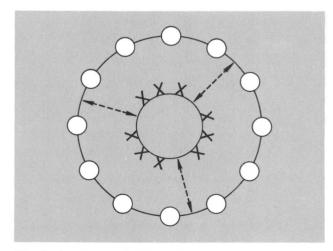

Fig. 4—4. Double ball handling.

basket, the more successful the shot. This shot can be executed while cutting toward the basket after a pass or dribble. If dribbling, the last dribble should be a hard one while approaching the basket, so that the ball will rebound high and prevent the necessity of bending over to pick it up. The shot (from the right side) is more of a high-jump technique and the take-off from the floor should be with the left foot. The ball is held in both hands, with the left hand underneath and the right hand on back and slightly to the top. The ball is aimed on the backboard at the center of the rim so it will rebound through the basket. The palm of the right hand should be facing the backboard when the ball is released. The body should turn inward while in the air so that, in landing on the floor, the player is ready for a rebound or fast break.

Two-hand Chest Shot

The ball is held in the cushions of the fingers with the hands spread over the sides, fingers extended. The body should be in a relaxed position with the elbows in and the ball in front of the body. In executing the shot, the player moves the ball downward toward his chest, keeping his weight evenly distributed on both feet, his knees slightly bent, and his eyes on the rim of the basket. With an upward motion of the arms and hands, the wrists are uncocked, and the ball is released toward the basket while the player executes a forward and upward jump. The eyes should remain on the target until the shot and follow-through have been completed.

Foul Shooting

Foul shooting is important because many close games are won or lost at the foul line. A natural movement in basketball is an underhand movement, and the underhand technique is probably the best way to shoot free throws. However, a player should shoot in the manner he likes best. For the underhand shot, a player stands on the foul line with his feet comfortably spread, holding the ball downward at arm's length, the hands well spread and behind the ball slightly, the ball resting on the cushions of the fingers. When ready to shoot, the player should be relaxed and concentrating on the basket. The shot is begun by bending the knees slightly and gradually swinging the arms upward. The ball is released about eye-level, and a follow-through with the palms of the hands facing the basket completes the movement. Other styles of shooting free throws are the two-hand chest shot and the one-hand push shot (described under shooting techniques).

Variations of Basic Shooting Techniques

Hook Shot. The hook shot is usually a pivot man's shot. However, forwards or guards can also execute the shot. It is a good shot to use when guarded closely from the rear. If the player is shooting with the right hand, he should fake his opponent to the right with a body fake and shift his weight to the right foot. He should then step with the left foot and push hard off the right, keeping the ball well out in front of the body and away from the guard. He must keep both hands on the ball and, as he turns toward the basket, drop the left hand off and continue the upward movement with the right arm, hand on the ball, using a sweeping motion until the shot is made. At the highest point of the raised arm, the ball is released with a flip of the wrist. As the ball leaves the shooting hand, the body faces the basket and should be in a balanced position to either follow the shot or be in a position for the rebound. A hook shot that hangs lazily around the basket can often be tipped in.

Jump Twist. The jump-twist shot is started with a fake to draw an opponent off-balance. The shooter then takes a long step either left or right, according to which way he turns for the shot; as he takes this step the weight shifts, a spring is made high into the air, the body is turned toward the basket, and the ball is swept to a full-arm extension over the head. At the height of the jump, with the ball over the head, the shooter flips the ball with one or both hands.

One-Hand Push. The one-hand push shot is a popular shot either from a set position or on the move. This shot is used at a distance of from 12 to 18 feet from the basket. If the player is a right-handed shooter, he should hold the ball tightly in position in the right hand, keeping his left hand over the ball. He should control the ball with the fingertips and not in the palm of the hand. The shooter begins by pushing the ball upward, extending the arm, and at the same time getting a lift from the right leg as he comes up on the ball of his right foot. He releases the ball with the shooting hand and follows through with the coordination of the leg, arm, and wrist, giving smoothness and accuracy to the shot.

In any type of shot, the player should not release the ball with too much force when trying for a basket. A medium arch should be used on all shots other than a lay-up. It is better to overshoot the basket than to undershoot it. The ball should be in control at all times on the cushion of the fingers. Hurried shots to rid oneself of the ball should be avoided. A player should at all times know his position on the floor, as well as the score and the time left to play in the game.

When executing one-hand shots or lay-up shots, the player should take off from the floor with the foot opposite the shooting hand.

Shooting Drills

1. (Fig. 4-5) The column on the left side of the court has the ball. #1 passes it in to #9 on the foul line and cuts by him. As #1 cuts from the left side of the court, #5 on the right side cuts by #9 on the foul line behind the first cutter (#1). #9 gives the ball to either #1 or #5, or turns and shoots the ball.

2. (Fig. 4-6) #1 man in the group at the center line passes the ball to #9 on the foul line. The #4 man in the group at the side cuts by #9. As he cuts by #9, #1 cuts behind #4. #9 gives the ball to either #1 or #4, or turns and shoots the ball.

3. (Fig. 4-7) #1 passes the ball to #4; then #1 guards #4 until he has attempted a shot. #4 retrieves the ball

and passes to #2. #2 does the same as #1, changing lines after each try.

4. (Fig. 4-8) #5 starts the ball to either side, #1 or #9, as #1 or #9 moves toward the basket. #5 cuts behind the man he passes to. The other end man cuts for the basket. #1 or #9 then passes the ball to #5, who shoots.

Dribbling

There are two types of dribbles—*high dribble* and *low dribble*.

Low Dribble

The low dribble is executed at close quarters. The dribbler should have his hand cupped around the ball for best control; when hard pressed by the guard, he should drop the inside shoulder and try to keep his body between the ball and the defensive man.

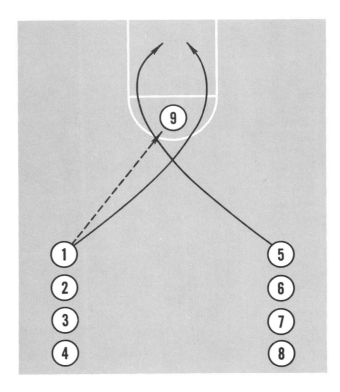

Fig. 4–5. Shooting drill no. 1.

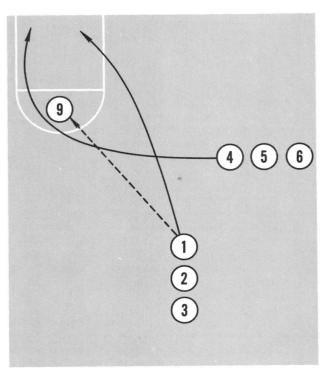

Fig. 4–6. Shooting drill no. 2.

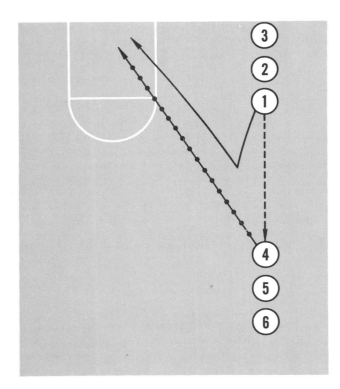

Fig. 4–7. Shooting drill no. 3.

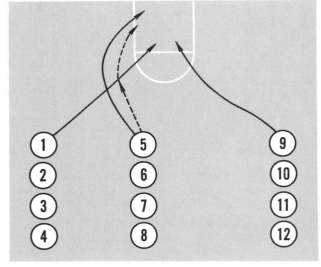

Fig. 4–8. Shooting drill no. 4.

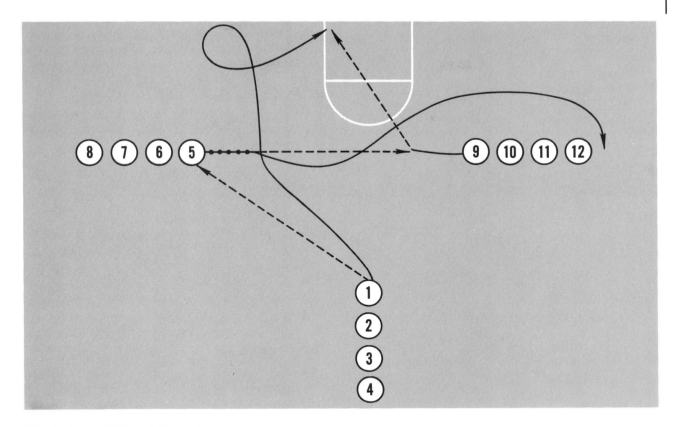

Fig. 4—9. Dribbling drill no. 1.

High Dribble

The high dribble is used when driving hard toward the basket or when bringing the ball up court slowly without defensive interference. The body is in an upright position on the high dribble, with the hands cupped on the ball, the leverage coming from the elbow down. The dribbler should lean forward when dribbling and keep his head erect.

Dribbling Drills

1. (Fig. 4-9) #1 starts the ball to his left, #5, and cuts in front of #5. #5 takes two dribbles and passes to #9. #5 cuts in front of #9. #1, after passing to #5, goes into the corner, pivots, and cuts toward the basket. #9 passes to #1 for a shot.

2. (Fig. 4-10) #1 starts the dribble around #2, #3, on through #7, weaving in and out, using either hand to dribble. When #1 comes to the end of the line, he passes the ball to the head of the line and remains at the end of the line. Each man moves forward one position as the dribbler goes by. If a team is limited to a small number, chairs can be used instead of men.

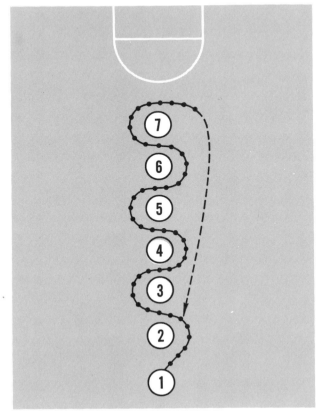

Fig. 4—10. Dribbling drill no. 2.

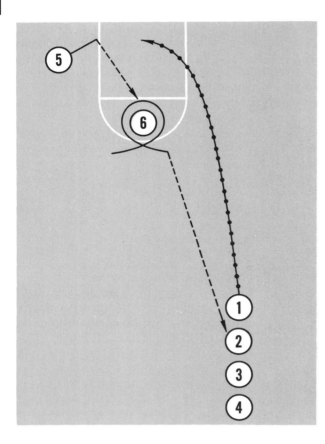

Fig. 4—11. Dribbling drill no. 3.

3. (Fig. 4-11) #1 dribbles in for a shot. #5 retrieves the ball and passes to #6, who makes a reverse pivot and throws the ball to #2, who follows #1. #1 will take #5's place and #5 will take #6's place. #6 will go to the end of the line.

4. (Fig. 4-12) #1 dribbles to the center, pivots, and gives the ball to #4. #4 dribbles to the center, pivots, and gives it to #3. #3 repeats to #2, and #2 to #1.

OFFENSE

Offense comprises those techniques which enable the player to pass, shoot, rebound, or dribble despite his opponent's defensive tactics. Individual offense involves faking with eyes, head, shoulder, use of voice, or a combination of these; also, cutting toward the basket or cutting toward the ball and changing of direction.

Team Offense

Basketball is essentially a passing game. Although it is true that scoring of points wins a game, the skills of dribbling and passing are necessary to move the ball into scoring position. Team offense is no longer composed of a center, two forwards, and two guards. When a team has possession of the ball, five forwards are needed; however, when the other team has

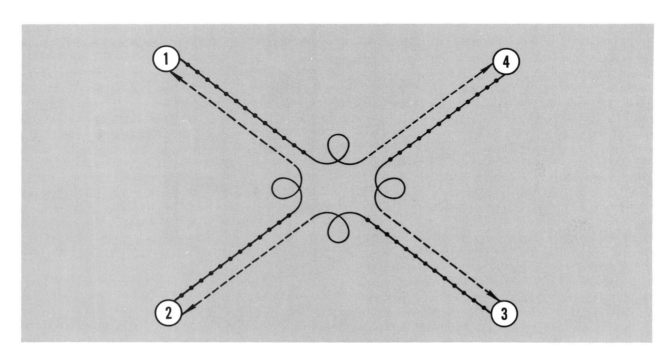

Fig. 4—12. Dribbling drill no. 4.

possession, five guards are required. The team that controls the ball usually wins the game.

Generally speaking, there are two types of attack—the slow or deliberate attack and the fast-break attack.

The slow or deliberate attack is used when the offensive team is big and slow of foot. It is also used near the end of a game by a team when it has a commanding lead. The deliberate attack involves extensive use of set screens, cutting, and ball control.

The fast break is used when a team can outrun its opponents. Also, it is used near the end of a game by the team that is behind. The fast break means simply beating the opponent down the court. Upon obtaining possession of the ball, a team immediately changes from defense to offense. A score is then attempted by moving the ball down the court as fast as possible with a minimum of passing or ball handling.

Slow Break—Set Offenses

Double-Post Offense. This offense is most effective and most often used if there are two good jump shooters near the basket, or possibly if there are two big men who are good rebounders but rather slow. From this setup the big men are near the basket and should get into rebounding position rather quickly. The high post is the position around the free-throw line, and the low post is that near the base line around the basket. Variations of personnel arrangement of the two post men can be made, as well as of that of the other three players.

Slow Break (Fig. 4-13). #1 passes the ball to #4 and screens for #2 as #2 cuts to his left toward #4, who gives #2 the ball. As this takes place, #5 steps forward and screens for #3, who cuts toward the basket down the foul line. #2 either shoots or passes off to #3 for a shot.

Slow Break (Fig. 4-14). #2 passes to #1 as #4 and #5 exchange places. As #2 passes he screens for #1 as #1 passes to #5 and cuts by #2. #5 drives in toward the basket or gives the hand-off for a jump shot to #1.

Fast Break Offense

(Fig. 4-15). One form of the fast break is the three-lane method, which is made practicable when a team out-rebounds their opponent.

If #3 gets the rebound, he passes out to #1, who has cut for the sideline. As #1 cuts for the sideline, #2 cuts for the middle of the court. #1 passes to #2 and cuts behind #2 for a hand-off down the middle of the court. As this is being executed, #4 cuts down the sideline. #3, who passed the ball to #1, cuts down the sideline. Three lanes are covered, one each to the sidelines and one down the middle. #2 and #5 are trailers. If #4 receives the rebound, the swing is to the other side. If #5 receives the ball, he can throw to either side and the lanes are filled in the same way.

DEFENSE

Body control is essential to good defensive play. A player must achieve a good stance so that he can start quickly, stop suddenly, and change his direction fast. There are two positions a defensive man can take to reach this goal. If the offensive man is moving forward or backward, the defensive man should stand with one foot forward, knees bent slightly, hips in a crouched position, stomach in, head up, and eyes on the opponent.

The outside hand should be up and in front of the opponent's eyes, the inside hand down and turned out.

If the offensive man is moving in a lateral direction, the defensive stance is changed slightly by altering the

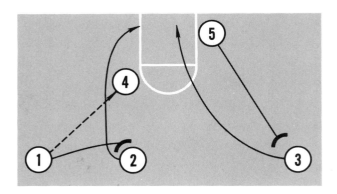

Fig. 4—13. Slow break—double post.

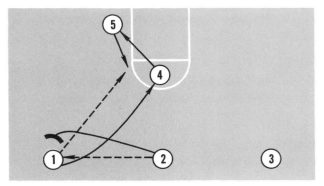

Fig. 4—14. Slow break—double post.

feet and the arms. It is started by placing the feet together, then moving either foot laterally until they are shoulder width apart. The position of the arms should change so that the elbows are close to the body, with the forearm held 90° to the upper arm, the palm of the hand facing the opponent and the extending fingers pointing laterally, left and right.

The head, shoulders, and back should be in a straight line, with the weight on the balls of the feet, heels on the floor.

Points to remember: The player should not stand flat-footed at any time. He should play his opponent in a position where the opponent can be blocked as he cuts for the basket. One hand should be kept up to block the shot, and one hand down and out to block or intercept a pass. He should try to force the opponent to shoot from "outside" or from the sidelines.

Always be in a position to see your man and the ball.

Drills

1. The guard stands, holding the ball, in the free-throw area near the foul line. The offensive player stands midway between the foul line and the center of the court. The drill starts when the guard throws the ball to the offensive player, who attempts to score while the defensive man attempts to guard him.

2. At least five players form a circle with a diameter of 12 feet. As the ball is passed around the circle, the player in the middle tries to intercept or touch the ball.

3. Players form two parallel lines extending across the court, facing a man out in front who has the ball. The man with the ball starts to dribble and move in any direction. As he moves about with the ball, the others respond as if they were guarding. If the dribbler moves forward, the lines retreat; if the dribbler moves backward, the lines advance; if he moves to the right or left, the lines move likewise.

4. A defensive man is placed midway between two offensive men who are 10 feet apart. The offensive players pass the ball back and forth while the defensive player attempts to gain possession of the ball. The offensive players are permitted one step in any direction in passing the ball. They are not allowed to arch the ball over the defensive player's head. The defensive player moves in a lateral direction only in attempting to gain possession of the ball. When he deflects or gains possession of the ball, he exchanges places with the player who passed the ball.

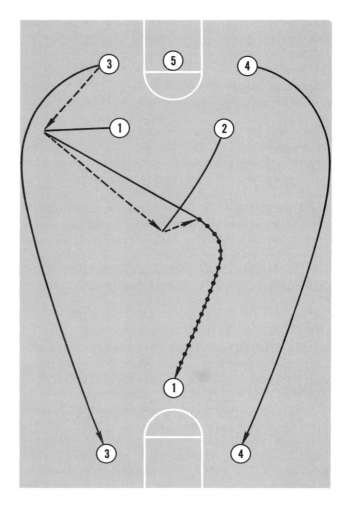

Fig. 4—15. Fast break.

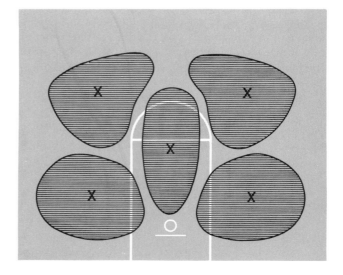

Fig. 4—16. Zone defense, court coverage.

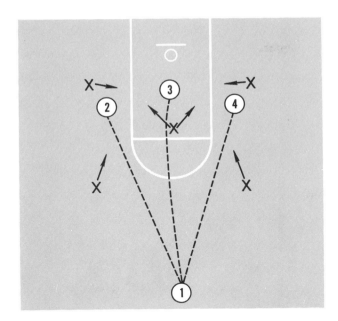

Fig. 4—17.

Movements of players in zone, ball in middle.

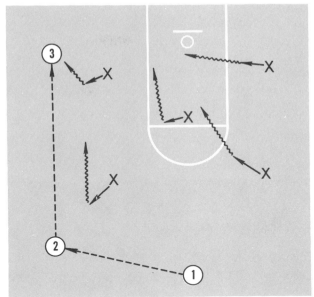

Fig. 4—18.

Movements of players in zone, ball to corner.

Team Defense

Team defense is either man-to-man, zone, or a combination of man-to-man and zone.

Man-to-man defense is executed by each defense man staying with and guarding an opponent. A basic rule, in general, for man-to-man defense is to stay between the basket and the offensive man at all times. *Points to consider:* (1) In man-to-man defense it is possible to match speed with speed and skill with skill. (2) Screens and blocks are effective against man-to-man defense. (3) There is a tendency to commit more personal fouls when using this type of defense. (4) The movements of the defensive player about the floor are determined by the movements of the offensive players.

In the zone defense the defensive player is assigned a specific area which he must cover and protect (Fig. 4-16). In a zone the team works as a unit, and at all times the players keep their eyes on the ball and move about the floor as dictated by the movement of the ball.

If the ball is in the center of the court, the position of the defensive players in a zone defense is illustrated by Fig. 4-17.

If the ball is passed to a player in either corner, the players in a zone defense shift to that side, as illustrated in Fig. 4-18. The players move as indicated by straight lines when the ball moves from (1) to (2). When the ball moves from (2) to (3) the defensive players move as indicated by the crosshatched lines. If the ball is returned to the center of the court, the players return to the original position.

BIBLIOGRAPHY

Barnes, Mildred J., *Women's Basketball.* Boston: Allyn and Bacon, Inc., 1972.

Basketball Rules—A.A.U. New York: Amateur Athletic Union of the United States.

Basketball Rules—DGWS. Washington, D.C.: American Association for Health, Physical Education and Recreation.

Bennington, John, and Newell, Pete, *Basketball Methods.* New York: The Ronald Press Company, 1962.

Cooper, John M., and Siedentop, Daryl, *The Theory and Science of Basketball.* Philadelphia: Lea and Febiger, 1969.

Cousy, Bob, and Power, Frank, Jr., *Basketball: Concepts and Techniques.* Boston: Allyn and Bacon, Inc., 1970.

Jucker, Ed, *Cincinnati Power Basketball.* Englewood Cliffs, N.J.: Prentice-Hall, Inc., 1962.

McGuire, Frank, *Defensive Basketball.* Englewood Cliffs, N.J.: Prentice-Hall, Inc., 1959.

National Federation of State High School Athletic Associations, *Basketball Rules—High School.* Chicago: The Federation.

Official NCAA Basketball Guide. Phoenix, Ariz.: College Athletics Publishing Service, 349 East Thomas Road.

U.S. Naval Institute, *Basketball.* Annapolis: The Institute, 1943.

Wooden, John R., *Practical Modern Basketball.* New York: The Ronald Press Company, 1966.

Records indicate that forms of bowling may be traced back 7,000 years. Implements have been found in Egypt, dating as far back as 5,000 B.C., providing evidence that a game similar to the modern game was played. The game may also be traced in early times through Europe and northern Italy, where wooden balls replaced the spherical stones formerly used. Later the nine-pin game developed in Germany, with Martin Luther as a leading enthusiast. During this time the pins were set in a diamond shape and the basic rules of the game were developed. Records indicate that, after many years, a tenth pin was added and the pins were set in a triangular shape.

Bowling was brought to America by the Dutch, who settled in New Amsterdam, New York; the first alleys, which were outdoor clay strips, were established in 1623. In 1895 the American Bowling Congress was organized.

Today, bowling is the most popular indoor sport in the United States. More than 30 million participants bowl on more than 70,000 lanes each year.

TERMINOLOGY

Alley—The surface upon which the contest is played. It is usually made of maple at each end and pine in the center.

Anchor man—The last bowler on a team. This is usually the bowler who maintains the highest average.

Approach—That part of the lane upon which the bowler gets his body into position to release the ball. This area must be not less than 15 feet in length.

Baby-split—The 2-7 or 3-10 pins are left standing.

Balk—Crossing the foul line without delivering the ball.

Bed post—The 7-10 pins are left standing.

Big ears—The 4-6-7-10 pins remain after the delivery of the first ball.

Big fill—Knocking down at least eight pins on the first ball rolled.

Blind—The score awarded a team having an absent member. This score represents his "average score." Sometimes the award is limited to — (average score minus ten pins).

Blow—Any spare "leave" that is not converted.

Body English—Motions of the bowler's body after the ball has been released.

Bridge—The distance between the two finger holes in the ball.

Brooklyn—A ball that strikes the pins to the left of the head-pin.

CC—a 200 game.

Cherry—Knocking down the front or back pin in a spare leave.

Creeper—An excessively slow, rolling ball.

Double—Two successive strikes.

Double-ball—Rolling the second ball before the first ball has been returned.

Double-wood—One pin directly behind another in a spare leave.

Error—Failing to convert a spare leave.

Fast alley—A highly polished alley surface that will not allow a hook ball to perform correctly.

Foul—Any part of the foot, hand, or arm touches or crosses the foul line.

Frame—One-tenth of a game which is registered in the box on the score sheet.

Gutter ball—A ball that leaves the alley proper and falls into the channels.

Handicap—A method of predetermining extra points to an individual or team with a lower average.

Kingpin—The five pin.

Lane—Same as alley.

Lead-off—The first bowler in a team line-up.

Leave—Pins standing after the first ball has been rolled.

Line—A game which is ten frames.

Mark—Clearing the pins with the first or second ball. Making a strike or spare.

Miss—Not making a spare leave.

Open frame—Not making a strike or spare.

Pocket—The space between the 1-3 pins for a right-handed bowler, and the 1-2 pins for a left-handed bowler.

Railroad—A split.

Setup—The entire ten pins in triangular formation.

Shadow-ball—Practice bowling without aiming at any pins.

Sleeper—A pin hidden by another pin.

Spare—Clearing all ten pins with two balls.

Split—The first ball rolled leaves two or more pins standing, with the width of a pin between them. The headpin must be down.

Strike—Clearing all ten pins with one ball.

Strike pocket—Target for making a strike. The space between the 1-3 pins for right-handers; between the 1-2 pins for left-handers.

Tap—A pin or pins remain standing after a near-perfect hit.

Three-hundred—A perfect game consisting of 12 strikes.

Turkey—Three strikes in a row.

Woolworth—The 5-10 split.

Working-ball—A ball that creates a lot of action among the knocked down pins.

RULES

1. A line or game is composed of ten frames.
2. A player is entitled to roll two balls per frame unless a strike (pins cleared with one ball) is scored.
3. If a strike is made in the tenth frame, the bowler completes the game by rolling two more balls. When all pins are cleared with the second ball rolled in a frame, a spare is scored. If this occurs in the tenth frame, one extra ball is rolled.
4. It is a foul when any part of the bowler's foot, hand, or arm, while in contact with the alley, touches or crosses the foul line. The pins knocked down do not count as legal pin-fall, and all pins are reset. The foul shall count as a ball rolled by the player. In team play if there is negligence by the foul judge or if the automatic foul detector fails to function properly and a foul is noticeable by both team captains or by one or more members of each team, a foul shall be recorded.
5. A ball is declared dead when:
   a. One or more pins are missing from the setup.
   b. Any interference occurs before the ball reaches the pins.
   c. In team play a bowler rolls out of turn or bowls on the wrong lane.

If a dead ball is declared, the bowler must reroll the ball in question.
6. The following situations may occur where the ball rolled and pins cleared do not count:
   a. A ball rebounds from the rear cushion.
   b. A ball leaves the alley and returns to knock down pins.
   c. A foul is committed.

7. There shall be no unreasonable delay in the progress of a game.

SAFETY

Bowling Courtesy and Common Sense: Rules of conduct on and off the lanes in bowling are, like traffic rules, based mostly upon common courtesy. The best general rule is "consider the other fellow."

1. Assuming a heroic or "professional" pose on the approach does nothing to improve your score and wastes valuable time. Take all the time you need for a smooth accurate delivery, but don't monopolize the alley.
2. Give the other fellows a chance to bowl when you have completed your match. The score can be tallied just as easily for you and your opponent if you leave the alley area.
3. In bowling, as in traffic, the man on the right has the right-of-way. If he has taken his stance, wait until he completes his delivery before you start. The bowler on your left will do the same for you.
4. As soon as you have finished your delivery and follow-through, move away from the foul line. This courtesy allows the bowler next to you to make his approach without being distracted.
5. When the bowler ahead of you has completed his delivery and is stepping off the approach, you should be ready to take his place. Making him tell you it is your turn merely wastes time.
6. When a person is bowling with a particular ball, even if it is supplied by a bowling establishment, it is considered to be his personal property at that time. Don't use it without his consent.
7. Be considerate of the management and your fellow bowlers, and keep food and drinks out of the playing area.
8. Use regulation bowling shoes at all times. Improper shoes can hinder your form and scar the approach.
9. Before attempting to bowl, check the approach thoroughly for slippery or rough spots.
10. To guard against injury to your fingers and hands, pick your ball up from the outside and parallel to the ball rack return.

EQUIPMENT

The modern bowling lane has a 16-foot approach, ending at the foul line. The lane is 60 feet long from the foul line to the headpin or number one pin, and is usually constructed of maple and yellow pine or similar wood. The area upon which the pins are set is called the *pin-deck*. This area is 3 feet in length. At the extreme end of the lane is a drop-off called the *pit*.

The width of the lane is 42 inches. Along each side of the lane are semicircular channels called *gutters,* which are approximately 9 inches wide.

There are ten pins spotted on the pin-deck in a standard trianglar position, 12 inches apart.

The regulation tenpin is 15 inches high and 2-1/4 inches in diameter at the base. A regulation pin must not weigh more than 3 pounds 10 ounces, or less than 2 pounds 14 ounces.

The first pin is called the *headpin* or number one pin. The remaining pins are numbered consecutively in their specific rows from left to right.

The bowling ball is constructed of a mixture of natural and highly vulcanized rubber. A regulation bowling ball must not exceed 27 inches in circumference. The weight of the ball may range from 10 to a maximum of 16 pounds.

There is no specific regulation for the number of holes in the ball; however, today most balls are bored with either two or three finger holes of varying sizes. The three-finger-grip ball is the most popular.

For right-handed bowlers the shoes have a rubber sole on the right foot and a leather sole on the left foot. For left-handed bowlers the shoe soles are reversed.

SCORING

The score in bowling consists simply of the cumulative record of pins knocked down in each of ten frames. It is a means of comparing the performance of the bowlers within a possible perfect total score of 300. Each game or line consists of ten frames, with a maximum number of two balls rolled each frame. The total possible score in each frame is 30 points.

If a strike is made—all 10 pins with the first ball—a score of 10 in that frame, plus the number of pins cleared with the next two balls rolled, is recorded.

If a spare is made, a score of 10 in that frame, plus the number of pins cleared with the next ball rolled, is recorded.

If a strike or spare is not made, record the number of pins cleared from 0 to 9.

⊠ A Strike
⊘ A Spare
⑧ Pins cleared first ball

⑧ A Split
– A Miss
F A Foul

A Sample Game

1	2	3	4	5
7 2	9 –	F ⊘	9 ⊘	⊠
9	18	37	57	87

6	7	8	9	10
⊠	⊠	⑧ –	⊠	6 ⊘ 7
115	133	141	161	178

Frame 1. Seven pins on the first ball, leaving a spare leave. Player cleared two pins on second ball. A score of nine is written in frame 1.

Frame 2. Nine pins on the first ball. Player missed single pin. Add nine pins to count in frame 1.

Frame 3. A strike. Player fouled. The pins must be reset. Player cleared all 10 pins with second ball. A spare is recorded. Frame 3 cannot be scored because count on spare is not complete.

Frame 4. Nine pins on first ball. Frame 3 score can now be scored. A spare was made in frame 3; thus, the player gets ten pins plus count on next ball delivered, which was nine pins. The score of 19 pins added to the 18

pins in frame 2 is recorded in frame 3, for a total score of 37 pins. On the second ball delivered the player made the single pin for another spare. The count for frame 4 cannot be scored until the first ball is rolled in frame 5.

Frame 5. A strike. Frame 4 can now be scored. The spare in frame 4 counts 10 pins plus next ball delivered, which was 10 pins or a strike. The bowler is entitled to 20 pins added to 37, which is the score in frame 3. The score is 57. This frame is not complete because a strike counts 10 pins plus count on next two balls delivered.

Frame 6. A strike. Frames 5 and 6 are not completed for score yet. There is one more ball to be rolled before count can be made for frame 5. This frame has two more balls to be rolled before frame can be scored.

Frame 7. A strike. Frame 5 can now be scored with 30 pins. This is the maximum number of pins possible for any frame. The score for frame 5 is 87. Frame 6 now has 20 pins plus whatever count is made on next ball rolled. Frame 7 cannot be scored yet.

Frame 8. Eight pins on the first ball, leaving a split. Frame 6 can now be scored. Having had two deliveries after the sixth frame strike, the player is entitled to 28 pins in frame 6, for an accumulated score of 115. Frame 7 cannot be scored as count on this strike until the second ball has been rolled. Player misses both pins on second ball rolled. Frames 7 and 8 can now be scored. Frame 7 is entitled to 10 pins for making a strike, plus count on next two balls delivered in frame 8, which was a total of 8 pins. Therefore, a total of 18 pins is scored in frame 7. Since no strike or spare was made in frame 8, the player is entitled to the 8 pins made.

Frame 9. A strike. Frame cannot be scored until next two balls have been rolled.

Frame 10. Six pins on first ball rolled. On the next ball rolled, player clears remaining pins and is credited with a spare. Frame 9 can now be scored. A total of 20 pins is added to 141, which is recorded in frame 9. A spare has been made in the tenth frame. One ball will be rolled, and the number of pins cleared will be added to the 10 pins already received in frame 10 for making a spare. Player cleared 7 pins on this roll. Game is now complete. Final score is 178.

FUNDAMENTALS

Selecting Ball

The weight, size, placement of the holes, and number of holes bored in the ball are of prime importance in selecting the right ball (Fig. 5-1).

A three-finger hole ball is recommended because it is easiest to roll, and is especially recommended for beginners. The finger holes should be large enough to allow the fingers and thumb to slide out easily.

In order that the ball may be properly carried in the approach to the foul line, the span between the thumb and finger holes must be spaced correctly to fit the hand. To check for proper span, place the thumb deeply into the thumb hole, and place the palm of the hand on top of the ball naturally across the finger holes. For a correct span, the first joint of the middle and fourth fingers should extend a quarter inch beyond the inner edge of the holes. The two fingers are placed into the finger holes. If the span is correct, there should be no undue strain on the thumb or fingers when carrying the ball. When suspended in the hand, the ball should hang so that a pencil will fit snugly between the palm of the hand and the ball.

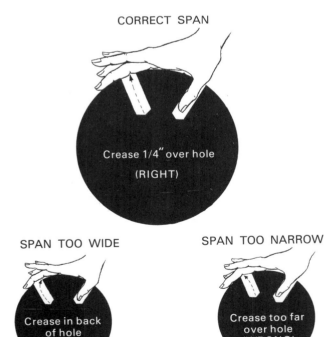

CORRECT SPAN

Crease 1/4" over hole
(RIGHT)

SPAN TOO WIDE

Crease in back
of hole
(WRONG)

SPAN TOO NARROW

Crease too far
over hole
(WRONG)

Fig. 5—1. Selecting the ball.

This is an excellent test for proper ball fit (span). If the span is too narrow or too wide, the ball will feel much heavier than it actually is.

The physical strength of the individual is also a factor in selecting the correct weight of the ball. A ball that is too heavy will cause the shoulder to drop and upset balance before releasing the ball.

The size, shape, and strength of the hands determine the *pitch,* which is the angle for the finger holes and the direction in which the holes are placed in relation to each other to assure comfort and control.

Grips

There are three common grips used by bowlers: the *conventional,* the *semifingertip,* and the *full-fingertip.*

For the beginner, the conventional grip is recommended. The thumb is completely inserted into the thumb hole, and the fingers are placed in the finger holes up to the second joint.

In the semifingertip grip, the thumb is inserted in the same manner, and the fingers reach to between the first and second joints in the finger holes.

In the full-fingertip grip, only the fingertips fit into the holes, with the thumb placed in the same manner as for the other grips.

The semifingertip and full-fingertip grips are used by more experienced bowlers because more spin can be placed on the ball.

Approach

The approach toward the foul line is a series of rhythmic and balanced walking steps, in coordination with body movement, arm swing, and finger position, which enables the bowler to place the ball into motion with a minimum of effort.

The steps taken in the approach vary from three to five. In the three-step and five-step approach, a preliminary step is taken with the left foot before the ball is placed into motion. The four-step approach is recommended for beginners because the ball and feet go into motion at the same time.

In the approach the bowler determines the starting point best suited, depending upon the individual's length of a natural step, so that every approach is the same.

Bowlers of average height should take a position approximately 12 to 15 feet back of the foul line. To determine a more accurate point, "pace off" from the foul line toward the end of the approach the desired number of steps plus a half step for the slide. Turn about and face the pins, with the shoulders parallel to the foul line.

Fig. 5—2. Four-step approach.

After the starting point has been determined, support the ball with the left hand and insert the thumb and fingers into the proper finger holes. Hold the ball waist-high, with the elbows firmly in as close to the body as is comfortable.

Stand fairly erect, with your feet together or one foot extended slightly forward. The knees should be flexed. The weight of the body should be evenly distributed over the feet. The eyes should be fixed directly on the target, which may be the pins or a set spot on the lane.

Four-step Approach (for right-handed bowlers) (Fig. 5-2)

After the stance has been assumed, shuffle forward beginning with a short half step with the right foot and push the ball naturally forward and downward in a smooth motion, removing the left hand (the left arm now acts as a counterbalance for the ball in the right hand) from the ball. Continue the forward motion of the body as the left foot shuffles forward with a slightly longer step than the first step. The body is now leaning forward, with the knees slightly bent as forward momentum increases. The ball begins the arc to the rear, and reaches the lowest point in the backswing when the weight of the body has been transferred to the left foot. The path of the ball continues in an arc as a step is taken with the right foot. The arm, acting as a pendulum, swings free at the shoulder, with the wrist and the elbow locked in a straight line. After reaching the highest point (no higher than shoulder level) in the backswing, the ball begins the forward motion and the body weight moves forward. At the same time the left foot comes forward and executes a short slide. The left foot and the ball come to the foul line at the same time. The ball passes close to the left ankle and is lifted smoothly and naturally over the foul line 6 inches out on the lane. The thumb comes out of the ball a "split second"

sooner than the fingers as the ball is released. The right arm continues a forward swing, with a straight arm to shoulder level. The shoulders are parallel to the foul line and the left toe is pointed straight forward toward the target.

Releasing the Ball

There are three types of releases, each of which results in a different action of the ball: *straight ball, hook ball,* or *curve ball* (Fig. 5-3). The release has a marked effect upon the direction of the ball and the ultimate devastating action upon the pins.

The Straight Ball

The straight ball is generally best suited for beginners. Aiming for the strike pocket, the bowler rolls a straight ball from an angle near the right side of the approach. To roll a straight ball, the bowler makes his thumb and index finger form a "V," with the thumb at a 12-o'clock position. This hand position is assumed in the stance and is maintained throughout the approach. The wrist is straight and firm, with no wrist twist in the push-away, backswing, forward swing, or follow-through. During the follow-through the palm is opened upward, with the thumb and fingers pointing toward the target.

The Hook Ball

The hook ball is the most effective type of release because the action of the ball as it spins at an angle into the strike pocket creates greater pin action. When rolling for the strike pocket, the bowler releases a hook ball 6 to 8 inches from the right gutter and well out on the lane. In the hook ball release, the thumb is placed at a 10-o'clock position. The fingers impart the spin with a sharp lift. For this reason, the thumb must come out of the thumb hole before the lift is made. As

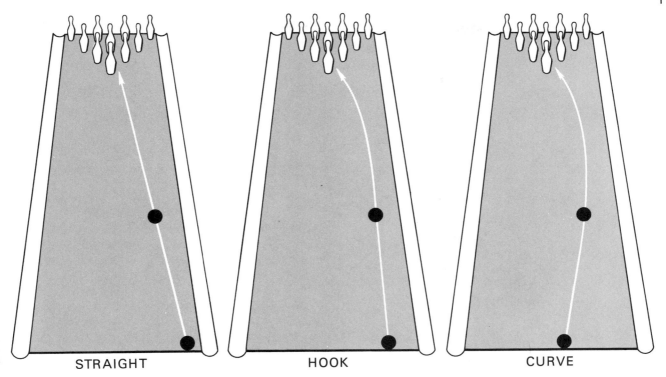

STRAIGHT   HOOK   CURVE

Fig. 5—3. Action of the ball.

with the straight ball, the position of the hand and ball should remain the same from the stance through the approach. The amount of hook may be increased by a stronger lift and a higher pull at the point of release.

The Curve Ball

There is very little distinction between the hook ball and curve ball. There is more striking power in the curve ball; however, it is much more difficult to control than a hook ball because of the marked arc as it rolls down the lane. The curve ball is released slightly to the right of the center mark of the lane, and rolls out to the right and then left to form a wide arc to the strike pocket.

To roll the curve ball, hold the thumb at the 9-o'clock position and apply much more spin-lift with the fingers upon the ball at the time of release.

"Picking Up" Spares

Getting a strike is the primary objective in bowling; however, no one gets a strike every time. To be a better than average bowler, it is absolutely necessary to convert spare leaves.

In making a spare leave, the fundamental rule is to angle across the lane or use most of the width of the

lane. If pins remain on the left side, start the ball from the right-hand side of the approach. For a spare leave on the right side, roll the ball from the left side of the approach. When a spare leave involves the number five pin or middle cluster of pins, roll from a strike position.

The bowler's type of release and number of pins left standing determine the degree of angle necessary to convert the spare. The fundamentals of the stance, approach, and release are the same regardless of the spare leave.

Aiming

When the fundamentals, timing, and rhythm of the approach have been thoroughly mastered and the ball is released at the same place and in the same direction every time, the bowler is ready to concentrate on aiming. There are three common methods of aiming: *spot, pin,* and *line bowling.*

Spot Bowling. In using this method of aiming, the bowler selects a specific target near the foul line or a short distance beyond it on the lane, then aims the ball to roll over the target. During the approach, the bowler sees no part of the pins; the eyes are fixed

firmly on the target spot. One advantage in spot bowling is that the bowler may find it easier to roll over a spot 12 feet away from his eyes than out 60 feet, which is the distance of the pins.

If the ball goes to the right or left of the target, it will be necessary either to move the target spot or to change the position at the foul line where the ball is released.

Pin Bowling. The theory of pin bowling is simple. Instead of aiming at a target spot, which is a close-range sighting, the bowler sets his sight 60 feet down the lane at the final target, which is the pin or pins to be cleared. This means fixing the eyes on the target while establishing an imaginary line from the stance to the target.

Line Bowling. Line Bowling is defined as modified spot and pin bowling. Any number of targets may be selected. An imaginary line is drawn through the selected targets, which might be a point at the foul line, another halfway down the lane, and another at the base of the pin or pins to be cleared. The objective is to roll the ball over each spot. If the ball fails to cross any spot, the bowler must adjust the starting point or select a new set of targets.

Points to Remember:

1. It is not necessary to keep score each time one bowls.
2. Practice correct fundamentals, and the score will take care of itself.
3. Experiment with the stance, approach, release, and follow-through to determine what is best for you as an individual.
4. Concentrate and work on one point at a time; master it and move to the next fundamental.
5. Any style of personal clothing worn should allow complete freedom of movement.
6. Selection of a correctly fitting ball is a "must."

It Is Important:

1. To develop proper mechanical habits in the stance, push-away, backswing, forward swing, and follow-through.
2. To check the starting point and use the same spot each time.
3. To keep the shoulders parallel to the foul line during the approach.
4. To walk in a straight line in the approach to the foul line.
5. To keep the wrist and arm straight during the backswing and forward swing.
6. To check the timing in the approach so that the left foot and ball come to the foul line at the same time.

7. To take the thumb out of the ball a split second before the fingers in the release.
8. To place the ball out on the lane six inches beyond the foul line.
9. To concentrate on a straight-arm follow-through to shoulder level.
10. To determine the target and keep the eyes fixed on that spot, whether it be pin, spot, or line bowling.
11. To learn to keep score as soon as possible.
12. To play safe—consider the other fellow, too.

BIBLIOGRAPHY

Bellisimo, Lou, *The Bowler's Manual.* Englewood Cliffs, N.J.: Prentice-Hall, Inc., 1965.

Casady, Donald R., and Liba, Maria R., *Beginning Bowling.* Belmont, Calif.: Wadsworth Publishing Co., 1962.

Day, Ned, and Raymer, Milton, *Bowling, Instructor's Guide.* Chicago: The Athletic Institute, 1953.

Martin, Joan, *Bowling.* Dubuque, Iowa: Wm. C. Brown Company, Publishers, 1966.

McMahon, Junie, and Goodman, Murray, *Modern Bowling Techniques.* New York: The Ronald Press Company, 1958.

National Bowling Council, *The Guide to Teaching Bowling.* Chicago: The Council.

Raymer, Milton, *The Teaching of Class Room Bowling.* Chicago: Spencer-Walker Press, 1958.

The first record we have of boxing is that it was part of the ancient Greek Olympian games of about 900 B.C. There were few rules, but sportsmanship was one of the guiding principles.

At first, hand wraps were used to protect the fighter's hands. However, when the peoples of the Roman Empire made men fight for the enjoyment of spectators, the fighters used spiked metal covers on their hands so that they could permanently injure or kill an opponent.

When boxing came to England during the seventeenth century, it developed into a more acceptable sport, though it was still brutal. This was the bare-knuckle era of boxing. The introduction of the Broughton Code in 1743, and the Marquis of Queensbury Rules in 1865, helped make boxing a sportsmanlike activity.

Boxing came to America from England and, though very popular, was still a brutal sport. The last bare-knuckle fight of any importance in the United States occurred in Mississippi between John L. Sullivan and Jack Kilrain in 1889. In 1892, John L. Sullivan and James J. Corbett fought the first world heavyweight championship fight in which boxing gloves were used. James Corbett won by a knockout in 21 rounds. From these beginnings, gloved boxing has evolved into the sport as we know it today.

TERMINOLOGY

Blocking—Catching the opponent's punch on your hand, shoulder, or arm.

Combination—Throwing two or more punches in sequence.

Countering—Striking an opponent who has thrown a punch.

Ducking—Lowering the body by bending the knees and dropping the hips. (The boxer may also bend forward at the waist at the same time.)

Feinting—A movement of the shoulders, head, hands, hips, or feet that is designed to confuse the opponent or move him into a position so that a punch can be landed.

Guarding—Any motion which is made to avoid a punch.

Kidney punch—Any punch which is delivered from behind the area of the kidneys.

Leading—Initiating the offensive action by striking with either hand.

Neutral corner—A corner which does not belong to either contestant.

On-guard position—The basic offensive and defensive position in boxing.

Parrying—Redirecting an opponent's punch with the hand or arm.

Rabbit punch—Any punch which is delivered to the back of the neck.

Rolling—Moving the head or body with a punch in order to reduce the force.

Shadow boxing—Fighting an imaginary opponent. This is valuable when done in front of a mirror because the boxer can see his strong and weak points.

Slipping—Moving the head to the side in order to avoid a punch. This is the most desirable method of avoiding a punch, since it places the fighter in an excellent position to launch his own offensive.

Striking—Hitting an opponent by using one of the punches in boxing.

Telegraphing—Any movement a fighter makes that informs his opponent of his intended action.

Throwing a punch—Directing a blow toward an opponent by using one of the punches in boxing.

SAFETY

1. The ring floor must be adequately padded with material having great resiliency. Gloves must also be padded.
2. Sixteen-ounce gloves should be used for class purposes.
3. To protect the teeth and jaw, a custom-fitted mouth-piece should be used.
4. Head gear is comprised of a padded face mask and chin guard.
5. Obtain medical aid at once for any injuries.

6. *Remember:* It is not necessary that the knockout be an objective in amateur boxing, or that any bodily harm befall a contestant. Boxing is a test of skill, as are other sports.

SKILLS

On-Guard Position

The on-guard position is fundamental to all offensive and defensive maneuvers in boxing. (The positions described are for the right-handed boxer.)

Technique:

1. Stand in an erect position, with the feet set about shoulder width apart.
2. Raise your right hand until it is in front of the right side of the chin. Keep the hand loosely open, in order that it may be used defensively to catch or deflect punches.
3. Step forward with your left foot until the legs are spread a comfortable distance from front to back. (This distance will vary because of the difference in height of each individual.)
4. Toe in slightly with the left foot. This enables you to keep your balance when you throw your right hand.
5. Make a fist with the left hand. Put the fist against the top of your left thigh, with the little finger touching the top of the thigh. Raise the fist until it is just above shoulder height.
6. Turn the shoulders on a diagonal with the opponent (either imaginary or real).
7. Lower your head so that, as you look at the center of the opponent's chest, you are seeing it from the top of your eyes. When your head is in this position, it is between the shoulders and is therefore not vulnerable. Looking at the opponent's chest enables you to see all of your opponent without dwelling on any one point, and reduces the possibility of your being feinted.

Footwork

The basic principle in footwork is: first, move the foot which is closest to the direction in which the boxer intends to move, e.g., forward—move front foot first. Move from one place to another by sliding the feet across the surface of the floor. The boxer should move 8 inches or less each time he slides his feet. Each time the basic foot position is disturbed, it should be restored immediately. Care should be taken not to get the feet any closer together than they are in the original on-guard position.

Fundamentals of Punching

There is a saying that "you punch with the seat of your pants," which means that this is where the punch originates. In delivering a punch, the hips are rotated in the direction of the punch an instant before the arm moves out. The whiplike effect of this action gives a punch its tremendous speed and power. In other words, the hips are like the handle, the shoulders like the middle, and the fist like the end of the whip. It is important for the boxer to be sure that the hips and shoulders rotate only slightly ahead of the release of the arm.

As the punch begins, the feet must be in a firm position on the floor so that the boxer's balance is good and none of the power from the blow "leaks out" through the feet. The foot pivot is made on the balls of the feet. The feet pivot with, and in the same direction as, the hips when any punch is thrown.

When a straight punch is thrown, care should be taken not to raise the elbow to the side because such action reduces the force of the blow. It is well to have a beginner rotate his hand only 45 degrees when throwing a straight punch; unless one has had much practice, the elbow will go to the outside, thus losing power and driving across the target rather than straight through it. Rotating the fist 90 degrees (palm down) would surely cause the inexperienced boxer to move his elbow **too far to the outside.**

Punch *through* the target instead of at the target.

From a defensive point of view, it is important to remember that when a punch is thrown, the shoulders pivot, but the head remains in its original position, with the shoulder protecting the chin from possible counterattack by the opponent. In other words, the shoulders move around the head.

Straight Left to the Head (left jab and left lead)

Technique:

1. Assume the on-guard position.
2. Start the punch by pivoting the hips in a clockwise direction.
3. **Pivot the shoulders in the same direction as the hips immediately after the hip pivot has started.**
4. Extend the left arm straight from the shoulder immediately after the shoulder pivot. The palm of the fist is rotated so that it is at a 45-degree angle to the floor (90-degree angle for advanced students).
5. Bring the left arm straight back to its original position quickly or keep punching with a combination of blows. Do not drop the left hand while returning it to the original position. This action

would allow the opponent to throw a countering right hand to the head.

Straight Left to the Body

The straight left is thrown to the body in the same manner in which it is thrown to the head, with one exception. The knees are bent far enough to place the left shoulder on a level with the target. Punches thrown at the body are usually directed at the pit of the stomach, which is located in the center of the abdominal region just below the rib cage.

Left Hook to the Head

The left hook, the right hook, the left uppercut, and the right uppercut are bent-arm blows. The most important principle to remember in the execution of these punches is that of range: the boxer must be close to his opponent in order to throw a bent-arm blow effectively. This is true because if, for instance, a boxer initiates the hook with his striking hand at a distance greater than approximately one foot from his chest, he loses much power and leverage.

The left hook, the straight left, and the straight right are the most important punches in boxing. The left hook has a great deal of power and is, generally speaking, an easier punch to land than the straight right, since it is thrown with the lead hand. For these reasons the left hook must be developed and refined by anyone wishing to become a skilled boxer.

Technique:

1. Assume the on-guard position.
2. Start the pivot of the hips.
3. Raise the left elbow to the outside so that the left forearm is almost parallel to the floor and the palm of the fist is toward the face. The left elbow is in a slightly lowered position so that the force of the punch is not only from the side, but slightly upward as well.
4. Simultaneous with this action, pivot the hips slightly, then the shoulders. When the shoulder pivot is approximately half through, release the arm and hand and terminate the punch with a quarter turn of the hips and shoulders. The hand continues on for about 6 inches so that the principle of punching through the target is followed.

Left Hook to the Body

The left hook is thrown to the body in the same manner that it is thrown to the head, except that the knees are bent in order to put the left shoulder on a level with the target.

Right Hook to the Head

The right hook is thrown in almost the same manner as the left hook, the difference in the punches being the distance the feet are allowed to pivot. Since the left leg is in a position in front of the right, the pivot from right to left is limited. The right foot may pivot about 25 degrees toward the left, while the left foot may pivot very little. It will be remembered that in the on-guard position the left foot is toed in slightly to enable the boxer to stay on balance when throwing the right hand. If, while throwing the right hand, the boxer does not keep the left foot toed in slightly, he defeats the fundamental principle of balance. For this reason, while throwing the right hook or straight right, the left foot pivots only slightly.

Right Hook to the Body

The right hook is thrown to the body in the same manner as to the head, except that the knees are bent enough to place the shoulder on the same level as the target.

Left Uppercut

The uppercut is usually thrown to the body, and only occasionally to the head. This is a powerful punch and difficult to block. The boxer should be conscious of the fact that when he prepares to throw an uppercut, part of his head is left in a vulnerable position because the left hand has been lowered to a position at waist level. If a counterpunch by an opponent is thrown to the head before the uppercut is thrown, the boxer should evade the blow by putting the free hand (in the case of a left uppercut, the right) across the face to catch the blow; by slipping the blow; or by catching the blow on his shoulder.

Technique:

1. Assume the on-guard position.
2. Drop the left hand, palm up, until the forearm is parallel to the floor.
3. Bend the knees slightly, simultaneously with the action in #2. This will enable the boxer to "lift" into the punch.
4. Throw the punch by pivoting the hips about one-eighth of a turn, whipping the arm up (while leaving the elbow joint bent at 90 degrees) and lifting with the legs.

Right Uppercut

The right uppercut is thrown in the same manner as the left uppercut, except that it is the right hand that delivers the punch while the left hand protects the head from a countering left-hand blow.

Straight Right to the Head

In most instances the straight right to the head is the strongest punch a boxer possesses. However, it is true that some boxers punch as hard, or harder, with the left hook. Perhaps the greatest mistake made in throwing the straight right hand is to restrict the movement of the left shoulder. When the right hand is thrown, the left shoulder must be allowed to move back in order to complete the shoulder pivot. A good rule to use in throwing the straight right is that anything that can be reached with the left hand can be hit with the right hand, since the shoulders change position when the right hand is thrown.

Technique:

1. Assume the on-guard position.
2. Start the hip pivot toward the left, follow with the shoulders, the arm, and hand in order to get the whiplike effect from the punch.
3. Make the hand into a fist as it approaches the target. The palm of the fist is rotated so that it is at a 45-degree angle with the floor on contact with the target (90 degrees for advanced students).

One of the more skilled maneuvers in boxing can be used when throwing the straight right to the head in combination with the straight left or the left hook. The straight left is thrown to the head. As the left arm starts to recoil, the boxer slides his left foot slightly to the left and forward, which puts the right shoulder directly on line with the target. From this position the right hand is thrown to the head.

The straight right is thrown under three circumstances: in combination with the left, as a counter punch, or after having feinted the opponent into an opening. Occasionally this punch is thrown as a lead. This may prove disastrous, however, since the man throwing it is open for a countering left hook or right to the head from his opponent.

Straight Right to the Body

The straight right is delivered to the body in the same manner as to the head, with one exception. The knees are bent in order to put the right shoulder on the same level as the target.

Basic Defensive Techniques

There are many defensive moves that one must know in order to become a good boxer. The use of these moves varies with the type of offensive punch.

Defense Against Straight Punches to the Head

1. *Slipping the Punch:* Move the head and trunk slightly right or left without twisting the body, causing the opponent's punch to go past the side of the head. This maneuver is the most desirable of all defensive tactics, since the body is left in proper position for immediate offensive action.
2. *Ducking the Punch:* Bend the knees, thus lowering the level of the head. The body may also be bent forward at the waist. Keep the hands high in order to avoid further punches that might be aimed at the head. Keep your eyes on your opponent.
3. *Parrying the Punch:* As the opponent punches, redirect the blow by flicking the opponent's glove as it nears the head. Blows to the head are parried by lightly slapping the approaching glove aside with a snap of the wrist. If the opponent punches with the right hand, the parry is with the left, and vice versa.

Defense Against Straight Punches to the Body

1. *Parrying the Punch:* As the opponent punches, lightly tap the blow aside using the inside of the elbow As the elbow moves inward, the hand remains in the original on-guard position. The parry should be made just before the opponent's glove reaches the midsection. If the opponent punches with the right hand, the parry is with the left, and vice versa.
2. *Blocking the Punch:* To block straight punches to the body, hold the elbow close to the side of the body to which the blow is directed and rotate the body slightly so the impact of the blow is caught directly on the protecting arm. If the opponent punches with the right hand, the block is with the left, and vice versa.

Defense Against Hooks to the Head

1. *Ducking the Punch:* Use the same technique as described for ducking straight punches to the head.
2. *Slipping the Punch:* To slip inside a hook, move the head and body slightly forward by bending at the waist. Greater success may be obtained by also sliding forward slightly with the front foot. This causes the punch to pass behind the head. To slip outside the punch, bend slightly backward at the

waist. In this case, the stride may be lengthened by sliding the back foot backward, causing the punch to pass in front of the head. In the event that the offensive boxer should continue to hook when the defensive boxer bends backward, the defensive boxer should launch a counterattack, slip to one side or the other, or clinch. It is extremely dangerous to be caught between the hooking hands of the offensive man when pulling back from a hook.

3. *Blocking the Punch:* A properly directed hook to the head will always approach from the side. To block these punches, cup the hand, fingers resting slightly above the temple, elbow extended slightly away from the body. The blow should strike the back of the hand, and the hand and wrist should serve as a spring to absorb the force of the blow. If the opponent punches with the right hand, the block is with the **left, and** vice versa.

Defense Against Hooks to the Body

In order to remain in the proper position for launching an immediate counterattack, move the hips backward quickly, with the feet remaining stationary. Blocking hooks to the body places the defensive man in a poor position to counter quickly. The clock is made in the same manner as that used in defense against straight punches.

Defense Against Uppercuts

As in the defense against hooks, the best defense against uppercuts is pulling back from the punch and maintaining a good offensive stance. To block the uppercut, chop downward briskly with the forearm and glove as the blow approaches the body. The block should be made with the left arm for right uppercuts—the right arm for left uppercuts.

AMATEUR RULES

The Ring

The ring must be at least 18 feet square. The ring apron must extend at least 2 feet beyond the ropes. Ropes, posts, and turnbuckles must be padded. There must be a 2-inch thick felt padding between the canvas and ring floor.

The Boxing Gloves

The weight of the boxing gloves varies according to the weight of the boxer and the organization sponsoring the competition. The thumb should be attached to the glove with a leather web.

Handwraps

The contestant may use no more than 10 yards of gauze per hand.

Rounds

There will be three rounds of 2 minutes' duration, with a 1-minute rest between rounds.

Officials
Referee

1. The referee votes at the conclusion of a bout if he is the only official, or if there are one or two judges. If there are three judges, the referee does not vote.
2. The referee may stop a bout at any time if he considers it to be too one-sided.
3. He may deduct points for rule infractions.
4. He may disqualify a contestant who fouls and award the bout to his opponent.

Judges

1. The judges watch the bout and record their decisions by rounds.
2. Judges may deduct points only when instructed to do so by the referee.

Timekeeper

1. The timekeeper indicates the beginning and end of each round by ringing a gong or bell.
2. He sounds a buzzer or blows a whistle to indicate there are 10 seconds before the beginning of the next round.

Scorer

1. The scorer checks the score slips for addition and designates the winner.
2. In event of an error, he returns the card to the person making the error. If, however, the error has no bearing on the outcome of the contest, he makes the correction himself and initials the correction. After checking the referee's and/or judges' slips, the scorer gives the results to the announcer to broadcast.

Medical Officer

The medical officer has absolute medical supervision of the contestants. If, in his opinion, a man should not continue, he shall disqualify him and stop the match.

At the conclusion of the matches, all contestants shall be re-examined by the medical officer.

Weight Classifications

Flyweight—112 lbs.
Bantamweight—119 lbs.
Featherweight—125 lbs.
Lightweight—132 lbs.
Light-welterweight—139 lbs.
Welterweight—147 lbs.
Light-middleweight—156 lbs.
Middleweight—165 lbs.
Light-heavyweight—178 lbs.
Heavyweight—over 178 lbs.

In order to compete in a weight classification, the boxer must weigh more than the class limit below, but no more than the maximum limit for the division in which he desires to compete.

Scoring

Ten points are available to the winner of each round. The loser shall receive less than ten points.

Point Allotment. Points shall be given for (a) attack and defense; (b) ring generalship; (c) aggressiveness.

Fouls

The referee may disqualify a fighter for fouling, or he may deduct points from his score. (If points are deducted, the referee must make it clear to all concerned that this has been done, so that the judges do likewise.)

Specific Fouls:

a. Holding opponent while hitting him.
b. Holding a clinch.
c. Failing to break clean from a clinch.
d. Pushing or butting with head, shoulder, or knee.
e. Hitting with the open glove.
f. Hitting with the heel of the hand, wrist, or elbow.
g. Wrestling at the ropes.
h. Striking from behind at the area of the kidney.
i. Rabbit punching.
j. Striking the opponent while holding the ropes.
k. A coach or second giving advice to a contestant during a round.

Down

A boxer is down when any part of his body other than the feet is touching the floor. When a contestant is down, his opponent must go to the farthest neutral corner of the ring.

A contestant being knocked down must remain there until the count of nine.

When a "down" contestant does not resume boxing before the ten count, the match is over.

These rules are generally accepted. However, there are minor differences in the several states, and among different organizations.

DRILLS

1. *Learning the Punches:* While learning the punches, the contestants should punch into one another's gloves, which are held in the proximity of the target area; e.g., if the punch is thrown to the head, the open glove is held to the side of the head. When punching into his partner's glove, a contestant should take his on-guard position relative to the target (glove), not the head of his partner.

2. *Learning the Defenses:* When learning the defenses, the man who is throwing the punch should punch only to the target, not through it. The defensive boxer is told which defense to use. The offensive boxer is told which punch to throw. The several defensive maneuvers for each punch are practiced in this manner.

3. *Controlled Boxing:* When men are learning to box, it is good practice to designate one man as the offensive boxer and the other as defensive, or to have both men on both offense and defense. The men should be cautioned to punch *to*, not *through*, the target.

BIBLIOGRAPHY

Boxing Rules—AAU. New York: Amateur Athletic Union of the United States.
Haislet, Edwin L., *Boxing.* New York: A.S. Barnes & Co., 1940.
LaFonde, G.V., and Menendez, J., *Better Boxing.* New York: The Ronald Press Company, 1959.
The Official NCAA Boxing Guide. New York: National Collegiate Athletic Bureau.
Silks, Donald K., *Boxing for Boys.* New York: Alfred A. Knopf, Inc., 1953.
Simmons, Roy D., and others, *Boxing.* Annapolis: United States Naval Institute, 1950.

DIVING | 7

Springboard diving offers an exhilarating thrill to the diver. It is a combination of skill and grace performed in the act of entering the water. It has aesthetic values for the performer and for the spectator. This section gives an introduction to the fundamentals of springboard diving.

Diving boards in years past were constructed of wood. However, aluminum boards in use today are much more flexible and require more balance and control. The AAU standard length of a diving board is from 14 to 16 feet. The AAU standard height for a springboard, from the upper side of the tip down to the surface of the water, is one meter (3-1/3 feet) for a low board, and three meters (10 feet) for a high board.

Just as a person should learn to swim before he takes up diving, he should learn to dive from a stationary low height before attempting to dive from a springboard.

Standing Forward Dive (with bend at hips)

Starting Position. Assume a standing position at the end of the board, toes hooked over the edge, arms extended forward at shoulder height and shoulder width, palms down, and fingers together. The head is held high, with the eyes looking straight ahead.

Take-off. The take-off is tarted by bringing the arms downward until the palms touch the thighs. From this point the arms are raised sideward to shoulder level as the diver rises on the balls of his feet. After a brief pause, the arms swing downward as the knees and ankles bend. This action depresses the board. As the hands in the swing approach the thighs, they are redirected forward and upward, shoulder width apart. The reach of the arms is coordinated with the straightening out of ankles and knees. The body extension adds extra height to the lift from the upswing of the board after it has been depressed.

Flight. The arms reach upward as the feet leave the board. The body should not be off-balance in a forward lean as it takes off. The lift is more upward and slightly outward. The arms should continue to reach upward until the body almost attains the peak of its lift. At this point, the hips and legs continue to rise while the body bends at the hips. The bend increases until the outstretched palms touch the extended ankles. This bending motion turns the direction of the dive from upward to downward. As the body approaches the water, it straightens.

Entry. For the entry, the line of flight should be at an angle of approximately 80 degrees to the surface. The body position for the entry should be with legs together and straight, toes pointed, upper arms pressing the ears, and hands together, thumbs interlocked. Muscles, especially of the torso, are tensed for the impact with the water surface, and this tenseness should continue for several feet below the surface until the legs and feet are well underwater.

A good dive carries the diver at least ten feet below the surface. While the diver is underwater, he breaks from the entry position as he approaches the bottom by lifting the head, separating the hands, spreading the fingers, and bending the hands back until the palms are almost parallel with the bottom. At about the time the hands contact the bottom, the knees are drawn toward the chest in a tucking action. The feet are placed on the bottom near the hands, so that the body is standing on the bottom in a crouching position. The hands are then lifted toward the face. The diver pushes from the bottom, reaching the hands upward and forward toward the surface.

Running Forward Dive from Springboard

Approach. The approach to the end of the board is an accelerated walk. The approach should have at least three walking steps and a jump to the end of the board. The last movement, called the "hurdle," is a lift of the body into the air.

Starting Position. To determine the starting position on the board, the diver stands with heels at the for-

ward end of the board and takes three natural walking steps and a jump toward the back end of the board. This spot on the board serves as a starting point for the diver in executing a running forward dive.

Stance. After the starting position has been determined, assume a stance with the heels together, flat on the board. Hold the heels as near each other as the formation of the body permits. Keep the knees straight without stiffness. Hold the hips level, body erect, chest lifted and arched, shoulders square and even. Let the arms hang straight down without stiffness, palms touching the thighs. with fingers together. Keep the head erect, chin drawn in so that the axis of the head and neck is vertical, with the eyes focused on the board's forward end.

The Walk. The diver starts the approach by stepping forward on either foot. However, the first step should be taken with the foot with which the diver can jump

the highest, because this same foot will be used for the "hurdle" step to the end of the board. In this illustration, he will begin with the left foot.

When the stance has been assumed, the diver takes a short step forward on the left foot, placing his heel and toe in sequence as in a normal walk, allowing the arms to move forward together. As the right foot comes forward, the stride is smooth and increases in length and intensity. The arms are moving backward together. As the left foot comes forward, the leg presses the board downward. The arms begin to extend upward, straight up and shoulders width apart. The right leg is bent, with the toes pointed. The body is lifted, or thrust, into the air. At the peak of the "hurdle," the diver glances at the end of the board to see that he will land safely and correctly as he descends from the "hurdle." During the descent, he gradually raises the eyes so that he is looking straight ahead when his feet come into contact with the board. At about the same time the feet touch the board, both arms are brought down sideward vigorously to press the board downward.

Flight and Entry. The flight and entry depend upon the dive being executed. There are four positions in which a diver may carry his body through the air: (1) tuck, (2) pike, (3) layout, and (4) free.

Tuck Position. The body is balled up, with the knees and hips bent, legs together, and hands holding on to the legs near the shins.

Pike Position. The legs are together, knees straight, and hips bent.

Layout Position. The body is straight and legs together.

Free Position. Any combination of the pike and layout positions.

Back Dive from Springboard

Starting Position. The diver takes a position facing the back end of the board. The heels extend away from the board, with half the sole of each foot touching the board. The heels should not be raised, but level. The toes should be separated about two inches while the ankles barely touch. Arms are extended forward at shoulder height and shoulder width, fingers together, palms down. The head is held high, with the eyes focused on the back end of the board.

Take-off. The arms are lowered deliberately until the palms touch the thighs. The diver rises on his toes, the arms are raised slowly sideward to shoulder level. At this point the arms descend from the position sideward at shoulder level, the knees bend, and the body bends at the waist in a "coiling" or crouching position. As the arms move downward, they move behind an imaginary line through the hips. The arms gain momentum as they describe an arc back, down, and then forward. As the arms pass close to the legs and begin to go upward, the ankles, knees, and hips begin to uncoil. The body extends into the flight and the arms reach sideward as they rise upward and slightly back.

Flight. The head position changes very little during flight. The head is held steady until the diver has gone over the peak of his flight. A slight and slow backward movement of the head raises the feet high enough for the entry. The arms are carried in line with the shoulders until just before entry.

Entry. The arms are brought together, the thumbs interlocked, and the fingers crossed immediately prior to entry. The upper arms press the ears as the body tenses for the impact.

BIBLIOGRAPHY

American Association for Health, Physical Education and Recreation, *Official Aquatics Guide.* Washington, D.C.: The Association.

Armbruster, David A., Allen, Robert H., and Harlan, Bruce, *Swimming and Diving.* St. Louis: C.V. Mosby Co., 1958.

Clotworthy, Robert, *The Young Sportsman's Guide to Diving.* New York: Thomas Nelson and Sons, 1962.

Fairbanks, Anne Ross, *Teaching Springboard Diving.* Englewood Cliffs, N.J.: Prentice-Hall, Inc., 1963.

Harlan, Bruce, and Hayner, Roy R., *How to Teach Diving.* San Francisco: Millwood Press, 1959.

Moriarty, Phil, *Springboard Diving.* New York: The Ronald Press Company, 1958.

Official AAU Swimming Handbook. New York: The Amateur Athletic Union.

Official NCAA Swimming Guide. New York: The National Collegiate Bureau.

Total fitness is best achieved and maintained by combining specific exercises with sports and recreational activities. It is sometimes necessary, however, to rely on exercise alone if time and facilities become limiting factors.

LOCOMOTOR EXERCISES

The following program of exercises can serve as a starting point for an individual exercise program. Start by doing each exercise with slow cadence, according to the number of repetitions and time allotment indicated in the chart. Increase the tempo and number of repetitions gradually to assure a steady rise in the tolerance level of the body for these exercises. It is recommended that they be done at least every other day, and every day if possible.

Muscle soreness may develop; this is the normal reaction of a body unaccustomed to exercise. If muscle soreness persists more than two days after exercising, this is a warning that the body is not recovering from the stress placed on the muscle tissue. The exercise load should then be reduced, to give the body a chance to rest muscle tissue and rid itself of fatigue products that result from exercise.

A record should be kept of the increase in the number of repetitions for each of the seven exercises. As the number increases the cadence will quicken so that more repetitions are performed in the time originally allotted for each exercise. All seven exercises should be completed in a total time of thirteen minutes.

Alternate Toe Touches (Fig. 8—1)

Starting position: Assume a stride stand, with your arms out at shoulder level.

Action:

Count 1— Touch your right hand to the left foot, with your left arm back, and your legs straight.

Count 2— Return to the starting position.

Count 3— Touch the left hand to the right foot, with your right arm back, and your legs straight.

Count 4— Return to the starting position.

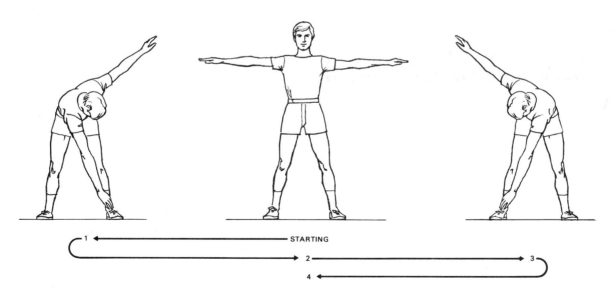

Fig. 8—1. Alternate toe touches.

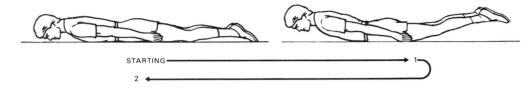

Fig. 8—2. Chest and leg raises.

Chest and Leg Raises (Fig. 8—2)

Starting position: Lie prone, with your legs straight and your hands on your hips.

Action:

Count 1— Raise both legs and the upper part of your body off the floor as high as possible.

Count 2— Lower the legs and the upper body to the floor.

Sit-Ups (Fig. 8—3)

Starting position: Lie on the floor with your knees up and together, the feet about twelve inches from the buttocks, flat on the floor and well-anchored. The fingers should be laced behind the head.

Action:

Count 1— Sit up, keeping the elbows back, and touch the chest to your thighs.

Count 2— Return to the lying position.

Hip Raises (Fig. 8—4)

Starting position: Sit on the floor, place your hands on the floor behind your hips, with the palms down and the fingers pointing in the opposite direction from the feet. The heels should be about nine inches apart.

Action:

Count 1— Raise the hips so that the body is completely extended, with the head bending backward.

Count 2— Lower to the sitting position.

Push-Ups (Fig. 8—5)

Starting position: Lie prone, with your hands on the floor, with palms down under the shoulders.

Action:

Count 1— Straighten your arms, raising the body to arm's length, keeping the body rigid.

Count 2— Lower your chest to the floor by bending your arms at the elbows. Keep your chin up.

Modified Push-Ups (Fig. 8—5a)

Starting position: Lie prone, with your knees bent, hands on the floor, with palms down under the shoulders.

Action:

Count 1— Straighten the arms, raising the body to arm's length so that the body is supported by the knees and hands.

Count 2— Lower the chest to the floor by bending the arms at the elbows, with the knees still in bent position. Keep the chin up.

RECORD OF EXERCISE ACHIEVEMENT

	Time Allotted	No. of Repetitions Starting	1st Increase	2nd Increase	3rd Increase
Alternate Toe Touches	2 min.	12			
Chest and Leg Raises	2 min.	4			
Sit-ups	2 min.	10			
Hip Raises	2 min.	4			
Push-ups	2 min.	10			
Squat Thrusts	2 min.	10			
Running in Place	1 min.	30			

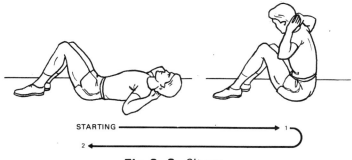

Fig. 8—3. Sit-ups.

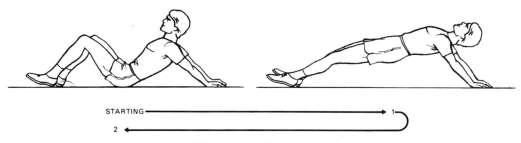

Fig. 8—4. Hip raises.

Fig. 8—5. Push-ups.

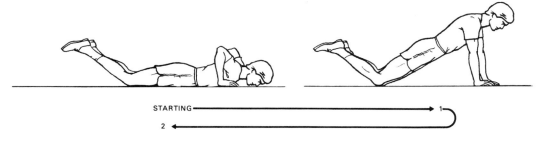

Fig. 8—5a. Modified push-ups.

Fig. 8—6. Squat thrusts.

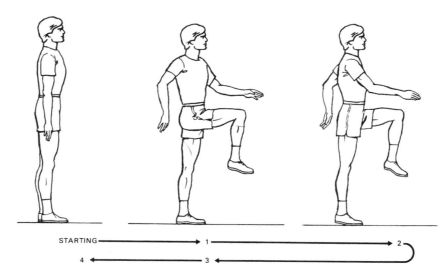

Fig. 8—7. Running in place.

Squat Thrusts (Fig. 8—6)

Starting position: Stand erect, with your arms at the sides.

Action:

Count 1— Bend your knees and place your hands on the floor, with palms down and arms straight, elbows inside the knees (squat position).

Count 2— Extend your legs backward so that the body is straight, resting on the toes and hands.

Count 3— Return to the squat position in one movement.

Count 4— Stand up.

Running in Place (Fig. 8—7)

Starting position: Stand up straight, with your arms at your sides.

Action:

Count 1— Lift the right leg to hip level, with the toes pointed downward.

Count 2— Lift the left leg to hip level, with the toes pointed downward.

Note: The runner lands on the balls of the feet.

Abdominal (Fig. 8—8)

Starting position: Sit on the floor, with the knees bent so that the heels are 12 inches from the buttocks. The feet should be anchored to the floor in this position. The fingers are laced behind the head and the elbows held way back. The trunk is lowered backward until the head is about 15 inches from the floor.

Contraction time: This position should be held for 10 seconds. As tolerance for this exercise builds up, a weight may be held behind the head.

Fig. 8—8. Abdominal.

Back (Fig. 8—9)

Starting position: Lie prone, with your legs straight. The fingers are laced behind the head and the elbows held up. Both legs and the upper part of the body are raised off the floor and held as high as possible.

Contraction time: The position should be held for 10 seconds.

Variations:

1. The trunk could be held down and just the legs raised off the floor and held for 10 seconds.
2. The legs could be held down and the trunk raised off the floor and held for 10 seconds.
3. Resistance to these positions could be offered by another person.

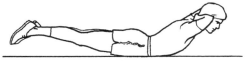

Fig. 8—9. Back.

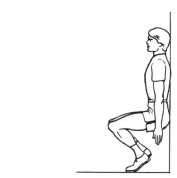

Fig. 8—10. Legs.

Legs (Fig. 8—10)

Starting position: Stand with your heels 15 inches away from a wall. Lean back until the buttocks, back, and head touch the wall. Rise up on your toes, and then lower the body until the thighs are parallel to the floor.

Contraction time: Hold this sitting position for 10 seconds.

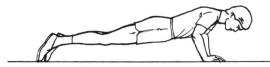

Fig. 8—11. Arms.

Arms (Fig. 8—11)

Starting position: Lie facedown on the floor. Place your hands under the shoulder joints. Keeping your body straight, lift it to a half push-up position.

Contraction time: Hold this position for 10 seconds.

Variation: As tolerance for this exercise builds up, place weight on your shoulders or have another person apply downward pressure on them.

Arms (Fig. 8—12)

Starting position: Hang from a bar. Raise the body to a bent-arm position.

Contraction time: Hold this position for 10 seconds.

Variation: As tolerance for this exercise builds up, have another person offer resistance to the body.

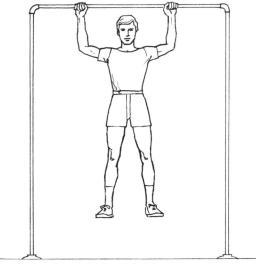

Fig. 8—12. Arms.

ISOMETRIC EXERCISES

Isometric exercises can serve as a *supplement* to the exercise program, because they are a simple and convenient method of developing muscle tone. The basis of isometric exercise is the contraction of muscles without apparent movement during short periods of time.

Suggested Isometric Program for the Home or Office

It is suggested that each exercise be performed only once a day. The resistance needed to perform isometric contraction can be found in any home or office, using a chair, desk, or wall. The exercises can also be done using a partner to offer the resistance needed.

Exercise 1 (arms)*

Standing in the doorway, with your arms bent and your legs straight, press against the top of the doorway.

Exercise 2 (legs)

Standing in the doorway, with your arms straight and pressing against the top of the doorway and your legs bent, press down against the floor.

Exercise 3 (legs)

Standing in the doorway on your toes, with your legs bent, and your arms straight and pressing against the top of the doorway, push down against the floor with the toes.

Exercise 4 (arms)

With your hands on top of the door and your arms bent, pull down on the door.

Exercise 5 (legs)

Sitting in the doorway, with your back against one side and your feet against the other side with the legs bent, straighten the legs.

Note: For proper position to execute Exercises 1, 2, and 3, it may be necessary to stand on a bench or chair.

Exercise 6 (neck)

Standing with your back against a wall and your feet 14 inches away from the wall, press the back of your head against the wall.

Exercise 7 (neck)

Standing facing a wall, with your feet 14 inches away from the wall, place the forehead against the wall and press.

Exercise 8 (shoulders)

Standing in the doorway, arms down and straight at the elbow, push outward against the sides of the doorway.

Exercise 9 (arms and chest)

Standing in the doorway, with your arms bent and your hands at shoulder level, push against the sides of the doorway.

Exercise 10 (abdomen)

Sitting in a chair with your feet flat on the floor, your hands on your knees, and your arms straight, press down with your hands and push up with your knees.

SUPPLEMENTARY EXERCISES

The following exercises can be used to supplement an exercise program, and they can be done at your office or at your home.

1. Lie on your back and stretch hard.
2. Stand or sit. Expand your chest, flatten your abdomen, then relax. Repeat several times.
3. Sit in a straight chair, and do these 10-second contractions:
   a. With your hands under the chair seat, pull up.
   b. With your hands on the chair seat, push down.
   c. With the fist of one hand in the palm of the other and your elbows at shoulder level, push your hands together.
   d. Lace your fingers behind your head. Force your head back and your hands forward.
4. Sit at a desk or table, and do these 10-second contractions:
   a. With your forehead on the table surface, press your head down.
   b. With your hands under the table, palms up, lift.
   c. With your hands on the table, press down.
5. Walk more, and at a faster pace.

FIGURE CONTROL

Often individuals are not motivated to practice or perform exercises regularly. Girls and women, especially, find conditioning and exercise programs unattractive and too strenuous. In order to encourage women to participate in this worthy activity, certain problem areas have been identified. Thus, women will be motivated to perform exercises which will enhance their appearance.

Abdomen:

The abdominal area is greatly improved by participation in:

1. Sit-ups (see Fig. 8-8).
2. Swimming—standing with your feet apart, use the overarm swim stroke: first to the center, then to the left, and then to the right.
3. Waist twists—standing with your feet apart and your arms outstretched, twist your body all the way around to the right, and then to the left.
4. Knee-nose stretches—on all fours, bring your left knee to your nose, then stretch your leg back and upward, raising the head at the same time.
5. Thigh rotations—sitting with your legs spread and leaning back on your arms, rotate your foot outward until the little toe touches the floor. Rotate the foot inward and carry the leg across your body, touching the big toe to the floor. Repeat this with the opposite leg.
6. Roll-outs—sitting up straight, with your legs straight and together, lower the head and round the shoulders, allowing the upper body to move backward toward the floor; hold this position for about five seconds about halfway down, and then proceed downward. Roll slowly upward, raising the head first.
7. Bicycle—resting on your elbows, circle your legs in bicycling motion. Then hold your arms in the air and continue the bicycling motion.
8. Stretch and shoulder flexibility—in a kneeling position, place your shoulder and ear on the floor,

thrusting your arm between the opposite hand on your knee. Swing the thrusted arm up and back, following with the head and eyes. Repeat this with the opposite side and arm.

9. Pelvic tilt—lying on your back with your knees bent and apart, arch back, keeping the shoulders and seat on the floor. Press your spine down against the floor, and hold for a count of five.

10. Running—do this outdoors if possible; if indoors, do it in place. Run very rapidly, with your knees high.

11. Running on all fours—place your hands on the floor and run in place with your feet. Later, use your arms and move across the floor.

Chest:

1. Swimming (see Abdomen, no. 2).
2. Waist twists (see Abdomen, no. 3).
3. Shoulder rotations—standing with your right arm out, turn your thumb all the way to the right, then to the left. Repeat this with your left arm.
4. Roll-outs (see Abdomen, no. 6).
5. Push-ups (see Fig. 8-11).
6. Shoulder shrugs—shrug your shoulders up as if trying to cover the ears. Hold and press your shoulders down, then forward, and then backward.
7. Stretch and shoulder flexibility (see Abdomen, no. 8).

Back:

1. Swimming (see Abdomen, no. 2).
2. Waist twists (see Abdomen, no. 3).
3. Shoulder rotations (see Chest, no. 3).
4. Push-ups (see Fig. 8-11).
5. Stretch and shoulder flexibility (see Abdomen, no. 8).

Neck:

1. Swimming (see Abdomen, no. 2).
2. Waist twists (see Abdomen, no. 3).
3. Shoulder rotations (see Chest, no. 3).
4. Knee-nose stretches (see Abdomen, no. 4).
5. Shoulder shrugs (see Chest, no. 6).

Hips (lower):

1. Knee-nose stretches (see Abdomen, no. 4).
2. Thigh rotations (see Abdomen, no. 5).
3. Bicycle (see Abdomen, no. 7).
4. Running (see Abdomen, no. 10).
5. Running on all fours (see Abdomen, no. 11).

Thighs:

1. Thigh rotations (see Abdomen, no. 5).
2. Bicycle (see Abdomen, no. 7).
3. Knee bends — standing with your feet together and your heels on the floor, bend the knees as far as possible, then rise slowly to a standing tiptoe position.
4. Running (see Abdomen, no. 10).
5. Running on all fours (see Abdomen, no. 11).

Calf and ankle:

1. Knee bends (see Thighs, no. 3).
2. Running (see Abdomen, no. 10).
3. Running on all fours (see Abdomen, no. 11).

HELPFUL TIPS

1. Exercise for shorter periods of time (15 minutes) at more frequent intervals (daily).
2. Exercise to music, both vigorously and slowly.
3. Use an overall exercise program with emphasis on specified problem areas.
4. Wear comfortable clothing and no shoes if you prefer.
5. Begin slowly, build up, and finish with the most vigorous activities.
6. Do not put off exercising until the last thing each day.
7. Exercise with someone else if possible.
8. *Have fun*—make a game out of it!

BIBLIOGRAPHY

Berger, Richard A., *Conditioning for Men.* Boston: Allyn and Bacon, Inc., 1973.

Cassady, Donald R., Mapes, Donald F., and Alley, Louis E., *Handbook of Physical Fitness.* New York: The Macmillan Co., 1965.

Prudden, Bonnie, *Improve Your Body.* New York: Knight and Gilbert, Inc., 1959.

Royal Canadian Air Force Exercise Plans for Physical Fitness. Mt. Vernon, N.Y.: This Week Magazine, 1962.

Wallis, Earl L., and Logan, Gene A., *Isometric Exercises.* Englewood Cliffs, N.J.: Prentice-Hall, Inc., 1964.

Wessel, Janet A., and MacIntyre, Christine M., *Body Contouring and Conditioning Through Movement.* Boston: Allyn and Bacon, Inc., 1970.

FENCING | 9

Originally, the sword was used in combat for the purpose of rendering the opponent helpless. In its earliest forms, the sword was a two-edged blade and, in some countries, two-handed. The heavy and cumbersome weapon evolved into lighter weapons as stronger metals were developed. The lighter sword brought about the present type of fencing, which depends upon skills of speed and technique of thrusting. As methods of warfare changed, the sword became an ineffective weapon. It remained, however, a military symbol of dignity and authority, and was used as a dueling instrument in defending an individual's honor. This, in turn, led to the adoption of dueling as a sport.

Modern fencing uses the épée, saber, or foil as a dueling weapon. Épée fencing involves the use of a triangular blade that tapers to a point with three small prongs. A point is scored on a thrust when contact is made on any part of the body. Saber fencing involves a triangular or Y-shaped blade, and a point is scored when a thrust or cutting contact is made with any part of the body above the belt line. However, the most popular of the fencing weapons is the foil, which has a rectangular blade that tapers to a blunted point. A point is scored by thrusting and making contact with the torso, which serves as a target. A knowledge of fencing with foils is considered basic to the skills needed for épée and saber fencing; therefore, this chapter will explain fencing with foils.

THE MATCH

The object of fencing is to touch the opponent within the legal bounds of the designated target. The target for foil fencing is from the top of the collar to the groin lines in front, and in the back from the top of the collar to a line which runs straight across from one hip to the other. The individual who scores five legal touches first is considered the winner. The time limit for a bout is 10 minutes. The contestants' playing area is a strip 40 feet long and 6 feet wide. The contest is begun by the crossing of the blades. A right-of-way is declared when one fencer takes the offensive by extending the foil. Before the defense can make a counterattack, the right-of-way movement must be parried (blocked). After a defender has parried the offensive attack, the defender may riposte (counterattack).

TERMINOLOGY

Engagement—The crossing of the blades.
Feint—A fake movement to trick the opponent.
Parry—A defensive movement with the foil to block or divert an offensive attack.
Riposte—The action taken by a defensive fencer after a successful parry. It is also called a *counterattack.*
Target—The area of the body which, if contacted by the blade, would be considered a legal touch.

SAFETY

Minimum equipment includes the mask, jacket, glove, and foil. The protective equipment worn by the fencer should be of the highest quality and in excellent condition. The mask should be examined before use, to ensure that it will protect the fencer should the foil touch the head area. *At no time* should the fencer oppose another fencer either in combat, practice, or demonstration without a mask. The jacket serves to protect against occasional hard touches and blades which might possibly break. As an additional precaution, the tip of the foil should be wrapped with adhesive tape to avoid injury. The blade should be discarded if found to be damaged or have flaws. A glove should be worn at all times, for protection and to ensure a better grip of the foil.

SKILLS

Grip. The handle of the French foil is slightly curved. The arched or convex side of the handle is placed in

the palm of the hand at the base of the thumb, just below the fleshy part. The thumb bends over the top of the handle, with the index finger curving beneath the handle and supporting the foil. The other three fingers curve around the handle and rest on the concave part of it.

Salute. The salute is executed as a ceremonial procedure before contact in a lesson or in a bout. Traditionally, it is also performed at the end of a bout, saluting the opponent and the judges. The salute is started from the initial position, which is an erect position of the body, giving the opponent a profile picture with the head turned toward the opponent. The feet are at right angles, with the right heel touching the left heel. The tip of the foil is held about 6 inches from the floor. The foil and arm form a straight line, with the thumb up and the tips of the fingers to the left. From this initial position, the foil is brought to a perpendicular position in front of the right shoulder by bending the elbow. Following a slight pause in this position, the foil is extended forward so that the weapon and arm form a horizontal line from the shoulder, saluting the opponent. After a short pause, the foil is brought back to the per-pendicular position from which other salutes may be made, or the fencer may go to the on-guard position for contact work or practice.

On-Guard Position. The position assumed by the fencers ready to engage in combat, either for attack or defense, is called the *on-guard position*. The feet are at right angles to each other, with the forward foot pointed at the opponent and about 20 inches in advance of the rear foot. The front foot should be in line with the rear heel. Each knee is bent so that it falls directly over the instep of the foot and the weight is distributed equally over both feet. The side of the body is presented to the opponent because it offers a minimal target. The body should be turned away from the opponent in a natural position, without any undue strain. The foil is raised until the elbow is bent and about 7 inches away from the body, with the hand about chest-high. The foil and the forearm form a straight line from the elbow to the weapon tip, which is aimed at the opponent's face. The left hand is raised to an arched position, with the upper arm on the same level as the shoulder. The hand is relaxed, with the fingers pointed forward.

Advance and Retreat. From the on-guard position, it is necessary to move toward the opponent in order to register a touch. The motion is called the *advance*, and is made by raising the toe and moving the forward foot toward the opponent. When the heel of the forward foot has touched the floor in its new position, the rear foot is moved forward the same distance that the forward foot traveled. In this motion, both feet are kept near the floor and the body is not moved up or down.

A *retreat* is made by moving the rear foot backward the desired distance, then moving the forward foot backward the same distance. The general procedure of advancing and retreating is identical, although the patterns of movement are reversed.

Lunge. The lunge is made by extending or straightening the right arm from the shoulder. The left leg makes a rapid extension and the right foot moves forward, landing on the heel first. The left foot is held stationary and flat on the floor. The left arm is straightened and brought down so that it is parallel with the left leg. The palm of the left hand faces upward. In the lunge position, the knee of the forward foot is directly over the instep, and the body is held erect but in line with the rear leg. The extension of the arm should precede the actual lunge of the body.

Recovery. The recovery from the lunge is made by a pull and a bend of the left leg and a push with the right foot, so as to return to the on-guard position. The left hand is raised to the arched position, with the upper arm on the same level as the shoulder. The hand is relaxed and the fingers are pointed forward.

Thrust. The *straight thrust* is the simplest of the attacking motions. It is executed by extending the arm as if to stab the opponent. This motion employs little deception, so speed of execution is an important factor.

Disengage. Another form of attack is moving the foil downward and under the opponent's foil and coming up on the unprotected side. This is called a *simple disengage*, and is used when the opponent is applying pressure to the side of your blade, trying to push it aside in preparation to attack. Actually, the tip of your foil goes through a "U" motion. The disengage motion should be executed by the wrist and fingers, with the arm held relatively still.

Double Disengage. As the attacker makes a disengage motion, an immediate retreat of the foil through the same path constitutes a double disengage. This

movement is effective if the opponent parries hard against a disengage movement.

Cutover. A disengage movement over the opponent's foil is a *cutover*. In this move, the action of the foil is controlled by the wrist.

Attack Against Blade. One attack is to force the opponent's blade by tapping it in such a manner as to permit you a thrust attack.

Another attack is to apply pressure to the opponent's blade so that you gain an opening toward the target.

Defensive Movements

The main defensive motion is the *parry*, which is simply a pressure or opposition to the attacking foil. It may be executed in either direction. Care must be exercised not to overprotect by too much motion in the parry. In defense of each target area the hand may be *supinated* (palm up) or *pronated* (palm down). The essential movement in the parry to protect the upper part of the target is to move the hand to the right or left, keeping the point of the foil pointed at the opponent's eye. The parry against the lower part of the target is to keep the hand in its normal position and to drop the blade through an arc or semicircle, forcing the attacker's blade to the inside or outside. The counter parry is executed by moving the foil in a small circle so that the attacker's foil cannot reach its mark. In this parry the fingers and wrist control the motion.

BIBLIOGRAPHY

Amateur Fencers League of America, *Fencing.* New York: The League.

——————, *Fencing Rules and Manual,* Miguel Decapriles, ed. New York: The League, 1957.

Bernhard, Frederica, and Edwards, Vernon, *How to Fence.* Dubuque, Iowa: William C. Brown Co., 1956.

Division of Girls' and Women's Sports, *Bowling-Fencing-Golf Guide.* Washington, D.C.: American Association for Health, Physical Education and Recreation.

Garret, Maxwell R., and Heinecke, Mary F., *Fencing.* Boston: Allyn and Bacon, Inc., 1971.

Miller, Maxine Muri, "Don't Let Fencing Foil You!" *Journal of the American Association for Health, Physical Education and Recreation,* Vol. 22, No. 10 (December, 1951), pp. 17-19.

Vince, Joseph, *Fencing.* New York: A.S. Barnes & Co., 1940.

There is evidence in early history that man found enjoyment in rolling stones at fixed objects and that he used tree branches to move stones around. These two activities are the forerunners of many of our modern sports such as field hockey. About 2,500 years ago, the Greeks played a game using sticks similar to the present hockey sticks, of which illustrations may be found in their works of art. Several centuries ago, the British observed the French playing a game that was called "hoquet." It appealed to them so it was taken to England, where it was called "hokay" after the French pronunciation. They spelled it "hockey" and later the pronunciation changed in keeping with the English orthography. It was not until after the development of the ice hockey game that the game of "hockey" was changed to "field hockey." Historically, the game of field hockey has had varying degrees of popularity, a fact which necessitated many rule changes and additions. In the early stages of development, the game was played exclusively by men; it was considered too rough for women. However, in 1887 women started playing field hockey and made modifications in the rules, which resulted in its becoming a very popular activity for women.

In 1901 Miss Constance Applebee, "Miss Hockey," of the British College of Physical Education, demonstrated the game at Harvard Summer School. After Harvard, Miss Applebee went to Vassar, Wellesley, Smith, Radcliffe, Mt. Holyoke, and Bryn Mawr introducing field hockey to very receptive groups of young women. The United States Field Hockey Association was formed in 1922 to govern the game for women. In 1930 the Field Hockey Association of America was formed as the governing body for men.

The ninth grade is the average level for introduction to this sport. During high school, a girl may participate on a varsity, junior varsity, and/or intramural team. After high school, she may participate on a college team or join a field hockey club open to noncollege students, college students, and graduates alike.

Hockey camps have been established in Pennsylvania and Maine, and day camps are also offered in the Philadelphia area.

The popularity of the sport among women is spreading and, as a result, a large number of young women are involved with this sport today. More than 150 clubs are now in existence in the United States.

TERMINOLOGY

Advancing—The use of the feet or legs, intentionally or unintentionally, to deflect or stop the ball.

Backing up—Playing behind a teammate who has the ball, or behind a teammate about to tackle an opposing player, so as to render help if needed.

Blade—The curved end of the stick (the head).

Bully—The bully is used to start play at the beginning of the game, the start of the second half, or after a goal has been scored. Two opposing players stand squarely, facing the side lines, with the ball on the ground between them. The players strike the ground on their side of the ball with the blade and then touch sticks over the top of the ball in the air three times. Each player then attempts to control the ball.

Corner [long]—A member of the attacking team is awarded a hit on the goal line, or five yards from the corner on the side line over which the defensive player caused the ball to go out-of-bounds.

Corner [short or penalty]—A member of the attacking team is awarded a hit not less than ten yards from the nearer goal post on the goal line when (1) fouled by a member of the defensive team, or (2) the defensive player intentionally causes the ball to go over the goal line not between the goal posts.

Covering—Being in a position to intercept a long pass, or in a position to tackle an offensive player.

Dodge—While in possession of the ball, an offensive player evades the defensive player.

Drawing—While in possession of the ball, the offensive player forces the defensive player to stay close.

Face—The flat side of the blade.

Fielding—The act of legally stopping the ball.

Goal—An attacking player within the striking circle touches the ball before it passes between the goal posts and under the crossbar.

Goal cage—The two goal posts are twelve feet apart and the crossbar is seven feet high. The area immediately behind the goal line is enclosed with a net.

Hit—Striking the ball with the face of the stick.

Interchange—Two players exchange position.

Marking—Guarding an opponent so that it is difficult for him to receive a pass, thereby getting into position to recover the ball by interception; or, if the opponent receives a pass, being in a position to tackle him.

Offside—A foul caused by a player advancing ahead of the ball on the offensive end of the field, with less than three opponents between the player and the goal.

Penalty bully—A bully taken five yards in front of the goal by the player who fouled an attacking team member, who in all probability would have scored a goal, and by any member of the attacking team. All other players remain outside the striking circle.

Penalty goal—A goal awarded the attacking team when the defensive team fouls during a penalty bully.

Reverse stick—The stick is rotated so that the toe is pointing toward the ground.

Sticks—Raising the stick above the shoulders at the start or end of a stroke. This constitutes a foul.

Tackle—To make an attempt to gain possession of the ball when the opponent has control of it.

Tackling back—A second tackling situation in which: (1) a defensive man initially fails to tackle successfully and recovers to try again; or (2) an offensive man loses the ball to a tackler, then tries to get it back.

THE GAME

Field hockey is played by a team of eleven players on a rectangular field (see Fig. 10-1). The players are: five forwards, three halfbacks, two backs, and a goalkeeper. The offensive objective of the game is to propel the ball through the opponent's goal from within the striking zone by means of a hit with the stick. The offensive team advances the ball by means of stick passes or dribbles. The defensive team attempts to prevent a goal from being scored by marking, tackling, and covering.

Start

The game is started when the center forward from each team bullies the ball in the center of the field. All other players must be between the ball and their own goal line, and further away from the ball than five yards until the bully is completed.

Roll-in

A ball that goes across the side line is put in play with a roll-in by an opponent of the player who caused it to go out-of-bounds. The player throwing the ball in must have both feet and the stick behind the side line, and he cannot touch the ball again until another player has touched it. All players must remain five yards away from the individual rolling the ball in. The ball must not have a spin or be bounced when rolled in from out-of-bounds.

Bully

A ball is put in play with a bully when: (1) a player of the attacking team causes the ball to go out-of-bounds over the goal line (not between the goal posts); (2) an attacking player causes the ball to go over the goal line between the goal posts from outside the striking area; (3) two opposing players cause the ball to go over the goal line (not between the goal posts), or (4) a defending player in the area between the goal line and the 25-yard line unintentionally causes the ball to go over the goal line. The ball will be put in play with a bully on the 25-yard line opposite the place where the ball crossed the goal line.

Fouls

It is illegal for a player to raise any part of the stick above the shoulders either at the beginning or end of the stroke. It is illegal to strike at the ball in a dangerous manner, e.g., swinging the stick wildly. It is illegal to advance the ball with any part of the body. The ball may be stopped with the hand, but the ball must drop to the ground in a vertical plane. The goalkeeper may stop the ball with the hand; if the ball merely rebounds, it is legal. The goalkeeper is permitted to kick the ball within the striking circle. It is illegal to touch the ball with the rounded side of the stick, interfere with an opponent's stick, or play without a stick. It is illegal to use personal contact such as to trip, push, charge, or use the body as a shield to prevent the opponent from playing the ball. If a foul is made by a member of the attacking team, the defending team is awarded a free hit, and vice versa if the defending team is outside the circles. If a foul is made by a member of the defending team *inside* the circles, a penalty corner or penalty bully is awarded to the attacking team. If a double foul is called, the umpire shall give a bully at the spot where the foul was made.

EQUIPMENT

Stick

The hockey stick consists of a straight shaft, and the blade. The part of the shaft nearest the blade is called the *splice*. The curved part of the blade is called the *heel*, and the end the *toe*. The left side of the blade is flat, while the right side is round. Left-handed sticks are illegal. The hockey stick should be selected by the individual, who considers the length and weight of the stick and the thickness of the handle in relation to his physical structure and the position he plays.

Ball

The official hockey ball is made of cork and string covered with leather. The weight of the ball is between 5-1/2 ounces and 5-3/4 ounces, with a circumference of between 8-3/4 inches and 9-1/4 inches.

Pads

Players should protect their legs with shin guards. If these are strapped on with leather straps, the buckles should be on the outside of the leg. A lightweight type of shin guard can be worn under the socks. Goalkeepers' pads should cover the entire leg from the thigh down to the instep. For added protection, sponge rubber should be used over the instep. Canvas hockey sneakers are recommended. These shoes have a canvas top with rubber cleats. Some players prefer a leather shoe with leather cleats. Shoes with metal cleats, metal spikes, or projecting nails must not be worn.

SAFETY

1. The stick should be free of splinters and sharp edges. The stick may be taped, but heavy taping should be avoided in order not to unbalance it.
2. Protective pads should be worn at all times.
3. Players who wear glasses should wear eye guards.
4. Sufficient time should be taken to warm up before a scrimmage or practice.
5. Players should be familiar with the rules, and abide by them. This is particularly true for the foul rules.

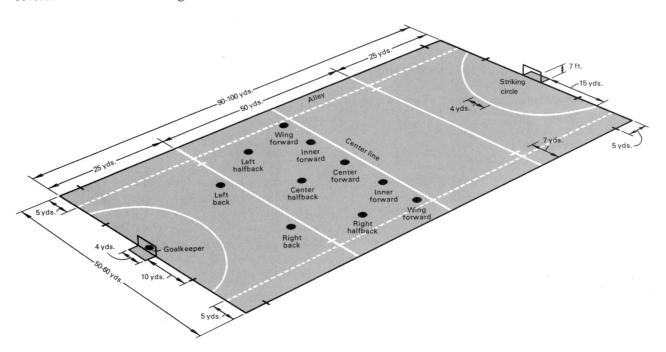

Fig. 10—1. Regulation field hockey field.

6. Mastery of the techniques of stick work and footwork will help to eliminate dangerous play.
7. Personal contact should be avoided at all times.

INDIVIDUAL SKILLS

Basic to the skills of hockey is the ability of the player to have the feet in proper relation to the ball when stroking the ball and tackling an opponent.

Carrying the Stick

When not playing the ball or running, hold the stick out in front, with its shaft parallel to the ground and its toe pointing upward. The left hand is placed at the top of the stick, the right hand about 18 inches down; flex both elbows slightly. In playing the ball, adjust the right hand upward or downward, depending on how the ball is to be played. The "V" formed by the thumb and index finger of each hand as it grasps the stick should be in line with the toe of the stick in the carrying position, as well as in the playing of the ball.

Dribble

The moving of the ball forward by a player is called a *dribble.* This comprises a series of short-distance taps while running slowly, or longer taps when running faster. In dribbling, hold the right hand about four inches down the stick from the left hand and keep the elbows away from the body. Hold the stick vertical and keep the wrist moving forward and backward while advancing the ball. With the body facing forward, play the ball in front of and slightly to the right of the right foot. It is important not to tap the ball too hard as it is dribbled, so that it may be kept in control at all times.

Drive

The drive is used to pass the ball to a teammate or to shoot for a goal. Therefore, more power is used in this stroke than in the dribble. Keep the hands close together, holding the stick in a vertical position. Carry the stick back in line with the ball about waist-high, making sure not to cock the wrists. As you bring the stick forward, transfer the weight to the forward foot (either right or left), with a follow-through. In a straight drive, play the ball in front of and to the right of the forward foot. Point the left side of the body in the direction that the ball is aimed. In a drive to the left, play the ball from in front of the body and near the left foot. As you bring the stick forward, it should

follow a thrust in the direction of the desired drive. For a drive to the right, play the ball to the right and farther behind the feet than in the other drives. Keep the right foot forward, and the shoulders and hips pointing to the right as the left shoulder moves in the direction of the pass. Move the stick forward to the right and step forward with the left foot as you shift the body weight.

Push Pass

For short passes in a situation where the motion of the stick is limited, or there is not time to execute a backswing, the push pass may be used. The stroke is used with either the left or right foot forward. Lower the right hand slightly from the fundamental position. As the ball contacts the blade, push the stick forward with the right hand and straighten the right arm. While the right hand pushes the stick forward, the left hand keeps the top of the stick ahead of the ball. Finish the stroke by pulling the left hand backward and allowing the right hand to act as a pivot point for the motion of the stick. The stick follows through, aimed in the direction of the pass, until the shaft is in position approximately parallel to the ground. At this point the left arm and stick should be in a straight line. This type of pass should cause the ball to roll along the ground.

Flick

The flick is similar to the push pass except that, at the time the ball leaves the blade, the wrists are snapped and the stick is rotated counterclockwise as the ball is lifted off the ground and starts in the desired direction. The flick pass is hard to stop, since the ball will rise from the ground. It is effective when passing to a marked, or guarded, teammate.

Scoop

From a dribbling position, lower the hands so that you can turn the blade upward. The ball should be in front of and slightly to the right of the forward foot. Place the toe of the blade under the ball. Raise the stick upward and forward with the right hand, and at the same time lower the left hand. This stroke is used to make a dodge, a short pass, or a shot at the goal.

Dodging

A player executes a *dodge* when he possesses the ball and wants to control it, and at the same time to progress toward scoring a goal. As an opponent approaches from in front and tries to get control of the ball, the offensive player must use effective ball handling and dodges to avoid losing it.

Right Dodge

An offensive player can often avoid an oncoming tackle by using a right dodge—hitting the ball around to the right of the defensive player, and then running in front of him to regain possession of the ball when it has gone beyond the opponent. The offensive player should not use the right-hand dodge constantly but should vary the type of dodge in order to confuse the defense.

Left Dodge

The left dodge is executed in the same way, but to the left. The move to the left should be made at the time the defensive player attempts to make contact with the ball. It is important for the offensive player to keep control of the ball and vary the speed of motion at various times during the dodge.

Triangular Pass

Pass the ball to a teammate, then receive it again. To avoid a would-be tackler, the offensive player passes the ball diagonally forward to a teammate. This pass may be to either the right or left. The passer then runs past and behind the tackler to receive the return pass.

Tackling

A player tackles to gain possession of the ball by taking it from an opponent. The tackle is made at the moment the opponent loses control of the ball.

Straight Tackle

As the offensive player moves forward, the tackler (holding his stick in the dribble position) moves forward to meet his opponent stick-to-stick. The tackler keeps his body to the left (offense's right) to avoid body contact. He watches the ball and the stick, and when he believes the ball may be taken away, he makes contact with the ball and dribbles it away.

Circular Tackle

The circular tackle is used when the defensive player is on the left of the offensive player and they are running in the same direction. The would-be tackler must be ahead of the offensive player. The defensive

player then circles to the right and gains possession of the ball, avoiding body contact.

Left-hand Lunge

When the defensive player is on the offensive player's stick or right side, facing him, the left-hand lunge is used to tackle. The tackler releases the right hand from the stick and lunges forward, in order to place the head of the stick in contact with the ball. The rear foot is brought up and a pivot to the left is made. The right hand is placed back on the stick and an attempt is made to control the ball. Players should learn to judge the distance from which they can effectively execute the left-hand lunge.

STRATEGY

Field hockey is essentially a team sport, and successful teams depend upon each player's carrying out his position assignment properly. Individual skills should be mastered by each player, then coordinated into team effort so that all players function as a unit.

Offensive Strategy

The purpose of the offense is to take the ball down the field and score. The responsibility for this lies with the forward line, whose members must therefore be alert and ready to play the ball at all times. Since the wings play near the side lines and can take the ball down the field without too much interference from other players, the inner forwards should attempt to get the ball to them as soon as possible. As the wings approach the 25-yard line, they should pass to the inner forwards, who have a better, less angled shot at the goal.

As the ball is moved down the field by the offensive team, they should move as a unit in a line until they near the striking circle, where they close up without getting in each other's way. Success at taking the ball down the field depends a great deal on the forwards' ability in ball handling and passing. In general, short passes are preferred because long passes may be intercepted more easily; however, there are times when long passes are desirable and can be used to advantage. The center forward should be a good shot, since he is in front of the goal and does not have to shoot at an angle. All shots at the goal should be followed up by the shooter and other forwards in the vicinity of the goal. On offensive plays, the fullbacks should not go as far down field as the halfbacks because they must be able to set up a defense should their team lose the ball.

The halfback nearest the point where a team is awarded an out-of-bounds should initiate the play. The roll-in should be executed as quickly as possible to prevent the defense from getting into position. The halfback should use finesse in putting the ball back in play by feinting and varying the direction of returning the ball to play.

The wing should execute the long corner, or penalty corner, by driving the ball hard to a forward who is waiting for the ball. *Under no circumstances should the ball go near the goal.*

Defensive Strategy

The purposes of the defense are: (1) to prevent the offensive team from scoring, and (2) to get possession of the ball. If a forward loses the ball to an opponent,

he should immediately tackle that player. However, the halfbacks and backs are the main lines of defense. In general, the left and right halfbacks cover the opponents' wings, the left and right backs cover the inners, and the center halfback covers the center. When possible, one back carries out his assignment by marking while the other back covers. In the event the offensive player gets away from the man who is marking him, he is picked up by the cover man. This switch is maintained until the original position can be regained without weakening the team play. Backs should never be in a position on the field to obstruct the view of the goalkeeper.

The goalkeeper has the responsibility of stopping the ball which has been shot at the goal. He should be in a line between the ball and the goal, remaining slightly in front of the goal line. The goalkeeper can use the stick, feet, or hands to stop the ball. When he makes contact with the ball, he should prevent it from entering the goal and get it to a teammate, preferably to the opposite side of the goal than that from which the ball was shot (or in front of the goal). If an offensive player is coming down the field and no one has tackled him, the goalkeeper may go out and tackle him. However, *under most circumstances the goal should not be left unprotected.*

BIBLIOGRAPHY

Barnes, Mildred J., *Field Hockey: the Coach and the Player.* Boston: Allyn and Bacon, Inc., 1969.

Field Hockey—Lacrosse Guide (DGWS). Washington, D.C.: American Association for Health, Physical Education and Recreation.

Haussermann, Caroline, *Field Hockey.* Boston: Allyn and Bacon, Inc. 1970.

Lees, Josephine T.. and Shellenberger, Betty, *Field Hockey for Players, Coaches, and Umpires.* New York: The Ronald Press Company, 1957.

Mackey, Helen T., *Field Hockey: An International Team Sport.* Englewood Cliffs, N.J.: Prentice-Hall, Inc., 1963.

Pollard, Marjorie, *Hockey for All,* New York: Thomas Nelson and Sons, 1957.

Potter, Arthur M., "Field Hockey for Boys and Men," *Journal of The American Association for Health, Physical Education and Recreation,* Vol. 28, No. 7 (October, 1957), pp. 8-10.

The game of gator ball was first introduced at Seabreeze High School at Daytona Beach, Florida in the fall of 1930.

D.K. Stanley, then a coach and physical education teacher, was confronted with the problem of having in one class large numbers of heterogeneously-grouped students, grades seven through twelve, for which was provided only one area about the size of a small football field. The game was evolved from some field games to which were added several basketball situations. As the skills of individuals increased and playing areas became available, refinements were introduced. The game, as now played at the University of Florida and many of the Florida public schools, is the product of the original "mass" participation sport.

The general playing regulations are that the ball can, under certain conditions, be kicked, carried, or batted in any direction within the playing area. The goals are the modified soccer type, and the ball can be thrown, kicked, or headed through the goal.

The most attractive feature of the game is that it provides that varying numbers of small and large, fast and slow, skilled and unskilled people alike can play together. While the game *can* be rough, this kind of participation is of the individual's own choosing. The ball moves enough so that everyone, at one time or another, can kick, punch, "swipe at," or run with the ball.

THE GAME

Gator ball is a team game combining the skills of soccer, touch football, and basketball, which has grown in popularity with students and teachers of physical education.

The skills and game situations presented by this activity fulfill the requisites of a team game designed to promote physical conditioning, as well as to provide for a high degree of competitive effort.

Playing Area. (Fig. 11-1) The playing area is a rectangle 80 yards long and 40 yards wide, with lines drawn across the field every 20 yards, dividing it into four equal areas.

A circle with a 10-yard radius is located in the center of the field. The goals on each end line are constructed of two uprights, 15 feet apart, with a crossbar 7 feet high. From each end of the goal, an arc with a 5-yard radius is drawn from the end line to a point directly in front of the goal posts. The tops of these two arcs are then joined by a straight line running parallel with the end line. Thus, the *goal restraining arc* is a minimum distance of 5 yards from any part of the goal.

Equipment. One soccer ball.

Players. A team is composed of from five to nine players.

Time Element. The game is played in two 20-minute halves, with a 5-minute rest between halves. Each team is allowed two 3-minute time-outs, during which the clock continues to run. No time-outs are allowed during the final 3 minutes of play except to remove an injured player.

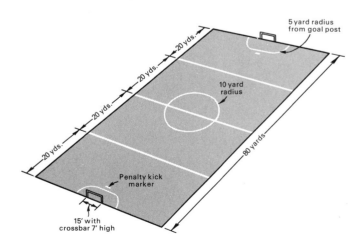

Fig. 11—1. Playing area.

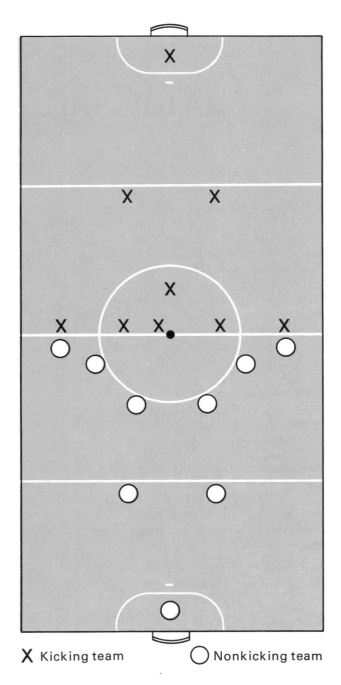

X Kicking team   ◯ Nonkicking team

Fig. 11—2. Starting lineup.

Kick-Off. The ball is put in play at the beginning of each half and after each goal by a place-kick from the middle of the center circle. When one team puts the ball in play at the start of the game, the other team shall put it in play at the start of the second half. On the kick-off, all players must be in their own half of the field, and nonkicking team players must stay out of the center circle. (Fig. 11-2) The kicker may stand anywhere in the center circle and kick the ball in any direction to put it in play—to the opponents or to his teammates; he may not play the ball again until it is touched by at least one other player.

After each goal, the team scored upon has the option of putting the ball in play with a place-kick, or of allowing their opponents to do so.

As soon as initial contact is made with the ball, all players may cross the center line or restraining circle and play anywhere on the field.

Fly Ball. A fly ball is defined as a ball in the air that has not touched the ground since touching a player. As soon as the ball becomes a fly ball, it should be played with the hands. When a fly ball is caught, it may be passed, run with, or kicked. When a player catches a fly ball and does not take more than one step, he must be defended against as a basketball player. That is, he may not be touched or overguarded and must not move the pivot foot. He may drop the ball to the ground and play it with his feet, but may not play it again with his hands until another player has caused it to become a fly ball. Ground or air dribbling with the hand is not allowed at any time.

Running. A player in possession of the ball may run with it at any time. If a player is tagged after taking more than one step with the ball in his possession, a free kick is awarded the opponent's team at the point where the tag is made. To avoid being tagged, a runner may drop the ball to the ground and play it with his feet, or pass it, or punt it.

Scoring. A team scores one point each time the ball legally passes completely over the opponent's end line between the uprights and under the crossbar in any of the following ways:

1. Kicked through the goal from any point on the field outside the goal restraining arc.
2. Thrown through the goal from any point on the field outside the goal restraining arc.
3. *Penalty kick*—the ball is kicked from a point 2 yards outside the goal restraining arc. The goalkeeper must stand 1 yard in front of the goal and must be the only player between the kicker and the goal. This kick is awarded only as the result of committing a flagrant personal foul or for unsportsmanlike conduct.

Fouls. The following constitute fouls:

1. Holding, pushing, tripping, hacking, striking, or violently charging.

2. Touching a ground ball with the hands.
3. Kicking a fly ball.
4. Playing a ball again on a kick-off, throw-in, free kick, or penalty kick before it has been touched by another player.
5. Making a dangerous kick, either by kicking into an opponent, or raising the foot dangerously in attempting to kick the ball.
6. Kicking a ball while inside the goal restraining arc.

Free Kicks. Fouls are penalized by awarding the opposing team a free kick at the point where the foul occurred, except for fouls that involve a penalty kick. A free kick is also awarded a team when one of its players tags an opponent who has taken more than one step with the ball in his possession. (*Note:* A modification of this rule may be applied if players deliberately tag the man who is in possession of the ball and who has not taken more than one step, and the tagging player wishes to provoke a free kick situation instead of allowing the man to pass the ball with his hands. Then the defensive players must stand not less than 5 yards away and allow the man in possession of the ball an opportunity to pass the ball or kick it, whichever he wishes.) On a free kick, all players of the opposing team must be *at least 5 yards* from the ball at the time it is kicked. In order to score from a free kick, the ball must touch another player before going across the goal line; i.e., a goal may not be scored directly from a free kick but must be touched by another player first.

Out-of-Bounds Ball. When a ball crosses a field boundary (other than to score a legal goal) it is put in play by a throw-in at the point where it crossed the line by an opponent of the player who last touched the ball before it went out. But if the attacking team has the ball out-of-bounds over the end line, the ball may be put in play only by a throw-in from the nearest corner. Any member of a team may throw the ball in, and he may use one or both hands to do so.

Held Ball. A held ball occurs when two opposing players: (1) cause the ball to go out-of-bounds, (2) gain possession of a fly ball, or (3) foul each other simultaneously. When any of these occurs, the ball is put in play by the team defending the nearer goal; one man takes the ball out-of-bounds at the nearer side line and throws it in.

Goalkeeper. One player on each team is designated as goalkeeper. The goalkeeper may play anywhere on the field. However, when he is in the 20-yard zone nearer his goal, he has the privilege of playing ground balls with his hands. When the goalkeeper assumes possession of the ball within the goal restraining arc, he is given 5 seconds to move the ball out of the arc by throwing, hitting, kicking, or carrying it. If he takes longer, the ball is awarded the opposing team out-of-bounds at the nearer side line.

Players of the attacking team must not cross the goal restraining arc under any circumstance.

RULES

Rules governing the game of gator ball are not inclusive, and reference must be made to specific rules governing each of the three activities included in the game. For example, when the ball is on the ground, being played with the feet, no player can touch it with his hands or arms, as indicated in the rules governing soccer. When the ball is deflected into the air and caught with the hands, the player in possession may choose not to take more than one step. This situation comes under the rules governing basketball, and defending players must not touch the player in possession of the ball. If a person chooses to run with the ball, the rules of touch football apply, and he may be tagged.

Officiating, conduct of the game, and interpretation of governing rules are for the sole purpose of providing for the safety and active participation of all the players.

SKILLS

There are three principal skills that need emphasis in learning and teaching the game of gator ball. Individual and team skills are closely interrelated, and are most easily learned with the members of the group working together.

1. *Lifting the ball into the air with the foot.* This is a skill almost unique to the game of gator ball, and it requires practice for persons not used to playing the ball with the feet. The ball is deflected into the air most easily by contacting it with the toe while the foot moves sharply forward and upward. If the ball is not moving, or is moving slowly, flexing the foot quickly and making the movement mostly upward will result in the ball being raised off the ground. It is advisable to create a fly ball situation whenever possible so that players may run with the ball or pass it with their hands, and thus be more sure of advancing the ball.

2. *Throwing and catching a fly ball with the hands.* This is a relatively easily acquired skill because of the early experience most children have in throwing and

catching balls. In the game of gator ball, the runs are usually short and the ball is carried in two hands. For this reason, most catches and throws are made with two hands. The exception is one-handed throws that are made in an attempt to score.

The two-handed chest throw is made with the fingers spread, and the hands behind the ball. The arms are extended forward at shoulder level, the wrrsts extending quickly as the ball is released. In any two-handed throw, the important thing is to extend the arms and hands toward the target and be moving toward the target if possible.

Of the one-handed throws, the most commonly used is the side-arm throw. Except in rare instances, the throw to score is made by a player who is running rapidly toward or parallel to the goal line. It is worthwhile, then, to become skilled in throwing one-handed from a variety of running positions.

Skill in catching the ball is increased by letting the hands "give" with the ball, i.e., moving the hands in the same direction in which the ball is moving. The hands and the front of the body may be used to trap the ball and thus be more sure of retaining possession.

One of the best ways of advancing the ball is to run with it until an opposing player is about to tag, then throw to a teammate. Team coordination is required in advancing the ball, in covering certain areas of the field offensively, and in being free to receive a throw when a teammate is about to be tagged.

3.*Advancing and maintaining possession of the ball by kicking it with the feet.* Skill must be developed in kicking the ball just hard enough to keep it ahead when running. (1) Short steps are used. (2) Best control is maintained by kicks made with the inside of the foot. This is done by turning the toe outward as the foot approaches contact with the ball. (3) Care

must be taken not to overrun the ball. (4) Kicking too hard often means losing possession of the ball by advancing it far downfield. (5) Kicking on the ground to a teammate is often accomplished by turning the toe inward and contacting the ball with the outside of the foot to move it sideward.

STRATEGY

Strategy, or concerted team effort, in the game of gator ball depends primarily upon both offensive and defensive coverage of all four areas of the field. The goalkeeper is a key player in the overall defensive setup. Some goalkeepers are aggressive, playing outside or around the goal restraining arc, keeping the ball from getting near the goal. Others stay right in the goal, depending upon quick reflexes and agility to deflect the ball out of the goal, or catch the ball before it enters the goal.

Common strategy calls for two players to act as guards, never leaving the 20-yard zone near their own goal. This prevents, in some measure, the possibility of a quick goal occurring as the ball changes possession around the middle of the field. In case one of the guards catches a fly ball and elects to run with it, another designated player on his team should drop back into the guard zone to take his place.

Very few situations occur in which teammates have a chance to work out offensive team strategy. Indeed, the basic design and rules are such that players of all skill levels and abilities should enjoy playing this game. The very nature of the game precludes the possibility of a few highly skilled players taking possession of the ball and not allowing players of less ability to actually play it.

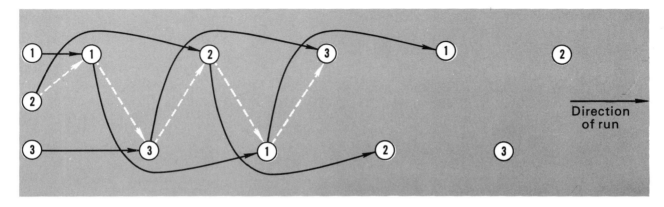

Fig. 11—3. Drill no. 1.

DRILLS

Inasmuch as gator ball involves skills of three different games, drills designed to develop the more important skills are described:

1. (Fig. 11-3) Throwing and catching the ball while running.

(1) Three men start on the same line. The middle man has the ball.
(2) Two side men advance.
(3) The ball is thrown to one advancing man (broken line). The man throwing the ball runs behind the man to whom he throws the ball and continues to advance downfield (solid line).
(4) Repeat the throw-and-run procedure, making sure that the man who throws the ball runs behind the man to whom he throws it and continues to advance downfield.

2. (Fig.11-4) Lifting the ball into the air with the foot.

(1) Form two lines of not more than five players each, facing each other, as indicated in the diagram.
(2) The end man in one line places the ball on the ground in front of him.
(3) After placing the toe of the kicking foot directly behind and in contact with the ball, he lifts it into the air to the man in the opposite line as indicated.
(4) As each man catches the ball with his hands, he places it on the ground and repeats the procedure.
(5) When the ball reaches the end man in the other group, the direction of the ball is reversed.

3. (Fig. 11-5) Advancing the ball on the ground by a series of short kicks.

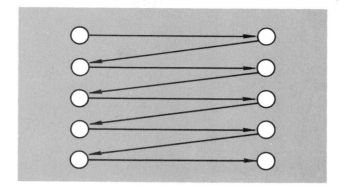

Fig. 11—4. Drill no. 2.

(1) Two single-file rows of men face each other at a distance of at least 30 yards. In line with them are two obstacles (X) that are 10 yards apart and 10 yards from the first player in each line.
(2) The first man in one line places the ball on the ground in front of him. He begins by advancing the ball toward the first object, using a series of short kicks. He must move the ball around the first object on one side and around the second object on the other side. He continues kicking the ball until it approaches the line of men opposite him (solid line).
(3) When the first man in the opposite line takes possession of the ball, the man finishing the drill moves to the end of that line of men (broken line).
(4) The procedure is repeated as many times as possible in the time allotted for this drill.
(5) Emphasis is on control of the ball with the feet, negotiating the course in the least possible time.

4. (Fig. 11-6) Throwing the ball through the goal.

(1) Divide the players at each goal into two equal groups—defensive and offensive.

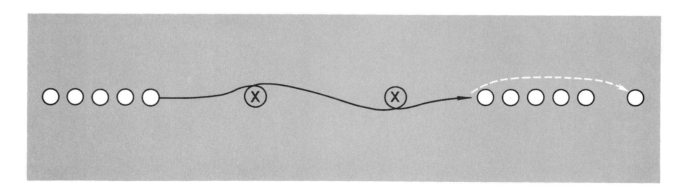

Fig. 11—5. Drill no. 3.

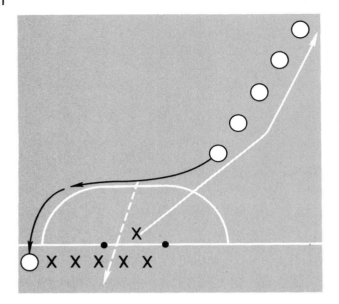

Fig. 11—6. Drill no. 4.

(2) Place one defending player in front of the goal as a goalkeeper (X).

(3) The offensive group stands on the field, with the first man at least 10 yards from the goal restraining arc and to one side of the center of the field (O).

(4) The first offensive man advances toward the goal, with the ball in his hands (solid dark line). He attempts to score by throwing the ball through the goal (broken white line) but is careful not to enter the goal restraining arc. The defending goalkeeper attempts to prevent the goal from being scored by catching or deflecting the ball.

(5) As each man throws for score, he goes to the end of the line of defensive men behind the goal (solid dark line).

(6) After each man defends the goal once, he goes to the end of the line of offensive men (solid white line).

(7) When each man has completed the cycle two or three times, the line of men on the field moves to the opposite side, and advances toward the goal at the opposite angle.

5. Kicking the ball through the goal (see Fig. 11-6: Throwing the ball through the goal).

(1) The players start in the position of drill 4.

(2) The same procedure is followed, except that the offensive man attempts to score by advancing the ball on the ground and kicking it through the goal.

One of the most popular games of all time, with almost universal appeal, the game of golf can bring great satisfaction to a player on one occasion and extreme frustration on another. One of the few things certain about golf is uncertainty. More than five million golf players toil our fairways in the United States, and their median score is 110 strokes for 18 holes.[1]

Golf courses (Fig. 12-1) are either 9 or 18 holes in length—a *hole* being the distance from the tee to the green. Depending upon their length, these holes are rated at three, four, or five *pars,* figures determined by the number of shots an expert golfer should take to negotiate the hole, assuming that two shots will be putts. In general, the length of par-three holes ranges up to 250 yards, par fours from 250 to 450 yards, and par fives 450 yards and over. The area from which the first shot is made is called the *tee.* The area at the other end of the hole is called the *green,* and contains the hole or "cup" into which the ball must be stroked. Greens are generally well-kept grass areas 60 to 90 feet in diameter. The cup can be located anywhere on the green, and should be moved about from time to time.

The intervening area is called the *fairway;* this area, while well-kept, contains hazards of contour, soil, trees, shrubs, and grass. Fairways are usually about 25 to 60 yards wide. Bordering the fairway is less well-tended land interspersed with trees, sand traps, and other natural hazards. These areas are called the *rough.*

HISTORY

Golf dates from the 14th or 15th century, depending upon whether one wishes to credit its origin to Holland or Scotland. Its growth was very slow for over two generations. In 1440 it began to intrigue the Scotch, which caused the King of Scotland to become alarmed. Golf was regarded as a menace to the

practice of archery, a compulsory national sport. A law was passed prohibiting the game; however, King James VI of Scotland in some manner got the golf "bug," and golf began to grow.

The first noted woman golfer of whom there is any mention was Mary, Queen of Scotland, who was the granddaughter of King James V. Queen Mary, who was educated in France, referred to the boy who served her on the golf course as a "cadet"—meaning someone who was learning the game. The pronunciation of the word in French is "caddy"; hence, the caddie of today. The first known golf tournament was played in 1860 at Preswick, Scotland.

John Reid, a Scotsman who settled at Yonkers, New York, in the 1880s, is called the "Father of American Golf." On December 22, 1895, four clubs in the East formed the United States Golf Association, which has been the ruling organization for amateurs ever since.

The professionals had no organization until 1916. Rodman Wanamaker was the leader in forming the Professional Golfers Association, or the PGA, on April 10, 1916, and the organization officially began its leadership.

TERMINOLOGY

Ace—A hole-in-one shot.
Approach—A stroke to the putting green.
Birdie—A score of one under par for a single hole.
Bogey—A score of one over par on a hole.
Bunker—A mound on the fairway; also sometimes used to indicate a sand trap.
Deuce—A hole made in two strokes.
Divot—A piece of turf cut out of the ground in making a stroke.
Dog leg—A bend in the fairway either to the left or right.
Dormie—The dormie player or team is winning by as many holes as there are holes left to play. In match play, the losing team can only hope to tie the leading team.
Double bogey—Two strokes over par for a single hole.

---

[1]Courtesy, National Golf Foundation.

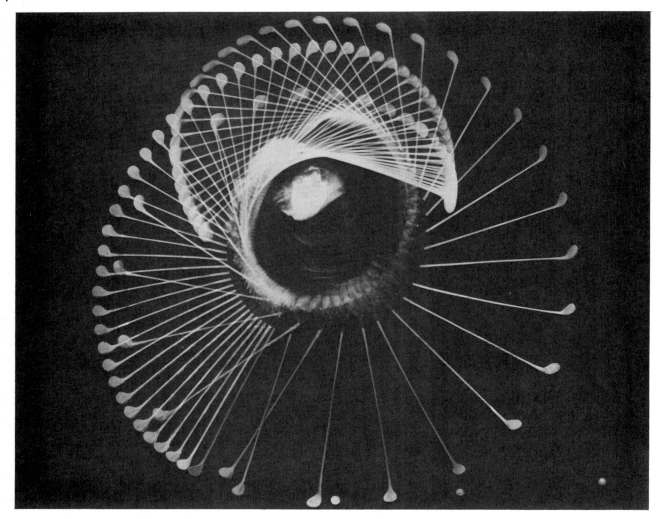

Double eagle—Three strokes under par for a single hole.

Eagle—Two strokes under par for a single hole.

Face—The hitting surface of the club.

Fade—A slight drift of the ball from the left to the right at the end of the ball's flight.

Fore—A warning cry to any person in the way of play.

Foursome—Four players playing together.

Halved—The hole is tied.

Handicap—Strokes given to equalize playing ability. The purpose of the handicap is to encourage poor players to enter tournaments.

Hole out—Putting or hitting the ball into the cup.

Hook—The opposite of a slice; with a right-handed player, it comes from a stroke that causes the ball to rotate counterclockwise and to curve to the left of the line from player to objective; with a left-handed player, a clockwise spin on the ball causes it to go to the right of the line from player to objective.

Lie—The position of the ball resting on the ground.

Par—The number of strokes a good player should need to play a hole, without mistakes, under ordinary conditions; it always allows for two putts on the green.

Pressing—Trying to hit the ball too hard.

Shanking—Hitting the ball with the heel and shaft of the club, causing it to go far right of the intended flight.

Slice—For a right-handed player, a stroke that gives the ball a clockwise spin, making it arc its flight to the right of the line from player to objective; for a left-handed player, a stroke giving the ball spin that arcs it to the left of the line from player to objective.

Smothered shot—The ball rolls on the ground after being hit, instead of going upward when distance is desired.

Sole—The surface of the club that touches the ground.

Summer rules—The ball must be played as it lies from tee to cup.

Tee—First, the peg on which the ball is elevated when it is to be struck from the teeing ground; second, the teeing ground itself.

Top—To hit the ball above its center.

Winter rules—The lie may be improved by a maximum of 6 inches, but the ball may not be moved nearer to the hole.

RULES

The official rules of golf are those approved by the United States Golf Association. There are two basic types of play: (1) *Match play,* in which the player winning the most holes wins the match; (2) *Medal play,* in which the player having the smallest number of strokes per round is declared the winner.

The basic golf rules are: (1) In the tee area the ball must be teed up between, but not in front of, the markers, and not more than two club lengths behind the markers. (2) Each swing at the ball counts as one stroke, even though the ball is missed. However, if the ball is accidentally knocked off the tee, it may be replaced without penalty. (3) Once the tee shot is hit, **the player whose ball lies farthest from the green plays first.** (4) If the ball goes out-of-bounds, the golfer must play another ball from the spot where he played the out-of-bounds ball. The penalty is one stroke. (5) When the ball is in a hazard, it must be hit before the ground can be touched with the club; example—a player may not set the club down behind the ball in a trap. (6) When the ball is lost and cannot be found after 5 minutes of searching, the golfer must go back to the spot from which he played the lost ball and play another one. The penalty is one stroke. (7) Where the ball is thought to be out-of-bounds, lost, or in a water hazard, a provisional ball is played from the same position. If the original is found later within bounds and is playable, the provisional ball must be picked up and the original must be played; no penalty is given. (8) If the ball comes to rest on the wrong green, it must be moved off the green and dropped as near as possible to where it lay, but not nearer to the hole being played. (9) If an artificial obstruction such as a hose or tee bench is in the lie of play, the ball may be moved within two clubs' length of the nearest point of the obstruction, but not nearer to the hole, and played without penalty. (10) A tee shot going into a water hazard is replayed, with a penalty stroke.

ETIQUETTE

(1) Never stand in the line of a player's shot. (2) Be still while a player is making a shot. (3) Be sure that all

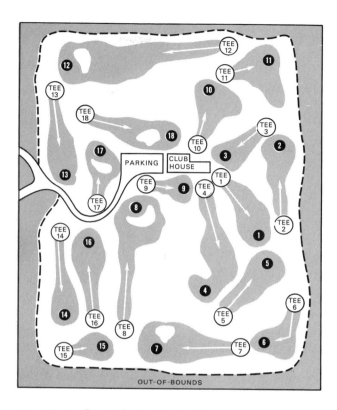

Fig. 12–1. Plan of a typical golf course.

players are off the green before making approach shots. (4) Replace all divots; simply press the grass down with the feet to help the grass grow better. (5) As soon as each player has completed putting, leave the green immediately. If there is any discussion as to how many strokes each player has had, this should be held off the green.

EQUIPMENT

The selection of golf clubs for personal use is largely a matter of preference. If a player is able to buy only a few clubs at one time, it is suggested that standard brands be purchased, so that at a later date the same brand can be acquired to complete the set. The beginning set should be composed of a number 1 wood, number 3 wood; 3, 5, 7, and 9 irons; and a putter.

The woods can be protected with knitted mittens, which should be replaced on the clubhead after each shot. This keeps the club clean and dry. The woods should be cleaned and waxed frequently. A regular floor wax can be used. Dents in the sole of the irons should be filed smooth and nicks in woods should be

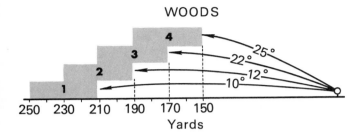

Fig. 12–2. Loft of woods.

filled with plastic wood and reshellacked. It is important to keep the clubs clean and dry. The shafts of all the clubs should be oiled occasionally.

The cost of the golf bag varies with its size, the material used, and the number of selling features. Most beginners will find the light "Sunday bag" adequate for their start in the game of golf.

Clubs

By rule, each golfer is allowed to carry fourteen clubs, but eleven or twelve are enough for the average golfer, and seven for the beginner. Starting with the number 2 iron, the faces of the irons are given graduated loft; the number 9 iron has the greatest loft. The wood clubs, starting with the driver, are likewise lofted to the number 4 wood. The purpose of lofted clubs is to provide height of shot, in order to overcome obstacles or to cause the ball to "stick" on the green with the desired limitation on roll after the ball strikes the green. The putter, of course, is used to roll the ball into the cup.

Use of Clubs

A complete set of clubs, together with a short explanation of their particular use, is listed here.

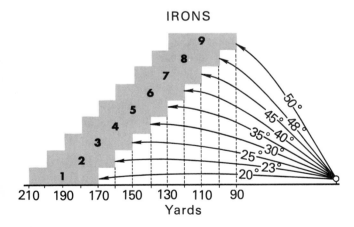

Fig. 12–3. Loft of irons.

Woods (Fig. 12–2):

Number   *Use*

1 Gives maximum distance and rather flat trajectory. Used for a tee shot only.
2 Shot off tee and for a good lie (when ball is high in grass) on the fairway.
3 Shot off tee on a short hole and for a close lie (when ball is touching dirt) on the fairway.
4 Shot off tee on a short hole and for a deep lie (when ball is in hole where divot has been taken) on the fairway.

Irons (Fig. 12–3):

Number   *Use*

2 Long shot from fairway, tee, low rough, or poor fairway lie.
3 Used in place of the midiron for less distance or where lie is bad.
4 Tee shot on a very short hole. Medium-distance approach shot, short roll-up shot (a low shot onto green where ball rolls after it hits the ground; also called "chip and run shot"), low rough, and bad lie on the fairway.
5 Occasionally for tee shot on a short hole. Fairly long, high shot from the fairway, rough, and bad lie. Pitch and run shot (a high shot to the green where ball rolls when it hits ground) when the distance desired is greater than can be obtained from short irons.
6 Pitch shot (a high shot to the green; ball does not roll when it lands). Difficult shot in bad rough.

Short Irons:

Number   *Use*

7) These short irons are used for
8} high pitch shots, in sand traps
9) or other hazards, and short approaches.
10—Putter   Used on green.

Ball

Golf balls are of two basic types— the *thin-cover* for securing distance, and the *thick* or *tough-cover ball* that will not fly as far.

The beginner should use the tough-cover ball, which is usually less expensive and will remain playable longer because it will not cut as easily as the thin-cover ball. In addition, the beginner has a tendency to lose balls in the rough and in water hazards.

Golf Course

An 18-hole course should comprise a minimum of 120 acres. The number 1, 9, 10, and 18 tees should be located near the clubhouse, so that players can play either a full 18 holes or stop conveniently after 9 holes. It is also best if the number 4 and 12 holes are close to the clubhouse, so that players can easily return in case of rain. Golf courses usually have drinking fountains and shelters in strategic locations on the course.

The type of grass for fairways and greens varies according to the climatic location in general, but bent grass is the most popular type for greens.

Dress

Comfort is the essential requirement in the selection of golfing attire. Clothes should provide freedom of movement, especially under and around the arms. Cotton, absorbent-type shirts are excellent, as are Bermuda shorts.

Probably the most important part of golfing attire is footwear. Proper shoes and socks are of vital importance. Socks should generally be of cotton or wool, and should be changed frequently for fresh ones. Shoes should be carefully fitted, and preferably should be spiked properly. Rubber-soled shoes with "ripple" design are acceptable for some persons. Because of the terrific strain on the feet, ankles, and knees in executing many golf shots, the player must be firmly anchored. Proper footwear should meet this need.

SAFETY

Generally speaking, golf is not a dangerous game; however, people have been killed from being hit by golf clubs and golf balls. All who play the game of golf should accept the responsibility of using the accepted safety precautions.

Adequate clearance should be available for each golfer when swinging in play or in practice; the one who is about to make the stroke, as well as those watching or waiting, should assume responsibility for clearing the area. Practicing should be done only on practice areas. When practicing long shots, the golfer should have ample range laterally as well as forward. A practice cage may be substituted for the range practice if facilities are limited. When playing on the fairway, the golfer should wait with his shot until the area in front is clear. If anyone is dangerously near to the range of the intended shot, the player should warn him of the play by calling, "FORE!" The player who

hears the warning should cover his head, turn his back to the call, and bend forward to avoid direct contact in a vulnerable spot on the body.

FUNDAMENTALS

Proper instruction: It is highly desirable that the prospective player first take lessons from a competent and experienced teacher. This reduces the risk of picking up bad fundamental habits at the outset. In addition, such lessons make the game more enjoyable because only experienced teachers can provide basic knowledge of the game, as well as teach the fundamental skills.

Grip

(Figs. 12-4, 12-5, and 12-6): First, place the handle of the club across the palm of the left hand, with the thumb crossing in front to the right side of the shaft. Second, take the right hand and overlap the small finger between the first and second fingers of the left hand. The thumb of the right hand should cross in front to the left side of the shaft. Third, the forefingers and thumbs of both hands from "V's" which point to the right shoulder.

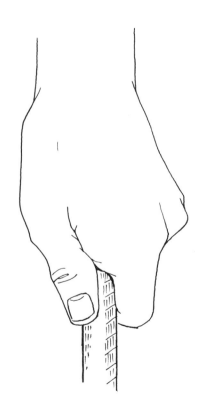

Fig. 12—4. Overlapping grip, left hand.

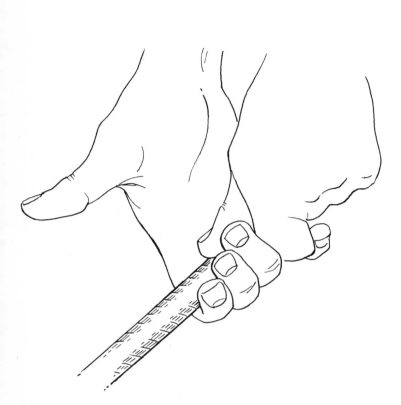

Fig. 12—5. Overlapping grip, right hand.

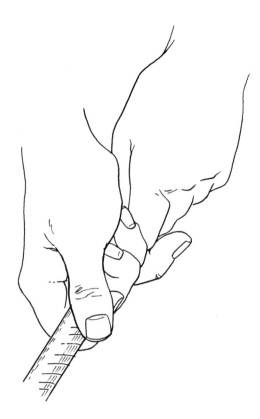

Fig. 12—6. Overlapping grip, complete.

Essentially, this is the grip—the shaft should be held very firmly in the fingers, but not so firmly as to cause a tensing of the muscles.

There is no relaxing of the grip at any time during the swing. Keep both hands fitted compactly together. They must coordinate the essential factors of left-hand control and right-hand power; unless they are working closely, your hand action will be faulty. The hands are the only transmitting power in hitting the golf ball, so learning the correct grip is one of the most important phases in mastering the golf game.

Full Swing (Long Game)

The Start of the Swing

The first phase in any skill is the position called the "ready" stage. The player must be in good balance, which means that the distance between the feet should be about the width of the shoulders; the knees should be flexed. Different woods require differences in the placement of the ball in relation to the body. (Fig. 12-7) When using the driver, the ball is played off the inside of the left heel. It is wise for beginners to use a square stance, for it is easier for them to learn to line

up for the shot by forming a right angle. This means that if an imaginary line were drawn from a parallel at the end of the toes and lined up with the intended target, the shot should be in line provided the clubhead is brought through in the correct position. The head is behind the ball; the shoulders should be tilted somewhat, with the right shoulder slightly lower than the left. The hands should hold the club firmly, but not with a tense grip. It is better for the player to learn what feels right to him, rather than to be told to hold the club firmly. What is firm to one may not be firm to another, so it is up to the player to learn for himself.

At the beginning of the backswing of the full swing, the hands, arms, legs, and shoulders act as a unit and must start back together. (Fig. 12-8) The arems and wrists go back until there is a pull on the left side of the body; by this time, the hips will begin to start the turn.

The beginning backswing of the full swing is a critical stage of the golf shot. (Fig. 12-9) The wrists do not cock consciously, and it is here the beginner gets into trouble. Once the pull is felt on the left side, the wrists will cock naturally; the player should not make

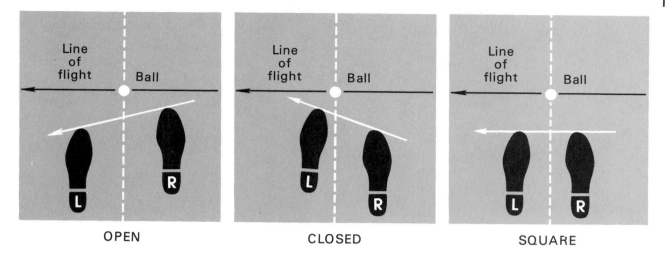

OPEN   CLOSED   SQUARE

Fig. 12—7. Golf stances.

any deliberate effort to break the wrists, for this will come naturally. The right elbow is kept close to the right hip, but even more important is the fact that the right elbow should be pointed downward, with the forearm perpendicular to the ground. The left arm is as straight as possible; it is not too important that the

left arm be locked, for some cannot keep the arm as rigid as others. The head is static, with the shoulders rotating around it. The knees remain flexed, to give freedom for the hips to turn. Both knees should be relaxed and flexed, to give the freedom necessary for a correct pivot.

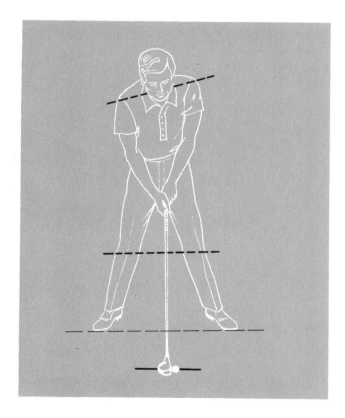

Fig. 12—8. Full swing: Position 1—start of swing.

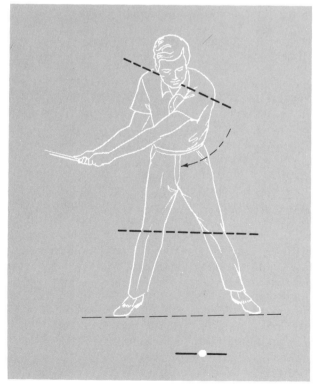

Fig. 12—9.
Full swing: Position 2—beginning of backswing.

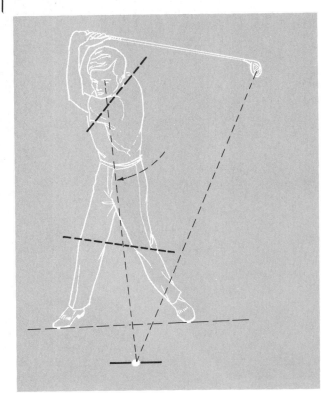

Fig. 12—10.
Full swing: Position 3—top of backswing.

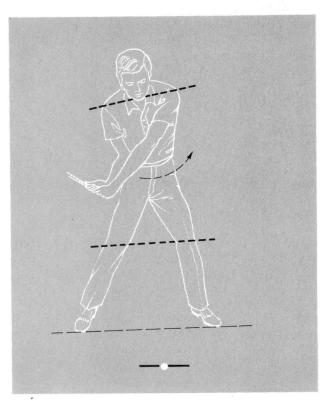

Fig. 12—11. Full swing: Position 4.

Top of the Backswing (Fig. 12—10)

The club shaft should be horizontal to the ground, with the face of the club square to the ball. This ensures that the wrists are in the correct position. The head and shoulders are behind the ball. The left arm is as stiff as possible; however, it is not necessary for the arm to be completely stiff. The right elbow is pointed downward. The hips will be in the correct position if the right hip is on the inside of the right foot. (At the top of the backswing, if the right hip is outside the right foot, the student is off-balance.) The body weight has been transferred over the right foot, and the inside edge of the left foot remains in contact with the ground. Actually, this position is considered the windup position for the full swing, and it is most important that the player be balanced at the top of the backswing position.

Through the Hitting Area (Figs. 12—11 and 12—12)

From the top of the backswing the arms, wrists, and shoulders initiate the downward motion. The time at which the hands and wrists come into the hitting area varies with the size of the individual; the player should remember that the hands do not uncock until the club

is only 10 to 12 inches from the ball. This gives the maximum speed to the clubhead. By the time the hands and arms arrive in the hitting area, the weight is shifted to the left side of the body. For beginners it should be stressed that the right elbow is pointed downward and that the left arm is straight. The knees remain flexed, with the weight of the right side beginning to turn to the left side of the body. Each player must get the feel of the weight coming correctly into the ball through experience. One extremely important point to remember is that when coming into the ball, the left arm should be pulling hard enough to keep the right hand and arm from overpowering the left hand. Most players are right-handed, and it is well established that the right hand often plays too large a part in the total swing pattern.

Finish of the Swing (Fig. 12—13)

The weight has transferred to the left side, with the right foot pushing off from the toes, giving the added power for the full swing. The hips have turned almost 90 degrees, with the arms and hands going clear around the shoulders. It should be stressed that practicing this form will result in better golf than can be achieved without proper follow-through. Many

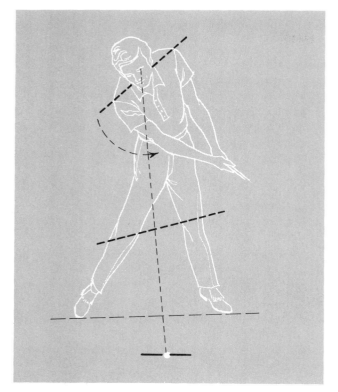

Fig. 12—12. Full swing: Position 5.

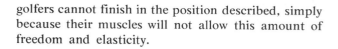

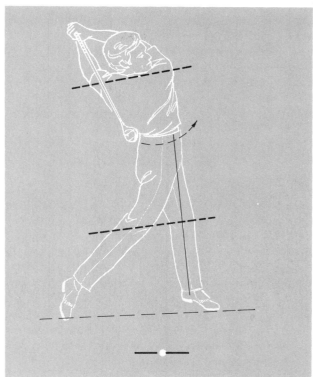

Fig. 12—13. Full swing: Position 6—finish.

golfers cannot finish in the position described, simply because their muscles will not allow this amount of freedom and elasticity.

Short Game

This is a variation of the full golf swing. Mechanics of a full swing and shorter swing are the same. The length of swing is determined mainly by the kind of club and the distance desired to project the ball. The shortening of the full swing to a smaller arc is often referred to as the "short game." A golfer must master both the long game and the short game to shoot par golf.

Putting

Putting is part of the short game, and is one of the most important strokes in golf. When it is considered that two putts are allowed for each green, it becomes apparent that putting comprises a major part of the total game.

The reverse overlap grip (Fig. 12-14) is used in putting. In this grip, the shaft of the putter is put in the palm of the left hand. Angle the shaft so that it crosses the forefinger between the base and the first joint. Close the left hand, allowing the shaft to angle across the fingers, with the pressure of the shaft more in the heel of the left hand. The thumb of the left hand extends down the shaft and parallel to it. The right hand then grips the club below the left hand, with the thumb going down the shaft to the club. The index finger of the left hand goes down and across the knuckles of the three fingers of the right hand. The club is then held firmly by the fingers of both hands, with a tighter grip by the left hand because it is executing the guiding motion.

The back of the left hand generally should go in the direction of the cup when the ball and the cup are on the same level. If the cup is on a lower level than the ball, the left hand does not lead to the cup; instead, it leads across the slope or uphill and, when the correct amount of force is applied to the putt, the ball should start off at an angle, then curve down to the cup. The contour of the green is a very important factor in determining the optimal starting direction for a putt, and a player can learn how to overcome it only by continued practice.

In putting, the ball is stroked by keeping the face of the club perpendicular to the line of the putt throughout the swing. The distance of a putt is governed by the amount of backswing. The club should follow through for a distance about equal to that of the backswing.

A correct mental approach to putting is extremely important. One factor that will help all golfers is confidence that the putt will go into the cup, no matter how long or short the putt is; a person must develop a positive approach in putting the ball.

REASONS FOR INCORRECT SHOTS

It is very difficult in the game of golf to know exactly what happens. The game is of such a nature that even the most experienced eye many times cannot tell why a shot went the way it did. The following explanations are listed to help you understand what causes incorrect shots.

Hooks are caused if you:

1. Use a grip that partially closes the club face (turns the face forward and toward the ground).
2. Use too closed a stance.
3. Play the ball too far back toward the right foot.
4. Put too much power in the right hand.

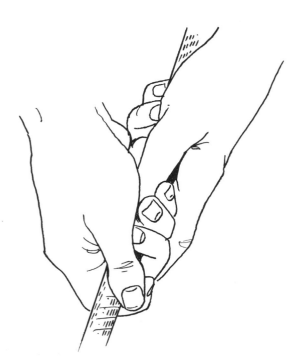

Fig. 12—14. Reverse overlap grip: Putting.

Slices are caused if you:

1. Use a grip which leaves the club face open at impact (face is turned upward).
2. Use too open a stance.
3. Lack proper foot and knee action in the swing.
4. Cut across the ball at impact (pull the club toward your body).
5. Have the body ahead of the hands in the downswing.

Smothered shots are caused if you:

1. Close the face of the club too much at impact.
2. Use poor wrist action, which closes the club face too much.
3. Get the body ahead of the hands in the downswing.

Shanked shots are caused by:

1. Gripping the club too tightly.
2. Bending the left arm too much during the backswing.
3. Failing to keep the head and body behind the stroke during the downswing.
4. Failing to keep the left arm close to the body in the downswing.
5. Attempting to guide or steer the ball at impact, instead of swinging the hands freely.

CHECKLIST

The following checklist has been devised to help the golf player analyze his swing. In using this checklist, start from the beginning and keep checking through the completion of the swing.

As you take the address position:

1. Check your grip.
2. Play the ball inside the left foot.
3. Use the square stance.
4. The left arm should be a straight line with the shaft of the club.
5. The chin should point to the right of the ball.

As you address the ball:

1. Start the swing—your feet, legs, arms, and back should be a unit.
2. Keep the head still.
3. Keep your weight on the inside of the ball of the feet.
4. Make sure your left hand pushes the club back.
5. Keep the left arm straight.
6. Roll the left foot inward (do not rotate the left ankle).

Top of the backswing:

1. The head remains static.
2. Your left shoulder should be pointing to the ball.
3. The right forearm is pointing toward the ground.
4. The club should be horizontal to the ground.
5. Both hands remain firm on the club.
6. The left hand controls the club.

As the downswing starts:

1. The hips initiate the downswing.
2. The left foot should be on the ground.
3. The head remains static.
4. The left arm remains straight.

Through the hitting area:

1. The left arm leads the right hand.
2. The head must remain static.
3. The right hip has turned into the direction line.
4. The right hand is the explosive power.
5. The left arm must be straight at the hit.
6. The weight is going forward; the left foot is on the ground.
7. The right shoulder is behind the hit.
8. The hands at the hit must control the club.

Following the impact:

1. The left arm has extended toward the line of flight.
2. The right side must be released.
3. The chest is turned toward the line of flight.
4. The head position is just beginning to turn.
5. The right hand crosses over the left hand.

The finish:

1. The arms finish high.
2. The weight is now all forward and on the left foot.
3. The right wrist and arm have crossed over.

STRATEGY

The two main problems of all golf shots are direction and distance. Actually, it may be said that there is only one fundamental principle in the whole game of golf: *The ball will go in any direction that is forced upon it by the face of the club.* Golf strategy is planned from the tee to the green by the individual player, according to his own skill. If the player has learned to swing the club squarely into the ball with the proper speed, he may proceed from the tee to the green according to the plan that he mapped out mentally before his first drive from the tee. Most beginners will need to plan new strategy after each shot because of the difference between the estimated and actual skill. Naturally, it is better to go down the middle of the fairway and to play for a position from which to enter the green safely and easily, than to take a short cut to the cup over the many dangerous hazards.

Distance is governed by the choice of the club. "Loft" results from the clubhead hitting down and through the ball; the ball is never scooped up to gain loft. Increase in the loft of a shot is gained by using a club with increased loft and playing it with a normal swing.

Direction is achieved by swinging the club through the ball in the desired line of flight. Any deviation of the swing from the line of flight will result in deviation from the desired placement.

BIBLIOGRAPHY

Bruce, Ben, and Davies, Evelyn, *Beginning Golf.* Belmont, Calif.: Wadsworth Publishing Co., 1962.

Cheatum, Billye Ann, *Golf.* Philadelphia: W.B. Saunders Company, 1969.

East, J. Victor, *Better Golf in 5 Minutes.* Englewood Cliffs, N.J.: Prentice-Hall, Inc., 1956.

Finsterwald, Dow, *Fundamentals of Golf.* New York: The Ronald Press Company, 1961.

Fossum, Bruce G., and Dagraedt, Mary, *Golf.* Boston: Allyn and Bacon, Inc., 1969.

Galvano, Phil, *Secrets of Accurate Putting and Chipping.* Englewood Cliffs, N.J.: Prentice-Hall, Inc., 1957.

Golf Magazine's Your Long Game. New York: Harper & Row, 1964.

Golf Rules—DGWS. Washington, D.C.: American Association for Health, Physical Education and Recreation.

Hogan, Ben, *Five Lessons* of *The Modern Fundamentals of Golf.* New York: A.S. Barnes & Co., 1957.

Morrison, Alex J., *A New Way to Better Golf.* New York: Simon and Schuster, Inc., 1932.

Nelson, Byron, *Winning Golf.* New York: A.S. Barnes & Co., 1946.

Rehling, Conrad H., *Golf for the Physical Education Teacher and Coach.* Dubuque, Iowa: William C. Brown & Co., 1954.

United States Golf Association, *Golf Rules.* New York: The Association, 1965.

GYMNASTICS | 13

The exact origin of gymnastics as a form of exercise and physical training is unknown. The histories of the ancient civilizations of China, India, Egypt, Greece, and Rome all contain references to the use of certain gymnastic activities in the training and education of youths for citizenship and for warfare. Prehistoric drawings and carvings depict tumbling and pyramid building; and there are many records from various periods of history that mention tumblers, leapers, acrobats, jugglers, and rope dancers. All of these records attest to early and sustained appreciation of gymnastic skill as an entertainment, a recreation, and a constructive athletic activity.

The gymnastics programs of today, however, received their start and early development in Germany under the leadership of Friedrich Ludwig Jahn and his followers. Jahn, who is often referred to as the father of modern gymnastics, founded the Turner organization and established the first turnplatz (outdoor gymnastic area) in 1811. Jahn and his pupils, through a process of trial and experiment, invented and constructed the apparatus, while also devising the tricks and routines that form the nucleus of the extensive variety of gymnastic maneuvers practiced today.

Under Jahn's leadership, gymnastics was enthusiastically received by the youth of Germany and soon spread to other European countries where, today, it occupies a most prominent place in their sports and physical education programs.

The introduction of gymnastics into the United States occurred with the immigration of Germans to this country in the early nineteenth century. Charles Follen, Charles Beck, and Francis Lieber are names prominent among those of Jahn's disciples who came to the United States and were active in the establishment of gymnastics in this country.

Our present-day diversified programs of physical education had their inception under the influence and guidance of these German turners, who brought with them to the United States an organized system of physical training. Turnvereins (gymnastics clubs) were established in many of our large cities wherever a large number of German immigrants had settled. The Turnverein has furnished, and continues to furnish, the important early training for many of our best gymnasts who compete on intercollegiate teams and represent the United States in international competition.

The YMCA, with fully-equipped gymnasiums and trained instructors in most of its organizations, has also made a significant contribution to the growth and development of gymnastics in the United States.

NATURE AND VALUES

Good Form

A unique characteristic of gymnastics is its emphasis upon good form. In other sports, form may be considered important only to the extent that better performance is achieved. In gymnastics, however, preciseness of position and movement, correct posture, and body mechanics are an integral part of every exercise and should be carefully observed by expert and beginner alike.

Style

While closely related to good form, style is a more elusive and intangible quality that distinguishes the performance of a *good* performer from that of one who merely is capable of the stunt. The gymnast is likely to have an audience whether he is performing in competition, exhibition, or merely in practice. He should strive to convey an impression of poise and confidence, while avoiding affectation and conceit. The extreme, unnatural, militarylike posturings of years past have been replaced by a more natural bearing which is neither sloppy and careless nor too stiff and formal.

Style and good form may be acquired through practice, through observation of outstanding performers in action, and through critical self-analysis.

Routines

A gymnastic routine usually consists of a mount, a series of tricks selected and arranged for continuity, and a dismount.

The development of routines calls for creativeness and physical endurance, and it supplies motivation for learning new tricks and routines.

SAFETY

Safety in gymnastics is largely a matter of common sense and good judgment. Experience has taught, however, that special consideration should be given the following:

(1) *Concentration:* Keep your mind on what you are doing; do nothing to distract others; no "horseplay."

(2) *Equipment:* Check equipment for security. Learn to adjust and handle it properly.

(3) *Progressive learning:* Learn fundamentals first. Progress from the simple and easy to the more complex and difficult.

(4) *Spotting:* Spotting or guarding refers to the assistance that one or more persons may render the performer during the execution of an exercise. Spotters must know what trick is being attempted, and place themselves so as to assist and protect the performer, while at the same time protecting themselves from injury.

(5) *Uniform:* Practice clothes should be clean and fit snugly. For girls and women, the leotard is the most appropriate uniform due to the close-fitting design. Lightweight shoes or gymnastic slippers should be worn. Omit rings and jewelry. The hair should be pulled back to prevent hanging in the eyes or obstructing movement in any way. Bright-colored leotards and subdued make-up are recommended for girls. Fingernails need to be well-trimmed.

(6) *Prevent slipping:* Keep the hands, body, and apparatus dry from perspiration. Carbonate of magnesia in block form (available at druggists), or powdered rosin (available at hardware or sporting goods stores) should be rubbed on the hands to ensure a secure grip.

(7) *Fatigue:* Avoid new or hazardous tricks, or long routines, when tired.

(8) *Warm-up:* Warm up before attempting strenuous exercise. Some of the recommended warm-up activities are push-ups, pullups, swinging to and fro on the bar, the front split, and the side split.

(9) *Physical condition:* Do not attempt difficult or hazardous tricks when in poor physical condition. After a "layoff," work gradually into top form by many repetitions of fundamental exercises.

(10) *Care of the hands:* Keep the apparatus clean from rust and caked magnesium. Stop before blisters burst or calluses are torn out. Reduce heavy, thick calluses by rubbing with a block of pumice stone (available at druggists). Treat open blisters and torn calluses to avoid infection.

(11) *Mats:* Place mats for dismounts and to reduce injuries from falls. Use several thicknesses where. needed. Pad the apparatus where needed.

(12) *Mechanical safety devices:* Use belts, wrist straps, and catch mats only under the supervision of an experienced gymnastics instructor.

(13) *Adjustable apparatus:* Lower the horizontal bar, rings, parallel bars, and horse whenever practical while learning new or hazardous tricks.

(14) *Proper mental attitude:* Don't change your mind in the middle of an attempt. Don't be too proud to take all obvious safety precautions. React sensibly to fear.

COURTESY

The general principles of courtesy and gentlemanly behavior are much the same regardless of environment. A respect for the rights and feelings of others is fundamental to all human relationships, and will naturally be observed in the gymnasium as elsewhere. However, breaches of etiquette may occur through lack of knowledge of the specialized requirements in a particular situation. Therefore, the following specific rules may serve as a guide:

(1) Do not monopolize equipment. Take your turn, then stand aside. Do not sit or lean on equipment while resting or awaiting your turn.

(2) Always leave the apparatus in safe condition. Wipe away perspiration and excess carbonate. Leave adjustment features properly secured.

(3) Do your part in placing and storing equipment.

(4) Do not enter the gymnastic area unless properly dressed for the activity. Spectators should remain on the side lines or in the grandstand.

(5) Try to help and encourage others, especially beginners. Sarcastic and derisive remarks do a great deal of harm, and should be avoided. A superior, aloof attitude on the part of more experienced performers has resulted in the discouragement of many a novice gymnast.

(6) Be neat and clean in both costume and person during practice sessions.

(7) Loud talking, whistling, eating, drinking, and "horseplay" are especially objectionable where gymnasts are attempting difficult and hazardous exercises that require close concentration.

COMPETITION

International competition, including Olympic gymnastics, is conducted under the jurisdiction of the International Gymnastics Federation (F.I.G.).

The following men's events are included: floor exercise (formerly free calisthenics), long horse vaulting, pommel horse, horizontal bar, parallel bars, still rings, and all-around (includes all of the above events). Women's events are: floor exercise, balance beam, uneven parallel bars, vaulting, and all-around (includes all of the above events).

Governing organizations for competitive gymnastics in the United States are the Amateur Athletic Union, the National Collegiate Athletic Association, and the United States Gymnastic Federation.

YMCA's, Turnvereins, Sokols, athletic clubs, and many high school athletic associations promote and conduct gymnastics competition on levels appropriate to their particular organization and situation.

With increasing emphasis upon international competition and greater public interest in gymnastics, the present trend is toward conformity to international rules at all levels of gymnastic competition in the United States. International rules call for one compulsory and one optional exercise in each of the international events; they also require that each team member compete in all events, thus encouraging the development of all-round gymnasts rather than specialists.

However, at the present time in many U.S. gymnastic meets, compulsory exercises are omitted and only optional routines are performed. Frequently, such special events as tumbling, trampoline, and rope climbing are included in the program. The flying rings is no longer a competitive event, but often it is included in the program of individual schools or organizations.

Scoring in competitive gymnastics is subject to change in detail from time to time; however, in general, exercises are graded by judges using a scale from zero to ten, graduated in tenths. Optional exercises are judged on the basis of difficulty, combination, and execution, while compulsory exercises, which are the same for each gymnast, are scored on execution alone. The vaulting events differ from other events in that a difficulty rating scale for the various vaults is provided in the rule book so that judges need consider only execution in scoring the one compulsory and one optional vault performed by each gymnast.

The all-around event is scored on the basis of a composite of points accumulated by the gymnast in the individual events.

Team scores are computed on the basis of points awarded for places won by individual team members in the various events.

SKILLS

In general, gymnastics stunts in most events can be done by both men and women. However, some stunts require exceptional muscular strength and are not appropriate for women to attempt. In competitive meets, the sex of competitors is specified for each event.

Fundamental to all phases of gymnastics, tumbling and balancing are probably the most beneficial and satisfying of the gymnastic activities. Fundamental training in tumbling and balancing will be of tremendous value in learning the advanced skills of other events, and are of equal importance for both men and women.

Balancing

Head Balance, Head and Hands on Mat. [a] *Kick-up approach.* Squat, place your hands on the mat shoulder width apart, fingers spread and pointing forward. Place your head on the mat beyond the hands so that the three points of contact form an equilateral triangle. Extend one leg backward and swing it upward. Allow the other leg to follow it so that your body assumes an inverted position. Your knees should be straight, your toes pointed, your feet together, your body arched, with the weight equally distributed on your hands and the front part of the top of your head (*not* on your forehead). Control your balance by increasing or decreasing the pressure on your hands. To recover to a standing position, draw one knee to your chest, swing the other leg downward and bring both feet to the mat. (*b*) *Curl-up approach:* Squat and place your head and hands as in (*a*). Press with your hands until inverted balance is accomplished, with your knees tucked in closely to the chest. Slowly extend your legs upward to the head balance position. Recover to a stand as in (*a*).

Head Balance, Head in Hands. Squat, place your head on the mat, clasp your hands around your head, fingers overlapping. Your forearms are on the mat so that an equilateral triangle is formed with the head and hands at the apex, the forearms on two sides and a line between the elbows as the base. Assume the inverted position as in (*a*) of the stunt above. Control your balance by pulling upward against the head if overbalanced (falling forward); bring your elbows closer together if underbalanced (falling back down).

Head Balance, Arms Folded. Squat with your arms folded and place your forearms on the mat. Place your head on the mat forward of the arms so that the head and elbows form an equilateral triangle with the head at the apex, and the folded arms as the base. Kick or curl to an inverted balance as in (a) or (b) of the basic head balance. Recover to a stand as in the basic head balance.

Squat Balance, "Frog Balance." Squat, with your knees spread; place your hands on the mat as in (a). Allow the hollow of the knee joints to rest upon the points of the elbows. Tip forward until your weight is supported upon the hands alone. Keep your head back and your toes pointed. Control your balance as follows: if falling forward onto the head, press hard on your fingertips and raise your head; if falling back toward the feet, lower your head slightly and pull your shoulders forward.

Forearm Balance. Squat, place your hands and underside of forearms flat on the mat about shoulder width apart; your hands are turned outward, with the fingers spread. Press your shoulders well forward and kick up to the inverted balance, with your weight supported on the forearms and hands only. Keep your head up and back. Control your balance as follows: if falling forward onto your face, press hard on your fingertips, raise your head and shift your shoulders back away from the hands slightly; if falling back down toward the starting position, dig in with your fingertips and pull your shoulders slightly forward over your hands.

Hand Balance. The hand balance is probably the most important single fundamental in gymnastics. The strength and control acquired in learning this trick are important in all phases of gymnastics and have proved valuable in other sports as well. The hand balance position is used extensively in advanced work on the parallel bars, horizontal bar, rings, floor calisthenics, and tumbling. Progress beyond the very elementary stages in gymnastics is dependent upon mastery of the hand balance. The beginner must be prepared to spend weeks and sometimes months of diligent practice.

The basic head balance (a) and the squat balance may be considered "lead-ups" to the hand balance, and should be learned first.

Practice against the wall has proved to be a useful learning device because it allows the beginner to remain in the inverted position long enough to acquire a sense of balance and to develop the necessary muscular strength.

Proceed as follows: squat; place your hands on the bare floor, about 6 inches away from the wall (this distance varies slightly with height and body build); the fingers should be spread, with the forefingers pointing straight forward. Do not place the palms and fingers flat, but rather flex the hands and fingers slightly, "gripping" the floor as if it were a bar or similar object. Keeping the arms straight, move the shoulders forward to a position directly over the wrists. With the head well back, either kick up or curl up to the inverted position as for the head balance and allow the heels to rest against the wall. Now, with the heels still resting against the wall, try to achieve a perfect hand balance position: elbows locked, shoulders directly over the wrists, head back, body slightly arched, feet and legs together, knees straight, and toes pointed.

To acquire a true balance and bring the heels away from the wall, it should be necessary only to press downward on the fingertips and raise the head slightly. Do *not* kick away from the wall. Balance is very delicate, so no sudden, rough moves should be made.

Much the same procedure should be followed when practicing without the wall. Use a mat for protection, but place the hands on the bare floor which provides a firmer, more responsive balancing surface. When practicing, do not walk or duck and roll when balance is lost; it is better to fall over and allow the feet to land on the mat. Maintain correct position and fight for balance all the way over.

Doubles Balancing

In doubles work the top man is usually referred to as the *topmounter* and the bottom man, who is usually the larger of the two, as the *understander*. The understander should control the trick and do most of the balancing. This type of work requires teamwork and timing. When two men become accustomed to working with one another, they should be cautious in working with strange partners.

Chest Balance. The understander takes position on his hands and knees. The topmounter stands beside him, then places his hands (palms upward) and forearms beneath the understander's chest and abdomen; the topmounter's shoulders and upper arms rest on the understander's back. The topmounter kicks to an inverted balance as in the head or hand balance.

Hands, Knees, and Shoulder Balance. The understander lies on his back, knees spread and fully bent;

feet flat on the mat; arms straight and extended forward and upward. The topmounter stands in front of the understander and bends forward, placing his hands on the understander's knees and his shoulders in the understander's hands. The topmounter then kicks to the inverted balance. Both men should keep their arms straight.

Low Arm to Arm Balance. The understander lies flat on his back with his legs straight, arms straight and extended upward. The topmounter stands astride the understander, facing him. The topmounter bends forward and grasps the understander's elbows. At the same time the understander grasps the topmounter's upper arms just below the shoulders. The topmounter kicks or curls to an inverted balance.

Feet to Thigh Stand. The understander stands directly behind the topmounter, squats, places his neck beneath the crotch of the topmounter and lifts him to a sitting position astride the understander's neck. The understander assumes a semisquat position and grasps the topmounter's thighs just above his knees, and stands up, leaning slightly forward. At the same time the understander ducks under the topmounter's crotch, straightens his arms, and sits back so as to counterbalance the topmounter's forward lean. The topmounter should stand with his legs straight, body arched, head erect, and arms extended sideward and upward. For the dismount, the understander straightens up, allowing the topmounter to drop to a stand directly in front of him.

Mount to Stand on Shoulders. The understander assumes a semisquat position, back straight, feet in line about 30 inches apart, heels flat on the mat, arms bent, hands alongside head, and palms upward. The topmounter approaches from the rear and slightly left, reaches with his left hand and grasps the understander's left hand. The topmounter places his left foot on the understander's left thigh near the hip, and steps up, bringing his right foot to the understander's right shoulder, grasping the understander's right hand with his own right hand. He immediately brings the left foot to the understander's left shoulder. As the topmounter places his right foot on the understander's shoulder, the understander should straighten up with a spring which, if timed properly, should assist the mount. The topmounter, before releasing the understander's hands and standing straight, should place his feet properly as follows: weight on balls of feet, heels together and slightly lowered. Upon releasing his hands, the topmounter should stand straight up, keeping his knees slightly

bent and his hips directly over the ankles. The understander should grasp the back of the topmounter's legs just below the knee joint, pulling forward and downward so that the topmounter's shins are against the understander's head.

To dismount, the topmounter squats slightly, the partners regrasp their hands, the topmounter jumps forward to a stand close in front of the understander, who squats slightly to assist the dismount. The handhold is released as the topmounter assumes a controlled stand on the mat.

Tumbling

Front Roll. Squat, reach forward, placing your hands on the mat about shoulder width apart, fingers pointing forward. Press forward with your legs, allowing the arms to bend so that the face approaches the mat. Duck your head (chin on chest), allowing the neck and shoulders to ease to the mat. Continue pressure with the legs, increasing forward momentum and roll forward onto the neck, shoulders, and rounded back; keep your knees tucked closely to the chest. As your weight comes onto the back, and *while still in motion*, grasp the legs just below the knees (catch the tuck), pull vigorously to complete the roll, and assume a straight standing position.

Front rolls may be performed in series. Variations of the front roll include the front roll with legs crossed, so that a half turn may be executed as the roll is completed, and the dive and front roll—which is not recommended for beginners because of the possibility of a serious head or neck injury.

Safety Hint. Never allow your weight to bear upon the head. Always place your weight first on the hands, then on the neck and shoulders.

Back Roll. From a straight stand, stoop forward reaching your hands toward the toes, head down (chin on chest). At the same time sit back with your hips and allow your buttocks to ease to the mat. As soon as the buttocks contact the mat, immediately tuck your knees to the chest; bend your arms and place the hands, palms upward, alongside the head; and roll backward onto your rounded back, shoulders, neck, and hands. As the weight comes firmly onto the hands complete the roll by a vigorous extension of the arms, bringing your feet to the mat and standing straight.

Back rolls may also be performed in series. A variation of the back roll is the extended back roll, in which a vigorous extension of the body and arms is executed at the halfway point in the roll so that a momentary hand balance is achieved. The trick is completed by a vigorous snap-down of the feet and legs to a straight stand.

Safety Hint. There is a strong tendency to throw the head back when attempting a back roll. This will not only slow or stop the roll completely, but will result in a painful blow to the back of the head. Keep your head down (chin on chest).

Headspring. This trick is more easily learned over a rolled mat or similarly elevated, padded object such as the top lift of a vaulting box, a tackle dummy, or a burlap bag filled with shavings. The procedure is the same, however, whether working over an alevated object or on the level mat.

Proceed as follows: squat, place your hands and head on the mat exactly as for a head balance. Straighten the knees, pressing forward through a momentary head balance position, forcing the hips over well beyond the shoulders. Fling your feet over your head by a vigorous extension of the hips, forcing an extreme body arch which should be maintained until the landing is accomplished. Just before the landing, push off vigorously with your hands and arms so that a straight standing position, with head erect and arms extended overhead, is assumed.

Headsprings may also be performed in series.

Learning Hints:

1. Delay the arm push until the very last instant.
2. Do not bend the knees for the landing.
3. Emphasize the leg fling (hip extension). The primary impetus comes from this motion, and it must be executed with great force. Knees must be straight for maximum power.

4. A short running approach will be helpful when using an elevated take-off.

Safety Hint. Place mats on both sides of the take-off point, especially when using an elevated take-off.

Neckspring (knip-up, snap-up, kip, upstart). This trick is quite similar to the headspring, except that the neck and shoulders are used as the pivot point instead of the head. The neckspring may be executed from either a forward or a rearward approach.

(a) Forward approach. From a stand, bend over, keeping your knees straight; place your hands on the mat as for a front roll, roll forward onto the neck and shoulders; hesitate for an instant, allowing the hips to move well forward. Then, as in the headspring, extend the hips forcibly; push hard with the arms, assuming a standing position, with the knees straight and the body maintaining an extreme arch.

(b) Rearward approach. From a straight stand, stoop forward and sit backward as for a back roll; roll backward onto the shoulders, neck, and hands, getting the feet well back of the shoulders; hesitate in this position for an instant. Then proceed as in (a), extending the hips, snapping the feet and legs forward, assuming a standing position. Variations of the neckspring include execution without the use of the hands or by.pressing with the hands on the front of the thighs.

The neckspring should be performed with knees straight throughout. Landing in a squatting position is considered poor form in the execution of this trick.

Front Handspring. The front handspring is similar to the headspring, except that the arms remain straight and the head does not touch. Also, the handspring is usually executed from a short running start and a one-foot skipping approach.

Proceed as follows: take a short run, execute a skip step on the right foot, swinging the left foot forward, raising both arms overhead, and alighting on both feet, with the left foot still forward. Immediately bend forward at the hips and place both hands on the mat in front of the feet. Swing the right leg overhead, followed immediately by the left leg, bringing the feet together, passing through the hand balance position, and continuing on over to a straight stand, body arched, and arms extended overhead.

Learning Hints:

1. Place great emphasis on the leg swing. As in the headspring, the primary impetus comes from this motion.
2. Keep the arms and legs straight, and the head back throughout the entire rotation, and for the landing.

The front handspring may also be executed from a square stance take-off and may be done in series. However, a series of front handsprings executed with speed and good form (arms and legs straight), is rarely seen even among top-notch tumblers.

Cartwheel. (*a*) From a standing start, proceed as follows: stand straight, with the left side toward the mat, legs spread, left arm extended sideward and right arm extended overhead. Bend sideward to the right as far as possible. Then swing vigorously to the left, placing the left hand on the mat to the left of the left foot. At the same time swing the right leg, followed immediately by the left leg, upward and over to the left, so as to pass momentarily through the hand balance position, as the right arm swings overhead and the right hand is placed on the mat beyond the left hand. Continue the rotation, bringing the right foot over and to the mat followed immediately by the left foot, and assume a straight stand with the legs spread and the arms extended sideward and upward. (*b*) From a running start, proceed as follows: take a short run; execute a skip step on the right foot and swing the left leg forward; make a quarter turn right so as to alight on both feet, the left side toward the mat, the left arm extended sideward and the right arm extended overhead. Taking full advantage of the momentum, swing immediately into a cartwheel as in the standing take-off.

Cartwheels may be executed in series, both in a straight line and in a circle, with great speed. When performing cartwheels in series, each succeeding cartwheel must be started before the preceding one is completed.

Learning Hints:

1. Keep the arms and legs extended and spread so as to simulate the spokes of a wheel.
2. Focus the eyes on the leading (left) hand when starting the trick.
3. Do not bend forward at the hips.

4. Try to follow a straight line down the center of the mat.

Roundoff. A roundoff is used in advanced tumbling to provide a running approach for backward tumbling tricks such as the flip-flap (back handspring) and the back somersault. A half twist is executed so that the tumbler alights facing in the opposite direction from that of his approach. Elements of both the running front handspring and the cartwheel are involved.

Proceed as follows: take a short run, execute a skip step on the right foot as for a front handspring, but with the arms in position as for a cartwheel. Bend forward and place the left hand on the mat directly in front of the left foot and swing the right leg, followed immediately by the left leg, upward and overhead. As the legs swing upward and join together, pivot on the heel of the left hand making a half turn, and place the right hand on the mat alongside the left hand so as to pass momentarily through the hand balance position. Immediately snap the feet and legs downward to the mat, at the same time pushing off vigorously from straight arms, and assume a straight stand, arms extended overhead, facing in the opposite direction from your initial approach.

Learning Hints:

1. Do not run too hard on the approach.
2. Fling the feet and legs straight up and over in a high arc. Do not allow them to swing to the side in a circular motion.
3. Emphasize the final snapping of the feet to the mat. The finish should be stronger than the start.

Vaulting

Vaulting is a gymnastic skill that consists of leaping over an obstacle, assisted by momentary support on the hands while clearing it. This fundamental skill will provide the beginner with an excellent introduction and orientation to gymnastics.

Vaulting is fun, and the elementary vaults that can be performed over the pommel horse, vaulting box, and buck are easily learned, yet valuable as fundamental training for a logical progression to the more difficult and strenuous demands of competitive vaulting. Also, the fundamentals of vaulting serve as the basis for many maneuvers, mounts, and dismounts in such events as pommel horse, parallel bars, horizontal bar, uneven parallel bars, and balance beam.

The following vaults are explained for execution over the pommel horse with pommels; however, they may be readily adapted to the vaulting box, buck, long horse, pommel horse without pommels, and vaulting bar (adjustable horizontal bar).

Either a standing or a running approach may be used. An elastic take-off board of the type presently specified in competitive rules for both men's and women's vaulting may be used if available, or the former regulation beat board (an inclined board approximately 36 by 21 inches, with the forward end elevated 3 to 4 inches) will suffice. The height of the horse should be adjusted to suit the age and ability of the vaulters. Competitive rules for vaulting events presently specify a height of 54 inches for men and 44 inches for women. The jump is made from both feet together (thief vault excepted) as the hands reach for the pommels. Mats should be placed on both the take-off and landing sides of the apparatus. Spotters usually stand on the landing side of the apparatus, facing the vaulter, or to one side away from the vaulter's feet. They should, however, be prepared to move in where needed.

Safety and Learning Hint: Most of the vaults can be learned more readily and with greater safety first from a standing take-off, later progressing to the running approach.

Squat Vault. (*a*) *The take-off:* Jump from both feet, straight forward and upward, hands grasping the pommels, shoulders directly above the supporting hands. (*b*) *Clearing the horse:* Bring the feet and legs forward between the pommels, with the knees tucked to the chest (squat position). Push off from the pommels, with the arms extended downward and backward. (*c*) *The landing:* Alight in a straight standing position, knees slightly flexed, arms extended sideward and upward.

Straddle Vault. (*a*) *The take-off:* Jump straight forward and upward, grasping the pommels, with the shoulders directly above the support hands; raise the hips high and spread the legs. (*b*) *Clearing the horse:* Bring the feet and legs forward over the horse, straddling the hands and pommels, "leapfrog" fashion. (*c*) *The landing:* Release the hands, flinging the arms sideward and upward. Straighten the hips, bringing the feet together, and alight in a straight standing position, facing forward with the knees slightly flexed, and the arms extended sideward and upward.

Squat-Straddle Vault (Wolf Vault). (*a*) *The take-off:* Jump straight forward and upward, grasping the pommels, with the shoulders directly above the supporting hands. Tuck the left knee to the chest.

Keep the right leg straight, flinging it upward and sideward to the right. (*b*) *Clearing the horse:* Bring the tucked left leg between the pommels; release the right hand, extending the right arm sideward and upward. Lean to the left so that the left shoulder remains directly above the supporting left hand. Keep the right leg extended sideward and upward above the horse. (*c*) *The landing:* As the feet and legs clear the horse, bring the right leg down to join the left leg, releasing the left hand and alighting in a straight standing position, facing forward with the knees slightly flexed, and the arms extended sideward and upward.

Side Vault (Flank Vault). (*a*) *The Take-off:* Jump straight forward and upward, grasping the pommels, with the shoulders directly above the supporting hands, flinging the feet and legs sideward and upward to the right. (*b*) *Clearing the horse:* Release the right hand, leaning to the left so that the left shoulder is directly above the supporting left hand. Body and knees remain straight, with the feet together and high above the horse. Face directly forward, keeping your body arched, with the left side toward the top of the horse (*c*) *The Landing:* Release the left hand as the feet and legs swing down to the mat, alighting in a straight standing position facing forward.

Front Vault. (*a*) *The take-off:* Jump from both feet, straight forward and upward, the hands grasping the pommels, with the shoulders directly above the supporting hands, flinging the feet and legs sideward and upward to the right. (*b*) *Clearing the horse:* Turn left so as to face directly into the top of the horse. The shoulders remain directly above the hands. The body is arched and extended upward to about a 45-degree angle above the horse. (*c*) *The landing:* As the horse is cleared, allow the body to swing downward, releasing the right hand. As your feet come to the mat, release the left hand, and alight in a straight standing position, facing left, with the knees slightly flexed, and the arms extended sideward and upward.

Rear Vault. (*a*) *The take-off:* Jump from both feet, straight forward and upward, the hands grasping the pommels, the shoulders directly above the supporting hands, flinging the feet and legs sideward and upward to the right. (*b*) *Clearing the horse:* Release the right hand, turning right so that the rear of your body is directly toward the top of the horse. The hips are bent to a 90-degree angle and the left shoulder is directly above the supporting left hand, so as to clear the horse in a sitting position, keeping the knees straight and feet together. (*c*) *The landing:* As the horse is cleared, bring the feet to the mat, releasing the left hand and

regrasping with the right hand. Alight in a straight standing position facing to the right, knees slightly flexed, right hand on the pommel, and left arm extended sideward and upward.

Thief Vault (Window Vault). (*a*) *The take-off:* From a running approach, jump straight forward and upward, striking the beat board with the left foot, swinging the right leg forward and over the horse between the pommels. As the left foot leaves the board, bring the left leg, with the knee tucked to the chest, between the pommels and over the horse. As the feet and legs pass between the pommels, reach your hands downward and slightly backward, alongside the hips toward the pommels. (*b*) *Clearing the horse:* Grasp the pommels for a momentary support, as your feet come together, and shoot forward with a full extension of the knees and hips. (*c*) *The landing:* Push off from the pommels as your feet approach the mat, arch your body slightly and alight in a straight standing position, facing forward, with the knees slightly flexed, and the arms extended sideward and upward.

Other vaults include the *sheep vault*— similar to the squat vault, except that the hips remain straight when clearing the horse; *stoop vault*—similar to the squat vault, except that the knees remain straight (jackknife position) when clearing the horse; and the *back straddle vault,* which includes a half turn on the take-off and a backward straddle of the buok or long horse.

Tumbling tricks such as the neckspring, headspring, front handspring, and cartwheel may be adapted to the vaulting apparatus. Very careful spotting should be observed when attempting these maneuvers, and as an added precaution a mat may be draped over the apparatus.

For variety, a quarter or half turn may be executed during the landing phase of the various vaults. Vaults may also be performed over the left section (neck), right section (croup), as well as the center section (saddle) of the horse. The side vault, front vault, rear vault, and squat-straddle vault may be executed to the opposite side from that described.

Parallel Bars

The parallel bars provide some of the finest exercise for muscular development available in the gymnasium. A variety of stunts, ranging from the simple, fundamental strength-developing exercises to the very difficult and sometimes hazardous routines of competitive caliber, are certain to challenge a gymnast of any level of ability.

Competitive rules require that the bars be set at a height of 64 to 68 inches and a width of 18 to 20 inches. However, for practice and class work, the apparatus should be adjusted to suit the individual's physical requirements, and also the specific skill being practiced.

It is very important that stunts be carefully spotted until the gymnast has thoroughly mastered them. Spotters must remember always to grasp or guide the performer from beneath the bars; the spotter should not reach above the bars because if the performer falls suddenly, the spotter's arms would be caught between the performer's body and the bars.

The uneven parallel bars have replaced the regular parallel bars in women's competition. As a physical education activity for women, however, the regular parallel bars are still an excellent event, with the exception of heavy or sustained exercises in the support position such as dips, dip swings, and the kip. The following skills are suitable for women and girls, as well as for men.

Dip Swing from Straddle Seat to Straddle Seat (Cross Riding Seat). Stand facing the end of the bars; jump forward and upward to a momentary straight-arm support (body between bars; weight on hands; one hand on each bar; arms along sides). Allow the legs to swing immediately forward and straddle both bars; straighten your hips; spread your legs wide; point your toes downward (straddle seat position). Reach well forward and grasp the bars in front of the thighs. Bend the elbows and lie flat on top of the bars, with your weight supported on the hands and thighs. Bring your feet and legs together; swing forward through the bent-arm support position. At the height of the forward swing, straddle the bars in front of the hands. Push up with your arms and assume the straddle seat position.

Front Uprise. Assume the upper-arm hang near the center of the bars (body suspended between bars, weight on the underside of the upper arms near the armpits; hands grasping the bars forward of the shoulders); swing, and at the height of the forward swing, snap the hips (hyperextend) upward above the bars; pull the shoulders forward over the hands, and rise to the straight-arm support position.

Back Uprise. Assume an inverted upper-arm hang (kip position—hips bent, feet over the head; hips and upper body level with the bars). Cast the feet and legs forward and upward, extending the body completely so as to obtain maximum swing. Swing downward and backward through the upper-arm hanging position.

At the height of the backward and upward swing, pull the shoulders forward over the hands and press to a straight-arm support.

Upper-Arm Kip. Assume an inverted upper-arm hang at the center of the bars. Vigorously extend the hips so as to snap the feet and legs forward and upward at a 45-degree angle. As the feet and legs swing downward, move the shoulders forward over the hands and come to the straight-arm support.

Rear Dismount. Swing in the straight-arm support at the center of the bars. At the height of the front swing, bend the hips; shift your weight to the right and perform a rear vault over the right bar. Clear the bar in a sitting position (legs straight); first release the left hand, then the right, shifting the left hand to the right bar, just back of the buttocks, as the bar is cleared. Alight alongside the bars, facing in the original direction, with the left hand maintaining its grasp on the right bar.

Note: When swinging in the straight-arm support, try to swing so that the axis of the swing is at the shoulders. Keep the hips straight and the shoulders directly over the hands.

Front Dismount. Swing in the straight-arm support at the center of the bars. At the height of the rear swing, lean your shoulders slightly forward; shift your weight to the right, and perform a front vault over the right bar. As the body clears the bar, shift the left hand to the right bar just in front of the right hand. Release the right hand and drop to a stand alongside the bars, with the left hand maintaining its grasp on the right bar.

Upper-Arm Balance (Shoulder Stand). (*a*) *Straddle seat approach:* Assume a straddle seat near the center of the bars. Grasp the bars just in front of the thighs; bend forward; turn your elbows outward, and place the upper arms on top of the bars just beyond the hands. Extend your hips, lifting the feet and legs upward, and assume an inverted balance on the upper arms. The hands grasp the bars, but support little weight. Keep your head back, your body arched, your feet together, your toes pointed, and your elbows pressed outward and downward. To recover—spread your legs, bend your hips, and lower to the starting position.

Safety Note: A spotter stands alongside the bars; he reaches *beneath* the bars, places one hand under the performer's shoulders and the other hand on the performer's lower back at the belt line. Two spotters may be used, one on each side of the bars.

(b) *Swinging approach:* Start from a medium-high swing in a straight-arm support, near the center of the bars. As the body swings through the vertical position and begins the rearward swing, bend the arms, and place the upper arms on top of the bars. At the same time, continue the rearward swing on upward and assume the inverted balance as in (a). To recover—allow your body to swing back down under control; straighten your arms, and come to the straight-arm support.

Spot as in (a).

Front Roll to Straddle Seat. From an upper-arm balance near the center of the bars, duck your head (chin to chest); bend the hips closely; alow them to move forward so that the body is momentarily counterbalanced in the bent position. Release the hands and clasp them at the small of the back, as in the military position of parade rest. Spread you legs, and roll forward over the forearms, which keep the hips from going down between the bars; come to the straddle seat position.

Spot as for the upper-arm balance.

Front Roll to Upper-Arm Hang. From an upper arm balance near the center of the bars, duck your head; allow your body to overbalance forward. Release the hands from the bars and extend the arms sideward so as to form an axle for the rotation. Keep your body straight and fully extended. Swing on around to the upper-arm hanging position. The hands regrasp the bars in front of the shoulders as the roll is completed.

Spot as for the upper-arm balance.

Dips

Note: The following items are classified as exercises rather than tricks. They should be executed in repetition for development of strength and endurance.

Still Dips. Start in a straight-arm support; bend the elbows and lower to a bent-arm support. Straighten the arms, reassuming a straight-arm support. Repeat.

Forward Swinging Dips. Obtain medium swing in a straight-arm support at the center of the bars. At the height of the rear swing, bend the elbows completely and swing forward in the bent-arm support position. Bend the hips slightly as the upward swing begins. At the height of the upward swing, straighten your hips and arms. Swing backward in the straight-arm support, and repeat.

Backward Swinging Dips. Obtain medium swing in straight-arm support at the center of the bars. At the

height of the front swing, bend the hips and arms; swing downward and backward through the bent-arm support position. Straighten the hips during the downward swing. Continue to swing backward and upward, straightening the arms at the height of the backward swing. Swing forward in the straight-arm support. Repeat.

Double Swinging Dips. This is a combination of the forward and backward swinging dips. The arms are straightened, and then quickly bent at the height of each forward and backward swing.

Horizontal Bar

The horizontal bar is one of the most popular gymnastic events, among gymnasts and spectators alike. Some of the most thrilling and spectacular routines in gymnastics may be seen in the horizontal bar event as performed in competition by outstanding amateur gymnasts. In the circus arena, the double and triple horizontal bar acts are acknowledged by professional gymnasts to represent gymnastic skill at its highest level.

The novice gymnast will find great satisfaction in perfecting the elementary skills presented here, and will see that they provide the fundamental training for a logical progression to more advanced and difficult work.

The extensive variety of movement, including the frequent changes from the hang to support positions that characterize horizontal bar work, provides some of the finest exercise available for muscular development in arms, shoulders, chest, and back.

A regulation horizontal bar for use in competition is made of spring steel shaft, 1-1/8 inches in diameter, 8 feet long, and set at least 8 feet above the mat. Professional bar performers use wooden or fiber bars, 1-1/2 to 2 inches in diameter. These bars are usually set two or three in a row, with tricks performed from one bar to another. The large diameter of wooden or fiber bars and the nature of the work done on them necessitate a grip with the thumb on top of the bar alongside the forefinger, while the smaller steel bar is grasped with the thumb underneath the bar, in opposition to the fingers. Wooden horizontal bars are occasionally found in older gymnasiums, and the women's uneven parallel bars are steel-core wooden bars, usually gripped in the same manner as the wooden horizontal bar which they resemble in size and flexibility.

An adjustable bar, which can be set at various heights for vaulting and to allow the novice to learn new tricks with greater safety, is recommended for class work.

The uneven parallel bar event for women and the horizontal bar event for men are alike in many respects. The following skills are similar and, in many instances, identical for the two events. Women and girls will find the adjustable horizontal bar especially useful in learning the fundamentals of the uneven parallel bars.

The Bar Snap for Distance. This is a low bar stunt that involves a forward swing under the bar, an extension of the body followed by a release of the hands, a flight through the air, and a landing as far from the bar as possible. In addition to providing an excellent activity for informal contests, the bar snap serves as a fine orientation to the horizontal bar for beginners.

Proceed as follows: With the bar set at about chest height, stand straight facing the bar, grasp it with a regular grip (palms downward), keeping the arms straight. Jump slightly upward, and as the feet leave the mat swing forward, bending the hips, and bring the feet directly to the bar. At the height of the front swing, extend the hips vigorously so that your body is forced into an extreme arch. As the body reaches full extension, release the bar, throwing the arms vigorously backward overhead, and try to "sail" through the air as fast as possible. Alight on both feet, facing forward.

When using this stunt for contests, measure the distance of the snap from a line directly beneath the bar to the landing spot. Adapt broad jump rules for fouls, etc.

Safety Note: It is extremely important that the arms remain straight for this trick. Bending the elbows may cause the performer to strike his head or face on the bar. As an added precaution, the center section of the bar should be padded.

The Fence Vault (Bar Vault). This is also a trick for the adjustable horizontal bar and, like the bar snap, makes an excellent event for informal competition. A side vault as described in the section on vaulting is usually used, and the following rules should be observed:

(1) A standing start, with both hands grasping the bar, must be used.
(2) The bar must be cleared in one continuous motion, without hesitation.
(3) Both feet must clear the bar at the same time.
(4) The head must not pass below bar level on the far side.

(5) No part of the body may pass beneath the bar at any time.

Set the bar about waist-high to begin, and as confidence is acquired and technique improves, increase the height gradually.

"Chin-high" may be considered a respectable height for this event; however, some men can clear the bar as high as they can reach.

The following tricks are described for execution on the high bar. However, by omitting or modifying the swing, they may be first attempted on the low bar.

Hip Swing Up to Front Support (Front the Bar, Belly Grind). Jump and grasp the bar, using a regular grip (palms forward). Pull up with the arms, and at the same time bend the hips, lifting the feet and legs forward and upward toward the bar. Continue pulling with the arms, allowing the feet and legs to pass beneath, beyond, then over the top of the bar. Bring the hips to the bar so that the front of the body rests on the bar at the hip line. As the feet and legs pass over the top of the bar, allow them to swing downward, and at the same time straighten the hips, raising the head and upper body to assume the front support position (weight supported on the hands; front of upper thighs and hips resting against the bar; arms and body straight; head erect; legs and feet together; toes pointed). Do not allow the feet and legs to swing around too far and pass under the bar.

Back Hip Circle from Front Support to Front Support. Start in a front support position; bend the hips, allowing the upper body to lean forward over the bar; the feet and legs swing forward under the bar. Then, immediately swing the feet and legs vigorously rearward (hyperextend the hips) to a momentary free front support (body not touching the bar). Allow the body to swing into the bar, and as the hips and upper thighs contact the bar, loosen your grip sufficiently for the hands to turn freely around the bar. Allow the body to rotate around the bar backward (head going backward and feet leading) and reassume the front support position. The hips should remain straight during this circle so that the body does not wrap around the bar.

A Free Back Hip Circle, in which only the hands contact the bar, is a more advanced skill that is begun in the same manner as the regular back hip circle. The body is not allowed to swing into the bar as the circle is started, and the hands are shifted around the bar by a vigorous hyperextension of the wrists at about the three-quarter point in the circle. This shift must occur before the feet pass over the top of the bar; otherwise,

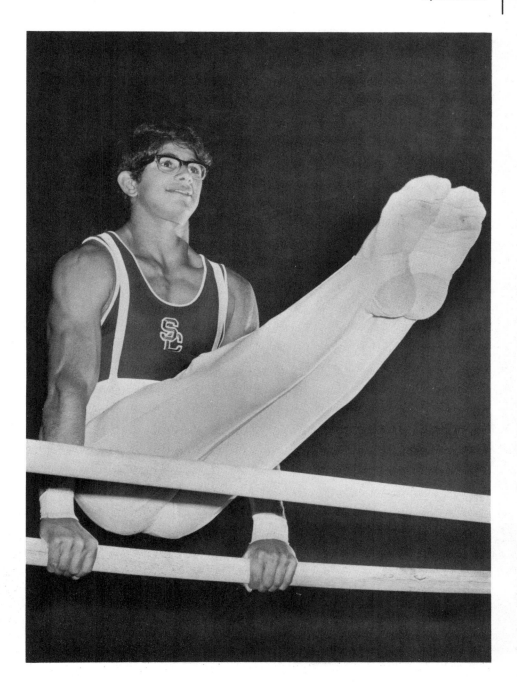

the body will fall into the bar before the circle is completed.

Both the regular and free back hip circles, which may be performed in series, are important in a logical progression toward learning giant circles (giant swings).

Short Underswing Dismount. This is simply a bar snap begun from the front support position, which serves as a neat and effective dismount from either the high or low bar.

From the front support position, drop back, bending the hips, lifting the feet to the bar, and allowing the hips to swing forward. Continue as in the bar snap, alighting in a straight standing position, facing forward.

This dismount may also be executed with a half twist upon the release so that the gymnast alights facing the bar.

A momentary toe touch (inverted jackknife position) just after the release adds a spectacular variation to this dismount.

Front Hip Circle from Front Support to Front Support. From the front support position lean slightly forward; bend and raise the hips so that the front of the thighs rest against the bar. To initiate the circle, lean farther forward, pushing the head and shoulders well forward and away from the bar. Circle forward, downward, and around the bar. Bring the hips to the bar and press downward with the hands to complete the last one-quarter of the circle and rise to the front support position.

Note: As a general rule, when circling forward, the reverse grip (palms upward) is used. The forward hip circle is an exception to this rule. The weight is primarily supported by the hips and thighs during this circle, so either a regular or reverse grip may be used.

A novel variation of the front hip circle is to release the hands from the bar as the circle is begun, and grasp the underside of the thighs just above the knees so that the bar is held between the thighs and forearms. Both this and the regular hip circle may be executed in rapid series.

The Long Underswing (Cast). Swinging back and forth pendulum fashion is poor form, may cause an awkward fall, and results in much unnecessary wear and tear on the hands. A preliminary swing is required for most horizontal bar work; therefore, the proper procedure for obtaining a swing is an important fundamental.

To obtain a swing, jump upward and grasp the bar. As the feet and legs swing forward, bend the hips and bring the feet up to the bar, while at the same time pulling up with the arms. As the feet approach the bar, immediately straighten the arms and hips, casting upward and outward away from the bar, so that the arms and body are completely extended before the downward and backward swing begins.

The height of the swing, which varies according to the requirements of the trick to immediately follow, may be controlled by the height above the bar that the feet attain on the initial cast or extension.

When practicing this cast, do not swing too high. Dismount at the height of the rearward swing, pulling downward with the arms, and bending the hips to bring the feet directly under the shoulders. Release and drop to a stand.

Single-Knee Swing-Up (Single-Knee Mount). Jump, grasp the bar with a regular grip and obtain a swing. On the forward swing, bend the hips and bring the feet and legs forward and upward toward the bar. At the height of the forward swing, bring one leg between the arms and over the bar. As the back swing begins, swing downward with the free leg, and rise at the height of the back swing to the front support position with one leg over the bar (front support astride).

The knees need not bend, nor the leg contact the bar, when this mount is timed properly and executed in good form.

A simplified version of this mount may be performed as follows: jump, grasp the bar with a regular grip and bring the feet and legs forward and upward. Hook one knee over the bar between the hands. Keep the free leg straight, swing it vigorously downward and rise to the front support astride.

Single-Knee Circles, both backward (use a regular grip) and forward (use a reverse grip), are frequently performed in conjunction with the single-knee swing-up. The procedure is similar to that for hip circles.

The Kip (Kip-Up, Upstart). The kip is one of the most important fundamentals on the horizontal bar, and its mastery is essential if progress beyond the novice stage is expected. The kip is used extensively in advanced routines, as an initial mount, and also whenever a quick change from a hanging position to a support position is required.

Proceed as follows: Jump, grasp the bar with a regular grip, and obtain a medium high swing. At the midpoint of the forward swing (hanging straight down from the bar), stop the feet at a point directly beneath the bar; thrust the chest and hips forward so that the body is extended in an extreme arch. Follow through, and maintain this arch until the forward swing is complete. Just before the backward swing begins, quickly bend the hips and raise the feet to the bar. Hold this position through the back swing. Then, as the backward swing reaches its height, kick or thrust the feet directly upward by a short, vigorous extension of the hips. The legs will swing downward and the body will rise to the front support position.

Learning Hints:

1. Place a chalk mark on the mat directly beneath the bar. Do not allow your feet to swing past this mark until the forward swing is completed.
2. Do not bend your arms. The impetus for the rise comes from the kick, which should be emphasized.

Simple conditioning exercises for muscular development that may be performed on the horizontal bar include:

1. Chinning with both a regular and a reverse grip.
2. Pulling up to the back of the neck.

3. Push-ups in the front support position.
4. Push-ups in the rear support position.
5. Suspended leg lifts.

Rope Climbing

The rope climbing event in competitive gymnastics is limited to hand-over-hand climbing against time. For the start the contestant sits grasping the rope with both hands. The legs are spread, fully extended, and astraddle the rope. Watches are started as the first pull is exerted, and stopped when a climber touches the tambourine, a plywood disk 24 inches in diameter, through which the rope passes. The tambourine is fastened securely to the rope, in a plane parallel to the floor at a height of 20 feet above the starting mat. Occasionally a 25-foot climb is used. Two climbs are allowed, the better time to count. The climber usually swings or kicks his legs, but may not use his feet or legs to grasp the rope and aid him in climbing.

Competitive climbing calls for great muscular strength and endurance, and rope climbers undergo intensive training programs for this event. The style of leg action and length of reach vary with the individual. When climbing for speed, quick reaches for each successive grasp are advised, rather than circular or looping motions that leave the weight suspended by one hand too long. Curling the hands and wrists too far around the rope should be avoided, as this technique causes the climber to rotate around the ropes and usually results in a poorer time.

In addition to competitive climbing, there are many interesting and novel rope climbing activities for both the single rope and the double ropes (two ropes suspended side by side, 18 inches apart). These activities not only offer a challenging and vigorous means of muscular development, but also provide safety skills which may prove invaluable for both men and women in an emergency.

Gymnasiums are usually equipped with regulation manila climbing ropes, 1-1/2 inches in diameter. However, cotton ropes and smaller-size ropes are satisfactory. Rope climbing equipment is readily improvised where standard equipment is not available.

Rope burns are painful and easily infected. When attempting the following rope activities, avoid uncontrolled sliding of the hands and other bare parts of the body on the ropes. Long pants and a long-sleeved jersey should be worn. Lightweight shoes or gymnastic slippers should be worn on the feet. Remember, when climbing, to conserve enough strength for a controlled descent. Thoroughly master holds, makefasts, and tricks a few feet from the floor before attempting them at greater heights.

Single Rope

The Stirrup Climb. Stand with the right side next to the rope. Reach as high as possible and grasp the rope, with both hands close together. Draw the knees up to the chest; place the sole of the right foot on top of the rope; hook the instep of the left foot beneath the rope and lift upward slightly with the left foot, to form a loop or stirrup for the right foot to stand in. Squeeze the feet close together to clamp the rope securely. Place most of your weight on the right foot; straighten the knees and hips, and at the same time pull hand over hand up the rope and regrasp with the hands close together, body and arms fully extended. Repeat this pattern until the desired height is reached. Descend, hand under hand with the rope between the feet, keeping most of your weight on the right foot. Keep both legs straight, moving the left foot slightly to the left to allow foot-hold to slip slightly during the descent. Descent may be slowed or stopped by squeezing the feet close together.

The Cross Leg Climb. Stand facing the rope. Reach as high as possible and grasp the rope, with the hands close together. Draw the knees up to the chest, with the rope hanging between the legs. Clamp the rope tightly between the knees and crossed ankles with a scissors hold, as in wrestling. Straighten the knees and hips, pushing the body up the rope; at the same time pull up, hand over hand, and regrasp with the hands close together. Repeat this pattern until the desired height is reached. Descend hand under hand, clamping the rope lightly between the knees and ankles.

Foot and Leg Lock Climb. Stand facing the rope. Reach as high as possible and grasp the rope, with the hands close together. With the rope hanging between the legs, entwine the right leg around the rope so the rope passes over the inside of the mid-thigh, diagonally downward, around the outside of the leg, and over the instep of the foot. Pull up as far as possible with both arms; place the sole of the left foot on top of the rope and press the rope against the instep of the right foot. Straighten the right leg and reach upward for another hand-hold. Repeat this pattern until the desired height is achieved.

Half Lever Climb. Climb hand over hand in the half lever position, with the hips bent to form a right angle between the thighs and body. Keep the knees straight, feet and legs together, and toes pointed. The rope hangs along outside of the thigh.

The Makefast. This is a stationary hold on the rope which may be used to give the hands and arms an opportunity to recover from fatigue.

(a) *Foot and Leg Lock Method:* From a straight-arm hang, with the hands grasping the rope close together, and the rope hanging between the legs, entwine the right leg around the rope as in the foot and leg lock climb. Straighten the right leg and place the sole of the left foot on top of the rope to press it against the instep of the right foot. Release the right hand and bring the right arm across the chest between the rope and the body. Then reach the right arm around in front of the rope so that the rope passes behind the right shoulder. Clamp the rope between the upper arm and body as close to the armpit as possible. Bring the right arm behind the body, and at the same time release the left hand and bring the left arm behind the body. Grasp the right wrist with the left hand and lock the elbows straight. Keep the head erect and lean the upper body back against the rope.

(b) *Cross Leg Method:* This method may be used when the lower end of the rope is anchored taut and cannot be entwined. Clamp the rope in a scissors hold as in the cross leg climb; keep the legs and hips straight. The arm hold is the same as for (a).

The Single Seat. This is done from a straight-arm hang, with the hands grasping the rope close together, and the rope hanging between the legs; assume a half lever position, with the rope between the thighs at the crotch. Cross the ankles to clamp the rope between the thighs in a scissors hold. Release the hand; reach down and grasp the rope below the thighs and bring the lower part of the rope up against the upper part to form a loop around the left thigh. The two parts of the long rope may be easily held together with one hand, providing a secure seat. The free end of the rope may be draped over the left shoulder, which eases the strain on the gripping hand.

Side Horizontal Lever. This is done from a straight-arm hang, with the left hand grasping the rope about 30 inches below the right hand; bring the knees up to the chest, and place the feet and legs between the hands. Pass the knees and hips to the opposite side of the rope and extend them so that the body lies fully extended horizontally, the left side toward the floor, and the buttocks against the rope between the hands. The left hip rests upon the left hand and wrist. Keep the knees straight, the feet and legs together, and the toes pointed.

The Inverted Hang. From a straight-arm hang, with the hands grasping the rope close together, pull up with the arms; swing the body upward to a bent-arm inverted hang, with the legs spread and astraddle the rope. Entwine the right leg securely in the rope which

passes along the inside edge of the foot, across the front of the ankle, around the outside of the leg, back of the knee, around the inside and front of the thigh, and hangs between the right arm and body. Release the left hand; extend the body downward; extend the left arm straight downward and grasp the rope, pulling it diagonally across the back and shoulders. Release the right hand and extend the right arm sideward. The left leg should remain straight and completely clear of the rope. To recover to a normal hang, regrasp first with the right hand and then the left. Disentwine the leg and lower the body to a straight-arm hang.

An inverted descent may be accomplished by sliding while in the inverted hang. Speed of descent is easily controlled with the left hand.

Double Ropes

Hand-Over-Hand Climb. Stand between the ropes, grasping them. Pull up alternately with the right and left hands. The legs may be swung alternately as in the competitive event, or a half lever position may be used.

Leg Lock Climb. Stand between the ropes, grasping them. Pull up to a bent-arm hang; spread your legs and straddle both ropes. Entwine the right leg in the right rope and the left leg in the left rope. Have someone pull down on the lower ends of the ropes to anchor them. To climb, bend the knees and hips, drawing the knees toward the chest. Push your body up the ropes by extending the knees and hips and reaching for a fresh hand-hold. The legs may alternate in the climbing motion, or they may operate in unison.

The Makefast. (a) With the lower ends of the ropes anchored, entwine the legs as for the leg lock climb; straighten the hips and knees completely. Reach forward between the ropes with both arms and extend the arms sideward so that the upper arms press backward against the ropes. (b) With the lower ends of the ropes free, and from a straight-arm hang, spread the legs and straddle *both* ropes. Entwine the right leg around both ropes, which are brought together; straighten the leg. Press the ropes against the instep of the right foot with the sole of the left foot. Reach forward between the ropes with both arms; extend the arms sideward so that the upper arms press backward against the ropes.

The Inverted Hang. From a straight-arm hang between the ropes, pull up with the arms and swing the body forward up to a bent-arm inverted hang, with the hips bent (kip position). Spread the legs and bring them forward so that the back of your thighs rest against the ropes. Entwine the right leg in the right rope, and the left leg in the left rope. Straighten the knees and hips. Maintain the original hand grip. A descent may be accomplished by sliding in this position. Speed of descent is controlled by the hand grip.

The Side Horizontal Lever. From a straight-arm hang between the ropes, swing the body forward up to a straight-arm inverted hang, with the hips bent (kip position). Spread the legs and straddle the left rope so that the back of the crotch rests upon the left hand and wrist. Bring the feet and legs together; pull up with the right arm, and roll sideward to place the body in a horizontal position, with the right side toward the floor. The right rope is placed behind the neck and held securely with the right hand.

The "Crucifix." Start in the makefast position, with the lower ends of the ropes free. With the arms hanging straight downward in front of the ropes, entwine the right arm in the right rope and the left arm in the left rope. Grip the ropes so that the palms are to the rear. Release the leg-hold and extend the arms sideward. The ropes should pass under the armpits, and encircle the arms and wrists.

Trampoline

The trampoline came into the physical education and competitive gymnastics programs by way of the circus, where performers used a bounding or trampoline net under aerial horizontal bar and casting acts. The "rube wagon," which was a circus wagon fixed up to resemble a hay rack, concealed a trampoline suspended in the wagon bed so that performers dressed as rustics appeared to bounce in the hay; it was a feature of many of the old-time circus parades.

George Nissen of Cedar Rapids, Iowa, developed the first commercially produced trampolines in the 1930s. These early models consisted of a rectangular canvas mat approximately 6 feet by 12 feet, suspended tautly with steel, coil springs, or rubber cables in a substantial metal frame approximately 40 inches high. Present-day models with greatly improved frames and an option of a more lively nylon web mat are fundamentally similar to the prototype.

During World War II, trampolines were used in the physical training programs in the armed services; and in the years following the war, trampolining underwent a period of very rapid development. The equipment was constantly improved by Nissen and other manufacturers, while at the same time performers of exceptional skills were quickly developed.

With the acceptance of the trampoline event into the competitive gymnastics program in the United States, tricks and routines formerly unheard of have become almost commonplace.

This extremely rapid evolution of the trampoline was not matched by the development of qualified instructors, and as a result too many unfortunate and serious injuries have occurred. Because of this situation, a great deal of criticism has been directed at trampolining, and its place in the gymnastics program has been seriously questioned.

The trampoline is fun, and is very good all-around exercise. Trampolining has a great appeal for almost everyone, partly because it appears to be very easy. The fact must be recognized, however, that trampolining is potentially more dangerous than other gymnastic events, owing to the great height that can be achieved by the most unskilled performer and to the suddenness with which dangerous rebounds may occur. The trampoline seems to attract more than its share of thrillseekers, daredevils, and others who may be in poor physical condition, lacking in aptitude, and often obtusely unwilling to learn the fundamentals before attempting more difficult tricks.

Therefore, in addition to the general safety precautions already suggested for other events, it is recommended that the trampoline be used only under the direction of a qualified, responsible person, properly authorized to supervise and control the activity; particular attention should be given to the following suggestions for the safe and proper use of the trampoline.

Instructions for the Performer

1. Mount and dismount from the trampoline safely, grasping the frame securely for support. Trick and fancy mounts and dismounts are occasionally used by proficient performers in shows and exhibitions, but even in top-notch competition, mounts and dismounts are not considered in scoring routines.
2. Master the fundamentals thoroughly before attempting somersaults ("flips").
3. Concentrate on good form and control rather than extreme height.
4. Dress properly. Long pants and a long-sleeved shirt will protect you from abrasions and at the same time protect the mat from excessive perspiration, which can become offensive to others and also will eventually damage the mat. Wear lightweight gymnastic slippers or at least clean sweat socks. Heavy shoes will damage the mat. Do not use the trampoline while barefooted.

5. Stay in the center of the trampoline. If you get too near the edges or lose control, "kill the bounce" (by a sudden flexion of the hips, knees, and ankles as the feet contact the mat, which absorbs the upward thrust of the mat so that no rebound occurs.)
6. Limit yourself to short sessions. One minute is long enough for one turn.
7. Do not jump from the trampoline mat to the floor.
8. Avoid doubles bouncing (two people in the same trampoline). This is for experts, and is dangerous for beginners.
9. Make use of the "mechanic" (suspended safety belt) when practicable.
   Note: Suspended safety belts are far from fool-proof. Their safe and effective use requires considerable training and practice. Don't trust your safety to an untrained belt holder.

10. Do not use the trampoline without spotters (safety men). Competitive rules provide for four spotters, one at each end and each side of the trampoline.
11. If the spotters have to assist you, don't struggle and fling your arms and legs about in such a way as to injure the spotters.

Instructions for the Spotters

The duty of the spotters is to prevent the performer from falling out of the trampoline, through the springs, or onto the frame. Spotting at the trampoline requires alertness, courage, presence of mind, and physical strength compatible with the size and weight of the performer.

1. Stand close to the trampoline, brace your feet in a stride stance, and do not back away if the performer bounds in your direction.

2. Try to anticipate dangerous rebounds and press the performer back toward the center of the mat. A word of warning will frequently suffice.

3. When reaching out to spot, keep the palms forward, with the fingers pointing upward, so that the hands and entire forearms may contact the performer and at the same time protect you from flying elbows and knees. A spotting position with palms upward and fingers pointing forward is ineffective, and may result in the back of your forearms being forced down against the trampoline frame.

4. If the performer bounds toward you in a standing or vertical position, reach high enough on his body to prevent his toppling over your head.

5. Be prepared to move quickly to the assistance of other spotters.

Trampoline Fundamentals

The Feet Bounce (Straight Jump). Mastery of the feet bounce is essential because all other tricks in the trampoline must be initiated with a feet bounce, and the jumping technique is much the same regardless of the trick being attempted. Height, balance, control, consistency, and the ability to stay over the center of the trampoline are important.

Proceed as follows: Stand in the center of the trampoline mat, with feet about shoulder width apart, head erect, eyes focused on the end of the trampoline mat, body straight, arms straight and lifted sideward. Swing the arms downward vigorously, and at the same time bend the knees and hips slightly and immediately thrust downward by a vigorous extension of the knees, hips, and ankles. Complete the downward swing of the arms and lift them forward and upward as you leave the mat. Bring your feet together and point the toes straight downward. At the height of the jump your body should be in a straight vertical line from the tip of your toes to the top of your head; the arms should be extended forward at about shoulder level, the head erect and the eyes still focused on the end of the trampoline mat. During the descent, as you approach the mat, position yourself for the next jump by lowering your arms to the starting position, spreading your legs, and flexing your hips, knees, and ankles.

Learning Hints:

1. Place great emphasis on ankle action. Contact the mat with the feet flat; then press vigorously downward with full extension of the ankles as you rise. Practice this skill by jumping in the trampoline with ankle action alone—do not bend the knees or hips, or swing the arms.

2. Be systematic in the use of the arms. Arms swing downward as you contact the mat and lift upward as you rise. To see for yourself the effect of correct arm action, stand motionless in the center of the mat and note the depression of the mat as the arms are swung vigorously downward.

Variations of the feet bounce which are good practice include: feet bounce with tuck, feet bounce with jackknife, feet bounce with straddle, and feet bounce with half and full pirouettes.

The following fundamental landing positions are described for execution following several preliminary feet bounces, to provide sufficient height for each trick.

Sit Drop. As you reach the height of a feet bounce, lift your feet and legs forward and upward, forming a right angle between the thighs and trunk. Drop to the mat in this sitting position, placing the hands palms downward, *fingers pointing forward,* on the mat alongside and slightly to the rear of the hips. Keep the head and body erect, the knees **straight, the feet** together, and the toes pointed forward. Push off on your hands as you rebound to a stand or to another feet bounce.

Knee Bounce. As you descend to the mat following a feet bounce, bend the knees and drop to the mat in a kneeling position. Spread the knees slightly for balance and keep the toes pointed so that the entire instep contacts the mat. Bend very slightly forward at the hips. When you rebound to a straight stand or another feet bounce, **carry the head and swing the arms** exactly as for a feet bounce.

Safety Hint: Be especially careful *not* to arch the body when landing in the kneeling position because a painful hyperextension of the back could result. Some performers and instructors, in order to preclude this possibility, prefer to substitute the HANDS AND KNEES BOUNCE, a variation of the knee bounce position in which the body is bent farther forward and the hands are placed on the mat in front of the knees, with the arms straight.

Front Drop. As you rise on a feet bounce, bend slightly forward at the hips, so that a semi-jackknife position is achieved at the height of the bounce. As you approach the mat on the descent, straighten the body, landing in a prone position. Extend the arms forward with the elbows slightly bent, so that the hands and entire underside of the forearms may press downward on the mat, keeping the upper chest from contact with the mat. Hold the head high and concentrate your weight onto the hips and upper thighs. Keep the legs straight, feet together, and toes pointed so that your entire instep will contact the mat. As you rebound, push off with the hands and forearms, and draw the feet and legs forward to a straight stand or another feet bounce.

Safety Hint: Many beginners have a tendency to dive forward as if going into the water. Avoid this by jumping straight upward and then descending in such a way that your hips contact the mat at the spot from which the feet took off. Strive for a level landing, with all parts contacting the mat simultaneously. Keep the bounce low while learning because a painfully sprained back can result from a poor landing.

Variations of the front drop include the execution of a full jackknife or a "swan" (body arched, arms extended sideward) at the height of the take-off bounce. The landing positions are the same as for the regular front drop.

Back Drop. As you reach the height of a feet bounce, tilt the body backward to a horizontal position and at the same time lift the feet and legs forward and upward, bending at the hips, but keeping the knees straight. Reach forward with extended arms and grasp your legs just behind the knees. Keep the head well forward (chin on chest) and descend, contacting the mat with the entire back from the shoulders to the base of the spine. Maintain this position until the height of the rebound is approached; then release the legs, raise the head, arch the body, and bring the feet to the mat to assume a straight stand or another feet bounce. An upward thrust with the feet and legs (slight extension of the hips) at the beginning of the ascent will assist in gaining greater lift on the rebound.

Safety Hint: Be especially careful to avoid jumping backward (traveling), lifting the feet and legs too high, or throwing the head backward. Any one, or a combination of these faults, may result in your turning over backward in an unintentional back somersault or falling out of the back end of the trampoline.

Combinations and Variations of the Fundamental Bounces and Landing Positions

When you have learned the fundamental bounces and landings with good form, control, and reasonable height, you may then put together in series an almost endless variety of combinations and variations of the fundamental tricks. Your imagination and creative ability should be put to work in forming routines involving the following suggested maneuvers.

Swivel Hips. As you rebound from a sit drop, push off hard with the hands, lift the arms vigorously overhead, and straighten the hips; as you approach the vertical position, twist the trunk and head to the left so that a half turn of the body around its longitudinal axis is accomplished. Descend to the mat in a sit-drop landing, facing in the opposite direction from that of the initial take-off.

Note: Do not allow the feet and legs to swing around in a big arc during the twist. The feet remain almost in one place over the center of the mat throughout the entire trick. If you achieve good height on your initial bounce, several swivel hip turns may be accomplished before returning to a stand or feet bounce.

Sit Drop; Front Drop; Sit Drop. As you rebound from a sit drop, lean forward into a front drop; push off hard with the hands and forearms from the front-drop landing and pull the legs through forward, to reassume the second sit-drop landing. Recover to a stand or feet bounce as from a regular sit drop. Try to achieve sufficient height so that the legs may be kept straight throughout this trick.

Sit Drop; Half Twist; Front Drop. As you rebound from a sit drop, push off hard with the hands, lie back into a horizontal position, twist the trunk and head to the left so that the body makes a half turn around its longitudinal axis, and descend to the mat in a front-drop landing; push off hard with the hands and forearms and recover to a stand or feet bounce.

Sit Drop; Full Twist; Sit Drop. As you rebound from a sit drop, push extremely hard with the hands, lie back into a horizontal position, twist the trunk vigorously, and turn the head to the left so that the body makes a full turn around its longitudinal axis. As you complete the twist, raise the upper body so as to assume the sit-drop position for landing. Descend to the mat in this position. Recover to a stand or feet bounce as from a regular sit drop.

Safety Hint (for both half and full twists): Be especially careful to take off from the exact longitudinal center of the mat and to rebound straight upward. Alert the spotters at the sides of the trampoline, as there is a tendency to throw sideways onto the springs and frame when first attempting these twists. Keep your legs together and your arms close to the body in order to avoid an eccentric twist.

Back Drop, Half Twist to Feet Bounce. As you rebound from a regular back drop and while the feet and legs are still thrusting upward, twist the trunk and head vigorously to the left so as to accomplish a half turn. Bring the feet to the mat, recovering to a feet bounce, facing in the opposite direction from that of the initial take-off.

Back Drop to Front Drop. At the height of the rebound from a regular back drop, tilt forward and descend in the prone position to a front-drop landing. Recover to a stand or a feet bounce as from a regular front drop.

Back Drop, Half Turntable to Front Drop. As you begin the rebound from a front-drop landing, push off vigorously with the right hand and forearm; bend the neck and trunk slightly to the left so as to initiate a spin of the body around its transverse axis in a leftward or counterclockwise direction. Maintain the face-downward position, keeping the back flat like a table top (hence the name turntable), and draw the knees toward the chest so as to spin in a tucked position. Extend the body and land in the regular front-drop landing position at the completion of a 180-degree turn, so that the head is pointing in the opposite direction from that of the take-off. Recover to a stand or feet bounce as from a regular front drop.

Front Drop, Full Turntable to Front Drop. Proceed as for a half turntable, but with greater height and a more vigorous push-off. Tuck tightly, clasping the legs just below the knees during the spin, so that you achieve a full turn of 360 degrees. Extend for the landing and recover as for the half turntable. Outstanding performers accomplish double turntables, and even an occasional triple turntable is seen.

Back Pullover. The back pullover is a modified form of the back somersault executed from either a tucked sit-drop position or from a closely folded, back-drop position. While it is strongly recommended that the feet-to-feet back somersault be learned with the aid of a suspended safety belt, the pullover may be attempted with alert spotters at the ends and sides of the trampoline.

Back Pullover from Tucked Sit Drop. Start about three feet forward of the center of the mat. At the height of a feet bounce, draw the knees to the chest in tuck position and clasp the legs just below the knees with the hands. As you descend, keep the head erect and the trunk vertical. Drop to the mat maintaining the tuck position so that the soles of the feet and the buttocks contact the mat simultaneously. As you rebound, throw the head back and somersault backward. As you complete the somersault, release the

legs, open your tuck and bring the feet to the mat to assume a stand or feet bounce.

Safety Hint: While learning the various forms of the back pullover, you may have a tendency to overturn and fall out of the back end of the trampoline. So, if possible, have two alert spotters behind you when practicing.

Back Pullover from Closely Folded Back Drop. Start two to three feet forward of the center on the mat and proceed as for a regular back drop, but fold into as close a bend as possible, clasping the back of the knees with the hands so that your legs remain straight; concentrate your weight on the lower back for the landing, rather than upon the upper back and shoulders, as in the regular back-drop landing position. As you rebound, thrust the feet and legs backward overhead and somersault backward to a stand or feet bounce. You may achieve greater height on the somersault by thrusting the feet and legs at a higher angle on the rebound.

Learning Hint: In order to get the "feel" of this second version of the back pullover, stand near one end of the trampoline mat with your back toward the opposite end. Then, without any bounce, jackknife forward and sit back into a straight-leg back roll exactly as in tumbling (see the section on tumbling). With several repetitions of this roll, gradually increase your momentum with a more vigorous spring-off from the feet as you sit back into the roll, and you will soon find that you are doing a low back pullover.

Twisting Back Somersault. The back pullover from a closely folded back drop is a valuable skill in learning a twisting back somersault, especially where a twisting safety belt is not available. The following twisting progression may be attempted with careful and alert spotting at the sides and ends of the trampoline.

1. Back pullover to front-drop landing.
2. Back pullover with half twist to sit-drop landing.
3. Back pullover with half twist to stand.
4. Back pullover with full twist to front-drop landing.
5. Back pullover with full twist to hands-and-knees landing.
6. Back pullover with full twist to knee-drop landing.
7. Back pullover with full twist to stand or feet bounce.

Front Somersault. You may learn the front somersault without the use of a safety belt by one of the following two progressions; however, careful and alert spotters at the ends and sides of the trampoline are essential.

Front Somersault, *First Method.* Stand on the trampoline mat about two feet back of the center line, facing the far end. Without any bounce, squat, place your hands on the mat, and perform a front roll exactly as in tumbling (see the section on tumbling). With several repetitions of this roll, gradually increase your height and the momentum of the forward spin by a more vigorous spring-off from the feet, so that the hands no longer contact the mat and a low somersault from the feet to a tucked back-drop landing is being accomplished. Gradually continue, with many repetitions, to increase your height and spin so that a sit-drop landing is achieved.

Safety Hint: Be especially careful when attempting the sit-drop landing to release the tuck and land in good sit-drop form, with your knees straight. Holding the tuck position for the sit-drop landing may result in your chin coming in contact with your knee with sufficient force to cause a painful injury.

The next and final step in this progression is the feet-bounce landing. To acquire a good, controlled landing, considerable practice is needed because you will not be able to see the mat. You must gradually learn to feel when to release the tuck and bring the feet to the mat for a straight landing. *Do not look downward* at the mat, or you will invariably overturn. Break out of a front somersault with the head and chest high, with the eyes focused straight ahead. A spotter or instructor can be of great help by shouting, "BREAK!" at the exact instant in the revolution when you should release the tuck and stop the spin. You should take off straight upward, initiating the forward spin by bending sharply forward at the hips as you rise. Your arm action as you prepare to leave the mat may be the same as for a straight feet bounce, or a better technique is just the opposite—to circle the arms forward and upward. This latter method is more adaptable for performing front somersaults in series or in conjunction with other tricks.

Front Somersault, *Second Method.* From a knee bounce or hands-and-knees bounce, somersault forward to a sit-drop landing. Next, progress to a knee-bounce take-off and feet-bounce landing; then, finally, from a feet-bounce take-off come to a feet-bounce landing.

Safety Hint: You may have a tendency to travel forward while learning the knee-bounce take-off so, if possible, have two spotters in front of you and take it easy, keeping the bounce low.

Front somersaults may also be performed in the pike position (knees straight, body bent) and in the straight-body or layout position.

Safety Hint: Trampoline somersaults must generally be done with "spotters"; that is, you must take off and land in the center of the trampoline. "Traveling" during a somersault, which is extremely dangerous, is usually caused by anticipating and leaning into the trick on take-off. You must take off as nearly straight upward as possible. Be especially careful not to overturn on a front somersault, or you may land on your face with sufficient force to cause a serious neck or back injury. While learning, "underturn" for a safe landing on your seat or back.

The Barani. The barani may be simply described as a half-twisting front somersault in which the eyes remain focused on the mat throughout the trick. To learn a barani, first learn the tumbling trick known as a *roundoff* (see the section on tumbling). Then get in the trampoline and try the roundoff either from a low feet bounce or from a knee bounce, or hands-and-knees bounce.

Note: The roundoff in tumbling employs a one-foot, skip-step approach, but in the trampoline a square-stance take-off is used.

Gradually, with many repetitions, increase your height on take-off until you can accomplish a roundoff without support on the hands. As you gain confidence and skill, the take-off and arm action will be similar to that of the front somersault.

Safety and Learning Hints: Keep all parts positioned directly over the longitudinal center line of the mat. Accomplish the twist while in the inverted position. Avoid the tendency to throw sideways. Throw the feet and legs straight over as in a handspring or straight somersault, avoiding any "wheeling" or sideward swing of the legs. Spotters at the sides of the trampoline should be especially alert to assist the performer in case of a sideward throw.

Balance Beam

The balance beam, now one of the events in women's competitive gymnastics, was undoubtedly one of the earliest forms of gymnastic apparatus. Balance beams are listed among the equipment of Jahn's first turn-platz and are mentioned in accounts of earlier programs. Like climbing and vaulting, the ability to balance and maneuver on a narrow walking surface represents a practical safety skill useful in occasional emergencies and important to hikers and others who venture into situations where narrow foot bridges are often improvised from logs or rails spanning narrow streams or gullies.

Poise, good posture, proper body mechanics and alignment, all essentials of balance-beam activities, are qualities important to everyone, and are especially highly regarded by girls and women for aesthetic reasons.

Competitive rules presently specify a solid or fabricated wooden beam, approximately 4 inches in width (walking surface), 6 inches in depth, and 16 feet in length; it is suspended horizontally at a height of 4 feet above the floor, on substantial supports placed near each end. Simple beams for elementary exercises are frequently encountered in gymnasiums. These beams are not of standard specifications, but are usually 2 inches in width (walking surface), 4 to 6 inches in depth, 12 feet in length, and not more than a foot high.

Exercises on the competitive beam include walking, running, jumping, and skipping along the beam, as well as leaps, turns, and pirouettes. Tumbling and balancing tricks such as head balance, hand balance, shoulder balance, cartwheel, front and back walkover and rolls—along with scales, splits, back and front bends, and movements and positions from the ballet such as are frequently seen in the floor exercise event—may all be adapted to the balance beam. Mounts are usually interrupted vaults or jumps ending with the assumption of a position on the beam. Dismounts may be vaults, jumps, or tumbling tricks such as cartwheels, necksprings, handsprings, baranis, and somersaults.

A competitive exercise on the balance beam is timed, and rules presently specify an exercise of 1 minute, 20 seconds', to 1 minute, 45 seconds', duration. The entire length of the beam should be used, and traversed several times during the course of the exercise.

The balance beam is not usually considered a particularly hazardous event; however, falls from and onto the beam are likely to be sudden and awkward, so all general safety precautions should be observed, along with the following specific suggestions:

1. Whenever practicable, adjust the beam to the lowest height while learning; or remove it from its supports and place it directly onto the mats. A line 4 inches in width painted or taped to the mat or floor to simulate the beam surface will be useful in learning new and difficult maneuvers.
2. Spotters on both sides of the beam move along with the performer as the beam is traversed.
3. Drape a mat over the beam when practicable.
4. Use the suspended safety belt for hazardous leaps, tumbling tricks, and dismounts.
5. If a take-off board is used for the mount, be sure to have an assistant remove it as soon as the mount is accomplished if a trick or exercise is to follow.

6. When learning a new trick or exercise, follow a logical progression from mat to bare floor, to low beam and, finally, to high beam.

Mounts

(a) Squat vault to stand. (b) Squat-straddle vault to stand. (c) Straddle vault to stand.

Note: See the section on vaulting for proper procedure for the above vaults. Use either a standing or running take-off. Approach the center of the beam from the side. A take-off board may be used for all mounts.

Fencer's Vault to Oblique Cross Seat. Approach the beam obliquely with a short run from the right; place the right hand on top of the beam, spring off from the left foot, swing the right leg forward and upward over the beam, followed immediately by the left leg as in the scissors-style high jump, and vault to an oblique cross seat, with both legs on the far side of the beam (sidesaddle style). Place the left hand on the beam in front of the left thigh, and the right hand on the beam behind the buttocks for balance.

Straddle Seat Mount. Approach the center of the beam from the side, place the hands on top of the beam, and jump to a front support (weight supported on the hands; front of upper thighs and hips resting against the beam; arms and body straight; head erect; legs and feet together, and toes pointed). Swing the right leg over the beam, executing a quarter turn to the left and assuming a straddle (cross riding) seat, with the hands grasping the top of the beam just behind the buttocks for balance.

Dismounts

Straddle Jump. From a side stand (shoulders parallel with the length axis of the beam), jump forward and upward off the beam. Spread your legs, lifting them forward and upward so that a right angle is formed between the thighs and body. Extend the arms forward and touch the toes at the height of your jump. Assume a straight stand as you descend to the mat. You may also execute this dismount from a cross stand (shoulders at right angles to the length axis of the beam) at the end of the beam.

Front-Vault Dismount. From a straight-arm, front-leaning support (push-up position) along the length axis of the beam, swing the right leg upward and backward, followed immediately with the left leg to a momentary free support, and shift your weight to the right and drop to a straight stand alongside the beam.

This dismount is similar to a front dismount from the parallel bars (see the parallel bars section).

Movements (Traveling)

Walking. (a) Walk forward: Swing your arms naturally and gracefully. Place your weight on the ball of the foot first. Don't look at your feet; keep your eyes focused on the beam well ahead of you and try to "feel" the balance with your feet. (b) Walk backward: Continue to watch the beam well in front of you; place your feet carefully and keep track of your distance so as not to step backward off the beam. (c) Walk with small knee dips: Bend or dip the knees slightly with each step as your weight comes onto the foot, allowing the free foot to drop below the beam as it swings forward.

Running. Keep your weight on the ball of the foot. Use a straight-leg running style. Acquire speed and longer stride gradually.

Jumping. (a) From a cross stand (facing the end of the beam), with one foot in front of the other, squat slightly, spring upward, and recover to a stand. (b) Same as (a), but reverse the position of your feet for the landing. (c) Same as (b), but travel forward or backward by a series of jumps.

Skipping. Same as on the floor, but with higher knee lift with your free leg.

Turning

Pivot Turn. From a cross stand, with one foot forward, pivot or spin on the balls of the feet so as to face the opposite end of the beam.

Pirouette Turn. Raise the arms overhead; at the same time lift one knee about waist high and turn or spin on one foot either through an arc of 180 degrees (half pirouette), or 360 degrees (full pirouette). Bring the lifted foot immediately back to the beam and lower the arms for the recovery.

Balances

V-Seat. Sit on the beam facing one end, lift the legs forward and upward and lean backward so as to balance on the buttocks, with the body bent at the waist in an open V-position. Keep the knees straight, the feet together, and the toes pointed. Grasp the top of the beam directly behind the buttocks, or extend the arms sideward at shoulder level for balance. Keep your head erect.

Front Scale. Stand on one foot, and bend forward at the waist so as to form a right angle between the body and the supporting thigh. Raise the other leg and thigh rearward to a position parallel with the beam. Arch the body, extend the arms sideward at shoulder level ("swan position"), keep the head well back and the knees straight.

Knee Scale. Similar to a front scale, but with support on one knee and leg instead of the foot. The knee is bent at a right angle, so that the entire lower leg and instep is in contact with the top of the beam for support.

Floor Exercise

Floor exercise is a competitive event in gymnastics for men and women. There is no time limit for men, but for women there is a 90-second maximum performance limit. Ballet and tumbling movements are used in this form of competition.

Floor exercises should begin on mats with spotters, and then move to the floor as the skill level is enhanced. Harmonious movement with grace and beauty is the objective. This objective is accomplished through different kinds of movements.

Ballet Movements

1. The *Ballet Touch* is accomplished through a controlled and relaxed position, with the right foot slightly in front of the left. Touch the forefoot with the right hand by bending gracefully, and then return to the original position. Repeat using the opposite foot and hand.
2. The *Toe Stand* is executed by extending the arms, palms downward, in a relaxed and graceful manner. The body, erect, rises to the toes. Lower the body to standing position, with the arms lowered to the side.
3. The *Pirouette* is a series of full body turns on the ball of one foot. Keep the head facing as far frontward as possible, then turn the head quickly to face frontward again.
4. The *Body Sweep* places the weight on the right knee and hand; then move the left arm forward, with the left leg extended. Full extension of the arm and leg should be attained.
5. The *Stop Leap* is executed by leaping high in the air, bringing the left foot up to touch the inner thigh of the other leg above the knee. The left arm should extend upward as the right arm extends to the side.

Tumbling Movements

1. The *Single Leg Balance* is performed by standing on the left leg, raising the right leg as high as

possible and grasping the instep with the right hand, then extending the leg. The opposite hand extends upward, palm up, in a graceful style.

2. The *Balance Stand* or the *Front Scale* is executed by standing on the right leg, bending forward and keeping your trunk parallel to the floor, with both arms forward. Extend the left leg backward, point the toes and raise the leg higher than the head to complete this skill. Keep your head up and your back arched.

3. The *Arabesque* is accomplished by moving the left leg backward and out from a standing position. Extend the right arm, with the fingers relaxed. The left arm moves to the side and a balanced position is maintained.

4. The *Jump to Headstand* is performed by jumping upward from a standing position, tucking the body, and landing on your hands. Slightly flex the elbow to serve as a cushion, then fully extend and lock the arms. Balance the body in full extension, and hold.

5. The *Needle Scale* is performed while standing on one leg with the arms extended forward. Bend the body slowly forward and downward until the palms rest on the floor and the forehead touches the front of the lower leg. The other leg is then extended upward.

6. The *Yoga Handstand* is executed by dropping the hips forward suddenly while in a handstand position. Jackknife the legs backward, bringing the head forward and keeping the back stiff, and hold.

7. The *Backover* is commenced from a standing position with a backward bend until the hands touch the floor. Kick the right leg up and over, followed by the left one. Finish in a standing position.

8. The *Front Walkover* is also begun from a standing position, then leaning forward to place the hands on the floor as in the handstand. Bring one leg slowly off the floor and all the way over, followed by the other one. Return to the original position by pushing with the hands.

9. The *Forward Drop* is performed by falling forward from a standing position, landing with the arms straightened, flexed, and supporting the weight. Extend one leg with the toes pointed as you fall, keeping the other foot on the floor.

10. The *Shoot Through* is executed by leaning forward on your arms, with the body fully extended. Flex the hips and bring the legs rapidly through the arms. Finish in a sitting position, with your legs and feet together and extended. The body should be tilted backward, supported by the hands held behind the shoulder line.

11. The *Supine Arch-Up* is begun from a supine floor position, raising the body by moving the hands from near the hips to the shoulder area. Straighten the arms, arch the back, and keep both feet close together on the floor.

BIBLIOGRAPHY

Amateur Athletic Union of the United States, *Gymnastics Year Book.* New York: The Union, 1965.

Babbitt, Diane H., and Haas, Werner, *Gymnastic Apparatus Exercises for Girls.* New York: The Ronald Press Company, 1964.

Baley, James A., *Gymnastics in the Schools.* Boston: Allyn and Bacon, Inc., 1965.

———, *An Illustrated Guide to Tumbling.* Boston: Allyn and Bacon, Inc., 1968.

Bedard, Irwin, *Gymnastics for Boys.* Chicago: Follett Publishing Co., 1962.

Burns, Ted, and Micaleau, Tyler, *Tumbling Techniques Illustrated.* New York: The Ronald Press Company, 1957.

DeCarlo, Tom, *Handbook of Progressive Gymnastics.* Englewood Cliffs, N.J.: Prentice-Hall, Inc., 1963.

Division for Girls' and Women's Sports, *Gymnastics Guide.* Washington, D.C.: American Association for Health, Physical Education and Recreation.

Drury, Blanche Jessen, and Schmid, Andrea Bodo, *Gymnastics for Women.* Palo Alto: The National Press, 1965.

Edmundson, Joseph, and Garstang, Jack, *Activities on P.E. Apparatus.* London: Oldbourne Book Co. Ltd., 1962.

Frey, Harold J., and Keeney, Charles J., *Elementary Gymnastic Apparatus Skills Illustrated.* New York: The Ronald Press Company, 1964.

Griswold, Larry, *Trampoline Tumbling.* St. Louis: Business Collaborators, Inc., 1948.

Gymnastics Rules—AAU. New York: Amateur Athletic Union of the United States.

Gymnastics Rules—NCAA. New York: The National Collegiate Athletic Bureau.

Harris, Rich, *Introducing Gymnastics.* Angwin, Calif.: Pacific Union College Press, 1964.

Hughes, Eric, *Gymnastics for Girls.* New York: The Ronald Press Company, 1963.

Kalakian, Leonard H., and Holmes, William R., *Men's Gymnastics.* Boston: Allyn and Bacon, Inc., 1973.

Keeney, Chuck, *Trampolining Illustrated.* New York: The Ronald Press Company, 1961.

Kjeldsen, Kitty, *Women's Gymnastics.* Boston: Allyn and Bacon, Inc., 1969.

Kunzle, G.C., and Thomas, B.W., *Olympic Gymnastics:* Vol. I, *Freestanding.* London: James Barrie, 1956.

Kunzle, G.C., *Olympic Gymnastics:* Vol. II, *Horizontal Bar.* London: James Barrie Books, Ltd., 1957.

————, Vol. III, *Pommel Horse.* London: Barrie and Rockliff, 1960.

————, Vol. IV, *Parallel Bars.* London: Barrie and Rockliff, 1965.

Ladue, Frank, and Norman, Jim, *This Is Trampolining.* Cedar Rapids: Nissen Trampoline Co., 1954.

Lienert, Walter J., *The Modern Girl Gymnast on the Uneven Parallel Bars.* Indianapolis: Indianapolis Printing Co., 1957.

Loken, Newton C., and Willoughby, Robert J., *Complete Book of Gymnastics.* Englewood Cliffs, N.J.: Prentice-Hall, Inc., 1959.

Official NCAA Gymnastics Guide. Phoenix, Ariz.: College Athletics Publishing Service, 349 East Thomas Road.

Rodwell, Peter, *Gymnastics.* New York: Emerson Books, Inc., 1959.

Ryser, Otto E., *A Teacher's Manual for Tumbling and Apparatus Stunts.* Dubuque, Iowa: William C. Brown Co., 1951.

Scannell, John A., *A Manual of Heavy Apparatus and Tumbling Stunts.* Minneapolis; Burgess Publishing Co., 1948.

Szypula, George, *Tumbling and Balancing for All.* Dubuque, Iowa: William C. Brown Co., 1957.

U.S. Gymnastics Federation, *Age-Group Gymnastics Workbook.* Tucson: The Federation, 1964.

U.S. Naval Institute, *Gymnastics and Tumbling.* Annapolis: The Institute, 1959.

Wachtel, Erna, and Loken, Newton C., *Girls' Gymnastics.* New York: Sterling Publishing Co., 1961.

West, Wilbur D., *Gymnast's Manual.* Englewood Cliffs, N.J.: Prentice-Hall, Inc., 1942.

Yeager, Patrick, *A Teacher's Guide for Men's Gymnastics.* Statesboro, Ga.: Wide World Publications, 1963.

Zwarg, Leopold F., *Apparatus and Tumbling Exercises.* Philadelphia: John Joseph McVey, 1928.

Handball was brought to this country from Ireland. It was also played in some form by the ancient Greeks, and down through the reign of Henry VIII of England.

The four-wall game originated in Ireland and was brought to this country by an Irishman named Phil Casey. The Amateur Athletic Union fostered its beginning in this country, and the first courts were built in Brooklyn, New York. During the early years only four-wall handball was played; however, other variations have come about in court designs, such as one-wall and three-wall, which have caused modifications in the game.

Much of the popularity of handball stems from the fact that it can be played by two, three, or four people on a single-, three-, or four-wall court. In addition, one does not have to be highly skilled to enjoy the game.

TERMINOLOGY

Ace—A point scored by a serve that the opponent is unable to reach.

Alive—Any ball that has not been declared dead.

Backcourt—That part of the court that lies behind the short line.

Base line—The back boundary line of court.

Blocking—Intentional interference with the play of the opponent.

Crotch ball—A ball that strikes at the junction of two walls, or of a wall and floor, or in the corner.

Dead ball—A ball out of play.

Doubles—A game in which each side has two players.

Fault—An infraction of the serving rule that deals with court position.

Front court—That part of the court in front of the short line.

Front wall—The wall against which the ball is hit.

Game—A regulation game requires one player or side to score 21 points. A two-point advantage is not required.

Get—the return of a ball.

Good—During play any ball that hits the front wall before hitting the floor.

Half volley—Hitting the ball on a short bounce near the floor. A pick-up shot.

Handout—The completion of the serving period of one player.

Hinder—Interference by one player with the play of his opponent or opponents. No penalty is involved, and no point is scored; the ball is replayed.

In play—A ball being served or returned.

Kill—A ball returned low on the front wall so it is unplayable.

Lane shot—A ball that is straight down the side wall.

Lob—Any ball that goes high into the air.

Long—(Four-wall): A served ball that rebounds from the front wall to the back wall without touching the floor. (One- or three-wall): A served ball that rebounds from the front wall beyond the back line without touching the floor.

Out-of-bounds—The area outside of the court.

Passing shot—A ball hit so that it is driven past the opponent.

Punch ball—Hitting a ball with a clenched fist.

Rally—When the ball is kept in play.

Receiver—The player who receives the service.

Service—Starting a game by putting the ball into play legally.

Short—When the ball rebounds from the front wall and strikes the floor between the front wall and the short line.

Side out—Loss of service by a player in singles or both players in doubles.

Volley—Hitting the ball in the air before it strikes the floor.

COURT

The four-wall handball courts shall not be less than 20 feet wide, 20 feet high, and 40 feet long; the back wall must be at least 10 feet high, or 12 feet high if possible. The one-wall court dimensions are usually 40 by 20 by 20 feet. In some areas of the country there are three-wall courts, comprising a front wall and two side walls.

In four-wall handball the short line divides the court in half. Five feet closer to the front wall is the *service line*. The space between these two lines is the *service zone*. A line 18 inches from the side walls and parallel to them is marked off in this service zone. In doubles play the partner of the server stands in either of these boxes, with his back to the side wall until the ball rebounds over the short line.

In single-wall handball, the short line is 16 feet from and parallel to the front wall. The service line is 9 feet farther from the front wall (25 feet away); it is not drawn the entire width of the court, but is merely indicated by a line or marker that extends 4 inches from each side line toward the center of the court.

EQUIPMENT

Handball regulations require gloves, an "official" black rubber ball, and a uniform of white clothing. The gloves can be a soft material, with fingers not webbed; there may be no hard materials in any part of the fingers or palm of the glove.

All players who wear glasses or contact lens should wear a protective mask or a shield.

THE GAME

A regulation game consists of 21 points; however, a game may be played to any score desired.

There are three types of games—singles, doubles, and rotation. The singles game pits one player against another; the doubles game, two players against two. In the rotation game the server plays against two players. When the server fails to keep the ball in play, he loses the serve and the players rotate clockwise, creating a new server who opposes the other two—this continuing until one player wins a game.

In all three types of game only the serving side scores points. The first player or side scoring 21 points is the winner. During play, as long as the ball hits the front wall before it hits the floor, it is good. A ball hitting any boundary line is inbounds.

Essentially, there is no difference between the fundamental skills of one-wall handball and four-wall handball. However, the strategy is slightly different because in a four-wall game there is emphasis on the

"passing game," whereas in the single-wall game the "kill shot" plays a much greater role.

FUNDAMENTALS

Serve

The zone between the service line and short line is the serving area. The server must start and complete his service between these two lines. In serving, the player drops the ball to the floor and hits it on the first rebound. The ball must strike the front wall first, after which it can strike either side wall on the return from the front wall, as long as it rebounds past the short line before hitting the floor. In doubles, one player serves while his partner stands in the doubles box; when the server is put out, his partner serves. However, only one man serves at the beginning of any one game; thereafter, each player serves his turn. When the original side comes back in to serve, the same man serves first who started serving at the beginning of the game.

While serving, if a ball lands outside the base line and hits between the two sidelines, it is a long ball and the server gets a second serve. A short ball is one that fails to rebound past the short line on the fly; the server gets a second serve.

A player loses his serve if: the ball fails to hit the front wall first; he serves two long or two short balls in succession, or one long and one short ball in succession; he is hit by his served ball as it rebounds; the ball hits his partner while the partner is outside the box; he strikes at and misses the ball on the serve.

When rallying the ball must hit the front wall before it touches the floor, but it may hit a side wall first. If the server fails to keep the ball in play, it is a "hand-out" and loss of service. In doubles when a player hits a ball that strikes him or his partner, it is a hand-out, whether the ball has hit the front wall or not. A ball that hits at the junction of the front wall and floor and bounces *upward* is not a fair ball; a ball that hits this junction and bounces *outward* is considered a fair ball.

Receiver

The receiver stands at least 5 feet behind the short line until the server has served; he may then move in any direction. The receiver does not have the option of playing a short ball, a long ball, or a foot fault ball.

When any of the above occur, the ball is dead. If a player does not have a fair opportunity to strike the ball because of his opponent, he may call a "hinder." In four-wall play each player, except on a serve, has the opportunity to play a ball he has once missed as long as it is alive. Only one hand may be used in striking the ball, but a player may use either hand. If the ball hits a player on the wrist or above, it is illegal. If a ball on the return hits an opponent on the way to the front wall, it is a hinder. In doubles, both partners have the right to hit the ball, and either one can call a hinder even though his partner plays the ball. The ball should not be interfered with until it is declared dead; if one player swings and misses, his partner may play the ball.

Use of the Hand

If a person can throw and catch, he should be able to play the game of handball. The first movements on a court should be to stand in the backcourt and to throw the ball against the front wall, then on the rebound to catch the ball on the first bounce or the fly. If a player can catch the ball, he will also be able to strike the ball with the hand.

The ball should be struck with a flat hand, cupped hand, or the fist. In executing the flat-hand shot, the fingers are together with the thumb alongside the index finger. The ball is struck on the cushion of the hand at the base of the fingers. For the cupped-hand shot, the fingers of the striking hand are curved slightly as if to pick up water. The fist shot is known as a "punch-ball" shot; it is used by the more advanced players. The punch shot is executed by contracting the hand into a fist, with the fingers covering the palm of the hand and the thumb placed against the index finger. This will provide a flat surface with which to contact the ball.

Basic Strokes

The four basic strokes are: the straight-arm underhand, the bent-arm underhand, the straight side-arm, and the bent-arm overhand.

Straight-arm Underhand

The straight-arm underhand stroke is executed with a motion similar to that of a pitcher in a softball game. The player stands with his feet in line about shoulder width apart, facing the front wall. From this position the right arm is swung in a backward direction. The initial forward movement is a shift of weight to the right foot and a step forward with the left foot. The

right is swung forward, contacting the ball with the right hand at about knee height so the ball will travel to the front wall. The player can bend his knees and his body at the waist according to the height at which the ball is to be played. He should follow through with the swing, shifting his weight from the back foot to the front foot while swinging the arm, then bringing the back foot up in line with the front foot so he will be in a starting position once again.

Bent-arm Underhand

The bent-arm underhand is really an imitation of the movement a person would use to "skip" a stone along the surface of a pond. The player stands facing the side of the court, with his feet spread slightly apart, in a comfortable position. The body is bent forward, the right shoulder is rotated backward, while the arm, bent slightly, is allowed to swing back high to ensure maximum power when striking the ball. The weight is shifted to the right foot. The arm comes forward in the same plane or line in which the arm was brought back, hitting the ball as a short step is taken toward the front wall with the front foot. The weight will naturally shift in the direction of the flight of the ball. If the player has a flexible wrist while striking the ball, it will not only add "zip" to the shot, but may make the ball hop either to the left or right.

Straight Side-arm Stroke

This stroke is used mostly as a defensive shot for keeping the ball in play when a player has been tricked by his opponent; it is somewhat of a "desperation" return. However, some players use the straight side-arm for serving the ball. There is power, but not too much control, in this stroke. The player stands facing the side of the court, with his feet spread comfortably apart. The body is fairly erect on this shot, with little or no bending at the waist. The arm, held straight, is raised to shoulder level in front of the body and brought backward parallel to the floor; the body rotates and the weight is shifted to the back foot. The arm moves forward in the same plane, and the hand meets the ball in front of the body with open palm as the player shifts his weight to the forward foot. On the follow-through, he brings the back foot forward and rotates his body so that he faces the front wall at the completion of the stroke.

Bent-arm Overhand Stroke

This stroke is used when the ball is higher than the shoulder. The ball should be struck with the same motion a catcher uses in throwing a baseball. The stance for this stroke is essentially the same as the stance for a straight-arm underhand. The player starts from a position facing the front wall, with the feet about shoulder width apart. The arm is bent at the elbow, with the hand moved up and behind the ear; the weight is on the right foot, with the knees slightly bent. The player shifts his weight and steps forward on the left foot as the arm is brought forward to strike the ball in front of the body. The snap of the wrist and the straightening of the arm produces power in the stroke. On the follow-through the arm is brought down across the body as is a baseball pitcher's on the follow-through of a throw. This stroke is extremely good for passing opponents on what is called "down the lane" shots. It can also be used in serving for variation and speed.

DRILLS

Handball can be practiced alone. The beginner should try to execute fundamental movements slowly so that coordination will come about gradually.

When coordination is achieved, the movements will be easier to execute and a player can add speed, power, and control without forming any bad habits or incorrect techniques.

The player should learn to throw the ball with the movements of the various strokes and practice with the "weak" hand; no player is any better than his weak hand. In throwing he should concentrate on accuracy, and speed will develop as he progresses. He should throw not only straight to the front wall, but also to the front and side walls, to the front and back walls, to the front wall and ceiling, to the front wall, ceiling, and side wall. After throwing the ball into these positions, he should learn to hit the ball in the same situations. A beginner should learn to serve with either hand hard enough to carry to the back wall in the air.

The player can practice his kill shot by playing a "percentage game," to see how many kills he can make out of 10 shots or 15 shots, etc. He also can play his left hand against his right hand. Two players, interested in developing their weak sides, can play against each other, using only the weak hand to return the ball. Players should remember at all times to keep their eyes on the ball. The walls of the court do not move—the ball *does*.

Specific Drills

1. Mark the back court into six equal squares and number each square. From a serving position, attempt to serve the ball into each square with the least number of strokes. Use either hand to serve.

2. Stand behind the short line facing the front wall. On command, throw the ball against the front wall; thereafter, continue to strike the ball with either hand. Use a time limit of one minute to record all legal shots against the front wall.

STRATEGY

When playing singles, a player should try to keep himself in a key position to play all shots by getting to the center of the court quickly after each shot. The player then has the advantage of court control and shot placement, and the receiver is forced to take one side or the other in returning the ball. The player must keep his eyes on a ball that passes him into the back court. However, when turning either to the right or left for this purpose, the respective arm should be up covering the face for protection. When a player is waiting to hit the ball, he should face the front wall, one foot slightly in front of the other, the weight on the balls of the feet, with his knees slightly bent, his body slightly bent at the waist, his hands up and ready to move in any direction.

In following the ball, the player should move on the court in anticipation of his opponent's shot. He must be on the alert for slow drives and lob or lane shots that are hit hard. He should try at all times to keep the ball away from his opponent and keep him on the defense. If his opponent is in close to the front wall, the player should lob the ball; if the opponent is in the back court, he should try to hit the ball low on the front wall; if the opponent has committed himself to one side or the other, the player should direct the ball away from him. The opponent should be kept running. A player should vary his game so that his opponent cannot *type* his style.

The stance and individual playing techniques are similar for both singles and doubles. However, the doubles game requires coordinated court coverage. The two generally practiced plans are: (1) Each player covers one-half the court from the front wall to the back; (2) When one player "moves up" he "stays up," while his partner stays back—until a point is determined or until a balanced position is achieved.

Advice to Beginners

1. Remember that your opponent is entitled to a free and unobstructed opportunity to play the ball. Unintentional interference constitutes a hinder;

intentional interference constitutes a point or side out as the case may be.

2. Concentrate on the one or two strokes that you use most frequently.
3. The bent-arm underhand stroke is to be preferred.
4. Play numerous one-handed practice games using only your weak hand.
5. Rather than attempt a "kill" on every ball, try an occasional passing shot.
6. Vary your style of game.
7. Remember that a well-timed wrist snap will greatly increase the speed of the ball.
8. "Follow" the ball until your hand strikes it.
9. Decide as you get ready to hit the ball whether it is to be a pass, kill, or lob.
10. Develop an effective serve. (Points are scored only by the serving side.)
11. Observe your opponent's strategy and get into the proper position to make each return.
12. When an opponent calls a "hinder," do not question the validity of his decision.

BIBLIOGRAPHY

Handball Rules—AAU. New York: Amateur Athletic Union of the United States.

National YMCA Handball Rules. Des Moines, Iowa: Champion Glove Mfg. Co.

Phillips, B.E., *Handball: Its Play and Management.* New York: The Ronald Press Company, 1957.

Robertson, Richard, and Olson, Herbert W., *Beginning Handball.* Belmont, Calif.: Wadsworth Publishing Co., 1962.

Shaw, John H., *Handball.* Boston: Allyn and Bacon, Inc., 1971.

United States Handball Association Rules. Skokie, Ill.: The Association.

Horseshoe pitching began as a barnyard activity. The shoes were those discarded from horses' hooves, and the stakes were improvised from pieces of pipe. Pitchers played by unwritten rules, and the pitching area was determined by setting two stakes an arbitrary distance apart.

Today the game has spread to the recreational areas, picnic grounds, and back yards of America. Well-defined rules and court layouts now govern the game, and an increasing number of people are being drawn to this enjoyable activity.

PLAYING AREA

The horseshoe court (Fig. 15-1) consists of two pitching boxes, 6 feet square, set flush with the ground. They can be made by nailing four 2- by 4-inch boards together to make a 6-foot square. A good base is made from part clay and part dirt, stamped down to form a surface flush with the top of the box. If clay is not available, the ground should be loosened in the box to allow the shoes to stay where they land.

A stake is driven into the ground in the center of each box until 14 inches remain above the surface. The stakes should incline toward each other so that when a perpendicular is dropped from the top of each stake, it will fall 3 inches from the base of each stake.

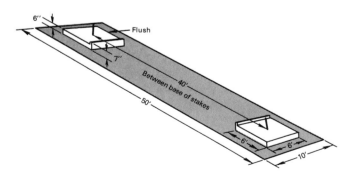

Fig. 15—1. Horseshoe court.

The court is laid out over level ground, with the centers of the boxes 40 feet apart.

According to rules governing tournament play, where two or more courts are laid out side by side, the front pitching box foul line should make a straight line across the entire area. Also, the stakes in adjacent courts shall be at least 10 feet apart.

Horseshoes are manufactured according to official specifications, and therefore most sets sold commercially are acceptable for play.

Each shoe has three "calks": one at the heel (the bend), and one on each end.

RULES

The important rules governing the game are:

1. Players shall in no way interfere with other players while actually pitching, and must remain to the side and behind the pitcher's box.
2. Players may not touch any shoes until all awarding of points is agreed upon.
3. An inning is completed when all shoes have been pitched from one end of the court. The players must wait until the end of an inning before walking to the opposite end of the court.
4. In pitching a shoe, a player must stand in the pitcher's box and behind the foul line until the shoe leaves his hand. If a player steps over the foul line in pitching a shoe, that shoe is declared a foul and is removed from play.
5. If a shoe lands in fair territory and breaks into two or more parts, it is removed and another shoe is pitched.
6. No shoe will count if it hits the ground outside a pitcher's box.
7. Measurements to determine points won are made with a straight edge and calipers.

THE GAME

A toss of a coin decides which player will pitch first. The player winning the toss has the choice of pitching

first or last. In successive games between the same two
players, the loser will have the choice.

The first player steps into the box and pitches two
shoes, one at a time. The second player then pitches
both of his shoes in the same manner. This completes
an inning. At the end of each inning, both players
walk to the opposite pitcher's box, agree upon points
won, and begin the next inning. In the case of no
points being won, or of a tie, the player pitching last in
the inning starts the next inning.

Scoring

The official game of horseshoes is won by the first
player scoring 50 points or more. However, the
number of points needed to win nonofficial or informal games may be agreed upon by the players prior
to starting a game.

A shoe must be no more than 6 inches from the
stake in order to score. *Note:* This rule may be
modified in certain situations. For beginners, unskilled players, the very young and very old, and
certain handicaps, it is advisable to score points for
shoes anywhere in the box if they are the nearest
shoes. This permits more rapid scoring and makes the
game more enjoyable for those who have not attained
a level of skill necessary to make a shoe stay 6 inches
or less from the stake. When individuals attain
adequate skill, and the scoring becomes quite rapid,
they will want to observe the 6-inch rule.

The final resting place of a shoe is the position that
is used to compute the score. When a shoe strikes the
ground, it often slides; the best pitch is one that
makes the shoe stick where it strikes.

The object of pitching horseshoes is to make
ringers. A *ringer* is defined as a shoe that encircles the
stake so that a straight edge can touch both ends of
the shoe and still clear the stake.

Shoe Positions	*Points Scored*
1. 1 closest shoe	1 Point
2. 2 closest shoes	2 Points
3. 1 ringer	3 Points
4. 2 ringers	6 Points
5. 1 ringer and 1 closest shoe	4 Points
6. 1 ringer by each player	0 Points
7. 2 ringers by each player	0 Points

Note: All points are scored at the end of each
inning, according to the position of the shoes after all
shoes have been pitched.

SKILLS

There are two common methods of pitching
horseshoes: one, by turning the shoe in a horizontal
plane with the ground (referred to as the "twist"); and
the second, by turning the shoe end-over-end (commonly referred to as "the flip").

The Twist Pitch

Preliminary steps in pitching "the twist" involve the
grip and the stance. The shoe is held with the calks
down and the open end toward the body. The right
thumb is on top of the right side of the shoe and the
fingers are held underneath. The pitcher stands to one
side of the stake at the rear of the pitcher's box. The
right foot is held slightly behind the left.

The twist pitch begins by the pitcher holding the
shoe up in front of the body, with the arm bent at the
elbow. He sights through or over the shoe to the
opposite stake and begins the backswing. At the start
of the backswing, the pitcher starts the forward
motion of the body with a short step forward on the
right foot. As the pitching arm reaches a full
backswing position, it will be about parallel to the
ground.

To begin the actual delivery, a full step is then
taken on the left foot, making sure that this foot
points directly at the opposite stake. At the same time,
the pitching arm begins the downward and upward
arc, at the end of which the wrist is extended, imparting a flat, clockwise, turning motion to the shoe.

Experience is the best guide in determining the
proper point of release for the shoe and how much
effort needs to be applied to give the shoe the correct
number of turns to bring the open end to the stake.
One of the most important points to remember about
pitching is: If the shoe is released too soon, it will
probably hit the ground in front of the opposite box,
not having enough height to reach the desired distance
or number of turns in the air. If released too late, it
will go too high in the air, fall short of the desired
distance, or make too many turns in the air. Once the
pitching motion is begun, the eyes should never leave
the opposite stake until the shoe falls.

The Flip Pitch

The flip delivery is different in two respects, the grip
and the release. The shoe is held with the index,
middle, and ring fingers, diagonally, underneath the
back of the shoe; the little finger is held straight and

supports from underneath. The thumb is held on top of the shoe (with calks down) and parallel to both sides. When the shoe is held in this manner, no calk is held or touched. The release is accomplished by keeping the palm up and imparting a flipping, end-over-end motion to the shoe. Again, experience will show how much flip is needed to bring the open end of the shoe to the stake.

Regardless of the method of pitching, three things should be true: 1. The open end of the shoe must point to the stake as the shoe lands; 2. The shoe should fall at the base of the stake; 3. The shoe should always land with the calks down.

SAFETY HINTS

The following simple safety rules will make horseshoe pitching safer and more enjoyable.

1. Never walk across a horseshoe court, always *around* it.
2. Always stand behind and well to the side of the pitcher's box when shoes are being pitched.
3. Do not walk toward the opposite box until all shoes have been pitched.

BIBLIOGRAPHY

General Sportcraft Co., *Horseshoes.* New York: The Company.

National Horseshoe Pitchers Association of America, *Horseshoes (Professional).* Crestline, Calif.: The Association.

St. Pierre Chain Corp., *The Game of Horseshoe Pitching.* Worcester, Mass.: The Corporation.

The game of ice hockey as played today is about 100 years old, and many claim it is the fastest team game in the world. The word "hockey" is derived from the word "hoquet," a French term for a shepherd's stick. Its actual origin is uncertain. However, it is an adaptation of the principle of batting a ball with a stick, which has been ascribed to many peoples and many lands. There seems to be little doubt that the related field game of "shinny" is the forerunner of the present game of ice hockey.

Historians disagree as to whether the first game (in about 1855) was played by the British regiments in Ontario or those in Nova Scotia. Regardless of the controversy, McGill University of Montreal, Canada, must be given credit for placing the game on a sound foundation by developing rules and regulations. The first rules used were known as the *Halifax rules* and were devised by W.F. Robertson during the winter of 1880, when several interclass matches were played by the McGill students. Within a decade, the game was introduced into the United States by C. Shearer, a Montrealer who was studying at the Johns Hopkins University in Baltimore.

The first organized hockey league played in Kingston, Ontario, on harbor ice. The league operated in 1886, and in 1890 the Ontario Hockey Association was founded. In 1896 the American Amateur Hockey League, composed of teams in the metropolitan district of New York, was formed.

Hockey was first introduced into Europe by G.A. Meager, then a champion figure skater. The first European team was formed in Paris. In 1908, mainly through the efforts of Louis Magnus of France, the International Ice Hockey Federation was formed. This organization conducted the first official European championships in 1910 on outdoor natural ice at Les Avantes in the Swiss Alps. In 1920 the first worldwide ice hockey and skating contests, which were held at Antwerp, Belgium, included Canada and the United States and were publicized in both the American and European press as the Winter Olympics. However, the results have never been recognized as official by the International Olympic Committee because the Winter Olympic games were not officially added to the program until 1924. With the 1932 Olympics scheduled to be held at Lake Placid, New York, the United States Olympic Committee in 1931 induced the Amateur Athletic Union to become the governing body of ice hockey.

TERMINOLOGY

Assist—A pass or a preliminary play to a teammate that enables him to score a goal.

Back check—A defensive tactic usually entailing skating back and covering opponents who are in an offensive situation.

Body checking—The art of using the shoulder or hip to physically stop or retard an advancing opponent.

Check—A defensive maneuver to stop the forward progress of an attacking player.

Clearing the puck—An offensive situation to move the puck out of the defending zone.

Crease—A zone marked off in front of the goalkeeper's cage.

Cross-checking—An infraction based on the misuse of the stick, in which a check is delivered when the stick is held with both hands and is off the ice.

Face-off—The means of putting the puck in play: the referee drops the puck between two players, who then attempt to gain control of it with their sticks.

Fore check—A defensive move using the stick and applied in the opponent's defensive zone.

Goal judge—The official who credits a legally scored goal, usually by turning on a red light. One goal judge is stationed at each end of the rink.

Killing penalties—Defensive play to use up time when a teammate is in the penalty box.

Line—An attacking unit comprising a center and two forwards.

Penalty box—A designated area where players are sent to serve out the time penalties specified by the referee.

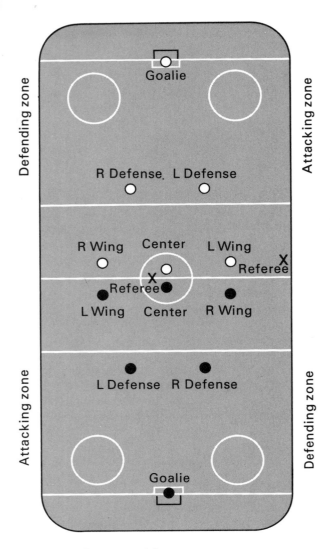

Fig. 16—1. Player positions.

Periods—A game is divided into three 20-minute periods.

Playing the point—Usually, a defenseman of the offensive team stationing himself on his opponent's blue line to aid in the offense.

Poke check—The art of poking the stick to get the puck away from opponents.

Power play—An offensive maneuver in which all five players move up the ice into the attacking zone, putting pressure on the opposing team. This is used especially when the attacking team has an edge in manpower.

Puck—A round, hard, rubber disc.

Ragging—To retain possession of the puck, usually by individual stickhandling.

Rink—An enclosed sheet of ice which may be naturally or artificially prepared.

Save—The act of a goalie stopping a shot.

Shinny—Disorganized play.

Spearing—An infraction based on the misuse of the stick, usually poking or jabbing with the blade part of the stick.

RULES

The object of the game is to propel the puck with the stick into the opponent's net. The game is started by a face-off at the center spot, with the player positions designated as shown in Fig. 16-1.

A hockey rink is 200 feet by 85 feet and is divided into three areas (the end or defending zone, the neutral zone, and the end or attacking zone) by two blue lines, each 12 inches wide. (See Fig. 16-2) From the blue lines to the goal line, the end zone is 60 feet long. Each team considers the end zone that they are defending to be the defending zone; they consider their opponents' end zone to be the attacking zone. The ice is bisected by a red line 2 inches wide that is known as the *center line*. Only the team defending the half of the rink on which play is centered is permitted to employ body contact—and then, only to the offensive man in possession of the puck. The wooden fence that surrounds the entire ice hockey rink is referred to as "the boards."

The face-off spot is the center of a circle with a radius of 15 feet; this is where the puck is faced when rule infraction or stoppage of play occur in that zone area. The referee drops the puck from knee height so that it lands on the "spot" between the sticks of the opposing players facing off. No other player may enter the restraining circle until this occurs.

The puck may be passed in any direction to a teammate in the defending and neutral zone. Players of an attacking team, however, must not precede the puck into the attacking zone.

A 2-inch-wide red line, called the *goal line*, crosses the mouth of each goal and is used to determine when a goal is scored and to call "icing-the-puck" infractions. When any player of a team shoots the puck from behind his own blue line (defending zone) beyond the red goal line of the opposing team and the defending team obtains possession first, the situation is known as "icing the puck." Play is then stopped and the puck faced off at the end or corner face-off spot of the offending team.

The goal is a framed net 6 feet wide and 4 feet high. The goal crease is an area 4 feet deep by 8 feet wide that is marked on the ice in front of each goal cage, as shown in Fig. 16-2. No attacking player, except the puck carrier, may enter the crease.

Players are penalized for infractions of the rules by being banished from the game for intervals of from two minutes to the balance of the game (actual playing time), depending upon the type of rule infraction. Three 20-minute periods constitute a game. Rest periods of 10 minutes are allowed between each playing period.

EQUIPMENT

Basic protective hockey equipment should include: shin pads, elbow pads, shoulder pads, gloves, helmet, tendon guards for the skates, and wide suspenders for the pants. Under the official NCAA Ice Hockey Rules, all players must wear headguards with chin straps fastened.

Skates

Skates are the most important item in the hockey player's equipment and should be selected with the greatest attention given to size, material, durability, and support for ankles and arches. Most hockey players have the blades of their skates "rockered" so that only a few inches are flat on the ice. The length of the rocker usually depends on the individual player. Generally a forward uses a shorter rocker than the defensemen. A longer rocker means more speed, but

less maneuverability. Skate sharpening must be done frequently. Usually skates can be used only three to five times before they need attention.

Skates for the goalkeeper are of special design. Their flat, low blade is constructed for better balance, to resist heavy knocks, and to stop pucks from passing between the blade and the foot. Most players lace the skates with cross (over and under) lacing using 72-inch semiwaxed lace.

Stick

In the selection of a proper stick, the individual must consider the length, lie, and face of the stick. The best quality stick is made from seasoned elm or white ash and is usually laminated. The length of the stick may not exceed 52 inches. The desired length may be gauged by standing the stick vertically; the end of the shaft should then reach the player's chin when the player is on skates. Some players use a shorter stick to facilitate stickhandling, especially when trying to control the puck along the boards.

The lie is the angle the blade makes with the shaft. The proper lie should be determined while on skates. The number range is usually from three to nine: the higher the number, the smaller the angle between the shaft and the blade of the stick. Most players use the average range of a five, six, or seven lie; the number is stamped on the shaft of the stick. The optimal lie for a

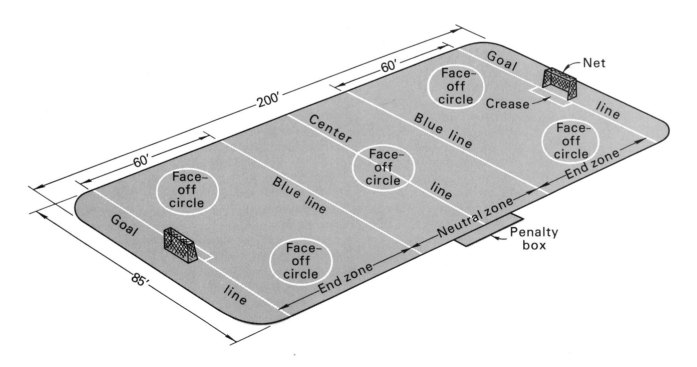

Fig. 16–2. Hockey rink.

player can be determined by how far from his skates he can carry the stick, keeping the blade flat on the ice, and still achieve maximum control of the puck. The lie used by goalkeepers ranges from 11 to 14, and its length is determined by the player's height and normal stance.

The blade of the stick is slightly curved upward, to aid in getting more blade contact on the puck. Generally, a left-handed person will pass and shoot right, and a right-handed person will pass and shoot left. There are three types of stick blades—left, right, and neutral (straight). In selecting a blade, the player must consider his position and his ability to raise the puck off the ice. Friction tape applied to the blade and upper end of the shaft will ensure better puck control and a more secure grip.

Puck

The puck is made of hard black vulcanized rubber, round in shape; it is 1 inch thick and 3 inches in diameter, and weighs from 5-1/2 to 6 ounces. It is advisable as a safety measure that pucks be rounded on the edges and chilled before using.

FUNDAMENTALS

Skating

Skating is the most important fundamental skill in ice hockey. A player must learn to skate frontward and backward and to turn clockwise and counterclockwise at varying rates of speed. Since skating is a bent-leg activity, good body position or weight distribution is the most important phase of skating.

The fundamental position of skating gives the appearance of a semisitting position. In forward skating, a comfortable forward body lean is made from the hips, and the knees are bent to a point just ahead of the skate. This body position places the center of balance in the hips, which are kept in a straight line with the middle of the skate.

Before the initial stride, place the skates 6 inches apart, having one skate slightly ahead of the other, with the rear skate turned out to a 45-degree angle. In beginning the stride, the weight is shifted from the rear skate to the front or gliding skate by pushing the inside edge of the rear skate blade against the ice and straightening the bent knee. At the same time, the arm and shoulder action is coordinated with the skate action by completing the shifting of the weight with a forward lean to the side and over the front or gliding skate. At the start of the stride, the blade of the skate is held straight. After a short glide, the inside edge of

the blade is pushed or shoved against the ice as the skate is turned outward. In making the stride, the knee is held flexible and is always ahead of the gliding skate.

In analyzing the rear or thrusting leg, it should be noted that the skate is brought forward quickly, close to the ice, and alongside the other skate with the blade straight; the knee is well bent. The weight shift now takes place to this skate as it begins another forward glide and stride. Most of the power in a stride comes from the weight shift and the straightening of the rear knee and leg against the ice surface. In free skating, the length of each left and right glide should be the same and comfortable. The length should be shorter when starting, or turning quickly, or changing direction. To increase the glide and momentum possible on ice, a lifting or hopping action of the arm and shoulders should be coordinated with each weight shift and gliding leg action.

Ice hockey requires that a skater learn to stop quickly and turn in either direction. The basic body position is quite similar in executing a stop and a turn. In stopping, most skaters use a single- or double-leg stop. Here the upper body, hips, and skates are turned quickly sideways or at right angles to the traveling direction. The skates are kept close together, and the knees bent in a stiffening action as the weight is shifted back to the inside skate of the turning direction.

Turning or cutting without the loss of speed is difficult, yet must be mastered if one is to become a proficient skater. Most skaters have their greatest difficulty in turning or cutting to the right. In performing a turn, the upper body initiates the movement by turning slowly over the front or gliding skate. The hips and leg then swing around, shifting the weight from the gliding skate to the cutting skate with a cross-over step. Speed can be increased in turning or cutting by coordinating a lifting and hopping action of the shoulders with the weight shift from the gliding to the cutting skate.

To improve balance and agility, backward skating must be added to the basic skating requirement for any hockey player. In backward skating, a lower sitting position is assumed and movement is derived from swinging the hips from side to side, while pushing and twisting as the weight is placed on each outside foot.

Passing

There is no easier or quicker way to move the puck than to pass it. Players should learn to pass well to either side. Before executing a pass, a player must look up for proper direction and timing. In most cases, the receiver is moving, so the passer should make his target a point ahead of the receiver's stick.

In passing, the stick is held comfortably and regarded as an extension of the arms and hands. Giving the stick a slight turn toward the puck causes the blade to have better puck contact and control. The upper hand is then worked against the lower hand, the latter acting as a lever in the snapping action. The blade of the stick is held flat on the ice and in line throughout the pass. There are several types of passes to meet particular situations. Basically, the four passes are the sweep pass, flip pass, slap pass, and drop pass.

The sweep pass is made by simply sweeping both hands forward, with the puck kept close to the middle of the blade either forehand or backhand. This type of pass is used primarily when the receiver is in the open and speed is not an important factor.

The flip pass is made with the puck held near the upper end of the blade. The puck is raised off the ice by twisting the wrists upward with a high follow-through. It is a slow pass, and is often used to clear the stick of an opponent in a congested area or as a lead pass (a pass to a spot that a teammate is heading toward).

The slap pass is made in the same manner as a slap shot (see the section on shooting that follows), but with less force. Here the wrists are snapped forward with a low follow-through to prevent any lift.

The drop pass is executed by placing the stick in front of the puck. The stick is held momentarily in this position and then moved away. The puck should stop on the spot desired. A player uses this type of pass when he wants to pass to a trailing teammate.

Receiving

The blade of the stick should always be carried close to the ice surface in preparation to receive a pass. The elbows are held high and away from the body to aid in a slight "give" of the stick when puck contact is made. The blade of the stick should be at right angles to the direction from which the puck is coming. Since the puck is usually rotating in flight, it is necessary to quarter-turn the blade in the direction of the pass to control and form a good puck contact or pocket with the ice.

Shooting

The stick is held firmly with one hand near the center of the shaft, the other hand on the upper end. The puck is kept close to the heel of the stick to add more power to the shot. The shot is started from behind the mid-line of the body, with the legs in a striding position and the shoulders facing sideways to the net. The shooting movement then begins with a sweeping motion of the stick as the rear leg, in thrust, transfers the weight forward. As the sweeping motion comes forward, the wrists are brought into play, ending in a snapping action. This snapping action is executed by having the top hand slightly ahead of the bottom hand, then bringing the top hand back toward the body while the lower hand pushes forward in a quick scissor movement.

The height of the shot is determined by the angle of the blade with the puck and the degree of follow-through. For a low shot, the handle of the stick is, at first, well ahead of the blade. Snapping the wrists forward with a low follow-through is essential. The ideal scoring shot is a quick low shot from about 15 feet out and in front of the net.

The four basic types of shots are: the wrist or forehand, the backhand, the flip, and the slap.

Wrist or Forehand Shot

The wrist shot is the fundamental shot in hockey. This is the basic shot described above and the one used most often. It can be performed with great accuracy and speed, and should be kept low. A low shot will give more rebounds and has less chance of being detected in flight. For this particular shot, the stick should finish below the level of the shooter's knees.

Backhand Shot

The backhand shot has a more sweeping than snapping action and is very effective, although not commonly used. In the backhand shot, the puck is brought behind the mid-line of the body in starting the shot. It is used primarily when there is no time to shift the puck to your natural shooting side.

Flip Shot

The puck is held near the middle of the blade and delivered from in front of the body plane. The lifting action is made by tilting the blade back and flipping the wrists upward with a high follow-through. It is used at close range to hit the upper part of the net.

Slap Shot

This is the most powerful shot in hockey, but it lacks the accuracy of the wrist shot. It is effective because of its speed and quickness of delivery. The puck is hit near the heel of the blade and delivered more from the front of the body than from the side. The slapping action is made by pulling the stick away from the puck, then slapping it down on the ice just behind the puck. The action is a short downward motion, made with the blade perpendicular to the ice. This type of shot is used not only for its power, but especially when speed of execution is an important factor.

Stick Handling

The most important skill in stick handling is the ability to control the puck on the stick without looking at it.

The puck should be kept under control midway on the blade of the stick. The correct stick lie should give the easiest control movement from all positions. The hands are held fairly close together on the shaft for a greater range of motion, and the shoulders are kept as square as possible to the path of the puck.

An integral part of stick handling is faking and shifting. Although players who shoot and pass left find it easier to shift to the right, much attention should be given to shifting in either direction. The ideal situation and stance from which to move is to be standing about 5 feet in front of the opponent with your skates parallel, so that you can cut in either direction. The continuous action in hockey has created many moves that are made instantaneously, which enables each player to give stickhandling techniques his own particular touch and variation.

Checking

Checking is a defense skill designed to enable a player to take the puck away from an opponent. The three basic means of checking are the stick check, the body check, and the skate check (back checking). Defensemen, especially, must excel in the basic methods of checking. The drills suggested for stick handling may also be used to practice checking.

Stick Check

Stick checking may be performed by a sweeping, hooking, or poking motion of the stick. The stick is held only with the upper hand in attempting any of these checking motions (the right hand is used to check a left-handed shot). A lifting action may also be used in stick checking, using both hands on the stick. Here the player places the stick under the opponent's stick, lifts it up off the ice, then tries to gain possession of the puck. In performing the basic stick checking movements, the approach should be made either from directly in front or from the side. A great number of

penalties are caused by the misuse of the stick in stick checking from behind. Stick checking can be most effective when the opponent is forced to turn toward the side boards, thus limiting his area of maneuverability and range of passing.

Body Check

Since ice hockey is a contact sport, body checking plays a very important role in defensive hockey. The two types of checks commonly used are the *shoulder check* and the *hip check*. In executing either check, the skates are kept well spread, with the knees bent, and the upper body in a distinct forward lean. Momentum in the step-in is gained by pushing off the rear skate in a short step-in movement. The ideal time to initiate the step-in is when the opponent is about a stick's length away. In the shoulder check, the lunge is made directly forward, the contact being about the middle of the body. The hip check requires a more swaying motion to the side, with the contact area preferably below the hips. As a safety precaution, checkers should perform body-checking drills with the use of their sticks; that is, instead of skating into an opponent's body, the checker should put his stick out in front.

Skate Check (back checking)

Back checking is the ability to skate back and cover an opponent who is in an offensive situation. In covering, a player should position himself between the opponent and the puck carrier, preferably between the puck and the goal. For a speedier recovery from back checking, the player should use a one-leg stop and a hopping skating action in picking up his opponent.

Goaltending

Other than skating, goaltending skills differ widely from the basic skills of an ice hockey player. There are no set ways to play the position; however, the goalie does have a few guiding principles:

1. Keep the eyes fixed firmly on the puck.
2. Stay as upright in the normal crouch (semisitting position) as possible.
3. Keep the body square to the puck so you can back up every shot.
4. Move across the net in a small semicircle, with the crease as the outside boundary.
5. Know how to play the angles by moving the body on the part of the semicircle nearest the puck.
6. Do *not* make the first move.

7. Catch the puck when possible, especially on the glove side for control of the shot.
8. Use the stick for low shots and when clearing the puck to the corner from in front of the net.
9. Freeze the puck with the body when having difficulty in clearing.
10. Always try to steer or deflect shots off the stick or pads to the corners.

DRILLS

The following suggested drills will provide the beginning player or coach with a fundamental program to follow in any classification of hockey.

Skating Push Drill. Players line up in pairs, one behind the other, at one end of the rink. Player number one places his hands, or his stick, on the hips or lower back of player number two and pushes him the length of the rink. When the players get to the end of the rink, they change places. This drill will help to develop the leaning body position, knee action, and push-off skating stroke.

Circle Skating Drill. Players are divided up into five face-off circles. When a whistle is blown, they begin to skate one behind the other, keeping on the circle line and using short chopping strokes. This drill is repeated in the opposite direction on a second whistle. This drill will develop cutting and balance skills and lateral mobility.

Figure Eight and Four Drill. Players skating behind one another take four gliding strides, then burst all out for four fast paces, then four glides, continuing this procedure around one goal cage and then back around the other, forming a figure eight. This drill helps to develop a player's ability to cut to both sides, as well as to quick-break and to change pace.

Scramble Forward and Backward Skating Drill. Players line up along the side of the rink. On command, they begin skating forward; at the second command, they stop and scramble back to the starting point; at the third command, they break (start) again, skating forward to the other side. At the fourth command, they return by skating backward to their original position.

Passing in Pairs Drill (stationary). Players are paired off, each pair having a puck. The players pass the puck back and forth. At first, short passes are used; then the distance between the players is increased and they make longer and longer passes. The progression from this drill would be lateral passing, with players skating the width and length of the ice.

Forward Line Passing Drill. The forward line forms a circle at face-off circles and skates around the circle, passing to each other from various angles. This drill will cause right-handed players to make backhand passes when going clockwise. On the whistle, the direction is reversed. This drill gives good practice in keeping the blade at right angles to the direction from which the puck is passed.

Stationary Shooting Drill. Players spread out along one side and take shots at the opposite side boards. Players then line up at the blue line and take turns shooting at the net from a stationary position. Progression from this drill would be receiving a pass and shooting at the goal. One player (feeder) could have a supply of pucks and keep passing them to the drilling players from one corner of the rink. Before passing, the feeder should check to see if the goalie is ready.

All-Purpose Drill. Players are lined up along both side boards at one end of the rink, with the coach or a feeder at the other end. The feeder and one line have a supply of pucks. On the whistle, a player and his opposite partner break down the ice, passing the puck back and forth and, upon approaching the cage, take a shot. After the shot, both players must stop, turn toward the center of the ice, receive a pass from the feeder, and continue passing and shooting on to the opposite cage.

Stick-Handling Maze Drill. Players line up at one end of the rink in a single line. Several other players are placed in positions 10 feet apart up the center of the ice, and remain stationary. Each player in the lineup takes a turn skating through the maze, carrying the puck without looking at it. Players who are part of the maze may make attempts to stick-check the puck carrier.

Pointed Stick-Handling Drill. Players line up along the sides of the rink, well spread out, each one having a partner on the other side. The players on one side are given a puck, and on command the puck-carrier tries to stick-handle past his partner who meets him in the middle of the rink.

Shinny Drill. Players are divided into three zones, with a puck in each zone. Each player has his turn to see how long he can maintain possession of the puck within his own zone.

Angle Drill (Goalkeeper). A number of players are spread 6 or more feet apart inside the blue line, each with a puck. Each player is numbered in sequence, and shoots at the goal only when his number is called out. The goalie may perform this drill without the use of the stick.

Rebound Drill (Goalkeeper). Two single-file lines are formed about 20 feet in front of the goal, one with a supply of pucks. The player with a puck skates for the goal and shoots a low shot, while a player from the other line trails in behind and plays the rebound. The shooter and trailer alternate lines.

BIBLIOGRAPHY

Amateur Hockey Association of the United States, *Ice Hockey Rules*. Atlantic City: The Association.

Caswell, B., and Life, J., *Coach's Manual*. Midland, Canada: The Midland Press, 1950.

Jeremiah, E., *Ice Hockey*. New York: A.S. Barnes & Co., 1942.

Official NCAA Ice Hockey Guide. Phoenix, Ariz.: College Athletics Publishing Service, 349 East Thomas Road.

Patrick, L., and Monahan, L., *Let's Play Hockey*. Toronto, Canada: The Macmillan Co., 1957.

Percival, L., *The Hockey Handbook*. Toronto, Canada: The Copp Clark Co., 1951.

R.C.A.F. Sports Series, *Coach's Manual Hockey*. Ottawa, Canada: The Queen's Printer, 1955.

Vaughn, R.E., and York, N., *Hockey*. Whittlesey Series. Toronto, Canada: McGraw-Hill, 1939.

Judo had its beginning at Kodokan Judo College, which was founded in 1882 by Professor Jigoro Kano, at Tokyo, Japan. Professor Kano took desirable techniques from jujitsu, added new techniques of his own, and developed the sport of judo.

Jujitsu is known as the "empty-handed trick," although the literal translation of the word jujitsu is "gentle practice." Originally conceived as a weapon of war, its major purpose was to inflict bodily injury on the opponent. As such, it could not be considered a sport. However, Professor Kano developed judo with a strict requirement of adherence to established rules; hence, its increasing popularity as a sport in Japan. In the early 1900s Professor Kano and several other judo experts visited the United States and Europe and introduced the sport to the Western world. Judo received its greatest impetus in the United States through the servicemen who were stationed in Japan immediately after World War II. These men have formed a strong nucleus for competitive judo in the United States.

TERMINOLOGY

Armlock—Putting pressure on the elbow joint, thus causing the opponent to submit.
Break—To put the opponent off-balance.
Choking—Cutting off the blood supply to the brain, thus causing the opponent to submit.
Dojo—The room in which judo is practiced.
Falling—The technique used to absorb the shock of a fall so the judoka is not injured as a result of being thrown.
Hold—A mat position in which the judoka controls his opponent.
Ippon—A full point.
Judo—"Gentle way"—this is a *sport.*
Judogi—The uniform worn by judoka.
Judoka—One who practices judo.
Jujitsu—"Gentle practice"—"empty-handed trick." This is a means of self-defense in which the object is to injure the opponent.

Mat grappling—Holds, chokes, and arm bars.
Off-balance—A position in which the opponent moves or is moved to enable the aggressor to attempt a throw.
Randori—Informal contest.
Stance—A position taken by a judoka which enables him to maneuver both offensively and defensively.
Throw—A technique used to get an opponent off his feet.
Uchikomi—Form practice.
Wazaari—A half-point.

RULES

The beginning of a judo match is marked by the exchanged formality of each contestant's bowing to his opponent. At the end of the match the same procedure is followed. In the United States the procedure of shaking hands is sometimes substituted for bowing.

The assigned time limit of a judo match is from 3 to 10 minutes.

The judoka must wear a judogi—a loose-fitting jacket and loose trousers of three-quarter length. He is to be barefooted, and must not wear glasses.

Scoring

There are two ways in which points may be scored:
1. If a contestant throws his opponent using a recognized judo throwing technique, and performs this technique expertly, he receives a full point. If a contestant throws his opponent and performs the technique not so expertly, he receives a half point.
2. If a contestant controls his opponent's body for 30 seconds, using a recognized judo holding technique, he scores a full point. If he holds his opponent for 25 to 29 seconds, he scores a half point. A hold of less than 25 seconds does not score.

A contestant is declared to be the winner of the match immediately upon scoring one point. This may be the result of having scored two half points.

A contestant may win a judo match in the following ways:

1. By executing a full-point throw.
2. By holding the opponent for 30 seconds.
3. By scoring two half points.
4. By causing the opponent to submit by means of a choke or an armlock (the only joint that may be twisted legally is the elbow joint).
5. By scoring one-half point within the time limit if the opponent does not score.
6. By being the object of foul play by the opponent. If a contestant in a judo contest displays poor sportsmanship, he is disqualified.

SAFETY

Strange as it may seem, judo is a relatively safe sport. The entire structure of the sport is such that, if followed correctly as explained below, it is quite safe.

1. *Falling techniques:* The judoka is thoroughly schooled in falling before he is ever thrown in any situation that is not rigidly controlled.

2. *Throwing techniques:* The judoka is taught always to consider the safety of his opponent first when executing a throwing technique. In many instances the judoka actually helps his opponent with his fall by pulling up on the sleeve of his jacket.

3. *Holding techniques:* The judoka may not squeeze the sides of an opponent's face with his arms or legs, because to do so might bruise the opponent. For the same reason, the defensive man may not push upon the side of his attacker's head or face while attempting to escape.

4. *Choking techniques:* The judoka may not use the "Adam's apple" as his primary point of pressure.

5. *Armlocks:* The judoka is taught to apply pressure to armlocks slowly, in order to eliminate the chance of injury. Pressure may be applied only to the elbow joint because this joint is quite durable and cannot be easily injured.

SKILLS

There are approximately 225 different techniques in judo. The ones herein described are essential to the person wishing to become a student of the sport.

First, one must learn to grasp the opponent's jacket. The normal position of the hands is with the left hand grasping the bottom of the opponent's right sleeve below the elbow and the right hand grasping his left lapel. This is a grasp for throwing the opponent on his left side; it is the natural position for a right-handed player. All throws described in this unit are done on the natural side for the right-handed player. A very skillful player is able to execute the throws in either the left-hand or right-hand way, and may use many different methods of grasping his opponent's jacket.

In the normal stance the legs should be spread about shoulder width apart, with the feet parallel, the knees slightly flexed, and the weight slightly forward on the balls of the feet. In order to assume a defensive stance, one must bend the knees and spread the feet. This places him in a strong defensive position but a rather weak offensive position.

Falling

Once the starting position is learned, the judoka must learn to fall. There are several different kinds of falls. The type described is the most useful. It may be used to take a fall from any of the throws described in this chapter.

Technique

First Phase:

1. Lie on the back, holding the head up (chin on chest).
2. Slap the mat with the left and right arms alternately, using a whiplike motion (the hand is in a

rigid position). The hand slap is at an angle of about 30 degrees from the side of the body.

Second Phase:

1. Lie on the back, holding the head up (chin on chest).
2. Roll to the left side so that the shoulders are at a 45-degree angle with the mat.
3. Place the straight left arm at a position about 30 degrees from the left side.
4. Bend the left leg slightly so that all of the surface of the outside of the leg is in contact with the mat.
5. Bend the right leg with the knee facing upward.
6. Place the ball of the right foot in contact with the mat, slightly to the right of the calf of the left leg.
7. Bend the right arm at a right angle and rest it comfortably across the chest.

Third Phase:

1. Lie on the back, holding the head up (chin on chest).
2. Roll quickly to the left, slapping the mat as described in the first phase and assuming the position described in the second phase.
3. Repeat the above to the right side, reversing the directions described in phases one and two.

Having learned the slap and the basic position of the fall, it is important to learn falls from judo throws. These are practiced in the order of the ease with which one can learn to fall—the easiest coming first, the hardest last.

When a judoka has learned to fall from the following three throws, he is well on his way to becoming proficient in falling.

Throwing

Any throw, in order to be effective, must consist of one rapid, flowing, continuous motion. Possibly the most significant part of a judo throw is the breaking of the opponent's balance. This is done in any one of eight different directions: front, back, left side, right side, left rear corner, right rear corner, left front corner, and right front corner.

Osotogari (literal translation—"major external reaping")

Technique:

1. Grasp the opponent's jacket in the normal manner.
2. Pull down on the opponent's right shoulder with the left hand, while sliding the left foot to a point

adjacent to the right side of his right foot. While performing these movements, the aggressor should have his knees bent and his weight forward.

3. Swing the right leg through the space between the left leg and the opponent's right leg.
4. While holding the right leg in a slightly bent, locked position, thrust it back against the back of the opponent's right leg. This action lifts his right leg very high to his front, causing both of his legs to come out from under him so that he falls on his back.

Escape:

1. Shift the weight to the left foot.
2. Raise the right leg forward.

Counter:

1. Shift the weight to the left foot.
2. Pull the opponent close to the right side of the body.
3. Sweep the opponent's right leg from under him with the right leg. This technique is also osotogari.

Taiotoshi (literal translation—"pulling the body down")

Technique:

1. Grasp the opponent's jacket in the normal manner.
2. Break the opponent's balance to the left front corner with the hands.
3. Step back with the left foot, while pivoting on the right. This places the attacker's back in front of the left side of the opponent's body and very close to him.
4. Continue the pull around with the hands. This action keeps the opponent from regaining his balance.
5. Anchor the toes of the right foot at a position just right of the opponent's right foot, so that the back of the leg below the calf is against the lower part of the opponent's right shinbone.
6. Turn the head to the left and move the shoulders in an arc to the left, using the large muscles of the trunk, while pulling down and around with the hands. This action will cause the opponent's body to describe an arc to the left and land on the left side of his back.

Escape:

1. Bend the knees.
2. Push behind the opponent's right knee with the right knee.

3. Put downward pressure on the opponent's right shoulder.

Counter:

1. Put your weight downward on the opponent's right shoulder.
2. Put the left leg behind the opponent's left knee.
3. Pull the opponent backward.

Ippon-seoinage (literal translation—"throwing down over the shoulder")

Technique:

1. Grasp the opponent's jacket in the normal manner.
2. Break the opponent to the front off-balance position.
3. Place the ball of the right foot in front of the opponent's right foot and slightly to the inside. Keep pulling the opponent forward and lifting him on his toes at the same time.
4. Pivot in a counterclockwise direction on the ball of the right foot.
5. Place the left foot in a position next to the right foot, so that both of the feet are inside the opponent's feet. The body is now in a position directly in front of and against the opponent. The knees are bent so that the hips are lower than the opponent's hips.
6. Simultaneously with the pivot, release the opponent's jacket with the right hand and bring the right arm under the opponent's armpit. Curl the right hand over the top of the opponent's right arm, grasping his jacket at a point just below his right shoulder.
7. Back into the opponent, with the hips slightly lower than the opponent's, and with the right hip slightly outside the opponent's right hip.
8. Straighten the legs. Simultaneously with this movement, pull down hard with the arms. This movement will cause the opponent to come straight over the right shoulder and land on the left side of his back.

Escape and Counter:

1. Put the weight on the left foot and bend the knees.
2. Pull back on the opponent.
3. Grasp the opponent's left collar with the right hand and choke.

Mat Grappling

Mat grappling consists of three parts: holding, choking, and bending or twisting the joints of an opponent.

Holding Techniques

When holding an opponent on the mat, the judoka is not required to pin his shoulders. However, he must maintain control of his opponent, using one of a number of holds. Probably the easiest hold to learn and secure is kesagatame.

Kesagatame (literal translation—"holding in the form of a slanting scarf")

Techniques:

1. Get the opponent on his back.
2. Sit along the opponent's right side. This is the natural position when the opponent has been thrown with a right-hand throwing technique.
3. Put the right arm under the opponent's neck. The right hand reaches to the top of his right shoulder, grasping his jacket.
4. Pin the opponent's right arm between the inside of the upper left arm and the left side of the chest.
5. Grasp the opponent's jacket at a point in back of the upper part of the right arm with the left hand.
6. Put the right side of the chest across the top of the opponent's chest.
7. Spread the legs, the right thigh being against the opponent's right shoulder with the knee slightly bent, the left leg moving toward the opponent's feet so that the knee is adjacent to the opponent's right thigh.

If the opponent should succeed in unbalancing the attacker by rolling toward him, the attacker may regain his balance by placing the palm of his open left hand at a point on the mat above the outside of the opponent's right shoulder. Immediately after regaining his balance, the attacker should regrasp the opponent's right arm. If the opponent should succeed in unbalancing the attacker by rolling away from him, the attacker may regain his balance by placing the palm of his open right hand at a point on the mat above the outside of the opponent's left shoulder. Immediately after regaining his balance, the attacker should regrasp the opponent's neck and shoulder with the right arm and hand.

Escape and Counter:

1. Turn to the right, causing the right shoulder to be on the mat in the same position as in the fall to the right side.
2. Reach across the outside of the opponent's left arm behind the elbow joint with the left hand, and join

it with the right hand, which has been pinned under the left arm of the opponent.
3. Pull the opponent's left arm toward the chest by applying pressure to the back of his left elbow with both hands.
4. Control the opponent's left arm by maintaining pressure with the right hand behind his elbow and holding his left arm to the chest, so that his hand is on the right side of the neck.
5. Push the opponent's head toward the feet. This is accomplished by pushing against the neck with the left hand.
6. Put the left leg across the left side of the opponent's neck.
7. Press on the back of the opponent's left elbow with both hands.
8. Arch the back, thus applying an armlock.

Yoko-shihogatame (literal translation—"lateral locking of four quarters")

Techniques:

1. Get the opponent on his back. The attacker is on the right side of his opponent.
2. Assume the top position, at a right angle to the opponent, so that the chest is on the lower part of the opponent's chest.
3. Reach under the opponent's left shoulder and upper body and grasp his belt with the left hand.
4. Reach between the opponent's legs with the right arm and grasp his pants under the left buttock, or grasp the bottom of his jacket or belt.
5. Spread the legs, keeping the toes in contact with the mat. If the opponent attempts to turn toward the attacker, the attacker may keep him on his back by pushing forward with his toes. If the opponent attempts to turn away from the attacker, the attacker may keep him on his back by moving slightly backward.

Escape and Counter:

1. Grasp the opponent's left arm under the elbow with the right hand. Grasp his elbow with the left hand.
2. Press the opponent's left arm up.
3. Move the feet and lower body toward the right, in order to assume a position parallel to the opponent.
4. Slide the head under the opponent's left arm. This is done simultaneously with the action in #3.
5. Slide under the opponent, forcing him to his right. Maintain control of his left arm. When this is accomplished, the opponent will be on his face.
6. Apply an armlock to the opponent's left arm.

Kami-shihogatame (literal translation—"upper four-quarter hold")

Technique:

1. Get the opponent on his back.
2. Assume a kneeling position in back of the opponent's head and lie on top of him, with the side of the head on top of his waist.
3. Spread the knees wide and point the toes to the side, causing the inside edges of the feet to be in contact with the mat, thus giving the attacker a solid position. This places the waist of the attacker on the head of the opponent, reducing his opportunity for movement.
4. Move both hands under the opponent's arms very close to his body and grasp his belt at the outside edges. Keep the arms in against the body. This restricts the movement of the opponent's arms. This hold may also be done with the legs stretched straight out to the rear and spread. This technique is very difficult to escape.

Escape and Counter:

1. Slide the right hand under the opponent's neck and grasp the left side of his collar.
2. Raise the right leg. Bend the right leg and place the side of the calf on the back of the opponent's neck.
3. Grasp the right ankle with the left hand.
4. Pull down with the left hand and to the right with the right hand, thus choking the opponent.

Choking Techniques

Chokes are legal in judo. The chokes that are used cut off the blood supply to the brain. They are not the punishing type which put pressure on the "Adam's apple." The choke is not usually dangerous because an opponent will submit when choked, rather than become unconscious.

The first choke to be explained is useful when attacking from the rear.

Hadaka-jime (literal translation—"bare choking")

Technique:

1. Assume a position behind the opponent.
2. Place the part of the right forearm immediately above the wrist on the "Adam's apple" of the opponent. The palm of the right hand is facing the top of the opponent's left shoulder.

3. Place the back of the left hand on top of the opponent's left shoulder. The wrist of the attacker's left arm is bent back, enabling him to push the back of his left forearm against the upper left side of the opponent's back. This keeps the opponent from turning to his left to escape.
4. Clasp the hands together, with the palms touching one another.
5. Lean the head forward, so that the face is slightly above the clasped hands and the right side of the head is against the left side of the opponent's head. This helps to keep the opponent's head in position.
6. Press the right shoulder against the back of the opponent's neck.
7. Hold the hands tightly in place and pull the right elbow back. This is an extremely powerful choke and, once gotten, is extremely difficult to break.

Escape:

1. Grasp the opponent's right arm behind the elbow with the right hand, and at the front of the forearm with the left hand.
2. Pull down and out.
3. Turn the head slightly to the right.
4. Push the opponent's arm up, thus freeing the head.

When applying any choke from the back while on the mat, it is helpful to hold the opponent in position by wrapping the legs around his waist and putting the feet inside his thighs.

Gyaku-jiji-jime (literal translation—"natural cross choke")

Technique:

1. Get the opponent on his back.
2. Assume the top position and straddle the opponent, while in a kneeling position.
3. Grasp the right side of the opponent's collar deeply with the right hand. The palm of the hand should face upward, with the fingers inside the opponent's jacket and the thumb outside.
4. Reach across and grasp the left side of the opponent's collar with the left hand, in the same position as described in #3.
5. Choke the opponent by holding his collar very tightly with the hands, pulling up, and spreading the elbows.

Escape:

1. Grasp under the elbow of the top arm with the hand.

2. Push the elbow up.
3. Move the head in the opposite direction, away from the elbow being pushed.

Okuri-eri-jime (literal translation—"sliding collar choke")

Technique:

1. Approach the opponent from the rear. To practice this choke, the opponent should be in a sitting position.
2. Slide the right hand along the front of the opponent's neck from right to left.
3. Grasp the left side of the opponent's collar deeply with the right hand. The palm should be facing downward, with the thumb inside the opponent's collar. The inside of the right wrist is against the left side of the opponent's neck.
4. Reach under the opponent's left arm and across his chest, grasping his right lapel.
5. Pull the right elbow back and around.
6. Pull the right lapel down.

Escape:

1. Grasp the opponent's right arm behind the elbow with the right hand, and at the front of the forearm with the left hand.
2. Pull down and out.
3. Turn the head slightly to the right.
4. Push the opponent's right arm up, thus freeing the head.

Armlock Techniques

An armlock is a submission hold. Armlock techniques are most often used while the defensive player is lying faceup on the mat. They are employed only occasionally while the contestants are standing. While playing judo, a contestant may use only armlocks that exert pressure on the elbow joint. Other types of arm bars might prove dangerous. The judoka is taught to apply pressure slowly when he has an armlock on his opponent.

Udegatame (literal translation—"armlocking")

This armlock is used when the opponent, while lying on his back, reaches for the attacker. Assume that the attacker has thrown his opponent with a right-hand technique, causing him to land on his back. The attacker is on the right side of his opponent.

Technique:

1. Kneel at the right side of the opponent, facing him.
2. Lean forward as if to grasp the opponent in kesagatame. As this is done, the opponent reaches up in order to push the attacker away, or in order to grasp his jacket.
3. Place the underside of the wrist of the opponent's outstretched left arm on the right shoulder beside the neck.
4. Place the palms of the hands (one on top of the other) on the back of the opponent's left elbow.
5. Press the hands toward the body, leaning slightly forward with the right shoulder. This puts pressure against the back of the opponent's elbow joint and at the same time against the underside of his wrist.

Jujigatame (literal translation—"cross-locking")

This armlock is made when the opponent has been thrown with a right-hand throw such as ippon-seoinage. At the completion of the throw, the attacker is on the opponent's right side. He maintains his grasp on the outside of the opponent's right sleeve. The attacker is in a standing position; the opponent is lying on his back.

Technique:

1. Grasp the opponent's wrist firmly. The fingers of both hands are in contact with the underside of the opponent's wrist. The thumbs are against the outside of the opponent's wrist.
2. Pull the opponent's right arm up.
3. Put the right foot under the right side of the opponent's back. This will keep him from rolling toward his right side in an attempt to escape.
4. Put the left foot on the left side of the opponent's neck. Keep the left foot firmly in place during the execution of the entire technique, as this keeps the opponent from raising his head and upper body in an attempt to escape.
5. Sit very close to the right heel. Continue to pull the opponent's straight right arm toward the chest.
6. Squeeze the thighs together, with the opponent's arm between them.
7. Bend the opponent's arm against his elbow joint, by pushing the underside of his wrist toward the right. This causes the back of the opponent's elbow joint to be pushed against the inside of the right thigh of the attacker.

Escapes for armlock techniques. Armlock techniques must be escaped before the pressure is applied to the elbow joint. To accomplish this:

1. Twist the wrist.
2. Bend the arm.
3. Pull the arm away from the opponent's grasp.

SKILL PRACTICE

A typical practice for a judoka should be as follows:
1. *Exercises:* The judoka should go through a regular routine of warm-up exercises, partly because he gains a certain amount of physical conditioning through formal exercise. More important, however, is the fact that he will be flexible when he starts the vigorous practice of throwing and falling.

2. *Form practice:* Judo is a sport in which the participants constantly strive for perfection. Therefore, the judoka must repeat each technique many times before it is mastered. The judoka should first practice the technique in parts, then perform the whole technique in one continuous movement. An example of this is the practicing of a throwing technique. First, the off-balancing of an opponent is practiced; next, fitting into position for the throw; and finally, the entire throw.

3. *Free play:* Having practiced the form of various techniques, the judoka should engage in an informal contest with an opponent so he can apply the techniques that he is striving to perfect. This is usually done under "semicontest" conditions.

BIBLIOGRAPHY

Gustuson, Donald I., and Masaki, Linda, *Self-Defense for Women.* Boston: Allyn and Bacon, Inc., 1970.

Harrison, E. J., *The Manual of Judo.* London: W. Foulsham & Co., Ltd., 1952.

Kobayashi, Kiyoshi, and Sharp, Harold E., *The Sport of Judo.* Rutland, Vt., and Tokyo: Charles E. Tuttle Co., 1955.

The Kodokan, *What Is Judo?* Tokyo: The Kodokan, 1952.

Official AAU-JBBF Judo Handbook. New York: Amateur Athletic Union of the United States, 1964.

Takagaki, Shinzo, and Sharp, Harold E., *The Techniques of Judo.* Rutland, Vt., and Tokyo: Charles E. Tuttle Co., 1957.

Yerkow, Charles, *Modern Judo: Vol. I.* Harrisburg: The Military Service Publishing Co., 1951.

LACROSSE | 18

The earliest explorers and adventurers in North America saw and marveled at this Indian game called bagahatuwitimi or bagataway, according to tribe and location. It was a stick and ball game that seems to have been enjoyed by many tribes. Many of the Indians referred to it as "little war," and it was played with vigor, speed, and roughness that undoubtedly provided its players with rigorous training for war.

When the French Canadian explorers and settlers saw the game played, they noted that the stick that was used resembled a bishop's crozier, so they named the stick "la crosse," which is the French equivalent term; eventually the game became known as lacrosse.

Lacrosse was at one time used as a "Trojan horse" by the Indians. When Chief Pontiac of the Ottawa tribe organized the "Conspiracy of Pontiac" for the purpose of capturing the British forts in the West, the plan he worked out was to have the Indians near each fort announce a game of lacrosse to be played on June 4, 1763, the birthday of King George III. The great day came, and the soldiers left the confines of the forts to see the games. The play was fast and furious, and gradually the players came nearer the fort. At a signal, the women who were standing nearby pulled muskets and other weapons from beneath their blankets and handed them to the players, who attacked and massacred the unsuspecting and unarmed soldiers. Eight forts were captured in this fashion, one of them being Fort Michilimackinac on what is now called Mackinac Island.

White men first played the game in Canada. In September, 1834, a game was played at the St. Pierre race track in Montreal. By 1840 lacrosse was played on an organized basis in Canada, and by 1867 it became the national game and soon spread to the United States.

Intercollegiate lacrosse had its beginning at Harvard in 1881, whence it spread to Johns Hopkins, Yale, Stevens, Princeton, Swarthmore, and other universities and colleges. It is now played in more than 135 colleges and 190 high schools. In 1926 the United States Intercollegiate Lacrosse Association was formed; it is now the governing body of the sport in this country, and is an affiliate of the National Collegiate Athletic Association.

Lacrosse for women came to the United States from England, and not from the United States men's game. The All-England Ladies Lacrosse Association sent players and coaches to introduce the modified rules of the game to the women of the United States.

With the game being played in various sections of the northeast, the United States Women's Lacrosse Association was formed in 1931. With the exchange of the British and American touring teams, and the annual national tournaments, clinics, and clubs held in various sections of the country, the popularity of the sport is growing significantly.

TERMINOLOGY

Attack—Those players who are charged with the offensive plays (three attack players and three midfielders).

Backing up—Team play for strengthening a defense and for promoting support to the teammate encountering the ball carrier.

Backing up the shot—Playing in position so that if your teammate does not get control of the initial pass, you will get it.

Ball—A call by a teammate meaning he will get the ball, and for you to body-check the man from whom he is taking it.

Body checking—The use of any legal body block upon an opponent who may be (1) in possession of the ball, (2) a potential receiver, or (3) within 15 feet of the ball.

Break—A call by the goalie to signify he has made a stop and wants defense to break out for a clearing play.

Brush-off—An offensive maneuver to get into the open by running your opponent into one of your teammates (sometimes called a "pick").

Check—A call by the goalie to signify you are to check your opponent's stick in the area near the crease.

Checking—Hitting an opponent's stick to dislodge the ball or to prevent his passing or receiving the ball.

141

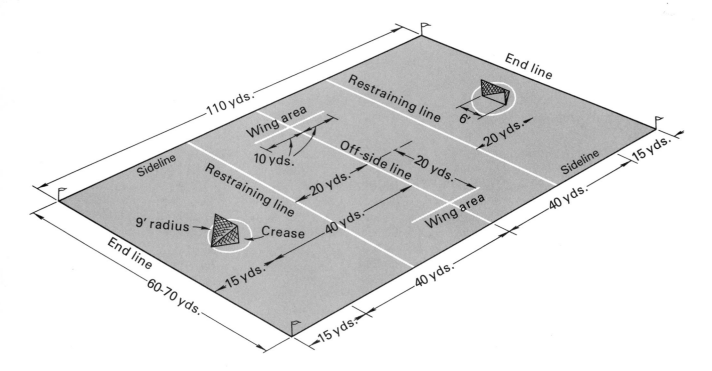

Fig. 18—1. Regulation lacrosse field.

Clearing—The launching of an attack by the defense immediately after they intercept or stop the ball in their defensive territory.

Crease man—The attack player that plays in front of the goal crease.

Cross-checking—The illegal use of that part of the stick between the butt and the throat in stopping an opponent with or without the ball.

Cutting—The action whereby, in a burst of speed or change of direction, one eludes an opponent in order to receive a pass from a teammate.

Extra man—A situation in which a team has an extra man on the attack on account of a dodge or because the other team has a man out of the game on a penalty.

Face-off—The ball put into play at the middle of the field at the start of the game, at the start of each quarter, and after each score; or when the official is not sure which team caused the ball to go out-of-bounds (sometimes called a "draw").

Field (See Fig. 18-1 for the men's game)—No strict rules govern the playing field dimensions for women, although the goals must be 90-110 yards apart and the minimum width should be 50 yards. The goal crease is 8-1/2 feet in radius.

Forcing—Making an attacking player with the ball retreat, so that he cannot make his pass.

Holding down—The holding of an opponent's crosse by one's own crosse, in the air or on the ground. This is unlike legal cross-checking, and is a foul.

Man—A call used on ground balls to signify to a teammate that you will body-check the opponent and he is to get the ball.

Midfielders—The three players who play both attack and defense.

Penalty box—The area where players put out of the game for rule infractions must stay until their penalty time expires.

Pick-up—A call by the goalie to signify you are to play the man.

Poke check—Keeping an opponent at crosse's length by poking at the butt of his crosse.

Riding—An action whereby a team, after attempting a shot or losing the ball, tries to prevent the defense from clearing the ball to their attacking unit.

Right back; left back—A call by the goalie to tell the position of the ball when it is behind the goal.

Right, left, etc.—A call by the goalie to signify the position of the ball (as seen by the goalie).

Scooping the ball—The skill necessary to get the ball off the ground into one's crosse.

Screen—When the crease man places himself between the goalie and the man with the ball, or when an attack player places himself in a position whereby a shot at the goal cannot be seen by the goalie.

Shift—A call by the goalie to signify a man has been dodged, and that the entire defense should slide toward the ball.

Slashing—Illegal use of the crosse upon an opponent's hand or arm.

Throw-in—Throwing the ball in play between two opposing female players when the players were equidistant from the ball as it went out-of-bounds.

RULES

1. A lacrosse team consists of ten players for men, and twelve players for women. *Men*—No player is set in his position, and may exchange with another as long as at least four players are on the defensive half of their field and at least three players on their offensive side of the field. *Women*—The players' positions are: attacking unit—center, right and left attack wing, third home, second home, and first home; defensive unit—right and left defense wings, third man, cover point, point, and goalkeeper. The distribution of players into areas of attack and defense is not compulsory.

2. Play begins with a face-off: the middle midfielders of the two teams place their sticks on the ground back to back and perpendicular to the sideline, with the ball lying between the nets of the crosse. When the whistle sounds, each attempts to move the ball in any legal manner he desires.

3. A ball going out-of-bounds is given to the team that did not cause it to go out, and the ball is put in play by running it onto the playing field or passing it. Opponents must stand 10 yards from the player putting the ball into play.

4. A ball going out-of-bounds *on a shot* is given to the nearest player (of either team) at the point where it left the playing field.

5. A ball going out-of-bounds on any occasion in the women's game is given to the nearest player of either team.

6. A player playing an opponent with the ball in his stick must use tactics of "body on body" or "wood on wood" in an effort to get the ball.

7. It is a foul to trip, hold, or body-check an opponent from the rear, or to strike his body with your crosse.

8. A ball that is on the ground or in the air is a "free ball" and an opponent's body or stick may be checked legally in an attempt to get the ball, providing the opponent is within 15 feet of the ball. No body contact is permitted in the women's game.

9. Penalty for a technical foul is either suspension of a player from the game for 30 seconds if your team does not have the ball, or loss of the ball to your opponents if your team had possession at the time of the foul. Technical fouls include: (1) a player within 10 yards of the ball when the opponents have the ball out-of-bounds; (2) off-sides—not enough players on the defensive or offensive ends of the field; (3) a player in the opponent's crease; (4) holding, pushing, or touching the ball with the hand; (5) lying on the ball; (6) thrusting the stick in an opponent's face.

10. The penalty for a personal foul is expulsion from the game from 1 to 3 minutes, and the ball is then given to the team fouled. Personal fouls include: (1) illegal body check; (2) tripping; (3) cross-checking; (4) striking the body with a stick; (5) striking an opponent on the head with a stick.

11. An expulsion foul is deliberate, intentional striking with the crosse or hand, or any malicious attempt to injure an opponent, coach, or official. The penalty is expulsion for the remainder of the game.

12. In the women's game, the wood wall of the crosse must be on the right side of the bridge; thus, left-handed crosses are illegal.

13. When an official blows the whistle for a violation, all female players must hold their positions until play resumes.

EQUIPMENT

Stick. Lacrosse sticks are made of hickory that has been seasoned for at least a year, and although aluminum and fiber glass sticks are being manufactured, hickory is still the best in the opinion of most experts. The world's largest lacrosse stick factory is located on Cornwall Island near Massena, New York, where Mohawk Indians produce 4,000 dozen lacrosse sticks annually. Fig. 18-2 shows the 15 main parts of a lacrosse stick or crosse.

The rules are very definite about the construction of the crosse; the main points are: (1) the crosse cannot be less than 7 inches or more than 12 inches wide; (2) the length of the crosse must be between 40 and 72 inches (except the goalkeeper's crosse, which may be of any length); (3) the pocket must be so constructed that a ball in the pocket will not show daylight at the wood wall when the crosse is held out straight. There are four sizes of crosses used: goalie, 12 inches; defense, 10 inches; midfield, 8 inches; and attack, 7 inches—with the measurements being the inside measurement across the head.

Helmet. A football-type helmet fitted with a face-mask is used, and must be worn at all times while playing.

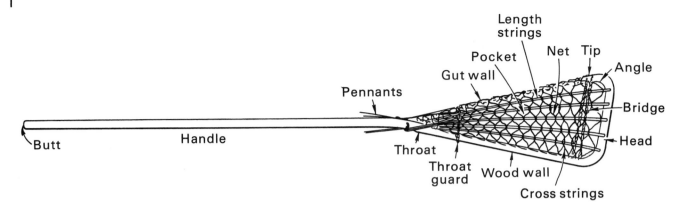

Fig. 18—2. Lacrosse stick.

Gloves. Ice hockey-type gloves are used to protect the hands and wrists.

Shoulder pads. A combination shoulder pad and arm pad is used to protect the shoulder girdle and arms.

Uniform. Each player should have a long-sleeved jersey that will hold the shoulder pads in place, a pair of shorts, and gym or football-type shoes.

Goalie's uniform. It is important that the goalie have a catcher's-type chest protector and that he wear a metal or plastic supporter. Although not necessary, the goalie may wear shin-guards.

INDIVIDUAL SKILLS

Holding the Crosse

The crosse should be held parallel to the ground, with the right hand near the throat of the crosse, palm up, and the left hand at the butt of the crosse, palm down. The thumb of the right hand should not be completely wrapped around the handle of the crosse, nor should either hand have a strong grip on the crosse.

Cradling

It is necessary to keep the ball in the pocket of the crosse. To accomplish this, the player executes a rocking motion using both the wrists and upper arms. The left hand remains close to the body in a fairly rigid position, while permitting the butt of the crosse to revolve in its loose grip. The right hand is held near the throat of the crosse and does all the cradling action with rotation of the wrist and forearm.

Overhand Throw

Throwing a lacrosse ball from the crosse involves almost the same body and arm movements as those used in throwing a baseball. The throw is made mostly with the right hand, while the left hand guides the crosse and adds a little power and speed. The complete throwing process involves these actions: Stand sideways, with the left foot forward and the feet pointing in the direction of the flight of the ball; hold the crosse up so that the right hand is about shoulder level, pull with the left arm, push with the right arm, and step with the left foot; have an exaggerated follow-through, so that the left hand finishes in contact with the right armpit.

The exaggerated follow-through of the left hand is not needed once a player gets the feel of throwing, but by keeping it in mind the novice will be able to progress rapidly.

Catching (right-handed)

A player must be prepared to catch the ball regardless of where it has been thrown, provided it is within reach of his crosse. At all times, a player should be in motion when catching; "Go to meet the ball" is a good axiom to follow. In catching a ball thrown above the shoulders, the crosse is extended forward, with the full face of the crosse in the path of the ball. As the ball hits the net, the player should give slightly with his right arm and hand, followed by a sharp inward rotation of his right wrist.

In catching a ball thrown between the shoulders and above the knees, the face of the crosse is extended directly in the path of the ball, but this time the rotation of the handle is upward as the ball hits the net.

If the ball is below the knees, the rotation of the handle is outward and upward.

A ball that is coming directly at the head is caught by putting the face of the crosse in the path of the ball; the head and shoulders drop to the left, and the crosse is rotated inward as the ball hits the net.

Finally, if the ball is on the left side of a right-handed player, he should bring the right hand across the body, putting the face of the crosse in the path of the ball. At the same time, he crosses the right leg over the left leg and his body makes a complete turn.

Scooping

As the player approaches the ball on the ground, he bends his knees and his body at the waist; he is holding the crosse with both hands, the hand near the throat in a loose grip and the other hand at the butt. The crosse is held to one side of the body, nearly parallel to the ground, and should slide along the ground within 12 inches of the ball; with a slight shovel motion, the player can easily scoop the ball off the ground. As soon as the ball enters the crosse, the player breaks (starts) to the right or left, getting away fast, and cradles the ball a few times. It is very important to remember to keep two hands on the crosse when scooping, and always to have the butt end of the crosse away from the mid-line of the body.

Dodging

The "extra man" is the fundamental scoring situation in lacrosse; the situation occurs when the offense has more men in the immediate scoring area than the defense; it is brought about by having an offensive player get by his guarding opponent. The offensive man dodges his opponent, then makes a fast break down the field as an odd man, so that there are four offensive men at the attack end of the field and only three defensive men. There are basically four types of dodges used to create the "extra man" situation: (1) face dodge, (2) change-of-pace dodge, (3) toss dodge, (4) force dodge.

Face Dodge. The crosse is brought forward as though to pass, and when the crosse is about even with the head, it is twisted through an angle of 180 degrees and brought sharply to the left side. When properly executed, the face dodge causes the defensive man to think the ball has been thrown. The offensive man then runs around his opponent by dropping his shoulders and head slightly to the left and bringing his right leg forward across the left leg.

Change-of-Pace Dodge. This dodge is done by running fast in one direction, suddenly stopping and reversing direction, and continuing the action until the opportunity arises to go by the defensive man.

Toss Dodge. This dodge is used when there is plenty of open field ahead of the offensive player. As the offensive player meets his defensive man, the ball is tossed into the air or on the ground. He runs past the defender and recovers the ball.

Force Dodge. The player with the ball approaches his defensive man with his back toward him and moves backward into the defender, causing him to retreat. As the offensive player fakes to the right and left, at the same time protecting his crosse from the defender, he waits for the defender to get caught off-balance, then breaks around the weak side.

SAFETY

1. Proper equipment should be worn at all times.
2. The crosse should not be cracked or otherwise in poor condition.
3. The crosse should be held at the side of the body in scooping up the ball, to avoid the butt of the crosse injuring the groin area.
4. Proper warm-up should be taken before any scrimmage or body contact.
5. Players who wear glasses should employ the proper kind of face masks.
6. Practice pivoting to avoid ankle and knee injuries.
7. Talk to your teammate. Be his extra pair of eyes. If he is being pursued from behind, tell him so.

PLAY OF THE GOALIE

The goalie is definitely the backbone of a team's defense and, as such, he must exercise positive leadership in directing and controlling his teammates. The goalie has three duties: (1) to stop the ball; (2) to direct the defense at all times (this calls for constant chatter on his part); and (3) to be the backbone of all clears.

The goalie's body position is with the feet set shoulder width apart, the knees bent, the body bent forward slightly at the waist, and his weight slightly forward on the balls of the feet, with the heels barely touching the ground. The eyes should be on the ball and crosse at all times, as the position of a player's crosse when the ball is shot will often tell the goalie where the ball is going.

The goalie operates on an imaginary arc about 3 feet in front of the goal; he moves on this arc with short glide steps, keeping himself always directly between the ball and the center of the goal. When the ball is behind the goal, the goalie remains on the same front arc but he favors the ball side. As the ball is passed from behind the goal to a cutter out in front, the goalie must turn so that he moves again into line between the ball and the center of the goal. He never turns his back on the ball.

The position of the goalie's crosse involves three points as the offensive man approaches: (1) 15-20 yards—the crosse is waist-high and on the right side; (2) 10-15 yards—the crosse is gradually raised as the shooter approaches; (3) 10 yards to crease—the crosse moves to the right side of the head to protect against high shots.

On a shot, the goalie steps into the ball with the foot nearest the ball and places his body directly behind the ball, with the entire head of the crosse facing the flight of the ball. The crosse is brought into position with a sweeping motion as the body moves to the ball. A good axiom to follow is to move your crosse and body as a unit.

ATTACK PLAY

There are four basic offenses used in lacrosse: 2-1-3; 3-1-2; 2-2-2; and 2-4.

In the 2-1-3 offense the players are around the goal, as illustrated in Fig. 18-3.

Each player in the 2-1-3 formation should know the function of each position and the options each position has with and without the ball. For example, if the ball is at #1, he may: (a) feed the crease man or cutters (the player "cuts" when he runs toward the

goal); (b) move toward position #2 and roll back to dodge or feed; (c) run through position #2; (d) pass to #2 and cut off (make use of) the brush-off put up by #6; or (e) pass to #2 and move inside to the screen. Thus, #2 could move inside to the screen, go outside for a flip pass, or swing inside to a clear position. Under no condition should #2 stand still as #1 approaches.

While the ball is in position #1, position #3, for example, would have the following options: (a) back up a feed to the crease; (b) cut off a brush-off by #4 or #5. If each offensive player knows the positions and thinks, then a fluid offense can be obtained without using set plays.

The 3-1-2 offense is illustrated in Fig. 18-4.

This is a variation of the 2-1-3 and 2-2-2, and can be very effective. Numbers 3, 4, and 5 are usually midfielders, and numbers 1, 2, and 6 attackmen. However, it is possible to use the crease man #6 at position #3, and the midfielder #3 at position #6. In this formation, position #3 plays always on the side away from the ball and always moves to back up passes.

The 2-2-2 offense is illustrated in Fig. 18-5, and is common to many teams.

This offense is used primarily if the team has a good feeder who can feed the crease man and if the midfielders have hard outside shots. However, the formation does not lend itself to cutting for the ball, because passes to cutters are difficult to back up.

The 2-4 offense is illustrated in Fig. 18-6.

The 2-4 offense features cutting, forces switches by opponents, and has excellent backing up power.

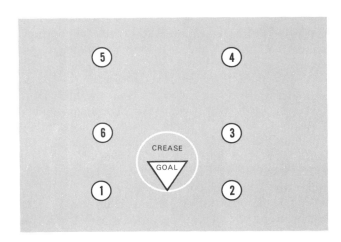

Fig. 18—3. The 2—1—3 offense.

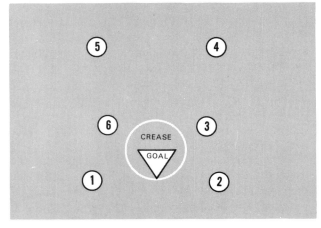

Fig. 18—4. The 3—1—2 offense.

Fundamentals

A good team, regardless of the formation being used, should adhere to the following basic principles of attack play:

1. Back up all shots and feeds.
2. Don't waste energy cutting when men behind the goal are not in position to feed the ball.
3. Keep a balanced field, as it is almost impossible to back up shots or passes unless you do so.
4. Move the ball around the attack in a correct manner, namely short, sharp passes to the outside.
5. Cut into the goal area and then out; keep the front of the goal uncongested.

Guides for Attack Player

1. Make your defense man play *you*, and you alone. Keep moving all the time so he must center his attention on you.
2. When you have the ball, do not stand still—keep moving all the time. If necessary, run backward and forward—but keep moving. When you are ready to make a pass, take one or two steps back quickly and throw.
3. All feed passes should be thrown directly overhand or directly underhand, and should be hard and accurate.
4. Move to meet every pass and circle away from the defense man.
5. When you have the ball, constantly fake passes—keep your defense man's stick moving.
6. When in possession of the ball, make the defense man play your stick. Watch his stick; the position

of it will determine the direction of your feed and the type of dodge you might try.

7. Do not make a pass to a man who is covered just to get rid of the ball.
8. If an attack man is being ridden hard and can't dodge or get away, the nearest man on each side goes to help him.
9. Whenever a player attempts a long shot, a teammate should be on the crease to recover the ball in case the shot does not score.
10. After receiving a pass, as the ball moves around the outside, look first at the man who threw you the ball to see what he is doing, then at the crease.
11. If you receive a pass after cutting and do not have a good shot, hold on to the ball.
12. Place all shots, usually for the far corner, and shoot hard. When within 5 yards of the goal, the shot should be for a top corner.
13. After picking up a loose ball, turn and face the crease immediately. If nobody is open, move in fast until you are picked up.
14. Do not try to dodge when men are in position to back up.
15. Never try to force in, with the ball or by a pass, if the defense is drawn in. Pull them out first.
16. Don't stand so close together that one defensive man can cover two attack men.
17. When there is a loose ball on the ground, go after it fast, bend low, and scoop.
18. Keep one, preferably two, men behind the goal to back up.
19. Do not try a pass to a man on the crease from any position other than one definitely behind the goal.

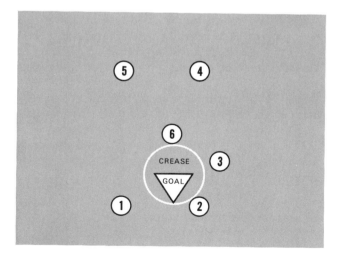

Fig. 18—5. The 2—2—2 offense.

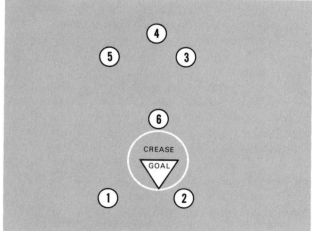

Fig. 18—6. The 2—4 offense.

20. Time your cuts; that is, don't cut if the man with the ball is not watching or is not in position to pass.
21. After a ball has been cleared, if you have a wide-open opportunity to dodge, do it; or if you are sure a man is open, pass to him. Otherwise, settle the ball down and don't rush; let your attack get set up. Remember that after the clear your midfield needs time to catch its breath.
22. When you lose the ball, RIDE. A close attack must ride, and ride hard until the ball is past midfield.
23. Don't rush at a man when riding; particularly behind the goal, force him to pass.
24. Remember that *teamwork* is the key to a good attack.

DEFENSIVE PLAY

The defense in lacrosse is made up of the three players called defense, the goalie, and the three midfielders. The purposes of the defense are: (1) to clear the ball to the attack; (2) to prevent shooting or scoring; (3) to block and intercept passes; (4) to gain possession of the ball.

As with any team game, there are only three defensive formations possible: (1) man-to-man; (2) zone; (3) combination of both. The man-to-man defense is not too effective, although it is sometimes used; most good teams prefer to use the zone, even though it is harder to learn and execute.

Fundamentals

When playing the man with the ball, the defense man must give him his undivided attention. He should keep forcing him by checking his stick at every opportunity. Try not to give the attack man a chance to get set, but be careful not to rush at him. Forcing means a cautious, deliberate method of driving the attack man back.

As the attack man prepares to pass, the defense man should attempt to block the ball by placing the face of his stick in line with the face of the attack man's stick. If the ball is passed, he should drop back immediately before looking to see where the ball has gone. This prevents the attack man from passing the ball and then immediately cutting for a return pass.

When the attack man runs with the ball, his defense man should follow him with sidesteps whenever possible. This enables the defense man to change his direction quickly and easily. A defense man should be careful not to rush at his opponent because a clever attack man can easily dodge when the defense man rushes.

Clearing

One of the most vital parts of defense play is clearing. It begins when a goalkeeper has made a stop or a defense man has intercepted a pass or a loose ball. Generally, after the goalie has stopped the ball, he finds it necessary to carry the ball behind the goal first. Two defense men immediately break with him, one to either side and about 10 yards away from him. A third defense man remains a few yards off the crease until the goalie has made his first pass, and then he breaks to that side to receive the second pass. Meanwhile, the three midfielders have broken up the field, one up the middle and the other two to either side. Passes should not be made to players directly in front of the goal.

Whenever it is possible, the goalie should carry the ball directly up the field. In this case, two midfielders break ahead of the goalkeeper, one on either side, in order to give him someone to pass to. This is, of course, the easiest clear, but it is not often possible.

Sometimes it is necessary to reverse the field. After the goalie has made his first pass, the receiver, seeing no one up the field to pass to, passes the ball back across the field to the other teammate closest to the goalkeeper.

Playing the Man on the Crease

When the ball is behind the goal, the defense man should play beside his opponent and face the ball carrier if the opponent plays close to the crease line. Keep your body in such a position as to enable you to best check your opponent's stick as he attempts to catch a pass. As the ball is carried (or passed) to the opposite side of the goal, be ready to quickly place yourself in the best possible position to prevent the attack man from making a quick break away from you.

If the attack man plays away from the crease, play between the man and the goal, but closer to the goal than the man.

When the ball is in front of the goal and the crease man is playing close to the crease, play beside him and generally on the side of the ball.

Guides for Defensive Player:

1. Never rush an attack man after he has caught the ball. If he is receiving a rather long pass and you are sure you can reach him before the ball, go

after him, checking his stick and hitting him with your shoulder.

2. As a pass is made to the man you are playing, move out to cover him as the ball is moving to him, so that you are in position as he catches it.

3. Once the attack man has the ball, worry him by flicking (making short, jabbing motions with your stick). Don't give him a chance to look over his field. Make him worry about you (there is a big difference between worrying a man and forcing or rushing him).

4. Never take a step into a man while playing him on defense; if you do this, you have made the first move.

5. When not flicking at a man who has the ball, keep your stick a little above the height of your attack man's shoulder.

6. Never carry the crosse at your side—keep it up.

7. When your man hasn't got the ball, play slightly to the ball side of him, so that you gain a step as he cuts toward the ball. If he cuts away from the ball, the pass must go over your head, which leaves you in good position to intercept or check.

8. There must be plenty of talk on defense. This is important. The following are the most important examples:

   a) The man on each side of the ball must let the defense man on the ball know he is backed up by saying, "I've got you backed right or left" as the case may be.

   b) If a man leaves to back up, he must let the defense know he is leaving, so they may shift to leave the man farthest distant semiopen.

   c) The man playing the ball must yell, "I've got the ball; who has me backed?" If no one answers, then call again, and continue to call until you get an answer.

   d) If a man cuts, the defense man playing him should yell, "man cutting," so he alerts the rest of the defense for a possible shift. The entire defense watches for the cutter.

   e) If a shift is necessary, the back man calls "shift," although both men should call it whenever possible. In general, the man who sees the pick coming should call "shift."

   f) The goalie must talk constantly. He is the key to the defense. Listen to him and react as he directs, regardless of your own opinions.

9. On loose balls scoop them quickly. If there is a crowd, go through and either kick it out or scoop it.

10. When you check, make your check short and hard across the opponent's stick and follow through

with your shoulder. Don't raise your stick high to check because this gives away the direction from which the check will come.

11. Don't pass a ball across the face of the goal.

12. After the man you are playing passes, step back two steps quickly and be ready for a cut.

13. If the ball is out front, and your man is behind the goal, play on the front edge of the crease on the side of the goal your man is on.

14. When the ball is behind the goal, if your man is also behind it (but isn't carrying the ball), go behind with him; this is only a general rule, and will change depending on the game situation.

15. If you ever switch, stay with that man until your team gets the ball or you have a very good chance to switch back.

16. On clears, make all passes sharp, away from the rider and, as a general rule, to the nearest open man.

17. On clears, if you can, run the ball out and go in on the offense until you are picked up.

18. The best defense is a good offense, and it is your duty to see that the attack gets the ball quickly in order to control it. The attack must have the ball if your team is to score.

DRILLS

1. *Throwing:* Throw a ball against the wall. Each man may have a ball, or one may throw and the other catch.

2. *Receiving:* With players in a circle about 10 yards apart, a ball is thrown around the circle, with players breaking into the circle, then out to receive the pass.

3. *Scooping:* Two lines take positions 20 yards apart facing each other, with the ball in the middle. One man scoops up the ball, carries it a few steps, and drops it; the other line continues in the same way.

4. *Man or Ball:* Three lines take positions about 3 yards apart, with lines #1 and #3 being the defense and #2 the offense. The instructor stands 15 yards from the lines and drops the ball. As he does so, the first man in each line tries to get the ball, with lines #1 and #3 cooperating by calling "MAN" or "BALL" and blocking off the man from line #2.

5. *Passing:* Two lines about 20 yards apart face each other, with a ball being passed to each man as he cuts out.

6. *Passing:* This employs the same formation as #5, but the man with the ball goes past the other line on his left, stops, and makes a lead pass as the other man breaks.

7. *Shooting:* One line faces the goal; the feeder behind passes the ball to another man as he cuts toward the goal. The lines can be moved to come in at various angles.
8. *Dodging:* The man with the ball plays keep-away with his opponent.
9. *Defense:* Three players form a circle with a 20-yard radius. Two players are offensive and try to maintain possession of the ball, while the third player is defensive and tries to get the ball. All players must remain in the circle.

STRATEGY

Attack

The various methods of getting a man free for a shot in lacrosse have been explained in dodging and passing, and one can see that the "give and go" situation is prevalent.

Play in lacrosse differs from many team games in that play is allowed from behind the goal, so the attack should take advantage of this fact because: (1) they can pass over the goal area to a free man who is facing the goal; (2) if control of the ball is lost behind the goal, the opponents must clear the ball the extra length of the field in order to get on the attack; (3) it is difficult for the defense to watch their man and the ball while the ball is behind the goal.

The "fast break" in lacrosse is seen when a mid-fielder gets ahead of his man and comes down the field as an odd man, thus creating a 4-against-3 setup for the defense. In this case, a quick scoring effort is made to take advantage of the extra man.

When no "fast break" has developed, the attack develops more slowly and forms in a circle around the goal so the defense men are forced to spread as far apart as possible. The attack then attempts to shake a man loose for a shot by: (1) dodging; (2) cutting; (3) screening.

Defense

If both teams do not have any players in the penalty box, then a man-to-man defense can be employed. One man plays the man with the ball and attempts to dislodge the ball from his crosse or block his pass, at the same time being cautious not to allow him to dodge by. Other defense men place themselves in a position to watch both the ball and their own assigned men, remembering that their first responsibility is *their man.* If the man with the ball dodges by, another defense man should be prepared to switch and cover him. When the defensive team is short a man, because one player is in the penalty box, they usually will play a zone defense in order to prevent a score.

BIBLIOGRAPHY

Moore, Alan C., and Waglow, I.F., "Fundamental Lacrosse Skills," *Scholastic Coach,* Vol. 24, No. 8 (April, 1955).

Morrill, W. Kelso, *Lacrosse.* New York: A.S. Barnes & Co., 1952.

The Official Field Hockey-Lacrosse Guide—DGWS. Washington, D.C.: American Association for Health, Physical Education and Recreation.

Official NCAA Lacrosse Guide. Phoenix, Ariz.: College Athletics Publishing Service, 349 East Thomas Road.

Stanwick, Tad, *Lacrosse.* New York: A. S. Barnes & Co., 1940.

Modern dance is a product of the twentieth century. In the beginning it was characterized by free and flowing movements based upon the natural movements used in everyday activities. Contemporary, interpretative, expressive, and creative dance were terms synonymous with modern dance in the early stages of this art.

This artistic form of dance was the result of a rebellion against the classical ballet and the traditional forms of movement necessary to ballet performance. The desire of a dancer to express human emotions and experiences in a freer form gave rise to this new art form.

Isadora Duncan. Isadora Duncan was the first person to gain public acclaim and acceptance of modern dance. Her contributions are found in three areas.

She began the expansion of the kinds of movements used in dance. While the ballet was emphasizing mainly the feet and legs, Miss Duncan was using *all of her body*, as did the ancient Greeks.

The ballet costumes included corsets, stiff ballet shoes, and tight costumes. Miss Duncan discarded these items for Grecian tunics, bare feet, and loosely styled hair.

Her taste in music also varied from the standard ballet music. She preferred the symphonies of great masters such as Beethoven and Wagner.

The Loves of Isadora is a film which portrays her exciting and eccentric personal life as a dancer.

Ruth St. Denis and Ted Shawn. Ruth St. Denis used the inspiration of the East and the Orient to influence movement based on the communication of ideas. She met and married Ted Shawn. Together they established the Denishawn Company, which paved the way for future dancers. The company came to be known as the "cradle for American Modern Dance."

Ted Shawn contributed the masculine image to modern dance, developing such themes as *Olympiad*. He used baseball, football, and basketball players, as well as wrestlers and track performers, in his dances in an effort to change the male image in dancing.

Mary Wigman. Mary Wigman was Germany's first modern dancer; following a brief career as a pianist and actress, she began the "new German dance." To this new art was applied the theories of time and motion. The new concept of the dancer's relation to space and to music was realized through the efforts of Miss Wigman.

Martha Graham. *Time* magazine described Martha Graham as the "high priestess of American dance." Miss Graham is credited with the technique built on the principle of the breathing cycle of the body, contraction and release. She has provided the most exact technique and the largest number of choreographic works.

Martha Graham entered Denishawn in 1916 and gave her first independent concert, "The Blessed Damoyel," in 1926. This public appearance began the American dance revolution.

Miss Graham utilizes the wide spectrum of life throughout her themes, many of which are of Greek origin. Her contributions to modern dance cannot yet be fully assessed; she has influenced two generations of dance artists and teachers.

Doris Humphrey. Doris Humphrey studied at Denishawn at approximately the same time as Martha Graham, and left there to establish her own school. She built dance around the principles of "fall-recovery"—or by periods of unbalance (the fall) and balance (the recovery). A third movement was the suspension held at the peak of recovery.

Charles Wiedman and Doris Humphrey. Charles Wiedman and Doris Humphrey teamed together, as they had when both were at Denishawn together. Mr. Wiedman contributed satirical dance works, and together they formed a branch of American modern dance.

Merce Cunningham. Since 1960 Merce Cunningham has been considered the most controversial figure in his field, as he choreographs *by chance*, with any

movement following any other movement. He has been both admired and rejected by audiences, depending upon their individual preferences.

Alwin Nikolais. Alwin Nikolais's most significant contribution is the visual effects and illusions which he has given audiences through props, costumes, films, slides, sound, and light surrounding the dancers. Abstract images and distorted or hidden bodies have been emphasized or suggested through the work of Nikolais.

Serge Diaghileff. The Diaghileff Ballet was directed by Serge Diaghileff, and under his direction ballet was radically changed. Modern dance had originally rejected ballet; however, ballet was now beginning to identify with modern dance.

Michel Fokine. Michel Fokine was a choreographer of The Diaghileff Ballet, and believed that all the elements of the ballet should represent the locale and time from which it came.

Vaslav Nijinsky. Vaslav Nijinsky became a choreographer for Diaghileff, and choreographed the controversial *The Rite of Spring* (danced to the musical composition by Igor Stravinsky). This work met with much opposition, owing to its unusual music and costumes and its uncodified movements and feet positions.

Eugene Loring. An American ballet choreographer, Eugene Loring actually used modern dance movements in ballet in his *Billy the Kid* (set to the music of Aaron Copland) in 1938. This was, and still is, considered one of the finest ballets using a native American theme.

The growth and development of a unique American dance idiom has flourished. Modern dance has a keynote of infinite variety—a trait which is both challenging and exciting.

TERMINOLOGY

Axial-locomotor—Axial refers to performance in place, and locomotor to changing location. In axial movements the body moves upon its own vertical axis. In changing location, the movement is across the floor.

Axial movements—Common motions of the body such as swaying, bending, stretching, swinging, twisting, rotating, turning, pushing, pulling, falling, and rising.

Bounces—Moving downward and rebounding upward, similar to a bouncing ball.

Brushes—Lifting the straight leg and returning, with the foot contacting the floor as long as possible. These are used to strengthen the ankles and legs.

Control-release—The Graham technique of shortening and lengthening of the muscles.

Dance walk—The reverse of walking, with the ball of the foot striking the floor first, followed by the heel and the turnout emphasized along with smoothness.

Fall-recovery—The Humphrey-Wiedman technique of pulling downward and returning upward, as a spiral.

First, second, third, fourth, and fifth positions—The positions of the feet and arms in classical ballet.

Flex-extend—Shortening and lengthening the muscles.

Half-toe—Raising the heel from the floor, with the body weight on the ball of the foot.

Locomotor movements—Patterns of moving across the floor such as sliding, skipping, running, hopping, jumping, leaping, etc.

Polka—Step, together, step, hop. The last step is long and the hop is short in duration, executed in an uneven rhythm.

Prance—A variation of running with the free leg lifted forward, the knee flexed, and the ankle extended.

Push-off—Pressure applied to the floor which adds to movement impulse.

Run—Execute action as in walking, but faster. During this action, there is a split second when both feet are off the floor. Carry the weight forward on the balls of the feet, and execute in an even rhythm.

Schottische—Execute three steps and a hop, in an even rhythm.

Skip—Execute a long step and a short hop on the same foot, in an uneven rhythm.

Slide—Step in any direction (backward, forward, sideward, or diagonally) and transfer the weight to that foot. Touch the advanced foot to the floor before starting to move the other foot; close the other foot up to it. Execute this in an uneven rhythm.

Step—Place either foot in any direction (backward, forward, sideward, or diagonally) and transfer the weight to that foot. Touch the advanced foot to the floor before you start to move the other foot.

Two-step—Execute a step, close the trailing foot to the forward foot, and step with a pause, in an uneven rhythm.

Turn-out—An outward rotation of the legs from the hip joint. increasing the ability of the legs to move.

Walk—Take steps from one foot to the other, in an even rhythm. Transfer the weight from heel to toe on each step.

Waltz—Step forward, sideward, and then close. The accent is on the first step. Execute this in an even rhythm.

MOVEMENTS

Locomotor

The following locomotor and derived locomotor movements are done to even and uneven rhythms. Movements made on each underlying beat are considered *even rhythms*. For example, a waltz has three beats to a measure and a step is taken on each beat. Movements employing a combination of quick and slow beats are considered *uneven rhythms*. For example, a two-step requires three steps to four beats of music. Therefore, there are two quick steps and a slow step to four beats of music.

Gallop—Step and leap with knee action and heel leading, using an uneven rhythm pattern.

Grapevine—Step sideward, then cross the other foot in back; step sideward, then cross the other foot in front, executing the movement in an even rhythm.

Hop—Spring from one foot to the same foot in place, executing it in an even rhythm.

Jump—Spring from one or both feet, landing on both feet with the knees bent, executing it in an even rhythm.

Leap—Spring from one foot, landing on the other; this is similar to a run, but higher, and is executed in an even rhythm.

Mazurka—Step, close up the trailing foot to the forward foot, hop on the trailing foot, bringing the forward foot across in front of the ankle of the hopping foot.

Nonlocomotor

Bending—This involves all or part of the vertebral column inclining in any of the planes, as in bending the neck or trunk forward, backward, or sideward. This may also involve a joint, as in a knee bend.

Falling—This involves the body descending to the floor, giving in to the pull of gravity.

Pulling—Exerting force so as to cause motion toward the force.

Pushing—Moving ahead or forward with steady pressure.

Rising—Making the body ascend to a higher position.

Stretching—Extending the limbs or body.
Swaying—Moving the entire body from side to side.
Swinging—Parts of the body making pendulum movements.
Turning—Revolving the body as a whole.
Twisting (Rotating)—Turning the trunk, or any of the extremities, on the long axis.

VALUES

Modern dance uses the body as the instrument of movement for artistic expression. This activity can contribute to the enrichment of your life by giving your movements grace and poise, along with a general sense of well-being from a body which is well-toned. An appreciation of music, art, and dance can be an outcome which will broaden your cultural activities and interests.

PREPARATION

Dress

Since clothing enhances movement, the dress for modern dance is specifically defined. Women should wear tights which cover the legs and hips, and a leotard which covers the hips and trunk. Underwear which is brief and fits well is recommended. The tights should be cut off at the ankles in order to bare the feet. Women should arrange their hair simply and neatly.

Men can wear a T-shirt and slacks, although dance pants or tights are recommended. A dance belt should be worn under the tights, to provide for firmness of the genitals and to help prevent ruptures. Suspenders are preferred over the belt, to hold the tights in place.

Tights and leotards come in many colors, and should be selected with the individual in mind. Severe color contrast between tights and leotards is not recommended. Dance clothes should be laundered after each use.

Warm-up

Warm-up methods vary from teacher to teacher, since some test results support warm-up while other tests do not.

Warm-up is worthwhile because it initiates movement, increases blood flow, and stimulates the muscles. Exercises should be simple, and should provide for movement of the entire body: from head rolls for the neck to rising and descending on the ball of each foot. Remember to *start slowly and simply.*

Music

Modern dance is performed to music, thus it is helpful for you to practice keeping time to various rhythms. Once you have developed a rhythmical sense, interpretation of the music (what moods or feelings are displayed by the composer) is the next consideration. Later, you may want to study known musical forms such as the waltz or polka.

TECHNIQUE

The traditions and techniques of modern dance grow and change when new ideas and new modes of expression appear. Technique is the craftsmanship or the vocabulary of dance movements but not the final art product of dance composition. Techniques do not have specific meanings, but rather are likened to practice drills or routines.

Technique begins with the warm-up exercises. Technique classes help to minimize sprains, strains, and other similar injuries.

Simple techniques should be followed for about 10 minutes, and then new or more challenging techniques can be experienced. The procedure depends upon the individual and his or her consciousness of the involvement of the total body. Complete control of your body, both physically and mentally, is a prerequisite to any movement. Locate the central point of your personal self. This can be accomplished from any position—standing, sitting, or lying. The objective is the assembly of oneself so that complete control can be realized.

Technique is also affected by placement, either static or dynamic. Each segment of the body needs to be in alignment, so that bodily unity is visible. *Static placement* refers to the motionless body, while *dynamic placement* is the moving body which must constantly adjust to the placement.

Breath control is a supporting feature of movement, since lift actions are enhanced through inhalation and the collapse is assisted by exhalation. Breathing takes place through the diaphragm, and *not* the chest.

Technical skill must be meticulously perfected. One must consider both single movements and their relationships to the *total* movement. He must acquire a sensation or feel of the technique. Techniques improve only with practice and self-analysis.

Technique analysis begins with the total body alignment, as one tries to acquire "good posture" while standing, sitting, or walking. Once this good posture has been assumed, begin stationary movements such as bending, rotating, or pushing. The leg, feet, arms, hands, head, or torso can bend. The head, shoulders, torso, and hips can rotate. The head, shoulders, rib cage, and hips can push while the body supports these stationary movements.

Movement in dance involves three lines: *vertical* and/or *horizontal* lines, *oblique* lines, and *curved* lines. When the body is upright or at a right angle, these lines are considered to be vertical and horizontal respectively. Oblique lines are acquired through slanted positions, while curved lines are in various positions as they combine with other oblique, horizontal, or vertical lines.

The positions of the feet, body, and arms are extremely important in technical skills. The feet may be together or apart, in a variety of positions such as heels together or toes together. The body may be standing, bending, sitting, kneeling, lunging, or curving. The arms may also be in a number of positions such as at the sides, straight from the shoulders, one arm raised, or both arms raised.

Other than in static positions, or nonlocomotor movement, technique is important to locomotor movements. Six types of movements are considered here. These are *descending* and *rising, outward* and *inward, turning* (either partially or with the whole body and traveling in patterns), and *falling* (either partially or entirely).

How an individual movement is performed is referred to as its *quality* or *dynamics*. Each pattern should convey both quality and its motivating forces, dynamics. Qualities or dynamics include four basic factors: *space, time, force,* and *flow.*

CHOREOGRAPHY

The art of arranging dance patterns is known as *choreography.* Dance composition is developed by the teacher for the beginning dancer; however, the ultimate goal is for the dancer to be motivated to create his own pattern of movements that are self-satisfying and entertaining.

Stage design is of two basic modes: *symmetrical* and *asymmetrical.* The first refers to balancing all sides equally by, for example, having two dancers on both sides of the stage. Asymmetrical design may have two dancers on one side of the stage and four on the other side.

In order to develop skill at stage design, one must first observe design, study pictures or paintings, and trace the lines of the movements. Then, he must study people by watching how they move.

Practice complete freedom of movement and limit yourself to two or three basic spatial patterns. Incorporate movements at varying speeds and use motions and ideas in your design. The use of common gestures or movements will enable you to initiate patterns; later, as your creative abilities increase, new movement patterns will come more readily.

The use of topic themes and background music will help you to begin a dance composition. Costumes, props, and scenery will enhance the quality or dynamics of your composition as it enters the final stages of its development.

SAFETY HINTS

1. Always warm-up completely prior to dancing.
2. Hot baths or showers should follow each class, for hygienic reasons and to assist in the prevention of muscular soreness.
3. Secure proper care for sprains, strains, shin-splints, and cramps.
4. Select proper, adequate, and regular diet habits.

BIBLIOGRAPHY

Cheney, Gay, and Connor, Janet Strader, *Modern Dance.* Boston: Allyn and Bacon, Inc., 1969.

Hawkins, Alma H., *Creating Through Dance.* Englewood Cliffs, N.J.: Prentice-Hall, Inc., 1964.

Pease, Esther E., *Modern Dance.* Dubuque, Iowa: Wm. C. Brown Company, Publishers, 1966.

Penrod, James, and Plastino, Janice G., *The Dancer Prepares.* Palo Alto, Calif.: The National Press Books, 1970.

Turner, Margery J., *Modern Dance for High School and College.* Englewood Cliffs, N.J.: Prentice-Hall, Inc., 1957.

RECORDS

Freda Miller Records for Dance. I—Accompaniment for Technique; II—Second Album for Dance; III—Third Album for Dance; IV—Music for Rhythms and Dance. Northport, L.I., N.Y.: Freda Miller Records for Dance.

Keig, Betty, and Nixon, Madeline, *Modern Dance.* "Music for Technique," L.P. #502; "Music for Composition," L.P. #503. Freeport, L.I., N.Y.: Educational Activities, Inc.

MOVEMENT AND BODY MECHANICS | 20

Several areas of emphasis in physical education have prevailed throughout different historical eras. Conditioning and training of the body for high fitness status has been emphasized, and the participation and involvement in many kinds of sports and games has been promoted. Now a new emphasis in physical education is being realized. This involves both the art and the science of human movement, voluntary and purposeful movement. Human movement in itself is not new; however, the teaching, training, and interpretation of human movement is relatively new.

Children innately respond to and with movement. Skipping, jumping, running and galloping are characteristic of the childhood ages. By the age of nine or ten, children lose some of their agility and freedom; however, the need for movement is still present. The loss of this movement is really a partial loss of communication with the outside world.

The elementary school child needs to move frequently with large muscle activity in order to promote better conditions for learning. The junior high student needs to move in order to satisfy both physical and emotional needs. The senior high student needs to move in order to release stored-up energies. The college student and other adults need to move for all the same reasons as does the school-aged child. Movement is a way of life. How we move, when we move, and why we move all have an effect upon our way of life.

THE "HOW" IN MOVEMENT

How do individuals move? Movement can be in directions—such as forward, backward, sideward, upward, and downward. Movement can be according to speeds—such as fast, slow, and varying degrees of each. Movement can be with different body parts—such as the hands, arms, legs, feet, head, or trunk. Movement can occur in relation to other persons or objects—such as throwing, catching, kicking, and dancing. Movement can be descriptive—such as wiggling, hot, bumpy, or shivering. How one moves

can be both creative and directive, depending upon the conditions of movement.

THE "WHY" IN MOVEMENT

The variety of reasons in movement are as numerous as the "how." One sometimes moves to cover a distance, as in walking or running; or, movement may be used to release emotional and nervous frustrations. One sometimes moves to perform an activity, as in dancing, games, or sports. One moves with the specific purposes of improving the condition of his body. Reasons for movement may be centered around expression and, again, may be either creative or directive.

THE "WHEN" IN MOVEMENT

The "when" to move is as flexible as the "how" or the "why" to move. An individual may move when told or allowed to do so, or for the relief of pain or discomfort. Participation in a specific activity such as a game will dictate to a participant when to move by certain cues. One may move when in danger, or when en route to a destination. Movement may occur when certain expressions or emotions need to be released, as in striking someone. The knowledge and interpretation of when to move is of utmost importance.

The "how," "why," and "when" definitely affects the performance of movement, as we can see; hence, these factors must be given every consideration when promoting learning through this media. This is known as the *cognitive phase* of movement: that which deals with the objectives of movement, the awareness of the need for movement, and the relationships inherent in it.

THE SKILL OF MOVEMENT

Although everyone has unique differences and specific styles for performing his own movements, the most efficient, functional, and proper methods of moving do exist. These methods vary from activity to activity, but can be identified in five major areas of activity: aquatics, dance, gymnastics, games and sports, and everyday activities. Fig. 20-1 shows these relationships.

As each of these areas, with the exception of everyday activities, is covered in specific chapters of this book, the everyday movement skills will be the concern of this chapter.

PERSONALITY AND MOVEMENT

Personalities may be identified by the way individuals move. Extrovert people display vigorous, confident motions as they stand, sit, or move, while introverted, shy persons reveal their insecurity with unsure actions. Sophistication is revealed through gracefulness and poise.

As one's personality is identified in the skill, movements may also suggest the personality, as seen through mimicry and imitation. Age, acceptance, and emotions can be portrayed through patterns of movement. Expressive moving is an art, and it can be learned with motivation and training.

STANDING

In order to move appropriately and beautifully, one must begin by standing properly. Balance the body over the base or feet, with the center of gravity slightly over the hips. Each body segment must be balanced over the feet, hips, and chest, or poor posture is the result.

Poor or improper posture contributes to impaired respiration and circulation, menstruation discomforts, fatigue, and constipation.

In good posture the shoulders need to be relaxed, held down and wide, and the eyes looking straight ahead. The chest should be relaxed and held high, with the rear and the stomach in. The knees are loose yet relaxed.

SITTING

The importance of sitting correctly needs to be emphasized, as the body is not designed to sit for any lengthy period of time. In order to avoid discomfort and fatigue, consideration should be given to the proper method of sitting.

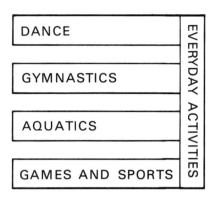

Fig. 20—1. Movement skills.

In the process of sitting, back close enough to the chair for the calf of one leg to touch the chair. The toes of the other leg should be placed under the chair.

To stand, move the feet close to the chair and push with the back leg as the weight is shifted to the forward foot.

When sitting, remember to sit up straight and not to slump forward; be relaxed and not tensed; keep the elbows close to the body; the back should always touch the back of the chair; keep your back straight when shifting or moving; the legs should cross at the ankles or knees; maintain balance, and select chairs and tables of proper height.

LOCOMOTOR MOVEMENTS

Walking is accomplished by transferring the weight from one foot to the other. The weight comes down on the outer side of the heel and travels along the outside to the ball of the foot. The big toe pushes the weight off the foot. At one point, both feet are in contact with the floor.

Running, of course, is faster than walking, with the weight carried on the balls of the feet. At one point, both feet are above the ground.

Leaping is walking or running with extended height. Both feet lose contact with the ground at the same time.

Hopping is transferring weight from one foot back to the same foot, in an even rhythm.

Jumping is accomplished by bending the knees and transferring the weight from one to both feet and landing on both feet. This movement may involve height and/or distance.

Galloping is performing by rapidly stepping and closing with the same foot in the lead at all times, in an uneven rhythm.

Sliding is stepping and closing to the side, using the same lead foot and moving in an uneven rhythm.

Skipping is performed by rapidly taking a long step and a short hop on alternating feet, in an uneven rhythm.

NONLOCOMOTOR SKILLS

Bending is the inclining of part or all of the vertebral column.

Falling is accomplished by the body relaxing and yielding to gravity.

Pulling is the imparting of body force toward the attracting force.

Rising is the ascending to a higher position.

Stretching is the lengthening or extending of the body and its parts.

Swaying is a side-to-side body motion.

Swinging is the result of pendulum movements of the body or its parts.

Turning or *rotating* is the revolving of the trunk or extremities on their long axes.

CREATIVITY IN MOVEMENTS

Freedom in movement may be expressed in any number or ways. Once individuals have been exposed to the different kinds of movements, performing any single skill or combination of skills becomes an easy and enjoyable task. Mimicry and imitation can be realized through the interpretation of animals, people, machines, and other things. Personalities can be displayed and emotions portrayed through the skills of moving.

Music enhances creativity, and gives clues and suggestions pertaining to the cognitive phases of movement. Every individual should be given the opportunity to overcome the barriers established by inhibitions and to move freely according to his own interpretations. This opportunity can be made available in the classroom, with either total freedom in moving or partial freedom through directed patterns of moving.

Values of movement sessions may include all of the contributions of a vigorous workout: the enhancement of good posture; the opportunity to release emotional frustrations; the performance of an activity rated high in carry-over values; and the learning of skills which transfer to every kind of movement need, such as in games and sports, gymnastics, aquatics, dance, and other everyday activities.

BIBLIOGRAPHY

Cratty, Bryant, *Movement Behavior and Motor Learning*. Philadelphia: W.B. Saunders Company, 1967.

Pye, Ruby Lee, and Alexander, Ruth H., *Physical Education Concepts*. The Maxwell Company, Middletown, Ky., 1971.

Rowen, Betty, *Learning Through Movement*. New York: Teachers College, Columbia University, 1963.

Schurr, Evelyn L., *Movement Experiences for Children*. New York: Appleton-Century-Crofts, 1967.

Wessel, Janet A., *Movement Fundamentals*, 2nd Ed. Englewood Cliffs, N.J.: Prentice-Hall, Inc., 1961.

Wessel, Janet A., and MacIntyre, Christine M., *Body Contouring and Conditioning Through Movement*. Boston: Allyn and Bacon, Inc., 1970.

The use of a paddle in place of a tennis racquet was advocated by Frank P. Beal in 1924 to start children playing. He was aware that many children did not have the strength and speed to play tennis, so he substituted a paddle and reduced tne size of a double court by half. It was not long after that innovation before the use of the paddle instead of the hand in striking the ball became popular on the handball court. A sponge rubber ball was used in playing paddle tennis, and it is interesting to note that the first ball used in paddleball was also a sponge rubber ball, followed by a tennis ball. Many modifications have been made in the kind of paddle used, such as shortening the handle of a tennis racquet and putting handles on various thicknesses of plywood.

As well as different kinds of material being used to make the paddle, the ball has also had many modifications, such as using a tennis ball, removing the cover on the tennis ball, and using sponge rubber balls. In 1952 the National Paddleball Association was formed.

COURT

The game of paddleball can be played on any standard four-, three-, or one-wall handball court either indoors or outdoors.

EQUIPMENT

Paddleball regulations require a paddle, a ball, and a uniform which meet certain specifications.

The rules state that the paddle may be wooden or plastic. The dimensions of the paddle should be approximately 8 inches wide and 15 inches long. The weight of the paddle should be approximately 16 ounces, and it must have a safety thong which is to be worn around the wrist during practice or play, to prevent the paddle from slipping out of the hand.

The General Tire-Pennsylvania Athletic Products Company of Akron, Ohio has been designated as the manufacturer of the official ball. This ball is 72 inches in circumference and weighs approximately 1.5 ounces. When the ball is dropped from a height of 6 feet it should rebound approximately 3.5 feet.

RULES

The object of the game is to keep the ball in play by returning it in the air to the front wall before it hits the floor or after it has bounced only once. The ball must go directly to the front wall after it is struck or hit another wall, and then go to the front wall. Failure of a team to return the ball properly results in a point for the serving team. If the serving team loses the point, the server loses the serve.

The game is started by a serve in the service zone. The ball is dropped to the floor in the service zone, and then struck with the paddle on the first bounce. The ball must go directly to the front wall and then rebound behind the short line into the back court. It is àn illegal serve in the four-wall game if the ball hits the back wall before hitting the floor. Two illegal serves in succession result in a side out (defined in the chapter on Handball).

After the ball has been served properly, the receiver must return the ball to the front wall either directly (in one- and three-wall) or—in four-wall—indirectly, by touching the side, ceiling, or back wall before touching the floor.

Players must be given a *fair opportunity* to play the ball without interference. If a player does not have the opportunity to play the ball without interference from an opponent, a *hinder* is called, and the point is replayed. A ball striking an opponent on the fly on its return to the front wall is also a hinder, and the point is replayed.

Twenty-one points constitutes a game, and points can be scored only by the serving side.

The game may be played by two, three ("cutthroat"), or four (doubles) players. In "cutthroat" games, each individual player competes against the other two. A score is made only upon service.

The side starting each game in doubles is allowed only one serve-out. After that, both players on each side are permitted to serve until each has had a serve-out.

SKILLS

The grip known as the "Eastern" in tennis is the most commonly used, and is described as "shaking hands" with the paddle.

The grip is taken by holding the paddle horizontally, with its face perpendicular to the floor. The palm of the hand faces the back side of the paddle, and the butt of the handle rests in the palm of the hand, holding the handle firmly but not too tightly so as to allow wrist flexibility. The forefinger may be advanced along the handle if desirable. The grip is essentially the same for both forehand and backhand types. Some players turn the hand slightly counterclockwise for the backhand grip, so that the thumb presses against the flat portion of the handle.

Ready Position

The waiting or anticipatory position is the stance taken while receiving a serve or preparing for a pivot for the basic stroke. The player faces the front wall. The feet should be approximately 12 to 15 inches apart, the weight on the balls of the feet with the knees slightly flexed, and the weight evenly distributed on both feet. From this stance, the player can move to a position to play the ball or pivot into a position to play the ball with either a forehand or backhand stroke.

Footwork

Footwork in paddleball requires the player to move forward, backward, and laterally, in order to have the body in proper position to play the ball. Movement of the feet to get into the proper position is similar to the type of footwork used in guarding in basketball. Usually short, shuffling steps with a sliding motion should be the pattern of moving. It may be necessary to move toward the ball with running steps forward, or to pivot and run to the ball if it is in back of you.

Pivots

The forehand stroke and backhand stroke require the front of the body to be facing the side of the court. For a right-handed player with the ball on the right, the front of the body faces the right sideline and the forehand stroke is used; for a right-handed player

with the ball on the left, the front of the body faces the left sideline and the backhand stroke is used. In either situation, if the ball is away from the body, the pivot is toward the front wall; if the ball is close to the body, the pivot is away from the front wall. (These pivots are illustrated in the Tennis chapter.) It is important to remember that the direction of the pivot and the appropriate stroke to use is determined by the location of the ball.

Stroke

The forehand and the backhand are the two basic strokes in paddleball. The player pivots into playing position with the foot nearer the front wall 3 to 6 inches forward of the rear foot and about shoulder width apart. The ball should be about arm's length away from the body. The knees are bent slightly and the arm brought back with the wrist flexed, in order to be in position to be brought forward to meet the ball. The stroke covers a short distance, with the weight moving over the forward foot as the paddle comes forward. A slight rotation of the body occurs, and the wrist is flexed. At the time the ball is about to be contacted, the flexed wrist starts a snapping or whiplike movement. The wrist action and the arm motion follow through in the path of the ball.

Serve

The strategy of the serve is to place the opponent on the defensive by making it difficult or impossible for him to return the serve.

The serve is executed by dropping the ball to the floor and allowing it to rebound to the desired height. The forehand stroke is usually used, modifying it slightly by varying the speed of the stroke and the height at which contact is made with the ball.

In serving the ball, the server should try to camouflage his motions so as to throw the opponent off-guard; he should also use various types of serves.

The placement of the serve in relation to the position of the server on the court determines the kind of serve used. A ball passing close to the server with very little angle on the front wall, and rebounding low from the front wall going either shallow or deep in the back court, is called a *drive serve*. If the server stands on one side of the court and serves to the other side, this is called a *crosscourt serve*. The *lob serve* may rebound directly overhead or crosscourt, depending upon where the server stands. The server hits the ball low, causing it to hit the front wall high and rebound in a high arc, so that it will fall near the back line or wall.

Playing the Ball

There are four fundamental shots used in playing the ball: (1) passing shot, (2) kill shot, (3) lob shot, and (4) drop shot. Each of these shots may be made with either the forehand or the backhand stroke, depending upon the position of the player and the ball.

The *passing shot* is a ball hit so that it is driven past the opponent. It is most effective when the opponent is in mid-court, so that the ball can be passed near the sideline on either side of the court. This shot should not be used if the opponent is playing in the back court.

The *kill shot* is a ball returned low on the front wall so as to be unplayable. It is executed by striking the ball as close to the floor as possible, with the *body* in a low, crouched position. The kill shot should not be attempted unless the body is in proper position to strike the ball.

The *lob shot* is a ball that goes high in the air so as to rebound high over the opponent. It is usually hit softly so as not to go to the back line. The main purpose is to drive the opponent to the back line so as to leave the center court open.

The *drop shot* is a ball hit so that, after hitting the front wall, it loses momentum and drops rapidly. This is effective when the opponent is in the rear of the court.

Receiving Service

The receiving player takes the ready position on the court, about 6 feet from the rear wall and midway between the two sidelines. In doubles, each player centers himself in his side of the court and 6 feet in front of the back wall. After the serve, the players move into positions side-by-side or forward and backward.

On the one-wall or three-wall court, the receiver takes the ready position outside of the court behind the long or end line.

Strategy

1. Control of the center of the court is essential.
2. Keep your eye on the ball at all times.
3. Assume proper position before playing the ball.
4. Keep your opponent guessing by varying the stroke and placement of the ball.

BIBLIOGRAPHY

Grambeau, Rodney J., *Official Paddleball Rules.* Ann Arbor, Mich.: Cushing and Mallory Printing Co., 1966.

Kozar, A.J., Grambeau, R.J., and Riskey, E.N., *Beginning Paddleball.* Belmont, Calif.: Wadsworth Publishing Co., Inc., 1967.

Although the exact origin of the game of shuffleboard is unknown, it is believed to have started in England. The modern game probably had its origin in two earlier games. One was played on a large, flat area, and consisted of shoving discs onto various scoring areas that were marked somewhat like a checkerboard. The other was quite similar to the modern game, except that each end of the court was marked with a line called the "deuce line." One point was scored for each disc closest to this line.

In England the early games were known by various names: shovel-groat, shove-groat, and shovel-penney; each game having individual characteristics. The game became known in America partly because of its popularity aboard the luxury liners that sailed between America and Europe.

In recent years the game has become more closely identified with an older and retired age group, particularly in the St. Petersburg, Florida area. Evidence of this is the large number of courts there that are used every day of the year. Also, the governing body for this activity, the National Shuffleboard Association, has its headquarters in St. Petersburg, and the annual winter tournament is played there.

Shuffleboard is played on a court 52 feet long and 6 feet wide (Fig. 22-1). Playing surfaces are of concrete, terrazzo, asphalt tile, or wood. The two scoring surfaces are located at opposite ends of the court and are identically marked. There are six scoring possibilities: one 10 area, two 8 areas, two 7 areas, and one 10-off area. Maximum width of the marking lines is 1-1/2 inches; minimum width is 3/4 inch. All dimensions are measured from the centers of lines.

In each 10-off area there is a separation triangle that divides the area in half; the triangle is 3 inches at the base and runs to a point at the front of each 10-off area.

The court is divided into three parts by two lines drawn parallel to the end lines, and 20 feet from each end of the court. These are called "dead lines."

EQUIPMENT

Equipment for the game consists of discs and cues. The discs are made of wood or composition and are generally manufactured to meet official specifications. A set consists of eight discs—four of one color (usually red) and four of a contrasting color (usually green). Care should be taken not to mix discs of varying sizes and weights in one set.

The cues must measure 75 inches or less in overall length, and are usually made of a lightweight metal such as aluminum.

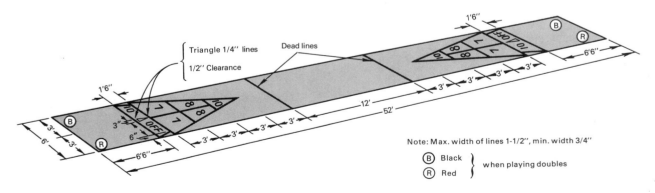

Fig. 22—1. Shuffleboard court.

FUNDAMENTALS

Singles

The play begins by selection of discs. This may be done by lot, the winner having his choice of colors.

For the purpose of ensuring proper starting and rotation of lead, one end of the court is designated as the head of the court and the other as the foot of the court.

Starting at the head of the court, a red disc is played first, on the right; then a green is played on the left, and play alternates until all eight discs are played. At the foot of the court the green is played first, on the right; then the red is played on the left, and so on.

To begin play, the discs are placed in the 10-off area and must not touch any line, including the separation triangle. The forked end of the cue is placed in contact with the disc to be played, and the cue is held with one hand, near the opposite end.

The discs are played alternately, until they have all been moved to the opposite end of the court. This constitutes a half-round. Players then walk to the foot of the court, decide the score by the position of the discs, place them in the 10-off area, and begin play back to the head of the court. When all eight discs have been played and scored at the head of the court, one round is completed. Play continues in this way until one person wins.

Doubles

The only exception to singles play is that partners play at opposite ends of the court, and the color lead does not change until one round is completed.

Scoring

Scores are computed at the end of each half-round, or after eight discs have been played. In order to score, a disc must be on a scoring area, and no part of it may touch a line. The disc that is properly positioned earns the score of the area that it rests on: 7, 8, 10, or minus-10. Most games are played on a 50-point basis; however, games of 75 or 100 points may be played. A match consists of two out of three games. In case of a tie score in doubles at game point or over, two more

rounds are played to determine the winner. In singles, only one more round is played. In case of further ties, repeat the above procedure.

SKILLS

Two factors are involved—the type of court and the type of discs used. In certain indoor areas, the courts are laid out on wood or in asphalt tile. If wax is used on these surfaces, it tends to build up on the bottom of the discs and causes them to drag, thus reducing the distance they travel. Accumulated wax should be scraped off.

The discs are moved by a smooth, continuous movement of the cue. The cue is held in a straight line with the target, and forward movement should continue through this line.

A disc should never be played straight down the center of the scoring area because the disc could then stop only in the 10 area or the 10-off area. Inasmuch as the 10 area in front is a vulnerable position, most scoring attempts are made into the seven or eight areas.

STRATEGY

Discs should have as much space between them as possible, in order to keep the opponent from moving two discs off the scoring areas with only one of his discs. Force the opponent to hit one disc or the other.

Some players prefer to place the first disc at the front part of the scoring area as a blocking disc, then slide the remaining discs behind it.

Defensively, the object is to clear the opponent's discs from the scoring areas whenever possible. Many players attempt only to clear the scoring area, hitting the opponent's discs as hard as possible to drive them off the court. In attempting to move your own disc out of the 10-off area, you must be sure to hit the disc off-center, in order to prevent the second disc from staying in the 10-off area after driving the first disc out.

RULES

1. Discs must be played from within the player's own half of the 10-off area, not touching any line, and must be played in a continuous motion.
2. Players must not step on or over the base line in playing a disc.
3. Players must not in any way interfere with the play of an opponent.
4. If a disc comes to rest between the base line from which it was played and the farther dead line, it is removed immediately.
5. A disc coming to rest just beyond the farther base line is removed to at least 8 inches beyond that base line.

BIBLIOGRAPHY

American Shuffleboard Leagues, Inc., *Shuffleboard Rules—Table*. Union City, N.J.: The Leagues.
General Sportcraft Co., Ltd., *Shuffleboard Rules— Deck*. New York: The Company.
National Shuffleboard Association, *Shuffleboard Rules—Deck*. St. Petersburg: The Association.

SKIING | 23

Historians disagree as to the actual origin of skiing. It has been ascribed to many lands as an ancient mode of locomotion, and is probably an outgrowth of the snowshoe. Certainly, the main impetus for present-day skiing has come from the Scandinavian countries. Skiing was introduced into Central Europe by way of Austria in 1590. The first known ski meet was recorded at Oslo, Norway in 1767, featuring the oldest ski event, the *biathlon*, which combined cross-country skiing and rifle shooting. Early Scandinavian settlers have been given credit for introducing skis to the United States, and in 1882 a group formed the first ski club at Berlin, New Hampshire. In 1904 ski enthusiasts of the Middle West formed the National Ski Association. However, the first ruling body for the sport was not formed until 1924, prior to the first winter Olympic games, and was known as the Fédération Internationale de Ski (FIS). The 1932 Winter Olympics at Lake Placid, New York and the 1960 Winter Olympics at Squaw Valley, California have given great impetus to skiing as a recreational sport. The most popular recreational skiing is the alpine or downhill skiing. Competitive skiing includes jumping, downhill, slalom, and cross-country. Downhill skiing is the only phase described in this text because of its wide interest and appeal.

EQUIPMENT

The most important consideration for the beginner is achieving both the right fit and right selection of quality equipment.

Boots

An important item of equipment is the boots, for it is through his boots that the skier controls his skis. The boots should be designed for the most popular kind of skiing, that being downhill skiing. This type should fit snugly, with no play around the heels, and should hold the ankles rigid to let the skier make a comfortable forward lean, the proper downhill skiing position.

When not in use, boots should be clamped in boot trees and occasionally polished with a good wax.

Binding

In addition to the boot, a good binding is needed. A conventional binding consists of a metal toeplate into which the boot tip is set, and a cable that circles the boot. When the cable is clamped forward, the toe is pushed firmly into the toeplate and the heel is pulled down tightly on the ski. The binding prevents lateral play and any lifting action of the heel on the ski. Release bindings or safety bindings are designed to release the boot and skier from the skis should there be a sudden forward or lateral twist during a fall. A desirable addition is a special strap attached to the binding and the boot to restrain a runaway ski if the binding is released in a fall.

Skis

Most skis are made of wooden laminations in a combination of wood and some metal. Both wooden and metal skis are graded either soft, medium, or hard—according to their flexibility. In general, if a skier is light for his height, a soft ski is preferable; if he is heavy, a hard ski. The skis should have steel edges for good control and durability. Plastic bottoms have also proved to be more resistant than wood. The emphasis on downhill skiing has tended to shorten skis. Cross-country skis are comparatively longer and narrower. For length, a rule of thumb is to stand the skis upright and stretch the wrist comfortably over the tip. A good skier may want a longer, stiffer ski; however, the beginner should use shorter skis for better control.

Ski Poles

Ski poles are used for balance and moving on the level or uphill. The poles should be strong, yet light, so as not to tire the skier. Poles may be made from bamboo, steel, aluminum, or fiber glass. They can also be

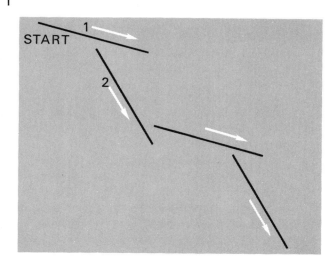

Fig. 23–1. Skating.

telescopic, so that the length can be adjusted. A suggested length for poles is from the ground to within a generous hand's breadth below the armpits.

Clothing

The skier's clothing should be designed to keep him warm and to give protection from the wind and wet snow. It should be light enough, however, and so styled as to avoid being clumsy.

SAFETY HINTS

1. Sufficient physical conditioning should be undergone before participating.
2. Master the fundamental skills, so that the skis are kept under control at all times.
3. Use release or safety bindings and well-waxed skis.

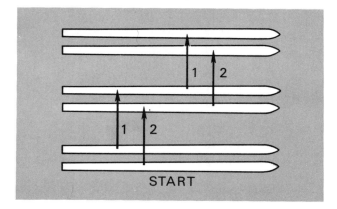

Fig. 23–2. Side step.

4. Observe the rules on riding the ski lift or tow.
5. Do not choose slopes or trails beyond your skill.
6. Never ski alone; use the "buddy" system.
7. Learn and observe the rules of the trail.
8. Be alert to changing snow and weather conditions.
9. Learn the technique of falling properly.
10. Improve the safety of the terrain, especially after a spill. Repair damage done to the ground or the snow as a result of the spill.

FUNDAMENTALS

The following instructions are brief and are directed to inform the beginner of the basic fundamentals of skiing.

Gliding

Gliding, or the basic walking step, is performed on level terrain. In the starting position the skis are together and kept parallel. In beginning the forward glide, the weight is transferred to the gliding ski, pushing the pole at the same time, using the right pole with the left foot, and vice versa. The arms and shoulders should swing upward alternately, and the pole is planted in the snow near the ski opposite the front or gliding foot.

Skating

Skating is a faster movement than gliding, and should help the beginner learn balance. It is usually performed on a slight downgrade too gentle to "run on." The basic movement is similar to the walking step. In beginning the skating action, the weight is transferred to the front ski; the inside edge of the rear ski is then pushed against the snow as the ski is turned outward, as shown in Fig. 23-1. At the completion of the initial glide, the rear ski is then lifted and placed in the gliding position. The arms and shoulders are coordinated with the leg action by swinging the left pole forward with the left ski, and the right pole with the right ski.

Turning on the Level

The two basic turns to change direction are the step turn and the kick turn.

Step Turn

This is a slow turn easily performed by taking short steps alternately, keeping the front or rear of the ski in one place, so that you are actually stepping around a central point until you reach the desired direction.

Kick Turn

This is the most widely used turn for changing directions. To begin the kick turn, the skis are parallel. The poles are planted behind the body about two feet from the skis, and are used for balance and support. The front ski or leg is kicked forward and upward, then turned out and down toward the direction desired. The skis are now parallel, but pointing in opposite directions. The weight is shifted to this front ski. The rear ski is now picked up and swung around until it is parallel with the other ski; at the same time, the arm and pole swing around, completing the body turn.

Falling and Getting Up

When a fall is inevitable, the skier should try to fall backward and to the side on as much body area as possible. Getting up on the hill is easier than on the level, but the basic movements are the same. The initial step is to roll so that the skis are free, parallel, together, and downhill from the body. The knees are bent and drawn in, getting the boots beneath the body. The poles are then placed together and held, with the hands well spread. The poles are planted into the snow on the uphill side near the hip. From this position, by leaning forward and pushing up with the poles, the skier pushes himself upright.

Climbing

The two basic techniques used in climbing are the side step and the herringbone. Of the two, the side step is easier and less tiring; it is used for fairly steep slopes.

Side Step

This climbing technique is performed by picking up and stepping to the side with the uphill ski and pole. The ski is kept horizontal to the slope and edged into the hill to prevent side-slipping. The downhill ski and pole are then brought alongside and in position to start the next step, as in Fig. 23-2. The side step is also used with the kick turn to climb a long hill.

Herringbone

This is a quick and efficient climbing technique. In performing the herringbone, the skis are in the "V" position, with the weight on the inside edges and the body leaning well forward. The poles are held behind the skis. The climbing steps are made alternately in the "V" position, as shown in Fig. 23-3, using the right pole with the left ski, and vice versa.

Downhill Skiing
Stance

The skis are parallel, with one foot about 6 inches ahead of the other for balance. The lower body is held upright, with a slight bend of the knees and ankles. The upper body is slightly bent and kept relaxed. When standing on a slope, the poles are planted in front of the body to keep the skis from slipping. On the level, the poles are held above the waist, with the tips or ends above the snow and behind the body.

Skiing Position

Once in motion, the skier assumes the new *comma position*. This position entails countermovement of the upper body against the lower body. The body is swayed in the shape of a comma toward the slope. The downhill shoulder is pulled back, the knees are kept close together, and the weight is on the downhill ski. This basic position is employed on most turns.

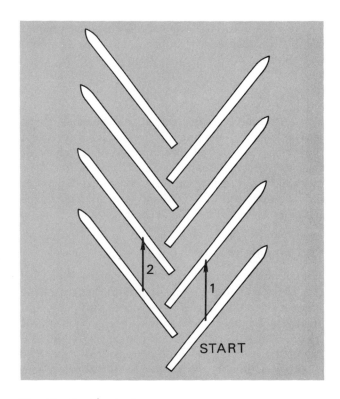

Fig. 23—3. Herringbone.

Diagonal Movements

The two basic techniques by which a beginner should move diagonally across the slope are traversing and side-slipping.

Traversing

This technique is performed with the beginner in the comma position, stepping diagonally across and into the slope. The uphill ski is lifted and advanced slightly, thereby transferring the weight to the downhill ski. Stepping action is continued diagonally into the slope until the skis are perpendicular to the fall line or line of steepest descent.

Side-slipping or Skidding

The comma position is assumed, with the skis parallel and horizontal to the slope. The upper edges of the skis are diagonally angled in the slope, with the weight mostly on the downhill ski. Side-slipping is performed by releasing and rolling the upper edges of the skis diagonally into the slope in a controlled slide. The skidding action is also employed in stopping and making a beginner's initial turn. The stopping action employs a heel thrust until the skis are changed from the diagonal angle to the position perpendicular to the fall line.

Basic Turns

The following turns vary in degree of difficulty, and should be perfected by every skier. These turns are made through the fall line or line of steepest descent. The four basic turns are the snowplow turn or double stem, the stem turn, the stem swing, and the parallel swing.

Snowplow Turn, or Double Stem

This turn is a safe, slow turn performed from the snowplow position. The plow position is also used in braking. It is achieved by having the tips of the skis close together and the rear of the skis spread, forming a wide inverted "V." The braking action is executed by keeping the knees close together and placing equal pressure on the inside edges of the skis in the above position. From this position, while traversing, the turn is executed with the comma position. The skis are kept in the inverted "V" position throughout, with the weight shifted to the uphill ski by leaning the body over this ski as the skier moves into the fall line.

Stem Turn

The stem turn resembles a half-snowplow. It is started with the skis together and the body in the comma position while traversing. The braking action is performed by shifting the weight from the downhill ski in the comma position to the uphill ski as it is angled to the other ski. The tips of the skis are kept close together throughout the turn, and the skis are brought parallel once they pass the fall line.

It is essential to learn the above turns in both directions, and they should be completely mastered by the beginner, since they are slow motions of the two turns mentioned below. Steering or braking is now eliminated in favor of a swinging motion.

Stem Swing

The stem is the most used turn in skiing. The stem uses initially the same technique as the stem turn, but is performed at a steeper angle and, consequently, at higher speed. On approaching the fall line, the inside or downhill ski is brought parallel to the uphill or stemming ski. The turn is completed by an outward controlled heel thrust, finishing in a new transverse position.

Parallel Swing

The parallel is the most graceful of all the turns, and is performed with the skis parallel throughout. The prime mover in the parallel is the controlled heel thrust, aided by the use of the pole. The parallel is started while traversing in the comma position. On approaching the fall line, the uphill shoulder is pulled back while the weight remains on both skis. The skier now performs the heel thrust, skidding the rear ends of the skis across the snow; he assists the turn by a lifting action of the arms after the downhill pole is planted. The turn is completed with the weight shifted to the downhill ski, with the body in a strong comma position.

BIBLIOGRAPHY

Bourdon, Robert, *The New Way to Ski.* New York: Universal Publishing and Distributing Co., 1961.

Bradley, D., Miller, R., and Merrill, A., *Expert Skiing.* New York: Holt, Rinehart and Winston, Inc., 1960.

Huber, E., and Rogers, N. G., *Complete Ski Manual.* Englewood Cliffs, N.J.: Prentice-Hall, Inc., 1946.

Kalakian, Leonard H., and Wayne, Cheryl L., *Skiing.* Boston: Allyn and Bacon, Inc., 1971.

National Ski Association of America, *Skiing (Downhill and Slalom International Rules).* Denver: The Association.

The Official American Ski Technique. Minneapolis: Professional Ski Instructors of America, 1964.

Official NCAA Skiing Guide. Phoenix, Ariz.: College Athletics Publishing Service, 349 East Thomas Road.

————, *Skiing (Jumping and Cross-Country International Rules).* Denver: The Association.

————, *Skiing (Downhill Slalom and Giant Slalom, NSA Rules).* Denver: The Association.

Prager, Walter, *Skiing.* New York: The Ronald Press Company, Inc., 1951.

Sports Illustrated, *Book of Skiing.* Philadelphia and New York: J.B. Lippincott Co., 1960.

SKIN AND SCUBA DIVING | 24

Man moved on or about the water for hundreds of years before going below the surface to a depth greater than that which can be attained on one breath of air.

Skin diving, the sport of swimming below the surface of the water while holding the breath, has been practiced for centuries by the pearl divers of the South Sea Islands and the sponge fishermen of Greece.

During the first half of the nineteenth century, Augustus Siebe developed the "close" dress diving suit. This allowed the diver to go below the surface of the water and have compressed air pumped to him through a flexible hose. The basic principle of supplying compressed air to the diver is being used today in scuba diving.

The development of self-contained diving equipment came about just before World War II. During the war it was used effectively by the Navy in its underwater demolition work.

Interest in skin and scuba diving is evidenced by the spectacular growth of underwater clubs and the large-scale production and sales of underwater equipment.

Skin diving and scuba diving are the names given to the sports of swimming below the surface of the water to explore, photograph, hunt, and exercise.

TERMINOLOGY

Breathing lung—A metal container of compressed air, a set of straps, an air regulator, a flexible rubber hose, and a mouthpiece.
"Buddy"—Individual pairing with another and working together as a unit on land and in the water.
"Close" dress suit—An airtight diving suit worn by the diver and connected to the surface air supply. The pressurized air is forced down to the diver wearing the suit.
Decompression chamber—An airtight chamber that allows the air pressure on the individual to be controlled in order to simulate pressures below the surface of the water.

Hyperventilating—Taking a series of deep breaths.
Open circuit—A breathing apparatus that supplies air to the diver as he inhales through the mouthpiece and then allows the exhaled air to escape into the water surrounding the diver.
Scuba diving—Swimming below the surface of the water using some type of breathing lung. The word scuba comes from the first letter of the words "self-contained underwater breathing apparatus."
Self-contained diving equipment—Equipment that carries an accessible supply of air that the diver can use as he swims "free" underwater.
Skin diving—Swimming below the surface of the water with the aid of swim fins and mask, while holding the breath.
Small craft—A small boat propelled with or without a motor.

EQUIPMENT

Basic Equipment—Skin Diving

Swim fins and a face mask are basic pieces of equipment for skin and scuba diving.

Swim fins are broad, flexible, rubber fins worn on the diver's feet. The fins should fit snugly around the feet and be comfortable. The purpose of the fins is to increase the efficiency of the leg kick.

The face mask consists of shatterproof glass, a stainless steel rim, and a rubber skirt to provide a watertight seal. The face plate can be of plastic; however, it should be noted that plastic will scratch and fog easily. The mask fits over the nose and eyes. The mask should seal itself when the diver inhales initially through the nose and exhales through the mouth. A strap is provided to keep the mask in place and to keep it watertight. The primary function of the mask is to keep water from the nose and eyes.

The third basic piece of equipment for a skin diver is the snorkel. This is a flexible, plastic tube that curves under the chin and has attached to it a rubber mouthpiece that is gripped by the teeth. The straight part of the tube is held close to the head by the strap of the face mask. The "J" type of tube is recommended. The snorkel resembles a periscope on a submarine, only it is for breathing instead of seeing. It allows the diver to breathe when at the surface of the water in a facedown position.

Scuba Diving Equipment

The essential difference between skin diving and scuba diving is the use of some form of breathing lung, which the diver uses to obtain oxygen below the surface of the water. Therefore, the essential equipment of the scuba diver is the face mask and swim fins, plus the breathing lung that replaces the snorkel of the skin diver.

The breathing lung consists of a tank or tanks, regulator, hose, and mouthpiece, that are used by the diver to furnish air while swimming underwater.

The tanks are strapped on the diver's back to permit mobility in the water. The number of tanks worn by the diver is a determining factor in the length of time he can stay underwater. Each tank, or cylinder, carries air compressed at about 2,100 pounds per square inch.

The regulator is located on top of the cylinders and keeps the air at a constant 60 pounds per square inch, allowing the air to be drawn out on demand. As the pressure changes at various depths, the regulator automatically adjusts the pressure of the air in the cylinder to the desired pressure for breathing. The regulator allows the diver to breathe in a natural manner as he descends or ascends.

To the regulator are connected two flexible, corrugated, rubber hoses that encircle the head and are attached to the mouthpiece. The mouthpiece is constructed so that the diver may grip it firmly between his teeth.

The better breathing lungs are equipped with a built-in warning device to warn the diver when his air supply is low. *Make sure the diving apparatus has this safety feature.*

Additional Equipment for Both Scuba and Skin Diving

1. *Exposure suit*—This piece of equipment allows the diver to maintain a more constant body temperature, thus allowing him to work longer in cold water.
2. *Weighted belt*—A belt with built-in compartments, holding chunks of lead. This additional weight helps the diver stay below the surface with less effort. It should be equipped with a quick-release buckle which can be operated with one hand, so that the attached weights can be dropped in an emergency. The belt should be the last piece of equipment put on before diving.
3. *Knife and Sheath*—The knife should be sharp and the handle broad. The knife should be attached to the diver's body with a lanyard. The knife is used primarily for cutting the diver free of any binding materials, such as weeds that grow underwater, tangled harness and rope, or for protection.

Care of Equipment

Check the equipment and care for it according to specific instructions of the manufacturer. The following general instructions refer to the open-circuit (demand-type) breathing lung.

1. After each diving operation, rinse all equipment with fresh water.
2. Allow equipment to dry thoroughly before storing.
3. Do not use any preservative on the rubber tubing or breathing lung.
4. For the care of the cylinders:
   a. Store the cylinders in a cool, dry area.
   b. Before refilling, allow some of the air to escape, thus blowing out any dust particles present.
   c. Do not fill the cylinders so fast that excessive heat is generated. If you do, your gauge will give a false reading of the amount of air in the tank.
   d. Never fill the tank with pure oxygen. Fresh air is used in most situations. Fill the tank with fresh air from the compressor.
5. Check all equipment for proper working order before using it.

SKILLS AND KNOWLEDGE OF SKIN DIVING

There is a hazard in holding the breath too long while swimming underwater. Sometimes the excitement of the activity will cause the diver to hold his breath too long, thus forcing him into a state of unconsciousness.

When a diver commits the common mistake of hyperventilating or "overbreathing" before swimming underwater, he depletes the body of carbon dioxide, which is the main factor controlling the urge to breathe. If this urge to breathe is delayed to a point where the oxygen supply is inadequate, the person will lose consciousness and, without some outside help, will drown. Never ignore the "urge to breathe."

Skills Necessary for Skin Diving:

1. Before attempting skin diving techniques, the individual should have a thorough knowledge of swimming techniques. In addition, he should have an excellent endurance capacity.

2. The mastery of swimming with equipment is essential. One of the basic skills involves the use of swim fins. When wearing swim fins, use a flutter-kicking action of the feet, with most of the power for the legs coming from the hips. The flutter kick with fins is similar to the flutter action of the feet in the American crawl swimming stroke; the main difference is that the kick with fins is slower and deeper.

If the hands are used along with the feet, the speed of the diver will increase. The action of the hands can be any of the following: a breast stroke arm pull; paddling action—moving both arms at the same time; or alternating the arm movement.

Endurance is an important factor in performing the arm or leg strokes for an extended period with fins.

3. Learn to use the face mask in the following way:
   a. Entering the water from a small craft: This skill is executed by leaving the boat and landing on the back in the water, keeping the impact of the water away from the face plate.
   b. Clearing the face mask of water or fog in the water: Tilt the face plate up, lift one corner of the mask away from the face, and blow through the nostrils. When the mask is clear, let it settle back, following the contour of the face, and breathe in through the nostrils.

4. Gain proficiency in the use of the snorkel. The necessary skills are:
   a. Swim in a facedown position, with the snorkel protruding above the surface of the water. *Remember, all breathing is through the mouth.*
   b. Go below the surface, submerging the upper end of the snorkel while holding the breath, thus keeping the water out of the mouth but still in the snorkel.
   c. Come back to the surface, keeping the face down, clearing the upper end of the snorkel above the surface. At this point give a strong gust of air through the snorkel, thus clearing the water from the tube and allowing regular breathing through the mouth once more.

Skills of Scuba Diving

Scuba diving allows the individual to breathe compressed air under the surface of the water, which is quite different from the normal process of breathing on land. Therefore, the techniques of breathing compressed air in water should be thoroughly understood. These should be practiced and mastered under the guidance of a competent instructor. Knowledge and application of the following points are also essential to a mastery of scuba diving:

1. The same swimming skills used in skin diving are applicable to scuba diving.
2. Follow the manufacturer's directions in the use of your breathing lung. Strict adherence to directions is essential for the proper functioning of your equipment.
3. Master the mechanics of handling the breathing lung.
   a. Put on your gear, making sure of a snug fit of all the straps.
   b. Place the mouthpiece firmly between the teeth, closing the lips tight around the outer portion of the mouthpiece.
   c. Turn the valve to the "on" position at the top of the tank.
   d. Breathe in through the mouth the air that travels through a flexible rubber hose from the tank.
   e. Exhale through the mouth, thus causing the valve on the tank to close and another to open, allowing the exhaled air to escape into the water or atmosphere. This operation will continue as long as you have air in the tank and you continue to breathe.
4. After mastering the breathing operation with the lung on land, move to shallow water or a swimming pool. Continue the same operation as above, keeping in mind that when you enter the water you will need the skills in the use of swim fins and face mask as described in skin diving.
5. As the scuba diver descends below the surface, with each "buddy" checking the other's equipment for leaks, etc., the diver breathes in a regular manner. The diver will have to remember that one of the disadvantages of the scuba diving equipment is the added effort placed on the muscles of the respiratory system in carrying on normal breathing and in opening and closing the valves of the regulator.
6. If pain is experienced in the ears as the diver descends, he should ascend a few feet and hold the nose, close the mouth, and blow out, thus forcing air into the middle ear and sinus to relieve the pressure. If the pain is relieved, continue on down; if the pain is not relieved, return to the surface.
7. If the diver goes to a depth of over 130 feet, he is subject to a condition known as "nitrogen nar-

cosis." This condition is caused by breathing nitrogen under pressure, and the symptoms are similar to those of alcohol intoxication. A person in this condition is prone to mistakes and poor judgment.

8. The discontinued use of pure oxygen eliminates the possibility of a condition known as "oxygen toxicity." The symptoms are similar to those of an epileptic having a seizure. Oxygen toxicity usually occurs when oxygen is breathed under pressure.

9. As the diver starts to ascend, he should remember that his body has been exposed to severe pressure and he should ascend gradually. One good rule is, "Never pass your smallest bubble." If he ascends too fast, the diver may develop a condition known as decompression sickness or "bends."

10. The diver should never hold his breath as he ascends to the surface. If the diver traps the air in his lungs as the pressure outside decreases, the air inside the lungs will expand, thus causing a condition known as "air embolism," which could be fatal.

KNOWLEDGES OF SCUBA DIVING

Laws of Physics Important to Underwater Activities

Air is compressible; water is incompressible.

Pressure in the air-containing cavities of the body must change to equal that of the surrounding water. When the air pressure in the cavities (lungs, sinuses, or middle ears) is not equalized with the surrounding water, a partial vacuum will exist. Distortion will take place or blood will fill the vacuum, resulting in pain and discomfort.

The volume of a gas varies inversely with the pressure.

In descending into water, the pressure increases on the diver at the rate of one pound for about every two feet of descent. This means that at 33 feet he has doubled the pressure or has added one atmosphere, compared with the pressure exerted at the surface. Relating this to the diver, a lung half inflated at a depth of 33 feet would be completely inflated at the surface. A fully inflated lung below the surface may rupture if the diver comes up without properly exhaling.

In a mixture of gases, the partial pressure of each component depends upon the proportionate number of molecules present.

Air is composed of approximately 21 percent oxygen and 78 percent nitrogen. The normal atmospheric pressure is 14.7 pounds per square inch. The pressure of the oxygen is 21 percent of 14.7, or 3.1 pounds per square inch. The pressure of the nitrogen is 78 percent of 14.7, or 11.5 pounds per square inch.

The partial pressure of each of these gases increases proportionately with increasing depth. The pressure of oxygen at the surface is 3.1 pounds per square inch, and will be increased to 14.7 pounds per square inch at a depth of 125 feet. This would be approximately the same pressure of oxygen that an individual would receive if breathing pure oxygen at the surface, and would have a toxic effect on the body.

The components of a mixture of gases in contact with a liquid will dissolve in direct proportion to their partial pressure.

The partial pressure of nitrogen is 11.5 pounds per square inch. At 33 feet the partial pressure of nitrogen will be 23 pounds per square inch. This results in twice the usual amount of nitrogen dissolved in the blood. Conversely, the blood will hold in solution half the volume of nitrogen that will dissolve at 33 feet. Therefore, when rising to the surface, the excess will come off as bubbles of gaseous nitrogen.

Hazards of Diving

1. *Nitrogen Narcosis:* The usual scuba diving depths for experienced divers range between 130 feet and 200 feet. Within this range, the diver will be subjected to "nitrogen narcosis," whose symptoms are similar to alcohol intoxication. When nitrogen is breathed under pressure, it has a depressing effect on the nervous system and often results in the loss of skill and judgment in carrying out the duties of the diver.

2. *Oxygen Toxicity:* It has been found that the breathing of pure oxygen under pressure has a toxic effect on the diver. It will produce a condition in the diver similar to that of an epileptic having a "seizure." For this reason, drowning would be a serious threat.

3. *Decompression Sickness (The Bends):* This condition is probably the most common of all diving ailments. As the diver leaves the surface going down, the pressure steadily increases, forcing more and more gas into the diver's tissues through his circulatory system. The deeper and longer the diver stays underwater, the more gas is forced into the blood and body tissues. As the diver ascends abruptly, the pressures change abruptly, and the nitrogen bubbles expand rapidly. This rapid expansion causes bubbles in the blood and body tissues to occlude capillaries, resulting in pain and discomfort. To remedy the

bends, it is necessary to recompress (descend) and then decompress slowly.

4. *Air Embolism:* This condition occurs when a diver suddenly ascends holding his breath, restricting the expanding gases from escaping and thus producing an overextension of the lungs and eventual rupture. This condition can and will be fatal unless the stricken diver is recompressed immediately. To remedy this situation, the diver should be taken to a decompression center for treatment.

SAFETY PRECAUTIONS

The more dangerous an activity, the more important the safety precautions. In the case of skin and scuba diving, remember the following safety points:

1. Proficiency in swimming is the first step in safety. Some skin divers rely too much on their equipment, and not enough on their own individual skill.
2. When wearing a face mask, always enter the water in such a manner as not to bring pressure directly on the face plate.
3. Mastery of scuba diving equipment before going below the surface is important. Get acquainted with all the valves and learn to use them.
4. A complete check of equipment should be made before each dive. Special care should be taken to wash all equipment with fresh water and dry it thoroughly.
5. Keep oil away from the rubber connections and oxygen valves. Oil deteriorates rubber and is a fire hazard when combined with oxygen.
6. The "buddy system" is a *must* when skin diving and scuba diving.
   a. Scuba diving in dark water requires that a line be attached to both divers, and that a set of communication signals be worked out.
   b. Where visual contact is available, hand signals for communication should be worked out.
   c. It is the responsibility of each buddy to inspect the other's equipment for leaks, tangled harness, etc., as they descend below the water.
7. Diving with ear plugs is taboo. The external pressure of the water can force the ear plugs

through the ear drums, causing permanent injury to the ears.

8. Diving with an infection in the upper respiratory tract is dangerous. If the diver goes below the surface and experiences pain, he should immediately return to the surface and cease his diving operations.
9. When the diver begins his ascent to the surface, care should be taken not to pass the smallest bubble. The depth, the length of time at that depth, and how fast the diver ascends will determine the severity of the decompression sickness that could occur.
10. Keep your dives shallow and enjoy yourself. The location and accessibility of the nearest decompression chamber should be known by all skin and scuba divers.
11. A spare breathing unit should be available at the diving area.
12. Don't trust homemade equipment. It is enough risk to place your life in the hands of someone who knew what he was doing and had the best materials on hand when he manufactured the equipment. *Get the best!*
13. When an emergency arises, think it out—*don't panic.* As a last resort, leave your air supply and make a free ascent.
14. As the diver makes the ascent, he should never hold his breath. Doing this will bring on air embolism.

BIBLIOGRAPHY

Borgeson, L., and Speirs, J., *Skin and Scuba Diver.* New York: Arco Publishing Co., Inc., 1962.

Empleton, Bernard E. (chairman), *The New Science of Skin and Scuba Diving.* New York: Association Press, 1970.

Lee, Owen S., *Complete Illustrated Guide to Snorkel and Deep Diving.* New York: Doubleday Co., Inc., 1963.

Roberts, Fred M., *Scuba, Self-contained Underwater Breathing Apparatus,* edited by Eugene V. Connett. Princeton: Van Nostrand Publishing Co., 1960.

Tassos, John, *The Underwater World.* Englewood Cliffs, N.J.: Prentice-Hall, Inc., 1957.

VanderKogel, Albert, with Rex Lardner, *Underwater Sport.* New York: Henry Holt and Co., 1955.

Soccer is a game of very early origin. The Greeks played a form of soccer called Harpaston which the Romans adopted and changed somewhat.

When the Romans invaded Great Britain, the British adopted the game; as they subsequently colonized new lands, the game spread around the globe.

At the present time soccer is played in some 141 countries, and in most of these it is considered a national game. Spectator crowds of 150,000 or more are common in Europe and South America. As early as 1830 a form of soccer was being played in American colleges and by 1860 most of the colleges along the Atlantic seaboard were playing soccer under one set of rules. At present, approximately 500 colleges and 2,100 high schools in the United States play soccer.

In 1919 Bryn Mawr College was the scene of the first soccer game for women. The rules, of course, were modified from the men's game and first printed in 1927. Since then soccer for both sexes has grown in the United States and abroad. The sun never sets on the game of soccer.

TERMINOLOGY

Back up—To follow closely a teammate who has possession of the ball in order to be in position to receive a pass. Also, to support a teammate when he attempts to get the ball from an opponent.

Behind—The term given to a ball that is forced over a goal line, but not between the goal posts.

Carrying—The act of the goalie in carrying the ball more than four steps.

Center—To kick the ball to the middle of the field and in front of the opponent's goal.

Charge—To put one's weight against an opponent, using the part of the body from the shoulder to the hip, in order to force the opponent off the ball.

Clearing—The team on defense moves the ball away from the goal they are defending when the area is congested with players. Clearing usually results in the start of an offensive movement.

Corner area—A quarter circle, with a radius of 1 yard, at each of the four corners of the field from which the corner kick is taken.

Cross—To kick a ball from one side of the field to the other.

Feed—To give a teammate a pass so he can attempt a shot.

Hand ball—To touch the ball with the hands or arms when it is in play; this does not refer to the goalie in his penalty area.

Marking—Keeping close to an opponent so he cannot make an offensive move if he should receive the ball.

Throw-in—The method of putting a ball back into play after it has crossed the touch line; the hands are used.

Touch—The space inside the field of play. A ball in play is in touch; if out of play, it is out of touch.

Touch line—The side boundaries of the field, running the length of the field.

THE GAME

Soccer is played by a team of 11 players on a rectangular field, as shown in Fig. 25-1. The women's field is 80-100 yards in length and 40-60 yards in width, with 6 yards between the goal posts.

The players are: one goalie; two fullbacks—right and left; three halfbacks—right, center, and left; five forwards—outside left, inside left, center forward, inside right, and outside right. The offensive objective of the game is to propel the ball into the opponent's goal. A goal is scored when the whole ball legally goes under the crossbar—between the goal posts and over the goal line. The ball must be kicked, headed, or played with the body by all players except the goalkeeper, who may use his hands on the ball within his own penalty area.

It is a foul in the women's game if the goalkeeper takes more **than** two steps or bounces the ball more than once. Women may use their arms and hands to play the ball, if they are in complete contact with the body.

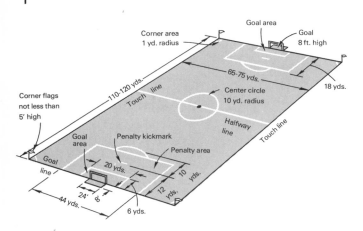

Fig. 25—1. Regulation soccer field.

Start

The game is started when a player kicks the ball into the opponents' half of the field a distance at least as far as the circumference of the ball. Every player shall be in his own half of the field, and members of the receiving team must be at least 10 yards from the ball until after the kick-off. The ball must not be played twice in succession by the player first kicking it.

Throw-in

When the ball has gone out-of-bounds, play is started again by a throw-in from outside the touch line. A player of the team that did not cause the ball to go out will throw it into play to a teammate. A ball thrown in from out-of-bounds cannot be touched again by the player who throws it in until another player has touched it. A goal can not be scored directly from a throw-in.

In the women's game, a ball going across touch lines is put in play by kicking, with the opponents at least 5 yards from the ball.

Corner Kick

When the defensive team touches the ball last before it crosses their own goal line, it is given to the opponents at the nearest corner area.

Goal Kick

When a ball crosses the goal line, having last been touched by the offensive team, it is put in play by the defensive team at their goal area by a goal kick. All opponents must remain outside the penalty area until

the kick is made, and the ball is not in play until it leaves the penalty area.

Offside

A player is offside if he is nearer his opponent's goal than the ball at the moment the ball is played unless: (a) he is on his defensive side of field, (b) two opponents are nearer to their goal than he, (c) his opponent last touched the ball, or (d) he received the ball directly from a goal kick, corner kick, throw-in, or dropped ball by the official.

In the women's game, offside is called if less than three defensive players are between the goal and the offensive player moving the ball.

Direct Free Kick

A direct free kick is a free kick from which a score may be made directly. All opposing players must be stationed at least 10 yards from the ball until the kick has been made.

Direct free kicks are awarded when a player has fouled by: (1) touching the ball with his hands or arms, (2) holding, (3) pushing, (4) tripping, (5) using his hands on an opponent in an effort to reach the ball, or (6) charging from behind, or kicking an opponent. All direct free kicks are awarded from the point of the foul, except those that occur within the penalty area, which are awarded as a penalty kick.

Penalty Kick

A penalty kick is awarded when an opponent commits any foul that ordinarily results in a direct free kick— but the foul must be committed within the penalty area. The player is awarded the ball in the middle of the field, 12 yards from the goal. The goalie is the only defensive player who can attempt to prevent the kicker from scoring a goal.

In the women's game, a penalty kick scores one-point, while a field goal counts two points.

Indirect Free Kick

An indirect free kick is a free kick from which a score cannot be made directly; the ball must first touch another player. Again, all opposing players must be stationed at least 10 yards from the ball until the kick has been made.

Indirect free kicks are awarded when a defensive man has fouled by: (1) playing the ball twice before it has been played by another player on a kick-off, throw-in, penalty kick, corner kick, or free kick; (2) (a goalkeeper) carrying the ball more than four steps within the penalty area; (3) (a goalkeeper) failing to get rid of the ball within five seconds; (4) coaching from the sidelines; (5) offside; (6) ungentlemanly conduct; (7) disputing the decision of an official; (8) dangerous play; (9) (a coach or player) entering the field of play without permission from an official. All indirect free kicks are awarded at the point of violation.

Roll-in

In the women's game, a roll-in is used when fouls occur simultaneously or two opposing players simultaneously cause the ball to go out-of-bounds. The two opponents stand 5 yards apart and 5 yards away from the official as the official rolls the ball between them. All players must be at least 5 yards away from the ball.

SCORING

(1) In the men's game, each point value is one.
(2) In the women's game:
    a penalty kick is worth one point;
    a field goal is worth two points;
    the score of a defaulted game is 3-0.

EQUIPMENT

The personal equipment of a soccer player consists of a shirt, a pair of short pants, shin guards, long stockings, and soccer shoes.

SAFETY

1. A warm-up should be taken before any vigorous kicking is started.
2. Weak ankles should be wrapped.
3. The playing field should be free of rocks, holes, and obstructions.
4. If soccer shoes are worn, all players should wear shin guards.
5. When falling to the ground, learn to relax and roll to avoid injury.

FUNDAMENTALS

Kicking

Straight Instep Kick

The straight instep kick is the most important kick used in soccer, and the most difficult to master. As the ball lies on the ground the player should, with eyes focused on the ball: (1) leap into a position so that the foot opposite the kicking foot is placed alongside or even slightly forward of the ball; (2) swing the kicking leg backward into kicking position, with the leg and ankle relaxed, until the kick is started; (3) with the body leaning forward, bring the kicking leg forward. The kicking knee is over the ball, with the toe pointed downward, so that the instep (shoe laces) contacts the ball. The power of the instep kick comes from a final snap of the lower part of the leg; not from the hip.

Outside-of-Foot Kick

This kick is made with the action of the instep kick, except that the foot is turned inward so that the ball is contacted in the area of the small toe. This kick will cause a ball to curve. It is used for deception, shooting for the goal when a curve is necessary, and on corner kicks to utilize a curve ball.

Pivot-Instep Kick

The pivot-instep kick is executed with the action of the instep kick, except that the foot opposite the kicking foot is placed about 12 inches behind the ball; the kicking leg is swung in a circular motion from the hip; and the body is more erect and leaning slightly in the direction of intended flight of the ball. This kick is used to center the ball to the middle of the field and on corner kicks.

Volley Kick

A volley kick is a kick made while the ball is in the air or after it bounces. The ball is contacted with the instep, the knee over the ball and the body well balanced.

Half-Volley Kick

The instep contacts the ball on the bounce just at the moment it begins to rise (as in a football drop-kick).

Trapping

Trapping is used for getting control of a pass or loose ball by stopping it or changing the direction of the ball to the player's advantage.

Trapping a Rolling Ball

Sole of the Foot. As the ball approaches, the trapping foot is raised about 6 inches from the ground, with the knee slightly bent. The toe is raised higher than the heel, so that the rolling ball is wedged into the "V" formed between the sole of the foot and the ground.

Shin. As the ball approaches, the knees are bent slightly. As it rolls between the ankles and bent knees, the knees are pressed over the ball, wedging the ball between the shins and ground.

Deflection. The trapping foot is raised and turned inward or outward, so that the ball contacts the side of the foot, causing it to rebound in the desired direction.

Trapping a Bouncing Ball

Sole of the Foot. This is executed as a rolling ball trap, except that the sole of the trapping foot is over the ball as the ball touches the ground. The ball strikes the foot (*not* the foot strikes the ball) and the knees should be well over the ball, with the toe slightly higher than the heel.

Shin. Execute this as for a rolling ball trap, except that the knees are pressed over the ball just as the ball contacts the ground.

Side of the Foot. This is similar to the sole trap, except that the foot is turned inward or outward, as desired, and at right angles to the ball. The knee is bent and relaxed, and the foot "gives" with the ball.

Relaxed Leg. The trapping foot is off the ground, with the knee bent 90 degrees and the inside of the leg at right angles to the oncoming ball. The ball is contacted with the thigh or calf muscles, with the leg relaxed.

Chest or Stomach. The body is bent well forward at the waist, so that a pocket is formed between the shoulder and waist; as the ball contacts the stomach, a slight movement backward is given to absorb the impact of the ball.

Trapping Hints:

1. Keep your eyes on the ball until contact is made.
2. Let the ball contact you.
3. Trapped balls should not roll more than one stride away from you. Don't trap the ball for your opponent.
4. Give with the ball as it makes contact with you.

Dribbling

Dribbling is the progression of the ball by one player using a series of slight kicks in order to keep it under his control.

Dribbling is executed by using either the inside or outside of the foot, or a combination of both. The kicking can be done by alternate feet.

Heading

Heading is used when the ball is too high to play with the feet or body. The head may be used to pass, to clear the ball from the goal, to shoot for a goal, or to put the ball in a clear area where the player can get control of it.

The ball is usually hit with the forehead, not the top of the head. The direction of the ball when headed is governed by the point at which the head meets the ball. If the ball is hit near the horizontal axis, it will go down.

A distinct feature in the women's game is the use of *any* part of the hands or arms in playing the ball, in order to protect their breasts. Thus, if an arm is held at the side close to the body or over the breast, and the ball strikes the arm or hand, no foul is called.

Forward

The head is brought back and then forcefully forward, hitting the ball with the top of the forehead. The eyes must be on the ball as long as possible, as the follow-through with the head is made by pushing it forward away from the body with the neck muscles. Jumping into the air as the above is executed is sometimes a good maneuver when an opponent is also playing the ball, but better balance is maintained if the player stays on both feet and the weight is transferred to the forward foot as the ball is headed.

Sideward

The head is cocked to one side before thrusting it against the ball, and the ball is hit with the side of the forehead.

Backward

This is the same as the above, except that the ball is struck with the top of the head, causing the ball to rebound backward.

Passing

As in many other sports, passing in soccer is the most important factor in good team play, and is the art of giving the ball to another player on your team who is placed so he can do something useful with it.

Long Pass

As described in kicking, the long pass is executed with an instep kick. An occasional long pass can open up the play when the defense begins to check the short passes.

Short Pass

Inside of the Foot, or Push, Pass. The kicking foot is turned outward, so that the ball is met with the side of the foot between the big toe and the heel. The leg is swung from the hip, and the ball should be well under the body. Such a pass should have a sweeping follow-through with the leg, so that the ball will roll and not bounce. It is used for diagonal passes and for shooting at the goal when accuracy and not power is needed. It has a weakness, in that the direction of the pass is obvious to the opponents unless good deception is used. The ankle should be relaxed, the eyes kept on the ball, and the pass made ahead of the intended receiver before an opponent is too close.

Inside of the Foot Lob Pass. This is the same as the above, only it is used on a bouncing ball, as a short pass over an opponent's head, or to get the ball past a defensive player.

Outside of the Foot Lob Pass. This is also the same as the above, except that the foot is turned inward and the ball is flicked or pushed rather than kicked. This is a good deceptive pass.

Sole of the Foot Pass. The sole of the foot is placed lightly on top of the ball, and by a quick flexion of the knee the ball is rolled backward. It is used to pass backward; if executed on the run, the player must jump and make the play in the air. Make sure your teammate is there to receive the pass. It may also be used to prevent a ball from going out-of-bounds or as a dribbling tactic.

Heel Pass. This is another method of making a backward pass. The leg is merely swung backward from the hip, with the knee flexed, and the heel meets the ball.

Overhead Pass. The ball is kicked with the instep, near the top of the toes, by a sharp straightening of the knee and flexing of the ankle. The ball should be kept low, just over the opponent's head, as the body leans backward. It is a longer pass than the lobs.

Hints for the Passer:

1. Conceal the direction of the pass until the last moment.
2. Look for a receiver, and then keep the eyes on the ball while making the pass.
3. Always pass in front of the receiver.
4. Keep a ground pass on the ground by a good follow-through, and give it the correct amount of speed.

Hints for the Receiver:

1. Get in the clear.
2. Run to meet the ball.
3. Glance quickly around, and instantly decide what to do with the ball when you get the pass.
4. Keep the eyes on the ball while receiving.

Tackling

The defensive fundamental of attempting to secure the ball from an opponent by using your feet is called *tackling.* It should be remembered that a player does not always gain possession of the ball by virtue of a tackle, but that he has accomplished a form of defensive tactic if he stops the dribbler, forces the dribbler to lose control of the ball, or forces a poor pass by his opponent.

Two-Leg

The heels of both feet are together, with the knees turned outward, the body leaning forward. The ball is trapped with the legs as the shoulder forces the opponent off the ball; the tackle is followed up by stepping forward with one foot and securing the ball with the other. This tackle is effective when the opponent is not ready to dodge the tackle, when he has limited room to dodge, or when he is directly in front of the defensive player and near the ball.

One-Leg

The inside of the tackling foot is put against the ball as the body moves forward, and the ball is trapped with this foot and the lower leg. The other leg is backward and serves as a brace while the shoulder charge is delivered. As the tackle is executed, the backward leg steps forward as the ball is pulled forward with the trapping foot. If the tackle is made with the left foot, the left shoulder makes the charge. It is important to remember to face the opponent, and not use a cross-body block on him. This tackle is useful in forcing an opponent to pass or lose control of the ball, to stop an opponent's dribble, or when the defensive player is directly or diagonally in front of an opponent.

Sole of the Foot

The leg executing the tackle is placed with the sole of the foot upon the ball, with the leg straight out, just as the opponent attempts to contact the ball. The defensive player must be directly in front of the ball, with the body well balanced and his weight forward. This tackle is effective to block a kick, prevent an opponent from getting possession of the ball, or when the defensive player is in front of the opponent.

The Pivot

This tackle is executed in the same general manner as the one-leg tackle, except that the body is turned toward the opponent by pivoting on the foot that is not tackling. It is necessary to be well ahead of the dribbler to allow time for the pivot; the degree of the pivot will depend upon the angle of approach of the defensive player.

Charging

Charging is the defensive fundamental used by a player making shoulder contact with his opponent in such a manner that his opponent is forced off the ball. As the charge is executed, the foot nearest the dribbler steps toward the ball as the opponent's outside foot contacts the ground, and the other foot gains control of the ball. The arms should be held close to the body, with the top of the shoulder contacting the opponent, and the arms or shoulders should not be moved as the charge is made. It should be remembered that the charge must not be violent and the ball must be played; under no circumstances may the charge be made from behind the opponent, unless the opponent is intentionally obstructing.

Throw-in

When the ball is forced over the touch line by a player, the other team puts the ball back into play by a throw-in at the point where the ball crossed the touch line.

The player throwing the ball in may take a stationary position behind the touch line facing the field of play, with the feet about 12 to 16 inches apart, or he may approach the touch line with a short run or a few walking steps.

The Throw

Place the hands on the ball, with the fingers spread on the back surface of the ball at the horizontal axis. Carry the ball back to a position behind the head and neck, with the elbows pointing forward, the knees bent, and the trunk arched backward toward the hands. The forward thrust is then made with the knees extending, while the trunk is swung forward from the hips; the arms swing forward sharply in an arc over the head; then, with a snap of the wrists, the ball is released at a point in front of the head. It must be remembered that a part of each foot must be in contact with the ground throughout the action of the throw-in.

The throw-in should be used as an offensive weapon, and all players should realize that the basic strategy of a throw-in is to start an offensive movement. Thus, the ball should be thrown to: (a) a predetermined player, (b) a teammate who is moving toward or away from the throw-in; or (c) to the goalkeeper if your team is on defense near its own penalty area. The throw-in should always be made so that the receiver is able to trap or control the ball with little difficulty.

DRILLS

Kicking—The ball is kicked back and forth between two parallel lines 15 yards apart.

Trapping—One man is in the middle of a circle, with a 10-yard radius. The man in the middle throws the ball to the players in the circle, and traps are executed.

Heading—Use a circle with a 10-yard radius, with one man in the middle. The man in the middle throws the ball to players outside the circle and the ball is headed back to his feet.

Dribbling—Five obstacles are placed 5 yards apart. Each man dribbles in a weaving fashion through the obstacles and back.

Throw-in—The lines form 20 yards apart; each player executes a throw-in to his partner, who executes a leg trap.

All-purpose—Three players are in a circle, with a 20-yard radius. Two players try to keep the ball away from the third player. All must remain in the circle.

STRATEGY

Soccer is essentially a zone-type game, and all players should stay spread out and play the ball only when it enters their zone. The zone is easily set if the forward line divides the field into fifths, the halfback line into thirds, and the fullback line in half.

Offense

The two popular plans of attack are the "W" formation (Fig. 25-2) and the "M" formation (Fig. 25-3). The "W" formation is strong offensively at midfield, but weak defensively against a fast-breaking attack. The "M" formation is very effective when the insides are good shots, but its real strength is on defense.

Defense

The two popular systems of defense used in soccer are the *two-back* (the two fullbacks) and *three-back* (two fullbacks and center halfback) systems.

Guiding principles for the two-back system are: (1) the two fullbacks cover the inside forwards, picking them up about 10 yards outside the penalty area; (2) the wing halfbacks cover the opposing wings; (3) the center halfback covers the opposing center forward; (4) the inside forwards cover the opposing inside forwards through the midfield and back on defense until the fullbacks pick them up; (5) switches are necessary (a) when a wing breaks fast on a wing halfback—the fullback and halfback switch men, and (b) when the opposing center forward plays deep—one of the fullbacks covers him, and the center half covers the inside forward; (6) the forward line must work out of a very deep "W," with emphasis on fast breaks by the wings and center forward. This system is advocated for large, slow fullbacks.

The guiding principles for the three-back system are: (1) the two fullbacks cover the opposing wings; (2)

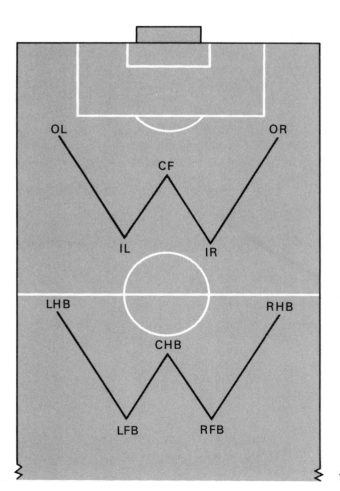

Fig. 25—2. The "W" formation.

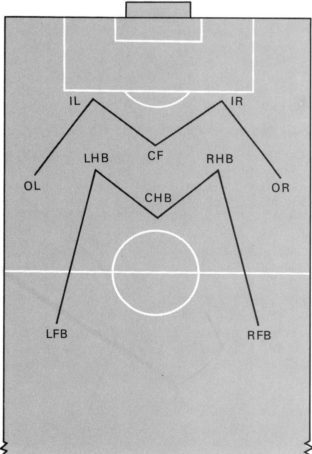

Fig. 25—3. The "M" formation.

the halfbacks cover the opposing inside forwards; (3) the center halfback covers the opposing center forward; (4) the emphasis is on offense as the wing halfbacks move up closely behind the inside forwards to create a seven-man line; (5) the three backs must play the opposing wings and center forward very closely. Fast backs are necessary for the success of the three-back system.

Basic Strategy Hints

1. Scores can be made from outside the penalty area; shoot often.
2. When in possession of the ball, advance until picked up by an opponent; then pass.
3. Spread the defense. The forwards should divide the width of the field into defensive fifths.
4. The three halfbacks should divide the field into thirds, while the fullbacks should divide it in half.
5. Forwards should keep in mind that back passing to the halfbacks opens up the defense.
6. The wing, inside forward, and halfbacks form a triangle combination that can use short passes effectively.
7. The goalkeeper should talk and guide his teammates on defense.
8. Use the throw-in as an offensive weapon; do not let your opponents get their defense set before you take the throw-in.

New Patterns of Play

The past ten years have seen the professional soccer teams of Europe and South America developing new patterns of attack and defense, with players distributed as follows:

1-3-3-4. One goalkeeper; a defensive line of three fullbacks; a supporting line of left halfback, inside right, and right halfback; a front line composed of left wing, inside left, center forward, and right wing.

1-3-3-3-1. One goalkeeper; a defensive line of three fullbacks; a halfback line of left halfback, inside left, and right halfback; a supporting line of left wing, inside right, and a right wing; a front line of a center forward.

1-3-1-3-3. One goalkeeper; a defensive line of three fullbacks; a middle left halfback who plays behind and to the right of the inside left and inside right; a supporting line of inside left, inside right who plays in the middle of the field, and right halfback; a front line of left wing, center forward, and right wing.

1-3-2-2-3. One goalkeeper; a defensive line of three fullbacks; a supporting defensive line of two halfbacks; a supporting line of inside left and inside right; a front line of left wing, center forward, and right wing.

1-4-2-4. One goalkeeper; a defensive line of four fullbacks; a supporting line of left and right halfbacks; a front line of left wing, two center forwards, and a right wing.

BIBLIOGRAPHY

Di Clemente, Frank F., *Soccer Illustrated*. New York: A.S. Barnes & Co., 1955.

Goldman, Howard, *Soccer*. Boston: Allyn and Bacon, Inc., 1969.

Official NCAA Soccer Guide. Phoenix, Ariz.: College Athletics Publishing Service, 349 East Thomas Road.

Official Soccer-Speedball Guide—DGWS. Washington, D.C.: American Association for Health, Physical Education and Recreation.

U.S. Naval Institute, *Soccer*. Annapolis: The Institute, 1953.

The most common position used in social dance is the *closed position*. The gentleman faces the lady and moves toward her, placing his right foot between the lady's feet, and his left foot a few inches outside his partner's right foot. The gentleman places his right hand firmly on the middle of his partner's back, keeping the fingers together. His right elbow is raised slightly to make contact with the lady's left arm. The gentleman's left arm is raised, so that the elbow is carried away from the body and gives the effect of being balanced with the right elbow. The fingers are held together, with the palm facing forward and slightly upward.

The lady places her left hand on the gentleman's right shoulder, so that her arm follows the line of her partner's right arm. She places the fingers of her right hand on the gentleman's palm and permits her thumb to curve around the base of her partner's thumb.

In this position, each dancer can look over his partner's right shoulder.

The directions given in this section are directed toward the gentleman. The lady moves with the opposite foot in the opposite direction. In a few instances, specific directions are given for the lady.

In all descriptions of social dances, the symbol "Q" represents the word "quick," and the symbol "S" represents the word "slow." Two "Q's" equal one "S."

Waltz

The waltz is done so that a step is taken to each beat of music. Essentially, a forward step is taken on the first or heavy beat of each measure. On the second beat, a side step is taken. On the third beat, the feet are brought together. With the exception of the hesitation steps, there is a weight change and step on every beat of music.

Basic Box Waltz (Fig. 26—1)

Forward Basic Step

Step Pattern	Time	Count
1. Step forward on left foot.	Q	1
2. Step diagonally forward on right foot.	Q	2
3. Close left foot to right foot.	Q	3

Backward Basic Step

4. Step backward on right foot.	Q	1
5. Step diagonally backward on left foot.	Q	2
6. Close right foot to left foot.	Q	3

Left Turn (Fig. 26—2)

Step Pattern	Time	Count
1. Step diagonally forward on left foot, pivoting one-quarter turn to the left.	Q	1
2. Step sideward on right foot.	Q	2
3. Close left foot to right foot.	Q	3
4. Step diagonally backward on right foot, pivoting one-quarter turn to the left.	Q	1

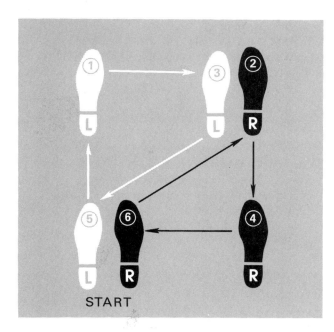

Fig. 26—1. Basic box waltz.

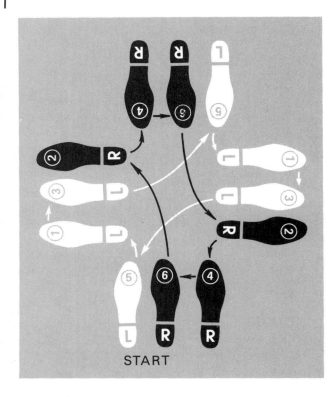

Fig. 26–2. Left turn—waltz.

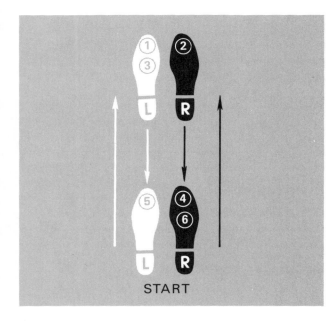

Fig. 26–3. Hesitation—waltz.

Step Pattern	Time	Count
5. Step sideward on left foot.	Q	2
6. Close right foot to left foot.	Q	3

Repeating the two steps above will return the dancer to the starting position.

Hesitation (Fig. 26–3)

Step Pattern	Time	Count
1. Step forward on left foot.	Q	1
2. Bring right foot up to left foot without exchanging weight.	Q	2
3. Hold above position.	Q	3
4. Step backward on right foot.	Q	1
5. Bring left foot back to right foot without exchanging weight.	Q	2
6. Hold above position.	Q	3

Fox Trot

The fox trot is considered to be a walking step that employs a series of slow and quick steps. By definition, a slow step takes two beats of music and a quick step takes one beat of music. Although these steps can be used in any combination, a consistent rhythm pattern adds to ease of leading and following.

Forward Fox Trot (Closed Position) (Fig. 26–4)

Step Pattern	Time	Count
1. Step forward on left foot.	S	1,2
2. Step forward on right foot.	S	3,4
3. Step diagonally forward on left foot.	Q	1
4. Close right foot up to left foot.	Q	2

Backward Fox Trot (Closed Position) (Fig. 26–5)

Step Pattern	Time	Count
1. Step backward on left foot.	S	1,2
2. Step backward on right foot.	S	3,4
3. Step diagonally backward on left foot.	Q	1
4. Close right foot backward to left foot.	Q	2

Sideward Fox Trot (Closed Position) (Fig. 26–6)

Step Pattern	Time	Count
1. Step in place on left foot.	S	1,2
2. Step in place on right foot.	S	3,4
3. Step to left on left foot.	Q	1
4. Close right foot up to left foot.	Q	2

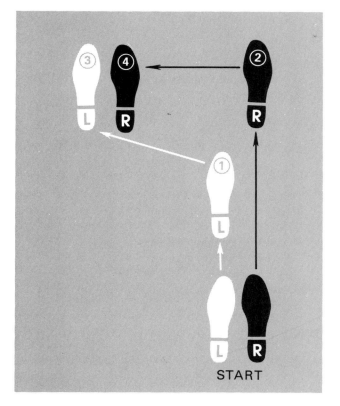

Fig. 26—4. Forward fox trot.

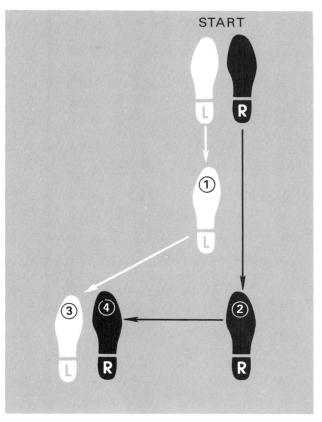

Fig. 26—5. Backward fox trot.

Open or Conversation Fox Trot (Open Position)

The man's right side and the lady's left side are adjacent, and both face the same direction. The man indicates this position from the closed position by applying pressure to his partner's back with the heel of the right hand and a slight forward push with his left hand. The lady then drops the right side of her body backward, remaining close to her partner with the left side.

The step is executed as a forward step. When the man steps on the left foot, the lady steps on the right foot; when the man steps on the right foot, the lady steps on the left foot.

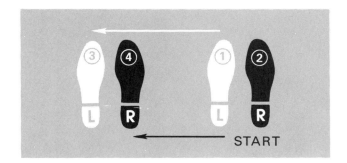

Fig. 26—6. Sideward fox trot.

Dip (Closed Position) (Fig. 26—7)

Step Pattern	Time	Count
1. Man: Steps back on left foot, pointing it at about a 45-degree angle. The knee is bent and the back is held erect.	S	1,2

Woman: Steps forward on right foot, bends the knee which is just inside of the man's knee.

	Time	Count
2. Step forward on right foot.	S	3,4
3. Step forward on left foot.	Q	1
4. Close right foot up to left foot.	Q	2

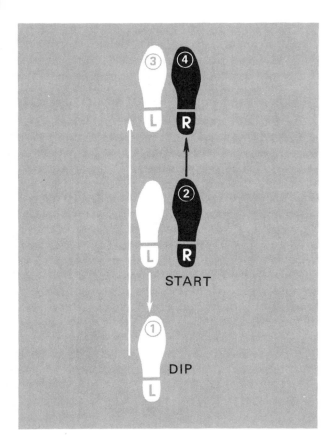

Fig. 26—7. Dip—fox trot.

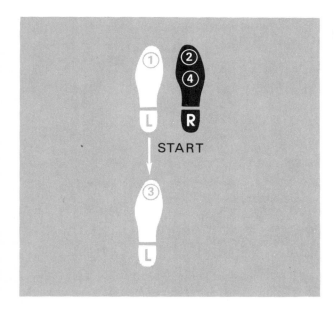

Fig. 26—8. Jitterbug.

Jitterbug or Lindy (Fig. 26—8)

Step Pattern	Time	Count
1. Step in place on left foot.	S	1,2
2. Step in place on right foot.	S	3,4
3. Step back on left foot.	Q	1
4. Step in place on right foot.	Q	2

Triple Lindy (Fig. 26—9)

Step Pattern	Time	Count
1. Step to the left on left foot.		
2. Step to the left on right foot.	S	1,2
3. Step in place on left foot.		
4. Step to the right on right foot.		
5. Step to the right on left foot.	S	3,4
6. Step in place on right foot.		
7. Step back on left foot.	Q	1
8. Step in place on right foot.	Q	2

LATIN AMERICAN DANCES

Samba

The samba is the liveliest of the ballroom dances having a fast tempo. In doing the forward step, the head and trunk lean backward; in doing the backward step, the head and trunk lean forward. The dancers execute the steps with a light and springy action.

Basic Box Step (Fig. 26—10)

Step Pattern	Time	Count
1. Step forward on left foot.	Q	1
2. Close right foot up to left foot.	Q	&
3. Step in place on left foot.	S	2&
4. Step backward on right foot.	Q	1
5. Close left foot back to right foot.	Q	&
6. Step in place on right foot.	S	2&

Walking Step (Fig. 26—11)

Step Pattern	Time	Count
1. Step forward on left foot.	Q	1
2. Step in place on ball of right foot.	Q	&
3. Step in place on left foot.	S	2&
4. Step forward on right foot.	Q	1
5. Step in place on ball of left foot.	Q	&
6. Step in place on right foot.	S	2&

As the step forward is made on the left foot, the left shoulder is brought forward. The left elbow is raised

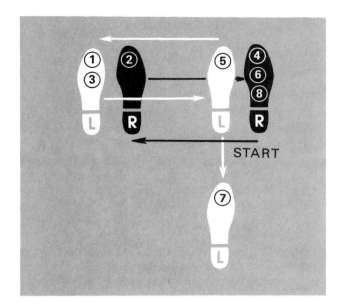

Fig. 26—9. Triple lindy.

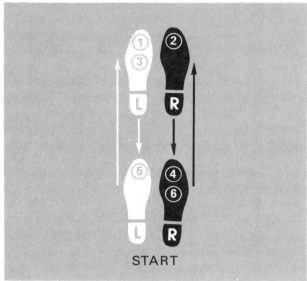

Fig. 26—10. Samba basic box step.

to shoulder height and rests on the back of the right hand. As the step forward is made on the right foot, the right shoulder is brought forward. The right elbow is raised to shoulder height and rests on the back of the left hand.

Rumba

The rumba is characterized by short steps, with the feet flat on the floor, and accompanied by a subtle swaying of the hips. Before attempting to learn the rumba step itself, one should learn the action of the hips.

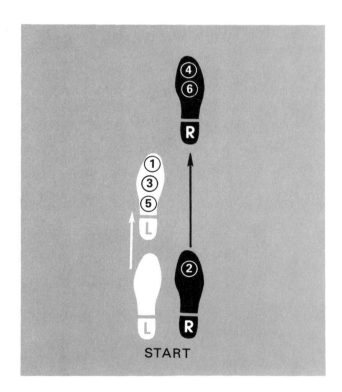

Fig. 26—11. Samba walking step.

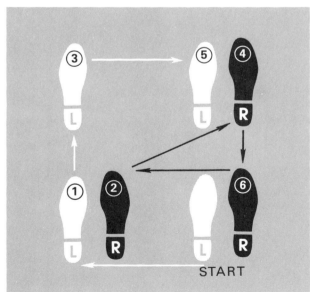

Fig. 26—12. Rumba basic step.

Rumba Motion

1. Shift the body weight to the heel of the left foot, permitting the left hip to be higher than the right hip.
2. Shift the body weight to the heel of the right foot, permitting the right hip to be higher than the left hip.

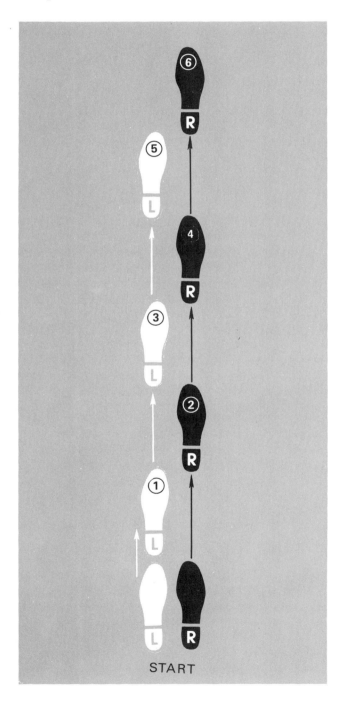

Fig. 26—13. Rumba walking step.

Basic Box Step (Fig. 26—12)

Step Pattern	Time	Count
1. Step sideward on left foot.	Q	1
2. Close right foot up to left foot.	Q	2
3. Step forward on left foot and hold.	S	3,4
4. Step diagonally forward on right foot.	Q	1
5. Close left foot up to right foot.	Q	2
6. Step backward on right foot and hold.	S	3,4

Walking Step (Fig. 26—13)

Step Pattern	Time	Count
1. Step forward on left foot.	Q	1
2. Step forward on right foot.	Q	2
3. Step forward on left foot and hold.	S	3,4
4. Step forward on right foot.	Q	1
5. Step forward on left foot.	Q	2
6. Step forward on right foot and hold.	S	3,4

Tango

The tango is executed in a slow and deliberate manner. This motion can be described as a stalking motion or a stop-and-go movement.

Basic Step (Fig. 26—14)

Step Pattern	Time	Count
1. Step forward on left foot.	S	1 &
2. Step forward on right foot.	S	2 &
3. Step forward on left foot.	Q	1
4. Step diagonally forward on right foot.	Q	&
5. Close left foot up to right foot, keeping weight on right foot.	S	2 &

Open Step

(Steps 1 and 2 are done in open position, as explained in the fox trot section.)

Step Pattern	Time	Count
1. Step forward on left foot.	S	1 &
2. Step forward on right foot.	S	2 &
3. Step forward on left foot. The man brings his partner around in front of him to a closed position.	Q	1
4. Step diagonally forward on right foot.	Q	&
5. Close left foot up to right foot, keeping weight on right foot.	S	2&

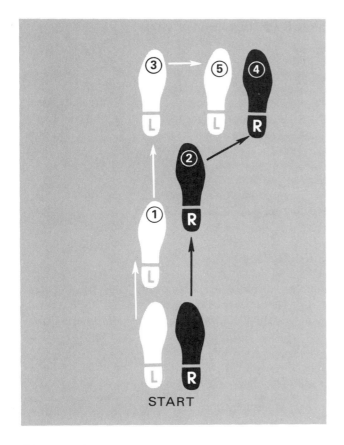

Fig. 26—14. Tango basic step.

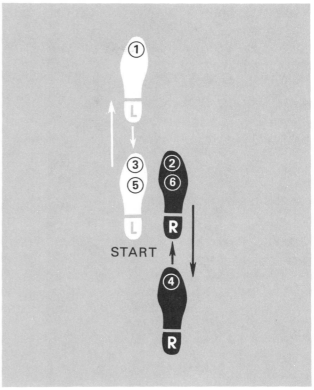

Fig. 26—15. Mambo basic step.

Mambo

The mambo has been described as the "jitterbug of the rumba." In dancing the mambo, the body action is not restricted to any particular motion, since the dancer moves to a syncopated type of rumba music.

Basic Step (Fig. 26—15)

Step Pattern	Time	Count
1. Step forward on left foot.	Q	1
2. Step in place on right foot.	Q	2
3. Step back on left foot.	S	3,4
4. Step back on right foot.	Q	1
5. Step in place on left foot.	Q	2
6. Step forward on right foot.	S	3,4

Side Step (Fig. 26—16)

Step Pattern	Time	Count
1. Step sideward on left foot.	Q	1
2. Step in place on right foot.	Q	2

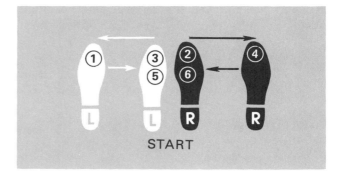

Fig. 26—16. Mambo side step.

3. Close left foot up to right foot.	S	3,4
4. Step sideward on right foot.	Q	1
5. Step in place on left foot.	Q	2
6. Close right foot up to left foot.	S	3,4

Cha Cha Cha

The cha cha cha is based on the mambo step, with the dancer executing three steps to the slow count rather

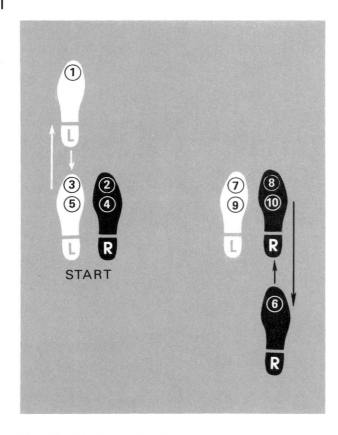

Fig. 26—17. Basic cha cha cha.

Basic Step (Fig. 26—17)

Step Pattern	Time	Count
1. Step forward on left foot.	Q	1
2. Step in place on right foot.	Q	2
3. Step back in place on left foot.		3
4. Step in place on right foot.	S {	&
5. Step in place on left foot.		4
6. Step backward on right foot.	Q	1
7. Step in place on left foot.	Q	2
8. Step back in place on right foot.		3
9. Step in place on left foot.	S {	&
10. Step in place on right foot.		4

BIBLIOGRAPHY

Fletcher, Beale, *How to Improve Your Social Dancing.* New York: A.S. Barnes & Co., 1956.

Heaton, Alma, and Heaton, Israel, *Ballroom Dance Rhythms.* Dubuque, Iowa: William C. Brown Co., 1958.

Hostetler, Lawrence A., *Walk Your Way to Better Dancing.* New York: A.S. Barnes & Co., 1952.

Kraus, Richard G., and Sadlo, Cola, *Beginning Social Dance.* Belmont, Calif.: Wadsworth Publishing Co., Inc., 1964.

Turner, Margery J., *Dance Handbook.* Englewood Cliffs, N.J.: Prentice-Hall, Inc., 1959.

Waglow, I.F., *Social Dance for Students and Teachers.* Dubuque, Iowa: William C. Brown Co., 1953.

Whites, Betty, *Ballroom Dancebook for Teachers.* New York: David McKay Co., Inc., 1962.

than holding the count. The tempo of the cha cha cha is slower than the mambo, and the rhythm section accents the dancer's slow count with three distinct beats.

The game of softball originated from the need of professional baseball players to practice and keep in condition during the winter months. They played the game indoors.

About 1930 interest and participation led to a rapid growth in the United States, as a result of amateur players starting to play outdoors. In 1933 the Amateur Softball Association was formed, and today, the Association and the International Joint Rules Committee on Softball make up the governing body for the game. Sectional tournaments and a "softball world series" are held annually in the United States.

The American Physical Education Association adopted softball for girls and women in 1927, when Gladys Palmer drew up the rules for the National Section for Girls' and Women's Sports (now **DGWS**). Softball is one of the few team sports which lends itself to informal corecreational settings or to both men and women with a variety of skill and experience levels.

Much of the popularity of softball is due to its wide sponsorship by industrial concerns, businesses, churches, and city and county recreation departments. Additionally, the game is played by ever-increasing numbers of women's teams.

TERMINOLOGY

Assist—Credit awarded to each player handling the ball in any play that results in a runner being put out.

Batting average—The batter's number of turns at bat divided by the number of his hits.

Double—A two-base hit.

Double play—Two outs resulting from one continuous action.

Earned run—The point scored by a runner who arrived safely at first base other than on an error.

Error—An avoidable misplay of the ball resulting in base advancement or a lengthier batting life.

Fielder's choice—The option of the fielder to retire a base runner other than the hitter.

Hot corner—Third base.

Infield fly—A high ball hit into the infield.

Inning—One of the seven divisions of the game, in which both teams have offensive turns. (Professional baseball, on the other hand, employs nine innings—or more, if the score is tied after nine innings.)

Keystone sack—Second base.

Line drive—An aerial ball hit directly into the infield.

No-hitter—A game with no safe hits by one or both teams.

Sacrifice—A bunt, hit, or fly intended to advance the base runner, with the hitter subjecting himself to being put out.

Single—A one-base hit.

Squeeze play—The third base runner coming home on a bunt.

Stolen base—Advance of a base runner unaided by a hit, error, or put-out.

Triple—A three-base hit.

RULES

For detailed rules governing the game of softball, reference should be made to the book of official softball rules published by the International Joint Rules Committee on Softball.

The game of softball is actually a modification of the game of baseball, and therefore the rules are generally the same for both games.

Basic rule differences governing play involve:

1. *The delivery of a pitch*—in softball, the pitcher must use an *underarm* motion. The pitching arm must move straight forward past the body, with the hand below the hip and not farther from the body than the elbow.
2. *Base runner*—the base runner is entitled to advance only after the ball has left the pitcher's hand in his delivery of a pitch. If he steps off a base any time prior to the release, he is declared out.
3. *Strikes* occur when a:
   batter swings and misses a pitched ball.

pitched ball is delivered over home plate between the top of the knees and the armpits of the batter.

batter, with less than two strikes, is hit by his own batted ball.

fly foul ball is not caught, with less than two strikes on the batter.

foul tip remaining lower than the head of the batter is caught by the catcher.

4. *Balls* occur when balls:

are pitched so as not to go over the plate in the strike zone and the batter does not swing.

touch the ground before reaching home plate.

are pitched illegally.

5. *Fair balls* are balls:

touching or settling in fair ground in the infield.

touching first, second, or third base.

landing in fair territory in the outfield between the lines from home to first base and home to third base.

traveling on or over fair ground and settling behind a fence or in the stand at a distance of more than 200 feet.

going out of the infield on fair ground.

6. *Foul balls* are balls:

settling in foul territory before reaching either first or third base.

first touching foul beyond first or third base.

bounding past first or third base on or over foul ground.

7. *A batter is out* when:

a fly ball is caught.

a third strike is caught by the catcher.

there are three strikes, less than two outs, and a runner on first base.

he swings and misses the third strike and the ball touches him.

he bunts foul after the second strike.

a foul ball is legally caught.

an infield fly is hit with runners on first and second base or on first, second, and third base with less than two outs.

8. *A runner is out* when:

he is touched with the ball by a fielder before he reaches base.

first base is tagged by a fielder with the ball before the runner reaches base, or when he is not in contact with the base.

he causes interference with a player fielding the ball.

he runs more than 3 feet outside a base line.

he is forced out at a base.

he passes another runner.

he leaves his base before the ball leaves the pitcher's hand.

he fails to return to the base before the ball, following a fair fly ball that is caught.

he is hit by a directly batted fair ball while off-base.

PLAYING AREA

The playing area, commonly called the "diamond," is in fact a 60-foot square, with the bases located within the corners of the square. (Fig. 27-1)

The distance from home plate to the pitcher's plate is 46 feet for men, and 40 feet for women.

The batter's box is 3 feet by 7 feet (there is one on each side of home plate), the inside lines being 6 inches from home plate. The front line is 4 feet in front of the center of home plate.

The entire playing area should be as smooth and even as possible, with no obstructions that might interfere with a ball or player.

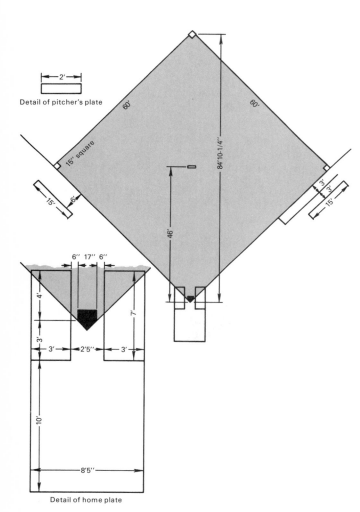

Fig. 27—1. Softball playing area.

The bases are 15 inches square. The pitcher's plate is 6 inches by 24 inches. Home plate is 17 inches wide.

EQUIPMENT

Bat. The softball bat is a single piece of round wood not more than 34 inches in length and not more than 2-1/8 inches in diameter at its largest part.

Ball. The softball is between 11-7/8 inches and 12-1/8 inches in circumference, and weighs between 6 and 6-3/4 ounces. The cover is leather and is filled with Kapok or a mixture of rubber and cork.

Gloves. Softball gloves are made of leather, usually with a larger pocket than a baseball glove. The connecting leather thong between the thumb and forefinger must not measure more than 4 inches.

Mask. The catcher should always wear a protective mask. It is usually a leather-covered metal frame with horizontal metal bars across the front, allowing good vision.

SAFETY

Situations that demand caution in order to prevent injury include the following:

Base Running. Base runners must be skilled in sliding into base, to prevent leg and arm injuries. They must also avoid colliding with defensive players at bases.

Batting. The cardinal safety rule for batters to observe is: *Never lose control of the bat.* The bat should always be dropped, not released during the swing.

Fielding Fly Balls. Players fielding fly balls must use caution to prevent colliding with each other, and also to prevent running into fences or walls surrounding the playing area.

Fielding Ground Balls. Defensive players should always play hard hit ground balls with the gloved hand. This will prevent finger injuries to bare hands.

BASIC SKILLS

Throwing a Ball

There are several steps in the throwing process which must be integrated into one smooth, coordinated motion.

The body faces approximately at a right angle to the target. The ball is held in the throwing hand, and the eyes are on the target.

The sequence of steps is:

1. The ball is brought back below hip level.
2. The body begins to turn toward the target.
3. The throwing hand comes to shoulder level, with the wrist extended; the opposite arm and body weight move toward the target. The lead foot points at the target.
4. The throwing arm moves toward the target, with the elbow leading until it reaches the shoulder line. At this point the forearm extends toward the target, the wrist flexes quickly, the **fingers extend, and the** ball is released at shoulder height.

Catching a Ball

The following factors are involved in catching a ball:

1. The eyes should follow the flight of the ball until it is caught in the glove.
2. If possible, the body should be directly in the path of the ball.
3. If the ball is caught above waist height, the thumbs are inward, toward each other. If the ball is caught below waist height, the thumbs point away from each other.
4. When the ball hits the glove, the ungloved hand covers the ball.
5. The glove should be moving in the same direction as the ball when contact is made, thus cushioning the impact and helping to prevent the ball from bouncing out of the glove.

DEFENSIVE PLAY

In defensive play, the players should be alert to the movements of each other, so as to function as a unit. At all times they should be ready to back up a teammate in any playing situation.

Infield

The two essential skills of infielders are fielding ground balls and throwing to a base.

Fielding Ground Balls:

1. Practice getting into the path of the ball rapidly, keeping the body in front of the ball.
2. Learn to start the catch with the glove low, and come up to meet the ball. This prevents the ball from going under the glove and into the outfield.

Throwing the Ball to a Base:

1. The most important factor involved is that of knowing which base will be the target before the ball is actually caught. There is not sufficient time after the ball is caught to decide where the target is.
2. Infielders must be able to throw from a variety of body positions without taking an extra step. This is especially true if a player must go very far to either side and does not have time to set himself in a favorable body position for this catching-throwing motion.

Infield Positions

First Base. Because in softball base runners are not allowed to leave the base prior to the delivery of a pitch, the first baseman assumes his defensive position about 3 yards from his base toward second base. Usually he stands about 2 yards behind a line from first to second base. In the event a left-handed batter is hitting, the first baseman moves closer to the first base line.

The defensive stance is:

1. The feet are about shoulder width apart, with the weight evenly distributed.
2. The body is slightly flexed at the knees and hips, with the head up and the back straight.
3. The body must be free to move quickly in any direction—especially toward first base, where most of the first baseman's defensive plays are made.

Second Base. The second baseman assumes his defensive position to the left of second base, about 5 yards toward first base.

The defensive position is assumed according to the position of base runners. If first base is occupied, the second baseman must be ready for a defensive play to second base in case the ball is hit on the ground to an infielder. He must also be ready to relay the ball to first base.

The second baseman must be able to move to his right to field ground balls hit over the pitcher's plate, and then throw to first base.

Shortstop. The shortstop plays between second and third bases, slightly closer to second base. His usual defensive position is deep, about 4 or 5 yards behind a line drawn from second to third base.

He assumes the defensive stance as the pitch is about to be delivered.

Third Base. The third baseman assumes his defensive position about 4 yards inside the third base line and 4 yards behind a line drawn from third base to second.

If third base is occupied, the third baseman is in the most important defensive position to assist in preventing a score by the offensive team. The distance from home plate to third base is quite short, and many right-hand hitters pull their hits sharply toward third base. Thus the third baseman should play his position fairly deep, so he will have time to react and play sharply hit balls.

If a bunt situation is apparent, the third baseman must advance his defensive position closer to the third base line and just in front of a line drawn from second base to third base.

General:

1. All infielders must be skilled in being able to keep a foot touching the base while catching the ball. This is especially true of the first baseman, who executes this skill for the majority of put-outs made in the infield.
2. When a play will be made to first base, the first baseman should be astride the base on the inside. If the ball comes directly to him, he can move either foot back to the base. If the throw is to his right, he steps in that direction with his right foot, touching the base with his left foot. If the throw is to his left, he steps in that direction with his left foot, touching the base with his right foot.

Outfield

For defensive purposes, the outfield is divided into three areas, each one assigned to an outfielder.

The *right fielder* plays in what is the right side of the outfield as viewed from home plate. He has the longest throw from his position to halt the advance of base runners.

The *center fielder* plays the deepest outfield position, on approximately a line drawn from home plate through second base. He should be the fastest runner because he has the greatest area to cover.

The *left fielder* plays in what is the left side of the outfield as viewed from home plate. He will handle more balls hit through the infield, so he must be able to field ground balls; have a quick, accurate throw to the infield; and handle many of the fly balls hit to the outfield.

All outfielders must be careful to assume a position from which they can see every player on the field, especially the batter.

The primary skills of the outfielder are: catching fly balls, returning the ball to the infield rapidly and accurately, and backing up plays being made in the infield.

1. The most important skill an outfielder must attain is catching fly balls. An outfielder must watch every playing situation as it develops. He must be able to cover his field rapidly, getting under the ball quickly. He must be in motion as soon as the ball is hit, judging accurately how deeply the ball will travel into the outfield.

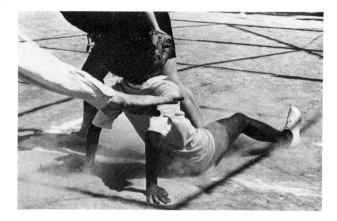

2. Outfielders must know where the ball should be thrown before it is actually caught, and be able to throw the ball a great distance in a straight line.
3. In case an infielder lets the ball get through his position, an outfielder must be in position to field the ball and thus prevent base runners from advancing.

Pitching

The softball pitch begins with the pitcher facing the batter squarely, with both feet in contact with the pitcher's plate. The ball is held in both hands, in front of the body.

Start the forward movement of the body with the left foot striding toward home plate. As the body movement starts forward, the ball is released by the gloved hand. The pitching arm, in an extended position, begins a forward and upward motion. The pitching arm continues a full circle movement, coming down and then directly under the right shoulder.

Speed is imparted to the ball by flexing the wrist sharply as the hand passes the right thigh below the hip as the ball is released.

The softball pitcher must have all the skills of a baseball pitcher: control, speed, and variety.

1. The primary skill of the pitcher is to pitch the ball across the strike zone without letting the batter hit it. This demands ability to put the ball across the corners of the plate, which makes it difficult for the batter to hit the ball squarely.
2. Most successful softball pitchers have an extremely fast ball as their most effective weapon. The fast ball takes only a fraction of a second to reach the plate, making it difficult for batters to decide whether it will cross the strike zone, then get the bat in motion and contact the ball. The decisive factor in a fast-ball pitch is a hand-wrist snap as the ball is released.
3. Variety in the speed and direction of the pitch is a distinct advantage, assuming the pitcher can control his pitching.
4. Different types of pitches are called fast balls, curves, knuckleballs, and change-of-pace balls. The grip on the ball determines which way it is likely to travel, and variety is attained by varying the way the ball is released.

The grip for a *fast ball* or *curve* is essentially the same. The index and middle fingers are on the bottom seam, and the thumb is on the top seam. The other two fingers are bent toward the palm along the ball. To release a fast-ball pitch, the palm is turned toward the pitcher and the ball rolls off the tip of the index finger last. For the out curve, the palm is turned down and away from the pitcher, and the thumb and index finger impart a spin to the left.

A *knuckleball* is held with the extended thumb and little finger, the other three fingers being bent sharply so that the fingernails are wholly against the ball. The ball is released with the palm up.

A *change-of-pace ball* can be any of the above grips and releases, the only exception being that the pitching motion is slowed or stopped as the hand passes the thigh and the ball travels slowly toward home plate. An important element is that the pitcher must deliver every pitch with the same preliminary motion, thus preventing the batter from anticipating the type of pitch from variations in the pitching motions.

Catching

The several responsibilities of the catcher are: To catch every pitch delivered by the pitcher; to direct the defensive play and strategy employed by the team; to know the weaknesses of all the opposing batters and call for appropriate pitches.

1. The catcher uses a special mitt and, in a squatting position behind the batter, calls for and catches pitches delivered by the pitcher. He must have quick reflexes, ability to throw accurately to any base, and be fleet enough to back up plays made at first and third bases.
2. The catcher is in the best position to direct the play of the defensive team. Because he knows the characteristics of each batter, and knows what type of pitch will be delivered and where, he can indicate changes of position for defensive players.
3. The most important defensive function performed is that of the catcher, when he directs the type of pitch to be delivered and sets his mitt as a target for the pitcher.

OFFENSIVE PLAY

Offensive play depends upon the ability of the player to get "on base"; and when he gets there, to run the bases.

Batting

Batting is the major offensive weapon of a softball team. Batting skill depends upon ability to hit a pitched ball that passes across any part of the strike zone.

The batter should assume a comfortable stance in the batter's box, facing the plate. He holds the bat near the handle end, with his hands at about shoulder level. The bat must be held in a position from which it may be swung horizontally in order to meet the ball as it crosses the strike zone.

The most important things the batter must do are: get the ball in his vision as soon as possible; decide whether or not the ball will cross the strike zone and, if so, get the bat into motion. This sequence takes approximately one-half second or less, and therefore the batter must establish a smoothly coordinated motion which is triggered reflexly. Experience in hitting against a number of different pitchers helps to develop ability at the plate.

Throughout the swing, the weight is evenly distributed between both feet. If a stride is taken, the new foot position becomes the base of the shoulder and hip turn, and consequently of the center of gravity.

Most common errors in batting include: "chopping" or swinging downward at the ball (this often results in hitting the bottom part of the ball, which in turn means an easily caught fly ball); not looking at the ball from the time it leaves the pitcher's hand until it enters the strike zone; not being ready to swing when the pitch is delivered; starting the swing too quickly and not being able to "hold up"; and finally, swinging too hard.

A specialized type of batting called "bunting" is sometimes used. As the pitch is delivered, the top hand slides up the bat and the bat is held out to meet the ball. At the time the ball meets the bat, the batter must still be in the batter's box, but should be beginning his move toward first base.

Base Running

Once a batter has reached first base safely he is considered a base runner, and becomes a potential scoring player. Base running skills include: ability to start and stop rapidly, running fast, sliding, and an intimate knowledge of all possibilities within the rules to advance one or more bases.

In softball, because the base runner must stay on the base until the ball leaves the pitcher's hand, he must be able to sprint from a still position on a base to advance safely to the next base.

There are several ways to slide into a base safely. The most common is the *hook slide*. This allows the base runner to touch the base while staying a maximum distance from the defensive baseman. The hook slide should be made to the side opposite that on which the ball arrives. If the left foot is to touch the base, the left leg is flexed fully at the knee and extended at the ankle. The opposite leg is extended at the knee and the body leans away from the base.

The straight-in slide is made with one leg flexed under the body so that if, during the slide, the base runner decides to straighten and continue running, he can do so by extending the flexed leg.

Base runners are guided by the base coaches. Hand signals indicate whether the base runner is to slide, slide and stand up (get up immediately), stand up to the base (don't slide), make the turn and stop, or keep going to the next base.

STRATEGY

The outcome of a softball game is often determined by the strategy employed. Offensive strategy is basically a plan for getting runs, while defensive strategy is a plan for preventing the opponents from getting runs.

Strategy is frequently based on the unexpected, and consequently, does not always produce the desired results.

Offensive

The most important element of offensive strategy is to push base runners around to second and third base as rapidly as possible. This puts them in scoring position. When men are on first and third bases with one or no outs, for example, the man on first can often advance to second quickly, because on a slow or bad throw to second the runner on third may score.

A *hit and run* is a means of advancing a base runner by having the batter hit a certain pitch. At the signal, the runner starts at the pitch; if the hit is a single, the runner may be able to advance two bases.

A *sacrifice fly* is called for when a runner on third represents a crucial run with one or no outs. The batter attempts to hit the ball deep into the outfield.

Once the ball is caught, the runner sprints for home plate.

A *sacrifice bunt* means that the batter must bunt the ball in order to advance a runner already on base. If the batter is also a fast runner, this strategy is increased in value because the defensive players have less time to decide and act; thus the situation may end with two base runners instead of only one.

A *squeeze play* is a bunt situation when the offensive team needs a crucial run and has a man on third base. The batter bunts the ball, and the runner on third starts toward home plate as the ball leaves the pitcher's hand.

Defensive

In softball, the main concern of the defensive team is to make three outs as quickly as possible before the offensive team can score.

The Double Play. The double play usually involves the first and second basemen and the shortstop.

If first base is occupied, a ground ball hit to the infield forces the base runner to advance to second base. This makes possible a force-out at both second base and first base.

If the shortstop fields the ground ball, the second baseman makes the put-out at second base by taking the throw from the shortstop as he crosses the base. To avoid contact with the base runner, he steps on second base, takes one step toward third base, pivots, and throws to first base. When the shortstop must go to his right to field the ball, the additional time may necessitate the second baseman eliminating the step after he touches the base. This means that the second baseman must pivot in the air and make the throw at the same time.

If the second baseman fields the ball, the shortstop must make the put-out by taking the throw, stepping on and across second base, pivoting, and throwing to first base.

If the shortstop is right-handed, the pivot and throw is difficult to master if he steps toward right field. The relay is much easier if the shortstop has time to approach second base on the inside, on the pitcher's plate side. The touch is made with the left foot as the throw is made.

All members of the defensive team must be alert to every situation as it develops. The defensive situation changes with each pitch, each out, the number and location of men on base, the number of runs scored, the inning, and depends on which batters will come to bat in a particular inning.

Infielders must play deep or close in, depending on the kind of batter they are defending against. Outfielders must know at all times where base runners are and where they must throw a ball that is hit over their head or a ground ball that gets through the infield. If outfielders know that a particular batter usually hits to left field, they shift their positions to allow for this hitting pattern.

SCORING

The score is recorded by innings, with a final score totaled at the end of the game. One point or run is scored each time a runner rounds first, second, third, and then home bases in a legal procedure.

The team with the highest number of runs at the close of the game is declared the winner.

SLOW-PITCH SOFTBALL

The rules established by the International Joint Rules Committee on Softball are the most commonly used rules for slow-pitch softball.

The major rule differences are:

1. The pitcher must deliver the ball with moderate speed *underhanded*, below the hip, with an arch of at least 3 feet prior to reaching home plate.
2. Ten players constitute a team. A short fielder is added between center field and second base.
3. The batter is called out if he bunts or chops the ball.
4. Stolen bases are illegal.
5. Gloves and mitts are not used if a larger than official-sized ball is used.

BIBLIOGRAPHY

Amateur Softball Association, *Softball Rules (12"—fast and slow pitch)*. Newark, N.J.: The Association.
Kneer, Marian, Lipinski, Dan, and Walsh, Jimmy, *Softball, Instructor's Guide*. Chicago: The Athletic Institute, 1953.
Norden, Arthur T., *Softball*. New York: A.S. Barnes & Co., 1947.
Softball Rules—DGWS. Washington, D.C.: American Association for Health, Physical Education and Recreation.
Umpires Protective Association of Chicago, *Softball Rules (16")*. Chicago: The Association.

Marjorie A. Larsen of Stockton, California experimented for nearly ten years to develop a lead-up game to hockey. Speed-a-way was developed as this lead-up activity, and stands as a vigorous, competitive, and skillful game for all levels of ability. Many girls have the need to play a game entailing football skills, which can be fulfilled through this activity. Speed-a-way has been introduced in Canada, England, and India in addition to the United states.

TERMINOLOGY

Aerial ball—A ball which may be legally passed, run with, kicked, or reconverted to a ground ball.

Blocking—The use of the body to change the progress of the ball. The goalkeeper may use his hands on a ground ball.

Dribble—A succession of controlled kicks used in advancing the ball.

Dropkick—A ball dropped and kicked by the player as it strikes the ground.

Field-goal—Any attacking player kicking a ground ball or executing a dropkick from within the striking circle causing the ball to pass between the goalposts below the crossbar.

Free kick—Any opportunity, usually following a foul which has been committed against the kicker, to kick or lift the ball with all other players at least 5 yards away.

Holding the ball—Maintaining possession of an aerial ball for longer than 3 seconds.

Penalty corner—An award to the attacking team when a foul is committed by the defending team in its own striking circle.

Place kick—Kicking the ball from a stationary ground position with no use of the hands.

Punt—A ball kicked after being dropped by a player and prior to touching the ground.

Shouldering—Volleying a ball with the front, top, or back of the shoulder.

Tagging—A defending player placing one or both hands on the back of the offensive player carrying the ball. A legal tag results in a free kick for the tagger.

Tie ball—A ball caught and held by two opponents simultaneously. A toss-up follows.

Trapping—Stopping and gaining control of the ball using a foot, leg or legs, and the ground.

Volleyball—Playing the ball with any part of the body except the hands.

THE GAME

The rules and skills of touch football, basketball, soccer, fieldball, field hockey, and speedball are combined in this active game.

Two teams of eleven players each advance the ball toward the opponent's goal. Scoring is accomplished by means of kicking, passing, or running the ball into the goal area. The defensive team attempts to prevent the offensive team from scoring.

The positions and play resemble hockey, as each team has five forwards (center, left and right inners, left and right wings), three halfbacks (center, left, and right), two fullbacks (left and right), and a goalkeeper.

A game consists of four quarters of 8 minutes each, with 2-minute rest intervals after the first and third quarters, and 10 minutes for halftime rest.

FACILITIES AND EQUIPMENT

The speed-a-way field is approximately 100 yards in length by 60 yards in width. A minimum standard is 75 yards by 45 yards.

The striking circle at each end of the field is described by a 4-yard line parallel to the goal line and 15 yards from it. Two quarter circles are drawn from the ends of the 4-yard line to a point 15 yards from the goalposts on each side.

The goal is located in the center of the goal line, with the posts 4 yards apart and connected by a crossbar 7 feet high. Four feet behind each goal, two other posts and crossbars are joined to the goalposts and covered with a net or wiring.

A regulation soccer ball is used. The goalkeeper needs to wear some kind of identifying clothing or device.

SKILLS

Running and Dodging. Running is necessary to adequately move the ball or to defend the goal from the attacking team. Dodging is necessary in order to avoid being tagged and coming in contact with other players.

Blocking. This involves using the legs, hips, stomach, shoulders, and chest to stop the ball as a player advances it down the field. The arms and hands should be folded across the chest.

Tackling. This technique is used to take a ground ball from an opponent. From a front or side position, the tackler moves a foot toward the rolling ball and quickly moves the ball away from the opponent.

Trapping

1. A one-foot trap is executed with the sole of the foot. The trapper moves into the path of a moving ball and raises one foot, keeping the heel closely to the ground. The ball of the foot is placed firmly on the ball.

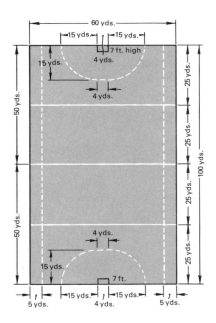

Fig. 28—1. Speed-A-Way court.

2. A one- or two-leg trap is used to gain control of a faster moving ball or a low bouncing ball. With one leg slightly forward, the shin of the rear leg comes into contact with the moving ball and the shin closes down on the ball. The inside of the leg can be used to trap the ball by allowing the right hip to rotate outwardly; the knee and calf must then force the ball to the ground.

3. A two-leg trap is executed with the feet closed and parallel. The body weight lowers as the shins trap the ball to the ground. Balance is gained by extending the arms comfortably at the side, with the weight on the balls of the feet.

Tagging. The tagging team can gain possession of the ball by legally tagging a runner.

Dribbling. With the legs rotating slightly outward, the ball can be safely played off the center of the body by tapping with the inside of the foot, alternating feet with the steps.

Passing. Hand methods (passes are executed as in basketball) include one- and two-hand chest, underhand, shoulder, overhead, and hook.

With the feet (using the inside of the foot not supporting the weight), the ball can be passed across the front of the body.

Running. By holding the ball securely with both hands and/or using the body, running can be advantageous when the field is open and no pass receivers are available.

Place Kick. This skill is executed by kicking a stationary ground ball with any part of the foot.

Dropkick. This skill can be used in returning an out-of-bounds ball or in scoring. The ball is dropped and kicked with the instep of the foot just before the ball rebounds from the ground.

Punt. This skill is used to advance the ball an excessive distance in a single play, and is executed by dropping and kicking the ball with the instep of the foot prior to the ball touching the ground.

Lifting

1. A lift to a teammate is used for kickoffs, free kicks, out-of-bounds play, and a free ground ball. This skill is executed by pointing the toes of the foot not supporting the weight toward the ground under the stationary ball. By using the instep of this same

foot, and by keeping the knee flexed, the ball is lifted rapidly into the air as the knee straightens and the leg follows through in the direction of the receiver.

2. A lift to oneself is executed with either both feet or one foot. By holding the stationary ball between the feet, using the inside of the foot and the ankles, the player jumps into the air, sending the ball upward as the hands reach to meet it.

3. A one-foot lift is executed by placing the toe of the lifting foot on top of the ball and quickly applying pressure to the ball, pulling the toe backward and downward. The lifting foot moves under the ball and quickly raises the ball into the air as the hands reach to receive it.

4. Lifting a moving ball is accomplished by placing the toes of the lifting foot in a downward position, with the leg slightly extended. The approaching ball rolls up and over the toe, and is lifted by the leg into the hands of the lifter.

RULES

Scoring

Field Goal. This is scored by drop-kicking or kicking the ball from within the striking circle over the goalposts and under the crossbar. The point value is three.

Touchdown. This is scored by running the ball across the goal line outside of the goal cage area, or by completing a forward pass from an attacking player in the field to a teammate across the goal line but not behind the goal cage area. The point value is two.

Dropkick. This may be used outside the striking circle to score if the *optional scoring rule* applies. If hockey crossbars are used, this dropkick is not legal, as the crossbars are too low. If speedball, soccer, or football goalposts are used, then a dropkick from outside the striking circle may be used for scoring. The dropkick may be executed from any place on the field from without the striking circle, and must travel between the goalposts and over the crossbars. The point value is three.

Fouls:

Infringements of the rules are:

1) picking up a ground ball (except for the goalkeeper);
2) knocking or grabbing the ball from an opponent's hands;
3) holding an aerial ball longer than 3 seconds;
4) two or more guards on the opponent with the ball, disallowing an opportunity to move the ball in any direction;
5) kicking an opponent or kicking the ball dangerously;
6) scoring directly from a free kick, toss-up, or throw-in;
7) not completing three passes prior to a touchdown following a penalty corner or throw-in taken between the 25-yard line and the goal line;
8) standing closer than 5 yards to a player taking a penalty corner, throw-in, or free kick;
9) an individual playing the ball more than once in succession following a throw-in or penalty kick;
10) tripping, shoving, pushing, charging, or striking an opponent (the runner with the ball is the only one who may be tagged);
11) tagging a player receiving the ball or prior to the elapse of 3 seconds after gaining possession of the ball.

Penalties:

1) A free kick is awarded for infringements occurring outside the striking circle.
2) Infringements occurring within the striking circle against the attacking team awards a free kick to the defending team at any point within the circle.
3) Infringements occurring within the striking circle against the defending team awards a penalty corner on the end line where the circle bisects the line to the attacking team. A punt, place kick, dropkick, or throw-in may be used. Defending backfielders must be behind the goal line and other defending players behind the 25-yard line. All attacking players must be outside the striking circle.
4) A double foul results in a toss-up at the place where the foul occurred, except when the foul occurred within 5 yards of a boundary line. The toss-up must be executed at least 5 yards from any boundary line.
5) A tie ball results in a toss-up at the place where the tie occurred, under the same conditions as in Number 4.

Out-of-bounds:

1) Throw-ins result for side out-of-bounds balls, and are executed by an opponent of the player last touching the ball inbounds.
2) Throw-ins, punts, place kicks, or dropkicks are used to put the ball in play after an end line out-of-bounds.

3) Intercepting a forward pass by a defensive player results in an end line out-of-bounds.

4) Two opponents simultaneously touching a ball and thereby sending it out-of-bounds results in a toss-up 5 yards from the line opposite the spot where the ball went out-of-bounds.

5) Throwing the ball between the goalposts is an end line out-of-bounds.

6) Drop-kicking outside the circle below the crossbar is an end line out-of-bounds.

STRATEGY

1. Forwards should move the ball downfield as quickly as possible.
2. Inners should move the ball to the wings and help disperse the defense opening the scoring area.
3. The center forward directs the attack.
4. The wings should move quickly downfield and should be skilled in catching touchdown passes.
5. The center halfback backs up the forward line on the attack and intercepts ground and aerial balls on defense.
6. The left and right halfbacks guard the wings of the attacking forward line and follow up forwards on offensive play.

7. The fullbacks are aggressive defensive players assisting the goalkeeper in guarding the scoring area.
8. The goalkeeper has additional playing privileges as he or she tightly defends the scoring area.
9. The defensive team attempts to secure possession of the ball and to prevent the offensive team from scoring.
10. The offensive team attempts to maintain possession of the ball and to score.

SAFETY

1. Necessary warm-up activities should be taken.
2. The playing field should be free of rocks, holes, and other obstruction.
3. Proper attire should be worn.
4. Rules should be strictly enforced.

BIBLIOGRAPHY

Larsen, Marjorie S., *Speed-A-Way Rules*. Stockton, Calif. 95204: 1754 Middlefield.

———, *Speed-A-Way, A New Game for Girls and Boys*. Stockton, Calif. 95204: 1754 Middlefield, 1960.

In 1921 Elmer A. Mitchell created the game of speedball to be included in the men's intramural program at the University of Michigan. Women immediately began to play the game as well, and in 1930 DGWS, then the National Section of Women's Athletics, made the necessary rule changes to meet the needs of female participants. A combination of football, basketball, and soccer skills is present in this challenging activity.

TERMINOLOGY

Aerial ball—A ball which is legal to play with the hands; the ball is raised into the air from a kick or a pass when it has not yet touched the ground.

Dodges—Tactics used to avoid tacklers.

Feints—Deceptive tactics used to confuse the opponents.

Ground ball—A moving or stationary ball on the ground.

Interchanging—A defensive tactic used in changing positions among defensive players.

Marking—A defensive tactic to stay close enough to the opponents to intercept the ball.

Trapping—Stopping a moving ball with the body or feet.

Volley—Playing the ball with the head or any part of the body except the hands, forearms, and feet before the ball touches the ground.

THE GAME

A rectangular field of 100 yards in length and 60 yards in width is used for the game of speedball (see Fig. 29-1). High school play may use a field 80 x 40 yards. A regulation soccer ball is used.

As in soccer, the object of the game is to advance the ball down the field for the purpose of scoring.

Start

The game is begun with a kickoff or a place kick in the center of the field, with all players approximately 5 yards away from the ball. Kickoffs are used at the beginning of each quarter and after each score.

Lifting the Ball

(1) *Lift to a teammate.* The individual lifting is approximately 1 foot behind the stationary ball. With the weight on the left leg and the right leg forward, the knee flexed, and the toe pointed downward, the ball is lifted as contact is made with the instep of the foot, accompanied by rapid movement of the leg. The leg follows through in the direction of the receiver.

(2) *Lift to oneself.* An individual lift is accomplished through any of three methods:

  a) *One-foot lift of a stationary ball.* From a behind position, a player places the toe of the lifting foot on top of the ball, applies pressure, pulls the ball backward and, with the toes of the same foot under the ball, lifts the hands.

  b) *Lift of a moving ball.* With one foot extended, the heel off the ground, and the toe pointing down, the ball rolls up and over the toe. The leg is lifted quickly and the knee bends outward. The body leans forward to catch the ball.

  c) *Lift-up with both feet.* Holding the ball between his feet by the inside of the feet and ankles, the player jumps and bends the knees outward to raise the ball within reach of the hands.

RULES

(1) Eleven players constitute a team, with substitutes entering or reentering the game any number of times.

(2) Four 8-minute quarters constitute a game, with 2-minute rest periods between quarters and a 10-minute rest between halves.

(3) The team winning the toss has the choice of the kickoff or the goal to defend.

(4) A ground ball may be advanced with the feet, head, or body.

(5) An aerial ball may be air-dribbled, passed, punted, or dropkicked.

(6) Ground balls may be converted to aerial balls by any lift-up method.

(7) Aerial balls touching the ground become ground balls.

(8) A throw-in is used to put the ball in play following a sideline out-of-bounds.

(9) A punt, place kick, throw-in, or dropkick is used to put the ball in play following an end line out-of-bounds. This is executed on the goal line opposite the spot where the ball left the playing field.

(10) Two opponents catching the ball at the same time and thereby causing it to go out-of-bounds, or committing a double foul, results in a tie ball. The ball is put in play by a toss-up between the tieing players.

(11) When fouls are committed a free kick is awarded.

(12) When a team or individual foul is committed to an attacking player within its own penalty area or behind the goal line, a penalty kick is awarded.

(13) *Individual fouls* are—blocking, delaying the game, using the hands or arms on a ground ball, charging, air dribbling more than once in succession, holding, tagging, pushing, tripping, employing roughness, traveling, holding the ball over 5 seconds in or out-of-bounds and over 10 seconds for a penalty kick, drop-kicking for a goal or attempting a forward pass for a touchdown within the penalty area, and threatening the eyes of an opponent.

(14) *Team fouls* are—illegal substitutions, too many players on the field, and using more than three time-outs.

STRATEGY

Offensive play should utilize the following concepts:

(1) maintain possession of the ball;
(2) pass to the front of the intended receiver;
(3) pass to the sides of the field when nearing the goal;
(4) master the skills of passing, dribbling, kicking, and scoring;
(5) play the ball to open spaces rather than closely guarded areas;
(6) play your own positions;
(7) utilize such skills as feinting and dodging;
(8) make changes from offensive to defensive play quickly;
(9) execute free kicks and throw-ins quickly;
(10) utilize all advantages such as wind or weaknesses of the opponents;
(11) employ an aerial game to move the ball faster.

Scoring

(1) *Field goal*—This is made as the ball advances across the goal line between the goalposts and under the crossbar. The value is 2 points.

(2) *Touchdown*—This is made when the ball is thrown by the offensive team from a point outside the penalty area and is caught by a teammate behind the opponent's goal line. The value is 2 points.

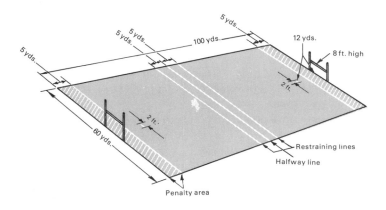

Fig. 29—1. Speedball field.

(3) *Dropkick*—This is scored by dropping and kicking the ball, after it strikes the ground, over the crossbar between the goalposts. The kick must be taken from outside the penalty area. The value is 3 points.

(4) *Penalty kick*—This is scored by drop-kicking the ball from behind the penalty kick mark. The ball passes between the goalposts and over the crossbar. The value is 1 point.

(5) A goal cannot be scored directly following a kickoff, throw-in, or a catch from a toss-up.

Tackling

As in soccer, tackling is a technique used in taking the ball from an opponent by use of the feet. A successful tackle causes a dribbler to overrun the ball, make a poor pass, or lose possession.

(1) *Front or straight tackle.* After the dribbler has contacted the ball, the tackler reaches with one foot to stop the ball by placing the sole of his foot on it.

(2) *Side or hook tackle.* This tackle is executed from a position to the side of the opponent. The tackler places the body weight on the stationary leg, then allows this leg to bend deeply as the opposite leg extends toward the opponent with the ball. With the ankle flexed and the side of the foot downward, the ball is hooked toward the tackler. The stationary leg straightens.

(3) *Split tackle.* By dropping to one leg and extending the other leg toward a ball which is nearly out of reach, the ball is blocked. The tackler must immediately regain playing position.

Defensive play should utilize the following concepts:

(1) the nearest defensive player should guard the attacker with the ball;

(2) utilize interchanging opportunities;

(3) maintain a defensive line and a goalkeeper between the attacking team and the goal;

(4) be aware of your opponents' weaknesses;

(5) shift from ground defense to aerial defense tactics rapidly;

(6) stand behind the end line opposite the opponents on a penalty kick.

PLAYERS

The Goalkeeper (one) plays near the goal, within the penalty area, in front of the end line, to prevent the opponents from scoring. He leaves his position only when a fullback can cover for him or her.

The fullbacks (two) defend one-half the width of the field around the penalty area.

The halfbacks (three) play the entire field, marking attackers on defense and following forwards on offensive play.

The forwards (five) play from their own halfback line to the opponents' goal, and are responsible for advancing the ball in an attempt to score.

BIBLIOGRAPHY

D.G.W.S.—*The Official Guide for Soccer-Speedball.* Washington, D.C.: American Association for Health, Physical Education and Recreation.

D.G.W.S.—*Soccer-Speedball Rules.* Washington, D.C. 20036: Division for Girl's and Women's Sports, 1201 Sixteenth St., N.W.

Though many parts of our square dances have come from foreign countries, square dancing is basically American in origin. It has expanded from the simple patterns based on dances of other countries, with hand clapping for music, to the more intricate forms that are popular today. Square dancing now has traveling callers, square dance bands, clubs, clothes, conventions, television programs, magazines, record companies, and important programs in our physical education, recreation, and rehabilitation programs.

Though square dancing originated in America, it is now done throughout the world, and thanks to the traveling caller, magazines, and record companies, the dances are practically standardized. A person who learns square dancing in the United States should be able, with a few minor adjustments, to participate in a square dance anywhere in the world.

In about the twelfth century the English, Irish, and Scots used dances as part of a religious ceremony in an attempt to ensure the success of their newly planted fields. These religious rites were restricted to men; only the healthiest and strongest were selected to participate, since it was believed that these men symbolized prosperity. Through the years the significance of these dances changed and they became more a seasonal recreation. Subsequently, women were allowed to participate, the seasonal connection was lost, and folk dancing became a familiar expression of the joy of living.

At the start of the seventeenth century these dances were borrowed by the courts of Western Europe, where they were modified to suit local tastes. When the Pilgrims landed on the shores of New England in the early 1600s, they brought with them a sampling of the different steps and variations of the dances of the British Isles. Immigrants from other countries also brought new patterns that contributed to the development of our square dance. As settlers moved West, one of their most enjoyable types of recreation was the dancing of these figures blended into an entirely new form. The more fortunate groups had musical instruments, but many had to improvise their music by singing, clapping, or beating on boxes and barrels. One member of the group who knew the figures was designated to call the instructions to the dancers. The caller generally prompted, chanted, sang, or kept up a running patter of the directions, depending upon his individual skill and ability to extemporize humorous rhythmic remarks in time with the music.

For many years, square dancing remained popular with the country people, but it was not until the start of the twentieth century that urban populations started to learn more about it. Vacationers spending their summers in the country saw the local citizens enjoying themselves in this activity; many continued their square dancing by forming clubs when they returned to the city.

The big impetus to square dancing was provided during World War II by the United Service Organization. In need of mass recreation and entertainment, the USO adopted square dancing as one of its recreational activities. It was easy to learn, enjoyable, and could be taught to a large group in a minimum amount of time. When the war ended, these soldiers returned to their home towns and organized clubs, became callers, and actively promoted square dancing on a national level.

Today, there are square dance clubs throughout the world, and practically every town of any size has a club of its own. The dances we now use which were, in a sense, adopted from other countries, are now, in turn, flowing back to all the other continents. Present-day American square dancing has created a large number of enthusiasts all over the world.

TERMS AND MOVEMENTS

Active couple(s)—Those designated by the caller to take the action.

All around your left-hand lady—The ladies go to the center of the set and drift toward their *corner's* position. The gentlemen walk behind their corners, passing each other's right shoulders, and turn to the center of the set. The ladies back into place and the gentlemen walk toward their partners, passing in front of their corners.

Allemande left—The *corners* join their left hands and, using these hands as a pivot, walk around each other counterclockwise back to their original positions.

Allemande thar—With either the gentlemen or ladies in the center making a right-hand *star* and backing up, they hold their partners' left hands as they walk forward.

Arch—The hands joined and raised by any designated dancers.

Around one, two, etc.—The active person or persons moving around the nonactives as directed by the caller.

Balance—With couples facing, they hop on the left foot, cross the right in front of the left, hop on the right and cross the left in front of the right. This movement is done with the dancers (or couples) holding right hands, and is often referred to as a *two-step balance*, or an *Eastern balance*.

Balance and swing—With couples facing and the gentleman holding the lady's left hand in his right, both rock back on their left foot and point their right. They then pull toward each other and *swing*.

Bar—Home position.

Bend the line—A line of dancers separate in the center of their line and, as a unit, turn 90 degrees to face the center of the set. Two new lines will be formed facing each other.

Box the flea—Partners join their left hands and the lady makes a right-face turn under the gentleman's raised left arm as he walks forward and does a half left-face turn.

Box the gnat—Partners join their right hands and the lady makes a left-face turn under the gentleman's raised right arm as he walks forward making a half right-face turn.

Break—To release hands or let go.

Break and trail—The change from a *circle* to a *promenade single file*.

Break to a line—From a *circle*, the dancer designated by the caller will break from the circle and, leading the rest of the dancers, form a line facing into the *set* or whatever direction the caller gives.

Buzz step—A type of step used in the swing. (See *Swing.*)

California twirl—Partners take their inside hands and change places and direction with each other by raising their joined hands, while the gentleman walks around the lady in a clockwise direction and the lady walks forward under their joined hands to make a left-face turn.

Call—The direction given to the dancers.

Caller—The person giving the directions to the dancers.

Center—The middle of the *set*.

Chain—*Ladies chain*—Two ladies, as designated by the caller, form a right-hand *star*, pass their right shoulders, and give their left hands to the opposite gentleman, who *courtesy-turns* them in place. *Ladies grand chain*—The ladies move clockwise in a right-hand star, pass one gentleman, and give a left hand to the opposite gentleman, who courtesy-turns them in place. This is also called a *four ladies chain. Four men chain*—This is the same as a *grand chain*, except that the ladies turn the gentlemen with a left forearm turn instead of the courtesy turn.

Circle—The dancers join their hands and move in a circle to the left or right. In circling, the action is a walk, with the lower portion of the body aimed in the direction of the circle and the upper portion facing into the center of the circle.

Contra—The dancers are shoulder-to-shoulder, facing the same direction.

Corner—The lady immediately to the gentleman's left; the gentleman immediately to the lady's right.

Courtesy turn—The gentleman takes the lady's left hand in his, and places his right arm around the lady's waist. While standing side by side, they both turn as a unit counterclockwise to face back to where the lady came from.

Cross over—To move to the opposite side of the *set*.

Cross trail thru—The *active couples* pass their right shoulders with their opposites, and the lady (or person on the right) crosses in front of her partner moving to the left, while the gentleman (or person on the left) crosses behind moving to the right. This is sometimes called *trail (on) thru*.

Dive thru—To go through an *arch*.

Dixie chain—Two couples meet single file and pass each other as in a *grand right and left*, using alternate hands. The couples can be in any combination, with the first person always starting with the right hand, the second with the left, and they should end up in single file awaiting the next call.

Don't slow down—Directions to keep *promenading* even if *home* is reached.

Do-paso [Dopaso, Dopas-o]—The dancer, using a left *forearm hold* with a designated person, walks around that person in a counterclockwise direction. Going to the corner, he turns this person clockwise with a right forearm hold and then back to the first person for the next direction or a *courtesy turn*. This movement is called a *do-si-do* [Doceydo, Docido, Dos-i-do] in some parts of the country.

Do-sa-do [dosados, dos-a-dos]—Two dancers face each other, advance, and pass their right shoulders. They move to the right behind each other and, without turning, they pass their left shoulders as they back into place.

Double pass thru—Two couples face each other, with a couple behind each of them facing in the same direction. All four couples move forward and pass their right shoulders with the couples they are facing.

Eight chain thru—With four couples lined up across the floor, the two men on the inside are back to back facing the two couples on the outside, who are facing in. The couples on the inside do a *right and left thru* with the outside couples. The couples on the outside, having given a right hand to the inside couples, *pull by*, give a left to the next, pull by, and do a right and left thru with the outside two. The couples always *courtesy-turn* on the outside and pull by in the center. With all couples working simultaneously, the figure is completed when they reach their starting positions.

Elbow swing—To walk around the designated person by hooking the right or left elbows.

Ends turn in—In a line of four facing out, the center couple forms an *arch*, allowing the end dancers to come forward, around, and through the arch.

Ends turn out—In a line facing in, the center couple forms an *arch* and the end dancers come around and through the arch.

Face (to) the middle—A call directing the *active couples* to change their present facing direction and make a quarter turn toward the center of the *set*.

Face those two—The designated persons will face new partners, generally those two with whom they have been working.

Forearm hold—This hold is accomplished when each dancer places the palms of his hands against his partner's forearms. The dancers do not grip each other; the slight friction of the hand on the arm is sufficient.

Four in line—The dancers line up in fours.

Frontier whirl—Another name for a *California twirl*.

Full turn around—This directs the dancers to go more than the ordinary half turn in either the arm turns or the *courtesy turn*.

Go all the way around—Extending any movement from a half to a full movement.

Grand right and left—The partners take their right hands and pass each other, right shoulder to right shoulder. They go to the next person, giving him a left hand and passing left shoulders, and continue on, alternating hands, until they meet their original partners.

Grand square—A simultaneous movement, wherein the original head couples are doing one movement and the side couples are doing another. The action for the heads is to move forward into the center of the square (4 steps), turn a quarter to face their partners and back away to the side of the square (4 steps). Facing the opposite direction, they back away to the corner of the square (4 steps), and turn to face their partners and walk to home (4 steps). Without turning, the action is reversed. The heads back away from their partners (4 steps), turn a quarter, and walk forward to the opposite direction (4 steps). They turn a quarter and walk forward into the center toward their partners (4 steps), and turn a quarter to face the opposite way and back up to their starting positions (a total of 32 steps). While the heads are moving through their pattern, the sides start by facing their partners, backing up, turning to face the opposite way, and continuing the same pattern as the heads.

Half sashay—See *Sashay*.

Hand over hand—Grand right and left.

Hash—A type of patter call with no predescribed pattern.

Home—The dancers' original starting positions.

Honors—An acknowledgement. The gentlemen bow and the ladies curtsy.

Inactive couple(s)—Those couples not designated by the caller to be active.

Indian style—To promenade in a single file.

Inside out——outside in—From a *star promenade*, those on the inside swing out to the outside, and those on the outside swing in to form a new star. This is done by pivoting around a point between the two dancers.

Ladies chain—See *Chain*.

Lead out—Directions to a person, couple, or couples to go to a designated area.

Line—The dancers are shoulder to shoulder, facing the direction indicated by the caller.

Ocean wave—A line of alternate-facing dancers, with their hands joined, rock forward two steps, then back two steps.

On to the next—An active person, couple, or couples move one position counterclockwise.

Partner—The lady to the right of the gentleman; the gentleman to the left of the lady.

Pass thru—Two couples, facing each other, pass their right shoulders with the opposite person and await a further call.

Patter—A type of call that includes a great deal of rhyming and fill-ins with the directions.

Promenade—(1) This is *performed in couples,* with the man on the lady's left in a counterclockwise direction unless otherwise specified by the caller. The dancers walk in rhythm with the music.

> *Skaters' position* (also called *Western promenade*)—The gentleman holds the lady's left hand in his left hand, and the lady's right in his right, crossed over the left hand and in front of the dancers.
>
> *Varsouvienne position* (also called *Butterfly position*)—The lady's left hand is in the gentleman's left in front of them, and her right in his right, over her right shoulder.
>
> *Eastern position*—The lady's left hand is in the gentleman's left in front of him, and her right hand in his right on her hip; his arm is around the lady's waist.

(2) This can also be *performed in single file* by dancers, in any number designated by the caller.

Promenade half—The indicated couple(s), in promenade position, move halfway around the outside of the *set.*

Prompt—A type of call that is only directional.

Pull her by—While holding their right or left hands, exchange positions but continue to face in the same direction.

Quadrille formation—A *set* or a *square.*

Reverse—To turn the movement or the action in the other direction.

Right and left thru—Two couples, facing each other, advance and give their right hands to their opposites. They pass their right shoulders and give a left hand to their partners for a *courtesy turn.*

Right-hand lady—The lady in the right-hand couple.

Roll back (from *promenade*)—In couples, the indicated persons turn away from their partners and move in the opposite direction. In a single file, the indicated persons turn away from the center and move in the opposite direction.

Sally Goodin—The right-hand lady.

Sashay—Originally, this was a short, sideways, sliding step. Today, it is performed very much like a *do-sa-do,* with the dancers facing the center of the set.

Half Sashay—While facing in the same direction, the dancers exchange positions by the lady turning counterclockwise in front of the gentleman as he steps behind her and into her original place. The gentleman is holding her left hand in his right,

and as she turns in front of him he drops her left hand and picks up her right in his left.

Resashay—Reversing the movement of a half sashay.

See saw (*pretty little taw*)—This is a left shoulder to left shoulder walk-around movement executed by partners.

Separate—Two dancers, working in a couple, turn back to back and go in different directions.

Set—A set consists of four couples, each with their backs to one of the four walls, and approximately 9 feet between opposite couples (Fig. 30-1). The couples are numbered 1, 2, 3, and 4 around the set to the right, or counterclockwise, starting with the couple whose backs are closest to the caller. The lady is always to the right of her partner.

> Heads—Couples one and three.
> Sides—Couples two and four.
> Opposite—The person directly across.
> Opposites—The couples facing each other.

Shoot that star—From an *allemande thar* or *wrong way thar*, the partners' holds are retained but the *star* is released, and the dancers walk forward around each other 180 degrees and await the next call.

Shuffle step—The basic step of square dance: a short, sliding step, with the balls of the feet remaining on the floor.

Singing—A type of call in which the directions are sung, generally to the tune of a popular song.

Single file—The dancers trail each other in a designated direction.

Square—A set.

Square thru—Two facing couples, in any combination, take the opposite's right hand, pass their right shoulders, and pivot 90 degrees to face their partners; they take their partner's left hand, pass their left shoulders, and pivot 90 degrees to face their opposites; they take their opposite's right hand, pass their right shoulders, and pivot 90 degrees to face their partners; they take their partner's left hand, pass their left shoulders, and continue facing the same direction, awaiting the next call.

> *Half square thru*—This is reached after the dancers pass two dancers, or two hands.
>
> *Three-quarter square thru*—This is reached when the dancers pass three dancers or three hands.
>
> *Left square thru(s)*—All of the combinations reached with the *square thru,* starting with the right hand, can also be executed by starting with the left hand.

Star thru—With two facing dancers, the gentleman's right palm touches the lady's left palm as they walk toward each other. The joined hands are raised and the lady walks under the joined hands, making a quarter left-face turn. The gentleman walks around the lady, making a quarter right-face turn, to end up side by side with the lady on his right, facing the same direction.

Stars—The dancers place the indicated hand in the center and walk forward in a circle.

> *Star by the right*—A clockwise movement.
>
> *Back by the left*—Those in the star release their right-hand holds and place their left hands in the center. They now move counterclockwise in a circle to their starting positions.

Star promenade—The couples promenade, with the inside dancers forming a star.

> *Swap*—To exchange partners.

Substitute—With two couples facing in the same direction, one in front of the other, the one in front makes an arch and backs over the other couple. The couple in the back ducks under the arch and becomes the *active couple.*

Swing—A manner in which couples move around each other, holding a stationary position on the floor. All swings are clockwise.

> *Waist swing*—The couples stand right hip to right hip facing in opposite directions, the lady's right hand in the gentleman's left, his right arm around her waist, and her left hand on his right arm or shoulder.
>
> *Arm swing*—This is executed by joining arms in a *forearm hold* and walking around each other.
>
> *Walk around*—The dancers, stepping in rhythm with the music, walk around each other in the swing.
>
> *Buzz step swing*—The right feet of the dancers are next to each other as they stand right hip to right hip. As the right foot pivots or moves in a small circle, the left foot moves in a larger clockwise circle with larger steps. The action is similar to pushing a scooter.

Taw—A gentleman's partner.

Those who can—A call for those that are situated in such a manner that only they can execute the figure.

Throw in the clutch—From an *allemande thar* or *wrong way thar*, those in the center retain their *star* but release their arm hold with those on the outside. The inside dancers then change directions and walk forward, while those on the outside continue to move in the original direction. The

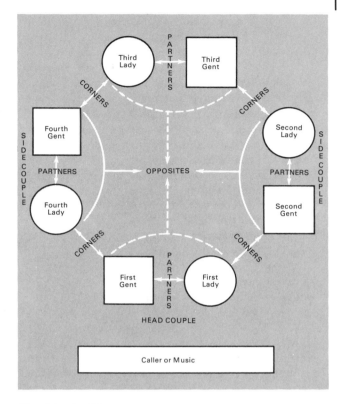

Fig. 30–1. The set.

inside dancers will be starring in one direction, and those on the outside will be walking in the other direction, to such positions or persons as the caller directs.

Tip—The sequence by which square dances are called. Commonly it includes a patter call, a singing call, and then a break, but it can be any combination.

Turn alone—See *U-turn back.*

Turn back—Those indicated by the call reverse their direction to a new call.

Turn under—A designated person or couple moves under an *arch.*

Twirl—A movement in which a lady turns under the gentleman's raised arm.

> *Twirl from swing to promenade*—The gentleman's left hand retains the lady's right. As he starts walking forward, keeping to the inside of the set, the lady makes a right-face turn once and a half under the raised hands, until she faces the same direction as the gentleman. The hands must then be changed to get into the promenade hand position.
>
> *Twirl at the end of a promenade*—The lady is turned to the right under the gentleman's raised right arm.

Twirl from a grand right and left to a promenade—The gentleman takes the lady's right hand in his and turns her once and a half clockwise under his raised right hand. He then takes her left hand in his for a promenade.

U-turn back—An individual about-face.

Walk—A shuffle done to the beat of the music.

Weave the ring—The same as a *grand right and left*, except that the dancers do not touch hands.

Wheel and deal—From a line of four dancers, the right-hand couple will wheel to the left, with the inside person holding the pivot. Meanwhile, the left-hand couple will move forward and wheel in behind the other couple.

Wheel around—From a promenade, the designated couples turn as a unit and reverse their direction. The gentlemen walk backward and the ladies forward, using their hands as a pivot point.

Wrong way—The opposite from the normal or accepted direction.

Wrong way thar—Those in the center are in a left-hand *star* and backing up, while those on the outside are walking forward, holding their partners with a right-arm hold.

FORMATIONS

Square dancing can be done in a circle or line formation as well as in the set, and these formations vary in popularity throughout the country. The following is a brief description of these formations and some of the dances that can be performed in them.

Circle

The dancers form a large circle, with the lady to the right of her partner. This formation is used by many teachers and callers to teach basic skills such as circle left, promenade, swing, do-sa-do, and honor. From this formation there are dances that can be enjoyed by dancers at all levels of skill.

Appalachian Running Set (or Kentucky Running Set)

This formation is often called the *odd-and-even-couple* formation, and is also used by many teachers to introduce certain skills to the dancers such as stars, chains, do-paso, and leading out. The dancers are in a large circle, and the couples are alternately numbered one or two. The "ones" are the visiting or traveling couples, and the "twos" are the home or stationary couples. The odd-numbered couples move counterclockwise and circle left with the even-numbered couples. From this position certain dances can be done; at the completion of this figure the odds again move one position counterclockwise to the evens, and start by circling left.

Line

Line dances, or *contra dances* as they are commonly called, are popular with square dancers in many areas of the United States. The dancers start the dance in lines facing each other, and execute many of the figures performed in the set formation. Probably the most popular of all the contra dances is the Virginia Reel. There are many variations of the Virginia Reel, and the following is one of the more popular forms of the dance:

Virginia Reel

(Gentlemen and ladies are in separate lines, facing each other, with the gentlemen's line to the caller's right.)

Everybody go forward and back.

Forward again with a right-hand around.

Forward again with a left-hand around.

Forward again with two hands 'round. (Circle to the left with your partner.)

Forward again with a do-sa-do.

Head couples sashay down the set and back.

Head couples start the reel. (A right hand goes to their own and a left to the next person down the line of the opposite sex, going around each one in turn.)

All the way down the set you go.

Sashay back, separate, and lead around.

Ladies go to the right, gents go left.

Form an arch and under you go. (The head couple forms an arch at the foot of the line, and the rest promenade through and form new lines, with the head couple taking a new position at the end of the line.)

(Repeat from the beginning for each couple.)

Set

This formation is the basis of the most popular form of square dancing throughout the world. From this formation the caller can weave his dancers through stars, lines, circles, and any of the patterns from the other dances. There are countless numbers of patterns that can be performed from this formation because every time a new skill is introduced, it can be combined with all of the other known skills to form a new challenge for the dancers.

TIPS

There are many things that dancers can do to make the dance completely enjoyable to all concerned.

Styling and etiquette are of the utmost importance in square dancing. Different areas of the country differ on styling, but certain aspects of square dancing are accepted almost throughout.

On all turn movements, for example, the dancers should take a forearm hold instead of the conventional hand grip. While making a turn, the forearm hold keeps the size of the set smaller and the dancers won't have to take large steps to get around.

Whenever dancers circle, it is an accepted rule that the gentlemen keep the palms of their hands facing up and the ladies, facedown. The ladies place their hands on the gentlemen's palms, and no actual grip takes place. In a star formation, the gentleman generally grasps the wrist of the man directly in front of him, while the ladies merely place their hands in the center of the star.

Etiquette

1. Be quiet when instructions are given.
2. Be patient with new dancers.
3. Take only your allotted space on the floor.
4. Thank your partner and the others in the set after the tip.
5. Don't be rough with anyone in the set, and at all times be courteous to the rest of the dancers.
6. Listen to the caller; he's trying to direct you.
7. If a mistake is made, pick up the dance from a point that is familiar to all the dancers in the set.
8. Above all, *have a good time!*

BIBLIOGRAPHY

Harris, Jane A., Pittman, Anne, and Waller, Marlys S., *Dance A While*. Minneapolis: Burgess Publishing Co., 1964.

Kraus, Richard, *Square Dances of Today*. New York: A.S. Barnes & Co., 1950.

Sets in Order Handbook Series, "Basic Movements of Square Dancing." Los Angeles: Sets in Order, 1963.

————, "Square Dancer's Indoctrination Handbook." Los Angeles: Sets in Order, 1963.

Shaw, Lloyd, *Cowboy Dances*. Caldwell, Idaho: Caxton Press, 1939.

The game of squash racquets had its beginnings in about the seventeenth century in England. During its early history, the game was played by hitting a soft rubber ball against any available wall with a racquet. Later, however, the playing area was enclosed by four walls. The name is derived from the fact that the soft rubber ball makes a particular noise described as a "squash" sound when striking the wall. The likeness to racquets accounts for the inclusion of that term in the name.

Before 1923 the game was played using the rules of racquets as a basis for play. However, later that same year the Tennis and Racquet Association evolved a specific set of rules for squash racquets. The availability of courts has limited the number of individuals who play this game, but where courts are available it has become a very popular game. There are many factors about the game that appeal to people of all ages; it is not strenuous to the point of requiring exhausting play, and there is much reliance placed on skill and strategy. The possibility of playing the game year-round contributes to the enjoyment of squash racquets.

COURT

The court consists of an area measuring 32 feet x 18-1/2 feet, enclosed on four sides. Further description is

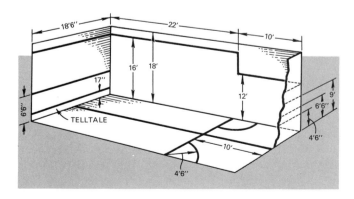

Fig. 31—1. Squash court.

given in Fig. 31-1. A piece of sheet metal the width of the court and 17 inches high is secured 1-1/2 inches from the front wall, and is called a *telltale*.

The telltale is not part of the playing area, and the ball becomes dead, or out of play, when it strikes the metal.

The four walls and floor are painted white, so that the players will be able to see the ball easily. Players should dress in white, so that the ball will not be lost because of distracting colors. Since the floor is painted white, it is desirable that the sneakers not leave visible marks on the floor.

EQUIPMENT

The squash ball is a black, hollow rubber ball having a circumference of 1-3/4 inches. In comparison with a child's rubber ball of the same size, it has much less bounce. However, as the ball warms up during play, it does "liven up" considerably.

The squash racquet is similar to, but smaller than, a tennis racquet and it possesses a longer handle. It is suggested that the beginner purchase a good racquet. However, a beginner may be careless and strike the wall with it, thus damaging the racquet, so a steel racquet with steel strings is suggested for beginners. A racquet should be kept in a press when not in use, and stored in a dry place. In order to keep breakage at a minimum and reduce the possibility of striking someone else with a racquet, players should use caution in swinging the racquet during play.

RULES

The object of the game is for the players to keep the ball in play by returning it in the air to the front wall after it has bounced only once on the floor. It may strike the back wall, or the side wall, before hitting the front wall, but it must go to the front wall without hitting the floor after it is struck. If he chooses to, a player may return the ball to the front wall (directly or by way of another wall) without letting it bounce once. If either player fails to return the ball to the front wall—after one bounce or with no bounce—a point is awarded to the opponent.

The game is started by a serve from either the right or left server's box. After the first serve is made, the serve always alternates between serving boxes, regardless of which player is serving. The server must keep one foot in the server's box as the serve is made. The ball must hit the front wall above the service line and then rebound on the floor of the opposite court to be a legal serve. If the ball hits the side wall or back wall after hitting the front wall legally, then bounces on the floor in the proper box, it is a legal serve. If the ball is not legally served, such as failure to hit the front wall above the service line or failure to land in the proper court, it is a *fault*. The server may take the serve over, but if his second serve is also a fault, the opponent is awarded the point and the serve. Failure of the server to win the point also gives the opposing player the point and the serve.

After the ball has been properly served, the receiver must return the ball to the front wall by hitting it in the air or after it bounces once in the proper court.

If the ball being returned by a player strikes the opponent, a decision must be made as to whether or not the ball would otherwise have reached the front wall in a legal manner. Technically, the point is awarded to the player returning the ball if it is decided that the ball would have reached the front wall had the opposing player not been hit with it. If the decision is that the ball would not have reached the front wall, the point is replayed. It is suggested that the interpretation given this rule be that whenever a player is hit with a ball, the point be replayed.

A *hinder* occurs when a player is unable to return the ball properly because his swing at the ball has been restricted by his opponent. (The server repeats the serve from the same box, and no point is awarded.) A player should always give his opponent every chance to play the shot without interfering with the swing.

Fifteen points constitute a game. In the event that the score reaches 13-13, the player who reached 13

first makes a decision to keep the game at 15 points, extend the game to 16 points (set to three), or extend the game to 18 points (set to five). If the game becomes tied at 14 points, the player who reached 14 first may choose to keep the game at 15 or play three extra points.

In doubles, only the serving team is awarded points when the point is made. A partner continues to serve as long as he continues to win points; when his side loses a point, his partner begins to serve. When his partner loses a point, the opponents begin to serve. The team starting the game has only one serve; when they get the serve again, the original server serves first, then his partner serves after they lose a point.

SKILLS

Grip

There are many acceptable ways of holding a racquet, such as the Eastern grip, the Continental grip, and the Composite grip. The *Eastern grip* (Fig. 31-2) is the most commonly used and is described as "shaking hands with the racquet." The grip is started by holding the racquet horizontally, with its face perpendicular to the floor. The palm of the hand faces the back side of the handle near the end, and then the hand is wrapped firmly around the handle. The junction of the thumb and first finger is on top of the handle so the "V" opening can be seen from above. The same grip is suggested for the forehand and the backhand, and in each stroke the grip must be firm so as to have control of the racquet.

Strokes

In making the forehand stroke, the player, if right-handed, should be facing the right wall, and on the backhand stroke the player should be facing the left wall; the reverse is true for left-handed players. The ball is played off the forward foot, with the body weight shifting over the forward foot as contact is made with the ball. Players should face the front wall while waiting for the ball to be played. In this position the weight is distributed equally over both feet, with the knees bent slightly. In moving into position to play the ball, small shuffling steps are taken. Cross-over steps are permissible if the player can move sufficiently fast to execute them.

The elbow is kept close to the body in the stroke, so that the forearm and wrist play the major role in the swing. The backswing is started as soon as the flight of the ball is evident. The backswing begins by moving the racquet back, using the elbow as a pivot point, and

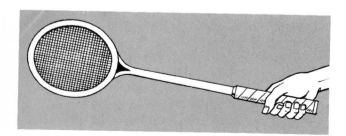

Fig. 31-2. Side view of grip.

cocking the wrist so as to bring the racquet head higher than the wrist. The racquet is then brought down to the level at which contact will be made with the ball on the forward swing. The racquet head is carried higher than the wrist, and it continues forward after contact with the ball in the path intended for the ball to follow. The swing should be smooth throughout and executed with a continuous forward motion of the forearm and wrist. At the time the ball is contacted, the racquet head is perpendicular to the floor. The wrist action continues along the forearm motion as the racquet head follows through in the path of the ball.

Serve

The strategy of the serve is to place the opponent on the defensive by making it difficult or impossible for him to return the serve.

The underhand serve has the greatest utility value and is used most. It is executed from either the right or left service box to the opposite court. When the server is in the right court, he keeps his right foot in the server's box and places his left foot ahead and to the left or center of the court. The racquet is held low, and the ball is dropped from waist height over a spot in front of the left foot. The racquet is brought forward and upward across the front of the body. Contact with the ball is made at a point slightly below the waist. The ball should hit the front wall in a way that will keep it close to the left wall on the rebound. In addition, it should have a trajectory high enough so that it will bounce on the floor a short distance from the back wall, thus making a return shot very difficult. This serve is executed in the same manner from the left server's box, with the same footwork and motion of the racquet. The one exception is that after hitting the ball the racquet must follow the path of the ball toward the front wall, to prevent it from striking the left wall on the follow-through.

The overhand and side-arm smash serves rely upon the use of force for their effectiveness. The ball should hit the center of the front wall just above the service line. This serve will be effective if the ball rebounds with force to the back wall close to the floor, so that it will have speed and a low-to-the-floor rebound bounce. If the ball does not hit the rear wall before hitting the floor, this serve will be less effective. A ball that hits first the floor and then the rear wall will have a high rebound, making it easier for the opponent to return it. If possible, the opponent will play this serve in the air before it has had a chance to hit the floor at the back wall. Another possible play with this serve is to make the ball strike the front wall near a side wall,

causing it to rebound to a side wall before hitting the back wall. This makes the receiver turn his body around to watch the ball in flight. The execution of the overhand smash is similar to the tennis serve, while the side-arm smash is similar to the forehand drive but made above the waist-line.

Playing the Ball

There are two fundamental shots used in playing the ball: (1) alley shot and (2) crosscourt shot. Each of these shots may be made with either the forehand or the backhand stroke, depending upon the positions of the player and the ball.

The *alley shot* is made close to one wall, and on its rebound from the front wall it continues to remain close to that same wall. For this shot to be effective, the ball should hit just above the telltale, so that its rebound will be low and it will have to take two bounces on the floor in order to reach the back wall. In making this shot, the player should let the ball drop low before playing it, so that the angle of rebound from the front wall will be small and the ball will return in its backward flight along the same path that it made in going forward to the front wall.

The *crosscourt shot* is made so that the ball rebounds from the front wall to the opposite side of the court from which it was played. Similar to the alley shot, this shot should be low and hard, so that the rebounding ball first bounces on the floor and then hits the side wall.

The *corner shot* and the *reverse corner shot* are also effective when made with either the forehand or backhand strokes, depending upon the positions of the player and the ball. The corner shot is made by first sending the ball to the front wall, from which it rebounds to the side wall as close as possible to the corner. The reverse corner shot is made by playing the ball to the side wall first, from which it rebounds to the front wall as close as possible to the corner. These corner shots can be made to either the right or left side of the court.

The *drop shot* is effective when executed in such a manner as to make the opponent assume that the ball is going to be driven hard. The normal backswing is executed at full speed, but as the racquet approaches the ball, the swing slows down and the wrist moves forward with the racquet head, so as to place the ball just above the telltale, permitting very little rebound of the ball from the wall. This shot is usually made when the intention is to play the ball to the forecourt while the opponent expects it to be played to the back court.

At times it will be advantageous to play the ball before it has bounced. Playing the ball in the air in this manner is called *volleying*. Care must be taken not to play the volley with too much force. In the volley, the backswing is reduced and the grip is tightened, allowing the racquet to meet the ball as if to block it from going by.

Receiving Service

The player stands in the receiving court near the line that separates the right and left courts, a few feet behind the service line, with his body facing the closer side wall. The receiver should keep his eyes on the server and the front wall, in anticipation of any moves that the server might make that would give away the type of serve he intends to make. After the ball has been served, the receiver keeps his eye on the ball and follows the ball around the court until it has been played.

STRATEGY

Control of the center of the court is very important.

Shots should be varied. Alley shots, mixed with crosscourt shots, will keep the opponent running.

The ball should be kept low. A high ball permits the opponent plenty of time to get into position to play the ball.

When possible, screen the shot with your body, thus obscuring from the opponent the kind of shot being made. This is particularly important for the drop shot.

When on the defense, try to anticipate the opponent's moves. Keep your eye on the ball and try to anticipate how and where it will be played by watching the opponent's moves.

BIBLIOGRAPHY

Cowles, Harry, *The Art of Squash Racquets*. New York: The Macmillan Co., 1935.

Debany, Walter, *Squash Racquets*. New York: A.S. Barnes & Co., 1950.

Squash Racquets. New York: The Association.

U.S. Squash Racquets Association, Inc., *Official Guide*. New York: The Association.

Swimming is undoubtedly one of man's earliest athletic activities. Pictures of swimmers were carved on the rock walls of caves in the Libyan Desert in the era of about 9000 B.C. Some historians believe man learned to swim in order to survive. It is surmised that man was forced into the water by wild animals. Then, in order to stay afloat, he extended his arms, paddled the water, and kept his legs moving in a running fashion.

In 1538 Nicolaus Wynman, a German professor, wrote what was probably the first book on swimming. In 1696 a Frenchman named Thevenot wrote a more specific book about swimming. However, the greatest development of swimming styles has been very recent. It has been only since the latter half of the nineteenth century that very much written material has appeared on swimming.

WATER SAFETY

Safety in swimming is mostly a personal matter. Training in the principles of safe swimming seems to be the best answer for safety in, on, or about the water.

Personal Safety in Swimming

1. Make a serious effort to learn to swim before engaging in activities involving the water.
2. Swim only in supervised areas, in the presence of others—*never swim alone!*
3. Remain in waters well within your own capabilities.
4. Fatigue comes about more readily in the first swim of the season; therefore, distance swims should be avoided at that time.
5. When entering cold water, a swimmer should adjust gradually by splashing water over the body.
6. The length of time the bather stays in the water is governed by a sense of physical comfort.
7. Should cramps occur and the swimmer is unable to get out of the water, he should roll to a facedown position in the water, lungs fully in-flated, grasp the cramped area, and apply pressure firmly with one or both hands.
8. A swimmer caught in any type of current should never attempt to "buck it." Swim diagonally across the current with its flow (the longest way home may mean the safest way home).
9. The swimmer should avoid forcibly blowing water from the nose.
10. Individuals with skin disease, inflamed eyes, nasal or ear discharge, cuts, scratches, or any communicable disease should refrain from swimming.
11. "Horseplay" in, on, or about the water is unwise.
12. A swimmer should always "stop, look, and listen," before entering the water.
13. Don't overestimate your ability as a swimmer and take foolish chances in the water. Learn to respect the water.

Suggested Rules for Pools

1. All persons should take a soap bath or shower before putting on a bathing suit.
2. Upon entering and leaving the pool area, the swimmer should use the foot bath.
3. No swimmer should use the pool unless a lifeguard is on duty.
4. Persons with body rash or skin infection should not use the pool during the course of the infection.
5. No "horseplay" should be permitted in or around the pool.
6. No swimming should be allowed under the diving board.
7. There should be no expectorating in the pool. The overflow trough should be used for this purpose.
8. Only one person should be allowed on the diving board at a time.
9. Street clothes or shoes should not be worn around the pool deck.
10. Throwing objects should not be permitted.
11. Articles such as bottles, glasses, cans, or any material which might cause injury should not be allowed.
12. Gum chewing while swimming is undesirable.

13. The control of the pool should be entirely in the hands of the lifeguards.

Safe Bathing Places Should Have:

1. A good bottom that is smooth and slopes gently toward deep water.
2. An approach to the water that is free from rocks, stumps, sudden "step-offs," and sunken logs.
3. An absence of currents, whirlpools, and the like.
4. Some form of lifesaving equipment located nearby.

FUNDAMENTALS

Beginning Swimming

The ultimate goal of the beginner is, of course, to propel himself along the surface of the water. The methods used to obtain this goal have varied greatly. There are, however, certain basic skills that should be achieved, and a logical order in which to achieve them.

Getting Used to the Water

The purpose of this phase is for the beginner to become physically and mentally adjusted to the water.

Standing in waist-deep water, submerge repeatedly up and down in the water to chin level. "Rinse" water in the face, and run forward and backward until a sense of balance has been achieved.

Remember to:

1. Keep the arms forward, fully extended.
2. Splash water in the face.
3. Wash the face and blow water out of the hands.
4. Make the adjustment gradual.

Breath control and face in water

The beginner should learn to inhale and exhale through the mouth, and to place and keep his face in the water for at least 10 seconds with the eyes open.

The starting position is with the feet apart, the hands on the hips, in waist-deep water. Bend forward at the waist and place either the right or left ear in the water. Take a deep breath of air through the mouth and roll the face beneath the surface of the water. Hold the breath for approximately 5 seconds, then start to exhale underwater and continue exhaling until the face has rolled back to the starting position. Repeat, holding the breath, with the face submerged, a little longer each time.

Remember to:

1. Have the feet well apart for balance.
2. Inhale before rolling the face beneath the water.
3. Continue exhaling until the face is completely out of the water.
4. Open the mouth about one-quarter of normal size when exhaling.
5. Keep the hands on the hips at all times.
6. Open the eyes beneath the water.
7. Exhale through both the mouth and nose.
8. Stand with the feet separated and one foot about 6 inches in front of the other, if needed, to aid balance.

Jellyfish Float

This skill will help the beginner develop a sense of balance and serve to determine the buoyancy of the individual.

The starting position is a standing position in waist-deep water. Bend forward at the waist and place the side of the face and the ear in the water. Place the right hand on the right thigh, and the left hand on the left thigh. Take a deep breath of air and roll the face down into the water. Slide the right hand down the right leg until the ankle is reached. Maintain this position for 10 seconds. To return to the starting position, slide the right hand up to the thigh, roll the face from beneath the water, and exhale through the mouth and nose. Repeat, using the left hand and the left leg.

Assume the same starting position, slide both hands, at the same time, down to the ankles. Remove the hands from the ankles and hang suspended in this position for 10 seconds. To recover to a standing position, slide the hands up the legs to the thighs and roll the face from beneath the water and exhale.

Remember to:

1. Slide the hands up and down the legs slowly.
2. Roll the face into the water before the hands move from the starting position at the thighs.
3. Bend the knees slightly, if necessary, as the hands move down to the ankles.
4. Make an effort to keep the feet on the bottom when executing the skill for the first time (it may be surprising to discover that this is sometimes difficult to do). The natural buoyance of the body tends to make the feet rise from the bottom.

Turtle Float

The purpose of this skill is to develop a sense of balance and to gain confidence.

The starting position is assumed by standing in waist-deep water, with the feet 10 to 12 inches apart. Bend forward at the waist until the chest is resting on the surface of the water, and place the side of the face in the water, with both hands placed on the right thigh. Take a deep breath of air, roll the face beneath the water, and slowly slide both hands down the leg to a position just below the knee. Pull the right knee tightly toward the chest. Maintain this position for at least 10 seconds. To recover, press the leg back to the bottom and slide the hands up the leg to the thigh. Then, extend the arms forward, and as the arms press downward, roll the face from beneath the water and stand. Repeat, using the same process with the left leg only.

Assume the same starting position as before, except that now the right hand is placed on the right thigh and the left hand is placed on the left thigh. Inhale, roll the face beneath the water, and slowly slide both hands to a position just below the knees. Slowly raise the legs from the bottom and pull both knees to the chest; maintain this position for ten seconds before recovering to a standing position. Recover by lowering the feet, sliding the hands up to the thighs, and extending the arms forward along the surface of the water. Roll the face from beneath the water as the arms are pressed downward.

Remember to:

1. Roll the face down in the water before the hands start to slide down the thighs.
2. Make slow, deliberate movements.
3. Recover to a standing position by reversing the procedure used in doing the skill.
4. Assume the turtle-float position even though the natural buoyancy is not sufficient to keep the body at the surface.
5. Do not become alarmed when a slight forward motion occurs just after the feet leave the bottom.

Rhythmic Breathing

This skill must be learned thoroughly, so that the beginner can develop a specific pattern for exhaling and inhaling while making progress through the water.

The starting position is assumed by standing in waist-deep water, with the feet apart and the hands placed on the thighs. Inhale through the mouth and bend forward until the face is in the water; exhale for 3 seconds. Raise the head and inhale. Continue this process until a definite breathing cycle has been established.

Assume the same starting position and turn the face to the side, with either ear placed in the water. Inhale and roll the face into the water. Exhale for 3 seconds and roll the face back to the starting position. Repeat until there is no difficulty in inhaling and exhaling.

Remember to:

1. Begin exhalation with the face out of the water.
2. Turn the head to the side, keeping the "low" ear in the water.
3. Place the face in the water so that it is submerged to a point 1 inch above the eyebrows.
4. Spend a great deal of time on this skill because it is one of the most important factors for good swimming.
5. Practice walking through the water and executing the skill.
6. Practice breathing on both sides until the natural side is found. One side will usually seem more natural.

Prone Float

The purpose of this skill is to assume another type of floating position and a sense of relaxation and balance while in a prone position.

Stand in waist-deep water, with the feet placed 8 to 10 inches apart, the hands resting on the thighs. Take a deep breath of air and execute a turtle-float position. After this position has been assumed, extend the arms forward and directly in line with the shoulders. As the arms are being extended forward, the legs are slowly extended backward to a position at or near the surface of the water. The legs are held firmly together, with the toes pointed. Maintain this position for 10 seconds before recovering to a standing position.

Remember to:

1. Keep the arms fully extended and directly in line with the shoulders.
2. Keep the face in the water, with the chin pinned to the chest.
3. Recover to a standing position· by reversing the process (back to a turtle-float position) and stand.
4. Keep the arms extended forward but not "stretched."
5. Keep the eyes open when the face is beneath the water (to help maintain balance and a sense of direction).

Back Float

The purpose of the back float is to develop a sense of balance and relaxation while on the back.

A standing position is assumed in waist-deep water, with the feet a comfortable distance apart. Sit down in the water until the shoulders are just below the surface. Drop the head back so that the ears are in the water. While the arms remain under water, raise them to a side extended position about shoulder level, with the palms up. Slowly lean backward until the chest and hips are at or near the surface. To recover to a standing position, drop the chin forward, draw the knees toward the chest, scoop the hands down and forward at the same time.

Remember to:

1. Keep the head back, ears in the water, and look directly overhead.
2. Extend the arms to the sides, with palms up.
3. Make no effort to raise the feet from the bottom. If the feet come off the bottom. it should be a result of the lifting of the hips.
4. Be sure the water covers the shoulders before dropping the head backward.
5. Inhale through the mouth, and exhale through the mouth and nose in a definite rhythm. If it is necessary for a "buddy" to support the upper part of the body, the buddy will take a position at the face and support the back of the neck with one hand and the small of the back with the other hand.

Prone Glide

The prone glide is the first propulsive movement made in the water. The beginner must develop a sense of balance and relaxation while moving through the water.

The starting position is in waist-deep water. Bend forward at the waist until the upper part of the body is flat on the surface, with the arms extended forward and directly in line with the shoulders; rest the side of the face on the water, with the ear under water. Take a deep breath of air and turn the face down into the water. Bend the knees, then straighten the legs and push with the feet from the bottom; slide along the surface of the water in a prone position and glide. As the glide ends, draw the knees to the chest and recover as in the turtle float.

Remember to:

1. Be sure the face is in the water before going into the glide.
2. Concentrate on regaining a standing position.
3. Keep the legs straight and the toes pointed.

4. Remain at or near the surface of the water at all times.

Back Glide

The purpose of the back glide is to develop a correct body position while gliding on the back.

Assume a starting position in chest-deep water. Lean back until the hips are as near the surface of the water as possible, with the hands and elbows pinned tightly to the sides of the body. Drop the head back into the water until both ears are beneath the surface; bend the knees, then slowly straighten the knees and push off into a back-glide position. As the glide stops, recover to a standing position as in the back float.

Remember to:

1. Wait until the hips are near the surface before pushing off from the bottom with the feet.
2. Keep the arms at the sides of the body, and the legs fully extended backward and together, with the toes pointed in the glide.
3. Lift the hips to the surface rather than the feet from the bottom.
4. Inhale and exhale through the mouth in a natural pattern.

Prone Glide and Kick

The purpose of this skill is to develop the ability to make progress through the water by use of the legs alone. The beginner should develop and establish a correct body position flat on the surface of the water.

First, execute a prone glide. As the glide slows, start an alternate thrashing of the legs in an upward and downward motion. The knees are slightly stiffened as the leg starts the downward motion. A bending movement develops as the pressure of the water affects the knees. Stretch the leg in the upward motion and sweep backward and upward to the surface of the water. The initial force of the legs is from the hips. That part of the leg below the knee is as relaxed as possible. At the end of the prone glide and kick, draw the knees into the chest and recover as in the turtle float.

Remember to:

1. Have the heels just break the surface of the water.
2. Bend the knees as the leg drops.
3. Keep the face beneath the surface at all times.
4. Lift the heel toward the surface, straighten the leg and point the toes. On the downward movement of

the foot, the water pressure is on the instep. On the upward movement, the water pressure is on the sole of the foot. If there is difficulty in making forward progress, check for the following mistakes:

a. Uneven kick
b. Too wide or too narrow a kick
c. Bending knees too much

Back Glide and Kick

Execute a back glide; as the glide slows, start a thrashing of the legs in an upward and downward motion. The leg movement is similar to the kick on the front except for a slightly greater depth in the kick. Keep the legs as straight as possible, allowing them to bend only slightly at the knees. At the end of the back glide and kick, draw the knees into the chest and recover as in the back float.

Remember to:

1. Keep the hips close to the surface of the water.
2. Keep the chin tucked into the throat, and the eyes open.
3. Have the toes just break the surface of the water.

Elementary Arm Stroke (Front)

The purpose of this skill is to develop a method of moving through the water by using the arms alone.

Assume a front horizontal position, with the face beneath the surface of the water. Extend the arms forward, with the palms down. Keep the entire body as relaxed as possible. Make a glide through the water; as the glide stops, allow one hand to drift downward 3 inches below the surface. Pull the arm downward with a definite bend at the elbow until the hand is below the shoulder, then bring the hand to the mid-line of the body, with the palm up and the fingers pointed toward the toes. Slide the hand along the chest until it reaches the chin (the palm is turned down, elbow in); reach the arm forward to the starting position directly in line with the shoulder. Repeat, using the opposite arm.

Remember to:

1. Cup the hand, keeping the fingers together.
2. Keep the legs straight and together and fully extended backward, with the toes pointed.
3. Keep the arm that is not pulling directly in line with the shoulders and fully extended, palm down, until

the pulling arm completely recovers to the starting position.
4. Keep the face beneath the surface at all times.

Elementary Arm Stroke (Back)

The arm stroke used by the beginner on the back is called *finning*. The purpose of finning is to develop a method of moving through the water, on the back, using the arms alone.

Execute a back glide. The arms are straight, with the palms of the hands touching the thighs. As the glide slows, slide the hands upward along the thighs for about 10 inches. At this point turn the hands outward to form a 45-degree angle with the thighs, then press the hands back to the starting point. This is a "paired" movement of the hands; therefore, both hands do the same thing at the same time.

Remember to:

1. Keep the hands moving at all times.
2. Keep the arms close to the body while pressing the hands back to the starting position.
3. Keep the eyes open.

Elementary Arm and Leg Stroke (Combined)

The purpose of this skill is to coordinate the arms and legs while in a prone position, with the face beneath the surface of the water.

In waist-deep water, execute a prone glide. As the glide slows, start an alternate thrashing of the legs in an upward and downward motion, then add the elementary arm stroke (front) as previously described. The right arm should be forward when the left heel is at the surface. The process is a continuous one, with the left arm going forward and the right heel at the surface.

Remember to:

1. Keep the face beneath the surface of the water.
2. Use slow, deliberate movements.

Finning and Elementary Leg Stroke (Combined)

The purpose of this skill is to make progress, on the back, with a minimum of effort.

Execute a back glide. Start the alternating leg thrash with a greater spread than when performed on the front. Finally, add finning with the arms. At all times keep the back flat and the chin tucked into the throat. Breathe naturally at regular intervals.

Remember to:

1. Keep the hips at or near the surface of the water.
2. Keep the hands beneath the water.
3. Keep the eyes open, to assist in maintaining balance and a sense of direction.

Human Stroke

The human stroke, in prone position, is one of the oldest methods of making progress through the water with a minimum of effort. It is composed of an alternate thrash of the legs in a downward and upward motion, with an alternate arm thrust executed under water similar to the motion of a "dog paddle." Breathing is combined with the arms and legs by turning the face to the right while the left arm is extended forward and the right heel is at the surface. Take a breath of air and rotate the face into the water as the arms and legs change position. Repeat, concentrating on slow, rhythmical movements.

Remember to:

1. Breathe at the same time on each arm cycle.
2. Develop a long reach of the arm and pull toward the mid-line of the body.

Turning Over from Front to Back

As forward progress is being made through the water, start the turn to the back as one arm pulls toward the mid-line of the body. Roll in the direction of the opposite arm, which is fully extended and in line with the shoulder. Exhalation should take place throughout the turn. Pull the arm that was extended overhead to the side of the body, and start finning with the arms as the face comes clear of the water on the turn.

Turning Over from Back to Front

When turning from back to front, simply reverse the process used in the front-to-back turn and begin the human stroke as soon as a prone position is reached.

Remember to:

1. Drop the shoulder in the direction of the turn.
2. Continue kicking the legs throughout the process of turning.
3. Keep the hands and arms below the surface of the water at all times.
4. Continue exhaling until the face is clear of the water.
5. Keep the body at or near the horizontal position.

Changing Direction

Begin the human stroke, maintain the body at or near a horizontal position, execute a left turn by reaching with the left arm to the left, and at the same time turn the head and the body to the left. Execute the right turn by extending the right arm to the right, the head to the right, and the rest of the body to the right.

Remember to:

1. Keep the arms and hands below the surface of the water.
2. Continue a strong kick in the turn.
3. Maintain rhythmic breathing during the turn.

Jumping into Water

When jumping from a standing position, fully extend the body, legs closed, and press the arms against the side of the body. As the head slides beneath the water, spread the arms and legs, then swim up to the surface.

Beginner's Dive from a Sitting Position

Place the feet over the pool edge, with the knees apart; bend forward at the waist, with the arms extended overhead, the hands together, the head placed between the knees, with the chin on the chest. Lean forward until balance is lost. Return to the surface by raising the head and execute a prone glide and kick.

Remember to:

1. Keep the chin down.
2. Extend the arms overhead.
3. Keep the head down until the body goes beneath the water.

Beginner's Dive Kneeling on One Knee

The starting position is with one knee and the opposite foot on the deck. Bend the body forward, with the chin tucked well into the throat and the arms extended overhead, with the hands together. Lean forward until balance is lost. Return to the surface as before.

Remember to:

1. Keep the foot on the deck as long as possible.
2. Keep the arms extended forward until the head has returned to the surface of the water.

3. Keep the upper part of the arms pressed against the ears.
4. Keep the chin down.

Beginner's Dive Standing in a Semideep-Knee-Bend Position

The starting position is a semideep-knee-bend position, with the feet 10 inches apart, and the toes gripping the edge. Bend forward at the waist, with the chin tucked into the throat, the arms extended overhead, and the hands together. Lean forward until body balance is lost. Return to the surface as before.

Remember to:

1. Keep the chin down.
2. Push with the feet as balance is lost.

Beginner's Dive Standing Erect

The starting position is standing, with the feet together. Bend forward at the waist, the chin tucked into the throat, with the arms extended forward and the hands together. Allow the body to fall forward, and as balance is lost, push with the toes. Return to the surface as before.

Remember to:

1. Enter the water close to the side.
2. Push from the deck as balance is lost.

SKILLS

Elementary Back Stroke

This stroke is probably the easiest style of swimming to master. The elementary back stroke is very restful because the arms recover under the water and the face is at all times out of the water.

Starting Position

The entire body is on the back underwater, except the face. The chest is raised and the chin is tilted forward into the throat. The legs and hips are slightly lower than the chest.

Arm Movements

Extend the arms fully at the sides, with the elbows pinned close to the body. Move the hands, with the thumbs touching the sides of the thighs, up along the sides of the body to a point at the armpits, keeping the elbows as close to the body as possible. At this point, turn the palms of the hands down and fully extend the arms 6 inches above the shoulder line. When the arms are extended, turn the hands so that the little fingers are pointed toward the bottom with the palms facing toward the feet. Using the palms of the hands and the insides of the arms, press back to the starting point. (The arms are kept straight, and the hands move parallel to the surface of the water 4 to 8 inches below the surface.)

Leg Movements

In the starting position the legs are fully extended and together, with the toes pointed. The legs are 8 to 10 inches below the surface of the water. Draw the feet toward the buttocks, in line with the spine, the heels touching. Spread the knees sideward. At this point, turn the feet so that the toes are pointed to the side, with the heels still touching. Start pressing or pushing the feet out to an extended position and turn the knees inward. As a continuation of this movement and just before the legs are fully extended, start to press the feet toward each other. The extended legs are brought together at the starting point.

Combined Stroke

The starting position is assumed. Start moving the hands along the sides. As they reach the waist, draw the feet toward the buttocks in the recovery position of the leg movement. As the arms extend sidewards to a position for stroking, rotate the legs and extend outward to the position for pressing back to the starting point. Simultaneously, make the stroke and allow the arms, legs, and body to glide before the next cycle is started. The inhalation is taken during the recovery part of the stroke. Exhale through the mouth and nose during the thrusting and gliding portion of the stroke.

Breast Stroke

The breast stroke is one of the oldest strokes known to man. Executed properly, it is a very efficient stroke.

Starting Position

Assume a prone position, with the face in a normal position beneath the surface of the water and the shoulders at or near the surface. Angle the body downward until the heels are 8 to 10 inches below the surface. Outstretch the arms overhead and directly in line with the shoulders.

Arm Movements

In a front horizontal position, extend the arms fully, palms down. (The arms are directly in line with the shoulders.) Allow the hands and arms to drift downward 3 inches. Make the catch by turning the hands until the palms are facing outward and in a position ready to pull against the water. Pull the arms outward and downward, with the elbows slightly bent. Continue the pull until the arms are in line with the shoulders. Bend the elbows and bring the hands inward, with the thumbs leading; the hands meet in front of the chin. Continue to move the upper arms until the elbows are approximately 6 inches apart and directly under the upper part of the chest. At this point turn the hands so that the palms are down, the thumbs are together, and extend the arms slowly to the starting position.

Leg Movements

The legs are fully extended and together, with the toes pointed. The heels are approximately 8 inches below the surface of the water. Draw the feet, with the heels together, toward the body as the knees separate and extend sidewards. (At the point of maximum bend, the heels remain together and the toes are turned sidewards.) As a continuation of the previous movement, separate the feet. Without stopping, continue to move the legs by pressing the feet back. Just before the maximum extension of the legs is reached, start pressing the legs inward and backward to the starting point.

Combined Stroke

Assume the starting position, pull the arms to the side-extended position and in line with the shoulders. Begin to draw the legs in the recovery part of the leg action. Recover the arms and move to the starting position, while the legs complete the pressing movement of the leg stroke and return to the starting position. allow the body to glide a comfortable distance before the next cycle of the arms and legs is made. At the finish of the glide, exhale while the face is in the water; lift the face clear of the water and begin the inhalation phase as the arms press out and back. As the hands come together under the upper part of the chest, place the face back into the water and keep it in that position as the legs kick and the arms extend forward.

Side Stroke

The side stroke is used primarily for distance swimming when speed is not desired, or as a restful change from another stroke. It is the basic stroke for lifesaving carries.

Starting Position

The body is in a side horizontal position near the surface, with the back straight. Place the side of the face in the water and in line with the spine; the legs are fully extended and together.

Arm Movements

The starting position is fully on the side. Place the fully-extended underarm, palm turned down, beyond the head and in line with the shoulder. Extend the upper arm backward, with the palm of the hand resting on the thigh. Move the underarm, with the palm leading and the arm straight, in a vertical press to a position just below the shoulder. As a continuation of the previous movement, bend the arm at the elbow and lift it to a position just below the surface in front of the chin. Turn the hand so that the palm is down and the fingers point forward. Extend the arm forward to the starting position. Start the upperarm, fully extended, along the side of the thigh. From this point, draw the hand along the side of the body. As it passes the elbow it is extended, with the fingertips forward and the palm down, to a position just below the chin. The catch is made at this point. Pull the arm downward and backward until the starting point at the thigh is reached.

Leg Movements

The legs are fully extended and together, with the toes pointed. Draw the feet slowly toward the body and in line with the spine. Bend the knees, separating them approximately 4 inches to decrease resistance. Separate the legs when the knees have been drawn up a comfortable distance. Move the top leg forward 18 to 20 inches from the mid-line to the body, keeping the knees still slightly bent. Move the bottom leg backward the same distance, but with a greater bend in the knees. After the legs have been separated, and as a continuation of the movement, thrust the legs inward and backward to the starting position. Allow the body to glide a comfortable distance before the next cycle of the arms and legs begins.

Combined Stroke

Assume the starting position. The underarm catches and starts to pull. As it approaches the vertical position, begin to recover the upperarm and the legs. When the underarm completes the pull and starts to move upward to recover, the upperarm and the legs catch at the same time and drive through to the starting position. Inhale as the underarm pulls to the vertical, and exhale as the upperarm makes the pull and throughout the gliding portion of the stroke.

American Crawl

The American crawl is the fastest and perhaps the best known of all the styles of swimming. When executed properly, it is a very graceful and efficient stroke.

Starting Position

Assume a prone position, with the face beneath the surface of the water and the chin slightly forward. Extend the arms forward, at or near the surface, and in line with the shoulder. Fully extend the legs, together, with the toes pointed.

Arm Movements

Assume the starting position for the arms. Allow one arm to drift downward 4 inches below the water. Pull the arm downward toward the mid-line of the body, with the elbow slightly bent. As the arm passes the vertical, it begins to relax and is allowed to drift back to the thigh. Lift the shoulder at this point, bend the arm at the elbow, rotate the thumb toward the bottom, and raise the elbow out of the water. The hand then comes out of the water and is flung forward.

When the arm is two-thirds extended and in line with the shoulder, place the hand in the water, the fingers first and the elbow last, and slide forward to a fully extended position at or near the surface. To complete a full cycle of the arms, the opposite arm moves in the same manner as described above.

Leg Movements

Fully extend the legs to a nearly straight but relaxed position. Extend, but do not stiffen, the toes. Start the movement at the hips, with one leg executing a downward thrash. Slightly stiffen the knees. (A bending movement of the knees occurs because of the water pressure against the legs.) Press downward to a depth of 12 to 18 inches, with the water pressure on the instep. At this point, the upward motion of the leg begins. Stretch the leg and sweep it backward and upward to the surface of the water; the water pressure is on the sole of the foot. Alternately whip the legs up and down in the vertical plane.

Breathing

It is assumed that the swimmer takes air to the right. Extend the left arm forward in the glide and support position. As the right hand pulls the water, turn the face to the right until the nose and mouth are clear of the water. Take a complete inhalation until the recovering right arm, by the action of its forward thrust, turns the face down and forward for the exhalation. The legs continuously whip up and down in the vertical plane throughout the cylce of the arms.

BIBLIOGRAPHY

American Red Cross, *Swimming and Diving*. Philadelphia: Blakiston Co., 1938.

Gabrielsen, M. Alexander, Spears, Betty, and Gabrielsen, B.W., *Aquatics Handbook*. Englewood Cliffs, N.J.: Prentice-Hall, Inc., 1960.

Harris, Marjorie M., *Basic Swimming Analyzed*. Boston: Allyn and Bacon, Inc., 1969.

Lanoue, Fred R., *Drownproofing*. Englewood Cliffs, N.J.: Prentice-Hall, Inc., 1963.

Mackenzie, Marlin M., and Spears, Betty, *Beginning Swimming*. Belmont, Calif.: Wadsworth Publishing Co., Inc., 1962.

Official NCAA Swimming Guide. Phoenix, Ariz.: College Athletics Publishing Service, 349 East Thomas Road.

Torney, John A., *Swimming*. New York: McGraw-Hill Book Co., Inc., 1950.

The concept of swimming in a rhythmical artistic form is known as *synchronized swimming*. Water ballet was the original name for this activity. Norman Ross is credited with the origin of the name synchronized swimming; he used this term when announcing a water show prepared by Kathrine Curtis in the Chicago World's Fair in 1933. Although the activity is not of true American origin, it is more popular in the United States than in any other country. Germany, England, and Canada also have been known for competition in "ornamental" swimming for many years.

The popularity of synchronized swimming has resulted in the formation of the Association of Synchronized Swimming for College Women and the International Academy of Aquatic Art. Every four years the Pan-American Games schedule events in synchronized swimming, and the Amateur Athletic Union sponsors this activity at the Olympic Games.

TERMINOLOGY

Aquatic art—Swimming stunts and strokes integrated with music and dance.
Combined strokes—Performing two or more strokes in a series.
Hybrid strokes—Combining two or more standard strokes setting a pattern or rhythm.
Modified strokes—Adopting standard strokes for synchronized needs.
Sculling—Using the hands to propel the body while in water.
Synchronized swimming—Swimming techniques coordinated to music and to patterns.

SCULLING

Primary among elementary skills for beginners in synchronized swimming is sculling. Sculling is executed by movements of the hands and arms only, thereby supporting and propelling the body, main-taining body position and creating a sense of equilibrium in the water.

The body is in a supine position near the surface, with water barely trickling over the thighs. The legs are fully extended and straight, held together with the toes pointed. The hands and arms are approximately 8 inches below the surface and 10 inches away from the body. The palms face away from the body, with the thumbs down and the hands at a 45-degree angle to the thighs. The hands are cupped and the fingers held tightly together.

Analysis of hand movements: From the starting position the hands and arms (in a straight line) move outward about 15 inches. At this point, and with a continued application of pressure against the water, the palms are rotated inward in a circular motion until the little fingers are down and the hands form a 45-degree angle to the surface of the water. The pressure of the palms against the water is continued until the hands reach the starting point (10 inches away from the body); without stopping, the same outward-hand movement is executed as described above. There is some "play" in the wrists as the arms move back and forth in the horizontal plane. By varying pressure, bend of the wrists, and direction of the movement of the hands, the swimmer may change the direction in which the body is propelled and still maintain the horizontal position at the surface of the water.

STARTING BODY POSITION

There are several basic positions the body may assume before the execution of a figure.

1. *Front layout* (prone position): Assume a facedown position, with the arms extended forward and directly in line with the shoulders. The legs are extended backward in a position at or near the surface of the water. The legs are held firmly together, with the toes pointed.

2. *Back layout* (supine position): Assume the same position as for the front layout, except that the body is in a position on the back, faceup.

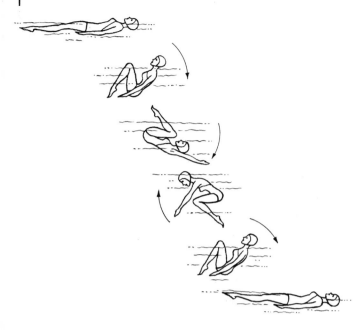

Fig. 33—1. Back tuck somersault.*

Figs. 33-1, 33-3, 33-4, 33-5, 33-7, and 33-8 are adapted from Andrews, Smith, Squance, and Russell, *Physical Education for Girls and Women*, 2d Ed. (Englewood Cliffs, N.J.: Prentice-Hall, Inc., 1963), by permission of the authors.

3. *Boat position:* Assume the same position as for the back layout, except that the arms are fully extended along the side of the body. The hands are in position for sculling.

4. *Tuck position:* The knees, held together, are drawn toward the chest with the toes pointed. The back is rounded, the head forward, with the chin tucked tightly into the chest.

5. *Pike position:* The body is bent sharply at the hips, with the legs straight and the toes pointed. The head is forward, with the back rounded.

ELEMENTARY FIGURES

Back Tuck Somersault (Fig. 33—1)

The body is in a boat position, with the hands executing sculling. Execute a tight tuck, press down and backward, with the hands and arms as far as the shoulders will permit, rotate the arms and circle them forward and continue circular movement of the arms until the starting tuck position is reached. At this point the body is stretched out into the boat position.

Front Tuck Somersault (Fig. 33—2)

The body is in prone position, with the hands executing sculling. Execute a tight tuck position. the hands are at the surface of the water, next to the

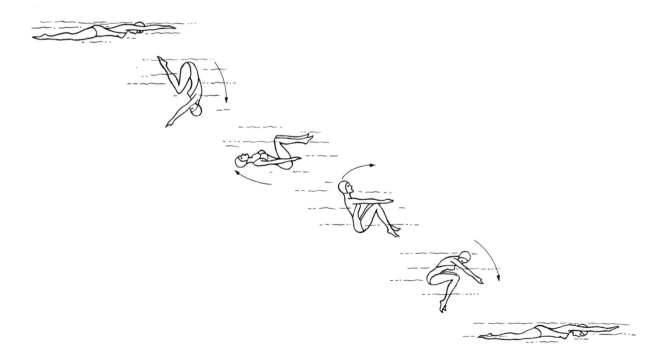

Fig. 33—2. Front tuck somersault.

Fig. 33—3. Back pike somersault.

ankles. Allow the hands and arms to drift downward 3 inches. Turn the hands until the palms are facing outward and in a position ready to pull against the water. Pull the arms sideward and downward until the arms are in line with the shoulders, and continue pressing downward and forward until the arms reach the starting position.

Back Pike Somersault (Fig. 33—3)

The body is in a boat position, with the hands executing sculling. Simultaneously, press down with the hands and bend at the hips into a tight pike position as the legs rise into the air, with the toes pointed. As the legs reach the overhead position, the roll backward is started. The chin remains tucked tightly into the chest throughout the figure. The arm movements are the same as described in the back tuck somersault. The figure is completed by returning to the boat position.

Front Pike Somersault (Fig. 33—4)

The body is in a front layout position. Tuck the chin tightly into the chest. Turn the hands until the palms are facing outward and in a position ready to pull against the water. Pull the arms backward and downward, and at the same time bend the trunk forward to a pike position. Press the arms downward and continue to circle until the somersault is completed. The figure is completed by returning to the front layout position.

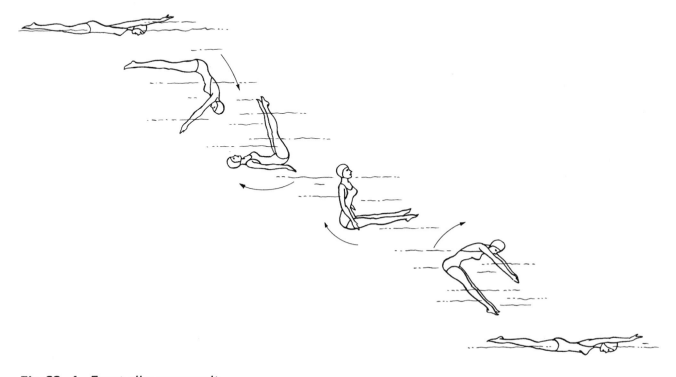

Fig. 33—4. Front pike somersault.

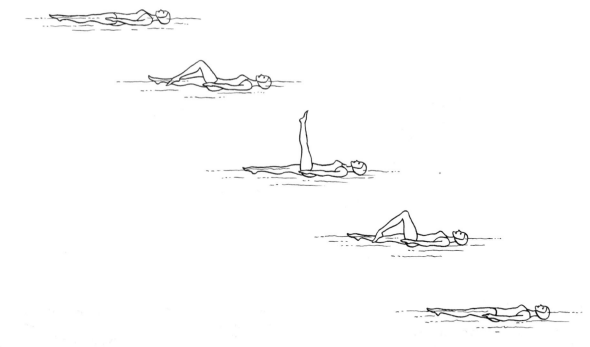

Fig. 33—5. Ballet leg.

Ballet Leg (Fig. 33—5)

The body is in a boat position, executing a forceful scull. Draw one knee up, until the thigh is in a vertical position. Keep the foot in contact with the inside of the straight leg. Extend the leg to a straight-up position above the water, with the toes pointed, and hold this position for 2 seconds. Bend the knee and return the foot to the inside of the straight leg at the knee. Slide the foot along the straight leg and return to the boat position.

Porpoise (Fig. 33—6)

Assume a front layout position. Drop the face forward and downward and, with an outward spreading movement of the arms, bend sharply at the hips as in a front pike somersault until the trunk of the body is in a vertical position. At this point the arms circle downward and inward as the weight of the lifted legs forces the body downward. The arms then extend forward and downward directly overhead.

Flying Porpoise

Begin with a vertical feet-first surface dive to the bottom of the pool. Push the body to the surface by flexing the knees and ankles. As the upper body rises above the water surface, a pike position is assumed so as to execute a porpoise. No break in the movements should occur.

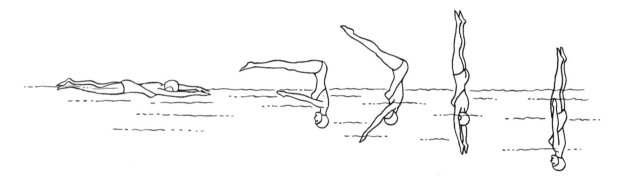

Fig. 33—6. Porpoise.

Fig. 33—7. Dolphin.

Dolphin (Fig. 33—7)

Assume a boat position and execute sculling. Drop the head back and arch the upper part of the back. Slide the arms sideward to an overhead position and begin a series of small circular pulls around and up (the knees do not bend and the body makes a complete even circle) until the body starts coming up, with the head leading. Then slide the arms to the sides of the body and scull until the boat position is reached at the surface of the water.

Flying Dolphin

Using a vertical feet-first dive, the body lifts halfway out of the water, executing a dolphin from the top of the lift.

Oyster (Fig. 33—8)

Assume a boat position and execute sculling at the sides of the body. Press the arms downward as far as comfortable; at the same time pike the body, raising the legs above the surface of the water to a vertical position. With a continuous movement of the arms, rotate the palms outward, sliding the arms overhead and pulling upward toward the feet, touching the ankles. The body is allowed to submerge below the surface in this position.

Shark

Beginning with the body in a side layout position, the body is arched and the top arm extended overhead in a continuing arc. Execute a shallow arm pull with the lower arm and pull the arched body in a wide circle with small scooping movements, locking the knees and extending the toes.

Ballet Legs

The body is in a layout position for a single ballet leg, and the hands perform a flat scull. Bend one knee toward the chest and extend the other leg at the

Fig. 33—8. Oyster.

surface of the water. The bent knee rises to a vertical position, then extend the knee and toe firmly. Bend the leg back to the chest and extend to the starting position. Alternate the legs and perform the same skill.

Double ballet legs is performed by pairing the leg movements.

Marlin

The arms are extended, with the palms up, from a back position. Turning left, the right knee bends to the chest and the left arm moves above the head. Rolling the body left, the right arm moves downward to the thigh. Keep the head up and extend the arms from the shoulders when on the chest. Roll in the same direction, pushing downward with the right arm. At the end of the roll the arms should be at shoulder level. Extend the leg. Both legs may be straightened, but at the completion of the roll, in either case, the feet should remain at the pivoted spot and the body has moved horizontally 90 degrees.

Catalina

Assume a right ballet leg position from a beginning back layout position. Dropping the head, turn under the left arm and maintain the ballet leg as the body reaches a vertical position, with the head downward. With the body arched, raise the left leg from the surface, meeting the right leg. Then, submerge and recover.

Submarine

From a back layout position, extend one leg vertically, with the hands moving backward and forcefully pressing toward the surface and side, pulling the body directly down. The leg may submerge, or a portion may remain above the water. Press downward with the palms and rise to the surface.

Kip

Begin in a back layout position, and draw the knees sharply to the chin. Roll backward from this tuck position by pulling the head downward and under the hips. The torso becomes vertical, and then the legs and head extend. Submerge vertically and recover as in a dolphin.

This can be altered to include a split or scissors, with the legs extended before submerging.

Somer-Sub

A pike somersault is begun from an extended prone position. The legs move to a parallel position with the surface of the water. The back is downward and the face upward toward the surface. One leg is extended in a vertical position, while the other leg is forward and parallel to the surface. With the vertical leg leading, rise to the surface. When on the surface, the vertical leg bends and is drawn to the chest. Now, lower this leg to meet the extended leg.

COMPETITIVE RULES

Competitive events recognized by the Division of Girls' snd Women's Sports through the Amateur Athletic Union are classified as solo, duet, and teams of four to eight swimmers. The routines are usually 5 minutes in length, and consist of three specific stunts and three optional stunts.

Execution of the strokes and stunts are rated, in addition to the styles of the stunts. Style is defined through structure, interpretation, and utilization of the pool. Variety, originality, and difficulty is also considered. The synchronizing of all these elements is of major consideration.

A scale of 1/2 to 10 points is the scoring range, with three to five judges rating on execution and style. In solo events 2 points are possible for synchronization, 4 for construction, and 4 for variety. In duet and team events, 4 points are possible for synchronization, and 3 for both construction and for variety.

BIBLIOGRAPHY

American Association for Health, Physical Education and Recreation, *Official Aquatics Guide.* Washington, D.C.: The Association.

Official AAU Swimming Handbook. New York: The Amateur Athletic Union.

Seller, Peg, and Gundling, Beulah, *Aquatic Art.* Cedar Rapids, Iowa: Pioneer Litho Co., 1957.

Spears, Betty, *Beginning Synchronized Swimming.* Minneapolis: Burgess Publishing Co., 1958.

Yates, Fern, and Anderson, Theresa, *Synchronized Swimming.* New York: The Ronald Press Company, 1958.

TABLE TENNIS | 34

The exact origin of this activity is unknown. However, in the 1890s the game was being played in various forms in England, Europe, and the United States. The first noticeable increase in its popularity came as a result of the manufacture of celluloid balls of uniform proportions and performance.

Commonly known as "ping pong," the game began to gain popularity in the United States in about 1927, and today it is considered a favorite among indoor recreational activities because it requires little space, is inexpensive, and affords the opportunity for keen competition. National and international championships are regulated by the United States Table Tennis Association and the International Table Tennis Association. Such championship contests are held annually.

EQUIPMENT

Table and Net

The table (Fig. 34-1) for this game is rectangular, measures 9 feet in length and 5 feet in width, and is usually made of wood. A table tennis ball, when dropped on the table from a height of 12 inches, should bounce up 8 to 9 inches. The whole table surface should be level and 30 inches from the floor. The playing surface is usually dark green, with a 3/4-inch white line around the outer edge. The 5-foot lines are called end lines, and the 9-foot lines are called sidelines.

The net is strung across the table, dividing it equally into two courts. The top of the net should be 6 inches from the table surface and extend 6 inches (3 on either side) outside the sidelines; the bottom of the net should be close to the table surface.

Ball and Paddle

The ball is extremely lightweight (37 to 39 grams), pale in color, and made of celluloid. The paddle may be of any size, shape, material, or weight. The surface of the paddle is usually covered with rubber (stippled) or with a very fine grade of sandpaper.

THE GAME

1. Twenty-one points constitute a game, unless the score is tied 20-20, in which case one player must win by a 2-point margin.
2. Play begins with one player serving and one receiving.
3. The server puts the ball into play by tossing it into the air from the palm of one hand and striking it with the paddle (held in the other hand), so that it hits his own court. The ball goes over the net and hits the receiver's court.
4. The receiver must return the ball over the net so that it hits the server's court. Only on the serve does the ball go from paddle to court, then over the net.
5. Play continues until one player fails to make a legal return. The opponent then scores one point.
6. The serve changes from one player to the other every time five points are scored, except when the score becomes tied 20-20. At that time the serve changes, and continues to change after each point until one player scores two consecutive points, thus winning the game.
7. When no official is present, the players must keep score of the game. The best way to keep an accurate score is for the server to call out the score before he serves each time, always calling his own score first.

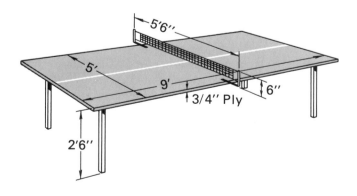

Fig. 34—1. Table tennis.

RULES

The more important rules for table tennis are:

1. In serving, the server's paddle must strike the ball behind the end line and between the sidelines (extended).
2. If a player touches the playing surface of the table with any part of his body or clothing, the point is won by his opponent. The same is true if a player should move the table by bumping against it.
3. In serving, the ball must be held in the palm of the hand, visible to the opponent and with no spin being imparted to it by the hand.
4. If the ball hits the net on the serve and goes over, it is a "let" and the server serves again. However, if the second serve is also a let, the player loses the serve and the point.
5. If a player misses the ball completely when he is serving, it is a point for his opponent.
6. A paddle can contact the ball legally only if the paddle is held in a player's hand.
7. If a ball is broken during actual play, a new ball is put into play and the point during which it broke is replayed.
8. The only way a ball can be legally hit is with a paddle or the hand holding the paddle.

Doubles Play

The most important rules governing doubles play concern rotation of the serve and hitting alternate shots.

The Serve

In doubles play, a line 3/4 inch wide divides the table lengthwise; it is 30 inches from each sideline. The first server on one team serves from his right half court into the right half court of the receiving team for the first five points. For the next five points, the partner of the first receiver serves to the partner of the first server. The third five-point series is served by the partner of the first server to the partner of the first receiver. The fourth five-point series is served by the first receiver to the player who was the first server.

Hitting Order

The server must make a good serve and the receiver must make a good return. The partner of the server must make the next good return, and the partner of the receiver must make the next good return. The returns must be over the net but may be placed anywhere on the opponents' court. This sequence of hitting continues in the same manner until one player fails to make a good return.

SKILLS

Successful table tennis players are able to hit the ball in a variety of ways: forehand, backhand, chop, and smash. Most success depends upon skill in putting different types of spin on the ball, thus making it react differently when it rebounds from the table or paddle.

The two most effective types of spin are backspin and topspin. Players must learn to judge which way the ball is spinning by the way it is hit with the paddle.

Backspin

This is imparted to the ball by hitting down and turning the hitting surface of the paddle up as it strikes the ball. A ball with backspin will rebound sharply downward if struck by a paddle held vertically.

Topspin

This is imparted to the ball by hitting up and turning the hitting surface of the paddle down as it strikes the ball. A ball with topspin will travel a greater distance in a horizontal plane if struck by a paddle held vertically.

One other way to impart spin to the ball is to rotate the paddle on a vertical axis to the left or right. If such a ball is returned in a normal manner, it will rebound sharply to the left or right, depending upon the direction of the vertical spin.

STRATEGY

In table tennis it is advisable to ferret out an opponent's weakness as soon as possible and to attempt to play that weakness as much as possible. It may be a weak backhand or an inability to observe spin imparted to the ball—but whatever it is, learn to take advantage of it. It is wise to learn a variety of attacks, serves, and serve returns, mixing them sufficiently to keep the opponent from anticipating them and devising proper defenses.

In doubles play, in addition to using singles strategy, it is well to take advantage of the fact that partners must alternate hitting the ball. Thus, many successful returns can be made by forcing one player to move rapidly from a position to allow his partner enough room to hit the ball.

BIBLIOGRAPHY

Carrington, J., *Modern Table Tennis*. London: G. Bell, 1950.
General Sportcraft Co., Ltd., *Table Tennis*. Bergenfield, N.J.: The Company.
Harvard Table Tennis Co., *Table Tennis* (*Teacher*). Cambridge: The Company.
United States Table Tennis Association, *Table Tennis Rules*. Newark, Del.: The Association.

Tennis seems to have its origin in the ancient game of handball, first played in Greece. Later it was a very popular sport in Ireland. It was a favorite pastime of the royal families of Europe for several centuries.

The first form of the racket used in modern tennis was a glove for protection of the hand. A small paddle was then introduced to increase the striking area. Eventually, the center of the paddle was cut out and replaced with some type of string. It is interesting to note that there are no rules to determine the size or shape of the modern tennis racket. There are, however, specific rules concerning the size and weight of the tennis ball.

Tennis as the game we know today was introduced at Staten Island by Mary Outerbridge after a vacation trip to Bermuda. The exact date seems to be in doubt, with some books showing 1874 and others 1875. The United States Lawn Tennis Association (U.S.L.T.A.) was organized in 1881, and is still the governing body of amateur tennis.

National championships in tennis are held each year, not only in the United States but in most of the other countries in the world. Tennis in Australia is as popular a sport as baseball is in the United States. International competition consists of the Davis Cup matches, which involve men's teams from the various countries of the world, and the Wightman Cup matches for women's teams from the United States and England.

During the past few years many have advocated changing the game of tennis, but basically the rules are the same as they were at the start of the twentieth century. Most of the pressure has been for changing the method of scoring and the advantage of the net rush after a "big serve."

Tennis is one of the few sports in which the rules are basically the same for men and women. The only difference is in the length of an official match and the rest period of ten minutes after the second set for women and after the third set for men.

Fig. 35-1 gives the dimensions of the tennis court.

A new type of tennis game was introduced at the University of Florida in the spring of 1953 through the cooperation of Edward D. Fales, Jr., of *Parade*, the Sunday picture magazine. The game is called *Florida Tennis,* and the first court was laid out on the campus of the University of Florida. The court is half as wide as a regulation singles tennis court, in order to eliminate most of the strenuous running and to present a game for people who feel they are too old to play the regular game but still want to compete in some type of tennis game. Studies showed that people of almost any age could play without a rapid increase in the pulse rate. The court can also be used for other family recreational activities, and is popular with children as well as adults.

EQUIPMENT

Good equipment is essential for the tennis player, but the cost of rackets, tennis balls, and clothing for

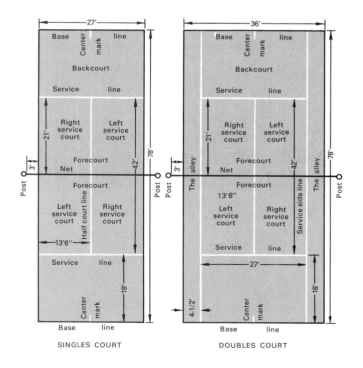

Fig. 35—1. Diagram of tennis court.

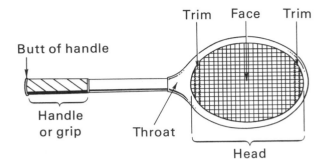

Fig. 35—2. Tennis racket nomenclature.

tennis is relatively inexpensive in comparison to the cost of equipment for many other sports.

Rackets and Balls

The beginning tennis player should select a racket frame of his own preference as to weight, handle size, and balance (Fig. 35-2). The weight of frames varies from about 12-1/2 ounces to 15 ounces, and the frames are classified as light, medium, or heavy. The handle size (circumference of the handle) varies from 4-1/2 inches to 5 inches at 1/8-inch intervals. The most popular racket for a majority of players has a handle size of 4-5/8 inches and is of medium weight. The balance of each frame is different because of the placement of weight in the handle shaft.

The frame should be strung with either nylon or gut strings. Nylon seems to be the most practical for the beginning or average player, since it will wear longer, is much less expensive, and is not affected by moisture. The advanced tournament player will favor gut, since it is more elastic and most players of this caliber claim the gut strings give them a better touch.

A press and cover are good investments, since the cover will protect the strings and the press will prevent the frame from warping when the racket is not in use.

The U.S.L.T.A. has devised definite specifications for the weight and size of tennis balls, and any balls meeting these specifications are acceptable for play. Tennis balls should always be bought pressure-packed in cans, in order to guarantee the proper internal pressure. If, when a can is opened, no release of air is heard, the tennis balls are not good and should be returned to the place of purchase.

Clothing

White is the accepted color of clothing for tennis players, since it is not distracting to the opponent and follows the tradition set forth over a period of years.

Rubber-soled tennis shoes are essential to ensure a good footing. High-top basketball shoes may be worn on hard-surface courts, but never on clay or dirt-type courts. Most players today use the oxford variety on all types of courts, and many use shoes with a scored surface instead of a smooth sole. White shirts and shorts complete the clothing, along with white socks. Two pairs of socks are helpful to prevent blisters when play is continued over a long period of time or on a hard surface. Some players like to wear a wrist band on the playing arm to prevent perspiration from getting on the handle of the racket and causing it to slip.

TERMINOLOGY

Ace—A legal serve not touched by an opponent.
Band—The strip of canvas attached to the top of the net.
Base line—The back line at each end of the court.
Center mark—The mark in the middle of the base line which indicates one of the sides of the serving area.
Center service line—The line that separates the right and left service courts.
Fault—A served ball that does not strike in the proper court or that is not properly served.
Foot fault—An infraction of the service rules, such as stepping on or over the base line before the ball is hit.
Game—The scoring unit next higher than the point. Game is reached when one side wins four points (unless the two sides had previously tied at three points; in that case, a team must gain a lead of two points to win the game).
In play—A ball is "in play" from the moment it is legally served until the point has been decided.
Let—A served ball that touches the net and lands in the proper court. Also, any point replayed due to an interruption.
Lob—A lofted ball over the head of an opponent in the forecourt area.
Match—For women, the best of three sets; for men, the best of five sets.
Net—The net barrier that divides the court crosswise.
Point—The smallest unit of the score. Four points scored generally win a game. (See *Game*.)
Post—One of the wooden or metal uprights that support the net.
Receiver—The player to whom the serve is directed.
Service or serve—The act of putting the ball into play.
Service line—The line 21 feet from the net that marks the back of the service courts.
Set—The unit of scoring next higher than the game; when a side has won six games, it wins the set

(unless the two sides had previously been tied at five; in that case, a team must gain a lead of two games to win the set).

Set point—The winning point in a set.

Side service line—The line that bounds the service courts at the right and left sides. On a singles court the side service lines are also the sidelines.

Sideline—The line that marks the outside edge of each side of the court.

Stroke—The act of striking the ball with the racket.

Toss—To spin the racket or throw it in the air for choice of serve or side.

Tournament—An official competition. In some tournaments, when the score is "all," a *tie break procedure* may be used. Tournament officials may rule that five out of nine points, or seven out of twelve points, will decide the winner.

Volley—A stroke made by hitting a ball before it has bounced once; it may be made at any point when the ball is in play except to return a serve.

Wide—A ball landing beyond the sidelines.

SCORING

The Point

The point is the first phase in scoring tennis.

Points	Name
1	Fifteen
2	Thirty
3	Forty
4	Game (unless the opponent has gained three points)

Deuce— When each side has won three points.

Advantage—The next point after deuce. When the serving side wins the point, it is "advantage in" or "advantage server." When the receiving side wins the point, it is "advantage out" or "advantage receiver."

The score returns to deuce when the next point after advantage is won by the player who is one point behind (e.g., when each player has four points). Two points in succession by the same player after deuce results in a game for that player.

The server's score is always called before the receiver's; e.g., if the server has two points, and the **receiver one—the score called is "30-15."**

Love—No points; e.g., if the server has no points, and the receiver three—the score is "love-40."

All—When the server and receiver have one point each or two points each—the score called is "15-all" or "30-all."

Players sometimes use abbreviations in scoring, but these are never used by an official umpire. Examples are "five" for fifteen, or "ad" for advantage.

The Game

The game is the second phase of scoring in tennis. The player wins the game when he wins four points without his opponent having won three points. Two points in a row by the same player are necessary in case of a deuce game.

The Set

The set is the third phase of scoring in tennis. A set is won when one player wins six games before the opponent wins not more than four games. (*Example:* 6-0, 6-1, 6-2, 6-3, or 6-4.) In case both players win five games, the set continues until one player wins two games in a row. (*Example:* 7-5, 8-6, 9-7, 10-8, 11-9, or 12-10, and so on.) There is no limit to the number of games that may be played in a set of this type.

The Match

The match is the fourth phase of scoring in tennis. A player wins a match by winning three out of five sets for men and two out of three sets for women. Most interscholastic, intercollegiate, and tournament matches for younger players also specify two out of three sets to win.

Scoring in tennis is the same for singles and doubles.

PROCEDURE

One player serves an entire game, and each side alternates during the set and match. In doubles, one player serves once every fourth game during the set, and each side serves alternately during the match.

The server starts the game from behind the right half of the base line, and is allowed two trials to serve the ball into the right service court (diagonal). The second point is started from behind the left side of the base line, and again two trials are allowed for the left service court (diagonal). If the server fails on the second attempt, his opponent gains a point.

A served ball touching the top of the net and going into the proper service court is served again ("let" ball). However, except for served balls, balls touching the net and going over are considered in play and must be returned. Also, balls landing on or inside the boundary lines are considered in and must be played.

The receiver must let the ball bounce once and return it over the net into the proper area in order to keep the ball in play. Thereafter, the ball *may* be played in the air; it *must* be played after no more than one bounce. The player failing to do this loses the point (his opponent gains it).

FUNDAMENTAL SKILLS

Grips

There are three grips used by tennis players today. The type of playing surface and whether the player received any instruction when learning to play seem to determine the grip used. Many players use a variation of one grip, and some use a combination, such as an "eastern" forehand and a "continental" backhand.

The *western grip* is used by players on rough, hard-surfaced courts. It is excellent for balls bouncing high, but very awkward for low-bouncing balls. To try this grip: lay the racket on the court, reach over and pick up the racket, with the base of the palm of the hand at the butt of the handle. Lift the racket, with the thumb and fingers grasping the sides of the handle. After the racket has been lifted, the thumb and fingers are wrapped around the handle so that the thumb and last three fingers hold the handle firmly. The same side of the racket is used for the forehand and backhand. The wrist is rotated counterclockwise for the backhand as the body turns to the left with no change on the grip.

The *continental grip* is used by players on fast-surface courts and is practical for low-bouncing balls, but out of place for balls bouncing above waist level. Place the racket on its side, with its face perpendicular to the court surface, and pick it up at the end of the handle, with the wrist directly above the handle. Grip with the last three fingers and the thumb; the first finger is separated slightly from the others, curved around the handle, and used as an added support. The same grip is used for the forehand and backhand drives by turning the body to the right or left. This grip requires a very strong wrist and may tire the arm after a period of time.

The *eastern grip* is the most widely used grip and should be used, since it is the most practical and adaptable to all types of court surface. This grip is used equally well with either the low- or high-bouncing ball. Its only disadvantage is that it requires a change from the forehand to the backhand, but this becomes automatic as you learn to play.

To get the correct grip for the forehand, hold the racket (the face perpendicular to the court surface) with the left hand, with the butt of the handle against the abdomen. The palm of the right hand is then placed on the string on the right side; as the left arm is extended, the right is drawn over the throat and along the handle until the leather butt at the end of the handle rests against the base of the hand. The palm of the hand should be flat against the broad side of the handle and more or less parallel to the face of the racket. The forefinger is separated slightly from the others, and the gripping is done with the other three fingers and thumb. Be sure the thumb is around the handle. Extend the right arm, holding the racket waist-high, and move the hand over in front of the left hip. Raise the head of the racket so that it is slightly higher than the handle and the racket is pointing straight ahead. The wrist is slightly behind the handle, and gripping firmly will help to keep the wrist locked. The racket face should remain perpendicular to the court surface.

To change to the backhand grip from the forehand requires a change in the position of the hand, involving approximately a quarter turn counterclockwise. Starting with the forehand grip, hold the throat of the racket with the tips of the fingers of the left hand chest-high, in front of the middle of the body. Flex both elbows, pull the left hand toward the left side of the body, and extend the right hand to the right side (relaxing the wrist until the racket is almost parallel to the body). Rotate the knuckles toward the eyes (about a quarter turn). The thumb is held tightly against the broad part of the back of the handle, either diagonally or straight for added support. The first finger is separated as it is in the forehand grip, and pressure is applied with the last three fingers and thumb. Take the left hand off the racket and extend the right arm waist-high in front of the right hip. Raise the head of the racket slightly above the handle; the back of the hand should be reasonably flat. The wrist is now slightly behind the handle.

Footwork

Footwork in tennis is very important, just as it is in other activities requiring quick movement forward, backward, and laterally. The ball never bounces to the same height or comes from exactly the same direction, and in singles the player must cover the entire court. The body must be put in the proper position for each stroke, and this can be accomplished only by shifting the feet. Short shuffling steps, with a sliding motion for short distances and sprinting steps to cover longer distances, should be the pattern. Movement of the feet to get into the proper position is similar to the type of

footwork used in boxing or in guarding a man in basketball. The more efficient the movement of the body for correct body position, the more likely a correct stroke will be.

The waiting or anticipatory position is the stance taken while receiving a serve or before the pivot for the basic strokes. The player faces the net. The feet should be a comfortable distance apart (approximately 12 inches to 15 inches apart), the weight on the balls of the feet, with the knees slightly flexed and the weight evenly distributed on both feet. The racket is held with the forehand grip (beginners) in the right hand, with the left hand holding the throat of the racket with the fingertips. (Advanced players may prefer to use the backhand grip, since most of the serves they receive will be to the backhand.) The

racket is held slightly diagonally to the left, with the racket head above the handle (exaggerate), and the elbows lifted from the sides to prevent a cramped motion and free the body for quick action.

Fundamental Pivots

Since most strokes in tennis require that the side of the body be turned to the net, the fundamental pivot is essential for achieving correct body position. For a ball approaching on the right, the body is turned to the right (forehand position); for a ball approaching on the left, it is turned to the left (backhand position). In both cases, if the ball is away from the body, the pivot is toward the net; if the approaching ball is close to the body, the pivot is away from the net.

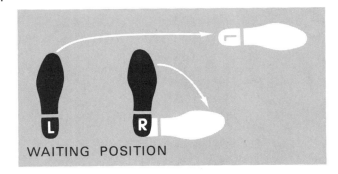

Fig. 35—3. Forehand pivot. Ball away from body.

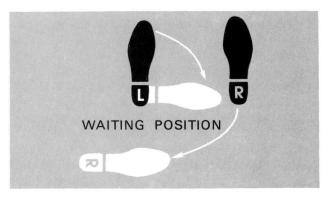

Fig. 35—4. Forehand pivot. Ball close to body.

Forehand Pivot—Ball away from body: Pivot on the ball of the right foot, making a quarter turn to the right, and bring the left foot toward the net and in front of the body. Bring the racket back for a backswing at the time of the pivot (Fig. 35-3).

Forehand Pivot—Ball close to body: Pivot on the ball of the left foot, making a quarter turn to the right, and move the right foot away from the net and behind the body (Fig. 35-4). Bring the racket back for a backswing at the time of the pivot.

Backhand Pivot—Ball away from body: Pivot on the ball of the left foot, making a quarter turn to the left, and step toward the net and in front of the body with the right foot (Fig. 35-5). Change to a backhand grip and bring the racket back for a backswing at the time of the pivot.

Backhand Pivot—Ball close to body: Pivot on the ball of the right foot, making a quarter turn to the left, and step away from the net and behind the body with the left foot (Fig. 35-6). Change to a backhand grip and bring the racket back for a backswing at the time of the pivot.

Forehand Drive

The forehand drive (along with the backhand drive) is considered the basic stroke in tennis. Many players prefer the forehand to the backhand, but equal emphasis must be placed on both strokes in order to develop a sound game.

Start from the waiting position and pivot to the forehand position. The left foot should be 3 to 6 inches in front of the right foot, with the knees slightly flexed. The racket arm is extended and brought back waist-high for the backswing, and the weight shifts to the right foot. There should be no movement in the wrist or elbow, with the shoulder initiating the move. The arm is in line with the body, and the head of the racket is slightly behind the handle and above the wrist. The left arm and hand are raised for balance about waist-

high, on the left side of the body. The forward swing is accomplished by bringing the hand and arm forward (the elbow away from the body) with movement still in the shoulder, and the weight shifted to the left foot. The point of contact for the ball is directly in front of the left hip, and the racket face should be perpendicular to the court surface at that point. The follow-through completes the stroke by relaxing the elbow and wrist and lifting the racket up and over the left shoulder, with the racket pointing high in the direction the ball has gone. The body weight is completely on the left foot as the follow-through is finished, and the pivot to the waiting foot should not be made until the stroke has been completed.

Backhand Drive

The importance of the backhand drive increases as the player improves in ability. Since this stroke is considered to be weaker than the forehand for most players, the advanced player will probably return more balls with the backhand during a match than with any other stroke. For this reason, the backhand drive must be mastered. The backhand drive is similar to a left-handed swing in baseball. To get the feeling of the stroke, swing the racket with both hands, with the right side of the body to the net. Keep the racket waist-high on the backswing, rather than shoulder-high, as is the case when a bat is used.

Start from the waiting position and pivot to the backhand position. As the pivot is made, the grip should be shifted to the eastern backhand grip. The backswing is accomplished by pulling the racket back with the left hand (the first two fingertips and thumb about halfway between the throat and the handle) and relaxing the right elbow and wrist. The right elbow is raised slightly on the backswing, and the racket is held waist-high at all times. The weight is shifted to the left foot on the backswing, and the eyes should be

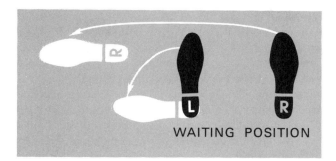

Fig. 35—5. Backhand pivot. Ball away from body.

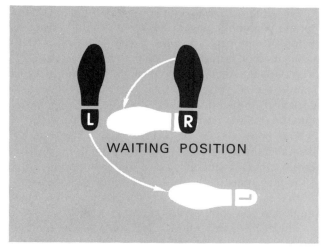

Fig. 35—6. Backhand pivot. Ball close to body.

looking over the right shoulder at the approaching ball. The right elbow and wrist straighten out on the forward swing, with both becoming rigid just before reaching the point of contact with the ball. The left hand releases its hold on the racket just before the ball is contacted, and the weight is shifted to the right foot on the forward swing. The follow-through is completed by lifting the racket high over the right shoulder, with the racket pointing high in the direction the ball has gone. The left arm should follow through naturally, and pointing with this hand in the general direction of the ball's flight increases the pace of the backhand stroke. The left arm is often neglected or used incorrectly, throwing the balance of the body backward rather than in toward the net. There is more body rotation in the backhand drive than in the forehand drive, and the ball should be contacted about 6 inches in front of the right hip. The result may be improved by getting the feeling of hitting out and around the outside portion of the ball, away from the body.

Serve

The Serve is a very important aspect of the game of tennis, since it is the stroke used to put the ball in play at the start of each point. The serve should be a potent offensive weapon, and requires a great deal of coordination between the toss and the swing for the proper results.

The three essentials of a good serve are:

Placement—Deep in the service court, to the disadvantage of the opponent.
Speed—Fast enough to keep the opponent back and off-balance.
Spin—Ball spin makes the ball harder to return accurately.

Placement is by far the most important element, because the other two, speed and spin, have little

effect if the ball does not land in the proper area. Serving in tennis can be related to pitching in baseball; variety and change of pace will be effective means of strategy to keep the opponent from knowing just where the ball is going and how to get set for a good return.

There are many different types of serves; the three most popular are the American slice, the American twist, and the flat or cannonball serve. Others are variations of these three.

American Slice

This serve is recommended for beginners. It is accurate, with a certain degree of speed and ball spin, causing the ball to curve to the left on the serve, going to the opponent's forehand. This type of serve is used by most average players.

American Twist

This serve has a great deal of top and side spin, resulting in a high bounce to the opponent's backhand. It is used by practically all of the better players as a second serve in singles and as the serve in doubles, since it is relatively slow and gives the server a chance to advance to the net following the serve. It is quite difficult to master, however, and is not recommended for the beginning player.

Flat or Cannonball

This is a fast, hard serve, hit with the face of the racket flat. It is used to "ace" the opponent or when a change of pace is desired.

Since the American slice serve is the most practical for the beginning player, this serve should be learned before attempting any other. The "whole" or full-swing method is desired in learning the serve, and only if this swing cannot be coordinated with the ball toss should the player revert to starting with the racket cocked over the shoulder or bringing up the racket into the striking position before the ball is tossed.

The body should be at an angle, with the left shoulder pointing to the desired service area. The left foot is closest to the net, and the feet are about 12 to 15 inches apart, with the weight evenly distributed on both feet. The sides of the feet are at more or less right angles to the shoulders.

The grip for the American slice can be the same as for the forehand, or the player may prefer to use the service grip, which is halfway between the eastern forehand and backhand, with the wrist on top of the handle. The service grip will make the racket contact the ball at more of an angle, producing more spin. This may make it difficult for the beginner to control the ball; he may be less confused by not learning another grip until he gains control and is ready to work on speed and spin in addition to placement.

The serve requires coordination of the left arm for the ball toss and the right arm for the striking motion. The toss is very important, and is often underestimated even by experienced players. The ball to be tossed should be held between the thumb and first two fingers of the left hand. The second ball is held in the palm, partially enclosed by the other fingers. Some players prefer to hold three balls; if this is the case, the second ball is pushed toward the base of the thumb, with the third ball held between this ball and the last two fingers. Every player should learn to hold at least two balls for the toss.

The toss starts at a position about halfway between the waist and chest, with the hand fairly close to the body. The hand with the ball is pushed up to the proper height, with the arm fully extended at the end of the toss as the ball leaves the hand. The ball toss should be high enough to allow enough time for a complete circle swing of the right arm. The approximate height can be determined by holding the racket above the head with the extended serving arm. If the toss is accurate and not hit, the ball should land about a foot in front (toward the net) of the front foot (left foot). A high toss is preferred to a low toss, which will hurry or cause a cramped motion. If the toss is too high, the timing can be corrected by a pause in the swing with the racket behind the back preliminary to the extended striking motion.

The right arm holds the racket with the proper grip (the service or eastern forehand), waist-high in a comfortable relaxed position, with the racket and arm pointing in the direction of the intended serve. The arm is relaxed and dropped close to the body so that the racket is pointing toward the court surface. Body weight is shifted to the back (right) foot as the arm comes down. The arm is rotated outward so that the face of the racket is open. The arm is brought up behind the shoulders, with the elbow and wrist in a relaxed position and the head of the racket pointing at the court surface at the level of the small of the back. The wrist and elbow are extended in a high throwing motion and the body weight is shifted to the front (left) foot. There is a definite wrist snap during this motion, since the serve is hit and not stroked as it is in the forehand or backhand drive. The racket arm is fully extended at the point of contact with the ball, with the racket face at about a 45-degree angle to impart spin to the ball. The stroke is completed with a follow-through by bringing the extended arm down on the left side, with a rotation of the body toward the net. The body weight is completely on the front foot, and balance is maintained by a step forward with the back (right) foot.

To master the complete motion (toss and striking motion), stand as if you are starting to serve and practice bringing the right arm down as the left arm pushes up the ball for the toss. If the complete swing seems difficult to master, start with the racket in the striking position (behind the back pointed toward the court), toss the ball, and serve from this position; gradually develop the full motion until it becomes natural and the timing is perfected. The feeling of "throwing the racket" into the proper service court is helpful to get the desired feeling of the complete serve. An old racket can be used on a soft surface such as grass or sand to get the desired motion.

Volley

The stroke used to play the ball before it strikes the court is called the *volley*. The ball may be volleyed at any time during the play after the return of the serve. This stroke has grown in importance during the past ten years, with the development of a more aggressive type of game. Volleying is usually done when the player is near the net, and the odds are much greater for making a point in that position than in the back-court area.

The volley can be made with either the forehand or the backhand. The racket is held in the same grips as for the forehand and backhand drives for beginners. The advanced player usually prefers to use the service or continental grip, since the exchange or return of the ball is quicker and there is not time to change grips from the forehand to the backhand in this type of game.

The volley is a punch against the ball rather than a full stroke. The body should be turned to the right for a forehand volley, and to the left for a backhand volley. The left foot steps toward the net on the forehand, and the right foot on the backhand. This step should be toward the net post as the body is turned. In case the step cannot be made, the body is turned on the balls of both feet. The knees are flexed, and many times it is necessary to jump to one side in order to keep the ball from coming directly at the body.

The backswing for both the forehand and backhand volley should be short and shoulder-high. The head of the racket is held well above the handle, and the racket face is perpendicular to the court surface. The racket comes down on the follow-through with a short punching motion. In case the ball is low, the body is dropped by bending the knees to get down to the level of the ball, not by dropping the racket head.

The half-volley has nothing in common with the volley, and is played just as the ball bounces. The racket head is dropped and the racket face is closed slightly to keep the ball from going too high.

Lob

The lob is a lofting type of stroke made with the forehand or backhand. A lob is usually made from the backcourt area, and should land as close as possible to the base line in the opponent's court. It can be used as a defensive weapon when drawn far to one side of the court to gain time to recover court position, or as a point winner by lifting the ball over the opponent's reach when he has come to the net. The height of this stroke depends on how high the opponent can reach and jump with his outstretched racket. The grips used should be the same as for the forehand and backhand drives. The backswing is the same, and at the last moment the racket head is dropped slightly. The ball is lifted and the follow-through is high. A slight amount of top spin is effective to make a ball run toward the fence when it bounces, and prevents the player at the net from running back and playing the ball. This stroke should be camouflaged as much as possible, so that the opponent at the net will not know whether to expect a passing shot or a lob.

The lob is often underestimated by younger players in favor of forceful drives. This stroke is a very important one in doubles play, since it is often the only way to dislodge the opposing players from the net.

Overhead Smash

The overhead smash is the stroke used to counteract a short lob, and requires a high degree of timing. It is the most spectacular stroke in tennis and a definite point winner. The overhead smash is made much like the serve (without the toss), except that the racket face may be a little flatter when the ball is contacted.

The body is turned to the right, with the weight on the balls of the feet and the feet moving in a shuffling motion, in order not to "get set" or "frozen" to the court at the wrong spot or too soon. Many players jump off the court to reach a high lob. The forehand or service grip may be used, and the racket is brought back in the ready position as the body is turned. The backswing may be just like the serve, although some players prefer to bring the racket up in front of the body. Many players prefer to use the left hand to point and follow the flight of the ball. At the desired moment, the racket contacts the ball with the motion similar to the serve. An angle shot should be made, and if close to the net, enough force should be used to bounce the ball into the top of the backstop. If the lob is high and close to the net, let the ball bounce; otherwise, strike the ball before it bounces. Overheads from the backcourt area are very difficult for even the advanced player, and should be played with caution.

Chop and Slice

The chop and slice are strokes to impart spin to the ball. The chop causes backspin and the slice sidespin, and both produce an unnatural bounce to throw the opponent off-balance. The grips and footwork for these strokes are the same as for the forehand and backhand drives.

The chop is used as a defensive stroke when it is impossible to make a full backswing in receiving a very fast serve or forceful drive. Along with the slice, it can be used as an offensive weapon to drop the ball just over the net with a low bounce when the opponent is deep in his court. This is called a "drop shot" and is effective on clay or grass, but not on hard-surface courts.

A short axe-like motion is used to execute the chop, with a backswing similar to the volley. The racket comes down with the face open slightly in a pushing motion, completed with a short, low follow-through. The slice follows the same pattern, with a lower backswing, and with the racket head dropped and open. The body should almost face the net for the slice, and the ball is contacted at knee height close to the body.

DRILLS

How to Practice

Learning to play tennis well requires a great deal of practice. The various strokes should be developed through drills and work on fundamentals before attempting to play too much. Working with other people wanting to learn how to play tennis is an excellent method, since their interest will be the same. Although a more experienced player can easily detect mistakes in stroke fundamentals, even beginners can correct each other while working together.

The most important thing in learning to play tennis is to *keep your eye on the ball.* Start with a ball in one hand, drop it, and catch it after one bounce with the other hand. Repeat this several times, and concentrate on watching the ball at all times. Pick up a racket and bounce the ball on the court surface, trying to keep the ball in the center of the face of the racket. These two simple drills should be repeated each time before the first few practice sessions.

Footwork Drills

The fundamental pivots can be practiced by starting in the waiting position and having someone call out, "forehand—ball away from body"; "forehand—ball close to body"; "backhand—ball away from body"; or "backhand—ball close to body." As each command is given, execute the pivot as shown in the footwork diagrams; bring the racket back for the backswing, complete the stroke, and return to the waiting position. Mix up the commands, and try to stroke an imaginary ball each time.

Forehand and Backhand Drills

The first step in learning the forehand and backhand drives is to stroke a ball which has been dropped to the court surface. Stand with your left side to the net, with the left foot on the base line. Reach out with the racket to show the approximate place the ball should be dropped. As the racket starts back for the backswing, the ball is dropped from shoulder height;

as it rebounds from the court, the racket comes forward to stroke the ball at waist level. If the foot is on the base line and the ball is dropped on the line, this will ensure that the ball is contacted in front of the left hip. Concentrate on watching the ball and the proper stroke, rather than the result.

The same drill is used for the backhand by having the right side to the net and the right foot on the base line. The ball drop is made about 6 inches in front of the line, since the backhand stroke should contact the ball slightly ahead of the right hip.

The ball drop for either forehand or backhand practice may be made by the person practicing the stroke, but better results are usually attained by having someone else drop the ball.

The next step is to stroke a ball from a short toss; for the forehand, the ball should come at an angle on the right side of the player, and for the backhand, it should come at an angle from the left. This drill should be practiced without footwork, with the body in the side position before the toss. It will be necessary to take short sliding steps to play the ball at waist level each time.

Next, start from the waiting position just behind the base line and stroke a toss from the opposite side of the net which lands about halfway between the service line and base line. Pivot as soon as the tosser's arm goes up, and move into position to stroke the ball. Play a certain number on the forehand, then the backhand, alternate, and then have the tosser mix them up.

Use the same type of drill by having the toss made to the corners of the court; practice returning to the center of the court behind the base line after the stroke has been made.

The last drill is to rally from the base line and work on stroking the ball properly by letting the ball bounce once or twice, and not worrying about always playing the ball on the first bounce. See how many times you can hit the ball back and forth over the net without making an error. Do the same thing later by always playing the ball after one bounce, as in a game situation. Work on hitting certain areas of the opponent's court as you gain confidence and your strokes improve.

Service Drills

Start by going through the serving motion without the ball toss. After this feels natural, put the racket down and practice the toss. Stand in the serving position, and draw a circle or place a target (a racket placed on the court can be used) at a point where the ball should land if tossed properly. See how many times you can

hit the target; reasonable success should be attained before attempting the complete serve.

Start serving by standing behind the base line; see how many balls you can serve over the net into the entire court. Next, practice serving into either service court; finally, serve into the proper service court. As your serve improves, mark off an area in the backhand corner of each service court and aim for that area. When a high degree of accuracy is reached, begin to serve harder and experiment with spin. A certain number of serves into each service court should be the start of each practice session in tennis.

Volley Drills

Practice the volley by playing a toss shoulder-high from the opposite service line while standing halfway between the service line and the net on the center service line. Volley a number of times on the forehand, and then the same on the backhand. Start from the side position (after a pivot), and then include footwork by starting from the waiting position. As you become more proficient, alternate the forehand and backhand. and then mix them up. Volley down and aim for a service court as a target.

After the volley has been developed, an excellent way to practice is to stand in the forecourt area and volley balls played by another player with forehand and backhand drives from the backcourt area. Advanced players work on the volley by standing just in front of the respective service lines and keeping the ball in play as long as possible by using the volley and half-volley.

Lob Drills

Practice the lob by standing behind the base line and playing a toss from the other side of the net which lands about halfway between the service line and the base line. The tosser can hold up a racket to help you judge the correct height. Aim first for the opposite backcourt area, and gradually decrease the area by drawing a line or laying down a rope 2 or 3 feet inside the court and parallel to the base line. The lob can be practiced in a rally situation by having one player work on the overhead smash and the other the lob.

Overhead Smash Drills

Practice the overhead smash by standing halfway between the service line and the net. Play the ball tossed high in the air from the opposite base line. The ball is struck overhead and aimed for the area just beyond the net in either service court. As the stroke improves, move back to the service line, and finally to the center of the backcourt area. The drill described in conjunction with the lob is excellent for advanced players.

Chop and Slice Drills

Stand just inside the base line and play a ball tossed from the opposite side of the net which lands just beyond the service line. The ball should just clear the net and have a certain degree of backspin. As the chop and slice develop, practice dropping the ball just over the net in a controlled rally by using a "drop shot" on any ball which lands on your side in the forecourt area.

Aids in Learning and Practicing Tennis

A backboard with a line the height of the net is an excellent place to practice regardless of ability. The forehand, backhand, volley, and serve can all be practiced with excellent results.

A basket of some type with a large number of practice balls is useful for drills to save time. The condition of tennis balls is not as important when learning to play as it will be for actual game competition.

A chart showing improvement may prove to be a compelling motivation and will show items needing the most attention. A record of serving (first into the entire service court, and later into areas of the service court) should also be beneficial.

Automatic ball-tossing machines are excellent for developing the fundamental strokes. These can be used on any level surface, even if a regular tennis court is not available. These machines have been improved a great deal during the past few years, and it is possible to vary the pace and height of the toss for practicing the various strokes.

A rope stretched across the court above the net which can be adjusted to various heights is an excellent practice aid. Stroking the ball from one backcourt area to the other under the rope is good practice for the forehand and backhand drives. Lob and chop practice is implemented by use of the rope.

Marks and targets on the court will be an incentive to learning and will help in charting individual progress. Chalk or rope can be used to mark off target areas or make circles for tossing. Towels, boxes, or even tennis ball cans can be used as targets for more advanced players.

Conditioning cannot be overlooked even when learning to play. To become a good or great tennis player, a person must be in excellent physical con-

dition. A jump rope for skipping should be a part of every young player's tennis equipment. Wind sprints and distance running will help build up endurance and increase the ability for the quick starts which are necessary in tennis. Weight training for tennis players is still in the experimental stage, and will probably prove helpful to many future champions.

STRATEGY

The Singles Game

Competition in tennis becomes more enjoyable by using strategy which will work to your advantage. A player may have excellent strokes, footwork, and the physical attributes necessary to be a great player, but unless he has a knowledge of good strategy and tactics, the other factors may be of little value.

The strategy for the beginning player is based on the three-stroke game—serve, forehand drive, and backhand drive. Play should be from the backcourt area, with control more important than speed. Most players just starting to play tennis have a weakness (usually the backhand), and most balls should be directed to this weakness. Run the opponent as much as possible, and keep pressure on him by deep returns which will allow you more time to get back into the proper position. Remember your court position at all times, and return to the center position (behind the base line) after making a shot from the side of the court. Stay just behind the base line or go to the net. Don't stop in the area around the service line. Two serves of moderate force are considered to be better than one very hard serve which goes into the service court only occasionally and an easy serve on which the receiver can put pressure in returning the serve. Most points in the beginner's three-stroke game are won on the opponent's errors.

By adding the volley and lob to the beginner's game, the player is able to play the net and defend himself against a net-playing opponent. This is a more aggressive type of game, and should not be attempted until the three-stroke game has been mastered. The addition of the overhead smash, chop, and slice makes it possible for the player to be at home at any place on the court. This player can change the pace of his drives and use spin to his advantage. This is a more spectacular type of game, and should be attempted only by the more advanced player.

Strategy of advanced players is more complex, and requires extreme concentration at all times to think ahead and have a definite plan of attack. The serve should be deep to the backhand, with an occasional attempt to "ace" the opponent on the forehand. Pace and the use of spin should be varied, not only on the serve but on the drives as well. The position of receiving the serve should be varied occasionally to throw the opponent off-balance, and the return should be a pressure shot rather than just a return over the net. During a rally, the balls should be returned deep to the corners of the opponent's court to keep him away from the net. The net advance should be made on any short return by the opponent, followed by a forceful shot. This is usually to his backhand, and the advance is made to the right of the center service line to cover the center of the angle of his possible return. If the forceful shot is made to his forehand, the advance is made to the left for the same purpose. Press the net attack and stay with the net game until it has been given a fair trial. Volley with pressure and crowd the net on short returns. Never change a winning game, and don't wait too long to change a losing one. Remember the score and *play to it*. Gamble when you are ahead, and keep the ball in play to force errors when behind. Try to play the ball on the rise, and use backspin against the opponent who favors the use of top spin. Play with a purpose and definite plan of attack by *thinking ahead*. Move the opponent from side to side and up and back to carry out this plan.

The Doubles Game

Doubles in tennis is definitely a game of teamwork, involving more than just increasing the number of players. Different strokes such as the volley, lob, and overhead smash take on greater importance, and good doubles play is considered more spectacular and enjoyable to watch by most ardent tennis spectators.

There are different formations for receiving, depending on the ability of the players. For beginners, both players should stay back, regardless of which one is receiving the serve. In more advanced competition, the player not receiving the serve should move in to be in a better position to volley for a placement on the return of the first shot by the serving team. This is usually a volley or half-volley by the server, who advances to the net after the serve.

The *parallel theory* of play (each player covering his half of the court from the net to the base line) is advocated by practically every tennis authority. The serve should be slower (with spin), in order to enable the server to advance to the net, which is essential in doubles play. The position of the net man varies with the ability of the individual player. For beginners, the net man should straddle the singles boundary line on the left side, or have his foot on the singles line on the right side. In both cases he should be just far enough

from the net so he can take a full swing at a ball and not touch the net. In more advanced doubles play, the net man moves back and more toward the center for more court coverage, since he knows his partner will keep his serve deep to the opponent's backhand with a slight hop.

The server stands close to the center mark when serving to the opponent's right service court, and moves 4 to 6 feet out when serving to the left service court to cut down the angle of return as he advances to the net after the serve.

The return of a serve should be directed at the server's feet as he advances to the net, or lobbed over the net man's head. In any event, it should be kept out of the net man's reach. Partners should call *"YOURS!"* or *"MINE!"* when in doubt as to who will play the ball, and cover any area left open when one player goes wide to play a ball. In most cases, use the lob to force the opponents back from the net, rather than trying to drive the ball between them. Volley at the opponent's feet in an effort to make him volley up, permitting a more forceful placement to win the point.

The player with the best serve should serve first in each set, since he may have the opportunity to serve more games during the set. It is essential that the first serve be good most of the time, in order not to waste energy advancing to the net on faults.

Choose a partner you can get along with, and stick with him. Teamwork and confidence can be the determining factors in good doubles play.

ETIQUETTE

Tennis is a game requiring extreme concentration, and certain rules of etiquette should be observed by both participants and spectators.

Good sportsmanship should be the first rule of tennis. Control of temper and language are essential. Players should not be critical of opponents, themselves, officials, or spectators. Movements or mannerisms to distract an opponent are to be avoided. When competing without the benefit of officials, players must make the decisions on their side and accept the decisions of the opponent without question. It is most important that all players know the rules of tennis and adhere to them at all times.

Points of Etiquette for the Player:

1. Clothing should be white, clean, and appropriate for tennis.
2. Be on time for any scheduled match or appointment to play tennis.

3. Be ready to receive your opponent's serve. The server should be sure his receiver is ready.
4. Play should be continuous during a match. Stalling or intentional delay are to be avoided.
5. Play a "let" on any questionable ball.
6. Don't become upset by a break in the game or by what you consider a poor call by an official.
7. Never throw your racket or hit a ball over the fence or into the net to show a flare of temper.
8. Don't make excuses if you lose.
9. Shake hands with your opponent at the completion of the match.

Points of Etiquette for the Spectator:

1. Be quiet and still while the ball is in play.
2. Applaud good plays after the point is finished. Never applaud errors.
3. Accept the official's decision.
4. Never walk behind or between courts while the ball is in play. If you have to leave, wait until a game is completed or, preferably, until the players change sides.

SAFETY

Since tennis is a noncontact sport, it is one of the safest games which can be played. However, certain precautions should be taken to prevent injuries while participating.

Before starting to play or practice, the court surface should always be checked for any rocks, broken glass, or similar objects. Backstops and side fences are not always placed according to regulations, and if they happen to be closer than the required distance, this should be called to the attention of anyone using that court. Benches or chairs along the sides of the court often present a hazard, and should be moved.

Proper court coverage and correct tactics are helpful in preventing head injuries in doubles play. Calling *"YOURS!"* or *"MINE!"* may eliminate a painful blow on the head when there is a question as to which partner will play the ball.

Jumping the net at the end of the match has been a tradition in tennis, but should be eliminated as a safety precaution. Some injuries have occurred because of this unnecessary practice.

Many players have been plagued with blisters on the hands and feet. Two pairs of socks and a skin toughener on the hands and feet often eliminate blisters.

Beginning players often put one or two tennis balls near their feet on the court surface when serving. This is dangerous, since it is very easy to sprain an ankle by stepping or tripping on a tennis ball.

Proper warm-up is important in tennis and very essential when practicing the serve. To prevent muscle strain, the movements should be slow and deliberate at the start and only gradually increased.

BIBLIOGRAPHY

Armbruster, David, Irwin, Leslie, and Musker, Frank, *Basic Skills in Sports,* 3d Ed. St. Louis: C.V. Mosby Co., 1963.

The Athletic Institute, *How to Improve Your Tennis.* Chicago: The Institute.

Barnaby, John M., *Racket Work: The Key to Tennis.* Boston: Allyn and Bacon, Inc., 1969.

Budge, Lloyd, *Tennis Made Easy.* New York: A.S. Barnes & Co., 1945.

Driver, Helen, *Tennis for Teachers.* Philadelphia: W.B. Saunders Co., 1940.

Everett, Peter, and Dumas, Virginia, *Beginning Tennis.* Belmont, Calif.: Wadsworth Publishing Co. Inc., 1962.

Hillas, Marjorie, and LeFeure, John R., *Tennis.* Dubuque, Iowa: William C. Brown Co., 1955.

Kramer, Jack, *How to Win at Tennis.* Englewood Cliffs, N.J.: Prentice-Hall, Inc., 1949.

Leighton, Harry, *Tennis, Instructor's Guide.* Chicago: The Athletic Institute, 1951.

Tennis Rules—DGWS. Washington, D.C.: American Association for Health, Physical Education and Recreation.

United States Lawn Tennis Association, *Tennis Rules.* New York—The Association.

———, *Tennis Rules* (includes guide). New York: The Association.

———, *Tennis Umpire's Manual* (includes rules). New York: The Association.

TOUCH FOOTBALL | 36

Touch football in some form has been played by boys and men of practically all ages since its introduction in the nineteenth century. Because many students do not have the opportunity for varsity football participation, they find touch football a very good substitute activity. It provides many of the experiences of the regular game and involves most of the fundamentals—such as passing, pass catching, running, carrying the ball, and kicking. Touching, or tagging, is substituted for tackling, and blocking is modified or excluded in touch football. Many of the injuries of tackle football are eliminated; and because it is a team game, the participants acquire the benefits of the social, emotional, mental, and physical values of cooperative athletic activity.

Touch football has become one of the most popular intramural sports in colleges and universities; it is also a popular activity in elementary, junior, and senior high schools. Playgrounds and industrial recreation programs usually include the game because it is inexpensive, safe, and requires little in the way of facilities.

RULES

There is very little uniformity in the rules of touch football as it is played today, either in schools or on an informal basis. The age of the participants, facilities available, and objectives desired are all factors to be considered, and the rules presented here are merely guides and should be modified or selected to suit the individuals involved.

The official rules of football should be used, with the following modifications:

Players. The number of players may vary from two (usually at least five) to eleven on a side.

Length of Game. It is played in four quarters, 8- to 12-minute quarters for older players, and 6- to 10-minute quarters for younger players.

The Field. It should be a regulation football field or smaller (40 by 80 yards is often used).

THE GAME

The object in playing touch football is to advance the ball legally across the opponents' goal line by running, passing, or kicking it.

In touch football, the defensive tactic to stop the ball carrier is touching with one or two hands, rather than tackling as in tackle football. The blocking maneuver is also modified. Therefore, protective equipment for the players is not needed.

The ball is put in play at the beginning of the game, at the start of the third quarter, and after each touchdown and field goal by a place kick (kicking the ball that rests on the ground) from one team's 40-yard line to the opponents' half of the field. The receiving team is spread out to receive the ball.

Line of Scrimmage

The *line of scrimmage* is an imaginary line that runs through the forward point of the ball, parallel to the yard lines. In order to prevent body contact, the teams line up, before the play starts, on their respective sides of the line of scrimmage. In touch football the defense lines up 5 yards, or 2 yards, from the line of scrimmage (or as in football if blocking is permitted).

Downs

From the line of scrimmage, the team in possession of the ball is allowed a certain number of plays to advance the ball. Each play is referred to as a *down*. Any of several different systems of downs can be applied. Failure to meet the requirement of the downs system in force for any particular game results in the loss of the ball to the opponents. The following are some suggested forms of downs:

(1) Teams are allowed four, five, or six downs (depending on the size of the field) to cover the distance to the opponent's goal line.

(2) Four zones are used (20 or 25 yards each), with four downs used to progress from one zone to another in order to keep the ball.

(3) Two zones are used (the field is divided in half), with four downs used in each half.

(4) Four downs are allowed to cover a certain number of yards (10, 15, or 20) from the point where the downs began. A chain or measuring device is needed for this method.

Passing

Any one of the following alternatives can be applied to the rules that govern passing:

(1) Forward passing is permitted only from behind the line of scrimmage.

(2) Passing is permitted from any position on the field any number of times, if the first pass is thrown from behind the line of scrimmage.

(3) No forward passes may be thrown if the ball is first run across the line.

Blocking

The rules that determine permissible blocking methods can be any of the following:

(1) Blocking should be restricted, in that a player may not use his body or leave his feet to block an opponent. Pushing with the shoulder or bumping is permitted with this type of blocking.

(2) Blocking that is similar to screening in basketball is permitted to maintain position or to screen the ball carrier. The defensive man must go around the blocker.

(3) No contact is allowed, and the offensive player may not run interference for a ball carrier.

Punting

To *punt* is to drop the ball from the hands and to kick it before it touches the ground. The alternatives concerning punting that are permitted in touch football are as follows:

(1) A punt must be declared, and the defense may not block the kick.

(2) Punt formation is permitted only on the fourth down, and the defense may rush.

(3) A punt can be attempted on any down, with rushing permitted.

Fumble

A *fumble* occurs when possession of the ball is lost during a play. The alternatives resulting from a fumble are as follows:

(1) A fumble is declared dead as soon as the ball hits the ground, and the ball goes to the player who last had possession of it.

(2) A fumble is played as in football.

Time-out

A time-out is called when a team requests suspension of play. Each team is allowed two time-outs in each half of the game. The referee may also call time-outs in several situations—for example, when enforcing a penalty. A time-out stops the clock and is not charged to playing time.

Touchback

If the offensive team kicks or passes the ball and it is intercepted by the defensive team over the defending team's goal line, the ball can be declared out-of-play. In this case, there is no score and the defensive team is awarded the ball on its 20-yard line. The ball is not declared out-of-play if the defensive player who catches it is able to stay on his feet and run with it.

Scoring

Touchdown

Six points are awarded for carrying or successfully passing the ball over the goal line.

Point-after-touchdown

After a touchdown has been scored, the ball is placed on the 2-yard line, and the same team that scored a touchdown tries for the point-after-touchdown. One point is awarded for carrying or successfully passing the ball over the goal line, or kicking the ball between the goalposts and over the crossbar. *Note:* The goalposts are located 10 yards behind the goal line, 18 feet 6 inches apart, and at least 20 feet high, with a crossbar 10 feet high. Often, local playing rules or situations omit the use of goalposts.

Safety

If the offensive team causes the ball to go behind their own goal line and the defensive team touches the offensive player, a safety, for two points, is awarded the defensive team. The team scored against must then kick off from their own 20-yard line.

Field Goal

Three points are awarded for kicking the ball between the goalposts and over the crossbar by a place kick.

INDIVIDUAL SKILLS

Offensive Stance

The most practical stance for the offensive player (both lineman and back) is the three-point stance. The feet are on a line and one hand rests on the ground in front of the feet, so that the body will naturally assume a comfortable semisquatting position. The body weight should be evenly distributed on the hand and the balls of the feet, with the back parallel to the ground. Offensive backs usually prefer to use a semicrouch standing position, since it is more practical for touch football.

Defensive Stance

The semicrouch stance is recommended for touch football for both linemen and backs when blocking is not allowed. The weight is evenly distributed on the balls of the feet, with the trunk of the body forward to enable the player to start quickly. One foot should be slightly ahead of the other (usually the foot closest to the expected blocker), the rear foot being used to push off in the direction of the charge.

The three-point stance may be used by defensive linemen if blocking is allowed. In this situation, the arm and hand closest to the expected blocker should protect the vulnerable defensive area (from the knee to the chest).

Blocking

Good safety practices eliminate the use of blocking in most touch football games. If blocking is allowed, the shoulder block is most adaptable.

The block in the line is executed from the three-point stance, with an explosive charge at the opponent's hip. Contact is made with the desired shoulder and forearm. The neck is locked and the back of the blocker is parallel to the ground. The block is completed with a pushing motion, with the feet well apart, and using short digging steps.

Passing

Forward and lateral (backward) passes are the basic offensive weapon in touch football.

Forward Passing

The ball is gripped or laid in the curved palm of the hand. (Better control is gained by gripping, although this may be difficult for players with small hands.) The fingers should be spread apart, with the little finger approximately near the center of the lacing and the index finger close to the rear end of the ball. The ball is raised with both hands to a position slightly behind the ear on the throwing side, with the arm cocked. The nonthrowing arm is released for balance. The body is turned slightly to the side, with the feet a comfortable distance apart. As the pass is made with a snap of the arm, the weight is transferred from the back foot to the front foot, which is pointing in the direction of the intended pass. The throwing arm continues through, completing the motion with the fingers pointing at the ball. On short passes, the ball is thrown parallel to the ground; on long passes, the flight is arched by raising the nose of the ball as it is passed. The receiver should be led; i.e., the ball should be thrown to the spot *where he will be*, not to where he is when the pass is thrown. A *spot pass* is a pass that is thrown to the place the receiver should be. The passer should watch the receiver, or a decoy, and try to disregard defensive players attempting to block the pass.

Lateral Passing

There are two types of lateral passes most adaptable to touch football.

(1) *The Two-handed Basketball Pass.* This type of pass is most effective in the open field when the offensive team has two players to the defense's one. The player making the pass should turn the head and shoulders quickly to see the intended receiver. The pass is thrown from the hip level with both hands when thrown behind the line of scrimmage, and from shoulder level in the open field. The pass should be crisp and travel parallel to the ground, but not hard.

(2) *The One-handed Spiral Pass.* This pass is thrown with an underhand pitching motion, starting at hip level. A short sliding step is used, and the pass is thrown from a crouched position. The pass is aimed at the hip of the receiver, and the passer should drop his rear knee close to the ground to maintain balance after the pass is released. The lead is essential in lateral passing just as it is in forward passing.

Receiving

Several factors are essential in receiving a football, whether thrown or kicked. The receiver should disregard the opponent and keep his eye on the ball at all times. The hands are stretched loosely toward the ball and must give slightly on contact, to prevent it from making the natural rebound from a firm surface. The hands then guide the ball into the body.

Receiving Thrown Passes

The receiver should attempt to fake the defender out of position. One method is to run to a point, stop, then start again quickly to get behind the defender. A second offensive tactic is to run directly at the defensive man and execute a sharp turn to the right or left. The *reverse-pivot-and-step-away,* or *buttonhook* maneuver, is excellent for short passes, since the defender's view is screened from the ball. Long passes should be received over the right or left shoulder, and not directly over the head. The hands are close together, with the fingers separated slightly and pointing upward, and the palms facing the ball. (Short passes should be thrown high, and the receiver pulls the ball close to the body as soon as it is caught.)

Receiving Kicked Balls

The receiver should wait with the feet spread, the knees flexed slightly, and the body weight on the balls of the feet. The hands are held shoulder-high, with the palms upward. The fingers are separated slightly, and the hands are dropped immediately on contact with the ball as the ball is pulled into the body.

Centering

The center pass in touch football usually is a direct pass to the back directly behind the center. The ball should be gripped with the throwing hand as for the forward pass. The other hand is placed on the opposite side at the rear end of the ball, and is used to guide the ball. The feet are spread apart, with the knees flexed, and the trunk bent forward, parallel to the ground. The body weight is on the feet, not on the ball. Long center passes, such as for a punt, require a wrist snap to apply force to the pass.

Some players may want to use a *T-formation pass,* but this is not practical in touch football unless the defensive line is required to be a certain distance from the line of scrimmage. If this is the case, the head of the center is held high in the center stance used for the direct pass, and the ball is merely handed between the legs to the back standing directly behind the center.

Kicking

(1) *Punting.* The punter stands with the kicking foot slightly advanced, the body weight forward, the eyes on the ball, the hands pointing toward the center, and the palms open and facing each other about a foot apart. The ball is caught with the hands near the center of the ball. The right hand is placed so that the middle finger is resting along the bottom seam of the ball. The hand should be forward on the ball far enough to have control of the ball, so that it may be dropped in the same manner each time the punter kicks. The left hand serves to balance the ball, and is placed lightly against the left front side of the ball. The laces of the ball are usually on top, but this is not necessary. The nose of the ball should be slightly lower, so that if the ball were dropped and not kicked, it would bounce backward. As the ball is caught and placed in the hands, a short step is taken with the kicking foot and a natural stride with the other. The kicking leg comes forward and upward as the hands drop the ball. At the time of impact, the kicking leg is locked up and the point of contact is made with the top of the instep. The toe is pointed and the follow-through is completed by driving the kicking foot high and raising the arms.

Quick Kicking. Quick kicking is used as an element of surprise. The fundamentals are the same as for the punt. The kick should be faster and started from the same position as for a running or passing play. The end of the ball should be contacted, to increase the possibility of a good roll.

(2) *Place Kick.* The holder lines up about 7 yards behind the line of scrimmage, with both knees on the ground, at about a 30- to 40-degree angle on the kicking side. The hands are outstretched in front of his body, to give the center a target for the pass. The holder gives the signal for the ball snap after making sure the kicker is ready. The ball is caught with both hands and placed perpendicular to the ground, with the index finger on top of the ball. The kicker stands behind the spot where the ball is to be placed, with the kicking foot slightly advanced and both feet pointing straight ahead, with his eyes on the spot. A short step and a half is used for a place kick as the ball is placed down by the holder. The first step, or half-step, is with the kicking foot, and the other foot steps as the kicking foot is brought back for contact. The ball should be kicked about midway between the center of the ball and the ground. The ankle and knee must be locked at contact, to get a leg snap by creating pendular motion from the hip. The foot should drive through the ball and not stop on contact, with the head remaining down. For a kickoff, the kicker stands back 8 or 10 yards and runs toward a ball, either held by a player or placed on a kicking tee.

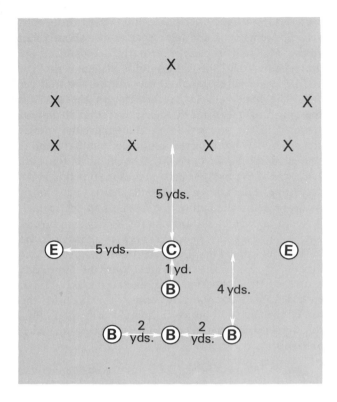

Fig. 36—1a. Offensive formation—T.

Fig. 36—1b. Offensive formation—Single wing.

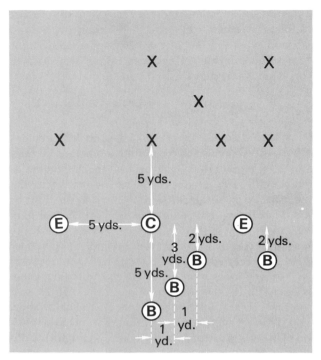

Running

(1) *Fade-away.* As he approaches the defensive player, the runner feints with the front foot and swings it across the body to the opposite side as far as possible. The weight is on the back foot; as the front foot touches the ground, the momentum is gained again by a vigorous push with the back foot, and the runner continues in his original direction.

(2) *Side Step.* As the ball carrier approaches the defensive player, he plants the inside foot and pushes off this foot with a long step directly to the outside and shifts the weight to this foot. The inside foot is pulled quickly toward the outside foot, and the ball carrier continues in his original direction.

Tagging

Some rules call for a one-handed tag, others for a two-handed tag, either on the entire body or below the waist. Regardless of the type of tag or the portion of the body to be tagged, the fundamentals are the same. The defensive player, or tagger, should attempt to make the ball carrier commit himself as soon as possible as to intended direction. The tagger's stance

should be with the feet apart, one slightly in front of the other, and with the weight evenly distributed on the balls of the feet.

Covering Pass Receiver

Defending against a pass utilizes the fundamental footwork skills used by the defensive man attempting to tag a ball carrier. The defender should usually stay behind the receiver, and not be influenced by any fakes or maneuvers used by him. After the pass has been thrown, the defender should attempt to follow the flight of the ball and jump to intercept the pass. In most situations, the ball should be caught, if possible.

TEAM SKILLS

Offense

A number of offensive formations are adaptable to touch football just as they are to regular football (Figs. 36-1 a-d). Since the number of players on a team varies according to the rules used, the type of formation should be in line with the total number of players on a side. For example, if there were six on a side, three players would line up on the line of scrimmage and three in the backfield. As the number on a team increases, the backs will increase to four and the linemen to seven.

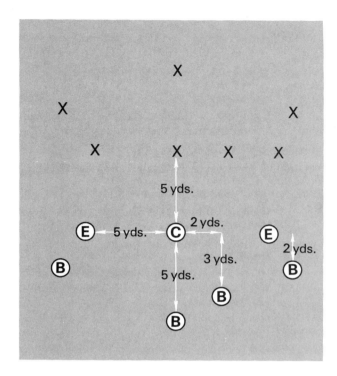

Fig. 36—1c. Offensive formation—Double wing.

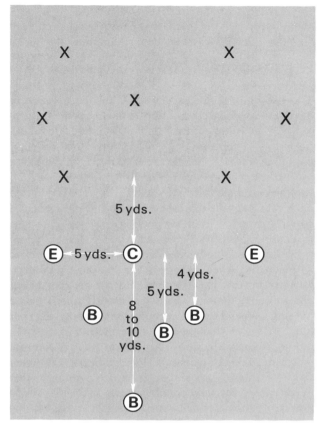

Fig. 36—1d. Offensive formation—Punt.

Basic running, passing, and punting plays should be developed with a signal system numbering the plays (Figs. 36-2a-d). A starting signal is needed which can be varied to keep the defense from knowing when the ball will be snapped. There should be a variety of plays used, both running and passing, but they should be kept as simple as possible, Passes should not be thrown to the same receiver all the time because this practice causes loss of interest and effort among the other players.

Defense

The type of defense used in touch football is also dependent on the number of players the rules allow. If blocking is not allowed, fewer linemen will be needed to rush. Linemen should know which ones are going to rush the ball carrier and which ones should cover wide running plays or drop back in the event of a pass.

Pass defense can be a *zone defense*, in which each man covers a given area; *man-to-man defense*, in which each defensive man has a certain offensive player to cover; or a combination of both. The best defense against long passes is to rush the passer. The defensive back should usually stay behind the receiver until the ball is thrown, and then go after the ball. In general, defensive formations should be flexible and changing constantly to meet new offensive situations.

How to Practice

Indidivual skills can be developed by working in pairs or through drill situations in small groups. Offensive and defensive plays require entire team coordination, to perfect the basic plays used on both offense and defense.

Blocking and defense can be practiced by each team member working with another player on each fundamental.

To practice passing, start a short distance apart and simply pass the ball to another man. Move back and increase the distance, then pass to a moving receiver. Coordination between the passer and receiver can be developed by working on basic receiving maneuvers such as run and cut, and run and stop; either turn quickly for the short pass or continue for a long pass.

Centering can be practiced by centering each other at various distances necessary for passing, punting, and place kicking.

Kicking, for distance and accuracy out-of-bounds, can be practiced objectively by increasing the distance as skill develops. Game drills, such as drive back (the players drive an opponent back behind a line by kicking from the point where the punt is received), are excellent and interesting to participants.

FLAG FOOTBALL

The use of flags instead of tags has been a recent development, and flag football has replaced touch football in many school and university intramural programs. The first flags used were handkerchiefs tucked in the belt at the back of each player. The type most common today is a belt with three colored flags that are fastened with snaps. One flag is fastened on each side, and one on the back. The flags are released when grasped by a defensive player.

There is less body contact in flag football, and officiating becomes easier. There is no question as to whether the player is tagged. The small, shifty player, because he can run with the ball, is given a better chance to participate, since touch football is largely a passing game. In flag football, the running game is more effective than in touch football.

Flag football was introduced in the intramural program at the University of Florida in place of touch football. Scoring increased to at least three touchdowns per game, and there was less friction between players and officials. Fewer injuries occurred, and the game became one of the most popular in the entire program.

Rules for Flag Football as Used by the Intramural Department of the University of Florida: Regular

National Federation of State High School Rules will govern, with the following exceptions:

1. No spiked or cleated shoes of any kind will be allowed.
2. Each player shall wear a set of three flags.
3. The grabbing of an offensive player, or his clothing, by the defense in order to remove his flag, or the deliberate pushing of a ball carrier out-of-bounds, is an infraction—a 20-yard penalty is incurred.
4. Any deliberate attempt by the ball carrier to stiff-arm, shield his flags, or deliberately run over the defensive player, is an infraction—a 20-yard penalty is incurred.
5. Any charging or attempt to block by the offense is an infraction—an offensive player may take a natural stance or position, making the defensive man go around him.
6. A legal touch is made when one detaches one flag from the ball carrier.
7. The offensive team must have three men on the line of scrimmage.
8. Each member of a team is eligible to receive a pass.
9. The kickoff will be made from the 30-yard line. Three men from the receiving team must not be closer than 10 yards nor more than 15 yards from the kickoff spot.
10. There shall be a 5-yard restraining line for the defensive team, unless the offensive team is within

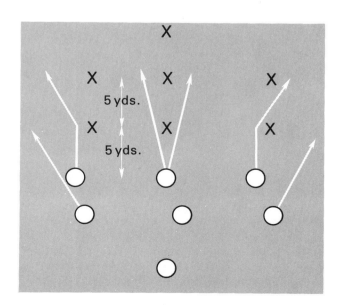

Fig. 36—2a. Play—Split safety pass or run.

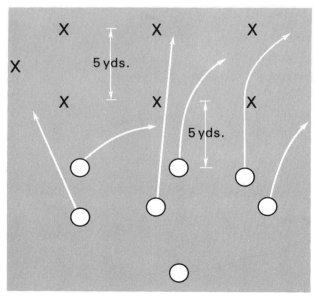

Fig. 36—2b. Play—Overload right.

its 5-yard line; then the defensive restraining line shall be 1 yard.

11. The ball shall be placed on the 10-yard line after any touchback or safety.
12. Any time-out will be limited to 1 minute. No team will be allowed more than two time-outs per half.
13. The game will consist of two halves, of 12 minutes each, with 2 minutes between halves. Goals will automatically change at the half.
14. There shall be a try for the point-after-touchdown by a pass or a run from the 5-yard line.
15. Teams have four downs to make 20 yards and a first down. *Exception*: When a team begins a new series of downs on the opponent's 20-yard line or within the opponent's 20-yard line, the team with the ball shall have four downs to make 10 yards for a first down. When a new series begins within the opponent's 10-yard line, the ball is put in play at the spot where the ball carrier is touched.
16. First downs count one point each, and shall decide the game only in case of a tie.
17. In case of a tie, both in score and first downs at the end of the game, the ball shall be placed on the 40-yard line and each team will be given a series of four alternating downs. The team gaining the most yardage will be declared the winner.
18. The size of the field shall be 40 X 80 yards, with a 10-yard end zone.
19. All infractions (with the exception of rules 3 and 4) shall incur 10-yard penalties.
20. Free substitution is allowed.

SAFETY

Injuries can occur in touch football if certain precautions are not taken by participants and officials do not recognize the problems involved. Most injuries to the participants are to the ankles or knees, due to the necessity of sharp turns and quick starts.

Many injuries can be prevented by taking a proper warm-up before activity is started. Bending and stretching exercises, along with quick starts, will decrease the possibility of an injury, especially at the start of the game.

The playing field should be checked for any uneven areas, rocks, glass, or other debris. Benches should not be placed close to the sidelines, nor warm-up clothing placed on or along the playing area.

Colored jerseys are helpful, so that players can easily identify teammates. Rubber-soled shoes should be required of all participants, and players should never be allowed to play without shoes.

All rules should be strictly enforced by competent officials. Rough or illegal tactics should never be tolerated. If they occur, the player responsible should be penalized immediately or eliminated from the game.

Flag football seems to be a safer game than touch football. Much of the rough tagging is eliminated by knowing immediately whether the ball carrier has been tagged.

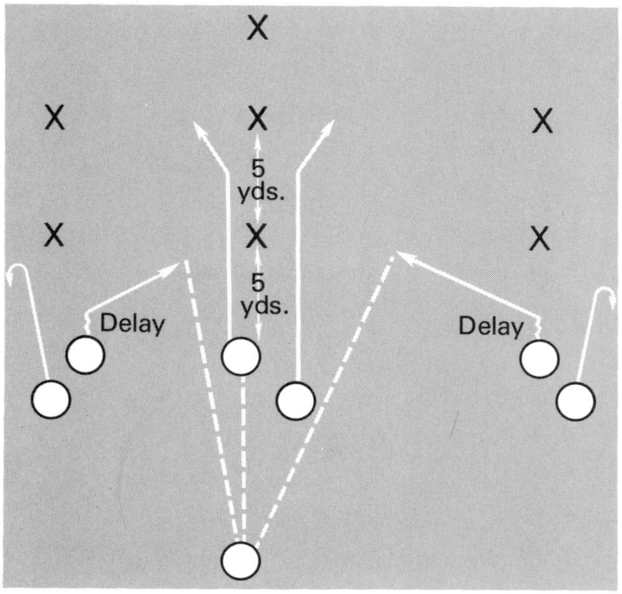

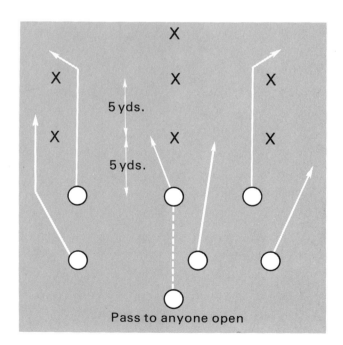

Fig. 36—2c. Play—End quickie.

Fig. 36—2d. Play—Basic pattern.

BIBLIOGRAPHY

Allen, George, with Weiskopf, Donald, *Inside Football: Fundamentals, Strategy, and Tactics*. Boston: Allyn and Bacon, Inc., 1970.

The Athletic Institute, *Official National College Touch Football Rules Handbook for Physical Education Service Classes and Intramural Programs*. Chicago: The Institute, 1953.

Bateman, John F., and Governali, Paul V., *Football Fundamentals*. New York: McGraw-Hill, Inc., 1957.

National Federation of State High School Athletic Association, *Touch Football Rules (High School)*. Chicago: The Federation.

Nelson, David M., *Football: Principles and Play*. New York: The Ronald Press Company, 1962.

Van Brocklin, Norm, in collaboration with Hugh Brown, *Norm Van Brocklin's Football Book*. New York: The Ronald Press Company, 1961.

The Greeks, through their Olympic games, were the first people to organize track and field events. It was a high honor to be an Olympic champion, for the Greeks regarded track and field events as a demonstration of strength and as an excellent preparation for the life of a soldier. They also considered a beautiful body a great accomplishment and something to be admired. Their sculptors carved the bodies of athletes in marble for all to admire and emulate.

The first track and field meet between two universities was held in 1864 between Cambridge and Oxford Universities. Subsequently, at the turn of the century, athletic clubs were formed in the northeastern part of the United States by immigrants to America. In 1876 the Intercollegiate Association of Amateur Athletics of America held their first championship meet; 1921 marked the date of the first National Collegiate Athletic Association championship.

Relay races were made popular by the Pennsylvania (Penn) Relays, which were first held in 1895. The revival of the Olympic games in 1896 again popularized track throughout the world. It is interesting to note that the five rings in the Olympic emblem indicate five continents joined together by a common bond of amateur athletic competition.

In the past American women have not responded well to this challenging activity, but interest and popularity in track and field is growing at a significant rate. Although American women have not attained the proficiency of Asian and European women, progress is being noted each year.

The Division of Girls' and Women's Sports is the governing organization for this activity for women. The D.G.W.S. *Track and Field Guide* identifies all rules and makes all recommendations for events and the age groups participating in these events.

TERMINOLOGY

Anchor man—The fourth or final runner on a relay team.

Baton—The "stick" that is passed between runners on a relay team.

Box or planting pit—The slot in which to plant the vaulting pole prior to a jump.

Breaking—Leaving the starting line before the starting pistol is fired.

Breasting the tape—Contacting the finish yarn with the chest at the finish of a race.

Checkmark—A point used by jumpers, javelin throwers, and relay men to get maximun results. This is usually a mark on the runway to indicate the proper stride.

Chute—An extension of the straightaway on an oval track to make it possible to run races of 220 yards or less without going around a turn.

Circle—The area from which the discus, shot, and hammer are thrown.

Dead heat—When two runners finish exactly together.

Exchange—The passing of the baton in a relay race.

Exchange zone or passing zone—An area that is 20 meters long and one lane wide, within which relay runners must pass the baton.

Field—A group of competitors entered in an event.

Field events—All events that are not running events—the jumping and throwing events.

Flight—A group of competitors competing at the same time in field events.

Flyaway—A term used to describe the push-away of a vaulter at the height of his jump.

Foul—An infraction of the rules by a competitor.

Heats—Preliminary trial races to reduce a large field of runners.

Hurdles—Barriers that are used in hurdle races.

Jog—An easy bouncing stride.

Jumping foot—The foot that transmits the jumping force.

Kick—The final burst of speed at the end of a race.

Lane—A strip or alley on the track within which a runner must stay to run a race legally.

Lap—The full distance of an oval track.

Lead leg—The first leg over a hurdle or over the crossbar in high jumping.

Lead-off man—The first man to run on a relay team.

Pace—To run at a specific rate.

Pole—In races, it is the lane by the inner border of the track. It is also the device with which the vaulter hoists himself.

Pulled muscle—A tearing apart of the fibers in a muscle.

Pull-over force—The force that it takes to knock over a hurdle.

Qualify—To win the right to participate at a more competitive level in a field or track event.

Record—The best time or distance in an event for a specific period of time.

Relay race—A track event in which a team of four men run successively, each passing a baton to his successor.

Scratch line—The line in the javelin throw and the broad jump, beyond which a competitor must not set foot.

Shin-splint—A strain of the muscles of the front section of the lower leg.

Shot—The metal sphere used in the shot put event.

Staggered start—A type of start used to compensate the distances on an oval track.

Starter—The official responsible for all runners getting away fairly at the start of the race.

Starting blocks—Steps placed on the surface of the track to ensure good traction when a runner starts.

Team race—A track event in which a group runs simultaneously as a team and each member scores points that correspond to his position at the finish. The low score wins. Cross-country is scored as a team event.

Toe board—A board used in some field events to help a competitor remain within the legal limits.

Trial—One of a specified number of attempts required in order to qualify for a field event.

Tying up—A condition that causes a runner to noticeably slow down and tighten up as he is running.

Warm-up—A group of exercises or any other method that a competitor may use to loosen up for competition.

Wind sprints—Short runs of 40-60 yards, done in rapid succession to develop speed and stamina.

TRACK SKILLS

The Start

The Crouch Start

There are two general ways of starting, the *crouch start* and the *standing start*. The crouch start can be

performed in three ways that differ only in the spacing of the feet in the "on-the-marks" position. The three types are the bunch, the medium, and the elongated.

The Bunch Start. To get in the "on-the-marks" position, set the starting blocks so that the rear foot is approximately 30 inches from the starting line and the front foot about 20 inches. Get into the starting blocks by standing in front of them and backing into the blocks. Bend forward, place the feet against the blocks, and the hands behind the starting line. Hold the arms straight at shoulder width. Shift the body weight forward, with the rear knee and arms supporting the body. More weight seems to be on the hands than on the feet. Look down at the track about 2 to 3 feet in front of the starting line.

At the command "SET!" raise the hips by extending the legs. The shoulders are lower than the hips. The arms are still held straight. Look at a point on the track about 15 inches in front of the starting line. The body weight is on the hands and feet.

At the pistol shot, drive out of the blocks with the forward leg. Thrust the opposite arm forward and take the first step with the rear foot. The body is kept low, with a forward lean from the hip. Take short, quick steps for the first 5 yards. This type of start is best for the short, stocky sprinter.

The Medium Start. The rear foot is placed 35 inches from the starting line. The front foot is on a line even with the knee of the back leg. The hands, arms, and head are kept in the same position as described in the bunch start. All other positions in this start are the same as in the bunch start, except that the legs are not extended as far in the set position. This has a tendency to distribute more of the weight to the legs than to the hands. The medium start is not as fast as the bunch start but it allows greater relaxation in the set position.

The Elongated Start. Set the blocks so that the rear foot is 40 inches from the starting line, and the front block about 2 feet ahead. The elongated start is comfortable for runners with very long legs.

The Standing Start

This start is generally used in the longer races, where a quick start is not imperative. In the "on-the-marks" position, place the forward foot close behind the starting line. The rear foot is about 20 inches behind. The body has a slight forward lean. The arm on the same side as the forward foot is bent and held out in front, with the hand at about shoulder height. The opposite arm is held down and to the rear, with the hand at about waist height.

In the set position, the body is rocked slightly forward and the weight is shifted mainly to the forward foot. The arms are extended slightly farther than their position held in "on-the-marks."

At the report of the pistol, drive forward with the forward foot, and at the same time thrust the rear arm forward and upward. The step taken by the rear foot is about 20 inches in front of the starting line. Get into a running style immediately.

The Stride

In running the knees are picked up and the arms are carried close to the sides in a bent-arm position. The body leans forward slightly. The arms are swung alternately straight forward and backward, not across the front of the body. The power comes from pushing from the rear foot. The ball of the foot touches the ground, while the heel touches it very lightly. As the rear leg straightens and the foot extends for the power, the other leg recovers by pulling the knee forward. Momentarily, after the final drive of the rear foot, both feet are off the ground. As the body moves forward, the leg is brought down so that the foot touches the ground ahead of the center of gravity of the body. Throughout the run, the feet point forward.

The Finish

The finish of a race is important, particularly in the short sprints and hurdles races. The runner must "gather" for a supreme effort about 20 yards from the finish. Maintain a forward lean in the final effort to breast the tape. Lunge forward but maintain balance. Do not throw the arms up and put the chest out at the finish. Continue to run past the finish line.

TRACK EVENTS

Sprints (Dashes)

Any race up to and including the 440-yard distance is considered a sprint. The best way to improve sprinting time is to improve the start. This phase of the race decides most short sprints because there is little time to think and use strategy.

The 440-Yard Dash

This race is considered a long-distance sprint. Start this race running hard enough to get into a favorable position through the first turn. Never start too slowly, as it is important to be in a front-running position in this race. Much energy will be required to catch the "field." "Float" at the halfway mark, and allow the forward momentum to carry the body for about 10 or 15 yards. Never allow anyone to pass while floating. Drive for the finish line and pick up speed on the last stretch to the tape. If running on a track that has two turns in the 440-yard run, run at top speed coming off the final turn.

The Half-Mile or 880-Yard Run

This run is not a dash, nor is it considered a distance run. To compete in this race one must possess speed, stamina, and a good sense of pace or timing. In a well-paced 880-yard run the runner will use a little less than half the total time of the race in running the first 440 yards. In the half-mile run it is necessary to work on stamina and pace. Use any form that comes most naturally. Start out like a quarter-miler, and then settle into a predetermined pace. As the halfway mark is passed, the runner floats for a short period of time, running at about three-fourths effort. Drive to the tape at full effort.

Distance Races

The distance races consist of any race longer than a half mile. The arms should be carried somewhat lower

than in the shorter races, thereby letting the runner remain more relaxed. Do not stay up on the toes, but allow the heels to come down and contact the track. The procedure is to contact the track with the toes first, then the heels, and then rock back up on the toes. Use a minimum amount of leg-lift and kick-back. This means that the feet stay close to the ground during the stride.

In the distance runs the first half of the race is faster than the last half. Get a good start and get into a favorable position immediately. The pace at the start is determined by conditioning. A time schedule for each quarter mile of the race is predetermined in practice. It is not until the last quarter mile that a distance runner steps out and makes an all-out effort to the finish.

Cross-Country Races

Cross-country running is a type of distance race that is unique in that a runner must run over a variety of terrain. One cannot maintain an even pace; the style of running will change to meet the changes in the course. Cross-country runners set a fast pace at the start of the race, using the "toe-heel-toe" stride. For a hill, the runner must get up on the toes, shorten and quicken the stride, and increase the forward lean of the body. When going downhill, the runner should not hold back, but should lengthen the stride and allow the forward momentum of the body to force it to move. When crossing sandy or soft ground, negotiate it as fast as possible by getting up on the toes and driving hard.

Relay Races

Relay races vary in length from a total of 440 yards (4 X 110) to the 4-mile relay (4 X 1 mile). There are also *medley relays* (in which the distances vary for each runner), and *shuttle relays* (in which each runner must run a flight of hurdles during his leg of the race).

The relay races require that a baton be passed between the successive runners on a team. In the shuttle hurdle relay no baton is used. The exchange must be made in a zone 20 meters long. It is permissible for the successor to stand 10 meters behind the exchange zone in the 440- and 880-yard relays, but the exchange must still be made in the 20-meter relay exchange zone.

There are two general types of exchanges, the *nonvisual* (Fig. 37-1) and the *visual* (Fig. 37-2). The visual exchange requires that the runner receiving the baton watch the oncoming runner, and it is his responsibility to make sure he gets the baton. This

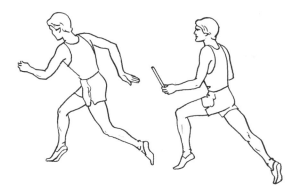

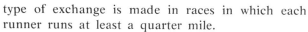

Fig. 37—1. Nonvisual or blind pass.

type of exchange is made in races in which each runner runs at least a quarter mile.

The nonvisual or "sprint-type" exchange makes the oncoming man responsible for getting the baton to the next runner. The receiver does not look back but "takes off" when he feels that the oncoming man can catch up to him. At this point he places a hand back as a target for his teammate to reach. The chances of a dropped baton are greater than in the visual exchange. However, the sprint pass is faster and less time is wasted.

The Baton Pass

Generally, the baton is passed to the right hand of the new runner from the left hand of the oncoming runner. However, this procedure is not used in races when the baton is passed on a turn, as in the second and fourth legs of the quarter-mile relay. In this type of race, the receiver keeps the baton in the receiving hand and passes to his next teammate, who will have the opposite hand out. The advantages of this are that the passer can hug the inside of the lane and the receiver can maintain better arm action after he gets the baton. The receiver has less chance of dropping the baton, since he does not have to switch it to his other hand during the race.

Sprint passes are nonvisual, so the receiver should offer as large a target as he can to his teammate. In one exchange the receiver will place his thumb against the side, at hip height. The palm of the hand is turned to the rear, with the fingers closed together. The inverted "V" formed by the thumb and fingers is the target. The oncoming runner slides the baton up into the "V".

In another sprint pass the tips of the fingers of the right hand just touch the right hip, the palm of the hand facing upward. The target is now a loop formed by the receiver's torso, arm, and hand. The oncoming

runner places the baton in the loop and brings it down into the receiver's hand. In the above two passes, a little distance is sacrificed to obtain a better target.

The most widely used sprint pass is the exchange in which the receiver extends his right arm to the rear, at about a 45-degree angle with the body. The thumb of the right hand is held away from the index finger to give the inverted "V" target, and the palm faces to the rear. This pass can be made visually or blind. The approaching runner passes the baton by bringing it up into the "V" target. The advantage of this exchange is that it sacrifices no speed or distance, and the baton can be switched by the receiver to his hand-off hand without any difficulty.

The visual pass, used most often, requires that the receiver wait for his teammate to hold the baton out at shoulder height. The receiver is turned slightly to the rear as he reaches back, and takes the baton by snatching it from his teammate. This pass is used generally in the distance relays, in which the oncoming runner is tired.

Fig. 37—2. Visual speed pass.

Hurdles

There are 10 hurdles or barriers to be cleared as rapidly as possible. The hurdles vary in height from the low hurdle (30 inches high) to the collegiate high hurdle (42 inches high).

The form for hurdling is learned best by assuming the correct position on the ground. First, sit with both legs extended straight out in front. To get the rear or trailing leg in position, place it so that, as seen from above, the thigh is at right angles to the front leg and the lower part of the trail leg is in a position parallel to the front leg. The toes of the front foot point forward and upward, and the toes of the trailing foot point out. The hand and arm opposite the front leg are stretched out directly in front of the body, and the opposite arm is held downward and slightly to the rear. This reaching-forward position puts the hurdler in a forward lean that helps him clear the hurdle.

Start a hurdle race by sprinting to the first hurdle. The optimal number of steps to the first hurdle in a high-hurdle race is eight, with three steps between hurdles. In a low-hurdle race it is ten steps to the first hurdle and seven between hurdles. Learn to hurdle so that the same leg position is used to clear each hurdle.

Upon approaching a hurdle in a race, prepare for it with a forward lean of the body. Extend the forward leg and opposite arm straight out in front. The body position over the hurdle is the form for hurdling described above. From this point the lead leg is pulled down as the opposite arm is brought back, and the trailing arm comes forward. The rear leg is brought forward from the hip and the lower leg dropped to prepare for a stride. The whole body pivots about the lead foot as it makes contact with the track, and the trailing leg is brought forward for the first step. The runner is now in position to run to the next hurdle and repeat the process. The higher the hurdle, the more the runner must lean forward in order to clear the hurdles with the trailing leg.

FIELD EVENTS

Running Long Jump

In long jumping the checkmark is extremely important because it determines the point from which the jumper will start the run. In a practice session, the jumper locates the checkmark by placing one foot against the edge of the take-off board that is closest to the pit, and simulates his run and take-off in the reverse direction from the actual event. The spot is marked, and the jumper, starting from this check-mark, tries a jump. By trial and error, slight adjustments are made until the precise spot for a perfect take-off is found.

Long jumping requires about a 100-foot approach run. A good jump requires that the jumper be running at close to top speed when addressing the take-off board with the jumping foot. The stride is shortened slightly on the last stride. This gives the jumper the ability to gather for the take-off.

Bring the arms forcibly upward at the same time as the opposite leg is lifted from the hip and bent at the knee. The head is held high and slightly back, and the hips are forward. The take-off is a rocking forward motion from heel to toe of the take-off foot.

During the jump it may be necessary to kick the legs as though running through the air to maintain balance, but this is not always necessary. Keep the head high and the feet forward, in a jackknife position. Upon landing the arms and head are brought forward and downward; this action will cause the body to fall forward. (To get the best distance, concentrate on getting up into the air, letting your speed take care of the distance.)

The Triple Jump

This event is also known as the hop-step-and-jump. It is again very important to determine a checkmark from which the jumper will start the run. The method used is the same as in the long jump, since the initial phase of this event is exactly the same as that for the long jump.

The contestant in the triple jump must take off from behind the forward edge (the side nearer the pit) of the take-off board. For this event, the take-off board is much farther away from the pit than it is for the long jump. However, the take-off from the board is made in the same manner as for the long jump but with less effort because the landing must be made on one leg—the one used to make the take-off. As the contestant is about to land, he drops the arms and take-off leg. The other leg is cocked and slightly behind the body. When contact is made with the ground, the take-off leg bends slightly, and the other leg swings forward in conjunction with the arms to make the stride or step. The take-off now must be taken with this foot, and a long jump is made into the pit. Landing in the pit will be the same as in the long jump.

In this event care must be taken not to overdo the first phase. If the jumper exerts too much effort on the hop, he will find it physically impossible to land on one leg and take off again from it to make the step.

High Jump

The style most commonly used by jumpers is the "straddle." In this style of jump the competitor uses the foot closest to the bar on his approach as his take-off or jumping foot. The jumper crosses the bar facedown, and lands on his back. This type of jump is preferred because the jumper does not have to jump as high to clear the bar as in the "western roll," and the jumping leg does not get as tired because the opposite leg is used to land.

The western roll is performed with the jumper clearing the crossbar on his side, and now landing more or less on the jumping foot. This style is now more or less obsolete.

Checkmarks are necessary for an efficient jump. The take-off checkmark is determined in this way: stand in front of the bar, facing it obliquely at a 45-degree angle; kick the closer foot up toward the bar; if the foot just clears the bar, then the toes of the foot on the ground are at the correct take-off mark. Turn, run back eight steps, and set checkmarks from which to start the running approach. Minor adjustments are made by taking a few practice jumps to determine if the steps are precisely correct.

In the straddle jump, the approach to the bar is at a 20- 30-degree angle. On the last step, rock back on the heel of the take-off foot as the arms are extended upward above the head; the leg furthest from the bar is kicked from the hip up toward the bar. As the forward leg starts to clear the bar, drive the same arm down and turn the take-off leg, which is bent at the knee, out. The jumping leg will then clear the bar, with the inside of the thigh facing the crossbar.

The "Fosbury Flop" is a new style of high jump that is gaining recognition. It should not be taught to youngsters until an adequate landing pit is available, since a person may injure the neck when landing.

Pole Vault

In learning to pole vault it is necessary to first locate the hand-hold on the vaulting pole. A beginner should start out by holding the pole about 6 inches above the height that is to be cleared. A vaulter who has become proficient will grasp the pole at the height that he finds through experience has given him best results (Fig. 37-3).

The take-off mark is located by placing the vaulting pole in the planting slot, and gripping the pole in the way it will be gripped for the vault. The pole is held overhead, with both hands together; the vaulter's feet will be at the take-off mark.

The vaulter now turns from the take-off mark, holds the pole in the running position (Fig. 37-4), and

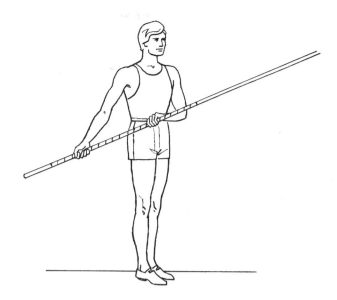

Fig. 37—3. Carrying the pole.

runs a distance great enough to bring him to top running speed (usually about sixteen strides from the take-off). The point at which he attains this speed is the starting checkmark. The vaulter should make a few practice runs to see if his checkmarks are accurate.

To start a vault, stand at the starting checkmark and face toward the pit. Grip the vaulting pole as previously determined for this jump; hold the pole over the head, allowing the end of the pole to rest on the runway. The hand that is directly overhead is the top hand. The other hand is placed lower on the pole, in front of this hand. In this position, the fingers of both hands are closer to the front end of the pole than are the thumbs, and the palms of the hands face each other. (Without releasing the pole, bring it down to hip level on the same side as the top hand.) The forward hand slides forward and lifts the end of the vaulting pole from the runway until the pole is raised slightly above hip level.

During the run toward the pit, the pole is held in approximately a horizontal position, and the end of the pole is kept in a line of sight from the eyes to the vaulting slot. Approximately three strides from the point of take-off, the vaulter lowers the tip of the pole toward the slot and shifts the pole forward. On the next step the pole is shifted overhead, and the top hand on the pole is directly overhead when the tip of the pole makes contact with the end of the slot. The hands remain 16 to 24 inches apart.

A sharp tug on the shoulders at take-off is an indication that the take-off is too close to the slot. A

Run   Plant   Take off   Rock back   Flyaway

Fig. 37—4. Pole vault sequence.

feeling that the pole has momentarily collapsed is an indication that it is too far away. The correct planting distance will impart a slight tug to the shoulders as the vaulter lifts into the air.

The take-off is made by stepping past the pole with the same leg as the top hand, and on the same side of the pole. The rear foot gives impetus to the vault by a forward thrust from the toes. Keep the body behind the pole by keeping the head on the opposite side of the pole from the side on which the vault is being made. After take-off rock the body back by using a high knee lift of the lead leg, and allow the head to tilt back slightly.

Gather in the legs at the hips and bend them slightly at the knees, raising the hips and feet above the head. Bring the same leg as the top hand over the opposite leg, and simultaneously turn the head in the same direction. This turns the vaulter over on the stomach as he clears the crossbar.

As the hips clear the crossbar, straighten the legs with a quick downward thrust of the lower leg. Push away from the vaulting pole by straightening out the arms. Release the pole, first the lower hand, then the upper. This action turns the vaulter slightly and gets the arms clear of the crossbar.

As the crossbar is raised higher the standards that hold the crossbar will have to be moved toward the slot. At maximum heights the crossbar is only about 12 inches from the end of the slot, and at low heights it is about 24 inches. Check this distance by placing the end of the vaulting pole in the small end of the slot, and hold it in a vertical position. The standards can then be moved to the desired distance. Some vaulters may have to change their handgrip to a higher position on the vaulting pole as the crossbar is raised. The handgrip can be checked by this method also.

Shot Put

The shot is put from a ring 7 feet in diameter; at the front edge of the ring is a toe board that is 4 feet long and 4 inches high. The shot must be put with one hand, and may not be swung behind or below the shoulder.

A right-handed person should take a position at the back of the ring, with his back toward the toe board (Fig. 37-5). The feet are about shoulder width apart. The shot is nestled in the palm of the right hand, with the fingers held close together. The thumb is slightly to the side of the shot. While holding the shot in this manner, place it against the neck just under the right cheek. The right elbow is down and at comfortable distance from the side. The left arm is held high and bent at the elbow, so that the forearm is parallel to the shoulders at the chest level.

Start the put by bending forward at the waist, lifting the left leg up and cocking it in the forward position. Thrust the left leg to the rear and hop backward on the right foot. Keep the body moving in the direction of the toe board, and start the body turning to the left. The left foot contacts the ground. In one coordinated explosive movement, push the right arm forward and upward as the right leg pushes backward. The left leg imparts a forward and upward thrust as the shot is allowed to roll from the palm to the fingers. A flick of the right wrist delivers the final force to the shot.

Complete the put by reversing the direction of the body, by stepping with the right foot toward the toe board. The left side of the body will end up being toward the center of the circle.

Discus Throw

The discus is thrown from a circle 8 feet 2-1/2 inches in diameter. All throws must fall within a 60-degree sector.

A right-handed discus thrower should grasp the discuss in such a manner as to have the first joint of his fingers just on the edge of the discus. The thumb is placed on the top for balance. The fingers are spread; however, some throwers prefer to keep the index and middle fingers together.

As in the shot put, the discus thrower will take a position at the rear of the ring, facing away from the direction of the toss (Fig. 37-6). The legs are separated so that the feet are planted about shoulder width apart. The knees are slightly bent, and the body is erect. The toss is started by bringing the discus down and behind the body in a pendulum movement; the left arm is allowed to swing up and across the front of the body. The spin starts as the discus thrower steps backward, with the left leg toward the center of the ring, while pivoting on the right foot. Then, the right foot swings across in front of the body, while the left foot pivots. The right foot comes down, pointing in the direction of the toss. The spin picks up speed as the right foot pivots and the left foot is planted. At this point the right arm starts to come through, and the left arm is pulled sharply downward and to the rear. The right hip is thrust forward and into the toss. The release is made at about shoulder height, and the discus comes off the front edge of the hand as the wrist is snapped toward the release. All of these movements must be precisely coordinated and the pivoting must be continuous and smooth, in order to get a good throw. The right leg will finish up with a cross-over step, which prevents the thrower from leaving the ring.

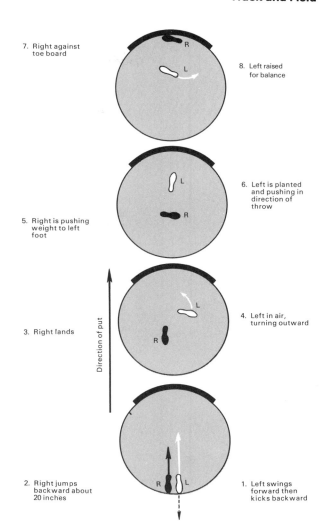

Fig. 37—5. Footwork for shot put.

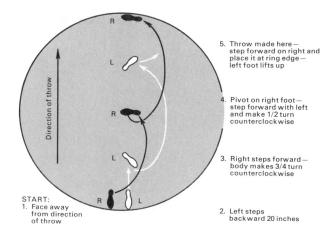

Fig. 37—6. Footwork for discus throw.

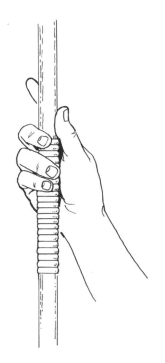

Fig. 37—7. Hand hold for javelin.

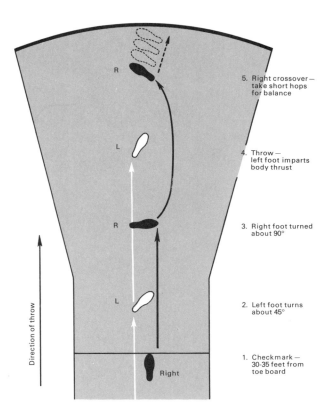

5. Right crossover — take short hops for balance

4. Throw — left foot imparts body thrust

3. Right foot turned about 90°

2. Left foot turns about 45°

1. Checkmark — 30-35 feet from toe board

Right

Direction of throw

Fig. 37—8. Footwork for javelin throw.

Javelin Throw

In this event the competitor must throw a javelin weighing 1.764 pounds from behind a restraining arc 4 meters long, with a radius of 8 meters. The javelin must strike the ground point first in a sector bounded by extensions of the lines running from the center of the circle and through the ends of the restraining arc. The thrower cannot pivot through a full 360 degrees during delivery, and his throwing hand must be touching the cord grip section when he releases the javelin.

The checkmark is established in the same manner as for the pole vault and the jumps; the throwing pattern is run in the opposite direction from the restraining line to find the proper starting point.

To start the run, place the feet at the starting checkmark and face the direction of the toss. Hold the javelin out in front in the vertical position, point down (Fig. 37-7). A right-handed person should place the right hand on the upper part of the javelin, and slide the hand down until the bottom three fingers are grasping the cord grip; the index finger and thumb are on the upper end of the cord grip. The index finger is separated from the other fingers and along the line of the shaft. (If the javelin fails to strike the ground point first when thrown, slide the index finger further around and under the javelin.)

Bring the javelin up to a comfortable position by holding it nearly horizontal over the right shoulder, the tip facing forward.

Run toward the scratch line, holding the javelin in this position. At a point approximately 30 feet from the line, the left foot will be planted at about a 45-degree angle to the right (Fig. 37-8). The javelin is brought down and out to the rear by lowering the right arm. Take a short step with the right foot across in front of the left, and place it down at a 90-degree angle to the right. The head is turned to the right and slightly to the rear, and the left arm is brought up and cocked in a slightly bent position in front of the chest. The javelin is pointing slightly upward. The tip should not be above the top of the thrower's head.

To release the javelin for the throw, the left leg is brought forward and the right arm is cocked by bending it at the elbow and throwing the javelin. The left arm is pulled forward and downward and the head is turned forward with the throw, which is made by uncocking the forearm in an upward and slightly side-arm throw. The complete movement will bring the whole body into the throw. The left leg imparts a thrust to the body. The release should start the javelin in an upward flight at about a 30-degree angle.

To complete the throw make a half forward pivot on the left foot as a cross-over step is made with the right.

A few short hops on the right foot are made as the thrower stops at the restraining arc.

BIBLIOGRAPHY

Canham, Don, *Track Techniques Illustrated.* New York: A.S. Barnes & Co., 1952.

Cretzmeyer, F.X., Alley, L.E., and Tipton, C.A., *Track and Field Athletics* (7th Rev. Ed. of Bresnehan and Tuttle's basic text). St. Louis: The C.V. Mosby Co., 1969.

Division for Girls' and Women's Sports, *Track and Field (243-07594).* Washington D.C.: American Association for Health, Physical Education and Recreation.

Doherty, J.K., *Modern Track and Field.* Englewood Cliffs, N.J.: Prentice-Hall, Inc., 1953.

Gordon, James A., *Track and Field: Changing Concepts and Modern Techniques*, 2nd Ed. Boston: Allyn and Bacon, Inc., 1972.

National Federation of State High Schools, Athletic Association, *Track and Field Rules (High School).* Chicago: The Association.

Official NCAA Track & Field Guide. Phoenix, Ariz.: College Athletics Publishing Service, 349 East Thomas Road.

Thompson, Donnis H., *Women's Track and Field.* Boston: Allyn and Bacon, Inc., 1969.

Track and Field Rules—AAU. New York: Amateur Athletic Union of the United States.

Volleyball is a team sport that is steadily gaining in worldwide popularity, as is shown by the development of so many recreational, industrial, city, and church leagues. It is a game that has few rigid requirements, for it can be played in a limited area with limited equipment, on almost any type of terrain, by young and old, men and women, unskilled and skilled. Many groups modify the rules to fit their own individual skills, facilities, equipment, or group size.

HISTORY

In 1895 William G. Morgan, the physical director of the Holyoke, Massachusetts, YMCA, invented the game of volleyball. Morgan felt that an indoor game was needed to provide his businessmen's classes the opportunity for competition and recreation at a not too strenuous level. Equipment for the new game was a tennis net raised across the gymnasium floor to a height of 6 feet 6 inches, and a basketball bladder that was batted by any number of players the space could accommodate. This ball proved to be unsatisfactory because it was too light while a regular basketball with its leather cover proved too heavy. A.G. Spaulding & Brothers made the first volleyball for trial use, and it is interesting to note that the official volleyball used today closely resembles the original ball made by Spaulding.

Volleyball, for no known reason, was originally called Minonette, and was confined almost exclusively to Holyoke—specifically to the YMCA gymnasium where Morgan was physical director. At Springfield, Massachusetts, during a demonstration between two teams from Holyoke, Dr. A.T. Halsted suggested that the name be changed to volleyball, since the basic idea of the game was to volley the ball back and forth over the net.

A set of rules was adopted in 1900 by the Physical Directors' Society of the YMCA. The new rules standardized ball handling, raised the net to 7 feet 6 inches, and eliminated phases of the game that tended to make it slow. In 1917 the NCAA and YMCA conjointly prepared the first complete Volleyball Guide. The United States Volleyball Association, which governs volleyball, was organized in 1928, and now publishes an annual official rule book and reference guide which helps standardize volleyball throughout the United States. In 1947 the International Volleyball Federation was formed, and by 1960 its membership included 58 countries.

Even though volleyball was being played by girls and women soon after it was devised, special rules were not published until 1926. At this time the "two-volley" game with a maximum of six contacts on a side was used. The D.G.W.S. now publishes the standards, rules, and guides for women's volleyball. Through recent cooperative efforts the United States Volleyball Association and the Division of Girls' and Women's Sports have developed rules more similar than previously.

Volleyball was recognized as an Olympic event for women in 1964, in Tokyo. This game is now one of the fastest growing team games for women in the United States.

Volleyball has progressed from a slow ball-tapping sport to a fast, highly competitive, and exciting game. The serve is no longer a means of merely putting the ball in play, but can be a hard-driven, well-placed, curving ball, with or without spin. The passes, setups, and spikes are all hit to predetermined areas, and players now use signals and plays to outmaneuver their opponents. The spike has been clocked at over 100 miles per hour, and teamwork has proved to be as important in volleyball as in any other team sport.

TERMINOLOGY

Attack—The offensive team attempting a score.
Block—A defensive play used to intercept a hard-driven spike. Players generally leap with their arms outstretched in front of the spiker, in an attempt to deflect the ball either back to the spiker's court or to one of their own players.
Crosscourt—A play in which the ball crosses the net diagonally.

Dig—A one-hand, clenched fist recovery shot.

Dink—A fake following preparation for a spike. The ball is tapped and falls close to the net on the opponent's side.

Double foul—Both teams committing a foul on the same play.

Foul—A violation of the rules.

Game—One team reaches 15 points, or 8 minutes elapse and one team is at least 2 points ahead.

Holding—A foul which allows the ball to rest on the hand or hands momentarily.

Lifting—A foul which allows the ball to rest on the hand or hands as the ball is carried upward.

Pass—To bat the ball to a teammate.

Placement—Hitting the ball to an intended spot.

Play over—The point is replayed without a point or sideout being declared.

Point—A score made by the serving team.

Pushing—A foul when a two-hand chest volley is not clearly batted.

Rotation—A movement of the players to a new position in a clockwise direction.

Screening—An illegal move in which the serving team conceals the serve by obstructing the opponents' view of the serve.

Service—The initial hit that puts the ball in play.

Setup—A high pass, close to the net, hit so that the spiker can drive the ball into the opponents' court.

Side out—Failure of the serving team to score.

Simultaneous contacts—Two players contacting the ball at the same time; either player may play the ball next.

Spike—Hitting a ball in play at net level or above, so that it is driven downward over the net.

RULES

The court (Fig. 38-1) is a rectangle 60 feet long and 30 feet wide, with a line 4 inches wide under the net separating the court into two equal areas. The net is 32 feet long and 3 feet high. The top of the net is 8 feet from the floor for men, and 7 feet 4-1/4 inches for women. The service area is bounded at the front by the end line, and at the sides by extensions of the sidelines. It must be at least 6 feet in depth from the end line.

The ball shall be spherical, with a laceless leather cover not less than 25 inches or more than 27 inches in circumference.

Essentially the volleyball rules for men and women are the same. However, there are some differences,

and a comparison is made in an article appearing in the book *Selected Volleyball Articles* (See the bibliography listing).

RULE DIFFERENCES
DGWS

1. The overhead clearance is 20 feet.
2. No spiking line (the front line players are the only spikers) is acknowledged.
3. No rotation is permitted on the first serve for a side out.
4. The hand and forearm are the only contacts.
5. The follow-through is permitted on a spike but reaching over the net to play a ball is not permitted.
6. The serve may be taken anywhere behind the end line.
7. The ball may be held or unsupported at the moment of service.
8. The players must play in their own area on the service and during the game.
9. A player may have two entrees into a game, including the beginning of the game.
10. Multiple blocks must be identified prior to playing the game.

USVBA

1. The overhead clearance should be 26 to 30 feet.
2. A 10-foot spiking line (back players may spike in front of this line) is acknowledged.
3. Rotation takes place on the first service following a side out.
4. Any part of the body from the waist up may be used to contact the ball.
5. A follow-through across the net is legal, and a player may reach for the ball after the opponents have played it.
6. A player may enter the game three times.
7. The service is allowed within 10 feet of the right sideline and behind the end line.
8. Multiple blocks are permitted (front line players only).
9. Players may shift their positions immediately following the service.

Suggested Coed Rules

1. Net heights:
   Senior high schools—7 feet 4-1/4 inches
   Junior high schools—7 feet
   College and adults—8 feet

2. A team consists of three girls and three boys placed in alternating positions on the floor.
3. The ball must be played alternately by boys and girls when contacted by more than one individual on a side.
4. Any part of the body may be used to contact a ball, except on a service.
5. Blocking is done by players on the front line at the time of service.

The Service

The toss of a coin shall determine courts or service.

A "service" is the putting of the ball in play by the player in the "right back" position. He bats it over the net into the opponents' court in any direction with one hand (open or closed), while keeping both feet fully behind the back line of the court until after the ball is struck.

The ball must go over the net between the markers on the net that are directly over the sidelines.

Only the serving team can score.

At the moment the ball is contacted for the serve, all players, with the exception of the server, shall be within the court boundaries in their correct serving rotation (see Fig. 38-1), with all forward players in front of their corresponding back line players.

After the ball has been hit for the serve, the players may move from their respective positions, but must return to their original serving order before the start of the next serve (by either team).

After a side out, the team receiving the ball for service shall immediately rotate one position clockwise.

When a served ball touches the net, passes under the net, or touches any player, surface, or object before entering the opponents' court, a side out shall be called. If the service lands on the playing surface other than in the opponents' court, it shall also be ruled a side out.

It is a side out when a player serves out of turn. All points won during this serve shall be declared illegal and shall be forfeited.

The Ball in Play

Basically, each team is trying to receive the ball and pass it to its setup man at the net (first play), who sets it up to the spiker (second play), who in turn spikes the ball into the opponents' court (third play). A team is entitled to three hits or less on the ball before returning it over the net. No player may hit the ball twice in succession, except in playing a hard driven spike. The ball may be played with any part of the body above and including the waist. Any player who touches or is touched by the ball shall have legally played it.

The ball must be clearly batted or hit. When the ball momentarily comes to rest in the hands or arms of a player, he shall be considered as having played the ball illegally.

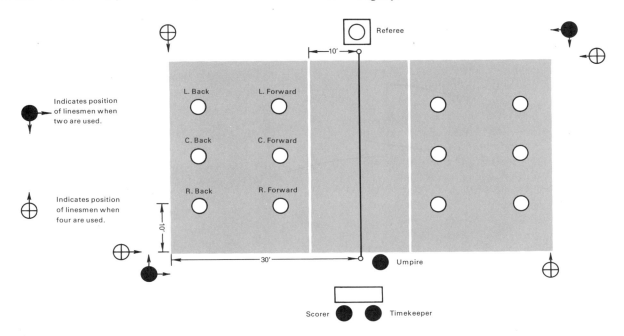

Fig. 38—1. Volleyball court.

A ball contacting the boundary line is fair. Any ball contacting an object or the ground outside the boundary lines is declared "out-of-bounds." A player may play the ball outside the boundary lines as long as he does not cross the center line or an extension of this line. However, after playing the ball he may cross the center line extended. Within the court, a player may step on but not over the center line.

It is a foul to enter the opponents' court while the ball is in play. Reaching under the net while keeping the feet in one's own court is legal, as long as there is no contact or interference with the opponent's play. A player may not touch the net, but may follow through over the net provided that the contact with the ball was made on the player's side of the net.

If a ball in play hits the net and goes over into the opponents' court, it is still considered to be in play, except on a serve.

A back line player may spike a ball, provided that he takes off behind the 10-foot line.

Scoring and Fouls

The head official of a volleyball game is the referee. He is assisted by an umpire, a scorer, a timekeeper, and two or four linesmen.

The first team scoring 15 points, or the most points in 8 minutes of play, wins the game, provided that it leads by 2 points.

A match consists of the best two out of three games.

The teams must change courts for each game. During the third game, they must change sides when one team reaches 8 points, or at the end of 4 minutes of playing time. The teams alternate serving first in each game.

A player is allowed to reenter the same game twice, but only in his original position. Players may change positions at the beginning of each game.

Front line players may unite in a block.

The ball is declared dead after a point, a side out, or any other decision that temporarily suspends the play.

A "double foul" during one play makes the ball dead, and the point is replayed.

SKILLS

The offensive attack is limited to four skills: the serve, pass, setup, and spike. The mastery of these skills alone does not constitute the entire attack because too many elements can vary the procedure for winning the point. But the team well schooled in the execution of these four basic skills will have a definite advantage over its opponents.

Serve

Since only the serving team can score in volleyball, it is imperative that each individual master the serve. Serving is more than just a means of putting the ball in play, and a player must "put something" on his serves. If the serve can cause the opposition to make an erratic pass, then their attack is weakened and the possibility of a hard return is diminished considerably. A player must learn to serve so that the ball has (1) "spin" on it, (2) a floating motion, (3) considerable speed, or (4) some action that will cause the opposition to have trouble returning it. It is recommended that the beginner employ the easiest and safest serve before he attempts the more difficult serves. Too many players, in their attempt to hit a serve that may cause their opponents some trouble, hit the ball into the net or out-of-bounds. It must be remembered that the team that cannot serve cannot score.

Careful consideration must be given to the placement of the serve as well as to the spin and speed of the ball. It is advisable to pick out an opponent who has trouble playing the serve and generally serve to him. If the opposition has two weak players, a well-placed serve between them can cause considerable trouble. Serving the ball between two aggressive players can also be very effective. If the opposition does not have a weak position to which to direct the serve, it is advisable to serve the ball deep, in order to force the opponents to make the long pass to the setup at the net.

There are many ways of serving the ball. Serves can be executed with an opened hand, closed hand, overhand, underhand, or side arm. Players should experiment with the different methods of serving, to determine which is most effective for them to use.

Underhand Serve

This is probably the simplest of all serves to learn but it offers the opposition very little difficulty in playing it. The player (right-handed) should face the net, with the left foot slightly forward and pointed toward the net. The left knee should be slightly bent, with the right knee either straight or bent, whichever feels more comfortable to the server. The ball is held in the palm of the left hand, at arm's length and in front of the right knee. The right arm is extended backward and brought forward in a line perpendicular to the net, hitting the ball out of the open palm of the left hand. The ball should be hit below the center with the heel of the hand, or with the heel and knuckles. The serve should be executed in one complete, smooth action. On the backswing of the right hand the weight is transferred to the right foot. As the right arm moves forward, the weight transfers to the left foot, and at the point of contact the weight is largely on the left foot. As the right arm follows through toward the net, the server steps forward with his right foot into the court and continues toward his position.

Overhand Serve

The overhand serve has become one of the most popular serves in competitive volleyball because of its versatility. Besides being a safe punch serve, it can also be hit with a great deal of spin, speed, dip, or floating action. Today, volleyball players spend considerable time practicing the overhand serve because, when mastered, it becomes a safe offensive weapon, and increases the overall attacking effectiveness of the team. The manner in which the hand strikes the ball and then follows through will determine the action put on the ball. A ball hit slightly to the right of center will cause it to spin and curve to the left. A ball hit to the left of center will cause the ball to spin and curve to the right, and a ball with the follow-through over the ball will cause it to dip. If the server desires a floating action to the ball, he should strike its center; placing the valve of the ball facing the net and in the lower panel of the wall will increase its floating action. Since the weight of the valve slightly distorts the arc of the ball's flight, the ball reaches the net in a dead float and then swerves or dips in an unpredictable manner, as does a knuckleball in baseball. By the time the ball reaches the net, the valve will have started a swerve from one side, causing the ball to react as it does. By snapping the wrist forward as the ball is hit, additional speed is imparted to the ball. Before a player attempts any of these serves with action on the ball, a considerable amount of time should be spent in practicing them. A safe serve that can be returned is always better than a power serve or spinning serve that often hits the net or falls out-of-bounds.

To perform the overhand serve, the right-handed server should face the net with the left foot slightly in front of the right foot. The right foot should be turned somewhat to the right, so that the server will be better balanced. The ball is held with the fingers of the left hand, and the right hand rests lightly on top of it; it is carefully thrown with both hands to a position slightly higher than the head and directly in front of the right shoulder. The server's weight then transfers to the rear foot as the right hand is drawn back behind the head. The hand then comes forward past the right ear, and contacts the ball while it is still above the head and in front of the right shoulder. The weight transfers forward as the ball is struck. The right elbow should be bent until the follow-through.

Roundhouse Serve

The roundhouse serve is a fast serve with a downward spinning motion. The ball is tossed up 3 to 4 feet overhead, and is hit with a sweeping arc of the hand. The heel of the hand hits the center of the ball and the fingers curve around the top of the ball; this kind of contact gives the ball its downward spinning force. The ball should be hit as the hand moves upward and outward.

The Pass

The handling of the pass has been found to be the key to successful volleyball. A team that cannot pass will have trouble with its setups, which in turn will affect its attack. The pass is considered by many experts to be the most important skill in volleyball, and many hours should be spent on its perfection.

The player should await the ball with his hands at face height, his fingers spread, with the index fingers and thumbs of both hands forming a triangle. The elbows should be pointing out, the wrists tilted backward, and the hands slightly cupped. The feet are in a stride stance, with the knees slightly bent and one foot a little in front of the other. With the body slightly crouched, the player should situate himself under the ball so that the contact is made about a foot over his head and in front of the face. The ball should be contacted only with the fingertips and thumbs, and never with the palms of the hands. After the ball is contacted, the fingers and hands follow through in the direction of the intended pass. The pass should be aimed to a spot approximately 15 feet in the air, about 4 or 5 feet from the net, and directly above the head of the intended receiver. The ball should be hit so that it has little or no spin. Every possible effort should be made to play the ball over the head, even if the player must fall to his knees to do so. It is easier to control the ball when it is over the head, and also, there is less chance of playing it illegally.

Bump Pass

The ball below chest level is played by using the bump pass. It is executed by having the palms of the hands facing each other. The fingers of the left hand are folded so as to make a fist, with the thumb of the left hand folded over the index finger of the left hand. The fingers of the right hand are folded around the fingers of the left hand, and the thumb of the right hand placed alongside the left thumb and parallel to it, resting on the upper part of the left index finger. The lower arms are held close together, with the elbows straight and rotated inwardly. It is best to have a flat, straight surface of the arms from the thumbs to the upper arms, so that the ball can be contacted with the wrist or forearms.

The feet are parallel to each other, with the weight on the balls and one foot slightly forward of the other, with the legs flexed, so that the body is in a slight, crouched position.

In receiving a hard line drive serve, or a ball in flight above chest level, an "inverted bump pass" technique is used. It is executed by holding the hands in the same position as for the bump pass, with the elbows bent, so that the hands are just in front of the face. Contact is made by striking the ball with the little finger side of the hand.

Dig

This involves the playing of a low ball with one hand on either side of the body. With the palm facing up, the fingers are closed to make a fist, with the thumb closed over the lower part of the index finger. The knees are bent and the body weight is over the balls of the feet. The fist, wrist, and forearm are areas by which the ball may be legally played.

Setup

A good setup man can make the attack work perfectly. If the setup is not executed properly, the spiker cannot put the ball where he wants it. The setup man should know his spikers perfectly, and be able to place the ball in the exact spot where the spikers want it. It is important that the best ball handlers on the team be the setup men. Basically, the ball handling of the pass and the setup are identical. The setup man faces the direction from which the pass is coming. As the ball comes down to him, he pivots, turning his side to the net so that he faces one spiker and has another spiker behind him. Then, arching his back, he can either set the ball up for the spiker he is facing, or set the ball up over his head for the spiker behind him. The setup should be passed to one of the front corners of the court, at approximately 12 feet high and 2 feet from the net. By keeping the ball at the corners of the court, the defense will have to spread their blockers and the overall effectiveness of the spike is increased. Through the use of signals, a setup man can vary the heights of the setups for quick plays. Signals also help the team know which player is going to spike the ball and into what area of the court.

Spike

There is no standardized method for spiking the ball. Some players will approach the net facing it and leap into the air from 2 feet away. Others will approach the net parallel to it and leap from 1 or 2 feet, while still others will use little or no approach. Some players like the ball close to the net, and others like it as much as 4 feet from the net. The spiker is faced with the difficulty of leaping to a maximum height, hitting a moving object, and placing the ball into an intended area. No other game places such difficult coordination requirements on its participants.

The 2 foot take-off approach is the method most frequently used. The spiker approaches the net almost straight-in, times his leap to meet the ball at the proper angle, and drives it forward and downward over the net. As the ball is being passed to the setup man, the spiker should be situating himself in the exact position to start his approach. Generally this distance is about 10 to 12 feet from the net.

The type of running approach can vary with the spiker. Some players use short running steps, some use long steps, and others sliding steps. The spiker starts his take-off from both feet with his knees bent to a crouch, and his body positioned behind the ball instead of under it. The arms drive upward on the leap, with the upper body and shoulders turned sideways away from the net. Then, the hitting arm is brought back and the other arm is extended forward for better balance. As the spiker reaches his maximum height, he drives his forward balance arm downward and brings his shoulders around square and parallel to the net. The spiking arm then whips forward, with the elbow leading, and straightens out as the wrist snaps the hand into the ball. The elbow should act as a pivot that holds the forearm and hand to a short arc that will not reach the net. The spiker should be prepared to play his blocked spike that will return very rapidly and may just clear the net. The most effective method of hitting the spike is with the butt of the hand, with the wrist snapping the fingers over the ball and imparting downward spin. Some players cannot attain enough height to hit the ball with the butt of their hands, and must make the spike shot with their fingers; this method will not drive the ball as hard, nor will it impart any spin on the ball.

When the player lands after the spike, he should absorb the impact by letting his knees bend slightly; he should assume a half-crouched stance and keep his elbows near his body. This means of landing will help to keep him from falling forward over the center line.

The spiker can outmaneuver the blockers by leaping at one end of the net and angling the spike. Or, he can aim to hit the outside arm of the blocker and cause the ball to go out-of-bounds. An occasional low setup directly over the center of the net can be driven quickly into the opponents' court with successful results. The spiker who is consistently being blocked can fake his block; then, as the blockers are falling back from their attempt, he can tap the ball over their outstretched arms. The spiker should vary his attack to offset the effectiveness of the block. By driving hard between the blockers, angling to the sides, hitting over the short man in the block, hitting the tips of the blockers' fingers, aiming for the outside arm of the blockers, and changing the speed of the drive, the spiker can break through the blockers and score.

Switching

The rules of volleyball allow players to switch positions after the ball leaves the server's hand. This helps a team keep its best spiker or setup man in a front line position that will be most beneficial to the team. Players may switch to any place on the court. All players must return to their original positions of rotation at the start of the next serve, by either team.

Defensive Play

Because only the serving team can score, and theoretically it gives the ball to the opposition on the serve, the serving team must devise an adequate defense to regain possession of the ball and make its attempt to score. Any time the ball is in the opponents' court, the opposing team is on the defense, and must prepare itself to stop the opponents' attack and take possession of the ball.

Blocking

The best method of stopping the opponents' hard driven spikes is for the defensive players to intercept the ball as it crosses the net. The blockers should start their block about 3 feet from the net and move to the spot where the ball has been set and is going to be spiked, by taking short sliding steps. The blockers should then watch the spiker, to determine how and where he is going to spike the ball. They should also delay their jump, allowing the spiker to leap first. Then, as if they were going to spike, the blockers jump into the air with their arms extended over their heads and slightly forward. The fingers should be well spread and the hands tilted backwards. For a block to be effective, the blockers should all reach the same height with their hands and have them adjacent to each other. This jump is made about 2 feet from the net. A block should not be a return spike, but a deflection of a hard-hit ball. Many blockers, in anticipating the hit, throw their hands forward and

thereby foul by either hitting the net or going over it. In modern volleyball, three players unite at the net for the block.

Recovery from the Net

Many points can be saved by the alertness of the players in handling balls driven into the net. A ball hit into the bottom of the net will momentarily hold and then spring out. A ball hit into the center of the net will come off the net more rapidly and will not spring out as much. A ball that hits the top of the net will drop rapidly and is the most difficult to recover. The player should crouch with his side to the net, and wait until the last possible moment before playing the ball. The closer the ball gets to the ground, the more time the player will have to execute his shot, and the better possibility he will have of making a good play. The player's primary concern should be with saving the ball. He should try to bat the ball high to one of his teammates, who will return it over the net. Many good players will go down to their knees to get a ball out of the net. Some players become quite proficient at saving the ball from the net, and can even set this ball up to a spiker.

STRATEGY

Team strategy in volleyball calls for one man to receive the serve and pass it to a predetermined setup man at the net; he, in turn, sets it up to a predetermined height and distance from the net for a spiker who usually is to hit it to a predetermined area in the opponents' court. Every player on the team should know to whom and where he is going to hit the ball if it should come to him. When on defense, the team also should know where they are going to situate themselves and what type of defense and switches to

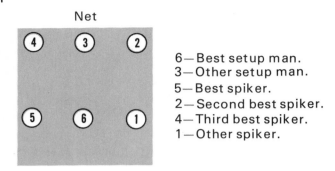

Net

6—Best setup man.
3—Other setup man.
5—Best spiker.
2—Second best spiker.
4—Third best spiker.
1—Other spiker.

Fig. 38—2. Players' positions at start of game.

use. Good blockers, by continually blocking the spikes, can cause a good spiker of the opponents to become erratic in his attack and can force him to resort to less effective maneuvers in his desire to penetrate the defense. It is advisable for the blockers not to try to block "just the ball" every time. Some spikers will hit the ball to the outside of the block, hoping to glance it off the blockers' hands so it will go out-of-bounds.

If the blockers are alert, they may be able to detect where the spiker intends to hit the ball by the way in which he approaches it. The players on the ends of the block should turn their hands in toward the spiker, so that a ball driven to the outside will be deflected back into the court rather than glanced out-of-bounds. To defend against a strong spiker, the blockers should try to block the ball back into the opponents' court by holding their hands straighter and more rigid. Generally, if the ball is set up closer to the net, a harder spike can be expected. All hard spikes should be blocked back into the opponents' court. If the setup is deep away from the net, the blockers may

have to delay their jump in order to meet the ball at the net.

The backcourt players should be on the alert to get all balls that are deflected off the blockers' hands. The center back generally moves within 3 or 4 feet of the blockers, and is in position to help stop and set up any ball that may be deflected or tapped past the blockers. Any player from the backcourt may move up to assume this position, but the well-trained team knows which players will unite in the block and which players will back up the spike.

There are many offensive formations in volleyball and many different patterns that can be used, depending on the skill of the players. At one time volleyball was made up of three setup men and three alternating spikers. The disadvantage of this pattern was that at one point in the rotation there would be only one spiker at the net, with a setup man on each side of him. This situation was easy for the blockers to defend against, so a different formation today is that which comprises two setup men and four spikers. This assures the team of always having two spikers and one setup man at the net at all times. Fig. 38-2 illustrates the positions that the players take at the start of the game.

After one rotation takes place and the number two man becomes the server, it will be necessary for numbers three and four to switch positions after the serve, so that the setup man is in the middle, with a spiker on each side. Every time the setup man is on the end, he will switch with the spiker in the center after the serve.

When a team receives the serve, they should station themselves so that the setup man does not receive the serve but is in position to take the pass from his fellow teammate who does receive the serve. Fig. 38-3 shows

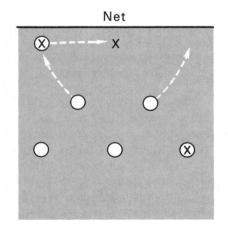
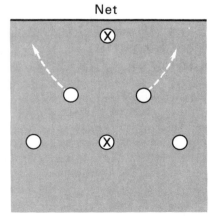
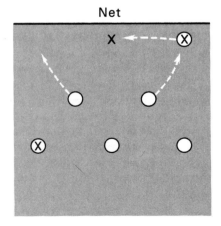

Ⓧ Indicates setup men

Fig. 38—3. Players' positions after rotation.

the formations with the setup man in the three forward positions. When he is situated at the right or left end, he should quickly switch to the center and receive the pass at that position.

DRILLS

Passing

1. The players are in two parallel lines 10 feet apart, with a double-arm interval between each man. A player in the middle tosses the ball to each player in turn. The receiver catches the ball when he is in the position that he would be in to pass it. He catches the ball and lifts it back to the middle man. This procedure should be followed until the feeling of the ball on the fleshy part of the fingers is obtained. The middle man now tosses the ball to each player, and the ball is clearly batted back. Emphasize to the players that they must move directly under the ball before playing it (Fig. 38-4).

2. This drill is generally used for the warm-up prior to a volleyball match. The players form a circle approximately 15 feet in diameter, and bat the ball to each other either around or across the circle. The purpose is for the player to be able to receive from any direction and to keep the ball in the air, passing it to a player at whom he aims. This is a good drill for practicing ball handling (Fig.38-5).

3. The players form a circle, with a 5-foot interval between them. Each player faces clockwise and passes the ball to the man directly in back of him. The player must pivot under the ball in order to make a pass, so that he faces the direction in which he is passing. Pivoting makes it possible always to face the player for whom the pass is intended (Fig. 38-6).

4. The squads are arranged in a straight line, with one player designated as a leader. The leader will toss the ball high into the air. The player whose turn it is to play the ball must shift his position enough to get his nose directly under the ball before returning it to the leader. The leader should alternate the throws, making some short so that the players will have to move forward, and others long or to the side so that they must move for the ball (Fig. 38-7).

5. The players are in straight lines facing each other. The first man of one line passes the ball to the first man of the second line, who hits it back to the first line, where the second player is now set to hit the ball. When a player hits the ball, he moves to the end of his line. This drill should first be done slowly, keeping the ball high. As the players become more skilled, the height of the ball is lowered, causing the players to move faster (Fig. 38-8).

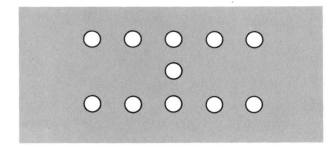

Fig. 38—4. Passing drill no. 1.

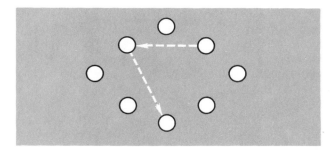

Fig. 38—5. Passing drill no. 2.

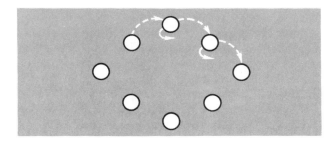

Fig. 38—6. Passing drill no. 3.

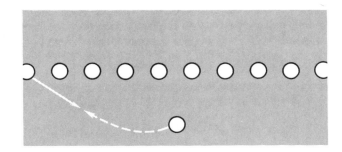

Fig. 38—7. Passing drill no. 4.

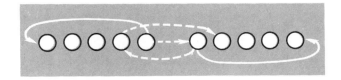

Fig. 38—8. Passing drill no. 5.

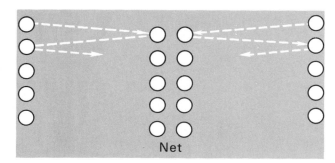

Fig. 38—9. Serving drills no. 1 and no. 2.

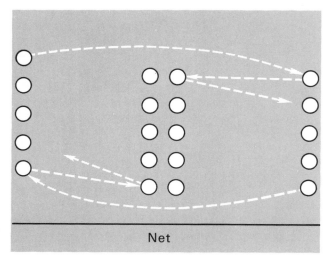

Fig. 38—10. Serving drill no. 3.

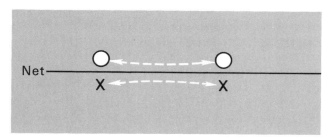

Fig. 38—11. Setup drill no. 1.

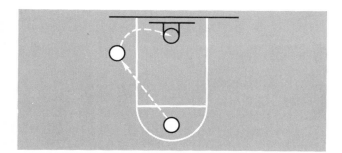

Fig. 38—12. Setup drill no. 2.

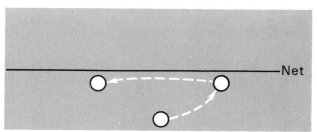

Fig. 38—13. Setup drill no. 3.

Serving

1. The players are divided into two groups, one on each half of the court. Half of each group is at the net, with their backs to it; the other half is at the base line, facing the net. Each group practices as a unit: the players serve back and forth to each other, in order to get the feel of the serve. The emphasis is on controlling the ball and serving at the intended target (Fig. 38-9).

2. The same formation is used as in the previous drill, except that the men at the net are eliminated and the ball is served back and forth over the net.

3. The same line formation is used as in the previous drill; the ball is served over the net to a group of players on the base line, who in turn pass or bat the ball to a group of players at the net. The pass receiver catches the ball and tosses it back to the server (Fig. 38-10).

Setup

1. The ball-handling skill of the setup is basically the same as that involved in the pass. The method of hitting the ball is the same; the target is different. Since the skill is practically the same, any drill used in passing can also be used in the setup. One variation is to place the players close to the net and have them set the ball up as close to the net as possible without hitting the net or letting the ball go over it (Fig. 38-11).

2. A player is stationed next to a basketball backboard and outside the free throw line. Another player, standing on the free throw line, lobs the ball to the first player, who sets it up so that it comes down on or through the top of the basketball rim. The ball should not hit the backboard (Fig. 38-12).

3. A player situates himself at the net, with a spiker at his side. Another player, standing at backcourt, passes him a ball and the player at the net sets the ball to the spiker. He should get himself under the ball and

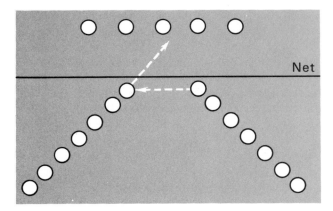

Fig. 38—14. Spiking drill no. 1.

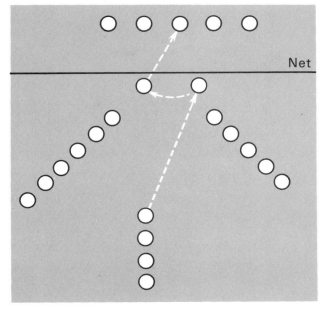

Fig. 38—15. Spiking drill no. 2.

turn to face the direction in which he will set the ball. As soon as the player has mastered this setup, another player should be stationed at his other side; then the setup man should practice setting the ball to him over his head as well as to the one he is facing (Fig. 38-13).

Spiking

1. A player situated at the net tosses a ball into the air for another player at the net to spike into the opponents' court. The players should rotate positions after a few attempts by each player to spike the ball (Fig. 38-14).

2. Using the same formation as in the previous drill, add another player to act as a passer. This player throws the ball to the setup man, who must set the ball to the spiker so he can drive it into the other court (Fig. 38-15).

3. The passer lobs the ball to the setup man at the net, who sets the ball to a predetermined position. The passer then becomes the spiker and must charge the net, leap, and spike the ball (Fig. 38-16).

Blocking

1. Since it is necessary to have a spiker in blocking drills, any of the drills used in the spike can be used as drills for blocking by placing three players side by side on the other side of the net and letting them attempt to block the ball (Fig. 38-17).

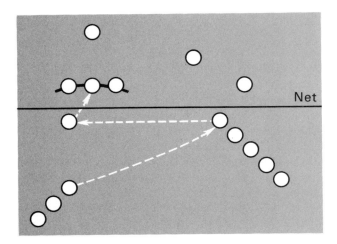

Fig. 38—16. Spiking drill no. 3.

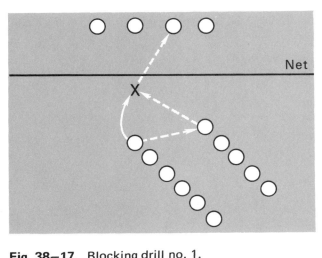

Fig. 38—17. Blocking drill no. 1.

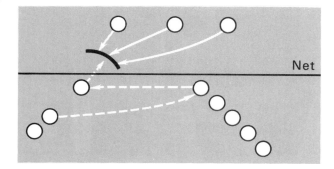

Fig. 38—18. Blocking drill no. 2.

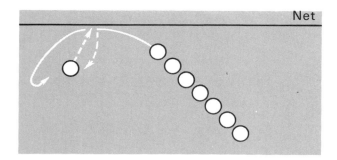

Fig. 38—19. Recovery from net drill no. 1.

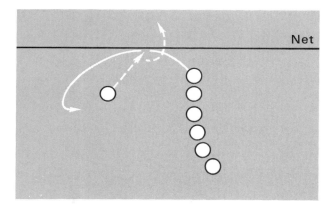

Fig. 38—20. Recovery from net drill no. 2.

2. Situate players in their positions at the front line, and have them move quickly in front of the setup. They should then attempt their block and be prepared to recover the ball should it fall on their side of the net. By using two spikers it would also give the blockers practice in shifting from one spiker to the other as the setup man varies the attack (Fig. 38-18).

Recovery from the Net

1. A player tosses the ball into the net. Another player, who is standing about 10 feet from the net and to the right of the ball tosser, moves forward to recover it. He should approach the ball in a low, crouched position, and "bat" the ball back to the ball tosser. He then forms a new line to the left of the ball tosser, so that he will be moving in a different direction when he attempts to recover a ball from the net the next time. The player who is doing the tossing should toss all the balls low into the net the first time around, high the next time, and mix them up after that (Fig. 38-19).

2. This is the same as the previous drill, but this time the players should assume that their attempt to recover the ball will be the third hit and should practice trying to get it over the net. (Fig. 38-20).

BIBLIOGRAPHY

Eastrom, Glen H., and Schaafsma, Frances, *Volleyball*. Dubuque, Iowa: Wm. C. Brown Company, Publishers, 1966.

Emery, Curtis, *Modern Volleyball*. New York: The Macmillan Co., 1953.

Laveaga, Robert E., *Volleyball, A Man's Game*. New York: A. S. Barnes & Co., 1945.

Lockhart, Aileene (ed.),*Selected Volleyball Articles*. Washington, D.C.: American Association for Health, Physical Education and Recreation, 1955.

Odeneal, William T., and Wilson, Harry E., *Beginning Volleyball*. Belmont, Calif.: Wadsworth Publishing Co., Inc., 1962.

Scates, Allen E., *Winning Volleyball: Fundamentals, Tactics and Strategy*. Boston: Allyn and Bacon, Inc., 1972.

Scates, Allen E., and Ward, Jane, *Volleyball*. Boston: Allyn and Bacon, Inc., 1969.

Slaymaker, Thomas, and Brown, Virginia H., *Power Volleyball*. Philadelphia: W.B. Saunders Co., 1970.

U. S. Volleyball Association, *Volleyball Rules*. Berne, Ind.: USVBA Printer.

Volleyball (DGWS) Guide. Washington, D.C.: American Association for Health, Physical Education and Recreation.

WATER SKIING—MOTORBOATING | 39

Skis dating back 4,000 to 5,000 years have been found by scientists in both Norway and Sweden. Since the days of these early skis, countless thousands have enjoyed the thrills of skiing on snow-covered slopes.

Water skiing, one of America's fastest growing sports, is a direct outgrowth of snow skiing. The American Water Ski Association, founded in 1939, has had a great share in the development of water skiing. It has established leadership training schools, and it awards certificates to successful graduates. It has also formulated the official tournament rules which govern national and regional tournaments.

SKIING EQUIPMENT

The necessary equipment for water skiing includes a motorboat, a towline, skis, a bathing suit, and a ski life jacket.

The boat preferably should be a runabout with a good planing bottom and sufficient width, particularly at the transom. It should be at least 14 feet in length for ordinary skiing. An all-purpose ski boat should be at least 16 feet long. It is desirable that a tow bar be attached to the boat, and that it be at least 3 feet high. It is usually installed in the center of the floor, between the middle of the boat and the transom. It is very important for trick skiing and jumping. The bar, called a *towing pylon*, keeps the line high so that it will not drag in the water or get tangled in the propeller.

The motor should be powerful enough to tow the desired number of skiers at a fast pace. For slalom skiing and jumping, this may be up to 35 miles an hour. The motor should have remote controls; if possible, these controls for shift and throttle should be of the single-lever type.

The towline should be approximately 75 feet in length. It may be of manila hemp or braided polyethylene. Since more than one type of handle is used, it is recommended that this line be in two sections, about 65 feet and 10 feet in length. A ring and snap attachment then permits interchanging the single bar, trick bar, and slalom, or double, handles.

The skis should be selected in relation to the weight of the skier. Manufacturers supply charts which provide ski length and width for each weight classification.

The bathing suit should be tight-fitting and of strong material. It should be of the brief type which gives a snug fit to the upper part of the thighs without binding. This is particularly important for jumping or trick skiing.

The ski life jackets should be worn during all instruction periods, and preferably at all times, except by advanced skiers during certain show activities. The jackets not only provide maximum safety but also combat fatigue, particularly for beginners in the early stages of learning. The vest type is the best, since it provides free movement yet affords the protection needed in the event of a spill.

SKIING SAFETY

Safety while skiing can be achieved by taking definite precautions. Among them are:
1. Don't ski without protective equipment.
2. Don't ski in crowded areas.
3. Don't ski close to others, the shore, or obstructions.
4. Don't ski after dark.
5. Don't hang onto the handle after a spill.
6. Don't ski in shallow areas or in water known to have obstructions beneath the surface.
7. The ski boat should have a competent driver and an observer.
8. Leave extra passengers on shore while skiing.
9. Only the skier should give signals, not a spectator.
0. Come into the dock or shore parallel, rather than head-on.
11. Have a safe, maximum speed suited to the particular type of ski activity.
12. Look out for other skiers who may have taken a spill.
13. Avoid showing off near fishermen, sailboaters, or those in canoes. They have water rights also.

FUNDAMENTAL SKILLS OF SKIING

Elementary skills which should be taught to skiers include:

1. Putting on the skis.
2. Gripping the handle.
3. The correct starting position in shallow water.
4. Weight control.
5. Bending the knees.
6. The correct riding position.
7. Dock starts.
8. Deep water starts.
9. Learning to fall.
10. Turning.
11. Crossing a wake.
12. Jumping a wake.
13. Signaling.
14. Landing.

In putting on skis, care should be taken to avoid jamming the feet into the bindings. The feet should be wet, then shoved as far forward into the bindings as they will go. The heel pieces then should be slipped over the heels.

Three holds are common in gripping the handle. One is the overhand with palms down, another the reverse grip with the palms up, and the third a combination of one palm up and one palm down. All three should be tried, to determine which is the most comfortable. The first and second joints of the fingers, rather than the entire hand, should be used in gripping, and the thumb should be pressed over the first and second fingers.

In getting a shallow water start from a crouching position, the ski tips are kept above the water. As the skis begin to plane, the skier rises slowly, keeping the weight evenly distributed on both skis and leaning slightly forward. With the knees bent, and the arms and back straight, the beginner lets the boat do the pulling. Correct posture provides balance, and maneuvering becomes easy without strain. Once turning is learned, the skier is ready to practice crossing and jumping the wake.

For weight control the weight should be distributed equally over both the skis. Leaning too far to the side, forward, or backward results in falls.

Keeping the knees bent enables the skier to take shocks better and to maintain balance more easily. To prevent the skis from spreading, the knees must be kept close together rather than far apart. They should never be farther apart than the width of the shoulders.

In the riding position the head, knees, and feet are kept in line, with the head slightly in advance of the feet. The arms are kept straight at all times.

In making a dock start, the skier should sit with the tips of his skis out of water and face the stern of his boat. With the tow handle in both hands and with several coils of the rope beside him on the dock, the skier times his **call of "HIT IT!"** with the forward movement of the boat. As the last coil unwinds, he transfers his weight from the dock to his skis and leans backward to offset the pull of the rope. By keeping his knees bent and his tow handle low, he achieves the balance necessary for a good performance.

A deep water start calls for keeping the knees close to the chest and the ski tips out of the water. The rope should be kept between the skis, and the skier should be facing the stern of the boat. As the line tightens, the weight should be forward, while the skier sits on the backs of his skis. Standing up should be accomplished gradually, with the straight arms and back pulling the skier to the riding position. The skis should be kept parallel and not over 1-1/2 feet apart.

Learning to fall calls for relaxation and timing. The simplest fall, particularly at slow speeds, is to let go and topple backward. At faster speeds the proper technique is to perform a somersault or roll. This is done by covering the face with the forearms, lowering the head, and rolling into a ball. It is important to fall alongside, rather than over, the skis.

Turning is accomplished by leaning to one side, riding on the inner edges of the skis while raising their outside edges. The lean should be of the entire body, rather than just from the waist. The greater the speed, the more area is needed to make a turn.

Crossing a wake calls for a right angle or perpendicular approach to the wake. It should be a confident rather than a timid effort. The knees should be bent to absorb the shock, and the body kept low for better balance.

Jumping the wake is not as difficult as it might appear. The approach should be from far outside the wake, with a sharp cut toward its center. The skier should spring upward into the air as the skis touch the wake. In the jump the toes should be held up, and the knees should be bent to take the impact of landing.

Signals are necessary for coordination between the driver and skier. Some of the more common hand signals by the skier include:

Go faster—Point the thumb or palm up.
Go slower—Point the thumb or palm down.
Change direction—Point with the hand in the new direction.
Speed O.K.— The thumb and forefinger form a circle.

Skier not hurt—The skier waves the hand out of water after fall.

Stop—The finger is drawn across the throat in a cutting motion.

Three easily understood verbal signals of the skier are:

"In gear"—Put tension on the line by boat movement.
"Out of gear"—Disengage the gear immediately.
"Hit it"—Come to full acceleration at once.

A driver's signal universally used is a circling arm movement over the head, to indicate that he is preparing to change the boat's direction. This is the skier's cue to be in the middle of the boat's wake, ready for a new direction.

Landing should be done safely by estimating carefully the distance to the dock or shore. The approach should be parallel rather than at right angles. The faster the skier is traveling when he lets go of the handle, the further he will glide. If a misjudgment occurs and the landing is too fast, it is easy to sink down on the skis and let the hands act as a brake in the water.

With the mastering of these fundamentals, another skier has been born. The relaxation, the freedom, and the exhilaration of skiing are now his.

BIBLIOGRAPHY—WATER SKIING

American Water Ski Association, *Official Tournament Rules*. Winter Haven, Florida: The Association.

Anderson, John H., *Skiing on Water*. New York: The Ronald Press Company, 1960.

Dorwin, Tom and Janie, *Water Skiing*. Milwaukee: Evinrude Motors, 1960.

Prince, W.N., *Water Skiing for All*. Philadelphia: Chilton Co., 1959.

Scharff, Robert, *The Complete Book of Water Skiing*. New York: G.P. Putnam's Sons, 1954.

MOTORBOATING

The history of boating antedates Noah's ark. Through the centuries boating has met utilitarian needs as well as cruising pleasures. From the oars of galley slaves to today's marvelous outboard motor is a tremendous advance in boat propulsion.

In many areas the ownership of a boat has become a status symbol, similar to owning a second car or a lake cottage. As a result of the tremendous surge to the outdoors, and particularly to water, there has come a corresponding need for skillful and safe use of boats.

BOATING TERMINOLOGY

Aft—At or near the rear end of the boat.
Astern—Directly behind the boat.
Beam—A boat's breadth at its widest part.
Bow—The front end of the boat.
Bridge—A raised platform from which the boat may be steered.
Chart—The water version of a road map.
Cleat—The horned hardware fitting to which lines may be secured.
Draft—The depth from the waterline of the hull to the lowest point of a boat's keel.
Freeboard—The vertical distance from the hull waterline to the gunwale.
Galley—The boat kitchen.
Gunwale—The upper edge of a boat's rail or side.
Hatch—A cover over an opening through the deck.
Head—A marine toilet.
Hull—The main body of a boat aside from its superstructures.
Keel—A boat's backbone from stem to stern.
Leeward—Away from the wind.
Log—The boat diary.
Port—The left side, looking toward the front of the boat.
Starboard—The right side, looking forward toward the front of the boat.
Stern—The back portion of the boat's hull.
Transom—That part of an outboard boat from which the motor is hung.
Trough—The hollow formed by two waves.
Wake—The track of the boat caused by its movement.
Windward—Toward the wind.

BOATING RULES

To a welcome member of the boating family, it is important that the rules of the nautical "road" be known and practiced. Some of these rules are:

1. When two boats are directly approaching each other, each steers to its right.
2. When one boat is overtaking another, the faster moving boat must keep clear of the one being overtaken.
3. In crossing paths, the boat having another approaching its left side has the right-of-way.
4. Boats leaving piers or launching areas have no rights until they are entirely clear in open water.

5. Sailboats have the right-of-way over power boats, unless the sailboat is overtaking one under power.
6. Fishing boats, whether anchored or moving with equipment in use, have the right-of-way.
7. A small motor boat should yield the right-of-way to a less maneuverable string of barges under tow.
8. Boatmen should always go to the aid of those in distress, rendering all necessary assistance.

BOATING EQUIPMENT

Boating as a sport has a variety of purposes. Some of the most popular are cruising, fishing, skiing, skin diving, camping, and photography. Each has its own adherents.

Before selecting a boat, it is important to consider the purpose for which it is being purchased. Size, design, construction materials, and other factors must be weighed. Price should never be placed ahead of quality.

Over the years improved materials have become available for boat building. For centuries boats have been built of wood. Now, there are steel and aluminum boats, but as yet they are less common. A material being used more and more is fiber glass. Energetic competition has given each type of material strength, durability, adaptability, and even eye appeal not dreamed of a few decades ago.

When in doubt, it is generally safer and more satisfactory to buy a "large" boat. It is easier to add horsepower than to lengthen a boat. This is particularly true in obtaining a boat for more than one purpose or for several people to enjoy. The less skilled the operator, the more need for size. A larger boat is less apt to be overloaded or swamped when an unexpected squall comes up. It is especially desirable for a boat to have enough width in relation to its length. It is then less likely to capsize in big waves or when the load is distributed unevenly.

Another important point to consider is the ability of the boat to keep afloat. The modern boat should not leak, and it should have sufficient flotation built in or inherent in its material. Whether overturned or filled with water, the boat should be able to remain afloat with a maximum load of motor, passengers, and gear.

For the boat bought for a single purpose, such as fishing or water skiing, the selection problem is simplified. The three questions which usually need to be answered are: How many will use the boat? In what type of water will it be used? What type of hull is most applicable for the use the boat will receive?

When only two or three persons will normally use the boat, and in comparatively quiet inland waters

only, a 14- or 15-foot boat is indicated. For rough water or offshore conditions, with or without a larger load, a 16-foot boat is the minimum size. If the trip is for several miles out, a 17-foot boat or larger is much safer.

The type of hull selected greatly affects the performance and the pleasure to be obtained from a boat.

The two main types of hulls are the *displacement* and the *planing* types.

The displacement hull moves *through* rather than on *top* of the water. Since it is deeper in the water, it is slower and generally safer. It is usually round-bottomed or V-shaped throughout the length of the bottom. This type will roll, pound, or toss less, and in choppy water will provide a more comfortable ride.

The planing hull is usually flat or nearly so for most of the length of the boat. It may have a slight or semi-V shape up forward. The true planing hull is sought for speed, and is characteristic of fast-moving runabouts.

Regardless of the type, attention should be given to sufficient length, width, and depth for safety. Sufficient depth generally means enough freeboard or height from the boat's waterline to the gunwale. Such freeboard, together with a good transom height, minimizes the possibility of swamping and danger from a following sea. To be doubly safe in rough water, an adequate motor well should be standard equipment.

Essential to pleasurable and successful boating is a balanced outfit. The boat, motor, and trailer should be matched to each other. A motor too large for the boat can be dangerous. A boat not fitted properly to the trailer may receive undue stress and damage. A boat and motor too heavy for the trailer may result in frame, spring, or tire trouble, and a breakdown on the road may occur.

When equipment for boating is selected carefully, according to purpose and in line with suitable standards, the chances for happy, successful boating are immeasurably increased. Attention to important aspects at the beginning will ensure enjoyable, safe, and carefree hours on the water.

BOATING SAFETY

Safety on the water is a matter of common sense and courtesy. Respect for the power of wind and waves, as well as a regard for the rights of others, go hand in hand.

Safety precautions for boating include:
1. Learn to swim.
2. Don't leave an overturned boat and swim to shore.
3. Don't overload the boat.
4. Don't stand up in the boat while it is moving.
5. Proceed cautiously in water where logs, bars, or other obstacles may be present.
6. Travel with another boat when cruising, particularly when going a long distance from shore.
7. Slow down when approaching other boats.
8. Understand the use of resuscitation methods.
9. Keep alert to avoid collisions.
10. Maintain cleanliness and ventilation in boats which use gasoline.
11. Have a life preserver or safety vest available for each person aboard.
12. Keep the fire extinguishers in good condition.
13. Know the rules of the nautical "road," and practice them.
14. Keep a chart and compass on hand.
15. Carry along all necessary extra equipment. Examples are lights, an auxiliary motor, additional fuel, spark plugs, tools, a propeller, paddles, an anchor, rations, foul weather clothing, flares, and a first aid kit.

BOATING SKILLS

Boat handling skills which should be a part of each boatman's repertoire include the ability to:

1. Operate a motor.
2. Make emergency repairs.
3. Apply elementary first aid.
4. Use paddles or oars.
5. Approach a dock for a landing.
6. Recognize weather signs.
7. Read distress signals.
8. Use knots for mooring.
9. Launch a boat with a trailer.
10. Interpret the meanings of buoys.
11. Maneuver a boat in high waves or heavy current.
12. Use a chart and compass.

BIBLIOGRAPHY—MOTORBOATING

Allen, J.J., *Boating—A Beginning Guide.* New York: The Ronald Press Company, 1958.

Andrews, Howard, and Russell, Alexander, *Basic Boating: Piloting and Seamanship.* Englewood Cliffs, N.J.: Prentice-Hall, Inc., 1964.

Hewitt, F. David, *Fun with Boats.* Chicago: Popular Mechanics Co., 1960.

Morris, Everett B., *Outboard Boating Skills.* Milwaukee:Evinrude Boating Foundation, 1957.

Outboard Boating Club of America, *Outboard Seamanship Instructor's Manual.* Chicago: The Club, 1960.

Potter, Jim, *Power Boat Handbook.* Los Angeles: Trend Books, Inc., 1960.

Whittier, Robert J., *Guide to Equipping Your Boat.* Philadelphia: Chilton Co., 1959.

WEIGHT TRAINING AND WEIGHT LIFTING | 40

Legend has it that Milo, a great Grecian athlete of the sixth century, developed tremendous strength by repeatedly lifting a calf until it grew to maturity. As a result of this practice, Milo exhibited his great strength by carrying a live ox around the course at the Olympic games.

The lifting of weights has been practiced in many countries, although its exact history is relatively obscure. The Turnverein movement in Europe accepted the use of weights in its program. The immigration of many Europeans brought the Turnverein movement, together with the practice of weight lifting, to America. Development of interest in weight lifting was evidenced by the presentation of theater acts in which feats of strength were performed as entertainment.

The Amateur Athletic Union recognizes weight lifting as a competitive sport by sanctioning meets and awarding certificates for performance. Weight lifting was a part of the Olympic games in 1896, but it was not until 1932 that the United States entered a full team.

An aspect of weight lifting which has developed quite recently is weight training. Weight lifting is generally thought of as a competitive sport that indicates the individual's ability to lift weights. Weight training is an exercise program involving the use of weights to develop the overall strength of the body. There is a trend toward the use of weight training programs to improve performance in specific sports, such as football, track, and swimming. The use of weight exercises in the convalescent period of hospital patients recovering from injuries and operations has been found beneficial.

A recent aspect of weight training has been realized through the efforts of Martha E. Wetzel, who has developed an excellent progressive weight training program for girls at Thornton Community College in Harvey, Illinois. This program uses barbell and dumbbell equipment, and its main concern is with the theory of increasing the weight and decreasing the number or repetitions. Muscle tone, and not size, is the objective.

WEIGHT TRAINING

Equipment

Equipment for weight training consists of a bar 5 or 6 feet in length, graded weights, and two pairs of collars to keep the weights in place on the bar. This equipment when assembled as a whole is called a *barbell*.

Dumbbells, iron boots, inclined boards, and benches are also used in weight training programs.

Suggestions

In preparation for lifting weights, sufficient time should be spent in warming up the body with simple exercises or calisthenics without the use of equipment. After the body has been warmed up without equipment, it may be wise to go through the exercises with a few repetitions using just the bar to further warm up the body. The beginner should start his exercise program with the number of weights he can handle without undue strain. Emphasis should be placed on the correct execution of the movements of the exercises, particularly during the first two or three weeks of weight training. During this period repetition of exercises is more important than lifting heavy weights.

In addition to weight training exercises, various other types of physical exercises should be a part of the program. Flexibility exercises and endurance activities such as running are important. Physical activities which develop coordination and agility, particularly as they are related to a specific sport, should be engaged in to improve all-around body development.

Drills

The following exercises should be done every other day, or at least three days a week, with a day of rest between workouts. A minimum of one hour should be devoted to each workout period. Although the amount of weight for each exercise has been suggested, it may be necessary to reduce the load to suit the needs of the individual.

Fig. 40—1.

Exercise no. 1—Warm-up.

Exercise No. 1.—Warm-up (Fig. 40—1)

Purpose:	Warm-up
Starting Position:	Stand with the feet apart and the barbell resting on the floor. (The barbell should weigh 20 pounds.)
Action:	1. Bending at the knees, pick up the weight.
	2. Raise the weight over your head and put the bar back on the floor.
	3. Execute this exercise 10 times.
Variation:	1. In each exercise period, the number of repetitions is increased.
	2. When the exercise has been repeated 30 times, add 10 pounds and start again with 10 repetitions, working up to the desired number of repetitions.
	3. Increase the weights and repetitions as desired.

Exercise No. 2.—Side Bends (Fig. 40—2)

Purpose:	To develop the abdominal muscles.
Starting Position:	Stand straight, with the feet apart, and the barbell resting on the shoulder behind the neck. (The barbell should weigh 20 pounds.)
Action:	1. Bend sidewards to the right as far as possible.
Variation:	2. Repeat to the left side.
	Increase the weights and repetitions as desired.

Exercise No. 3.—Curl (Fig. 40—3)

Purpose:	To develop the arm muscles.
Starting Position:	Stand straight and hold the bar with the palms facing away from the body, and the arms held straight down. (The barbell should weigh 20 pounds.)
Action:	1. Raise the weight to the shoulders by bending at the elbows, and return.
	2. This exercise should be repeated 10 times.
Variation:	1. In each exercise period, the number of repetitions is increased.
	2. When the exercise has been repeated 30 times, add 10 pounds and start again with 10 repetitions and work up.
	3. Increase the weights and repetitions as desired.

Fig. 40—2. Exercise no. 2—Side bends.

Exercise No. 4.—Waist Bends (Fig. 40—4)

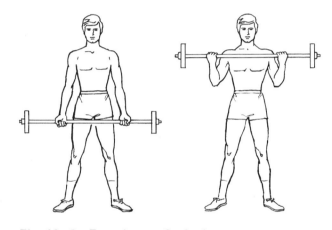

Fig. 40—3. Exercise no. 3—Curl.

Purpose:	To develop the back muscles.
Starting Position:	Stand straight with the legs apart, holding the bar with the palms facing toward the body (use an overhand grip) and the arms straight down. (The barbell should weigh 20 pounds.)
Action:	1. Bend forward and touch the weights to the floor outside the right foot, and return to position.
	2. Repeat to the left side.
	3. This exercise should be repeated 10 times to each side.
Variation:	1. In each exercise period, the number of repetitions is increased.
	2. The weights should be increased as desired, and repetitions started again with 10 repetitions to each side.

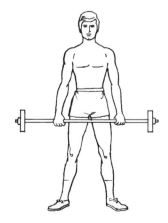

Fig. 40—4. Exercise no. 4—Waist bends.

Fig. 40—5. Exercise no. 5—Press.

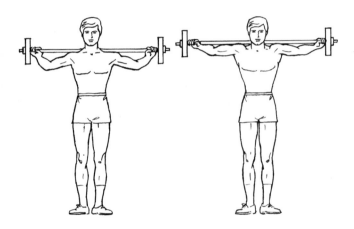

Fig. 40—6. Exercise no. 6—Shrug.

Fig. 40—7. Exercise no. 7—Dead lift.

Exercise No. 5.—Press (Fig. 40—5)

Purpose: To develop the shoulders and back muscles.

Starting Position: Stand straight with the heels together, and the barbell against the chest with an overhand grip. (The barbell should weigh 20 pounds.)

Action:
1. Raise the barbell over the head until the arms are straight, and return to the chest slowly.
2. This exercise should be repeated 10 times.

Variation:
1. In each exercise period, the number of repetitions is increased.
2. The weights should be increased as desired, and repetitions started again with 10 repetitions.

Exercise No. 6.—Shrug (Fig. 40—6)

Purpose: To develop the back muscles.

Starting Position: Stand straight with the heels together, and the barbell resting on the neck and shoulders. The arms are at full length, and the hands hold the bar with an overhand grip. (The barbell should weigh 20 pounds.)

Action:
1. Lift the shoulders high and allow them to relax.
2. This exercise should be repeated 10 times.

Variation:
1. In each exercise period, the number of repetitions is increased.
2. The weights should be increased as desired, and repetitions started again with 10 repetitions.

Exercise No. 7.—Dead Lift (Fig. 40—7)

Purpose: To develop the muscles of the lower back.

Starting Position: Stand with the feet apart, and the barbell resting on the floor. Bend over and grasp the bar with an overhand grip. (The barbell should weigh 20 pounds.)

Action:
1. Keeping the legs straight and the arms extended, raise the barbell until the body is erect.

Fig. 40—8. Exercise no. 8—Knee bends.

2. Lower the barbell until the weight is near the floor, and then return it upright.

3. This exercise should be repeated 10 times.

Variation:
1. In each exercise period, the number of repetitions is increased.
2. When the exercise has been repeated 30 times, add 10 pounds and start again with 10 repetitions.
3. Work up to the desired repetitions.
4. Increase the weights and repetitions as desired.

Exercise No. 8.—Knee Bends (Fig. 40—8)

Purpose: To develop the feet and leg muscles.

Starting Position: Stand with the feet apart, the barbell resting on the neck and shoulders, with the hands spread at a comfortable width and an overhand grip. (The barbell should weigh 20 pounds.)

Action:
1. Rise up on your toes, and then bend to a 3/4-squat position.
2. This exercise should be repeated 10 times.

Variation: Increase the repetitions and weights as desired.

Exercise No. 9.—Side Straddle Hop (Fig. 40—9)

Purpose: To develop the leg muscles and endurance.

Starting Position: Stand with the heels together, the barbell resting on the neck and shoulders, with the hands spread at a comfortable width using an overhand grip. (The barbell should weigh 20 pounds.)

Action:
1. Jump your feet apart, sideways and then together.
2. This exercise should be repeated 10 times.

Variation: Increase the repetitions and weights as desired.

Exercise No. 10.—Heel Raiser (Fig. 40—10)

Purpose: To develop the feet and leg muscles.

Starting Position: Stand with the feet apart, the barbell resting on the neck and shoulders, with the hands spread at a com-

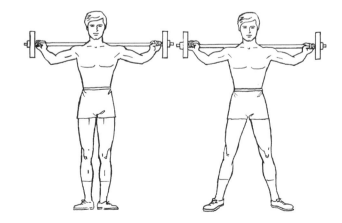

Fig. 40—9. Exercise no. 9—Side straddle hop.

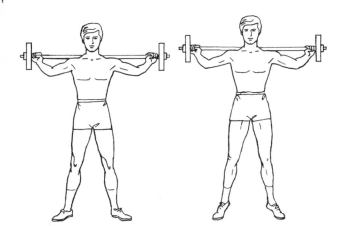

Fig. 40—10. Exercise no. 10—Heel raiser.

Fig. 40—11. Exercise no. 11—Leg lift.

Fig. 40—12. Exercise no. 12—Abdominal.

Action: 1. Stand erect by straightening the legs without moving the feet, the left hand grasping the bar in front of the body.
            2. Return the barbell within an inch of the floor slowly by bending the knees.
            3. This exercise should be repeated 10 times.

Variation: 1. Repeat the exercise with the left hand grasping the bar in front of the body, and the right hand grasping the bar behind the body.
            2. Increase repetitions and weights as desired.

fortable width and an overhand grip. (The barbell should weigh 30 pounds.)

Action: 1. Raise the heels to a tiptoe position, and then lower them slowly to the floor.
            2. This exercise should be done 10 times.
            3. Increase the repetitions and weights as desired.

Exercise No. 11.—Leg Lifts (Fig. 40—11)

Purpose: To develop the leg muscles.

Starting Position: Stand with the legs straddling the bar, with the right hand grasping the bar behind the body. (The barbell should weigh 30 pounds.)

Exercise No. 12.—Abdominal (Fig. 40—12)

Purpose: To develop the abdominal muscles.

Starting Position: Sit on a low box or stool, with the feet hooked under an immovable bar or held by another person.

Action: 1. Lean back so that the back of the head just touches the floor, and return to the sitting position.
            2. This exercise should be repeated 10 times.

Variation: 1. Increase the repetitions.
            2. Lean back and pick up the bar with the hands, holding it against the neck and shoulders. Repeat the exercise 10 times. Increase the repetitions.
            3. Place 10 pounds of weight on the bar, and start with 10 repetitions.
            4. Increase the repetitions and weights as desired.

Fig. 40—13. Two-hand clean-and-press.

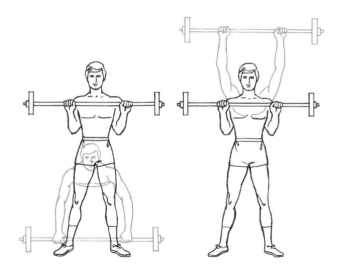

Fig. 40—14. Two-hand clean-and-jerk.

WEIGHT LIFTING

Rules

For competitive purposes there are three lifts: the two-hand clean-and-press, the two-hand clean-and-jerk, and the two-hand snatch. These are officially recognized as Olympic lifts.

The Amateur Athletic Union has a table of lifting awards given according to various body weight classifications. The body weight classes are: Bantamweight (123-1/2 lbs. and under); Featherweight (132-1/4 lbs. and under); Lightweight (148-3/4 lbs. and under(; Middleweight (165-1/4 lbs. and under); Light-heavyweight (181-3/4 lbs. and under); Middle-heavyweight (198-1/4 lbs. and under), and Heavyweight (unlimited).

Each contestant is allowed three trials in each of the three events in his weight class. The heaviest weight lifted in each event is summed to obtain a composite score.

The minimum increase of weight between trials is 10 pounds, except for the last trial, which may be 5 pounds. An increase of 5 pounds indicates that the coming lift will be the last lift of the contestant.

Competitive Lifts

The two-hand clean-and-press (Fig. 40-13) is executed in two phases: first, lifting the weight to the chest, and second, pushing the weight above the head (this is the part known as "pressing"). Bringing the weight to the chest should present no problem if it can be pressed at all, since the most difficult part of this lift is pressing the weight from the chest to the overhead position.

The first movement consists of placing the bar at the feet, gripping it with both hands in an overhand position, and bringing it up to and parallel with the shoulders in one motion, at the same time executing a split or bending the legs to get under the weight. From the squat position, the lifter comes to a standing position with the feet a comfortable distance apart. After a pause has been observed, the referee will give the signal for the second part of the movement. The second phase of the lift starts with the lifter pushing the weight over his head. During the lift the head must be erect, the eyes forward, and the heels on the floor. The body should not bend in any direction, and the arms should be pressing with equal force. This erect position must be maintained throughout the second phase of the lift. The lifter is not permitted to make any sudden or jerking motions while pressing. In pressing, most lifters release the grip of the thumbs, placing them alongside the fingers. The referee will give the signal to return the bar to the ground.

The two-hand clean-and-jerk (Fig. 40-14) requires exceptional skill and timing, since a great deal of effort is expended in executing this style of lift. The first phase is referred to as the "clean." This is executed by standing with the feet close to the bar, the body lowered, keeping the back flat and the head erect. The bar, grasped overhand with the hands shoulder width apart, is pulled straight up. When the bar is brought up to the shoulders either a split or bend of the legs is executed. The elbows are brought forward under the bar, with the bar coming to rest on the upper chest. With the bar at the chest, the feet should be returned to the same line, keeping the legs straight, before the jerk is begun.

The second phase is called the "jerk." This is executed by bending the knees slightly and keeping the body erect. The legs are then straightened, and the bar is brought just overhead. As it reaches its highest point, a lunge is executed and the arms are straightened overhead. From this lunge position, the feet are brought together so that the body is held in an erect position.

The two-hand snatch (Fig. 40-15) is executed in one continual motion from the time the barbell leaves the floor until the arms are extended overhead. At the start the feet are about a foot apart; the hands move down the bar, gripping it overhand about shoulder width apart, and raise the bar. The split or squat is executed, so as to get under the bar with the body. The body is then brought to an erect position to complete the lift.

PROGRESSIVE WEIGHT TRAINING FOR GIRLS

Weight training for girls can be offered anytime of the year as a separate activity, in combination with adapted programs, and in circuit training. Along with such an activity as weight training, there should be an alternative activity, so as to avoid lifting on consecutive days.

Martha E. Wetzel recommends that weight training not be offered to the freshman and sophomore girls in high school, due to possible injuries to the soft tissues near the epiphysis. Older girls are less likely to be affected by the extreme strain of lifting weights.

Equipment

The bar should be 5 feet in length. Solid dumbbells of 5 pounds are recommended. Plates purchased separately should be 1-1/4 pound in weight.

Classification

Initiating such a program involves the understanding that girls who weigh more than others will work with heavier weights, with the exception of the obese girl. The group is divided into groups of four to six students whose weight is similar. Lighter groups will remove the collars, and begin with a weight of 20 pounds. The heaviest group should add a plate of 2-1/2 pounds to each end, for a total of 25 pounds.

Activity

The curl (see Fig. 40-3), press (see Fig. 40-5), dead lift (Fig. 40-7), straddle lift (Fig. 40-11) and abdominal curl (Fig. 40-12) should be used.

After 10 curls and 10 presses are completed, then increase the weight by 5 pounds followed by 8 curls and 8 presses. Increase the weight 5 more pounds, and complete 6 curls and 6 presses.

The dead lift (Fig. 40-7) and straddle life (Fig. 40-11) use the same starting weight as the curl and press. Ten dead lifts and 10 straddle lifts are completed before increasing the weight by 10 pounds. Six dead lifts and 6 straddle lifts is the goal now.

After a girl can do 20 curls correctly, use the same weight and repetitions for the abdominal curl. Ten curls with body weight only, 8 curls with a 5-pound plate held at the sternum with one hand, and 6 curls

Fig. 40—15. Two-hand snatch—Continuous motion from floor to overhead position.

with a 10-pound plate held at the sternum is the pattern for this exercise (Fig. 40-12).

Safety Hints

1. Close supervision of this activity is of utmost importance, due to the possibility of injury.
2. Wear appropriate clothing, and *no jewelry*.
3. Equipment must be securely attached.
4. Use spotters.
5. Use your legs for lifting and lowering.
6. Work on mats.
7. Rest periodically.
8. Increase the starting weight not more than twice in eight weeks.
9. Alternate weight training days.
10. Breathe normally.

BIBLIOGRAPHY

Amateur Athletic Union of the United States, *Official Weight Lifting Rules.* New York: The Union.

American Association for Health, Physical Education and Recreation, *Weight Training in Sports and Physical Education.* Washington, D.C.: The Association, 1962.

Berger, Richard A., *Conditioning for Men.* Boston: Allyn and Bacon, Inc., 1973.

Counsilman, James E., "Does Weight Training Belong in the Program?" *Journal of Health, Physical Education and Recreation,* Vol. 26, No. 1 (January, 1955), pp. 17-18,200.

Hoffman, Bob, *Weight Lifting.* York, Pa.: Strength and Health Publishing Co., 1939.

Hook, Gene, *Application of Weight Training to Athletics.* Englewood Cliffs, N.J.: Prentice-Hall, Inc., 1962.

Sills, Frank D., and Evans, Lura, *Conditioning.* Belmont, Calif.: Wadsworth Publishing Co., Inc., 1962.

Wetzel, Martha E., "Progressive Weight Training for Girls? Yes!" *Johper:* 10:70. Washington, D.C.: American Association for Health, Physical Education and Recreation.

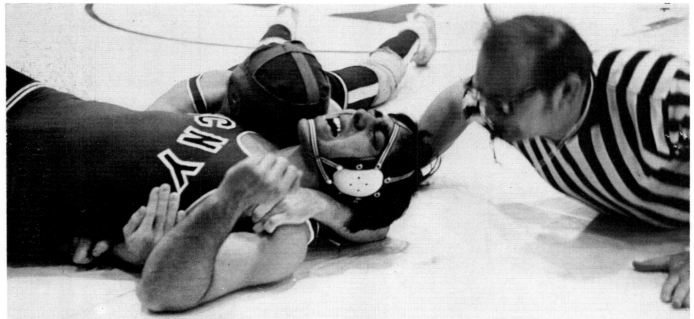

Wrestling, like boxing, is an ancient sport. We know from Egyptian writings and drawings that wrestling was practiced as long ago as 3000 B. C. The pentathlon, as practiced in the early Olympics, was an event in which each individual competed in five activities: running, jumping, wrestling, and throwing the discus and javelin. A large number of the principal characters in Greek mythology were outstanding wrestlers. Many years ago, before men started fighting one another with weapons, wrestling and hand-to-hand combat tactics were useful as a means of self-preservation.

There are three major forms of wrestling: *Greco-Roman*, which is done mostly with the arms and is most popular in Europe; *catch-as-catch-can*, or free style, which employs both the arms and the legs and is most popular in the United States; and *judo*, which involves both arms and legs and is the popular form in the Orient.

The University of Pennsylvania and Yale were the participants in the first intercollegiate wrestling match in 1900. In 1927 the National Collegiate Athletic Association organized a Wrestling Rules Committee. The standardization of rules had much to do with the growth and status of the sport.

Amateur wrestling differs considerably from professional wrestling, which has been popularized by television. As performed on an amateur basis, the sport involves considerable competitiveness in strength, skill, and strategy, and requires a high level of sportsmanship. All unsportsmanlike actions are grounds for defaulting a match. Professional wrestling, while requiring much physical finesse and skill, is often a well-rehearsed performance in which the outcome is not solely a result of the competitive action of the participants. As such, professional wrestling is more a stage production than an athletic contest.

TERMINOLOGY

Body press—Pressing the weight of one's body against a supine opponent in an attempt to secure a fall.

Break down from referee's position—Bringing the opponent to the mat from the referee's position while maintaining control of him.

Bridge—An arch which is executed while the wrestler is in a supine position. This is done by pressing the back of the head and the feet against the mat and raising the front of the body upward while arching the back.

Chain wrestling—Executing a series of offensive moves in order to oppose a defensive move.

Collar and elbow—A tie-up position used while standing. Each wrestler grasps his opponent's right elbow with the left hand and places his right hand behind the opponent's neck. The hand positions may be reversed.

Crotch pry—A maneuver in which the offensive man grasps his opponent's leg at or near the crotch.

Drag—Grasping the opponent's upper arm and pulling him to the mat.

Escape—A maneuver in which the wrestler moves from a disadvantage position to neutral.

Fall—Holding the opponent's shoulders in contact with the mat for one second.

Grapevine—A hold in which the offensive man entwines one or both of his opponent's legs with one or both of his own legs.

High bridge—The bridging position in which the head is bent back so that the face is on the mat. The weight is supported on the face, the hands, and the balls of the feet. The back is at least a foot above the mat.

Hold—Grasping the opponent in one of many ways. Each specific hold is usually named for the part of the body which is being held.

Lock—A hold in which the arm or arms grasp a part of the opponent's body or one or more appendages. For example: headlock, bodylock, armlock, wristlock.

Near fall—Holding both shoulders within four inches of the mat (but not on the mat) for one full second, or holding one shoulder on the mat and the other at an angle of forty-five degrees or less for one full second or more, constitutes a two-point near fall.

When the criteria for a two-point near fall has been met uninterrupted for five seconds, a three-point near fall is awarded.

Neutral position—Position in which neither man has an advantage.

Pinning combination—A hold which results in a fall.

Referee's position on the mat—A position in which the defensive wrestler is on hands and knees. The offensive wrestler is kneeling at the defensive man's side, facing the same direction. The offensive wrestler puts his nearest arm loosely around his opponent's waist and grasps his opponent's near arm at the elbow with the other arm.

Ride—Maintaining the position of advantage over the opponent who is attempting to escape.

Scissors hold—Locking the legs around any part of the opponent's body.

Sugar side—The side of the wrestler which is exposed in his stance. He can defend this leg better than the other and can counter when this leg is attacked.

Takedown—Bringing the opponent to the mat from a standing position while maintaining the position of advantage.

Wrestler's standing position—Upright position assumed by a wrestler from which he can most effectively attack or defend.

EQUIPMENT

Mats

The wrestling area of the mat shall be not less than a square 24' x 24' or a circular area 28' in diameter. A larger area is recommended.

Uniform

The uniform shall consist of:

a. Full-length tights, close fitting outside short trunks, and sleeveless shirt without fasteners at the shoulders and fasteners at the crotch.
b. Light, heelless gym shoes reaching above the ankle and laced by means of eyelets.
c. Contestants should be clean-shaven, with sideburns trimmed at earlobe level and hair neatly trimmed.
d. Headgear—a protective headgear should be a required part of the wrestling contestant's uniform.

RULES

A collegiate wrestling match consists of three periods. The first period is 2 minutes in length, while the last two periods are each 3 minutes long, unless a fall occurs during one of them. In the first period the opponents start the match from the standing position. If a fall does not occur during the first period, the wrestlers start the second period in the referee's position on the mat. The winner of a coin toss has his choice of top or bottom position. If the match goes to the third period, the relative positions of the wrestlers are reversed from those of the second period. No timeout is allowed except for injury. If a wrestler cannot continue the match because of injury, his opponent is declared winner by default provided the injury did not result from an illegal maneuver.

A fall or pin shall end the match in any period. In order to win the match by a fall, a wrestler must hold both of the opponent's shoulder blades in continuous contact with the mat for one full second. If no fall occurs during the 8-minute match, the winner is chosen by a point system.

Individual match points may be awarded in the following manner:

> 2 points for each takedown
> 2 points for a reversal of position of control
> 1 point for an escape to a neutral position
> 2 or 3 points for a near fall
> 1-2 points for riding time

In a takedown the wrestler must take his opponent to the mat from a neutral position and gain control of him in the same movement. Some good wrestlers take opponents down for 2 points and let them up, giving them 1 point for an escape. This maneuver repeated three times would give the takedown artist a lead of 6-3.

The wrestler who is in the bottom position, because of having been taken down or by virtue of the coin toss, can obtain points by reversal of positions or by escaping to the neutral position. A reversal shall be recognized and 2 points shall be awarded when the top man loses control and the bottom man gains control. One point is awarded for escaping from the bottom position without further influence on the opponent.

An escape to the neutral position is often good strategy if the bottom man is ahead on points and is in danger of being pinned. This is also a good maneuver if the bottom man is 2 points behind and is a good takedown wrestler. If he can escape for 1 point and take his opponent down for 2 points, he will win by 1 point.

Riding time can tie or win a decision, and so is quite important in wrestling. During the match a record is kept of the amount of time that the wrestler has control of his opponent. At the end of the match, if no fall has occurred, the total amounts of control time of the two wrestlers are compared; if one wrestler has at least 1 full minute more riding time than his opponent, then he is awarded 1 point. Only 2 points may be obtained in this manner.

In mat wrestling all holds which may choke or injure the wrestler are illegal, and points may be awarded to the offended participant. The top man (the wrestler who has control) may not lock his hands together except while standing or in a pinning combination on the mat.

A college team may consist of ten weight divisions. The following ten weight classes are standard: 118 lbs., 126 lbs., 134 lbs., 142 lbs., 150 lbs., 158 lbs., 167 lbs., 177 lbs., 190 lbs., and unlimited.

Team points determine the winner of the match, and are awarded in the following manner:

5 points for fall
5 points for a default
5 points for forfeit
3 points for a decision
2 points for a draw.

For a more complete picture of scoring, penalties, and illegal holds, the interested reader is referred to the current Official NCAA Wrestling Guide.

SAFETY

Although wrestling is a vigorous contact activity, it is quite safe insofar as major injuries are concerned. The most common injuries incurred in wrestling are strained muscles and mat burns. In order to lower the incidence of strained muscles, contestants should always warm up before practice or competition. Mat burns can be greatly reduced if the wrestlers wear tights. The mats should be of plastic foam material.

The ears are sometimes bruised, and if this occurs too often or too severely a condition known as "Cauliflower ears" may result. The ears should be lightly coated with vaseline in order to minimize the possibility of ear injuries. The rules require all contestants to wear headgear.

The mat should be sprayed with a disinfectant periodically in order to reduce the possibility of participants contracting infections. Mats should extend a minimum of 4-1/2 feet beyond the wrestling area. If the mat is next to a wall, the wall should be padded to a height of not less than 5-1/2 feet. Mat covers should be used if the wrestling mat has a rough surface.

SKILLS

Wrestler's Standing Position

Open Stance

1. Spread the feet 2-1/2 to 3 feet. One foot is approximately 10 inches in front of the other.
2. Bend the knees and flex the hips.
3. Let the arms hang loosely in front of the body to protect the legs.
4. Keep the back straight, and the head up.
5. Move by taking short steps in order not to expose the legs. Do not cross the legs or get them too close together.

Closed Stance

1. Grasp the opponent behind the neck with the right hand.
2. Grasp the opponent's right elbow with the left hand. (The hands may be switched in steps 1 and 2.)
3. Keep the back straight.
4. Hold the head up.
5. Stay relaxed.

The referee's hold may be varied by grasping both upper arms of the opponent just below the shoulders. (This eliminates steps 1 and 2 above.)

TAKEDOWNS

Speed, deception, setting up, and follow-through are essential for successful takedowns. These are a few of the many ways your opponent may be setup for a takedown:

1. Elbow pushups
2. Elbow pulldowns
3. Fake arm drags
4. Opponent pulling away from you.

After the proper setup, one of the following takedowns may be used:

1. *Single Leg Takedown*
   a. Drop to the knees—quickly moving in.
   b. Secure one leg at the ankle with your arms.
   c. Drive your shoulder into his shin bone as you pull his ankle toward you.
   d. Continue your drive as you move up into a ride.

2. Duck Under

a. Drive his right elbow upward as you apply downward pressure on the back of his neck with your right hand.

b. Move under his elbow as you jam it up.

c. Dip up and out (to the left of his right foot) on your right knee as you maintain the neck drag.

d. Spin behind your right knee and gain control.

3. Fireman's Carry

a. Start in a standing closed position.

b. Slip your left hand under your opponent's forearm and over it, regrasping his right arm tightly.

c. Pin his right arm against your body with your left elbow.

d. Clamp his arm tightly, duck under it, and reach between his legs with your other arm.

e. Begin your spin to the left (sitting on the left buttocks where your left foot was), then swing your right leg through as you spin (either between your left leg and the opponent's right, or between both of his legs).

f. Pull down with your left arm clamp, and lift up with your right shoulder under the opponent's right thigh, thus snapping your opponent to the mat in a rolling action.

Counters for Takedowns

For every maneuver in wrestling, there is an appropriate countermovement. All countermoves should become automatic responses. Protect your legs by keeping the elbows in close and the arms in front of the thighs. From this basic defensive position one of the following counters may be used:

1. Cross Face Sprawl

a. Drive your forearm across your opponent's face as you force his arm to the mat.

b. Move your legs back and spread them laterally.

c. As your opponent's arm drops, spin behind to gain control.

2. Snap Down Go Behind

a. Pull your opponent's shoulders to a point on the mat where you were originally standing.

b. Spread your feet laterally and move to the rear.

c. Spin behind, thus gaining control.

Breakdowns and Rides

The ability to ride (stay on top and keep your opponent under control after you bring him to the mat is most important in the art of wrestling. If you are unable to do this, you will not be able to win).

Try to maintain good balance, always keeping your weight bearing on your opponent.

Destroy your opponent's balance and work toward a pin. Make every attempt to keep him off his knees.

All breakdowns should be executed with force.

ESCAPES

In all the escapes discussed here, the wrestler in the position of advantage is on the right side. The escapes are executed by the wrestler in the defensive or bottom position.

1. Sit out to the side, or switch

a. Move the right hand to a position near the left hand.

b. Raise the left knee several inches and swing the right leg underneath the left leg, meanwhile lifting the left arm. Pivot on the right arm and left leg so that the body pivots from the front to the back.

c. Grasp inside the opponent's near thigh from underneath with the left hand, then swing upward and to his back.

2. Forward roll

a. Take the left arm from the mat and thrust it back between the legs, thus lowering the left shoulder.

b. Do a shoulder roll away from the opponent.

3. Armlock and roll

a. Reach back with the arm opposite the opponent, and lock his arm to your side.

b. Roll forward and sideward toward the locked arm (to the left), keeping the opponent snugly against your back.

c. Pivot quickly, coming face-to-face with the opponent as he nears the mat.

PINNING COMBINATIONS

1. Half Nelson and Crotch

a. Maneuver into a position in which the opponent is on his back and you are at a right angle, in a chest-to-chest position.

b. Pass the upper arm over the outside shoulder and under the neck of the opponent.

c. Pass the lower arm through the crotch and grasp under the opponent's buttocks.

d. Raise the opponent's lower body upward by lifting at the crotch. At the same time, push downward on the opponent's shoulders.

Escape from half nelson and crotch hold: The bottom man may escape from this hold by sliding his

free hand between his and the top man's chest and prying upward.

    2. *Double Armlock.* This pinning combination is executed from the referee's position, with the offensive wrestler on the right of his opponent.
    a. Move the right knee even with the opponent's right arm, keeping the back straight. The chest is held firmly over the opponent's near shoulder.
    b. Reach across in front of the opponent's arms and under his face, and grasp his left elbow with the right arm.
    c. Pass the left arm behind and grasp the opponent's right thigh.
    d. Throw the opponent on his left side by pulling his left arm forward and lifting his right leg.
    e. Grasp both the opponent's arms and secure them into the right armpit as he falls to the mat.
    f. Fall across the opponent's chest at a right angle. Your hands should then be locked together.

    g. Press downward against the opponent's shoulders.

    Block for double armlock: Do not allow the top man to reach the far arm: shove it outward beyond his reach. If an attempt is made at lifting the right thigh, extend the left leg to the side and stand up.
    3. *Farther Arm Bar:* This maneuver is executed from the referee's position, with the offensive wrestler on the left side. To apply the farther arm bar from this position, the top wrestler should be:

    a. From behind, reach between the opponent's body and right arm and grasp his right wrist with your right hand. Pull his wrist back toward his hip.
    b. Grasp the opponent's left wrist with your left hand and place your head firmly against the back of his left upper arm.

c. Pull on the opponent's left wrist while driving forward into the back of his upper arm with your head. This will cause the defensive wrestler to assume a position on his right side.

d. Maintain your grasp of the opponent's wrists as you apply pressure to the back of his left shoulder with your forehead and the front of your right shoulder.

e. Swing behind your opponent and assume a position at a right angle to him.

f. Raise your head and release his left wrist as you bar his arm by sliding your left arm, from the front, between his arm and body.

g. As you press the opponent onto his back, grasp his right wrist with your left hand while still maintaining the grip on it with your right hand.

h. Release his wrist with your right hand and lock your right arm around his head.

(The opponent's right hand is at the back of his right hip.)

i. Release his right wrist with your left hand and hook his left arm with your left arm, while moving your left hand toward the back of his left shoulder to join with your right hand.

j. Pull your opponent to you and press down, while stretching out and spreading your legs for balance.

Block for the farther arm bar: The elbows must be kept close to the body. Beware of reaching back for an opponent. Once the bar has been applied to the right arm, a good defense is to entwine the opponent's left leg with the left leg. Then hold him parallel until the left arm can be worked free. Avoid his securing a headhold at all costs.

BIBLIOGRAPHY

Gallagher, E.C., *Wrestling.* New York: A.S. Barnes & Co., 1951.

Keen, C.P., Spiedle, C.M., and Swatz, R.H., *Championship Wrestling.* Annapolis: U.S. Naval Institute, the V-Five Association, 1958.

Official AAU Wrestling Guide. New York: Amateur Athletic Union of the United States.

Official NCAA Wrestling Guide. Phoenix, Ariz.: College Athletics Publishing Service, 349 East Thomas Road.

Stone, Henry A., *Wrestling Intercollegiate and Olympic.* Englewood Cliffs, N.J.: Prentice-Hall, Inc., 1945.

U.S. Naval Institute, *Wrestling.* Annapolis: The Institute, 1943.

SOURCES OF OFFICIAL RULES*

Many sporting goods stores carry rule books on a wide variety of sports. Check your local sporting goods store when in need of them. If you are unable to obtain the books you are seeking from local authorities, they may be obtained by writing to the following sources. To save time, it might be well to enclose payment with your order. (*Note: Prices subject to change. Some prices include mailing charges.*)

The following list is not all-inclusive. Therefore, The Athletic Institute would appreciate receiving information which will make this list more complete, or which will help correct such data as may become outdated.

THE ATHLETIC INSTITUTE • MERCHANDISE MART • ROOM 705 • CHICAGO, ILL. 60654

Activity	Source of Rules	Cost
Aerial Tennis	Sells Aerial Tennis Co., Box 3042, Kansas City, Kan. 66103	(free)
Archery (Field) "N.F.A.A. Constitution, By-laws and Policy"	National Field Archery Assn. of the U.S. Inc. Rt. 2, Box 514, Redlands, Calif. 92373	$1.00
Archery Official Tournament Rules (Indoor-Outdoor)	National Archery Assn., Inc. of the U.S. 2833 Lincoln Highway E., Ronks, Pa. 17572	$1.25
Archers Handbook Official Rules (Indoor-Outdoor)	National Archery Assn., Inc. of the U.S. 2833 Lincoln Highway E. Ronks, Pa. 17572	$2.50
Official Shooting Rules—Field and Target International Archery Federation	National Archery Assn., Inc. of the U.S. 2833 Lincoln Highway E., Ronks, Pa. 17572	$1.50
Archery (Indoor)	American Indoor Archery Assn., P.O. Box 174, Grayling, Mich. 49738	$ .75
Archery (See DGWS listing, last page)		
Badminton	American Badminton Assn., Lester E. Hilton 15 Tanglewood Dr., Cumberland, R.I. 02864	$ .25
Badminton (Rules—other games rules included)	General Sportcraft Co. Ltd., 140 Woodbine St., Bergenfield, N.J. 07621	$ .25
Badminton (Rules)	Dayton Racquet Co., Inc., 302 S. Albright St., Arcanum, Ohio 45304	(free)
Badminton (Your Guide to Better Badminton)	Ashaway Line & Twine Co., Ashaway, R.I. 02804	(free)
Badminton (See DGWS listing, last page)		
Baseball Official Baseball (Nonprofessional Annual) (Annual w/rules)	National Baseball Congress, Box 1420, Wichita, Kan. 62201	$2.00
Baseball (Copyrighted Rules) (For Professional, Semi-Pro, Amateur & Youth Teams)	National Baseball Congress, Box 1420, Wichita, Kan. 62201	$ .25
Baseball (Constitution Tournament Rules)	All American Amateur Baseball Assn. R.D. 5, Box 316 A, Johnstown, Pa. 15905	(free)
Baseball (American Legion)	American Legion, Box 1055, Indianapolis, Ind. 46206	$ .25 or 5 for $1.00
Baseball, Babe Ruth (13-15)	Babe Ruth Baseball, 524½ Hamilton Ave., Trenton, N.J. 08609	(free)
Baseball, Babe Ruth (16-18)	Babe Ruth Baseball, 524½ Hamilton Ave., Trenton, N.J. 08609	(free)
Baseball, Boys 9 to 19 (Rules & Regulations)	National Hot Stove Baseball League, Inc. 210 East Main St., Alliance, Ohio 44601	(free)
Baseball (Khoury League)	George Khoury Baseball, 3222 Park Ave., St. Louis, Mo.	(free)
Baseball, Little League	Little League Baseball, Inc., P.O. Box 1127, Williamsport, Pa. 17701	$ .25

*Used by permission of the American Athletic Institute.

Activity	Source of Rules	Cost
Baseball, Little League (Umpire's Handbook)	Little League Baseball, Inc., P.O. Box 1127, Williamsport, Pa. 17701	$ .25
Baseball, Bronco-Pony-Colt	Boys Baseball, Inc., P.O. Box 225, Washington, Pa. 15301	$ .15
Baseball "Knotty Problems of Baseball" (Professional Rules Only)	The Sporting News, 1212 N. Lindbergh Blvd., St. Louis, Mo. 63166	$2.00
Baseball (Professional Rules Only)	The Sporting News, 1212 N. Lindbergh Blvd., St. Louis, Mo. 63166	$ .50
Baseball (See NCAA listing, last page)		
Baseball	American Amateur Baseball Congress, Stan Musial, Connie Mack Mickey Mantle and Sandy Koufax Divisions, P.O. Box 5332, Akron, Ohio 44313	(free)
Baseball, Rules in Pictures	American Amateur Baseball Congress, P.O. Box 5332, Akron, Ohio 44313	$1.25
Baseball, The Manager's Handbook	American Amateur Baseball Congress, P.O. Box 5332, Akron, Ohio 44313	$ .60
Baseball, The Scorer's Handbook (Does not include playing rules)	American Amateur Baseball Congress, P.O. Box 5332, Akron, Ohio 43313	$ .60
Baseball, Tournament Management and Operation	American Amateur Baseball Congress, P.O. Box 5332, Akron, Ohio 44313	$1.50
Baseball, The Umpire's Handbook (Includes playing rules)	American Amateur Baseball Congress, P.O. Box 5332, Akron, Ohio 44313	$1.50
Baseball (See High School listing, last page)		
Balanced Basketball (Height Equalization)	John L. McHale, 4 Montgomery Rd., Scarsdale, N.Y. 10583	$ .50
Basketball (See AAU listing, last page)		
Basketball (See High School listing, last page)		
Basketball (See NCAA listing, last page)		
Basketball (See DGWS listing, last page)		
Basketball (Biddy)	Jay Archer, 701 Brooks Building, Scranton, Pa. 18501	$ .10
Bicycling	Bicycle Institute of America, 122 E. 42nd St., N.Y., N.Y. 10017	(free)
Bicycling (Governing body of competitive cycling)	Amateur Bicycle League of America c/o James Grill, Box 285 Olive Street, Nehansic Station, N.J. 08853	$1.25
Billiards (Official Rules & Records for all pocket and carom Billiard games)	Billiard Congress of America, 717 No. Michigan, Chicago, Ill. 60611	$1.25
Bocce, Croquet, Darts, Deck Tennis, Horseshoes, Paddle Tennis, Shuffleboard, Table Tennis, Takraw Tether Ball, Tether Tennis—all in one book	General Sportcraft Co., Ltd., 140 Woodbine St., Bergenfield, N.J. 07621	$ .25
Bowling (Duck Pin)	National Duck Pin Bowling Congress 711—14th St., N.W., Suite 501, Washington, D.C. 20005	(free)
Bowling, Rubber Band Duck Pin (Tournament Rules and Regulations)	American Rubberband Duck Pin Bowling Congress 124 Odette St., Pittsburgh, Pa. 15227	(free)
Bowling (Ten Pin)	American Bowling Congress, 1572 E. Capitol Dr., Milwaukee, Wis. 53211	$ .25
Bowling, Women's (Ten Pin)	Woman's International Bowling Congress 1225 Dublin Rd., Columbus, Ohio 43212	(free)
Bowling (See DGWS listing, last page)		
Boxing (See AAU listing, last page)		
Casting: Tournament Fly & Bait Casting Guide	American Casting Education Foundation, P.O. Box 51, Nashville, Tenn. 37202	(free)
Corkball	Rawlings Sporting Goods Co., 2300 Delmar Blvd., St. Louis, Mo. 63166	(free)
Cricket (M.C.C. Rules)		
Marylebon Cricket Club	Secretary, Marylebon Cricket Club Lord's Ground, London, N.W. 8, England	1/-($ .12) plus postage
Croquet	General Sportcraft Co., Ltd., 140 Woodbine St., Bergenfield, N.J. 07621	$ .25
Curling	Laurie Carlson, P.O. Box 1465, Madison, Wis. 53701	(free 1 copy) in quantities, 10c each

Activity	Source of Rules	Cost
Dartball	Wisconsin State Dartball Comm. c/o E. Dorow Pres., 9333 W. Lincoln Ave., West Allis 19, Wis.	$ .50 Plus Postage
Darts	General Sportcraft Co., Ltd., 140 Woodbine St., Bergenfield, N.J. 07621	$ .25
Darts (History, Rules & Standards, Games, Tips on Good Play)	United States Darting Association 516 Fifth Avenue, New York, N.Y. 10036	$ .75
Deck Tennis	General Sportcraft Co., Ltd., 140 Woodbine St., Bergenfield, N.J. 07621	$ .25
Fencing Rules	Amateur Fencer's League of America, Dept. AI, 33—62nd St., West New York, N.J. 07093	$1.00
Fencing (See DGWS listing, last page)		
Field Hockey (See DGWS listing, last page)		
Field Hockey	General Sportcraft Co., Ltd., 140 Woodbine St., Bergenfield, N.J. 07621	$1.00
Floor Tennis	U.S. Floor Tennis Assn., 2030 W. Morse Ave., Chicago, Ill. 60645	(free)
Football (Touch & Flag)	The Athletic Institute, 705 Merchandise Mart, Chicago, Ill. 60654	$1.00
Football (Junior League)	Pop Warner Football 1004 Western Saving Fund Bldg. Philadelphia, Pa. 19107	$ .25
Football (Six-Man) (See High School listing, last page)		
Football (See High School listing, last page)		
Football (See NCAA listing, last page)		
Golf	U.S. Golf Assn., 40 E. 38th St. New York, N.Y. 10016	$ .25
Gymnastics (See AAU listing, last page)		
Gymnastics (See NCAA listing, last page)		
Gymnastics (See DGWS listing, last page)		
Gymnastics (National Compulsory Routines For Girls)	U.S. Gymnastics Federation, P.O. Box 4699, Tucson, Ariz. 85717	$1.50
Age Group Gymnastics Workbook		$3.50
FIG Code of Points for Men		$3.50
FIG Code of Points for Women		$2.00
FIG Measurements and Dimensions of Apparatus		$1.50
FIG Bulletin		$5.00/year Quarterly
Notes from Rome		$ .50
World's Games Compulsories		$ .25
Modern Gymnast Magazine		$5.00/year Monthly
Handball (See AAU listing, last page)		
Handball, Guide & Directory (Includes Rules)	U.S. Handball Assn., 4101 Dempster St., Skokie, Ill.	$1.00
Handball (Court Specifications & Rules)	U.S. Handball Assn., 4101 Dempster St., Skokie, Ill.	$2.00
Horseshoes	General Sportcraft Co., Ltd., 140 Woodbine St., Bergenfield, N.J. 07621	$ .25
Horseshoes (Professional)	National Horseshoe Pitchers Assn. of America Donald Koso, 803 East 12th St., Falls City, Neb. 68355	(free) Not in quantity
Ice Hockey (See NCAA listing, last page)		
Ice Skating	Amateur Skating Union, Edward J. Schmitzer, 4135 N. Troy St., Chicago, Ill. 60618	$1.00
Indoor Hockey	Cosom Corp., 6030 Wayzata Blvd., Minneapolis, Minn. 55416	$ .25
Lacrosse (See DGWS listing, last page)		
Lawn Bowls	John W. Deist, Secretary, 10337 Cheryl Dr., Sun City, Ariz. 85351	(free) 1 copy & each add'l. copy $1.00
Lawn Bowls	General Sportcraft Co., Ltd., 140 Woodbine St., Bergenfield, N.J. 07621	$1.00
Marbles Shooting	National Marbles Tournament, Cleveland Press Bldg., Cleveland 14, Ohio	(free)
Outings (See DGWS listing, last page)		
Paddle Tennis (Rules—also for other games)	General Sportcraft Co., Ltd., 140 Woodbine St., Bergenfield, N.J. 07621	$ .25
Paddleball	Rodney J. Grambeau, Sports Building, University of Mich., Ann Arbor, Mich.	$ .50

Activity	Source of Rules	Cost
Platform Tennis	General Sportcraft Co., Ltd., 140 Woodbine St., Bergenfield, N.J. 07621	$ .25
Racquetball (Rules)	International Racquetball Association, 4101 Dempster St., Skokie, Ill. 60076	$1.00
Riding (See DGWS listing, last page)		
Roller Hockey	National Roller Hockey Assn., of the U.S., 97 Erie St., Dumont, N.J.	$ .50
Roque	American Roque League, Inc., 4205 Briar Creek Lane, Dallas, Texas 75214	$ .35
Rugby (The Rugby Football Union Handbook)	Chicago Lyons Football Club Richard W. Smith, 1940 Lake Avenue, Wilmette, Ill. 60091	5/6 ($.66)
Rugby (Why the Whistle Went)	Chicago Lyons Football Club, Richard W. Smith 1940 Lake Ave., Wilmette, Ill. 60091	2/- ($.24)
Rugby (Laws of the Game and Notes on the Laws)	Chicago Lyons Football Club, Richard W. Smith, 1940 Lake Ave., Wilmette, Ill. 60091	1/6 ($.18)
Scoopball (Rules for 26 different games)	Cosom Corp., 6030 Wayzata Blvd., Minneapolis, Minn. 55416	$ .25
Shooting (See National Rifle Assn. listing, last page)		
Shuffleboard (Deck)	General Sportcraft Co., Ltd., 140 Woodbine St., Bergenfield, N.J. 07621	$ .25
Shuffleboard (Table)	American Shuffleboard Leagues, Inc., 533 Third St., Union City, N.J. 07087	(free)
Shuffleboard	Dimco-Gray Company Mr. C.F. Dearth, 207 E. Sixth Street, Dayton, Ohio 45402	(free)
Skating (Figure)	U.S. Figure Skating Assn., 178 Tremont St., Boston, Mass. 02111	$3.00
Skating (Roller)	U.S. Amateur Roller Skating Assn., 120 W. 42nd St., New York, N.Y. 10036	$1.50
Skating (Speed)	William J. Kelly, 8941 Crest Oak Lane, St. Louis, Mo. 63126	$1.00
Skeet Shooting	National Skeet Shooting Assn., 212 Linwood Bldg., 2608 Inwood Rd., Dallas, Texas 75235	$ .25
Skiing (See NCAA listing, last page)		
Skiing (Downhill, Slalom, Jumping & Cross Country FIS and USSA Rules)	U.S. Ski Assn., 1726 Champa St., Denver, Colo. 80202	$3.50
Skindiving, Competitive (See AAU listing, last page)		
Smash	Smash, 1024 North Blvd., Oak Park, Ill.	(free)
Soccer (Rule Book)	General Sportcraft Co., Ltd., 140 Woodbine St., Bergenfield, N.J. 07621	$1.00
Soccer (See NCAA listing, last page)		
Soccer (See DGWS listing, last page)		
Softball (12"—fast and slow pitch)	Amateur Softball Assn., Suite 1351 Skirvin Tower, Oklahoma City, Okla. 73102	$ .75
Softball (Originators of 16" Slow Pitch Softball)	Edw. Weinstein, Chairman Rules Comm., Umpires Protective Assn., of Chicago, Apt. 710, 3550 Lake Shore Dr., Chicago, Ill.	$ .65
Softball (Rules by International Joint Rules Comm. on Softball)	International Softball Federation 1351 Skirvin Tower, Oklahoma City, Okla. 73102	(free)
Softball (See DGWS listing, last page)		
Speed-A-Way	Marjorie S. Larsen, 1754 Middlefield, Stockton, Calif. 95204	$1.75
Speedball (See DGWS listing, last page)		
Squash Racquets (Rules and court specifications)	U.S. Squash Racquets Assn., 470 Latches Lane, Merion, Pa. 19066	$3.00
Swimming (See AAU listing, last page)		
Swimming (See NCAA listing, last page)		
Swimming (Synchronized—See AAU listing, last page)		
Table Tennis	General Sportcraft Co., Ltd., 140 Woodbine St., Bergenfield, N.J. 07621	$ .25
Table Tennis (Instructions & Rules)	U.S. Table Tennis Assn., Box 8587 Kensington Station, Detroit, Mich. 48224	$ .25
Table Tennis (Rules)	U.S. Table Tennis Assn., Box 8587 Kensington Station, Detroit, Mich. 48224	(free 1 copy) in quantities 10c each
Table Tennis (Instructions & Rules)	Nissen Corp., 930 27th Ave., S.W., Cedar Rapids, Iowa 52406	(free)

Activity	Source of Rules	Cost
Tarkaw Game	General Sportcraft Co., Ltd., 140 Woodbine St., Bergenfield, N.J. 07621	$ .25
Tennis (Includes Guide)	U.S. Lawn Tennis Assn., 51 E. 42nd St., New York, N.Y. 10017	$3.00
Tennis (Rules Only)	Tennis Publications, Inc., 23300 Mercantile Road, Cleveland, Ohio 44122	$ .50
Tennis (See DGWS listing, last page)		
Tennis (Rules)	Dayton Racquet Co., Inc., 302 S. Albright St., Arcanum, Ohio 45304	(free)
Tennis Umpire's Manual (Friend at Court)	Tennis Publications, Inc., 23300 Mercantile Road, Cleveland, Ohio 44122	$1.00
Tether Ball (Inflated Ball)	W. J. Voit Rubber Corp., 3801 S. Harbor Blvd., Santa Ana, Calif. 92704	(free)/
Tether Ball (Inflated Ball)	General Sportcraft Co., Ltd., 140 Woodbine St., Bergenfield, N.J. 07621	$ .25
Tether Tennis	General Sportcraft Co., Ltd., 140 Woodbine St., Bergenfield, N.J. 07621	$ .25
Track & Field (See AAU listing, last page)		
Track & Field (See High School listing, last page)		
Track & Field (See NCAA listing, last page)		
Trapshooting (Amateur)	Amateur Trapshooting Assn., P.O. Box 246, Vandalia, Ohio	(free)
Volleyball (Rules for other games included)	General Sportcraft Co., Ltd., 140 Woodbine St., Bergenfield, N.J. 07621	$ .25
Volleyball (See DGWS listing, last page)		
Volleyball (Rule and Guide)	U.S.V.B. Assn., Printer, P.O. Box 109, Berne, Ind., or other: P.O. Box 554, Encino, Calif. 91316	$1.50
Water Polo (See AAU listing, last page)		
Weight Lifting (See AAU listing, last page)		
Winter Sports (See DGWS listing, last page)		
Wrestling (See NCAA listing, last page)		

NAIA (Rules)

National Assn. of Intercollegiate Athletics
126 W. 12th St., Kansas City, Mo.

NCAA Rulebooks and Guides

College Athletics Publishing Service
349 East Thomas Road, Phoenix, Ariz. 85012

Baseball	$1.50	Read-Easy Football Rules	$ .75
Basketball	$1.50	Soccer	$1.50
Football	$1.50	Swimming	$1.50
Football Rules Interpretations	$1.00	Track & Field	$1.50
Gymnastics	$1.00	Wrestling	$1.50
Ice Hockey	$1.50	Skiing	$1.00
Read-Easy Basketball Rules	$ .75	Basketball Rules	$ .75

DGWS OFFICIAL GUIDES FOR WOMEN'S SPORTS, INCLUDING RULES

Division for Girls' and Women's Sports
1201 Sixteenth St., N.W., Washington, D.C. 20036

Aquatics	$1.25	Soccer—Speedball	$1.25
Archery—Riding	$1.25	Softball	$1.25
Basketball	$1.25	Track & Field	$1.25
Bowling—Fencing—Golf	$1.25	Tennis—Badminton	$1.25
Field Hockey—Lacrosse	$1.25	Volleyball	$1.25
Gymnastics	$1.25	Winter Sports & Outing Activities	$1.25
Basketball Rules Reprint	$ .35		

HIGH SCHOOL ACTIVITIES

National Federation of State High School Athletic Assns.
7 South Dearborn St., Chicago, Ill. 60603

Basketball:		Football:	
Rules	$ .60	Rules (includes 6 & 8-Man)	$ .60
Casebook	$ .95	Casebook	$ .95
Player Handbook	$ .60	Player Handbook (includes touch)	$ .60
Official's Manual	$ .60	Official's Manual	$ .60
Rules Simplified & Illustrated	$1.00	Rules Simplified & Illustrated	$1.50
		Track & Field, Rules and Records	$ .80
		Wrestling, Official's Manual	$ .60
		So Now You're An Official	$ .50

Baseball:
Rules	$ .60
Casebook	$ .95
Umpire's Manual	$ .60

**OFFICIAL AAU RULE BOOKS
AND GUIDES**

Amateur Athletic Union of the United States
231 W. 58th St., New York, N.Y. 10019

AAU Handbook	$2.00	Judo	$2.00
Directory, 1970	$1.00	Swimming, Diving, Water Polo	$3.00
Basketball Guide '69-70	$3.00	Swimming Rules Manual	$1.00
Baton Twirling Guide	$1.25	Synchronized Swimming	$1.50
Boxing	$2.50	Track and Field	$3.00
Gymnastics	$2.00	Track and Field Supplement	$1.00
FIG Code of Points for Men	$3.50	Volleyball	$1.50
FIG Code of Points for Women	$2.00	Weightlifting	$2.00
		Wrestling	$2.00

**NRA AND INTERNATIONAL
SHOOTING UNION RULE BOOKS**

National Rifle Assn.
1600 Rhode Island Ave., N.W., Washington, D.C. 20036

NRA High Power Rifle	$ .30	ISU Constitution	$ .20
NRA Pistol	$ .30	ISU Free Rifle & Army	$ .20
NRA Smallbore Rifle	$ .30	ISU General Regulations	$ .20
NRA 10 Meter Precision Air Rifle and Pistol	$ .35	ISU Rapid Fire Pistol	$ .20
NRA Shotgun Rules for Clay Pigeon	$ .30	ISU Running Deer	$ .20
ISU Bound Vol. (All rules)	$3.00	ISU Running Roebuck & Boar	$ .20
ISU Center Fire Pistol	$ .20	ISU Skeet	$ .20
ISU Clay Pigeon	$ .20	ISU SB Rifle & Free Pistol	$ .20

APPENDIX

1 | ANGLING SKILL TEST

Purpose: To measure the student's accuracy in casting.

Equipment and Facilities: One rod, of any variety; a reel, equipped with a level-winding device in working order. The reel handle may be no less than 2-1/8 inches in length; a line, no smaller in diameter than .013 inches, unless it can tolerate a 9-pound pull on recognized fish scales; a plug, no more than 5/8 of an ounce in weight; ten randomly-scattered targets, consisting of ten rings or discs of not more than 30 inches in diameter, anchored at distances unknown to the caster. The furthest target shall be not more than 80 feet and not less than 70 feet from the casting point. Tilted targets may be used when the targets and the casting point are on the same level. The far edge of a tilted target may not be more than 6 inches higher than the near edge. The casting box shall consist of a space 4 feet square. The nearest target is between 40 and 45 feet from the casting point.

Procedure: The student casts twice at each of ten targets and is scored as follows: six points for a perfect first cast and four points for a perfect second cast. A cast is "perfect" if the plug falls on or within the target. The student receives no points if the plug falls outside the target.

The casting method is freestyle unless otherwise specified. Casters rotate, taking two casts at each target, from one to ten, in sequence. The student's total score is determined by taking the sum of his scores on each of the ten targets (maximum 100).

2 | ARCHERY SKILL TEST

The archery skill test involves averaging the student's three highest Columbia Round scores of the semester.

The Columbia Round consists of the following:

> 1st range: 24 arrows (4 ends) at 50 yards
> 2nd range: 24 arrows (4 ends) at 40 yards
> 3rd range: 24 arrows (4 ends) at 30 yards

48-inch target.
Scoring as follows:

	Points
Gold	9
Red	7
Blue	5
Black	3
White	1

An arrow that hits the target and bounces off, or goes completely through the target, counts 5 points.

An arrow that cuts the line between two colors counts as hitting the color with the higher value.

3 | BADMINTON SKILL TEST

Purpose: To determine the player's ability to control the shuttlecock when rallying against a wall.

Equipment and Facilities: A badminton racket, and shuttlecock; a wall space; a serving line marked on the floor, 6½ feet from the wall; a line representing the height of a net, marked on the wall, 5 feet from the floor.

Procedure: The student stands behind the serving line and, at the signal to start, puts the shuttlecock in play with a legal serve to the wall above the net line. He continues to play the shuttlecock by hitting it back to the wall above the net line.

If the shuttlecock goes wild, the contestant may retrieve it, return to behind the serving line, and execute a legal serve.

The serve and rally continue for 1 minute and the student is awarded one point each time the shuttlecock hits the front wall above the net line.

To measure accuracy in serving, the instructor should mark targets on the floor and ask the student to execute a legal serve to each of the target areas.

4 | BASKETBALL SKILL TEST

Under Basket Shot

Purpose: To measure short shot accuracy and ball control.

Equipment and Facilities: A basketball; a basket; and a stopwatch.

Procedure: The contestant stands near the basket with the ball. At the signal to start, the contestant shoots the ball at the basket, retrieves the ball, and immediately shoots again, trying to make as many baskets as possible in 60 seconds.

Dribble

Purpose: To measure ball-handling and dribbling ability.

Equipment and Facilities: Six chairs in a straight line, the first chair 6 feet from the starting line and the other chairs 6 feet apart; a basketball and a stopwatch.

Procedure: The contestant stands behind the starting line with the basketball. At the signal to start, he dribbles the ball around the right side of the first chair and the left side of the second chair, alternating around the remainder of the chairs back to the starting line. The ball must be dribbled legally and at least once between each pair of chairs. Timing begins with the command to start and stops when the player crosses the starting line after dribbling around all of the chairs.

Passing

Purpose: To measure ball control and passing speed.

Equipment and Facilities: A circular target, 10 inches in diameter, marked on a wall space 5 feet from the floor; a basketball and a stopwatch.

Procedure: The contestant stands behind a restraining line 10 feet from the wall. At the signal to start, the contestant, using a two-hand chest pass, throws the basketball at the target. The contestant must remain behind the restraining line while throwing the ball, but he may go over the line to retrieve the ball. The ball must strike the wall within the circle. The contestant gets one point for each time the ball strikes the wall in 1 minute.

Shooting

Purpose: To measure shooting ability.

Equipment and Facilities: A regulation court and a basketball.

Procedure: The contestant shoots fifteen foul shots: five underhand, five two-handed chest shots, and five one-hand push shots. The contestant must move both feet between each shot. One point is awarded for each basket.

5 | BOWLING SKILL TEST

To determine the bowling skill test score, average the student's score on three games bowled at the end of the semester.

In these games, the foul rule shall be observed. A bowler fouls when any part of his body touches or goes beyond the foul line or any part of the alley after the legal delivery of the ball. A foul counts as a ball rolled. Pins knocked down when a foul is committed do not count. If a foul occurs on the first ball, any pins knocked down on the first delivery are replaced before the second ball is thrown.

Only legal pinfall shall be scored.

6 | BOXING SKILL TEST

The nature of boxing is such that a student's skill can best be rated subjectively by his instructor. The instructor should ask the student to demonstrate various offensive and defensive movements with an imaginary partner, rating him on the basis of his performance.

7 | DIVING SKILL TEST

The nature of diving is such that it requires a subjective rating. This is true for both class instruction and/or formal competition. The instructor might ask the student to do a number of required optional dives which he would judge on a ten point scale, as in a competitive meet. For the optional dives, the degree of difficulty, as well as the judge's rating, should be considered in scoring the contestant.

9 | FENCING SKILL TEST

Purpose: To measure basic skills in fencing.

Equipment and Facilities: A stopwatch; a foil, target marked on wall, consisting of three circles with diameters of 4 inches, 8 inches, and 12 inches, using a point 4 feet from the floor as the target center. A starting line is marked 8 feet from the target wall.

Procedure: On the starting signal, the student advances from the on-guard position behind the starting line, lunges, strikes the target, and retreats behind the starting line. Scoring is based on the amount of time elapsed from the starting signal until the contestant returns behind the starting line. This is repeated five times.

Using the same action, the contestant remains in constant motion - advancing, lunging, striking the target, and retreating - until the target has been struck fifteen times. Points are awarded for accuracy, on the following scale: inner circle, ten points; central circle, eight points; outer circle, five points.

10 | FIELD HOCKEY SKILL TEST

Purpose: To measure the skills of shooting and dribbling.

Equipment and Facilities: Hockey stick, balls, and stopwatch; a goal area, divided into three areas with a rope placed vertically, 1 yard in from each of the goal posts. This provides a center target area 6 feet by 7 feet and an area on each side of 3 feet by 7 feet.

Procedure:

Shooting - A shooting line (36 feet from the goal) is marked off on the field. Two markers are placed along the shooting line at points 15 feet from that line's center. The contestant shoots ten times from the right of the right marker, and ten times from the left of the left marker. The player may aim at any of the three targets and he is awarded one point if the ball goes through the center target and three points for either of the outer targets.

Dribbling - Six barriers are placed in a straight line, with the first barrier 12 feet from the starting line and the others 10 feet apart. The contestant dribbles around the barriers, starting to the right of the first barrier, left of the second barrier, and then alternating around the others until he returns to the starting line. The time elapsed indicates the score.

11 | GATOR BALL SKILL TEST

The skill tests for dribbling the soccer ball and for passing the basketball can be used to measure these skills in Gator Ball.

12 | GOLF SKILL TEST
Putting Test

Purpose: To determine the student's putting ability.

Equipment and Facilities: Six golf balls; one putter; a tape measure; a green with a cup in the center.

Procedure: The student can score a possible two points for each shot. To gain two points, he must hole out in two putts from a distance of 25 feet. To gain one point, the student must hole out in three putts. Since not every student can take the test at the same cup, it is essential that the distance from tee to hole be exactly 25 feet. Each student can score a maximum of 10 points on this test.

Chip Shot

Purpose: To determine the student's ability to hit within a 5 ft. and 10 ft. radius of the cup from a distance of 45 ft.

Equipment and Facilities: One number five iron; six golf balls; a green with a cup in the center.

Procedure: The student stands at designated areas around the green. The total distance is 45 feet; at 40 feet, there is a restraining line which the ball must carry over before any credit is given. If the student hits the ball within a 5-foot radius around the cup, he is allowed two points. If he hits the ball into the 10-foot radius, he is allowed only one point. Beyond the 10-foot radius, the student is not allowed any points. The student can score a maximum of ten points on this test.

Pitch Shot

Purpose: To determine the student's ability to execute the pitch shot.

Equipment and Facilities: One 7 or 9 iron; six golf balls; a green with a cup and two circles, with radii 20 and 25 feet, drawn around the cup.

Procedure: The student stands 105 feet from the cup. Each shot is worth a possible two points. If the student hits the ball correctly within the 20-foot radius, he is allowed two points. If the student hits the ball correctly within the 25-foot radius, he is allowed one point. No credit is given for any shot that rolls all the way into the 20- or 25-foot radius.

Short Iron Shot

Purpose: To determine the student's ability to hit the ball in the air.

Equipment and Facilities: One 7 or 9 iron; six golf balls.

Procedure: The student stands 100 yards from the green. Each shot has a value of two points. Two points are awarded the student if he hits the ball 60 yards carry on a fairway that is 50 yards in width. The ball counts where it lands and not where it comes to rest. To gain one point, the student must hit the ball in the air 40 yards. No credit will be given if the ball hits the rear or side boundaries of the test area.

Wood Shot Test

Purpose: To determine the student's ability to hit the ball in the air 75 or 100 yards on a 100-yard-wide fairway.

Equipment and Facilities: Several drivers; six golf balls.

Procedure: The student is given six balls. The first shot is for practice only. The student can score two points for each shot if he hits the ball 100 yards in the air on a 100-yard-wide fairway. To score one point, the student must hit the ball 75 yards in the air on the 100-yard-wide fairway.

13 | GYMNASTICS SKILL TEST

Each trick in a course is assigned a point value in keeping with its difficulty, hazard, or fundamental importance. As the student accomplishes or learns to perform a trick, he may request that he be tested on that trick.

The instructor rates the performance on a scale of zero to ten on the basis of form and execution, a score of ten representing a perfect rating. This score is then multiplied by the difficulty value of the trick. For example, a trick valued at ten points

has a difficulty value of one; a trick valued at twenty points has a difficulty value of two; and so on. Therefore, if a trick valued at twenty points receives a rating of eight for performance (form and execution), eight is multiplied by two, to arrive at the complete score of sixteen out of a possible twenty. The student is awarded five of the ten basic points for mere execution. Additional points are awarded on the basis of the quality of his form.

Three or more individual tricks may be combined into routines suitable for testing. Extra points may be awarded for this by scoring each item of the routine separately, totaling this score, and adding one-third for the complete score.

The final or raw score on the skill test shall be the total number of points accumulated by the student in all his events during the semester.

14 | HANDBALL SKILL TEST
Kill Shot

Purpose: To determine the player's ability to make a straight kill shot and his ability to control the ball on low shots.

Equipment and Facilities: One handball; one handball court with a line marked across the front wall, 15 inches from the floor.

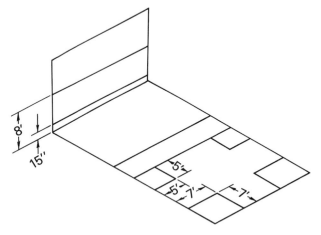

Handball court.

Procedure: The player stands in the service zone and tosses the ball against the front wall. As the ball rebounds from the wall, he attempts to hit it on the first bounce and send it into the area on or below the 15-inch line on the front wall. Twenty trials are allowed, and one point is scored and recorded for the contestant each time the ball hits on or below the 15-inch line before hitting the floor. The player's score for the test is the total number of good hits. Balls which hit the side wall and rebound into the area below the line are considered good.

In making his trials, the contestant may select the rebounds he wishes to hit, i.e., if the tossed ball does not rebound as he expects it to, he may refuse it and toss again.

If the player does not have one foot in the service zone when he hits the ball, no points may be awarded on that trial.

Lob Serve

Purpose: To test the player's ability to use the lob serve.

Equipment and Facilities: One handball; one handball court with 7-foot squares marked in the corners of the back court along the base line.

Procedure: The player stands in either half of the service zone and, using the server's bounce, attempts to serve the ball into the 7-foot square marked in the corners of the back court. He is allowed ten trials to the square directly behind him and ten to the opposite square.

One point is scored and recorded for each served ball which hits in the correct square or the lines forming square. The contestant will serve to the rear right square and then to the rear left square. Lob serve must be the legal serve.

Low Drive Service

Purpose: To determine the player's ability to use a cross-court, low drive service.

Equipment and Facilities: One handball; one handball court with 5-foot squares drawn in the corners of the front portion of the back court, along the short line.

Procedure: The player stands in one half of the service zone and, using a server's bounce, attempts to serve the ball with a low drive to the square on the opposite side of the court. He is given ten trials to hit to the square on the right side, from the left side of the service zone, and ten trials to hit into the square on the left side of the court, from the right. One point is scored for each ball that hits into, or on the boundary lines of, the correct square. The player's score for the test is the total number of points scored.

The serve must hit the front wall on or below a line drawn parallel to and 8 feet from the floor.

Rally

Purpose: To determine the player's ability to control the ball when rallying against the front wall.

Equipment and Facilities: One handball; one handball court.

Procedure: The player stands anywhere behind the short line, and, at the signal to start, puts the ball in play with a throw to the front wall. He continues to play the ball by hitting it back to the front wall. The ball must be returned in legal fashion; i.e., it must hit the front wall before it touches the floor.

If the ball goes wild, the contestant may catch it and throw to start the rally going again. If the ball does not rebound beyond the short line, the contestant may go and retrieve it; but before putting the ball in play, he must return to a position behind the short line.

The rally continues for 1 minute and one point is scored each time the ball hits the front wall in legal fashion. *Note:* The initial throw will count as one point but any throw thereafter will not count.

15 | HORSESHOE PITCHING SKILL TEST

Purpose: To measure ability to play horseshoes.

Equipment and Facilities: Horseshoes; horseshoe court with two circles, 6 and 12 inches in diameter, marked around one of the stakes.

Procedure: The contestant pitches the shoe at the stake fifteen times. Three points are awarded for a ringer, two points if the shoe falls inside the 6-inch circle, and one point if the shoe falls inside the 12-inch circle.

16 | ICE HOCKEY SKILL TEST

Purpose: To measure the skills of shooting, dribbling, and speed skating.

Equipment and Facilities: An ice hockey rink; a puck; one hockey stick; a stopwatch; six chairs; a goal area, divided into two equal vertical zones and three equal horizontal zones, which together form a grid of six scoring areas.

Procedure:

Shooting - A shooting line is marked on the ice 20 feet from the goal. Three shots are taken at each of the six areas. Three points are awarded if the puck goes into the designated target area, and one point if the puck goes into any of the other scoring areas.

Dribbling - The contestant starts from behind the goal line, dribbles the length of the rink, goes around the goalie's cage, and returns the length of the rink until he crosses the starting line. The time elapsed indicates the score.

Obstacle Skating - Six chairs are placed in a straight line, with the first chair 12 feet from the starting line and the other chairs 10 feet apart. The contestant dribbles around the chairs, starting to the right of the first chair, left of the second chair, and then alternating around the others until he returns to the starting line. The time elapsed indicates the score.

17 | JUDO SKILL TEST

The instructor rates the student subjectively as he executes certain offensive and defensive moves. Consideration of such factors as balance, timing, ability to execute the skills, and efficiency of motion will assist the rater to be objective.

18 | LACROSSE SKILL TEST

General Comment: The student should be equipped with helmet, shoulder pads, gloves, and stick as if he were participating in a game.

Goal Shots

Purpose: To determine the student's ability to score a goal.

Equipment and Facilities: Five lacrosse balls; a line drawn parallel to the goal, 20 yards in front of it.

Procedure: The student stands a few feet back of the 20-yard marker, with a ball in the pocket of his stick. He takes a few steps toward the goal and throws the ball without going past the restraining line. Two points are awarded for each goal scored.

Target Shots

Purpose: To determine the student's accuracy in throwing the ball from different angles at a stationary target.

Equipment and Facilities: 12 lacrosse balls; a wall with a target on it; the target consists of three semicircles, radii 17, 27, and 37 inches respectively, drawn from a point 5 feet 2 inches above the base line of the wall (line A). The base line of the semicircle is a line (line B) drawn through this point, parallel to line A. Another line (line C) is drawn on the ground, 40 feet from and parallel to line A. A perpendicular is dropped from the point on line A directly under the center of the semicircle, to line C. Two lines parallel to this perpendicular, lines D and E, are drawn on the ground through two points 11 feet six inches to the right and left, respectively, of the point of intersection of line B and the perpendicular.

Procedure: The student stands anywhere in area A and throws the ball at the target four times. Then he moves to area B and throws the ball at the target four times. He then moves to area C and throws the ball at the target four times.

Points are awarded for the accuracy of each throw as follows: five points for the center of the target, three points for the next area, one point for the next area, and no points if the ball hits outside the target area. The accuracy score is the sum made on the twelve trials. Balls hitting a line earn the higher score.

Scoop and Weave

Purpose: To determine the student's facility at scooping and cradling the ball.

Equipment and Facilities: One lacrosse ball; a stopwatch; five wooden barriers, 1½ inches by 1½ inches by seven feet in size. The barriers are driven into the ground at distances of five yards along a line. A mark is placed on the ground 5 yards in front of the first barrier. A line which will serve as a starting and finishing line is drawn 10 yards from the first barrier.

Procedure: The student stands at the starting line, runs to the ball, which has been placed on the ground 5 yards away, scoops the ball, cradles it as he weaves around each barrier, runs around the last barrier, weaves around each barrier on the way back, and finishes by running across the starting line.

If the ball drops to the ground, he must scoop it and continue to run through the course. The time that it takes the student to complete this event is taken as the score.

Dodge

Purpose: To determine the student's· facility at cradling the ball and executing dodges around the barriers.

Equipment and Facilities: One lacrosse ball; the same course as in the scoop and weave, except that the starting-finishing line is 5 yards from the first barrier.

Procedure: The student stands at the starting line with the ball in the pocket. As he comes up to the first barrier, he executes a dodge to the right side of the barrier and continues his dodge, alternating sides on the next three barriers. He runs around the last barrier and continues to dodge back, continuing to alternate sides from barrier to barrier.

The student executes the dodge by running up to the barrier, turning his back to the barrier, and spinning. This move is similar to the basketball pivot. If the ball drops to the ground, he must scoop it and continue to run through the course. The time that it takes the student to complete this event is taken as the score.

19 | MODERN DANCE

The student is required to perform the following tasks and movements. He is scored by his instructor on the basis of his skill and the quality of his presentations. Maximum score for each exercise appears in the right-hand column. Total score (maximum 65) is calculated by taking the sum of the scores for the individual tasks.

		Points
I.	Evaluation of static positions or non-locomotor movements.	
	a. Descending and rising	2
	b. Turning—inward and outward	2
	c. Falling—partially and completely	2
II.	Evaluation of elementary locomotor movements.	
	a. Walking	2
	b. Running	2
	c. Leaping	2
	d. Skipping	2
	e. Hopping	2
	f. Galloping	2
	g. Jumping	2
III.	Evaluation of a combination of any three or more nonlocomotor or locomotor skills.	10
IV.	Evaluation of a pattern of specific movements set to rhythm.	15
V.	Evaluation of choreography for completed pattern or routine, including such elements as design, drama, costumes, props, and scenery.	25

20 | MOVEMENT SKILL TEST

The student is required to perform the following tasks and movements. He is scored by his instructor on the basis of his skill and the quality of his presentations. Maximum score for each exercise appears in the right-hand column. Total score (maximum 50) is calculated by taking the sum of the scores for the individual tasks.

		Points
I.	Evaluate	
	a. Standing — including positioning of body parts, such as hips over feet and chest over hips, with shoulders back and relaxed.	3
	b. Sitting — including positioning of the feet and legs, hips and chest. This should also include the process of lowering and raising the body.	3
	c. Locomotor movements	
	1. Walking	2
	2. Running	2
	3. Leaping	2
	4. Jumping	2
	5. Sliding	2
	6. Hopping	2
	7. Skipping	2
	8. Galloping	2
	d. Nonlocomotor movements	8
	1. Bending	
	2. Falling	
	3. Pulling	
	4. Rising	
	5. Stretching	
	6. Swaying	
	7. Swinging	
	8. Turning	

Points

II. Understanding Movement
   a. Perform or create five movements which give information concerning how, why, and when.
   (Examples would include running because one is in a hurry, or pacing the floor because one is nervous.)   5
   b. Display an interpretation of these words through movement: (one each) 15

   1. Sophistication
   2. Fear
   3. Joy
   4. Anger
   5. Love
   6. Sadness
   7. Rejection
   8. Loneliness
   9. Enthusiasm
   10. Pity or sympathy
   11. Introversion
   12. Extroversion
   13. Jealousy
   14. Unconcernedness
   15. Scatterbrainedness

Total Points Possible   50

Suggested Scoring Range   46-50 — A
   41-45 — B
   36-40 — C
   31-35 — D
   0-30 — F

21 | PADDLEBALL SKILL TEST

Purpose: To measure the student's ability to play paddleball.

Equipment and Facilities: Paddleball court with markings similar to those on the court used for the handball skill test; regulation paddle and ball.

Procedure: Same procedure as skill test for handball.

22 | SHUFFLEBOARD SKILL TEST

Purpose: To measure the player's ability to control the disc.

Equipment and Facilities: Shuffleboard court; discs; cues.

Procedure: The contestant plays a disc, the score for that play is recorded, and the disc is removed from the court. This process is repeated ten times and the player's scores are added for a total score. If desired, a disc may be placed on each number 7 area and the contestant given three shots to remove it. The contestant may be awarded five points for each disc removed from the scoring area.

23 | SKIING SKILL TEST

Purpose: To measure the ability of the skier to ski downhill and to control his body as he maneuvers around barriers.

Equipment and Facilities: A complete set of standard skiing equipment; a zigzag downhill slalom course of a difficulty appropriate to the contestant's level of skill.

Procedure: On the command to start, the skier starts down the course, goes to the right of the first barrier, to the left of the second barrier, and continues this pattern until the course is completed. The elapsed time is taken as the score.

24 | SKIN AND SCUBA DIVING SKILL TEST

Purpose: To demonstrate the student's ability to clear his mask and to control breathing under water.

Equipment and Facilities: Full diving equipment, including a diving tank.

Procedure: The student enters the water fully equipped and demonstrates "buddy breathing" while submerged. He dives to 15 feet, removes all his equipment, surfaces, takes one breath, returns to the bottom, and puts back on his full equipment. Finally, he dives to 33 feet fully equipped and returns to the surface.

25 | SOCCER SKILL TEST
Kicking for Distance (Right Foot)

Purpose: To determine the student's ability to kick a soccer ball for distance and control.

Equipment and Facilities: Tennis or gym-type shoes; three soccer balls; an alley 60 yards long and

20 yards wide, behind which the student stands (see Diagram 1).

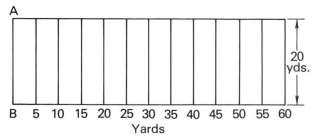

Diagram 1. Kick for distance.

Procedure: The student places the soccer ball anywhere on the line A-B, and kicks it (toe kick not allowed) so that it lands within the side lines, in the area marked off in 5 yard intervals (see Diagram 1). Three trials are given, and each distance the ball is kicked is recorded. The greatest distance is taken as the score. The score is estimated to the nearest yard.

Kicking for Distance (Left Foot)

The test is the same as above, except that the student kicks with his left foot.

Penalty Kick for Accuracy

Purpose: To determine the student's accuracy in the penalty kick.

Equipment and Facilities: Tennis or gym-type shoes; a rope or a two-by-four, placed 2 yards from each end of the goal, can be tied at the ground, with ordinary bricks used as anchors; a penalty kick mark 12 yards from the goal line (see Diagram 2); three soccer balls.

Procedure: The student places a soccer ball on the

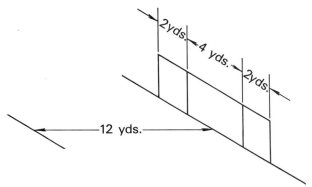

Diagram 2. Penalty kick for accuracy.

penalty kick mark and kicks three penalty kicks, as he would in a game situation.

A ball kicked into either of the 2-yard areas scores three points. If the kick goes into the 4-yard area, in the air, it scores two points. If it touches the ground and goes into the 4-yard area, one point is scored. If the ball fails to go through the goal, no points are awarded.

Corner Kick for Accuracy

Purpose: To determine the student's accuracy in the corner kick.

Equipment and Facilities: Tennis or gym-type shoes; regulation penalty area, with lines extended from each base of the goal post to the end of the penalty area, perpendicular to the goal line (see Diagram 3), that part of a circle, with radius 1 yard, center at the corner of the field, drawn inside the field of play between the goal line and the sideline; three soccer balls.

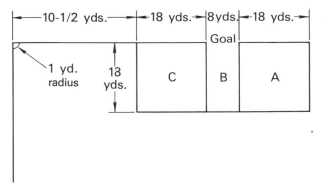

Diagram 3. Corner kick for accuracy.

Procedure: The student places the soccer ball at any point within the quarter-circle. Three kicks are allowed, with either foot. All kicks count in the scoring.

Two points are scored if the kick travels in the air and lands in the area (A) furthest away from the kicker. Three points are scored if the ball travels in the air and lands in the middle area (B). One point is scored if the ball travels through the air and lands in the area (C) nearest the kicker. If the ball fails to travel through or to land in one of these designated areas, no points are scored.

Heading for Accuracy

Purpose: To determine the student's accuracy in heading a soccer ball.

Equipment and Facilities: Tennis or gym-type shoes; a line marker 6 yards in front of the goal (see Diagram 4); six soccer balls.

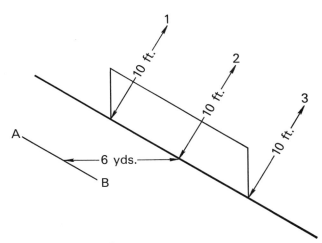

Diagram 4. Heading for accuracy.

Procedure: The student stands with both feet in back of line A-B, facing the goal. The instructor stands at least 10 feet in back of the goal at point No. 1 in Diagram 4. With both hands, he lobs the ball over the goal so that it reaches the student on its downward arc. The student attempts to head the ball into the goal. On the second trial, the instructor stands at point No. 2. On the third, he stands at point No. 3.

Three points are scored if the student heads the ball into the goal before it touches the ground. Two points are scored if he heads the ball into the goal after it has touched the ground. One point is scored if the ball passes over the top of the cross-bar. All three trials are scored.

Trapping

Purpose: To determine the student's ability to trap a soccer ball using the three basic traps: leg, stomach, and foot.

Equipment and Facilities: Tennis or gym-type shoes; four circles with radii of 3, 6 and 9 feet and one semi-circle with radius 24 feet marked on field (see Diagram 5); eight soccer balls.

Procedure: The student stands at the center of the circles. The instructor stands outside the 24-foot semi-circle and throws the ball three times at a point between the student's knees and waist. The student attempts to execute the leg trap. The in-

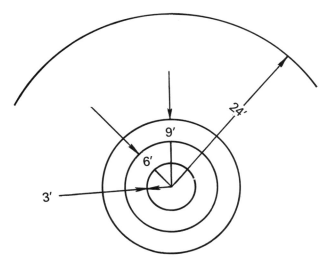

Diagram 5. Trapping.

structor then throws the ball three times at a point between the student's waist and shoulders. The student attempts to execute a stomach trap. Finally, the instructor rolls the ball three times at moderate speed on the ground, and the student attempts to execute a foot trap.

Three points are scored if the student traps the ball successfully within the circle of radius 3 feet, using the proper technique. Two points are scored if he traps the ball and brings it under control within the circle of radius 6 feet. One point is scored if he brings the ball under control within the circle of radius 9 feet. All trials count in scoring.

Dribbling for Time

Purpose: To determine the student's facility in dribbling a soccer ball through a series of five barriers.

Equipment and Facilities: Tennis or gym-type shoes; one soccer ball; a stopwatch; five wooden barriers, 1½ inches by 1½ inches by 7 feet, driven into the ground 5 yards apart. A mark, placed 5 yards from the first barrier, serves as a starting and finishing line (see Diagram 6).

Procedure: At the command "GO," the student dribbles the ball to the left or right of the first barrier and then alternates down to the last barrier. He then returns to the starting line in the same manner. Two trials are given the student, with his best time counting for score. The student may rest between trials.

The best score is recorded to the nearest second.

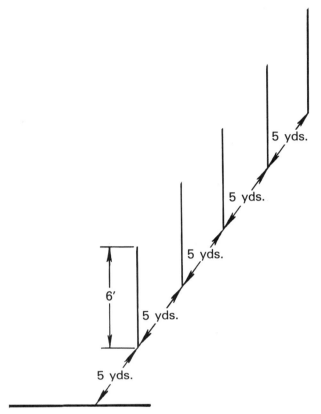

5 yds.

5 yds.

5 yds.

6'

5 yds.

5 yds.

Diagram 6. Dribbling for time.

26 | SOCIAL DANCE SKILL TEST

Purpose: To measure the ability to dance in time to various rhythms.

Equipment and Facilities: A tape recorder; the following rhythms, recorded on tape: waltz, tango, fox trot, jitterbug, rumba, and samba. The test tape should be composed of six selections of varying but similar duration, one for each rhythm to be tested, separated by a standard bridge four measures in length.

Procedure: The contestant stands on a target such as a chalk mark, on the floor. When the tape is started, he listens to hear what rhythm will be played and, when the appropriate rhythm begins, executes a forward and backward basic step in time with the music and continues to move until the music stops. The jitterbug is the only rhythm pattern that does not have a basic forward and backward step.

For each rhythm, the instructor counts the num-

ber of basic steps that the student has executed, and compares this with the correct count. For example, if twenty measures of waltz music are played, twenty basic steps should be executed. If the contestant does only eighteen basic steps, his score is −2; if he does twenty-two basic steps, his score is +2. To arrive at a final score, the instructor totals the scores for the individual rhythms, disregarding the negative signs. The lower the score, the more successful the student.

27 | SOFTBALL SKILL TEST

Accuracy Throw

Purpose: To measure the student's ability to throw the softball at a specific target.

Equipment and Facilities: A target consisting of three circles, 6 inches, 12 inches, and 18 inches in radius, with the center of the target 4 feet from the floor; two restraining lines marked 30 feet and 60 feet in front of the target.

Procedure: The contestant throws the ball five times from each distance. The final score is the total of the ten throws, with the inner circle having a value of 10, the central circle 5, and the outer circle 3.

Distance Throw

Purpose: To measure the student's ability to throw the ball for distance.

Equipment and Facilities: A field marked every 10 feet; a regulation softball.

Procedure: The contestant is permitted three trials. The distance of the throw is calculated on the basis of the last marker cleared by the airborne ball. The distance of the best throw is taken as the score.

Batting

Purpose: To measure batting ability.

Equipment and Facilities: An adjustable batting tee; a softball and several softball bats; a line drawn from home plate over second into center field.

Procedure: The contestant hits five balls off the batting tee into left field, and five balls into right field. Distance is measured to the nearest 10-foot interval that the ball clears on the fly. The average distance for each field is taken as the score.

28 | SPEED-A-WAY SKILL TEST

The student is required to demonstrate the following skills. He is scored by his instructor on the basis of his performance. Maximum score for each exercise appears in the right-hand column. Total score (maximum 85) is calculated by taking the sum of the scores for the individual tasks.

Points

I. Lifting Techniques:
   a. The student, using one foot, performs five consecutive lifts of a ground ball to a teammate. — 5
   b. The student makes five consecutive lifts, to himself, of a ground ball, by allowing the moving ball to roll up his toe and leg to his hands. — 5
   c. The student performs five consecutive lifts, to himself, of a ground ball, by holding the ball with his feet and ankles and jumping, tossing the ball to his hands. — 5
   d. The student performs five consecutive lifts, to himself, of a ground ball, by placing his toe on top of the ball and then spinning the ball onto the top of his foot and up his leg to his hands. — 5

II. Offensive Techniques:
   a. The student performs a series of dribbles a distance of 30 yards or more without a defense. — 2
   b. The student performs a series of dribbles a distance of 30 yards or more against a defense. — 4
   c. The student covers distance while he performs a legal juggle. — 2
   d. The student performs a series of short passes for a distance of 30 yards or more without a defense. — 2
   e. The student performs a series of short passes for a distance of 30 yards or more against a defense. — 4
   f. The student performs five consecutive punts covering a distance of 40 yards or more. — 5
   g. The student performs five consecutive drop kicks covering a distance of 30 yards or more. — 5
   h. The student performs one long pass over a distance of at least 20 yards. — 1
   i. The student performs five consecutive runs with the ball over a short distance of 10 yards or less against a defense. — 5

Points

   j. The student performs five consecutive runs with the ball over a distance of 10 yards or more, against defensive strategy. — 5

III. Scoring Techniques:
   a. The student performs five consecutive field goals, with a goalie defending the goal. — 5
   b. The student performs five consecutive touchdown passes, with a goalie defending the goal. — 5
   c. The student performs five consecutive touchdown runs, with a goalie defending the goal. — 5
   d. The student performs five consecutive drop kicks, with a goalie defending the goal. — 5

IV. Defensive Tactics:
   a. The student has eight opportunities to perform five successful side tackles. — 5
   b. The student has eight opportunities to perform five successful hook tackles. — 5
   c. The student performs five consecutive touchdown runs, with a goalie defending the goal. — 5
   d. The student has eight opportunities to successfully block five touchdown passes. — 5
   e. The student has eight opportunities to perform five legal tags on a ball carrier. — 5
   f. The student has eight opportunities to successfully block five field goals. — 5

Total Points Possible	105	
Suggested Scoring Range	94-105	A
	81-93	B
	68-80	C
	55-67	D
	0-54	F

29 | SPEEDBALL SKILL TEST

The student is required to demonstrate the following skills. He is scored by his instructor on the basis of his performance. Maximum score for each exercise appears in the right-hand column. Total score (maximum 85) is calculated by taking the sum of the scores for the individual tasks.

Points

I. Lifting Techniques:
  a. The student performs five consecutive lifts, with one foot, of a ground ball to a teammate.   5
  b. The student performs five consecutive lifts, to himself, of a ground ball, by allowing the moving ball to roll up his toe and leg to his hands.   5
  c. The student performs five consecutive lifts, to himself, of a ground ball, by holding the ball with his feet and ankles and jumping, tossing the ball to his hands.   5
  d. The student performs five consecutive lifts, to himself, of a ground ball, by placing his toe on top of the ball and then spinning the ball onto the top of his foot and up his leg to his hands.   5

II. Offensive Techniques:
  a. The student performs a series of dribbles a distance of 30 yards or more without a defense.   2
  b. The student performs a series of dribbles a distance of 30 yards or more against a defense.   4
  c. The student covers the prescribed distance while he performs a legal juggle.   2
  d. The student performs a series of short passes for a distance of 30 yards or more without a defense.   2
  e. The student performs a series of short passes for a distance of 30 yards or more against a defense.   4
  f. The student performs five consecutive punts covering a distance of 40 yards or more.   5
  g. The student performs five consecutive drop kicks covering a distance of 30 yards or more.   5
  h. The student performs one successful long pass over a distance of at least 20 yards.   1

III. Scoring Techniques:
  a. The student performs five consecutive field goals, with a goalie defending the goal.   5
  b. The student performs five consecutive touchdown passes, with a goalie defending the goal.   5

Points

  c. The student performs five consecutive drop kicks, with a goalie defending the goal.   5

IV. Defensive Tactics:
  a. The student has eight opportunities to perform five successful side tackles.   5
  b. The student has eight opportunities to perform five successful hook tackles.   5
  c. The student has eight opportunities to perform five successful passing interceptions or break-ups.   5
  d. The student has eight opportunities to successfully block five touchdown pass attempts.   5
  e. The student has eight opportunities to successfully block five field goal attempts.   5

Total Points Possible   85
Suggested Scoring Range   76-85   A
    66-75   B
    56-65   C
    46-55   D
    0-45   F

30 | SQUARE DANCE SKILL TEST

Purpose: To determine the student's facility in performing square dance routines.

Equipment and Facilities: A record player; those records used during the course of the semester; a small box containing slips of paper on which are written the names of those records danced to during the semester.

Procedure: The instructor rates each student as he performs to three different pieces of music. For each performance, the student is rated on the basis of rhythm, style, and response to caller. A five point scale is used to evaluate the student on each of these criteria: 5, excellent; 4, above average; 3, average; 2, below average; and 1, poor. The student may score fifteen points for each performance, or a total of forty-five points for all three.

To determine the musical selections to which he will dance, the student draws three slips of paper from the box described above.

31 | SQUASH RACQUETS SKILL TEST

Purpose: To measure the player's ability to keep the ball in play.

Equipment and Facilities: Squash court; squash ball and racquet.

Procedure: The contestant stands in the server's box, executes a legal serve, and then continues to strike the ball in a legal fashion. The rally is continued for 1 minute. The number of times the ball is legally played is taken as the score.

32 | SWIMMING

Beginners' Skill Test

The student is required to demonstrate the following skills. He is scored by his instructor on the basis of his performance. Maximum score for each exercise is ten points. Total score (maximum 100) is calculated by taking the sum of the scores for the individual tasks.

It is suggested that the Beginning Swimmer Skill Test be administered about a month before the last scheduled class meeting. This enables the students to obtain more practice and instruction than if they are tested at the completion of each instructional unit. Students swim the short courses (widths) of pool for instruction and test.

1. *Prone Glide:* The student demonstrates his proficiency in the prone glide for a distance of 10 yards. The student starts in the water, pushes off from the side of the pool, and extends his body fully, arms overhead and hands together, head between arms, and legs extended and together. No arm or leg action is allowed. One point is awarded for each yard, up to 10, that the student glides. Yardage is calculated to the furthest point touched by the student's hands.

2. *Back Glide:* The student demonstrates his proficiency in the back glide for a distance of 10 yards. The student starts in the water, pushing from the side of the pool, on his back, with his arms overhead, legs together, body fully extended. No arm or leg action is allowed. Award points from 0-10 with one point awarded for each yard (up to 10) that the student glides. Yardage is calculated to the furthest point touched by the student's hands.

3. *Kick Glide on Front:* The student demonstrates his proficiency in the kick glide on his stomach. The student pushes from the side of the pool, arms extended overhead and hands clasped together, head between arms. As the push-off glide slows, the student begins to flutter kick for propulsion over a 20 yard distance. In order to breathe during the kick glide, the student may lift or turn head, but arms must stay fully extended and *clasped together.* No arm action is allowed. One point is awarded for each yard the student kicks over 10 yards, up to ten points. Yardage is calculated to the furthest point touched by the student's hands.

4. *Kick Glide on Back:* The student demonstrates his proficiency in the kick glide on his back. The student pushes off on his back, from the side of the pool and either *places his hands on his thighs or extends his arms overhead, with his hands clasped together.* As the push-off glide slows, the student begins to flutter kick for propulsion over a 20 yard distance. No arm action is allowed. One point is awarded for each yard the student kicks over 10 yards, up to ten points. Yardage is calculated to the furthest point touched by the student's hands.

5. *Beginner's Crawl (Human Stroke):* The student demonstrates his proficiency in the beginner's crawl or human stroke for 20 yards. He pushes from the side of the pool in the prone position, with face in or out of the water, letting his legs trail or kick gently, and executes the arm stroke in series with his arms recovering above the water surface. One point is awarded for each yard the student swims over 10 yards, up to ten points.

6. *Change of Direction:* The student demonstrates his proficiency in making two 90 degree turns, one right and one left, while swimming. Any stroke on the stomach or side may be used. The student pushes from the side of the pool and swims 5 yards before making the first turn, and swims at least 5 yards between turns. The instructor awards 0-10 points based on ease of turning and relaxation.

7. *Jump in Deep Water:* The student demonstrates his proficiency in jumping feet foremost into water that is at least 10 feet deep, leveling off on the water surface, and swimming 20 yards, using any stroke. The instructor awards 0-10 points on the basis of the student's relaxation and his ability to surface, level off, and begin a coordinated stroke.

8. *Elementary Back Stroke:* The student swims 40 yards while demonstrating his proficiency in the elementary back stroke. The instructor scores the

stroke on proper form, without considering speed, awarding 0-10 points. The student starts in the water. He makes his push-off with his arms overhead and his legs held straight and together. As the push-off glide slows, only the arms are pulled, then, as the second glide slows, the arms and legs move in a coordinated stroke. On the recovery, the student's arms may be raised above his shoulders as he uses the inverted breast stroke kick. Scoring is based on correct body position, relaxation, coordination of arm pull and recovery, breathing, correct leg kick (inverted breast stroke kick) and recovery, and proper glide (sufficient glide for the stroke to be used as a resting stroke).

9. *Endurance Swim:* The student demonstrates his ability to stay on top of the water for 5 minutes. The student may swim (any stroke or strokes), tread water, or float. Two points are awarded for *each* complete minute (up to 5) the student stays afloat. The student's head must not go under water at any time. If his head goes under, the test is terminated. No points are given for fractions of a minute.

10. *Artificial Respiration:* The student demonstrates his proficiency in the back pressure — arm lift method of artificial respiration. Emphasis is placed on proper body position of the victim and the operator, smooth rhythm, and correct application of respiration techniques. The instructor awards 0-10 points to the student.

Advanced Skill Test

The student is required to demonstrate the following skills. He is scored by his instructor on the basis of his performance. Maximum score for each exercise is ten. Total score (maximum 100) is calculated by taking the sum of the scores for the individual tasks.

It is suggested that each skill be tested after it is taught and sufficient practice time has been allowed. Students will swim short courses (widths) of the pool for practice and testing.

1. *American Crawl:* The student swims 40 yards while demonstrating his proficiency in the American crawl. The instructor scores the stroke on the basis of proper form, without considering speed, awarding from 0-10 points. Emphasis is to be placed on strong flutter kick, correct arm pull and recovery, and proper breathing. The student may not stop and rest on the side of the pool while being tested.

2. *Back Crawl:* The student swims 40 yards while demonstrating his proficiency in the back crawl (racing back stroke). The instructor scores the stroke on the basis of proper form, without considering speed, awarding from 0-10 points. Emphasis is to be placed on a strong flutter kick (on the back), and correct arm pull and recovery. The student may not stop and rest on the side of the pool while being tested.

3. *Breast Stroke:* The student swims 40 yards while demonstrating his proficiency in the conventional style breast stroke (underwater arm recovery). The instructor scores the stroke on the basis of proper form, without considering speed, awarding from 0-10 points. Emphasis is to be placed on strong breast stroke kick, correct arm pull and recovery, proper breathing, and strong, smooth glide. The student may not stop and rest on the side of the pool while being tested.

4. *Side Stroke:* The student swims 40 yards while demonstrating his proficiency in the side stroke. The student's score will be determined on the basis of style.

The student will *start in the water* and use a regulation push-off for the start and the turn. The student pushes off into gliding position on his stomach, with his arms extended overhead, rolls on his side, and pulls his upper arm as the glide slows. No leg stroke is allowed on the push-off.

5. *Elementary Back Stroke:* The student swims 40 yards while demonstrating his proficiency in the elementary back stroke. The student's score is determined on the basis of style. The student starts in the water. He pushes off with arms overhead and legs held straight and together. As the push-off glide slows, the arms pull, and as this glide slows, the coordinated stroke begins. The student should use an inverted breast stroke kick. Arms may be raised above the shoulders on the recovery. No leg strokes are allowed.

6. *Tread Water:* The student treads water for ten minutes. 0-10 points are awarded, one point for each *full* minute completed. Floating, swimming, and bobbing are not allowed. The student's body must remain in a vertical position. No points are awarded for portions of a minute.

7. *Endurance Swim:* The student swims 500 yards using any stroke or strokes, swimming widths of the pool. Two points are awarded for each *completed* 100 yards. The swimmer may float or tread water but he may not hold to the side of the pool or stand on the pool's bottom. The regulation start begins the swim.

8. *Underwater Swim:* The student swims freestyle 20 yards, completely underwater. The

stopwatch starts with the student's first forward motion. Score (0-10 points) is based on the speed of completion. No score is awarded if the swimmer fails to swim the complete distance or if any part of his body comes to the surface before he has completed the swim.

9. *Sprint Swim:* The student swims 40 yards, freestyle, for time, from the *regulation start.* 0-10 points are awarded according to the time required to swim the 40 yards.

10. *Artificial Respiration:* The student demonstrates his proficiency in the back pressure - arm lift method of artificial respiration. Emphasis is to be placed on proper body position of the victim and the operator, smooth rhythm, and correct application of the respiration techniques. The instructor will award 0-10 points on the basis of the student's performance.

33 | SYNCHRONIZED SWIMMING SKILL TEST

The student is required to demonstrate the following skills. He is scored by his instructor on the basis of his performance. Maximum score for each exercise appears in the right-hand column. Total score (maximum 97) is calculated by taking the sum of the scores for the individual tasks.

	Points
I. The student is required to perform the following figures, and his instructor evaluates him on the basis of his style and synchronization.	
a. Elementary skills:	
Back Tuck Somersault	2
Front Tuck Somersault	2
Back Pike Somersault	2
Front Pike Somersault	2
Ballet Leg	2
Porpoise	2
Dolphin	2
Oyster	2
b. Intermediate skills:	
Flying Porpoise	3
Flying Dolphin	3
Shark	3
Ballet Legs	3

	Points
Double Ballet Legs	3
Marlin	3
Catalina	3
Submarine	3
Somer-Sub	3

II. The student performs a routine that combines three or more elementary skills. This routine may be performed to music or, if music is unavailable, to counts. This routine may be performed as a solo, a duet, or by a small group. — 15

III. The student, with a number of his fellows, performs a routine, to music or to counts, which combines three or more intermediate skills. — 15

IV. The student choreographs and performs, to music or to counts, a routine, of not less than 5 minutes duration. The routine, which may be performed by a group of any size, should combine several skills of the student's choice. — 24

Total Points Possible	97	
Suggested Scoring Range	90-97	A
	82-89	B
	74-81	C
	66-73	D
	0-65	F

34 | TABLE TENNIS SKILL TEST

Purpose: To measure the student's ability to keep the ball in play.

Equipment and Facilities: One half of a table tennis table pushed up against a wall, the height of a net (6 inches) marked on the wall above the table top; ball and paddle.

Procedure: The player serves and rallies. He gets one point for every legal play of the ball within a 60-second time period.

35 | TENNIS SKILL TEST

Equipment:
1. One tennis racket.
2. One dozen tennis balls of equal weight and pressure.
3. One rope, strung from one net post extension to other, 8 feet above the court surface.

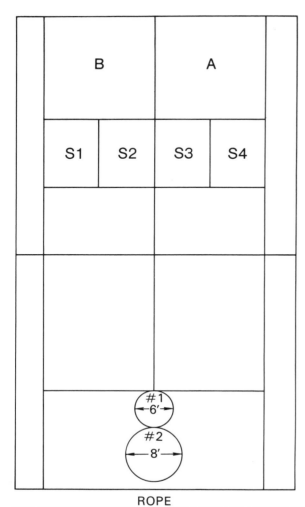

Placement areas for skill test.

Procedure:

1. On the following tests, the student is awarded one point for each placement into the proper area.
2. Where a toss is to be made, the instructor tosses from his shoulder with a pushing motion, to prevent spin on the ball. Only those tosses landing in the proper circle need be played. The student has the option of playing balls that miss the proper circle. If he plays such balls successfully, he receives credit; if not, he is given another chance . In the event of a bad bounce, the instructor will toss an extra ball.
3. Line balls are considered "in."
4. A recorder stands behind the test area in use and records scores, calling "in" or "out" on each shot. A ball that fails to go under the 8 foot tape (on any stroke except the lob) should be called "out over tape."
5. Balls with the same degree of wear should be used throughout the test.
6. Numbers in areas and colored lines between areas are helpful to the test administration.

Serve (40 Possible Points)

The student must use the full low backswing on each serve.

1. Position of the student: behind baseline and just right of center mark.
   Procedure: The student serves two balls for practice and ten for score into the area marked Sl.
2. Position of the student: same as above (1).
   Procedure: The student serves two balls for practice and ten for score into the area marked S2.
3. Position of the student: behind the baseline and just left of the center mark.
   Procedure: The student serves two balls for practice and ten for score into the area marked S3.
4. Position of the student: same as (3).
   Procedure: The student serves two balls for practice and ten for score into the area marked S4.

Forehand Drive (20 Possible Points)

The instructor stands at the net in the center of the court, on the side of the net opposite the student.

1. Position of the student: in front of the baseline at the center of the backcourt area, in the waiting position.
   Procedure: The instructor tosses one ball for practice and five for score into the circle and the student drives for area A.
2. Position of the student: same as above (1).
   Procedure: same as (1), except that all balls are driven into area B.
3. Position of the student: behind the center of the baseline, in the waiting position.
   Procedure: The instructor tosses one ball for practice and five for score into circle 2 and the student drives for area A.

4. Position of the student: same as above (3).
   Procedure: same as (3), except that the balls are driven into area B.

Backhand Drive (20 Possible Points)

The instructor stands at the net in the center of court, on the side of the net opposite the student.

1. Position of the student: in front of the baseline, at the center of the backcourt area, in the waiting position.
   Procedure: The instructor tosses one ball for practice and five balls for score into circle 1 and the student drives for area A.
2. Position of the student: same as (1).
   Procedure: same as (1) except that the balls are driven into area B.
3. Position of the student: behind center of baseline, in the waiting position.
   Procedure: The instructor tosses one ball for practice and five balls for score into circle 2 and student drives for area A.
4. Position of the student: same as (3).
   Procedure: same as (3), except that the balls are driven into area B.

Volley (5 Possible Points)

The instructor stands at the center of the court just behind opposite service line.

Position of the student: waiting position, with the heels on the service line and on each side of the center service line.

Procedure: The instructor tosses, at medium speed, six balls, one for practice and five for score, at a point below the student's shoulders and above his knees. These balls, which are tossed under the 8 foot tape, must be volleyed into the singles court playing area by the student.

Lob (5 Possible Points)

The instructor stands at the net in the center of the court, across the net from the student.

Position of the student: behind the center of the baseline, in the waiting position.

Procedure: The instructor tosses one ball for practice and five for score into circle 2 and the student lobs them, forehand or backhand, over the 8 foot tape into the backcourt area (area A or B).

Overhead Smash (5 Possible Points)

The instructor tosses the ball from just behind the baseline opposite the student's, in the center of the court.

Position of the student: waiting position, about half-way between the service line and the net in the center of the court.

Procedure: Instructor tosses one ball for practice and five for score over the 8 foot tape and the student plays the ball before the bounce with an overhead smash into the singles court area; the ball must be smashed so that it goes under 8 foot tape and bounces off the court on the first bounce.

Chop (5 Possible Points)

The instructor stands at the net in the center of the court, on the opposite side of the net from student.

Position of the student: in front of the baseline at the center of the backcourt area, in the waiting position.

Procedure: The instructor tosses one ball for practice and five for score into circle 1 and the student chops (forehand or backhand) under the 8 foot tape, into the forecourt area (either service court).

36 | TOUCH FOOTBALL SKILL TEST
Passing

Purpose: To measure the student's accuracy in passing the football.

Equipment and Facilities: A circle 5 feet in diameter, with its center 5 feet from the ground; a throwing line 60 feet from the target; a regulation football.

Procedure: The contestant stands behind the restraining line and throws the football at the target ten times. He is awarded one point for every hit.

Passing

Purpose: To measure the student's ability to pass the football for distance.

Equipment and Facilities: A field marked every 10 feet; a regulation football.

Procedure: The contestant is permitted three trials. His best pass is recorded to the last marker that the ball clears in the air.

Running with Ball

Purpose: To measure the student's ability to handle and run with the ball.

Equipment and Facilities: Regulation football; a field marked with a starting line and five lines 50 yards apart.

Procedure: The contestant stands behind the starting line, in a backfield stance. The ball is centered to the contestant, who runs 50 yards with it. The elapsed time between the student's receipt of the ball and his attainment of the finish line is taken as the score.

38 | VOLLEYBALL SKILL TEST

The volleyball court should be lined as illustrated in the diagram. The student may score a maximum of 100 points.

Serve

The student (O-Se) makes ten serves and, for each serve, receives the number of points marked on the area in which the ball lands. A ball which falls on a line counts for the higher area.

10 serves. Possible 40 points.

Passing

The instructor (I-P) stands at the corner of the passing area and, using an underhand throw, lobs six balls to the student at point A and six at point B. The first ball for each area is practice, the rest count. The student must use both hands and pass the ball *over* the clothesline and *into* the passing area. Each ball landing in the passing area counts two points. The instructor should throw the ball approximately 12 feet high and aim to drop the ball on the student's chest.

10 passes. Possible 20 points.

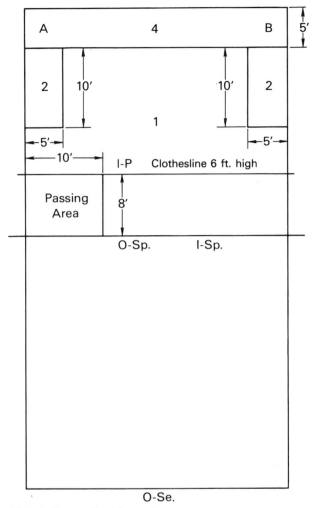

Volleyball court, lined for testing.

Spike

The instructor (I-Sp) lobs eleven balls to the student (O-Sp) at the center of the court. Each ball should reach a height of 12 to 15 feet, come to within 6 inches to 2 feet of the net, and fall in front of the student. The first ball is practice, the next ten count. The student must hit the ball *over* the net and *under* the clothesline, so that it hits in fair territory and bounces *off* the court on the second bounce. Each ball is worth two points.

10 spikes. Possible 20 points.

Setup

On a basketball court, instructor (I) lobs six balls to student at A and six at B. The first ball for each area is practice, the rest count. At the start of the throw, the student must have one foot outside the free throw lane. After the ball leaves the instruc-

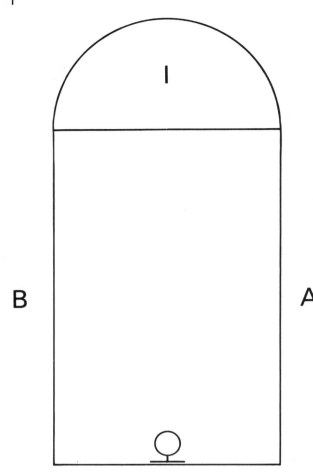

against the wall above the chalk line and between the vertical lines, or against the basketball backboard.

3. The player volleys the ball against the wall in this area. No restraining line is used.
4. If the player catches or holds ball, he must begin another volley as he began the first volley.
5. If the player loses control of the ball, he must regain control and begin another volley as he began the initial volley.
6. Only one volleyball may be used. The student must maintain control for the duration of the test. If the ball is held or if control is lost, the stopwatch will not be stopped while the ball is retrieved. However, the player does not lose credit for volleys executed prior to the loss of control or holding of the ball.

Scoring:

1. The player is awarded one point for each legal volley.
2. A throw prior to a volley does not score a point.

39 | WATER SKIING AND MOTORBOATING SKILL TEST

Rating the performer subjectively is the best available way of assessing the contestant in the various skills and maneuvers of water skiing and handling a boat.

40 | WEIGHT TRAINING AND WEIGHT LIFTING SKILL TEST

The instructor may evaluate his student by asking him to perform a series of specific exercises and rating him subjectively on the basis of his execution of these exercises. Weight lifting can be judged as a competitive activity on the basis of the combination of weights in competitive lifts.

41 | WRESTLING SKILL TEST

The instructor should rate the performance of the contestant as he executes certain offensive and defensive moves. Consideration of such factors as balance, timing, ability to execute the skills, and efficiency of motion will assist the rater to be objective.

tor's hand, the student may move anywhere to play the ball. The student may catch any ball that he does not wish to play. The setup must either hit the top of the basket's rim or go through the basket. The ball *must* be played with *two* hands. Each ball is worth two points.

10 setups. Possible 20 points.

The above skill test may be supplemented by the volleyball rally test, described below.

Rally

Equipment: A stopwatch; one volleyball; a smooth wall with a horizontal chalk line 5 feet long and 10 feet from the floor, and two vertical lines drawn through the end point of the horizontal line, perpendicular to it.

Test:

1. The player is allotted one minute.
2. The test begins when the player throws the ball